REPORTING
FOR DUTY

**U.S. Citizen-Soldier Journalism
from the Afghan Surge, 2010-2011**

Compiled & edited by Randy Brown
Middle West Press LLC
Johnston, Iowa

Copyright © 2016 Randy Brown
All rights reserved

Library of Congress control number: 2016914698
ISBN-13: 978-0-9969317-3-1
ISBN: 0-9969317-3-2

Middle West Press LLC
P.O. Box 31099
Johnston, Iowa 50131-9428

www.middlewestpress.com

Remember the Fallen

Spc. Brent M. Maher, Honey Creek, Iowa
KIA April 11, 2011

Spc. Donald L. Nichols, Shell Rock, Iowa
KIA April 13, 2011

Staff Sgt. James A. Justice, Grimes, Iowa
KIA April 23, 2011

Sgt. Christopher R. Bell, Saint Joseph, Mich.
Sgt. Joshua D. Powell, Tyler, Texas
Sgt. Devin A. Snyder, Cohockton, N.Y.
Spc. Robert L. Voakes, Jr., Hancock, Mich.
KIA June 4, 2011

Sgt. 1st Class Terryl L. Pasker, Cedar Rapids, Iowa
KIA July 9, 2011

TABLE OF CONTENTS

ABOUT THIS BOOK

This collection is intended to be a primary-source archive of the more than 180,000 words and photographs distributed to the public by the Iowa National Guard's 2nd Brigade Combat Team (BCT), 34th Infantry "Red Bull" Division (2-34th BCT) and related units. During its 2010-2011 deployment, 2-34th BCT was both reconfigured, and incorporated non-organic units. This amalgated unit was called "Task Force Red Bulls."

Most of these items are news articles and photo essays written by or about operations within Task Force Red Bulls' Area of Operations (AO), or that of Iowa's 1st Battalion, 168th Infantry Regiment (1-168th Inf.), which operated separately, and under a different brigade, as "Task Force Lethal." A few additional items, including press releases and news articles about events taking outside of AO Red Bulls and AO Lethal, have been included for reader context.

As a "first draft of history," this collection of public affairs journalism documents how citizen-soldiers spent time away from home, individually and collectively, during the biggest year of America's longest war.

Close observers will note thematic threads interweaving this coverage. Some of these reflect the "clear, hold, and build" themes intended by Army officials fighting a counterinsurgency campaign. Others, however, merely reflect the daily and seasonal routine of soldierly life on a year-long deployment. In addition to reports of patrols and battles, for example, there are visits by dignitaries and entertainers; memorial ceremonies for fallen soldiers; morale-boosting events and holiday celebrations.

With one exception, articles presented here are dated between November 2010 and July 2011—the approximate dates of the 2-34th BCT deployment to Afghanistan. These dates also coincide with the height of the "Afghan Surge," the shorthand term for U.S. President Barack Obama's 2010 deployment of an additional 33,000 U.S. troops to Afghanistan. Troop levels in that country plateaued at more than 100,000 troops in August 2010.

While public affairs soldiers submitted their stories and photos under deadline, soon after returning from missions they covered, military website editors often posted articles days or even weeks after the fact. Sometimes, this practice seems to have been aimed toward keeping the flow of published news steady and constant. Other times, the delay may have involved concerns regarding operational security (OPSEC) about a particular battle or troop movement. To better reflect the dates of events described within each article, rather than dates of release or publication, I have revised datelines and re-ordered articles into a more coherent chronology for readers.

Given the limitations of black-and-white photographic reproduction in trade paperback format, many images have been omitted from this collection.

Those that do appear are at admittedly lower resolutions than original—they are more like newspaper photographs than magazine- or monitor-quality images. They may also be cropped, reduced from their original dimensions, based upon available space on the printed page.

All photographs were originally published or posted in color. Photographs were selected for inclusion here based on a number of factors, including whether they contained information—both visual and in caption— not available in the related main article. Also, in the spirit of community journalism, preference was given to photographs that featured names of U.S. citizen-soldiers.

While released for public consumption at the times they were produced, these collected articles and photographs are often no longer available on-line. Indeed, with changes in units and missions in Afghanistan, websites such as "CJTF101.com" and "IowaRedBulls.com" simply no longer exist. Other websites, such as the Defense Video Imagery Distribution System (DVIDS, pronounced "DIV-ids"), continue to maintain articles and images from the deployment, but are not always easily accessed or searched by the public.

Headlines and text, with a few exceptions, generally appear as originally published. Acronyms, jargon, and other text have been edited or expanded, to improve understandability, uniformity, and ease-of-indexing.

For a glossary of acronyms, initialisms, and jargon, see page 630.

For further notes on how this collection was edited, see page 652.

— *Randy Brown, November 2016*

TASK FORCE
RED BULLS

Public affairs soldiers: Hometown journalists in uniform
By Randy Brown

Following a U.S. National Guard unit is like following a favorite sports team: Teams have uniforms. Teams have emblems. Teams have communities.

In each side of this metaphor—both sports and military—a group of uniformed representatives comes to represent the ideals and aspirations of a geographic place. There are individual records and championship seasons, newspaper clippings and books of statistics. There are flags and banners, mottos and mascots. In taverns and at reunions, there are oft-repeated stories of heroism and off-the-field hijinks. There can be hard-fought battles, once-in-a-lifetime wins, and heartbreaking losses.

Teams have stories.

Such tales might echo no further than the next day's chatter around the coffee shop or water cooler, of course, were it not for local newspapers, TV and radio stations, and even Internet bloggers. These sources record the life of a community—the names, events, dates, and details—what journalism professors like to describe as "the first rough draft of history."

Teams have histories.

In 2010, a generic U.S. National Guard brigade was made up of approximately 3,000 citizen-soldiers. In today's army, in addition to the infantry, cavalry, and artillery that people expect to see on the news and in the movies, each brigade formation also includes soldiers tasked with not-always-glamorous support functions—jobs like human resources, legal affairs, food service, transportation, vehicle maintenance, first aid and physical therapy. In a sports franchise, these might be labelled "front office" functions. In the army, these will often be found in a unit's "headquarters."

In every size of unit, soldiers performing such vital jobs can be found. In smaller units, those support soldiers may number in the single digits. In an army brigade, whole units—sections, companies, and battalions—may be devoted to support tasks.

The task of recording and telling stories, of creating a sense of community, of communicating with the followers of a particular team? In the army, that's called public affairs—sort of a hybrid mix of public relations and marketing, media relations, and plain-old news-editorial journalism. In the U.S. Army, the lowest-level unit with its own public affairs section is the brigade, and its soldiers are found assigned to the brigade headquarters company.

During the latter part of my 20-year career as a citizen-soldier with the Iowa Army National Guard, I had the honor of serving with the 2nd Brigade Combat Team, 34th Infantry "Red Bull" Division (2-34th BCT). In 2003, I was even deployed with 1st Battalion, 133rd Infantry Regiment (1-133rd Inf.) to a peacekeeping mission on the Sinai Penninsula, Egypt.

In my concurrent civilian life—after journalism school and before I went into magazines—I was first a reporter and editor in at a weekly newspaper in Osceola, Iowa, and later the senior reporter for the six-day afternoon newspaper in the river city of Muscatine, Iowa. Community newspaper life wasn't *The New York Times,* and it wasn't *The National Enquirer.* It wasn't about exposés and investigations, and it wasn's about scandals and celebrities. Instead, community newspaper writers learn to balance reporting the facts— good and bad—with equal amounts of civic pride and Chamber of Commerce boosterism.

I mention this personal history, because it has led me to this conclusion: As members of their own communities—both in their armories and in their hometowns—public affairs soldiers deliver a similarly wholesome and grounded journalistic product. Like community newspaper reporters, they tell the truth and report the facts, but they're also there to boost the home team.

Because someone has to tell the stories.

Serving God and Country—and Community

Two days a month, and two weeks a year, I served country and community wearing a U.S. Army uniform, and training to go to war. I myself wasn't a writer for Uncle Sam—instead, I specialized in helping to manage radio, computer, and telephone communications. Occasionally, however, like all National Guard soldiers, I had opportunities to directly help my neighbors. During responses to floods, blizzards, and other natural disasters, I learned that fellow citizens look at you differently—look to you for help and calm and safety—when you wear a uniform. Particularly one with an American flag patch on your sleeve.

Every soldier—whether reserve or active-duty—wears that flag, as well as a "U.S. Army" stitched in block letters. Every soldier also wears a unit patch on his or her left shoulder—their current team's emblem. Those soldiers who have at least once deployed to a war zone may wear another unit patch on their right. They wear the patch of the unit with which they personally went to war. That "combat patch" stays with them, throughout their careers.

Whenever I traveled in uniform more widely—in airports like Atlanta and Dallas-Fort Worth and Las Vegas—people chatted me up about my unit's "Red Bull" patch. They knew it represented the American Midwest as readily as if I had worn a Minnesota Vikings jersey or University of Iowa baseball cap.

Sometimes, people would talk about having served in "Red Bull" unit themselves—or having a grandfather, son, or niece who also wore the patch. Although unversed in sports, I became well-practiced making small talk about my home team in the Iowa National Guard. Luckily for me, the 34th Infantry "Red Bull" Division (34th Inf. Div.) boasts many stories, and provides plenty of material.

The division takes its name from the distinctive shoulder patch its soldiers wear on the sleeves of their combat uniforms: a red bovine skull, superimposed on the silhouette of a black Mexican water jug called an "olla." The symbol was designed by Pfc. Marvin Cone of Cedar Rapids, Iowa, a friend of famous Regionalist artist Grant Wood (who painted the famous farmer-and-wife portrait "American Gothic"), and himself an accomplished painter. The division was established in 1917, and originally comprised citizen-soldiers from Iowa, Minnesota, and North and South Dakota. The emblem is still worn by multiple units in Minnesota and Iowa. In each state, the symbol appears on everything from hats and T-shirts, to road signs and recruiting advertisements. To Middle Westerners, it represents a history, a geography, and a community—the home team.

Here's a quick bullet-list of other Red Bull talking points:

- Coming into port in Belfast, Ireland, the 34th Inf. Div. was the first U.S. division to arrive in European Theater during World War II.
- Also in World War II, the army's elite 1st Ranger Battalion was formed under the command of Capt. William Darby of the 34th Inf. Div. Some 80 percent of the unit's initial volunteers were drawn from the division. The resulting unit became famous as "Darby's Rangers."
- Arriving in the North Africa Theater, in the country of Tunisia, the 34th Inf. Div. was the first U.S. unit during World War II to fire artillery at German ground forces.
- Troopers of Iowa's 113th Cavalry Regiment, as part of 38th Cavalry Reconnaisance Squadron, were first to enter Paris in World War II. They didn't even stick around for the party, but drove on and kept going.
- The heroic "nisei" (second-generation immigrant) Japanese-Americans of the celebrated 100th Battalion/442nd Infantry Regiment fought as part of 34th Inf. Div. in World War II Italy. Members of the 100th Battalion painted the Red Bull on the front of their helmets.
- The 34th Ind. Div. was credited with more combat days than any other in World War II. One or more "Red Bull" units were engaged in actual combat with the enemy for 611 days. The 1st Battalion, 133rd Infantry Regiment (1-133rd Inf.)—the "Ironman" battalion—still holds the U.S. Army record for days in combat.
- While deployed to Iraq in 2005-2007, Minnesota's 1st Brigade, 34th Inf. Div.'s tour of duty was extended, caught up in the surge of U.S.

troops into Iraq announced by President George W. Bush in a televised speech Jan. 13, 2007. First mobilized in September and October 2005, the brigade's time in-country was extended to a record-breaking 17 months. This was the longest deployment of any U.S. Army unit during Operation Iraqi Freedom (OIF). Adding insult to injury, soldiers downrange first learned about the extension through the media. In the case of the Iowa's 1-133rd Inf., that moment was captured by a *60 Minutes* television crew who regularly embedded with the Iowa battalion during the deployment.

Of course, one of the most recent Red Bull war stories is the 2010-2011 deployment of 2-34th BCT to Afghanistan. Which brings us to this book.

The Big Event, the Big Story

Newspaper articles, press releases, and broadcast features unfailingly billed it as "the largest deployment of Iowa citizen-soldiers since World War II." From December 2010 to July 2011, operating as "Task Force Red Bulls," the unit was uniquely tasked with responsibility for the full-spectrum of combat, support, and other missions within its assigned geographic area of operations.

Task Force Red Bulls' responsibilities included the administration of Bagram Airfield (BAF)—the largest coaltion military base in the country, which was then home to an estimated population of more than 30,000—and the surrounding Parwan Province. The unit was also responsible for the provinces of Panjshir, Laghman, and a small portion of Nuristan.

In the 13-year history of Operation Enduring Freedom–Afghanistan (OEF–A)—from Oct. 1, 2001 to Dec. 31, 2014—only two other U.S. National Guard brigades can be argued to have been assigned such "battlespace ownership." The others were:

- The Vermont National Guard's 86th Infantry Brigade Combat Team (IBCT), operating as "Task Force Wolverine" (March 2009 to December 2010).
- The Oklahoma National Guard's 45th IBCT, operating as "Task Force Thunderbird" (August 2011 to March 2012).

In a Dec. 1, 2009 address to the cadets at the U.S. Military Academy in West Point, N.Y., U.S. President Barack Obama announced a surge of additional 33,000 U.S. troops to Afghanistan, bringing the total number of troops deployed there to approximately 100,000 by August 2010. Arriving in November 2010, the 2-34th BCT deployment occurred at the crest of this wave.

In June 2011, one month after the terrorist Osama bin Laden was killed in a nighttime helicopter raid in Pakistan, the president announced plans to begin withdrawing U.S. troops from Afghanistan, setting a target date of 2014 for handing over security operations to Afghan military forces. The drawdown began in July 2011.

Nearly simultaneous to the 2-34th BCT deployment, more than 60 Iowa Air and Army National Guard personnel deployed on a separate mission to Eastern Afghanistan's Kunar Province. A frequent symbol of the U.S. National Guard is the colonial minuteman—farmers, blacksmiths, printers, merchants who readied themselves to leave their civilian jobs, pick up their muskets, and answer their country's call. The citizen-soldiers of today have similar lives—farmers, teachers, cops, parents, business owners—and live for similar ideals.

Usually, despite the U.S. public's misperception that their mission is primarily one of response to natural disasters, National Guard soldiers train for war. "Technical and tactical proficiency," they call it. Soldiers' civilian jobs do not necessarily align with their jobs in uniform.

In a unique twist, however, from August 2011 to June 2011, the soldiers and airmen of the 734th Agribusiness Development Team (ADT) used both their civilian and military skills. Their mission? To help increase the capacity of Afghan farmers to raise, improve, and market their crops and cattle. They called themselves the "Dirt Warriors," and wore the Iowa National Guard's "Hawkeye" shoulder patch. The water-jug shape of the Hawkeye patch is derived from that of the 34th Inf. Div. "Red Bull" patch. In country, the 734th ADT was called "Task Force Hawkeye," and recognized by the hawk-head painted on the sides of its vehicles. Members report the unit was never attacked while out on agriculture-related missions.

While the 734th ADT was outside of 2-34th BCT's geographic area of responsibility, Agribusiness Development Teams from other U.S. states, as well as the more-common Provincial Reconstruction Teams (PRT), variously operated in each of the brigade's assigned provinces. These teams' efforts are an integral part of the nation-building, counter-insurgency narrative that underlay the "clear, hold, and build" counterinsurgency strategy then pursued by U.S. and coaltion forces: *Clear* their assigned areas of bad guys; *hold* the ground to prevent further insurgency; and help the Afghan government *build* infrastructure, services, commerce, and rule of law.

In short, both Iowa units—the 2-34th BCT and the 734th ADT—were uniquely positioned to help make history. It was the peak of the "Afghan Surge"—the height of U.S. troop involvement in Afghanistan. In the largest deployment of Iowa troops since World War II, the U.S. government mobilized as soldiers more than 3,000 Iowa citizens—a population equivalent to that of the town of Huxley, Iowa. Those troops went to Afghanistan to help stabilize the government of a foreign nation, and to help its people.

And public affairs soldiers were there to tell the story.

Soldier-journalists tell how they fight, why they fight
By Randy Brown

Like other units of its size, the Iowa National Guard's 2nd Brigade Combat Team, 34th Infantry "Red Bull" Division (2-34th BCT) headquarters includes a small staff of public affairs soldiers—military journalists who are trained and tasked to provide factual reporting from the battlefield.

Before they tell their stories, we should tell theirs.

Task Force Red Bulls Public Affairs soldiers mostly write for an audience of followers back home, including soldiers' friends and family. Sometimes, their words and pictures appear in civilian newspapers and television reports, complete with bylines and photo credits. Other times, their work inspires civilian reporters to cover the National Guard story in-depth. Finally, public affairs also serves as an informal channel for state and federal officials to keep informed regarding the U.S.-led coalition mission in Afghanistan.

Given their privileged perch, public affairs soldiers often have the inside scoop—and the constant task of using their access responsibly.

"We, as a governmental entity, have an obligation to tell the American public what we're doing," says Ashlee Lolkus. "The taxpayers, at the very least, need to know where their money is going. We try to be 'the first with the truth,' with 'maximum disclosure, minimum delay!'"

As a newly graduated psychology major from Iowa State University in 2010, Lolkus deployed as the Non-Commissioned Officer-in-Charge (NCOIC) of Task Force Red Bulls' Public Affairs team. It wasn't Lolkus' first deployment—she'd deployed to Kosovo in 2003-2004, and with Minnesota's 1st Brigade, 34th Infantry Division (1-34th Bde) to Iraq in 2005-2007. The Afghan deployment, however, was her first as a military journalist.

"Whenever I was talking to Joe Blow Snuffy, of course, I'd just tell them that I was 'here to make them famous'—to tell people back home what they're doing," she says.

Now Master Sgt. Ashlee Lolkus Sherrill, she is currently the public affairs NCOIC for the 34th Inf. Div., assigned to the division headquarters in Rosemount, Minn. In her civilian career, she is the Public Information Officer for the St. Paul (Minn.) Field Division of the Bureau of Alcohol, Tobacco, Firearms and Explosives.

If Lolkus' role was equivalent to managing editor of a community news organization, the Red Bulls' editor-in-chief and publisher was Michael Wunn of Clive, Iowa. Wunn is a 1991 graduate of the Drake University School of Journalism and Mass Communication, and a 2001 graduate of the university's School of Law. Wunn often jokes that he is a "recovering attorney," having practiced as a civilian lawyer before joining the Iowa National Guard full-time as a Public Affairs Officer in 2004. He is currently in charge of maintaining the Iowa National Guard's relationship to the Kosovo Security Forces via the U.S. government's State Partnership Program (SPP).

"In planning our coverage each week [in Afghanistan], we sought to link our story ideas to the brigade commander's Lines of Effort, which were nested within the division's campaign plan," says Wunn. "That meant for nearly every article, photo, or video we produced—from outside the wire, at least—we had some tie-in to Afghan governance, security, or civil infrastructure."

"As public affairs professionals, our focus was on telling the Army story," Wunn says. "That meant, in the context of our mission in Afghanistan, 'clear, hold, and build' was a matter of telling stories of 'governance, security, and development.'"

A former radio broadcaster and editorial director with more than 10 years of civilian agricultural journalism experience, Peter Shinn was a one-person public affairs team in Afghanistan. He was then a captain in the Iowa Air National Guard, and deployed with Iowa's 734th Agribusiness Development Team (ADT) to Eastern Afghanistan's Kunar Province. Shinn's coverage, unsurprisingly, focused on stories supporting the "development" narrative.

Because they were based outside of Area of Operations (AO) Red Bulls, Iowa's ADT members rarely crossed paths with Task Force Red Bulls personnel. Teams from other states, however, including those from Kansas and Kentucky, did operate within Red Bulls battlespace. And Oklahoma's 2nd Agribusiness Development Team, 45th Infantry Brigade Combat Team (2-45th ADT) was deployed to Paktya Province, the area of operations overseen by Iowa's 1st Battalion, 168th Infantry (1-168th Inf.).

The Agribusiness Development Team story is one unique to the U.S. National Guard, and one that deserves re-telling. More than five years after his deployment, Shinn has been promoted to major, and is on active-duty as a Florida Air National Guardsman. He's now the executive officer for the 601st Air Operations Center (601st AOC) at Tyndall Air Force Base, Fla. Shinn's ADT talking points, however, are still readily on the tip of Shinn's tongue:

"We communicated that the 734th Agribusiness Development Team was there doing the good work of counterinsurgency," he says, jovially. "That they were building the capacity of the Government of the Islamic Republic of Afghanistan. And that, through these efforts, they were improving the lives and the fortunes of the people of Afghanistan, so that they would be better able to take control of their own country, and feed their own people."

Meet the Task Force Red Bulls news team
Together, as Public Affairs Officer and NCO, Wunn and Lolkus formed the nucleus of Task Force Red Bulls Public Affairs team. Other 2-34th BCT public

affairs personnel during the deployment were either volunteers from other states, who joined the unit in summer 2010 at their mobilization station of Camp Shelby, Miss.; or U.S. Army Reserve and active-duty U.S. Army personnel, attached to Task Force Red Bulls only while in Afghanistan.

At various times during the deployment, then, the Task Force Red Bulls Public Affairs section included:

- Maj. Michael Wunn
- Staff Sgt. Ashlee Lolkus
- Staff Sgt. Ryan C. Matson
- Spc. Tim Beery
- Spc. Kristina L. Gupton
- Spc. James Wilton
- Spc. Adam L. Mathis

Each Task Force Red Bulls Public Affairs soldier had a "beat" on which to report regularly. That meant developing relationships, and a fluency with the units in their respective coverage areas.

"I rode my soldiers very hard," says Lolkus. "We notably had more releases than any of the other brigades, within either of the divisions we fell under during the deployment [101st Airborne Division and 1st Cavalry Division]. I usually required a minimum of two or three releases every week."

Ryan Matson, a patrol officer with the Metropolitan Nashville (Tenn.) Police Department in civilian life, was depoyed as a U.S. Army Reservist with the 210th Mobile Public Affairs Detachment (MPAD). A veteran of the Iraq War, he was attached to 2-34th BCT when the Iowa unit arrived in Afghanistan. Maston's journalistic beat was 1st Battalion, 133rd Infantry Regiment (1-133rd Inf.)—also known as the "Ironman" battalion. He, along with the battalion headquartes for Task Force Ironman, was based out of Forward Operating Base (FOB) Mehtar Lam, Laghman Province.

In the Task Force Red Bulls Public Affairs office at Bagram Airfield, Lolkus maintained a status board on which each member of her team was represented by a photo of a movie character. Matson's cinematic avatar was the flak-jacketed character "Animal Mother," from the 1987 Stanley Kubrick-directed film about the Vietnam War, *Full Metal Jacket.*

"Matson was an animal," Lolkus explains. "He ran up mountains, never ran out of breath. Went on mission, after mission. Never lost motivation. Never complained to me. He loved his job. He loved the Red Bulls. He loved how much sense of community he saw in our organization. Because he's a reservist, he'd never seen that before. How much of a familial tie we had in the National Guard, compared to active-duty or reserve."

At some point during the 2011 deployment—even Matson is now somewhat fuzzy on the details—he committed to a personal goal of writing more than 100 articles during his time downrange. "I think my motivation was, 'I've only got one year here. I want to make it count, and do the best I can, because the people I'm writing about deserve that,'" he says.

Matson remembers arriving at Combat Outpost (COP) Najil around Christmas 2010, to embed with Iowa's Alpha Company, 1-133rd Inf. Conditions there were remote, rough, and rustic. He knew the commander, Capt. Jason Merchant of Dysert, Iowa, only by reputation—and that reputation was tough. "Capt. Merchant asked me what I wanted to do up there, what my goals were," Matson says. "I told him I just wanted to tell the people back in Iowa what they were doing. As he was asking me stuff, I noticed that we were kind of sprinting up this mountain. I think he was kind of testing me, to make sure I could hang with them when they went out."

"Or maybe he just walks fast," Matson laughs. "Who knows?"

In the days to come, on his second or third patrol out, Matson found himself trying to gut through a conditions his fellow soldiers had nicknamed "Yeti HIV"—a week-long roller coaster of explosive diarrhea and other nasty symptoms. Nearly everyone else there had already been through it. "I remember confiding in one of squad leaders there, Sgt. [Kenneth] Cain—who I had known all of like, a week, but who I really liked—that I was worried about s---ing my pants out there or something. 'Don't worry, it happens,' he said." That put Matson's mind, if not his body, a little more at ease.

Later in that patrol, Matson—lightheaded, woozy, and practically hallucinating, the way he tells it—was taking photos when he looked down and saw a white lamp cord in the dirt. Finding such out-of-place items often leads to possible Improvised Explosive Devices (IED). Merchant and Cain, he says, were "stoked" at Matson's discovery.

After they'd found the cord, Merchant said, "Me and my guys will clear this ridge over here," and pointed at the area up from the valley where Matson had spotted the wire. Sick as Matson was, the commander's inclusive choice of words instantly and indelibly registered in his memory. He felt now officially one of Merchant's "guys."

"The Red Bulls really taught me how to treat people," says Matson. "I remember thinking to myself, 'Are there any jerks in Iowa?' Everybody, to a person, treated me well. I will never forget that. I can honestly say that the year I spent writing about the Red Bulls at war—and their higher headquarters, the 101st Airborne Division—was one of the best years of my life. And capturing the acts and images of American soldiers at war was one of the greatest honors."

Matson is still a police officer, but now specializes in crime scene investigation in the Metro Nashville Police Dept. His experiences as an Army writer-photographer, he jokes, pays off in his workaday documentation of crime scene evidence. He remains active in the U.S. Army Reserve, and has achieved the rank of sergeant first class. And he's a drill sergeant, training young soldiers during their first days in the military.

Tim Beery, a Utah National Guard volunteer, was the only member of Task Force Red Bulls Public Affairs trained as a broadcast journalist—in Military Occupational Specialty (MOS) job codes, he was a "46-Romeo."

"We tried to cross-train him, to some photos to do as much as possible.. That way, he could go out on a mission, release a couple of photos, and then work on his video," says Lolkus. "It takes a long time to cut a video release, and there wasn't a great venue for us to push his stuff to. We didn't really have access to [Armed Forces Network]. We had the radio, however—he loved doing radio—it takes personality to be a Romeo! And we often used his video stuff to motivate the troops."

In his on-air persona as the "Beer-man," Beery hosted an afternoon drive-time slot that served the greater Bagram Airfield metro area. "I'd play music, read emails to the station, take requests and just shoot the breeze. It was a lot of fun and the brigade seemed to love it. Not only because I was slightly irreverent on the air, but also because a Red Bull was on the air. That opportunity was typically reserved for active-duty public affairs soldiers."

Since the deployment, Beery completed an undergraduate degree in communications and media studies. He is now working in healthcare public relations in Northern Utah, while pursuing a related graduate degree.

Trained as a "25-Victor" combat documentation/production specialist, Kristina L. Gupton of Rocky Mount, N.C., was attached to Task Force Red Bulls from her home unit, 982nd Combat Camera (Airborne). The U.S. Army Reserve unit has a headquarters in East Point, Ga., and a detachment in Wilson, N.C. It is one of only two Combat Camera companies in the Army.

Combat Camera missions often focus on documenting battlefield conditions for historical records, after-action reviews, or damage assessments. Whenever she was not otherwise tasked to such missions, however, Gupton fell in with the Red Bulls' public affairs section.

"We are the commanders' eyes and the ears on the ground, and embed with every kind of unit, including scouts, snipers, Rangers, Special Forces," says Gupton. "We provide raw coverage, photos, and B-roll [unedited video] for the commanders. Commanders are often in the rear at the TOC [Tactical Operations Center]. So, using ComCam, commanders have visuals of how their troops operate in both hostile or peaceful areas. They're able to make observations themselves, and to better build and prepare for future operations."

Both on foot and while mounted on vehicles, the paratrooper-qualified Gupton often accompanied missions of Iowa's 1st Squadron, 113th Cavalry Regiment (1-113th Cav.) into the Bagram Security Zone surrounding the air

…it was also responsible for patrolling throughout the
…ce.

…c shooter," Lolkus says of Gupton. "You could give her a
…nd she'd come back with gold. [...] She would go on
…l walk and walk and ruck and not complain."

…s and contrasts the two military jobs: "Public Affairs
…at Camera doesn't write articles—but we do provide
…os," she laughs. "It's all 5Ws-and-an-H: 'Who, What,
…nd How.'"

…ed to Afghanistan at the military rank of specialist,
…ecretary for a North Carolina-based manufacturer of
…n is now a sergeant and full-time soldier with the U.S.
…Ordnance Company, Charleston, W.Va. She works in

James Wilton, a volunteer from the California National Guard, seemed to
thrive most in covering the comings-and-goings of the small metropolis that
was Bagram Airfield, pop. 30,000. Think of it as the "man about town" beat
found in some newspapers or magazines. "It wasn't that he was afraid to go on
missions, it was just his personality," Lolkus says. "He was more into the
lighter side of stuff—a fun-loving guy." Wilton even volunteered to stay in
Afghanistan, serving with Oklahoma's 45th Infantry BCT when that unit
replaced Iowa's 2-34th BCT in June 2011.

After leaving the Army in 2012, Wilton attended Code Platoon,
Chicago, Ill., an intensive computer-programming instruction course for
veterans. He continues to work in the industry.

Adam L. Mathis was occasionally loaned to Task Force Red Bulls from
17th Mobile Public Affairs Detachment, an active-duty unit based in Fort
Lewis, Wash, to help Task Force Red Bulls cover for vacancies while other
public affairs team members were on mid-tour leave. Before joining the Army,
Mathis had completed a graduate degree in church studies from Gordon-
Conwell Theological Seminary, South Hamilton, Mass.; and an undergraduate
degree in history and journalism from Murray State University, Murray,
Kent.

"Mathis was very particular about things," Lolkus remembers. "He came
with his own coffee ... thing. It wasn't a French press. It had its own grinder. It
was like a science kit, with which he'd make coffee everyday. There was like this
net, and this squeegee thing. It blew my mind."

Mathis' attention to detail paid off. After leaving the Army in 2013,
Mathis joined the staff of Stars and Stripes, a U.S. Department of Defense
newspaper for military personnel and families. He was assigned to cover news
out of Royal Air Force (RAF) station Mildenhall, England.

Other soldiers and airmen, deputized as "Unit Public Affairs Representatives" (UPAR, pronounced "YOO-par") in addition to their other duties, also frequently contributed news content to the Task Force Red Bulls news team. "Those UPAR positions changed frequently. Some people weren't able to do much," says Task Force Red Bulls' Lolkus. "People like Rasmussen, however, really stepped up, and really helped us out."

Nicholas Rasmussen, of Omaha, Neb., was a physical therapy graduate student at the University of Iowa, who took on UPAR responsibilities while assigned as the medical officer for 1-168th Inf. The battalion was attached to a different brigade's command to Paktya Province. There, the unit was known as "Task Force Lethal," a term taken from the battalion headquarters' radio callsign. While the unit was not part of Task Force Red Bulls during the duration of its time in Afghanistan, the 2-34th BCT headquarters still provided a public affairs channel and resource for Task Force Lethal.

Our developing story

The 734th Agribusiness Development Team was deployed to Kunar Province, also in Eastern Afghanistan, but outside of AO Red Bulls. The 2-34th BCT and 734th ADT deployments overlapped. The "Dirt Warriors" arrived in country first, in July 2010. The Red Bulls arrived in November 2010.

Agribusiness Devlopment Teams were ad hoc organizations first designed and deployed into Afghanistan by the Missouri National Guard in 2007. In popular tradition, citizen-soldiers are celebrated for putting aside their metaphorical plows at home, and picking up their muskets in their nation's defense. For the first time, however, the ADT program formally leveraged the civilian-acquired expertise of farmers, veterinarians, business owners, and others, in their missions as soldiers and airmen.

"In many ways, 2010-2011 represented the zenith of the Agribusiness Development Team concept," says the 734th ADT's PAO Peter Shinn. "It didn't last long. The first ADT went over there was a Missouri unit, that went over there around 2008. By 2013, the last of them were all gone. It was a brief effort, but in 2011, there were ADTs in about 13 provinces over there."

Approximately one-third of the unit was respectively made up of agricultural experts, security teams, and unit headquarters command and staff. The Afghan people understood that they were there to help. Perhaps because of that, Shinn says, insurgent fighters seemed to avoid attacking the Iowans while they were out on missions. (The 734th ADT's personnel, proud of their Iowa roots, had painted Hawkeye symbols on their military vehicles.)

While committed to the unit's purpose—"the only reason that I was effective in delivering these messages was that I believed them," Shinn says— he was also a realist regarding how much could be done during one deployment.

Shinn tells of one his first interviews in Kunar, one with the provincial official in charge of land management. The ADT hoped to install a demonstration farm with the official's help. "I'm interviewing this gentlemen named Zabihulla, but I don't speak Pashto," Shinn says. "But I've got [an interpreter] there, and we get by. I take the video back, and I get it translated. It turns out, he's saying, 'We have no infrastructure. We have no society. We need everything. Everything in this province needs to be built, or re-built again ...'"

"It was at that moment that I realized," Shinn says, "what we were going to do here was all very nice and good, but that unless we were going to stay for about 100 years, chances were this would only be a very small beginning."

An overview of Task Force Red Bulls, 2010-2011

By Maj. Michael Wunn
Task Force Red Bulls Public Affairs

June 2011—The Iowa National Guard's 2nd Brigade Combat Team, 34th Infantry Division (2-34th BCT), which is the commanding element for "Task Force Red Bulls," mobilized for active duty August 2010. This historical deployment was the largest single mobilization for the Iowa National Guard since World War II. It included 2,800 Iowa National Guard Soldiers drawn from more than 25 armories across the state, nearly 350 Nebraska National Guard Soldiers, and was augmented by approximately 100 service members from various other states' National Guard and federal Army Reserve units.

Upon mobilization, the brigade reported to Camp Shelby, Miss., where it underwent six weeks of intense training and preparation before heading to the National Training Center at Fort Irwin, Calif., for its comprehensive mission validation exercise. The three-week training rotation proved both beneficial and challenging for brigade, but the Red Bull Soldiers successfully achieved the required benchmarks and NTC deemed them ready to deploy.

In October 2010, the Iowa brigade's lead elements began arriving in Afghanistan to begin relief-in-place operations with the 86th Infantry Brigade Combat Team (Mountain), "Task Force Wolverine," and its subordinate units.

The 2-34th BCT contributed two battalions to other commands: The 1st Squadron, 134th Cavalry Regiment (1-134th Cav.), "Task Force Fury," was assigned to Regional Command–Capital; while Iowa's 1st Battalion, 168th Infantry Regiment (1-168th Inf.), "Task Force Lethal," was assigned under the 3rd BCT, 101st Airborne Division's (3-101st BCT), "Task Force Rakkasans" in Paktya Province. When Task Force Rakkasans was later relieved-in-place in January 2011, control of Task Force Lethal was assigned to 3rd BCT, 1st Infantry Division (3-1st BCT), "Task Force Duke."

Task Force Red Bulls assumed responsibility of Task Force Wolverine's area of operations Dec. 4, 2010. This area initially included the provinces of Bamyan, Panjshir and Parwan. The Red Bulls soon turned over responsibility of Bamyan Province, however, to 4th BCT, 10th Mountain Infantry Division (4-10th BCT), "Task Force Patriot," and assumed responsibility for Laghman Province and three districts in northwest Nuristan Province from 1st BCT, 101st Airborne Div. (1-101st BCT), "Task Force Bastogne," later that month.

Task Force Red Bulls provided command and control over approximately 6,000 Soldiers, Airman and Coalition Force military personnel throughout its area of operations. Included in the task force were ...

- Two maneuver units: Iowa's 1st Battalion, 133rd Infantry

Regiment (1-133rd Inf.), "Task Force Ironman"; and 1st Squadron, 113th Cavalry Regiment (1-113th Cav.), "Task Force Redhorse."

- One support battalion: Iowa's 334th Brigade Support Battalion (334th BSB), "Task Force Archer," which was augmented by the 2-34th Brigade Special Troops Battalion (2-34th BSTB).
- Three Provincial Reconstruction Teams (PRT), including those from the Republic of Korea's PRT Parwan, and the United States's PRT Panjshir and PRT Laghman.
- Three Agribusiness Development Teams (ADT), including two iterations from the Kentucky National Guard, which covered Parwan, Panjshir and Kapisa provinces; and another from Kansas National Guard, which covered Laghman and Nuristan provinces.
- Three Operations Coordination Centers–Provincial (OCC–P), one each in Panjshir, Parwarn, and Laghman provinces.
- One Combat Service Support Advise and Assist Team.
- One brigade Tactical Action Center located at Forward Operating Base (FOB) Gamberi.

Task Force Red Bulls' area of operations was unique and complex. From the beauty and tranquility of Panjshir Province, to the hustle and bustle of Bagram Airfield (BAF) in Parwan Province, to the key district and strategic Highway 7 corridor in Laghman Province, this was one of the most diverse areas of Regional Command–East. Using its enabling and maneuver forces together, Task Force Red Bulls worked hard to improve security, enhance the credibility of Government of the Islamic Republic of Afghanistan (GIRoA), and spur development throughout its area of responsibility. These efforts led to the identification of two geographic areas as early candidates for beginning the transition to full Afghan responsibility: Panjshir Province and the Mehtar Lam Municipality. The latter is the Laghman provincial capital.

During Operation Enduring Freedom X-XI, Task Force Red Bulls completed nearly 27 named operations, including seven air assaults, along with individual battalion task forces conducting more than 4,544 unit-level patrols in Laghman, Parwan, and Panjshir, as well as portions of Nuristan province. Task Force Red Bulls units also conducted 865 Key Leader Engagements (KLE) and shuras with local village leaders.

Task Force Red Bulls conducted more than 360 artillery missions, delivering 3,015 rounds of indirect fire, including 131 missions in support of troops in contact (TIC). These missions were provided by firing platoons employing M-198 and M-120 weapon systems from seven Combat Outposts (COP) and Forward Operating Bases (FOB), spread across three provinces and almost 16,000 square kilometers. Additionally, the brigade "Fires" cell coordinated more than 250 hours of Close Air Support (CAS), including 30 TIC responses and 104 priority requests; supported 14 brigade and battalion-level named operations; and delivered 42,500 pounds of ordnance on enemy fighting positions.

Task Force Red Bulls was among the first units in the Army to employ the new EQ-36 counterfire RADAR system in prototype testing, with one RADAR crew operating one EQ-36 and one Q-36 simultaneously. Task Force Red Bulls Fires personnel operated these systems, in conjunction with nine lightweight counter-mortar RADAR (LCMR) systems, and the counter-rocket, artillery, and mortar (C-RAM) sense-and-warn system. Task Force Red Bulls Fires cell conducted extensive cross-boundary coordination with Task Force LaFayette, a French brigade task force, incorporating French capabilities into Task Force Red Bulls' operations.

In support of Task Force Red Bulls counterinsurgency operations (COIN) and Afghan National Security Force (ANSF) partnership programs, the Soldiers of the 334th Brigade Support Battalion conducted 300 Combat Logistics Patrols (CLPs) transporting supplies, services, and equipment forward to nine FOBs and COPs covering more than 16,000 square kilometers.

Throughout the deployment, logisticians coordinated the delivery of more than 900,000 pounds of mail, one million gallons of fuel, and more than 50,000 pounds of miscellaneous cargo. They assisted in the management over 1.5 million gallons of Class III [the U.S. Army's class-of-supply designation for petroleum, oil, and lubricants], and were responsible for the distribution and accountability of more than one million rounds of ammunition, including small arms, mortars, and anti-tank munitions. They monitored and tracked more than 7,000 work orders, ranging from weapons to wheeled vehicles. They coordinated the recovery of 25 battle-damaged vehicles, and provided units with a mission-capable replacement vehicles to prevent delays in those units' mission readiness postures. Task Force Red Bulls monitored maintenance trends and quickly established corrective actions for negative trends, which resulted in the readiness rating never falling below 95 percent at any time during the entire deployment.

Task Force Red Bulls made good use of its Commander's Emergency Response Program (CERP) funds, completing more than 90 projects, totalling more than $13 million dollars, and oversaw an additional 107 projects valued at approximately $111 million dollars. In conjunction with its overall strategy, Task Force Red Bulls focused on smaller, big-impact projects—those geared more toward meeting the basic needs of the population.

Laghman Province & Northwest Nuristan

This area was the most kinetic within AO Red Bulls. The 1-133rd Inf., "Task Force Ironman," was the battlespace owner for this province, and was the main maneuver force responsible for working with the Afghan National Security Forces to help secure the population living there. Task Force Ironman worked with a number of enabling elements, including the Laghman PRT and Kansas ADT, to build confidence within the municipal and provincial governments and foster development throughout the area.

Task Force Ironman maintained elements at strategic locations throughout this area: COP Xio Haq, COP Kalagush, COP Najil, FOB Mehtar Lam, and in the Alingar and Qarghay'l district centers. Security in Area of Operations Ironman varied. The southern part of the area, including Qarghah'I and Mehtar Lam, was generally secure, although attacks along Highway 7 occurred sporadically. In the northern areas of the province, Task Force Ironman elements worked hard to expand security in and around their COPs and FOBs through clearing and holding actions. Working side by side with their ANSF counterparts, Task Force Ironman worked hard to expand security throughout its area of operations.

On the governance side, Task Force Ironman and its enabling units worked closely with Provincial Gov. Mohammad Iqbal Azizi to identify and prioritize the needs of people within the province, and to use available resources to assist the provincial government. The Laghman PRT worked closely with provincial-level line directors to strengthen Technical Working Groups in support of the Afghan system. With President Karzai's announcement that Mehtar Lam Municipality would transition during the summer of 2011, PRT Laghman began planning and partnering with Gov. Azizi to ensure a successful handoff of security and governance within the area.

One of the most dramatic developments within Laghman was the creation of the new Bad Pech District. This effort involved the largest air-assault operation conducted by the 101st Airborne Division, operating as Combined Joint Task Force–101, during its year-long deployment to Afghanistan. The operation was accomplished primarily using soldiers from the Iowa Army National Guard. "Operation Bull Whip," as the mission was called, began March 25, 2011, when nearly 1,200 coalition and ASNF soldiers were inserted by helicopter into the southern portion of the Galuch Valley. The purpose of the operation was to get a foothold in the Galuch area, and establish a new district center in order to connect the government with the Afghans living in that area.

As "Task Force Phoenix," the 10th Combat Aviation Brigade, 10th Mountain Division provided helicopter transport for the mission. Soldiers from Task Forces Ironman and Lafayette cleared the valley, with the French brigade also providing artillery support from nearby Kapisa Province. Soldiers from Task Force Redhorse provided overwatch from the ridge lines surrounding the valley. Two platoons from 1-133rd Inf., one each from Alpha and Delta companies, each teamed with an Afghan National Army company from the 2nd Kandak, 1st Brigade, 201st ANA Infantry Corps. Working together, these Afghan and U.S. units cleared the valley on both sides from north to south, while the scout platoon and another ANA company provided a blocking position on the Southern end.

Numerous insurgents were detained during this operation, including one who was a known High-Value Target. Task Force Red Bulls discovered 13 weapon caches during the operation and destroyed IED making material, landmines, weapons (including Soviet-made DShK and PK heavy machine guns, and Kalashnikov assault rifles) and ammunition reserved for enemy use. Coalition forces also destroyed communications equipment used by the insurgents and conducted numerous KLE's during the 6-day operation. The operation concluded with a large shura organized and executed by Gov. Azizi, where he took concrete steps to connect his provincial government with the people of the area.

The Kansas ADT also played an important role in helping to bring development to Laghman Province and Northwest Nuristan. Their efforts included: exploring the viability of fish farming in the village of Charbaugh; working to identify agribusiness and other agricultural training opportunities for the women of Laghman Province; assessing the viability of introducing new varieties of grape vines, and techniques for growing them sustainably; assessing the potential for a micro-hydroelectric plants; providing female-centric agricultural training; proposing the creation and development of small agricultural test plots as a model of food security; and highlighting the government's commitment to reforestation projects in the province.

Parwan Province

In Parwan Province, Task Force Red Bulls focused on securing the Bagram Security Zone (BSZ), protecting the population, and supporting the ANSF. The battlespace owner for this province was 1-113th Cav., "Task Force Redhorse." Overall security in this area was good, though there were some insurgent attacks against Bagram Airfield (BAF) and in the Pashtun-dominated Koh-e Safi District in the south of the province. Task Force Redhorse soldiers located forces at BAF, COP Pushtaysark, COP Pul-e-Sayad, and at a Vehicle Patrol Base (VPB) located at Dandar in Koh-e Safi.

In addition to proving security around Bagram and establishing a presence in the southern portion of the province, Task Force Redhorse also took part in a number of security operations, including proving a Quick

Reaction Force (QRF) to help secure a downed U.S. helicopter crew—a "fallen angel" recovery mission. Throught the spring of 2011, Task Force Redhorse conducted a series of operations to clear insurgents and expand security south of Bagram Airfield into Koh-e Safi.

The Kentucky ADT played an important role in helping revitalize agriculture in Parwan, Panjshir, and Kapisa. By improving agricultural practices and expanding agribusiness opportunities for Afghan citizens, the Kentucky ADT helped to improve the Afghan standard of living, the stability of district and provincial governments, and ultimately helped to discourage the local population from supporting the insurgency. They conducted nearly 500 missions and oversaw the execution of more than $2 million in funding on nearly 130 projects. Projects included: restoring irrigation canals; improving vocational and collegiate-level agricultural education; introducing poultry and beekeeping business skills to impoverished women; creating markets for soybeans; founding grower's cooperatives; expanding fish farms; reforesting eroded mountain slopes; and teaching pruning techniques.

Also operating in Parwan, was the Republic of Korea PRT, which helped establish the Charikar base. The location housed the PRT and U.S. Civilian Military Assistance Team. These entities worked closely with the Parwan provincial government, on projects such as: an ambulance donation program; midwife education classes; Afghan National Police (ANP) training; and operating the Korean Hospital and the Korean Vocational Technical School. The Korean voactinal school provided hands-on training in five disciplines: automotive work, construction, welding, electrical work, and computer systems. The midwife program focused on instruction in normal childbirth, neonatal care, pediatric care, and recognition of emergency situations during childbirth. The midwife program is part of an attempt by the government and coalition forces to decrease the maternal and infant mortality rates.

In Feburary 2011, the Parwan PRT and Task Force Redhorse conducted a three-week training course for 20 ANP officers and Afghan National Army (ANA) soldiers at Bagram Airfield. The course was geared toward preparing trainees for the eventual transition of security responsibility to the Afghan National Security Forces.

Panjshir Province

Panjshir Province was one of the most peaceful and tranquil areas in Regional Command–East. Coalition forces were able to move about and operate using reduced force protection measures. The improved security situation allowed the Panjshir PRT and Embedded Training Team (ETT) to focus on building capacity of Afghan governmental institutions, and development projects focused on meeting the needs of ordinary Afghans.

Iowa National Guard Soldiers of the Panjshir ETT, 2-34th BCT, worked with the regional Operations Coordination Center–Provincial (OCC–P) to improve the Panjshir government's emergency winter-response planning. The OCC–P team consisted of Afghan National Army, Afghan National Police, and National Directorate of Security (NDS) officials, who represent their respective agencies for Panjshir Province. The U.S. Army ETT supported this team by working with each staff section in plans development and operations. Using the "Emergency Decision Matrix," a summarized version of the Iowa Emergency Management Response Plan, the ETT helped the OCC–P staffs develop a step-by-step procedures on how to respond to different emergencies, including winter weather related issues.

Under the Task Force Red Bulls' rule-of-law program, the Panjshir PRT assisted in the opening of three law libraries. The libraries include Afghan law reference books to assist members of the public in need of judicial help.

The Panjshir PRT also assisted in the improvement of drinking water. Using "self-help" and small scale CERP projects, the PRT was able to increase access to healthy drinking water and irrigation among a number of Panjshir villages. The projects included the construction of micro-hydro systems, a bridge with a retaining wall, and an irrigation and micro-hydro canal.

The PRT also spent a great deal of time visiting provincial medical clinics to discuss medical issues with clinic personnel and advise medical staff on ways to optimize their operations.

In order to improve security facilities in the area, the U.S. Army Corps of Engineers (USACE) constructed five additional ANP stations in the province located in Shutol, Anaba, Rohka, Dara and Paryan.

The Pansjhir PRT provided construction oversight to ensure quality of work in built projects, and conducted a hands-on construction workshop for Afghan engineers from the province. Afghans from 13 construction companies received classroom and practical application training during the weeklong workshop.

The PRT helped the Dara Community Development Council members—a group of local Afghans who address the needs of their community—fund and develop a local girls' school. The school teaches more than 150 Afghan females and is a part of a three-school complex which includes a boy's school.

The Panjshir ETT's Police Mentor Team (PMT) section held validation exercises for the seven district police agencies in Panjshir Province. The exercises tested the agencies in proper traffic control procedures and checkpoint operations. Panjshir ETT also helped ANP and NDS personnel investigate shots fired at a local ANP officer in Khenj District.

Bagram Airfield

Task Force Archer's mission was to provide Base Support Operations for Bagram Airfield (BAF). Task Force Archer was comprised soldiers and units of the following:

- Headquarters and Headquarters Company (HHC), 334th Brigade Support Battalion (BSB)
- Alpha Company (Distribution), 334th BSB
- Bravo Company (Maintenance), 334th BSB
- Charlie Company (Medical), 334th BSB
- HHC, 2-34th Brigade Special Troops Battalion (BSTB)
- Bravo Company (Military Intelligence), 2-34th BSTB
- Charlie Company (Signal), 2-34th BSTB
- HHC, 185th Combat Sustainment Suport Battalion (CSSB)
- 134th Medical Company

The task force managed the efficient use of more than 3,700 acres of land; provided safe bed space for more than 32,000 permanent party and transient residents; and processed nearly 10,000 work and service orders on behalf of a diverse tenant population of military, Department of Defense civilians, and contractors. The team consistently sought ways to improve the base, and the quality of life of residents and members of surrounding communities. They collaborated with Combined Joint Task Force–101 staff, military and civilian environmental engineers, and others to:

- Disseminate a comprehensive recycling plan.
- Terminate use of open burn pits on BAF.
- Establish a solid-waste management facility.
- Establish a COIN-centric composting program.

Another success was the expansion of the bazaar near Entry Control Point 1 (ECP-1). The command worked with key leaders in Parwan Province to help build the marketplace footprint, which resulted in more than $1 million to the local Afghan economy. Charlie Company, 334th BSB provided first-class medical support to a countless number of military and civilian personnel, treating more than 7,000 patients.

NOVEMBER -
DECEMBER 2010

Parwan DAIL hosts deworming conference

PARWAN PROVINCE, Afghanistan, Nov. 8, 2010—U.S. Army Col. James G. Floyd, veterinarian with the Kentucky Agribusiness Development Team and resident of Shreveport, La., prepares a presentation for a conference on sheep deworming with the Directorate of Agriculture, Irrigation, and Livestock from Panjshir, Kapisa, and Parwan and other members of the Kentucky ADT. (Photo by U.S. Army Sgt. 1st Class Peter Ferrell, Task Force Wolverine Public Affairs)

By U.S. Army Sgt. 1st Class Peter Ferrell
Task Force Wolverine Public Affairs

PARWAN PROVINCE, Afghanistan, Nov. 8, 2010—The Afghan Provincial Directors of Agriculture, Irrigation and Livestock for Kapisa, Parwan and Panjshir provinces, and Kentucky Agribusiness Development Team members met for a conference with the Parwan DAIL to discuss and demonstrate the benefits of deworming sheep, Nov. 8.

This conference brought the three provincial DAILs together to exchange ideas and learn about the Kentucky ADT's sheep deworming plan. "We will solve many problems by having the three province DAILs sit together and learn from each other," said Mohammad Husain, the Kapisa DAIL.

U.S Army Col. James G. Floyd, a veterinarian with the Kentucky ADT and Shreveport, La., resident, started the conference by explaining how he planned to complete the study of the sheep. His plan calls for studying one flock from each of the three provinces. Each flock needs between 30 and 50 sheep that have not previously been dewormed. The flocks must be from different parts of the province and the recruiting area must be secure and accessible year round. "This has not been done systematically in Afghanistan in many years," said Floyd.

Floyd said the sheep would be weighed by portable scales provided to each DAIL by the ADT. Then each ewe would be marked with numbered ear tags for each farmer and given deworming solution orally. This would be done a couple weeks before lambing. The study is only effective if the dose is administered by weight and records kept by farmers on the effects of the medication. "This is a good idea to have a workshop for farmers to learn to keep records, it is good to have this kind of progress in Panjshir," said Hashmatular Enayat, the Panjshir DAIL.

Initially, Floyd planned to leave 15 ewes untreated in order to show the benefits of deworming. However, during the conference, Floyd learned it would be difficult to find flocks that had never been dewormed in any of the three provinces. "You can not find a flock in the province that has not been dewormed at some time," said Enayat.

After hearing this, Floyd changed the test model to have all the ewes assessed and recorded as to their present state of resistance to parasites by four visible indicators: assessing the eyes for pink conjunctive, examining the jaw for any signs of swelling (a condition known as "bottle jaw"), assessing the overall body condition and looking for any signs of diarrhea.

Once assessed, all the ewes will be treated with deworming solution. The next step will be to monitor the ewes for signs showing the success of the deworming. "Along with raising healthier sheep, the farmers will also learn how to keep a record on their sheep. The farmers will realize this will benefit them, but they will also be helping other farmers," said Floyd.

The last step in measuring success of the deworming is to monitor the new lambs. Each farmer will be given a sling and scale to weigh the lamb as close to birth as possible. The lambs will be ear-tagged with reference to their mother and monitored for signs of resistance to parasites, said Shamir Amiri, the Parwan DAIL. "We need someone to come every month to train the farmers and make sure the farmers are following the steps correctly."

Laghman PRT, C Company 1-133 assess school damage

LAGHMAN PROVINCE, Afghanistan, Nov. 10, 2010—U.S. Army Capt. Garrett H. Gingrich from Waterloo, Iowa, commander of Company C ("Commando"), 1st Battalion, 133rd Infantry Regiment, takes notes at the Alingar District center here. The "Commandos" were investigating an incident in the district where anti-government elements burned supplies, including more than 400 copies of the Quran, at a girls' school in the district. The soldiers operate out of Combat Outpost Kalagush in Nuristan Province. (Photo by U.S. Air Force Chief Master Sgt. Richard Simonsen, Nuristan Provincial Reconstruction Team Public Affairs)

Cavalry Soldiers visit vehicle patrol base

PARWAN PROVINCE, Afghanistan, Nov. 18, 2010–U.S. Army 1st Sgt. John Digby, the first sergeant of Troop C, 1st Squadron, 172nd Cavalry Regiment, Task Force Wolverine, of Swanton, Vt., points out important terrain to U.S. Army 1st Sgt. Douglas Wilkens, the first sergeant of Troop B, 1st Squadron, 113th Cavalry Regiment, Task Force Red Bulls, from Howarden, Iowa, at a vehicle patrol base in the Koh-e Safi District of Parwan Province. The Soldiers visited the VPB to familiarize the 1st Squadron, 113th Cavalry Regiment with their area of responsibility. (Photo by U.S. Army Staff Sgt. Whitney Hughes, Task Force Wolverine Public Affairs, 86th Infantry Brigade Combat Team (Mountain))

Task Force Lethal assumes authority of Paktya vfrom Task Force Avalanche

PAKTYA PROVINCE, Afghanistan, Nov. 22, 2010—U.S. Army Lt. Col. Stephen B. Boesen II from Ankeny, Iowa, and U.S. Army Sgt. Maj. Duane Hinman from Craig, Neb., uncase the colors for Task Force Lethal, 1st Battalion, 168th Infantry Regiment, 2nd Brigade, 34th Infantry Division, to mark both the Transfer of Authority of Patyka province and the official beginning of the unit's nine-month deployment at Forward Operating Base Gardez. (Photo by U.S. Army 1st Lt. Nicholas Rasmussen, Task Force Lethal)

By U.S. Army 1st Lt. Nicholas Rasmussen
Task Force Lethal

PAKTYA PROVINCE, Afghanistan, Nov. 22, 2010—As Task Force Avalanche cased its colors, a new set of colors from Iowa were revealed at Forward Operating Base Gardez.

This event marked not only the passing of battlefield control from Avalanche to its successor, Task Force Lethal, but also a beginning to a new chapter for Paktya Province.

Task Force Lethal, 1st Battalion, 168th Infantry Regiment, is part of 2nd Brigade, 34th Infantry Division (Task Force Red Bulls) of the Iowa National Guard, but falls under the command of the 3rd Brigade Combat Team (Task Force Rakkasans), 101st Airborne Division, while deployed.

Task Force Lethal assumed responsibility as the battlespace owner for all of Patyka Province. Its mission is to assist their Government of the Islamic

Republic of Afghanistan and Afghan National Security Forces partners to create an environment that sets the conditions for progress across all lines of operation: security, governance and development.

Deputy Governor [Abdul Rahman] Mangal, Deputy Provincial Police Chief Gen. [Ghulam] Dastagir, Paktya National Defense Security Chief Gen. [Nazar Shah] Safi and Chief of Police Brig. Gen. [Abdal Rahma] Safi, all from Paktya Province, attended the ceremony.

Mangal's speech addressed his enthusiasm about working with Task Force Lethal to continue the headway made by Task Force Avalanche that provided stability and safety to Paktya and its people.

"Task Force Avalanche set the bar high by working effectively with the Afghan National Security Forces, (Afghan citizens), and public officials throughout Avalanche's deployment," said Task Force Rakkasans commander U.S. Army Col. Viet X. Luong of Fort Campbell, Ky., commander of Avalanche's operational headquarters.

The Avalanche team dedicated significant time and effort toward successfully winning the hearts and minds of the Afghan people; a theme Task Force Lethal plans to perpetuate throughout its campaign in Paktya Province, Luong said.

U.S. Army Lt. Col. Robert Charlesworth of Jericho, Vt., Task Force Avalanche commander, said, after careful and scrutinous observation of Task Force Lethal, he had the utmost confidence in handing over control of the province. He said he knows the effort and work he and his team accomplished would not be wasted.

U.S. Army Lt. Col. Stephen B. Boesen II of Ankeny, Iowa, Task Force Lethal commander, said the task force plans to continue the course of action that Task Force Avalanche sustained with the ambition to attain a greater synergy between coalition forces, ANSF, local nationals and public officials in Paktya.

Boesen said a major goal of Task Force Lethal is to work closely with the Afghan National Army, Afghan United Police, Afghan Border Police (ABP) and all other ANSF forces to facilitate the safety, development and autonomy of the ANSF and local populace in Paktya.

After the remarks were complete, hands were shaken and embraces were made, Task Force Avalanche made its way from the Transfer of Authority ceremony to the flight line and Task Force Lethal officially assumed command of Paktya Province, picking up where its predecessors left off.

Afghans meet new Cav troop commander at Pul-e-Sayad

PARWAN PROVINCE, Afghanistan, Nov. 19, 2010—U.S. Army Capt. Jack Lehneman of Milton, Vt., commander of Troop C, 1st Squadron, 172nd Cavalry Regiment, 86th Infantry Brigade Combat Team, shakes hands with village elder Tela Mohammad of the Sayed village after a Key Leader Engagement at Joint Combat Outpost Pul-e-Sayad. Lehneman visited the JCOP to introduce soldiers from Task Force Red Bulls to Mohammad and to further discuss issues in the area. (Photo by U.S. Army Spc. Kristina L. Gupton, Task Force Wolverine Public Affairs)

PARWAN PROVINCE, Afghanistan, Nov. 19, 2010—U.S. Army Capt. Corey Langman of Des Moines, Iowa, commander of Troop A, 1st Squadron, 113th Cavalry Regiment, 2nd Brigade Combat Team, 34th Infantry Division, greets an Afghan National Army soldier [...] Langman met and discussed issues with the village elder Tela Mohammad. (Photo by U.S. Army Spc. Kristina L. Gupton, Task Force Wolverine Public Affairs)

Training equips Afghan women to use poultry as income source

PARWAN PROVINCE, Afghanistan, Nov. 20, 2010—An Afghan woman waits to receive chickens after a graduation ceremony held at the Department of Women's Affairs compound located near Charikar. The graduation marked a successful completion of a course that taught women how to properly raise chickens as an additional source of income for their families. (Photo by U.S. Army Staff Sgt. Whitney Hughes, Task Force Wolverine Public Affairs)

By U.S. Army Staff Sgt. Ashlee Lolkus
Task Force Red Bulls Public Affairs

PARWAN PROVINCE, Afghanistan, Nov. 20, 2010—Afghan women received chickens and supplies after a graduation ceremony held at the Director of Women's Affairs compound located near Charikar.

The graduation marked a successful completion of a course set up to teach women how to properly raise chickens as an additional source of income for their families.

Twenty-five women attended the five-day course coordinated by the DOWA, the Agency for Building a New Afghanistan and the Kentucky Agribusiness Development Team.

"These women are very poor and they came here for help," said Saleha Zareen, the Parwan deputy director of women's affairs.

Each woman graduating from the class received nine hens, a rooster, chicken wire, 80 kilograms of feed, a waterier and two vaccinations for each chicken. These supplies should provide the women with enough resources to grow their stock to produce eggs and eventually raise more chickens to sell.

"This is a big deal for the women and they are very appreciative of what they are doing," said Zareen. "They come from their homes for the training. They are farmers and they are very happy and very excited. They have 10 birds now, but I would like them all to have 100 birds."

"This was a great event and we were very happy to be a part of it," said U.S. Army Maj. Bobbie Jo Mayes, women's empowerment coordinator, Kentucky ADT, and a Lawrenceburg, Ky. resident. "These are truly amazing women and I know they will do a great job taking care of their chickens."

The event was attended by people of the community, local media and Samya Azizi Sadat, a representative of parliament.

The Kentucky ADT and DOWA are planning similar training events in the future.

Company A, 832nd Engineer Company conduct cordon and search

PARWAN PROVINCE, Afghanistan, Nov. 23, 2010—U.S. Army Capt. Christopher Brooks (far left), commander of Company A, 86th Brigade Special Troops Battalion, 86th Infantry Brigade Combat Team and a Walpole, N.H., resident conducts a mission brief to inform his Soldiers and the unit that will be replacing them, the 832nd Engineer Company, attached to 1st Squadron, 113th Cavalry Regiment on an upcoming mission Nov. 22. Brooks uses a sand table to demonstrate the layout of the village [...] which may contain possible homemade explosives and bomb-making materials. (Photo by U.S. Army Spc. Kristina L. Gupton, Task Force Wolverine Public Affairs)

PARWAN PROVINCE, Afghanistan, Nov. 23, 2010—An Afghan National Army soldier and U.S. Army Pfc. Corey Coburn, a combat engineer with Company A, 86th Brigade Special Troops Battalion, 86th Infantry Brigade Combat Team and a Corinth, Vt., resident, provide security for fellow Soldiers while they conduct a cordon and search mission in Parwan Province [...] to look for possible homemade explosives and bomb making materials. (Photo by U.S. Army Spc. Kristina L. Gupton, Task Force Wolverine Public Affairs)

Fallen Guardsmen honored at building dedication

By U.S. Army Staff Sgt. Whitney Hughes
Task Force Wolverine Public Affairs

BAGRAM AIRFIELD, Afghanistan, Nov. 23, 2010—U.S. Army Staff Sgt. Steven Deluzio and U.S. Army Sgt. Tristan Southworth, both infantryman with Company A, 3rd Battalion, 172nd Infantry Regiment (3-172nd Inf.), 86th Infantry Brigade Combat Team, will be remembered by future troop rotations on Bagram Airfield thanks to new buildings dedicated in their names.

Two long, yellow barracks that will house future rotations of Soldiers on Bagram Airfield had their names changed to Deluzio and Southworth Halls, in honor of the Vermont Army National Guard Soldiers.

Deluzio, 25, a Glastonbury, Conn., native, and Southworth, 21, a Walden, Vt., native, died of wounds sustained during combat operations in Paktya Province Aug. 25.

At a dedication ceremony attended by Soldiers of Company A, 3-172nd Inf., and 86th IBCT leadership, Deluzio and Southworth were remembered for their loyalty and commitment to the mission in Afghanistan.

"We will take the memories of Staff Sgt. Deluzio and Sgt. Southworth with us for the rest of our lives because they were both such incredible individuals," said U.S. Army 1st Lt. Micah Kidney, the Company A executive officer from Enosburg Falls, Vt. "It is very nice to know that part of them, and their memory, will be left here as well because this is the country where they gave the ultimate sacrifice."

Once they arrive, plaques engraved with the image of the two Soldiers will be mounted on the buildings. In the meantime, pictures of the designs were unveiled during the ceremony to show what they will look like once they are complete.

"It means everything to (the Company A Soldiers) that their fallen brothers are not forgotten, and their sacrifices were not made in vain," said U.S Army Lt. Col. Robert Charlesworth, the 3-172nd Inf. commander from Jericho, Vt.

Red Bull soldiers celebrate Thanksgiving

BAGRAM AIRFIELD, Afghanistan, Nov. 25, 2010—U.S. Army Maj. Eric Wieland of Algoona, Iowa waits in line at the Dragon dining facility located here. The line to enter the dining facility was uncommonly long as many service members came for the large Thanksgiving spread. (Photo by U.S. Army Staff Sgt. Ashlee Lolkus, Task Force Red Bulls Public Affairs)

BAGRAM AIRFIELD, Afghanistan—U.S. Army Sgt. 1st Class Todd Edler, a Anamosa, Iowa resident and the food service contract officer representative for Headquarters and Headquarters Company, 2nd Brigade Combat Team, 34th Infantry Division Brigade Support Battalion works with food service contractors to ensure the food served for the Thanksgiving Day meal at the Dragon dining facility was up to standard [...] (Photo by U.S. Army Staff Sgt. Ashlee Lolkus, Task Force Red Bulls Public Affairs)

BAGRAM AIRFIELD, Afghanistan, Nov. 25, 2010—U.S. Army Sgt. Trae Blessing of Headquarters and Headquarters Company, 2nd Brigade Combat Team, 34th Infantry Division and Ames, Iowa resident, orders dessert for the Thanksgiving meal served at the Dragon dining facility located here. (Photo by U.S. Army Staff Sgt. Ashlee Lolkus, Task Force Red Bulls Public Affairs)

BAGRAM AIRFIELD, Afghanistan, Nov. 25, 2010—U.S. Army Pfc. Chris Faber, U.S. Army Spc. Theodore Dvorak and U.S. Army Staff Sgt. Timothy Zediker eat Thanksgiving Day meal at the Dragon dining facility located here. The dining facility was extra busy as many service members came for the large Thanksgiving spread. (Photo by U.S. Army Staff Sgt. Ashlee Lolkus, Task Force Red Bulls Public Affairs)

Building dedicated in honor of fallen Vermont guardsman

By Task Force Wolverine Public Affairs

PARWAN PROVINCE, Afghanistan, Nov. 27, 2010—U.S. Army Spc. Ryan Grady, a combat engineer with Company A, 86th Brigade Special Troops Battalion, 86th Infantry Brigade Combat Team, was honored with a new dining facility dedicated in his name.

Grady Dining Facility, located at Camp Warrior on Bagram Airfield, will soon open to serve troops. Grady, 25, was killed during combat operations in Parwan Province July 2, 2010.

At a dedication ceremony attended by Company A Soldiers and other member of the 86th IBCT, leaders spoke about Grady as a Soldier and a man.

Grady really made a difference in the lives of the people of Parwan, said U.S. Army Capt. Christopher Brooks, Company A commander and Walpole, N.H., resident. "I was honored to serve with a Soldier of his caliber."

The Bradford, Vt., based Company A, assigned to Task Force Morgan, was responsible for security in the Bagram Security Zone. In addition to security patrols, Company A Soldiers actively participated in local shuras, which addressed issues in villages around Bagram Airfield.

Grady's picture is slated to be put in the Hall of Heroes back at the Vermont National Guard Headquarters in Colchester, Vt.

A picture showing the design of the plaque that will be placed in honor of Grady was unveiled during the ceremony.

Delta Company, 334th BSB takes supplies to JCOP in Jabal Saraj

PARWAN PROVINCE, Afghanistan, Nov. 27, 2010—U.S. Army Sgt. Christopher Gosch, a wheeled-vehicle mechanic and Sioux City, Iowa, resident with Delta Company, 334th Brigade Support Battalion, operates a forklift to unload supplies from a heavy-expanded tactical truck at the Joint Combat Outpost in Jabal Saraj District. Company D brings water and wood to the JCOP to continue to upgrade the base where they will be permanently moving within the next month. (Photo by U.S. Army Spc. Kristina L. Gupton, Task Force Wolverine Public Affairs)

U.S. ambassador visits Gardez, discusses education, development, security

PAKTYA PROVINCE, Afghanistan, Nov. 29, 2010—Karl Eikenberry, center, U.S. ambassador to Afghanistan, greets local Afghans at Paktya University in Gardez, Paktya Province. The meeting at the university allowed Eikenberry to see the improvements made over the past few years. (Photo by U.S. Army Sgt. John P. Sklaney III, 2-45th Agribusiness Development Team)

By U.S. Army First Lt. Nicholas Rasmussen
Task Force Lethal

and Sgt. John P. Sklaney III
2-45th Agribusiness Development Team

PAKTYA PROVINCE, Afghanistan, Nov. 29, 2010—U.S. Ambassador to Afghanistan Karl Eikenberry visited Gardez, to see the progress in areas such as public schooling, educational facilities and security conditions within Paktya Province.

"The United States' job is to help the Afghans help themselves with solving issues in areas they need assistance with," said Eikenberry.

A joint effort by Team Paktya, which included elements from Task Force Lethal, 1st Battalion, 168th Infantry Regiment; 615th Military Police Company; 2-45th Oklahoma Agribusiness Development Team; and Paktya Provincial Reconstruction Team ensured Eikenberry travelled safely to the various events throughout his visit in Paktya Province.

At his first stop in Gardez, Eikenberry spoke at a ceremony for the Peiran

School. The construction and completion of this school was a project Paktya PRT recently helped facilitate.

Paktya PRT worked with the Hameed Kochai Construction Company, a firm composed of 80 percent Afghan employees, half of whom live within a short distance of the project.

Alongside Paktya Deputy Gov. Abdul Rahman Mangal, Eikenberry handed out school supplies to one male and one female student at the end of the ceremony.

Eikenberry then spent a working lunch discussing the current security status of Paktya with leaders from provincial security forces. The ambassador dedicated most of the meeting to learning what the Afghan National Security Forces and Paktya's government of the Islamic Republic of Afghanistan officials need to better serve the province's people.

A tour of Paktya University to exhibit projects Paktya's Oklahoma ADT is developing was the last stop for the ambassador during his visit in Gardez.

"Future projects at the university include self-sustained generator power, Internet access throughout the buildings, incorporating female students, and a faculty exchange program with Oklahoma State University," said U.S. Army Spc. Mandy Kennedy, from Ellsworth, Wis., education specialist for the Oklahoma ADT.

Eikenberry toured the university grounds, hearing from officials about current and future infrastructure projects including bringing reliable power and internet to the school.

Culminating his time at the university, Eikenberry conducted a shura with local elders about governance, development and security issues. Topics ranged from the construction of the road between Khost and Gardez, the necessity and effectiveness of night time raids by coalition forces and general security conditions in the province.

In a press conference held outside the university's main building after the shura, Eikenberry highlighted the benefits of constructing the K-G Road.

"With that road comes better security," Eikenberry said. "With that road comes better education and healthcare. With that road comes better economy and commerce. With that road comes hope for the future. That's why the enemy doesn't want that road, because they fear hope."

Leaders from Team Paktya said the ambassador's visit was a success.

"This mission is crucial to showing the good the U.S. has been able to accomplish over the past few years," said U.S. Army Col. Robert Roshell, from Lawton, Okla., commander of the ADT.

"Ambassador Eikenberry's visit brings an increased visibility to exactly what can be accomplished, and help in revitalizing the Afghan agriculture in the province," Roshell said.

Kentucky ADT attends as 25 women graduate from poultry class

KAPISA PROVINCE, Afghanistan, Nov. 30, 2010—U.S. Army Col. Hunter J. Mathews, a Lexington, Ky., resident and commander of the Kentucky Agribusiness Development Team, speaks to the graduating class at the Kapisa Directors of Women's Affairs compound. Mathews congratulated the 25 women on their hard work and dedication in completing the five-day course that is designed to help them provide for their families for years to come. The course taught the women how to raise and sell chickens. They were given nine hens and a rooster to help jump-start their entrepreneurship. (Photo by U.S. Army Spc. Kristina L. Gupton, Task Force Red Bulls Public Affairs)

KAPISA PROVINCE, Afghanistan, Nov. 30, 2010—U.S. Army Maj. Bobbie Jo Mayes, Women's Empowerment coordinator with the Kentucky Agribusiness Development Team and a resident of Lawrenceburg, Ky., greets one of the teachers from the Agency for Building a New Afghanistan during a visit to the Kapisa Department of Women's Affairs. Mayes and other members of Kentucky ADT visited the DOWA to attend the graduation of 25 women from a five-day poultry class on how to raise and sell chickens. (Photo by U.S. Army Spc. Kristina L. Gupton, Task Force Red Bulls Public Affairs)

Task Force Morgan hands reins to Task Force Redhorse

PARWAN PROVINCE, Afghanistan, Nov. 30, 2010—Task Force Redhorse squadron and troop leadership and guidon bearers present arms while the national anthem is played during the Transfer of Authority ceremony here. Task Force Redhorse is primarily comprised of Iowa National Guard Soldiers from the 1st Squadron, 113th Cavalry Regiment based out of Sioux City, Iowa. (Photo by U.S. Army Sgt. Charles Espie, Task Force Wolverine Public Affairs)

By U.S. Army Staff Sgt. Ashlee Lolkus
Task Force Red Bulls Public Affairs

PARWAN PROVINCE, Afghanistan, Nov. 30, 2010—In a ceremony ripe with military tradition, 1st Squadron, 113th Cavalry Regiment of the 2nd Brigade Combat Team, 34th Infantry Division and the Iowa National Guard, provided relief in place to 1st Squadron, 172nd Cavalry Regiment, of the 86th Infantry Brigade Combat Team and the Vermont National Guard, during a Transfer of Authority hand-off on Bagram Airfield.

The units, also known as Task Force Redhorse and Task Force Morgan respectively, trained together for the past few weeks preparing Task Force Redhorse Soldiers for the missions that lie ahead of them. Task Force Redhorse assumes responsibility of Bagram Airfield and Parwan Province security.

"You have much to be proud of," said U.S Army Col. William F. Roy, Task Force Wolverine commander and Jericho, Vt. resident, addressing Task Force Morgan Soldiers. "Whether it was building bridges, both figuratively and literally, as well conducting combined operations with the ANSF... what you have done has truly made a difference here."

Throughout their deployment, Task Force Morgan accomplished many missions and reacted to numerous insurgent attacks, including the insurgent attack launched on Bagram Airfield May 19, where 16 insurgents were killed and five other detained.

"For Task Force Redhorse, I wish you the very best at your mission," said Roy. "Never forget, we are guests here, and our ultimate goal is to leave Afghanistan better than we found it."

"Task Force Redhorse mobilized with this mission in mind," said U.S. Army Lt. Col. David A. Updegraff, Task Force Redhorse commander and Wauconda, Ill., resident. "I believe that we are currently ready to take this mission and use the success that Task Force Morgan has shown as a spring board to further the coalition goals in Parwan and the BAF security zone."

The Iowa National Guard Soldiers will pick where the Vermont National Guard Soldiers left off in Parwan Province by working with and assisting Afghans to better the communities and provide security in the Task Force Redhorse area of operations.

Legal library opens in Salang District Center

PARWAN PROVINCE, Afghanistan, Nov. 30, 2010—Afghan students take a test in an outdoor classroom at the K-12 school in the Salang District Center here. The students and teachers of this school were invited to attend the dedication ceremony of a new legal library opening in the district center, which they will also be able to use for research and studying. (Photo by U.S. Army Spc. James Wilton, Task Force Red Bulls Public Affairs)

By U.S. Army Spc. James Wilton
Task Force Red Bulls Public Affairs

SALANG DISTRICT, Afghanistan, Nov. 30, 2010—The Afghan Ministry of Information and Culture held a dedication ceremony for a legal library in the Salang District Center here. The legal library was one of three that opened in the province this week.

Prominent Afghan figures in attendance included the Salang District police chief, members of the district police force, and local attorneys and judges to include Al Hajj Mului Abdul Satar Ghafari, a retired district judge who brought 80 copies of his new book to donate to the library. The district governor and shura members also attended. Teachers and students from the school located in the district center were invited. These students will be able to use the library for research and studying. U.S. Army attorneys from Task Force Wolverine were in attendance to support their Afghan counterparts in the legal sector.

"Libraries are a critical component in any society, creating a culture of literacy and learning, stimulating change and arming the citizenry with the power and tools necessary to fight corruption in its government," said U.S. Army Capt. Adam Bushey, from Syracuse, N.Y., a rule of law attorney for Task

Force Wolverine on Bagram Airfield. "Knowledge is power; with it, the Afghan citizens can hold the government responsible and accountable for their actions."

The ministries project plans for nine legal libraries in the provinces of Parwan, Bamyan and the first public library in Panjshir. The library project is intended to educate the Afghan people in the laws and rules that govern their country. This project puts the resources and tools necessary for education in the hands of Afghan people, often for the first time.

"Salang is one of the poorer districts and because of that we didn't have the same education opportunities in the past," said Maj. Gul Aba, the chief of police for the Salang District. "We give you the assurance that we are very interested in education. This opportunity is a good start for our youth to have this opening of the library."

The project receives funding from Task Force Wolverine's Commanders Emergency Response Program. The funding was used to purchase about 250 legal texts per library, and to provide shelves, tables, chairs and other materials used to refurbish the spaces. The dedication ceremony included a lunch provided to all in attendances.

SALANG DISTRICT, Afghanistan, Nov. 30, 2010— Barbalay Seddiqi, an Afghan attorney, and U.S. Army Capt. Adam Bushey, a Syracuse, N.Y., native and the rule-of-law attorney with Task Force Wolverine, cut a ribbon at the entrance of a legal library dedication in the Salang District Center in Afghanistan. The Afghan Ministry of Information and Culture held the dedication ceremony to celebrate the opening of the third legal library in Parwan (Photo by U.S. Army Spc. James Wilton, Task Force Red Bulls Public Affairs)

832nd Engineer Company conducts patrol in Dolatshi village

PARWAN PROVINCE, Afghanistan, Dec. 2, 2010—U.S. Army Sgt. Jody Ross with 2nd platoon 832nd Engineer Company, attached to 1st Squadron, 113th Cavalry Regiment and a Keokuk, Iowa, resident, poses for a picture with a group of young Afghan boys in the Dolatshi village where while Soldiers conduct a patrol. The platoon visited the village to conduct a patrol to ensure security within the village. (Photo by U.S. Army Spc. Kristina L. Gupton, Task Force Wolverine Public Affairs)

PARWAN PROVINCE, Afghanistan—U.S. Army Soldiers with 2nd platoon 832nd Engineer Company out of Mt. Pleasant, Iowa, attached to 1st Squadron, 113th Cavalry Regiment, conduct a patrol during a visit to the Dolatshi village. The platoon visited the village to conduct a patrol to ensure security within the village. (U.S. Army Photo by Spc. Kristina L. Gupton, Task Force Wolverine Public Affairs)

President Obama makes surprise visit to Bagram Airfield

BAGRAM AIRFIELD, Afghanistan, Dec. 3, 2010—President Obama made a surprise visit to Bagram Airfield, Afghanistan where he thanked all of the service members and civilians for their hardwork and dedication. The trip was part of an overall trip to meet with Afghanistan President Hamid Karzai. (Photo by U.S. Army Sgt. David House, 17th Public Affairs Detachment.)

BAGRAM AIRFIELD, Afghan, Dec. 3, 2010—President Barack Obama sends a holiday message to servicemembers during his surprise visit to Bagram Airfield. (Photo by U.S. Army Staff Sgt. Michael L. Sparks, 17th Public Affairs Detachment)

BAGRAM AIRFIELD, Afghanistan, Dec. 3, 2010—Sgt. Harold Dudley of Des Moines, Iowa, Task Force Red Bull, sings the national anthem during President Barack Obama's surprise visit to Bagram Airfield, Afghanistan. (Photo by U.S. Army Sgt. David House, 17th Public Affairs Detachment)

Red Bulls assume Wolverine's AO

BAGRAM AIRFIELD, Afghanistan, Dec. 4, 2010—U.S. Army Col. William F. Roy and U.S. Army Command Sgt. Maj. Forest Glodgett, both from Jericho, Vt., commander and command sergeant major of the 86th Infantry Brigade Combat Team, Task Force Wolverine, case the Task Force Wolverine colors during a Transfer of Authority ceremony at Bagram Airfield. The ceremony signified the 2nd Brigade Combat Team, 34th Infantry Division, Task Force Red Bulls, assumption of authority of Task Force Wolverine's area of operation in Regional Command–East. (Photo by U.S. Army Spc. James Wilton, Task Force Red Bulls Public Affairs)

By U.S. Army Spc. James Wilton
Task Force Red Bulls Public Affairs

PARWAN PROVINCE, Afghanistan, Dec. 4, 2010—The 2nd Brigade Combat Team, 34th Infantry Division assumed responsibility for full-spectrum operations in eastern Afghanistan from the 86th Infantry Brigade Combat Team during a Transfer of Authority ceremony at Bagram Airfield.

The ceremony marked the departure of Task Force Wolverine of the Vermont National Guard, and begins the rotation of Task Force Red Bulls of the Iowa National Guard in support of Operation Enduring Freedom.

The Soldiers were joined by U.S. Army Maj. Gen. John F. Campbell, commander of Combined Joint Task Force–101 and Regional Command–East, and distinguished visitors from Afghanistan including Gov. Abdul Salangi from Parwan.

Also in attendance was Maj. Gen Abdual Rahimi Jalil from the Operations Coordination Center–Provincial Parwan, and the commanders of the 1st Brigade, 201st ANA Infantry Corps, and the Parwan police district.

Campbell commented on the achievements and challenges Task Force Wolverine faced during its rotation. Task Force Wolverine worked with various Provincial Reconstruction Teams and Agribusiness Development Teams, coalition task forces and other enablers to build governance, improve the infrastructure and both train security forces and work with them to secure their area of operation. Their mission improved the quality of life for the Afghan people and the safety and security of the country.

"All of these successes were designed to build the capacity and capability of the Afghan National Security Forces and the local government so they could meet the basic needs of the Afghan people," Campbell said. "By creating the most secure provinces in Regional Command–East, Task Force Wolverine poised the leadership of these provinces for success."

Campbell wished Task Force Wolverine a safe trip home and welcomed Task Force Red Bulls to Afghanistan, stating his confidence in their ability build on the successes Task Force Wolverine had while here.

"I have seen many of the Task Force Red Bulls soldiers in my battlefield circulation and I can tell you first hand that they are well disciplined and well-trained," said Campbell. "I am confident standing here today that Task Force Red Bulls is exactly the right unit to continue the mission and the successes Task Force Wolverine carried on."

U.S. Army Col. William F. Roy, Task Force Wolverine commander, headquartered in Williston, Vt., addressed his counterpart U.S. Army Col. Benjamin J. Corell, a Strawberry Point, Iowa native and Task Force Red Bulls commander.

Roy stated his hope for Task Force Red Bulls to continue their mission of assisting the Afghan government in developing their capability and capacity to support the Afghan people.

"It is truly an honor to turn this mission over to you and your team," Roy said. "We have done all we can in the time we have had. But there is still much left to be done. I can think of no finer brigade to turn this mission over to than the mighty Red Bulls. We wish you the best of luck and Godspeed in the days ahead."

Corell spoke to the Soldiers about his expectations of the mission ahead and the importance of working together with the Afghans and other coalition forces to build a brighter future for the Afghan people and improve the quality for all Afghan citizens.

"Task Force Red Bulls, we start a new chapter in the history of this historic Red Bull division," said Corell. "As we take over the full weight of this mission, we know we can count on our coalition partners and Afghan brothers to help us meet our common goal ... Together, this team will continue the work of Task Force Wolverine and build on the successes that they have had."

BAGRAM AIRFIELD, Afghanistan, Dec. 4, 2010—U.S. Army Col. Benjamin J. Corell, commander of 2nd Brigade Combat Team, 34th Infantry Division, and a Strawberry Point, Iowa, native, speaks during a Transfer of Authority ceremony at Bagram Airfield. The ceremony marks the departure of the 86th Infantry Brigade Combat Team, Task Force Wolverine and begins Task Force Red Bulls' rotation in support of Operation Enduring Freedom. (Photo by U.S. Army Spc. James Wilton, Task Force Red Bulls Public Affairs)

BAGRAM AIRFIELD, Afghanistan, Dec. 4, 2010—U.S. Army Col. Benjamin J. Corell, 2nd Brigade Combat Team, 34th Infantry Division, Task Force Red Bulls commander and a Strawberry Point, Iowa, native, speaks with two Afghan generals [...] (Photo by U.S. Army Spc. James Wilton, Task Force Red Bulls Public Affairs)

BAGRAM AIRFIELD, Afghanistan, Dec. 4, 2010—U.S. Army Col. William F. Roy, 86th Infantry Brigade Combat Team, Task Force Wolverine commander, headquartered in Williston, Vt., shakes hands with Parwan Provincial Governor Abdul Salangi after being presented with a traditional Afghan robe as a gift [...] The governor's gift symbolized [Salangi's] thanks for the Task Force Wolverine's work to build the capacity and capability of the local government to better meet the needs of the Afghan people. (Photo by U.S. Army Spc. James Wilton, Task Force Red Bulls Public Affairs)

Breaking new ground: Red Bull engineers aid village mosque construction

PARWAN PROVINCE, Afghanistan, Dec. 6, 2010—U.S. Army Sgt. Shane Jobe, a combat engineer and team leader from Burlington, Iowa, with the 832nd Engineer Company attached to 1st Squadron, 113th Cavalry Regiment, Task Force Redhorse, loads a cricket set into the back of a Mine-Resistant, Ambush-Protected vehicle on Bagram Airfield here. The cricket sets were delivered to a school in Bajawri. (Photo by U.S. Army Staff Sgt. Ryan C. Matson, Task Force Red Bulls Public Affairs)

By U.S. Army Staff Sgt. Ryan C. Matson
Task Force Red Bulls Public Affairs

PARWAN PROVINCE, Afghanistan, Dec. 6, 2010—What do the towns of Keokuk, Iowa and Bajawri, Afghanistan have in common? For centuries, it was probably very little. But now, they are working together to construct a mosque in the village of Bajawri.

Soldiers from 2nd Platoon, 832nd Engineer Company, based out of Keokuk, Iowa, and attached to 1st Squadron, 113th Cavalry Squadron, Task Force Redhorse, traveled to the small village of Bajarwi here. The Soldiers went to the village to check the progress of a mosque being constructed that they were donating materials toward. The Soldiers are all part of the Iowa National Guard's 2nd Brigade Combat Team, 34th Infantry Division, Task Force Red Bulls.

"There was a project proposed by a local leader to help build a mosque in the village," U.S. Army 1st Lt. Benjamin J. Davis, 2nd Platoon leader and

Creston, Iowa, resident, explained. "The project was a carryover from the unit we replaced."

Several months ago, Company A, 1st Squadron, 172nd Cavalry Regiment, Task Force Morgan—the unit the 832nd replaced—met with local mailk Sayad Kareem. Kareem represents 19 villages east of Bagram Airfield. In the village of Bajarwi, Kareem said the villagers wanted to build a mosque to hold worship services.

"The people of Bajarwi did not have a mosque and were not able to get together and pray," Kareem said. "Everyone in the village is happy and appreciative that the coalition has been able to support the construction of the mosque. Our economy is not that good, and that is why we could not build it completely by ourselves and requested the help of the coalition."

Aiding in the construction of a mosque is a rather unique undertaking for coalition forces.

"It's very rare that U.S. or coalition forces would get to participate in the construction of a mosque," said U.S. Army Capt. Timothy A. Creasman, Boone, Iowa, native and 1st Squadron, 113th Cavalry Regiment, civil-military operations officer.

Creasman said the villages are more likely to approach the coalition for assistance in education and quality-of-life issues as opposed to religious needs. Both the citizens of Bajarwi and the Soldiers from the 832nd Engineer Company said they look at the mosque construction as a step in an improved partnership between the local citizens and coalition forces.

During their trip to the mosque Dec. 2, the 832nd Engineer Company took the opportunity to appraise the construction of the mosque, as well as to supervise the delivery of 100 additional bags of cement toward the mosque construction. A local Afghan contractor delivered the cement to the village.

The perimeter walls of the mosque are complete. They are made of red brick and mortar and laid by Bajarwi resident Mirzamin Ahmad-Zai. The walls exemplify Ahmad-Zai's craftsmanship and feature elaborate arches along the sides of the building.

"I did it in five months, a little at a time, and continued working as I got materials," Ahmad-Zai said. "This was my first mosque."

Ahmad-Zai also added that members of each household in the village donated money toward construction of the mosque, and those who could not contribute money, sent family members to help with the labor.

As they stared at the walls, the Soldiers said they were amazed at Ahmad-Zai's building skills.

To finish the mosque, Kareem said the building requires five tons of 16 millimeter rebar, which Creasman said the coalition will look into helping provide.

Abdul Rahim Mazai, Bajawri's malik, said the Red Bulls are carrying on the partnership of the village shared with Task Force Morgan and he cannot express the gratitude he and the villagers feel.

"The coalition forces came here and talked to us," he said. "They listened to our problems and provided us some assistance. This mosque was built by our people through the help of the coalition forces and the Red Bulls with materials. We hope to continue to work together, here and throughout Afghanistan."

Davis said 2nd Platoon meets with maliks and local villagers on an almost daily basis since they arrived here almost a month ago. The engineers, led by U.S. Army Capt. Scott E. Hansen, of Maquoketa, Iowa, have assumed responsibility for providing security to 120 villages, all of which fall within a 10-kilometer area of the Bagram District. Davis said the unit also tries to help the villagers with their daily needs and to improve their quality of life, as was the case with aiding in the mosque construction in Bajawri.

"We're trying to capture the human factor," Davis said. "We can't really understand what the people here need and how they operate without being amongst the people. They are getting more comfortable talking with us and realizing they don't need to be scared of us."

The Red Bulls engineers' visit did not end with the trip to the mosque. From there, the Soldiers walked with the villagers to the school at the opposite end of town.

U.S Army Capt. Joshua MacLean, 1st Squadron, 113th Cavalry Regiment information officer and Ottumwa, Iowa, resident, spoke with Kareem on a previous visit to Bajawri. Kareem mentioned there were 2,000 children attending the school, and that they enjoy playing cricket.

MacLean acquired eight cricket sets from the outgoing unit, complete with helmets, pads, balls and racquets, for the children of the school. The engineers delivered the sets to Nassar Ehmad, the school's principle.

"They like to play cricket," Davis said, "It shows them we are here to help."

Before the Soldiers left, Kareem told them he would set up further meetings whenever they wanted to meet with him and include the other maliks of the surrounding villages.

"We hope to have a great partnership with the Red Bulls," Mazai said, summing up the sentiments of the Soldiers and his townspeople.

PARWAN PROVINCE, Afghanistan, Dec. 6, 2010—U.S Army Capt. Joshua MacLean, 1st Squadron, 113th Cavalry Regiment information officer and Ottumwa, Iowa, resident, and Abdul Rahim Mazai, malik of the town of Bajawri, shake hands outside a mosque in the village here. The 832nd Engineer Company delivered 100 bags of cement to the village to help the citizens finish their mosque. (Photo by U.S. Army Staff Sgt. Ryan C. Matson, Task Force Red Bulls Public Affairs)

PARWAN PROVINCE, Afghanistan, Dec. 6, 2010—U.S. Army Sgt. 1st Class Todd Sackman, a platoon sergeant with the 832nd Engineer Company from Ottumwa, Iowa, shares a laugh with a group of Afghan boys in the town of Bajawri here. The 832nd Engineer Company delivered 100 bags of cement to the village to help the citizens finish their mosque. (Photo by U.S. Army Staff Sgt. Ryan C. Matson, Task Force Red Bulls Public Affairs)

832nd Engineers meet with leader, discuss development

PARWAN PROVINCE, Afghanistan, Dec. 7, 2010—U.S. Army 1st Lt. Benjamin J. Davis of Ankeny, Iowa, 2nd Platoon leader and combat engineer with 832nd Engineer Company, attached to 1st Squadron, 113th Cavalry Regiment, greets Hajji Asad at his restaurant. Asad was one of the representatives of the Qarah-Bagh Shura. The 832nd Engineer Company. visited to discuss economic development and projects to clean out irrigation canals in the Qarah-Bagh District. (Photo by U.S. Army Spc. Kristina L. Gupton, Task Force Red Bulls Public Affairs)

PARWAN PROVINCE, Afghanistan, Dec. 7, 2010—U.S. Army Sgt. 1st Class Todd Sackman of Ottumwa, Iowa, combat engineer with 832nd Engineer Company, attached to 1st Squadron, 113th Cavalry Regiment, uses Handheld Interagency Identity Detection Equipment to identify Afghans during a Key Leader Engagement in Qarah-Bagh District. The HIIDE system is a biometric identification database where Soldiers can easily input the local Afghan's information to identify them by scanning their iris and fingerprints. (Photo by U.S. Army Spc. Kristina L. Gupton, Task Force Red Bulls Public Affairs)

Campbell talks security, governance with Team Paktya

*PAKTYA PROVINCE, Afghanistan, Dec. 8, 2010—*U.S. Army Maj. Gen. John F. Campbell, Combined Joint Task Force 101 and Regional Command East commander, attends a briefing at Forward Operating Base Gardez Dec. 8. Base leaders briefed the commander about counterinsurgency operations conducted in Paktya Province. (Photo by U.S. Air Force Staff Sgt. Barry Loo, Paktya Provincial Reconstruction Team Public Affairs)

By U.S. Army 1st Lt. Nicholas Rasmussen
Task Force Lethal

PAKTYA PROVINCE, Afghanistan, Dec. 8, 2010—Maj. Gen. John F. Campbell, Combined Joint Task Force 101 and Regional Command East commander, visited Forward Operating Base Gardez to meet with Team Paktya's board of directors Dec. 8 to discuss counterinsurgency operations in Paktya and the future of the provincial governance.

Campbell had two main points to impress upon Team Paktya, which includes 1st Battalion, 168th Infantry Regiment, Paktya Provincial Reconstruction Team, Oklahoma Agribusiness Development Team, U.S. Department of State, U.S. Department of Agriculture and the U.S. Agency for International Development.

His first point was to provide guidance for project focus.

"You're doing a lot of good things here," Campbell said after hearing plans to establish different programs in Paktya, such as organized sports and courses on agriculture at Paktya University.

Campbell said he has seen units in the past spread their efforts on too many projects, leading to an overwhelming amount of work for the units and resulting in unfinished projects.

Campbell's guidance to the members of Team Paktya was to pick a few projects with good potential and focus to fully develop them.

"This will be a more effective way to engage and help the local population in the long run," Campbell said.

The second point Campbell made to Team Paktya was to ensure the people in control of governance in Paktya are right for the job.

To do this, Campbell said Team Paktya needs to work as a cohesive group. Herve Thomas of German Town, Md., a member of USAID on Team Paktya, said the future of the team is bright.

"More importantly," said Thomas, "there is a good understanding of what each unit is doing ... as demonstrated by the way the team comes together to solve issues."

Campbell offered the floor to the members of Team Paktya and listened as the members expressed what they feel needs to be done in the province to facilitate progress.

Team Paktya as a whole appreciated the opportunity to interact with Campbell and present their plans to help Paktya Province progress toward a better way of life.

"It was a great opportunity for Maj. Gen. Campbell to come out and amplify his guidance to Team Paktya to stay on azimuth with the (CJTF–101) campaign plan," said U.S. Army Lt. Col. Stephen B. Boesen II, Task Force Lethal commander from Ankeny, Iowa.

60 Panjshir families get healthy drinking water

PANJSHIR PROVINCE, Afghanistan, Dec. 8, 2010—Deputy Gov. Abdul Rahman Kabiri, Head of Panjshir Community Development Council Mawlavi Suleiman, Panjshir Director of Women's Affairs Mariam Panjshiri and Ahmad Shah Massoud's father-in-law, Tajuddin, cut a ribbon with Dah-e-Manjur villagers to signify the completion of a drinking-water project in Bazarak Municipality here. The project provides healthy drinking water to 60 families in the Dah-e-Manjur village. (Courtesy photo by Ahmad Siar Yousufzai)

By U.S. Air Force 2nd Lt. Ashleigh Peck
Panjshir Provincial Reconstruction Team

PANJSHIR PROVINCE, Afghanistan, Dec. 8, 2010—Thanks to a little self-help and the support of the Panjshir Provincial Reconstruction Team, 60 families in the Bazarak Municipality now have access to healthy drinking water.

The project, located in Dah-e-Manjur village, consists of a reservoir and a network of pipes more than 1,000 meters long. The villagers dug trenches 80 centimeters below the surface to prevent the pipes from freezing during the winter months, said Mawlavi Suleiman, head of Panjshir Community Development Council.

Panjshir Deputy Gov. Abdul Rahman Kabiri and Suleiman spoke during a ribbon-cutting ceremony in Bazarak Municipality here Dec. 8.

Dah-e-Manjur Mayor Bakshii, Panjshir Director of Women's Affairs Mariam Panjshiri, Panjshir U.S. Agency for International Development Ramp Up Team leader Khalil Rahmani, Ahmad Shah Massoud's father-in-law,

Tajuddin, Panjshir PRT members and local villagers attended the ceremony to celebrate the opening of the clean drinking water project.

Kabiri emphasized the importance of self-help projects during his opening remarks.

"We shouldn't wait for other people; we should wake up and be active. Instead of waiting for others, we need to build Panjshir ourselves together as Panjshiris," said Kabiri, through an interpreter.

"The drinking water project was submitted through the CDC and implemented in July. The villagers built the reservoir as a self-help project. The cement was paid for by PRT bulk funds," said U.S. Army 1st Lt. Hakan Togul, Panjshir civil affairs Officer-in-Charge.

"The contractor originally asked for $30,000 but with self-help, the cost of the project was less than $5,000," said Suleiman.

"Even in times of despair, Panjshiris always rise up to the challenge," said Suileman.

Following the day's events, Tajuddin hosted the deputy governor, village mayor, CDC and PRT members along with other guests in his home for tea.

PANJSHIR PROVINCE, Afghanistan, Dec. 8, 2010—The first home to gain access to the Dah-e-Manjur water well is connected after the ribbon-cutting ceremony in Bazarak Municipality here. The home belongs to Ahmad Shah Massoud's father-in-law, Tajuddin, and his home is one of 60 that now has access to healthy drinking water. The self-help project started in July after it was submitted through the Community Development Council. (Courtesy photo by Ahmad Siar Yousufzai)

Bravo Troop provides overwatch security

PARWAN PROVINCE, Afghanistan, Dec. 9, 2010—U.S. Air Force Staff Sgt. Chad Hutton, a Chillicothe, Ohio, resident and U.S. Air Force Staff Sgt. Mario Cantu, a Blairs, Va., resident, both of the tactical air control party with 169th Air Support Operations Squadron (ASOS), check their radios before heading out on a joint patrol with Bravo Troop, 1st Squadron, 113th Cavalry Regiment through the village of Dandar. Bravo Troop visited the village to conduct a patrol and to establish a relationship with the village malik and elders. (Photo by U.S. Army Spc. Kristina L. Gupton, Task Force Red Bulls Public Affairs)

PARWAN PROVINCE, Afghanistan, Dec. 9, 2010—U.S. Army Sgt. Brian Denery, a Cherokee, Iowa, resident and fire support specialist with Headquarters and Headquarters Troop on mission with Bravo Troop, 1st Squadron, 113th Cavalry Regiment, uses binoculars to scan his sector of fire during a dismounted patrol in the Khoe-Safi District. Denery provides overwatch security for fellow service members patrolling Dandar village. Bravo Troop visited the village to conduct a patrol and to establish a relationship with the village malik and elders. (Photo by U.S. Army Spc. Kristina L. Gupton, Task Force Red Bulls Public Affairs)

PARWAN PROVINCE, Afghanistan, Dec. 9, 2010—U.S. Army Pfc. Andrew Baldwin, a Sacramento, Calif., resident, and U.S. Army Spc. Gabe Lanz, a Boone, Iowa, resident, both mortarmen with Headquarters and Headquarters Troop, on mission with Bravo Troop, 1st Squadron, 113th Cavalry Regiment, practice gunnery drills with a 120 mm mortar, "Goliath" as the Soldiers call it, at Vehicle Patrol Base Dandar. (Photo by U.S. Army Spc. Kristina L. Gupton, Task Force Red Bulls Public Affairs)

Iowans recognize home station in traditional ceremony

BAGRAM AIRFIELD, Afghanistan, Dec. 9, 2010—Sgt. 1st Class David M. Bailey, Sgt. Tyler A. Smith, and Spc. Blake W. Phipps, Boone, Iowa residents and soldiers in Headquarters and Headquarters Company, 2nd Brigade Combat Team, 34th Infantry Division, prepare the U.S. flag to be flown Tuesday for a patch ceremony. The unit flew the City of Boone, Iowa flag to recognize their support of the citizen-soldiers that are stationed there when not deployed. (Photo by U.S. Army Staff Sgt. Ashlee Lolkus, Task Force Red Bulls Public Affairs)

By U.S. Army Staff Sgt. Ashlee Lolkus
Task Force Red Bulls Public Affairs

BAGRAM AIRFIELD, Afghanistan, Dec. 9, 2010—Soldiers of Headquarters and Headquarters Company, 2nd Brigade Combat Team, 34th Infantry Division, participated in a traditional patch ceremony at Bagram Airfield. For the ceremony, soldiers flew the City of Boone, Iowa flag to honor the city where the headquarters company is located.

The patch ceremony was held to recognize the unit's time in a combat zone, awarding soldiers the right to wear the Red Bull combat patch, and also to recognize the citizens of Boone for their continued support of their citizen soldiers.

Col. Benjamin J. Corell, 2-34th BCT commander and Strawberry Point, Iowa resident, received the city flag from John Slight, Boone mayor, during the send-off ceremony last summer at the Des Moines Area Community College in Boone.

"It is great to have such wonderful support by the Boone community, both when at home-station and deployed abroad," said Corell. "We wanted to include them in this significant ceremony to show our appreciation for everything they have done to support the soldiers of the brigade."

"I thought it was really cool that we could fly the Boone flag," said Sgt. Tyler A. Smith a communications specialist and Boone native. "I am proud to be able to have the Boone flag flying when we were awarded our combat patches."

Placed below the reversed American flag on the right shoulder, signifying American forces continuing to move forward, is the combat patch. The combat patch has a history dating back to World War II.

The unit patch is worn on the left shoulder sleeve signifying what unit the soldier is assigned. When deployed to a combat zone, 34th Infantry Division soldiers earn the right to wear the Red Bull patch on their right shoulder.

The Red Bull combat patch symbolizes not only serving with the 34th Infantry Division, but it is also a visible display of the hardships endured and commitments made by the soldiers while assigned to the unit.

Like many uniform decorations, it is an honor to wear the unique combat patch, a bond to the past that is shared with Red Bull soldiers who fought in previous wars.

BAGRAM AIRFIELD, Afghanistan, Dec. 9, 2010—U.S. Army 1st Sgt. Corey Westra of Elkhart, Iowa, is awarded the Red Bull combat patch placed by Capt. Dale Hight of Ankeny, Iowa, commander of Headquarters and Headquarters Company, 2nd Brigade Combat Team, 34th Infantry Division, Tuesday during a patch ceremony at Bagram Airfield. The unit flew the City of Boone flag during the ceremony to recognize their support of the citizen-soldiers that are stationed there when not deployed. (Photo by U.S. Army Staff Sgt. Ashlee Lolkus, Task Force Red Bulls Public Affairs)

Bravo strengthens relationship with Afghan people

*PARWAN PROVINCE, Afghanistan, Dec. 9, 2010—*U.S. Army Capt. Randall Stanford, a Clive, Iowa, resident and Bravo Troop commander, 1st Squadron, 113th Cavalry Regiment, Task Force Redhorse, meets with an Afghan villager during a patrol of the Koh-e Safi District. (Photo U.S. Army Spc. James Wilton, Task Force Red Bulls Public Affairs)

By U.S. Army Spc. James Wilton
Task Force Red Bulls Public Affairs

PARWAN PROVINCE, Afghanistan, Dec. 10, 2010—"As a commander and battlespace owner, I feel obligated to visit every village within the district so they all know we are here for them," said U.S. Army Capt. Randall Stanford a Clive, Iowa, native and Bravo Troop commander. "I also want to get an assessment of each village. What facilities they have and what they need: clean water, sewage issues and any other necessary infrastructure."

Stanford used the opportunity to ask villagers about security in the area, their essential daily needs and where they felt improvements were needed in the their villages. These issues were then brought up in a Key Leader Engagement conducted with ANP Col. Farzea Masoom the Koh-e Safi District ANP chief, Dr. Abdul Wahed Khan, the district subgovernor, and other Afghan leaders from the area held at the district center Dec. 9.

"Walking through the villages and meeting with the people is a very good idea," said Khan "By doing this, you get a good idea of what their needs are and what type of life they lead. Koh-e Safi people are a very poor people, and any help you can give them is much appreciated and by doing so it will keep your relationship strong."

The meeting also included status updates of current reconstruction projects like the court house being built in the district center. Bravo Troop hopes the district center becomes a symbol of governance and law for the Afghan people in Koh-e Safi.

"We hope the court house can be a physical representation for the Afghan people that the courts and police are working together to look out for the people and provide the security that is so necessary to their daily lives," said U.S. Army 1st Lt. Rodney Brock, an Ocean Springs, Miss., native and the Bravo Troop executive officer.

The meeting included coordination for joint patrols between the Soldiers and ANP in the following months, given more purpose due to a rocket attack on the Vehicle Patrol Base from insurgents the night of Dec. 9.

"Even though winter is coming, the enemy is still here and active, we need to work together to remove them from the area," said Masoom. "We have the same enemy, the same problem and we will fight them together."

"Let me know where they're at, and we'll go get them together," responded Stanford. "I trust the ANP, and I know if we go anywhere with you, that we will be safe."

The ANP members and Bravo Troop Soldiers conducted a joint patrol Dec. 10 to the point of origin of the rocket attacks and found a second device emplaced. Together, they disarmed and removed the rocket ensuring it would not harm Afghans or coalition forces.

The day concluded with a traditional Afghan meal where Bravo Soldiers and ANP members shared goat, Afghan bread, and vegetables. The goat was purchased by Stanford that day from a local Afghan and traditionally prepared by ANP officers.

PARWAN PROVINCE, Afghanistan, Dec. 9, 2010—U.S. Army Spc. Matthew Johnson (front), an Ankeny, Iowa, native, and U.S. Army Sgt. Drew Russell (background), a Dubuque, Iowa, native, both soldiers with Bravo Troop, 1st Squadron, 113th Cavalry Regiment, Task Force Redhorse, assist Afghan villagers with a vehicle they found stuck on the road during a patrol of the Koh-e Safi District. The mission gave Bravo Troop Soldiers a chance to get acquainted with the villagers in their new area of operations and address any issues or needs they may have. (Photo by U.S. Army Spc. James Wilton, Task Force Red Bulls Public Affairs)

Soldiers look for perfect holiday gift at Bagram bazaar

*BAGRAM AIRFIELD, Afghanistan, Dec. 11, 2010—*A shopkeeper stands by his store in the Bagram Airfield bazaar. The bazaar brings in more than $30,000 into the local economy on a typical weekend day. (Photo by U.S. Army Staff Sgt. Ryan C. Matson, Task Force Red Bulls Public Affairs)

By U.S. Army Staff Sgt. Ryan C. Matson
Task Force Red Bulls Public Affairs

*BAGRAM AIRFIELD, Afghanistan, Dec. 11, 2010–*U.S. Army Pfc. David Wagner and U.S. Army Spc. Manuel Chris Gomez, both ammunition specialists with the 592nd Ordnance Company out of Billings, Mont., entered the parking lot lined with connexes with the same goal in mind.

The two Soldiers were shopping at the bazaar Dec. 11 on Bagram Airfield for the perfect Christmas gift that symbolizes Afghanistan.

"I got my mom, dad, brother and sister a gift," said Gomez, a native of Murietta, Calif. "I'm just looking for something that represents Afghanistan to send back, so they see what we see here in a sense."

Almost an hour later, they each carried a couple bags in their hands with the treasures they had found.

"I bought some jewelry," said Wagner, from Wheatridge, Colo. "I've got a little lady back home. They're really good on bargaining here. I paid $34, and he started me off at $60." Even though they only bought a few small items, the Soldiers said just walking around and looking at all the items the bazaar had to offer was a lot of fun.

"Down there," Gomez said, motioning to a store at the far corner of the crushed stone lot, "they have a lot of really nice wooden boxes and chests; you can really see the work they put into each one."

Marble chess sets adorned with "United States" and "Afghanistan," hand-carved wooden chests, jewelry boxes and other items, traditional clothing, scarves, carpets and flags, leather jackets, purses and handbags, antique swords, knives, guns and other weapons, tea sets, weaved baskets, and embroidered patches are just some of the things servicemembers and civilians on Bagram Airfield can find at the bazaar.

The bazaar features more than 30 local vendors, most from Parwan Province. Wagner said he likes the fact that most of the vendors are from the local area.

"I like the culture," Wagner said, as he looked along the row of connexes around him. "When I came here, I didn't think we were going to have the opportunity to be part of a bazaar like this, and the culture here is something I definitely wanted to wrap my head around. This place definitely gives you an opportunity to do that."

U.S. Army Pfc. Anthony Weir, a medic with the 832nd Engineer Company, attached to the 1st Squadron, 113th Cavalry Regiment, Task Force Redhorse, was also shopping at the bazaar. He agreed that many Soldiers are seeking something that represents their time here when shopping at the bazaar.

"If it's something authentic, that was made here, that I couldn't find anywhere else in the world, that's what makes me buy it," said Weir, who lives in Monticello, Iowa.

U.S. Army Pfc. Chad Cosens, also a medic and with Headquarters and Headquarters Company, 334th Brigade Support Battalion, Task Force Archer, had his own strategy for Christmas shopping at the bazaar.

"I'm just looking around for Christmas presents, taking pictures of stuff and emailing them to my family to see what they like," said Cosens, from Madrid, Iowa. "I probably won't end up sending it 'til after Christmas, but it will still be nice to get them out a package."

Cosens said he enjoyed the antique weapons and currency, which he said one of his brothers may also enjoy, although his older brother is difficult to shop for.

"My mom, she'll probably like just about anything," Cosens said. "Maybe some jewelry ..."

U.S. Army 1st Lt. Timothy Halbur, Headquarters and Headquarters Company, 2-34th Brigade Special Troops Battalion, Task Force Archer, is the officer in charge of the bazaar. Halbur, from Cedar Rapids, Iowa, said Task Force Archer, which is made up of the 2-34th BSTB and the 334th Brigade

Support Battalion., is working to improve the infrastructure of the bazaar, which is run by the Army and Air Force Exchange Service. He said the task force inherited the bazaar from the 86th Infantry Brigade Combat Team.

"The real point of the bazaar is to form a counterinsurgency operation," Halbur said. "It's to bring local money to the locals in Bagram."

Halbur said the bazaar typically brings in about $15,000 on weekdays and more than $30,000 a day on weekends to the local economy.

Task Force Archer plans to make some changes and upgrades to the bazaar to improve it for the servicemembers, civilian contractors and local nationals who use it, Halbur said. He said among the improvements the unit is working on is the addition of a boardwalk around the shops lining the lot, so customers are walking on a solid surface rather than the crushed stone. Halbur also said the task force is working on adding a pavilion as well as a working bakery, so customers can buy food while shopping.

"You'll be able to come to the bakery here, buy some pastries and a coffee, and shopping here will be more of an enjoyable experience," Halbur said.

But with all of the things the bazaar offers, it seems Soldiers are happy to send a piece of Afghanistan back home for Christmas.

PARWAN PROVINCE, Afghanistan, Dec. 11, 2010—U.S. Army Chad Cosens, a medic from Madrid, Iowa, with Headquarters and Headquarters Company, 334th Brigade Support Brigade, looks at a ring in the jewelry shop at the bazaar on Bagram Airfield. Cosens said he was looking for Christmas presents for his family. (Photo by U.S. Army Staff Sgt. Ryan C. Matson, Task Force Red Bulls Public Affairs)

Kentucky ADT visits chicken farm entrepreneur

PANJSHIR PROVINCE, Afghanistan, Dec. 12, 2010—U.S. Army Lt. Col. Jeffrey Casada (left), Kentucky National Guard Agribusiness Development Team leader and London, Ky., native, and chicken farm entrepreneur Shanawaz Khan (right) speak through an interpreter in Khenj District. (Photo by U.S. Air Force 2nd Lt. Ashleigh Peck, Panjshir Provincial Reconstruction Team)

PANJSHIR PROVINCE, Afghanistan, Dec. 12, 2010—Some of the 800 chickens belonging to local chicken farm entrepreneur Shanawaz Khan are shown in Khenj District. (Photo by U.S. Air Force 2nd Lt. Ashleigh Peck, Panjshir Provincial Reconstruction Team)

BAF bazaar offers Afghan women merchants

BAGRAM AIRFIELD, Afghanistan, Dec. 12, 2010—Sulhaila Kohistani (left), U.S. Army Maj. Bobbie Jo Mayes, woman's empowerment coordinator with the Kentucky Agribusiness Development Team, from Lawrenceburg, Ky., and Saleha Zareen, stand in front of the women's stores at the Bagram Airfield Bazaar. Zareen and Kohistani were the first two Afghan women merchants to be contracted by the Army and Air Force Exchange Service in Afghanistan when they joined the bazaar. (Photo by U.S. Army Staff Sgt. Ryan C. Matson, Task Force Red Bulls Public Affairs)

By U.S. Army Staff Sgt. Ryan C. Matson
Task Force Red Bulls Public Affairs

BAGRAM AIRFIELD, Afghanistan, Dec. 12, 2010— At Bagram Airfield, you will find something you won't find anywhere else in Afghanistan—the first two Afghan women merchants contracted by the Army Air Force Exchange Service.

"You're number one!" said U.S. Army Maj. Bobbie Jo Mayes, women's empowerment coordinator with the Kentucky Agribusiness Development Team, from Lawrenceburg, Ky., as she put her arms around her friends, Sulhaila Kohistani and Saleha Zareen.

The AAFES and the 334th Brigade Support Battalion, 2nd Brigade Combat Team, 34th Infantry Division, run the bazaar on BAF. The bazaar is comprised largely of local vendors selling locally-made products. Servicemembers, as well as civilians, frequent the bazaar, which provides a boost to the local economy and is particularly busy this holiday season.

Since August, as a result of Mayes' relationships with Kohistani and Zareen, the bazaar also features five women vendors.

The five women's shops feature handmade clothes for men, women and children, blankets, rugs, shoes, jewellery, leather items and a slew of other products.

Mayes said she became involved with the bazaar after she was contacted by the 86th Infantry Brigade Combat Team, the previous unit in charge of the bazaar. They told her they had some open shops at the bazaar and would like to try to involve some female vendors.

"They couldn't find any local women who would come to it, and I told them I had two very strong women who own their own shops, and so I asked Miss Kohistani and Miss Zareen, and even though Miss Zareen had received death threats before this, they said, 'You know what, we'll come on base,'" Mayes explained.

Mayes was able to convince Kohistani and Zareen to open shops at the bazaar, while the 86th also added three female vendors of their own.

"They (Kohistani and Zareen) are the two highest women in the provincial government," Mayes said. "They came on base, and it's been a struggle, but that's how it came about. The threats they get are because they are so successful, and the men are not necessarily happy with that. But these women show women can make money and they can provide for their families. Eighty percent of the things these women sell go back to their families."

Mayes said she met Kohistani and Zareen through her work with the ADT as women's empowerment coordinator in the local area. Kohistani is the Parwan Deputy Director of Women's Affairs.

"These are the women who all the others come to for help," Mayes said.

One of the ways Zareen helps the other local Afghan women is through the Women's Handcraft Association of Parwan Province. Zareen said 800 women in the local area work for her to make the clothes, jewelry and other handiwork she sells at her store at the bazaar.

"We are very happy because Major Mayes is a very kind woman and she is helping all the women," Zareen said.

Even though there is risk involved, Mayes said the women are courageous pioneers, proving that everything can benefit from a woman's touch.

Task Force Redhorse honors fallen ANP EOD tech

PARWAN PROVINCE, Afghanistan, July 19, 2009—Afghan National Police officer, 1st Lt. Faridullah, does paperwork in an ANP office here July 19, 2009. Faridullah was killed Dec. 4, 2010 while attempting to disarm an Improvised Explosive Device near Bagram Airfield. His widow was given 109,500 Afghani, which equates to $2,500, Dec. 13 as a hero payment in honor of Faridullah's service to the coalition. (Courtesy photo)

By U.S. Army Staff Sgt. Ashlee Lolkus
Task Force Red Bulls Public Affairs

PARWAN PROVINCE, Afghanistan, Dec. 13, 2010—On a quiet, sunny day in a small rented space in the heart of Charikar's residential area, a woman's eyes welled up with tears. She sat on the red carpeted floor alone with her feet pulled in close and arms wrapped around her knees as she sobbed quietly into her bright purple scarf. She picked her head up out of the scarf in her hands to look up at two women interpreters of Task Force Redhorse with eyes red from burning tears.

As she stood up to greet them as best as she could, the interpreters swooped in to hold her, quickly and softly uttering words to console this new widow. Task Force Redhorse came to provide her a "hero payment" in honor of her husband who was recently killed while attempting to disarm an Improvised Explosive Device near Bagram Airfield Dec. 4.

U.S. Army Lt. Col. David A. Updegraff, 1st Squadron, 113th Cavalry Regiment, Task Force Redhorse commander and Wauconda, Ill., resident, arranged to give the widow of Afghan National Police 1st Lt. Faridullah, the son of Aminulla, a payment of 109,500 Afghani Dec. 13 at the family's home. Updegraff was accompanied by ANP Col. Abdul Rauf Uruzgani, chief of the ANP for Bagram District.

"I told my husband several times to leave this dangerous job," said the widow to the interpreters. "I told him I prefer to stay home and eat nothing, but he never accepted. Now he is gone."

Faridullah leaves behind a wife and three children ranging in age from 3 to 8. Shortly before he was killed, he bought property and was in the process of building a new home for his family.

"The money we were able to give to the widow will never replace her husband," said Updegraff. "But we hope it will help her along until the Afghan government pension kicks in. (The payment of) 109,500 Afghani equates to $2,500 in U.S. dollars, and is the maximum amount we are authorized to give for a hero payment."

"The hero payment," Updegraff continued, "isn't something we provide to every fallen ANP. Faridullah died attempting to disarm an IED which my Soldiers could have hit on the battlefield: he died in support of coalition efforts. Because he was helping the coalition, I felt it rose to the level of a hero payment."

Faridullah disarmed IEDs for three years as a member of the ANP explosive ordinance department. The IED he was attempting to disarm was rigged with dummy wiring. When he thought he had disarmed the bomb, he began the removal when it detonated, killing him.

The widow and family are now in the care of Faridullah's brother who plans to move them back to where the widow's family resides.

PARWAN PROVINCE, Afghanistan, Dec. 13, 2010 –U.S. Army Lt. Col. David A. Updegraff (left), 1st Squadron, 113th Cavalry Regiment, Task Force Redhorse commander and Wauconda, Ill., resident, stands with Afghan National Police Col. Abdul Rauf Uruzgani, chief of the ANP for Bagram District, outside the home of fallen ANP 1st Lt. Faridullah's widow in Charikar. [...] (Photo by U.S. Army Staff Sgt. Ashlee Lolkus, Task Force Red Bulls Public Affairs)

Bagram celebrates 374th National Guard birthday

PARWAN PROVINCE, Afghanistan, Dec. 13, 2010—U.S. Army Brig. Gen. Mandi Murray, the highest ranking National Guard Soldier on Bagram Airfield and the 46th Military Police Brigade, Task Force Peacekeeper commander, U.S. Army Command Sgt. Maj. Daniel Lincoln, 58, from Marshall, Mich., Task Force Peacekeepers command sergeant major and the oldest service member in attendance, and U.S. Army Pfc. Matthew Nickerson, 20, from Nevada, Iowa, a military police officer with the 1st Squadron, 113th Cavalry Regiment, Task Force Redhorse and the youngest service member in attendance, cut the first slice of birthday cake at the National Guard's 374th birthday celebration held on Bagram Airfield here Dec. 13. (Photo by U.S. Army Spc. James Wilton, Task Force Red Bulls Public Affairs)

ANSF, 615th MPs uncover homemade explosives lab in Chamkani

PAKTYA PROVINCE, Afghanistan, Dec. 14, 2010—Afghan Border Police and Afghan Uniformed Police forces search known insurgent cache sites during joint operations with coalition forces. The Afghan National Security Forces took the lead with the operation. (Photo by: 1st Lt. Nicholas Rasmussen, Task Force Lethal)

By U.S. Army 1st Lt. Nicholas Rasmussen
Task Force Lethal

PAKTYA PROVINCE, Afghanistan, Dec. 14, 2010—Afghan National Security Forces combined with the 615th Military Police Company to conduct a cordon-and-search mission of two known insurgent residences in the Chamkani District of Paktya Province, which resulted in the discovery of the remnants of a homemade explosive lab and a weapons cache.

The searches were conducted by Afghan Uniformed Police with soldiers from the 615th MP Company providing oversight during the operation. The AUP developed the intelligence, coordinated the planning, conducted the reconnaissance and executed the mission.

"We were confident because we had air and land support," said AUP Sgt. Fazal, Chamkani AUP Non-Commissioned Officer-in-Charge. "Our mission was to find and arrest a suspicious [Improvised Explosive Device] maker... Although we didn't capture him, we got his weapons.

"The operation was completely Afghan-led," said U.S. Army Staff Sgt. Kent Schooner of Gainesvill, Ga., a 615th MP squad leader. "The goal is for us to work ourselves out of the job."

The Afghan Border Police in the Chamkani area worked with their coalition forces partner, Company B, 1st Battalion, 168th Infantry Regiment, to establish security during the operation.

"[The ABP] has a great group of junior officers," said U.S. Army Sgt. Lucas Queck, Company B., 1-168th Inf., from Fontanelle, Iowa.

In order to facilitate continued ANSF progress, U.S. soldiers have to take a side seat and allow the ANSF to lead operations.

"You just have to sit back and watch," said U.S. Army 1st Lt. Michael Broderick, a 1-168th Inf. platoon leader from Clive, Iowa.

Broderick said the proficiency with which the AUP planned and conducted this operation is a positive indication of the progress being made to improve security in Paktya Province.

Kentucky ADT coordinates beehive project with DOWA

PARWAN PROVINCE, Afghanistan, Dec. 14, 2010—U.S. Army Maj. Bobbie Jo Mayes of Lawrenceburg, Ky., Kentucky Agribusiness Development Team women's empowerment coordinator, discusses bee classes with teachers from the Agency for Building a New Afghanistan during a visit to the Parwan Department of Women's Affairs. Mayes visited the DOWA to discuss a project to give 25 women a two-day class on bees. Once the women complete the class, they will receive a hive and bees in hopes to help them build additional income. (Photo by U.S. Army Spc. Kristina L. Gupton, Task Force Red Bulls Public Affairs)

PRT Civil Affairs Team visits Panjshir clinic

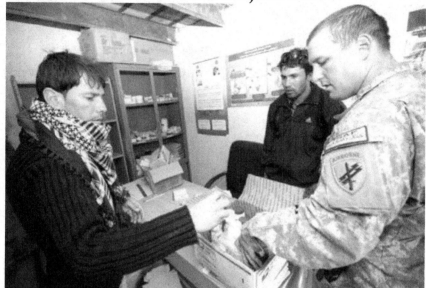

PANJSHIR PROVINCE, DEC. 14, 2010—Panjshir Provincial Reconstruction Team civil affairs specialist U.S. Army Sgt. Patrick Reilly of Troy, Mich., explains to a Kow Jan clinic leader how vitamins are used during a visit to the clinic. Upon learning that some local Afghans suffer from vitamin deficiencies during the winter, Reilly's friends and family took it upon themselves to send vitamins. (Photo by French Army Staff Sgt. Romain Beaulinette, Panjshir Provincial Reconstruction Team)

Engineers visit Bagram shura

PARWAN PROVINCE, Afghanistan, Dec. 15, 2010—Members of 832nd Engineer Company, attached to 1st Squadron, 113th Cavalry Regiment, discuss ongoing and future projects with village maliks and elders during a shura in Bagram District. (Photo by U.S. Army Spc. Kristina L. Gupton, Task Force Red Bulls Public Affairs)

PARWAN PROVINCE, Afghanistan, Dec. 15, 2010—U.S. Army Capt. Nick Poch, an Iowa City, Iowa, resident and engineer with Headquarters and Headquarters Company, 2-34th Brigade Special Troops Battalion, Task Force Archer, speaks to an Afghan who attended the Bagram shura about badging issues. Poch visited the Bagram shura to discuss access control issues for surrounding villages in Bagram District. (Photo by U.S. Army Spc. Kristina L. Gupton, Task Force Red Bulls Public Affairs)

PARWAN PROVINCE, Afghanistan, Dec. 15, 2010—U.S. Army Sgt. Adam Dean, a Morning Sun, Iowa, resident and combat engineer with 2nd platoon, 832nd Engineer Company, attached to 1st Squadron, 113th Cavalry Regiment uses a hand held metal detector to search local afghans before they can enter the Bagram shura, Parwan Province, Afghanistan. (Photo by U.S. Army Spc. Kristina L. Gupton, Task Force Red Bulls Public Affairs)

PARWAN PROVINCE, Afghanistan, Dec. 15, 2010—U.S. Army Staff Sgt. Adam Herman, a Newton, Iowa, resident and combat engineer with Headquarters and Headquarters Company, 2-34th Brigade Special Troops Battalion, Task Force Archer, speaks with Afghans about badging issues outside the Bagram shura. Herman visited the shura to address badging concerns for villagers in Bagram District. (Photo by U.S. Army Spc. Kristina L. Gupton, Task Force Red Bulls Public Affairs)

832nd engineers conduct water canal inspection in Dahn-e-Maidan

PARWAN PROVINCE, Afghanistan, Dec. 15, 2010—U.S. Army Capt. Scott E. Hansen (left center), a Maquoketa, Iowa, resident and 832nd Engineer Company commander, attached to 1st Squadron, 113th Cavalry Regiment, walks with village malik Shamudin (far right) walk through Dahn-e-Maidan village. Hansen and his Soldiers visited the village to inspect the progress on the water canal project. (Photo by U.S. Army Spc. Kristina L. Gupton, Task Force Red Bulls Public Affairs)

PARWAN PROVINCE, Afghanistan, Dec. 15, 2010—U.S. Army 1st Lt. Timothy Halbur of Carroll, Iowa, quartermaster officer with Headquarters and Headquarters Company, Brigade Special Troops Battalion, 2nd Brigade Combat Team, 34th Infantry Division, Task Force Archer, walks with and speaks to the Afghan boys of the Dahn-e-Maidan village. (Photo by U.S. Army Spc Kristina L. Gupton, Task Force Red Bulls Public Affairs)

PRT visits Panjshir clinics

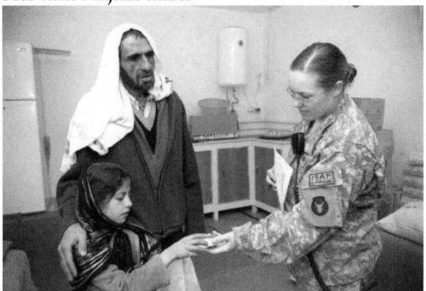

PANJSHIR PROVINCE, Afghanistan, Dec. 15, 2010—U.S. Air Force Tech. Sgt. Heather Lewis, Panjshir Provincial Reconstruction Team medical technician from Eagle River, Ala., checks an Afghan epileptic girl's medication in Charmagza clinic in Dara district. The medical team visits each clinic in Panjshir to discuss medical issues with clinic personnel and advise staff on ways to optimize their operations. (Photo by French army Staff Sgt. Romain Beaulinette, Panjshir Provincial Reconstruction Team)

Mullen brings USO tour to Bagram Airfield

BAGRAM AIRFIELD, Afghanistan, Dec. 15, 2010—Comedian and actor Robin Williams performs a stand-up routine during a USO tour on Bagram Airfield. In addition to signing autographs and posing for pictures, Williams acknowledged a servicemember's birthday. (Photo by U.S. Army Spc. Adam L. Mathis, 17th Public Affairs Detachment)

By U.S. Army Spc. James Wilton
Task Force Red Bulls Public Affairs

BAGRAM AIRFIELD, Afghanistan, Dec. 15, 2010—The USO sponsors holiday shows annually and performers get a chance to meet deployed personnel and thank them for their service. This time, troops were able to join [seven-time Tour de France winner Lance] Armstrong for a run around Bagram before the show.

"I had the most interesting experience today, I actually ran around the perimeter of this base," said Armstrong, who served as the master of ceremonies. "That is the nastiest run I have ever been on ... People call you hero for doing a lot of things ... but the reality is, you are the heroes and we're here to thank you for serving our country."

[Comedians Lewis Black, Kathleen Madigan, and Robin Williams were also part of the Annual USO Holiday Tour, as well as country musician Kix Brooks, formerly of Brooks and Dunn. Brooks performed with musician Bob DiPiero.]

While deployed, servicemembers often work long hours and events like these can provide a much-needed distraction or a moment to relax and decompress. The servicemembers voiced their thanks to the performers for taking the time to travel to Afghanistan.

"It's good for the welfare of the Soldiers," said U.S. Army 1st Lt. Timothy Halbur of Carol, Iowa, Task Force Archer, 334th Brigade Support Battalion, Iowa National Guard. "Most people work Monday through Sunday, no break, no days off and this is something to actually look forward to."

"I think it's an honor to be here and get a chance to see Robin Williams... I passed Lance Armstrong running and got some pictures of that, so that was pretty cool," said U.S. Navy Chief Bonnie Vermillion of Virginia Beach, Va., Combined Joint Interagency Task Force 435.

"A distraction is a good thing for a Soldier; the day-in, day-out routine can get boring after awhile," said U.S. Army Spc. Stephen Jaster of Davenport, Iowa, Task Force Archer. "This is great and it's nice of them to take some time out of their schedules and come do this for us."

The evening ended with servicemembers coming onstage to take group photos with the entertainers.

BAGRAM AIRFIELD, Afghanistan, Dec. 15, 2010—Lewis Black entertains servicemembers during a USO holiday show at Bagram Airfield. The show included comedy performances by Black, Robin Williams, and Kathleen Madigan, as well as a musical performance by Kix Brooks and Bob Dipiero. (Photo by U.S. Army Spc. James Wilton, Task Force Red Bulls Public Affairs)

Iowa National Guard medics treat girl, compare experience to life in U.S.

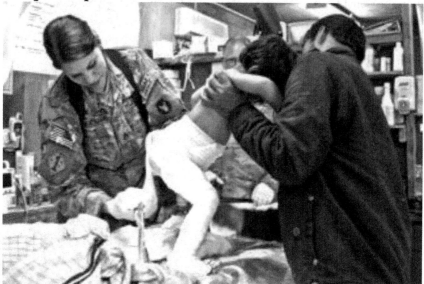

LAGHMAN PROVINCE, Afghanistan, Dec. 16, 2010—U.S. Army Staff Sgt. Jennifer Voegtlin, a combat medic with Headquarters and Headquarters Company, 1st Battalion, 133rd Infantry Regiment, applies fresh bandages to an Afghan girl after treating her burn wounds to her waist, left leg and foot at Forward Operating Base Mehtar Lam. Voegtlin, a paramedic in civilian life with the Des Moines, Iowa, fire department, who lives in Altoona, Iowa, said she is learning new medical techniques and treatments this deployment. (Photo by U.S. Army Staff Sgt. Ryan C. Matson, Task Force Red Bulls Public Affairs)

By U.S. Army Staff Sgt. Ryan C. Matson
Task Force Red Bulls Public Affairs

LAGHMAN PROVINCE, Afghanistan, Dec. 16, 2010—U.S. Army Staff Sgt. Jennifer Voegtlin cut a square piece of bandage from a section of petroleum gauze, while U.S. Army Spc. John Goebel held the outstretched bandage firmly in his hands.

The two Iowa National Guard combat medics with Headquarters and Headquarters Company, 1st Battalion, 133rd Infantry Regiment, were treating burn wounds to Kamela, a 3-year-old Afghan girl from the village of Alishang. The medics, beginning the third month of a year-long deployment to Forward Operating Base Mehtar Lam in Laghman Province, have been treating Kamela for two weeks for second-degree burns spanning from her waist to her right leg and foot.

"If we didn't treat her, these wounds would probably end up killing her," said Voegtlin, who lives in Altoona, Iowa. "She would get an infection from dirt in the burn, which could potentially be mortal." The medics treated Kamela every day for the first week and now see her every other day. They wash the wounds with sterile soap and water, cut off the dead tissue from her burned areas, administer antibiotic cream to the burns and then replace her old bandages with fresh ones. They said the wounds are painful, but they expect Kamela to heal fully, minus a few scars.

The medics said they try their best to reduce the pain and comfort Kamela when treating her burns. Due to the number of nerve endings around the burns, Voegtlin said any change in temperature is extremely painful to the child. The medics administer pain medicine to Kamela to help ease the pain of the treatments, as well as multivitamins to help her heal faster. They said they are also teaching Kamela's father how to care for her so he can eventually do it all himself.

Voeghtlin does not like that the girl cries every time she sees her, but it is all in a day's work for the medics.

"She's so adorable; I just wished she liked me!" Voegtlin laughed.

Goebel, who lives in Washington, Iowa, said his job in Afghanistan is worlds apart from his occupation back in Iowa, where he works on computer systems for the Riverside Casino and Golf Resort.

He said he originally enlisted in the National Guard as a radio operator/maintainer, but his unit was being mobilized and did not have any slots for communications Soldiers. They did, however, need medics and though he had knowledge in computers and communications equipment, Goebel said he was up for the challenge of learning to be a medic. He completed his medical training at Fort Sam Houston, Texas, and joined the aid station team for this deployment.

This is the first deployment for 30-year-old Goebel, who has been in the Army for two years.

Goebel said, like in his civilian life, he maintains the aid station's computers. He also ensures the water on the base is suitable for showering, adding chlorine to the tanks. But besides that, his day is largely working in his assigned job as a medic.

Voegtlin, a paramedic with the Des Moines, Iowa, fire department in the civilian sector, said her civilian job in the United States is similar to what she does as a medic in Afghanistan, but there are still many differences.

"I worked in a pediatric emergency room for a while as a paramedic, and I'm used to being able to communicate with the kids and saying, 'This isn't going to hurt, no owie,'" she said. "It's different when you can communicate with a child and say 'OK, we're going to give you a shot, and it's going to feel like a bee sting, but it's not going to hurt,' and then they're prepared for it."

She also said the types of treatment she administers here is different than those she did for the Des Moines Fire Department. "There, a pretty typical call would be cardiacs, difficulty breathing, seizures, diabetes and things like that," Voegtlin said. "Here, I'm learning about dermatology, suturing, and performing almost at the level of a physician ... it's pretty fantastic."

This is the third deployment for 31-year-old Voegtlin, an 11-year veteran of the National Guard. On her last deployment, to Iraq, Voegtlin served as a flight medic. She volunteered for this deployment, which gives her the opportunity to serve as the Non-Commissioned Officer-in-Charge of the 1-133rd Inf. aid station.

The aid station operates 24 hours a day, with eight medics working at the station, as well as a laboratory technician, doctor and a physician's assistant. Additionally, Voegtlin said medics from the aid station are serving with line units at other FOBs and combat outposts throughout the 2nd Brigade Combat Team, 34th Infantry Division's area of operation in Afghanistan.

Even though the deployment brings new challenges to the medics, both said they feel satisfaction from the work they are doing here, such as treating Kamela.

"The best thing here is being here and learning stuff," Goebel said. "I like that I can help people. I like knowing if the guy next to me goes down, now I can help to keep him alive."

Guardians of Peace program launched

By U.S. Army Sgt. Scott Davis
Regional Command–East Public Affairs

*BAGRAM AIRFIELD, Afghanistan, Dec. 16, 2010—*The Government of the Islamic Republic of Afghanistan, with the help of Coalition forces, launched a new campaign called Guardians of Peace in October to help improve security across Afghanistan.

The program allows Afghan citizens to anonymously report insurgent activity by either calling their local community safety lines or contacting Afghan National Security Forces or their village elders. Once the information is received, the callers are assigned a confidential number to protect their identity and ensure they are properly rewarded for their efforts.

"This program allows Afghan citizens to partner with their local government offices and help them provide protection for their villages by reporting any criminal or insurgent activity," said Maj. Gen. John F. Campbell, commanding general for Combined Joint Task Force–101 and Regional Command–East. "If the information they provide is beneficial to ANSF or coalition forces, they are eligible for a reward."

All rewards are based on the value of the information provided and can be money, food or other "in-kind" necessities. Individuals reporting the information are instructed to call back to see if the information they provided qualifies for an award. At that time, if the information was accurate and useful, the individual is rewarded.

"Guardians of Peace helps Afghan citizens to provide for their own security and connects the local population to their security forces and government," said Chief Warrant Officer Steven Mehl, RC–East rewards program manager. "Afghan citizens often have useful information regarding insurgent and criminal activities that can help the ANSF and GIRoA along with coalition forces. They just needed a place to share this information and the assurance of anonymity."

Advertising of the program began Oct. 22, airing on six television stations and 16 radio stations as well on the placement of billboards and posters throughout RC–East, Mehl said. The program has picked up momentum and, partnering with Ministry of Interior and Ministry of Defense, International Security Assistance Force is considering making Guardians of Peace a nationwide campaign.

"There's been a large increase in cache turn-ins in the last two weeks or so," Mehl said. "There was a slight increase in turn-ins since the program started but the numbers recently spiked and there's no doubt that there is a direct correlation between the increase in turn-ins and the program."

"Overall, the program has been very successful. The ANSF, GIRoA, and Coalition forces have received information that has led to five insurgent leaders being captured, over 50 weapons caches and numerous Improvised Explosive Devices turn-ins, four of which were made up of 200 pounds of homemade explosives," Mehl said. "Afghan citizens are using the Guardians of Peace to help secure their village and bring peace back to their families."

So far this year, 958 Afghans have been killed in insurgent attacks.

"At the end of the day, this program is about saving lives," Mehl said. "Not just the lives of ANSF or coalition forces but the lives of ordinary Afghan citizens. Insurgents target everyone who fights to improve Afghanistan and its future. This program has become a weapon to defend those people."

AUP, Task Force Lethal capture munitions cache in Jaji

By U.S. Army 1st Lt. Nicholas Rasmussen
Task Force Lethal

PAKTYA PROVINCE, Afghanistan, Dec. 16, 2010—The cache included more than 25 rocket-propelled grenades, multiple mortar rounds, bomb-making materials and ammunition for small arms.

The insurgents have used the area as a safe haven and as a hub to coordinate indirect fire attacks on Afghan National Security Forces and coalition forces throughout Jaji District.

"I knew there were [insurgents] living in that area," said AUP Lt. Mahboob, a platoon leader in Jaji.

Prior to the mission the villagers hadn't been receptive to coalition forces.

"Our predecessors told us [the village] was a bad place to go," said U.S. Army 1st Lt. Mark Lucas of Iowa City, Iowa, platoon leader with Co A., 1st Bn., 168th Inf.

The combined forces embraced the village with a friendly smile and treated the villagers with respect throughout the operation.

"The villagers at the end of the operation wanted us to stay. They wanted to have a shura and chai tea with us," Lucas said.

During the movement out of the area, the combined forces took RPG and small-arms fire. The group quickly gained fire superiority, managed to keep the insurgents suppressed and allowed the ANSF and coalition forces to move to safety.

PAKTYA PROVINCE, Afghanistan, Dec. 16, 2010 –A member of the Afghan Uniformed Police performs a search during an AUP-led operation with Company A, 1st Battalion, 168th Infantry Regiment, in Jaji District. The AUP searched a known insurgent safe haven while Company A Soldiers secured the area resulting in the removal of a weapons cache from insurgent possession and the detention of several insurgent fighters. (Photo by U.S. Army Sgt. Travis Tilley, Task Force Lethal)

AUP in Paktya learn new investigation techniques

PAKTYA PROVINCE, Afghanistan, Dec. 18, 2010—U.S. Army Capt. Bryan Anderson, 615th Military Police Company commander from Des Moines, Iowa, briefs 2nd Lt. Rayat Ullah, Afghan Uniformed Police platoon leader, prior to an operation to investigate reports of insurgent activity in northern Gardez District. Anderson and his company have mentored the AUP in Paktya Province since May. (Photo by U.S. Army 1st Lt. Nicholas Rasmussen, Task Force Lethal)

PAKTYA PROVINCE, Afghanistan, Dec. 18, 2010—Afghan uniformed police 2nd Lt. Rayat Ullah, a platoon leader for the AUP in Gardez District, explains the situation to a local villager while gathering a statement during an investigation of reports of possible insurgent activity in the area. (Photo by U.S. Army 1st Lt. Nicholas Rasmussen, Task Force Lethal)

Holiday mail run: Red Bulls Soldiers
get last-minute packages

By U.S. Army Staff Sgt. Ryan C. Matson
Task Force Red Bulls Public Affairs

LAGHMAN PROVINCE, Afghanistan, Dec. 18, 2010—It was a week before Christmas.

Some of the Soldiers of Company E, 1st Battalion, 133rd Infantry Regiment, talked of a snowstorm back home in Iowa. However, on Forward Operating Base Mehtar Lam in Eastern Afghanistan, they laughed as they tossed a University of Iowa Hawkeyes football back and forth on a beautiful, sunny, 70-degree day.

The Soldiers were relaxing before going on one of the last mail runs before Christmas. There are only a few hundred Soldiers on FOB Mehtar Lam, and even fewer on Combat Outposts Najil, Kalagush and Xio Haq, the places where some of the mail would eventually be delivered. The Soldiers, part of Task Force Ironman from the 2nd Brigade Combat Team, 34th Infantry Division, are responsible for running convoys of supplies back and forth between FOB Mehtar Lam and FOB Fenty, as well as to the smaller combat outposts.

"I enjoy getting mail as much as anybody else does, so it's kind of nice to bring some back to the other Soldiers," said U.S. Army Sgt. Cassidy Howard, a truck driver with the 2168th Transportation Company, attached to Task Force Ironman.

Howard looked over at the long line of pallets of mail lining the two flatbed trucks in front of him. There were 25 pallets of uni-packs completely filled with packages and tuff boxes on the trailer beds, the majority of which were holiday mail and care packages.

"When you deliver this much mail, there's probably something for you in there," said Howard, who works as a construction worker in Milford, Iowa. "I think that's kind of exciting; we've been waiting for it, too."

The Soldiers of Company E have been delivering a lot of holiday mail lately. The unit, based out of Waterloo, Iowa, typically does not handle mail. The majority of the mail is usually flown in by civilian contractors. However, U.S. Army 1st Lt. Clint Holtz, Company E executive officer from Walnut, Iowa, said there is currently a lapse in air-mail contracts, meaning Company E is picking up the slack. During this time of year, the volume of mail is even higher than usual.

"We always try to grab mail on our convoys, if we can," Holtz said. "But we're not used to grabbing so much!"

Holtz said Company E would usually conduct combat logistical patrols to transport supplies to the FOBs and COPs, as well as escorting Afghan vehicles on supply runs. The company does an average of two to three convoys a week between FOBs Mehtar Lam and Fenty, as well as to the COPs. The convoys are 20 to 45 miles each way. Holtz said in the three months they've been here, Company E has convoyed more than 1,300 miles and transported thousands of tons of supplies. But the company does much more than convoys.

He said Company E is a forward support company, meaning pieces of it can be found at FOB Mehtar Lam, as well as the smaller COPs in the Red Bulls area of operations. The company supports the 1-133rd Inf. by providing cooks, vehicle/equipment mechanics, fuelers and transportation Soldiers for the regiment.

U.S. Army Sgt. Shannon Osterholm is another truck driver from the 2168th Transportation Company, which is attached to Company E in support of Task Force Ironman. She said she likes driving trucks for the Army because of the places it takes her and also volunteered for this deployment.

"Back home, we drive all over the United States," Osterholm said. "I've seen so many states and different places being a truck driver."

Osterholm said driving trucks is also a nice change of pace from her civilian life, in which she works as a zookeeper with the Blank Park Zoo in Des Moines, Iowa.

"I like it," Osterholm, who lives in Des Moines but is from Mason City, Iowa, said. "It kind of breaks life up a little."

In addition, Osterholm said she has driven supplies on relief missions, such as to Louisiana after Hurricane Gustov.

After they had picked up all the mail at FOB Fenty, the Soldiers of Company E made the 42-mile trip back to FOB Mehtar Lam, where the mail was sorted to be distributed to the Soldiers there, as well as separated to go to the COPs. It was a busy day, and one the Soldiers knew they would repeat the trip again soon. Still, Holtz said his Soldiers like to be on the road.

"They get restless if they're sitting around on Mehtar Lam for too long," Holtz said. "They like to keep busy and be on the go."

LAGHMAN PROVINCE, Afghanistan, Dec. 18, 2010—U.S. Army Sgt. 1st Class Randy Rennison of Dubuque, Iowa, Headquarters and Headquarters Company, 1st Battalion, 133rd Infantry Regiment, 2nd Infantry Brigade Combat Team, 34th Infantry "Red Bulls" Division, Non-Commissioned Officer-in-Charge of the passenger terminal at Forward Operating Base Mehtar Lam, uses a Bobcat to push pallets of mail into the mail room. (Photo by U.S. Army Staff Sgt. Ryan C. Matson, Task Force Red Bulls Public Affairs)

Kentucky ADT II visits Panjshir 'green belt' sites

PANJSHIR PROVINCE, Afghanistan, Dec. 19, 2010—U.S. Army Lt. Col. Jeffrey Casada of London, Ky., Kentucky National Guard Agribusiness Development Team II leader, meets Gulam Sarware, manager of "green belt" workers in Rokha District. The project aims to plant 35,000 trees in Panjshir valley with 5,000 trees in each district. Rokha has planted 4,000 pine trees and 400 acacia. (Photo by French Army Staff Sgt. Romain Beaulinette, Panjshir Provincial Reconstruction Team)

*PANJSHIR PROVINCE, Afghanistan, Dec. 19, 2010—*Members of the Kentucky National Guard Agribusiness Development Team II meets with an Afghan worker in one of the seven locations where trees were planted in Rokha District. The ADT checks the ongoing "green belt" projects regularly. This project aims to plant 35,000 trees in Panjshir valley with 5,000 trees in each district. (Photo by French Army Staff Sgt. Romain Beaulinette, Panjshir Provincial Reconstruction Team)

PRT assists Panjshir villagers with civil cleanup

PANJSHIR PROVINCE, Afghanistan, Dec. 20, 2010—U.S. Army Sgt. Joshua O'Keefe, of Athens, Mich., Panjshir Provincial Reconstruction Team civil affairs, talks with Gulab Shah, Shutol district governor, and checks the delivery of materials to be used in the re-creation of a solid Dehe Kalan irrigation canal in Shutol District. (Photo by French Army Staff Sgt. Romain Beaulinette, Pansjhir Provincial Reconstruction Team)

PANJSHIR PROVINCE, Afghanistan, Dec. 20, 2010—U.S. Army Sgt. Patrick Reilly of Troy, Mich., Panjshir Provincial Reconstruction Team civil affairs, gives a hand to a local villager while delivering materials to assist in the recreation of a solid Dehe Kalan irrigation canal in Shutol District. Thanks to the common effort of villagers, the district governor and the PRT civil affairs team, a canal is planned to be rebuilt in the Shutol District before the winter weather prevents work. (Photo by French Army Staff Sgt. Romain Beaulinette, Pansjhir Provincial Reconstruction Team)

First Customers at Mehtar Lam PX

LAGHMAN PROVINCE, Afghanistan, Dec. 20, 2010—Pfc. Jeremiah Crisel, a chaplain's assistant from Sanborn, Iowa (left), Pfc. Gregory Shadlow, a supply specialist from Waterloo, Iowa, center, both from Headquarters and Headquarters Company, 1st Battalion, 133rd Infantry Regiment, look on as Command Sgt. Maj. Marcus Mittvalsky (right), also from HHC, 1st Battalion, 133rd Infantry Regiment, makes one of the initial purchases at the new post exchange at Forward Operating Base Mehtar Lam, Afghanistan. (Photo by U.S. Army Staff Sgt. Ryan C. Matson, Task Force Red Bulls Public Affairs)

By U.S. Army Staff Sgt. Ryan C. Matson
Task Force Red Bulls Public Affairs

LAGHMAN PROVINCE, Afghanistan, Dec. 20, 2010—When soldiers speak of a base in Afghanistan being "built up," there are several places on the base they typically mention.

First on the list, inevitably, is whether or not the base has a Post Exchange, or "PX," and how large that store is. If a base has a large dining facility or gym, soldiers will also often say it is "built up."

Forward Operating Base Mehtar Lam, home to a few hundred soldiers, most from the 2nd Brigade Combat Team, 34th Infantry "Red Bull" Division, took a big step toward being "built up" Dec. 20. It may not have all the amenities like you'll find at Bagram Airfield, but FOB Mehtar Lam now boasts a post exchange store.

At exactly 3 p.m., U.S. Army 1st Sgt. Brian Nichols, the Headquarters and Headquarters Company, 1st Battalion, 133rd Infantry Regiment first sergeant, cut the ribbon outside the connex trailer which houses the post exchange, officially opening it for business.

"One of the biggest things the post exchange brings is a morale builder for the soldiers," U.S. Army Capt. Shane Hunter, HHC, 1st Bn., 133rd Inf. Regt. commander, said.

"There are a lot of things you can't do over here that you can do in the States. One of the things people in the States take for granted is going out and spending money on something, even if it's only a dollar.

"This gives the soldiers the ability to feel a little more like they're at home, to go out and buy something like a cold drink, a sweat tea, or a Monster energy drink, even if it's only for a dollar."

Hunter, who hails from Grundy Center, Iowa, said when the 1-133rd Inf. assumed control over FOB Mehtar Lam in early November, bringing a PX to the base was one of the items on a list of ideas to improve the FOB from the previous unit. Before the PX, Hunter said soldiers would often have to travel to the larger bases at Bagram and Jalalabad to get things they need.

To make the idea of the PX to become a reality, Hunter said he and Nichols contacted various units to find out the process. They said they also drew up plans for the layout of the store together.

Nichols, who is from Boone, Iowa, said he then went to Bagram Airfield and attended a class given by the Army and Air Force Exchange Service, the company which runs PXs throughout the world. There, he said he learned how to order the products for the store and to run the cash register.

The FOB also offers a few stores run by local nationals, where soldiers can buy items representative of Afghan culture, as well as movies and electronics. The PX, however, offers more goods soldiers typically use on a daily basis, such as towels, shower shoes, foot powder, personal hygiene and feminine products, "Tuff boxes" to send things home in and clothes hangers. Pillows and refrigerated cans of Arizona sweet tea, which sold for a dollar each, were also among the day's top-selling items.

Hunter said he came up with the list of items for the initial order of goods for the PX based upon a survey of what soldiers in his company said they'd like to see.

He said the store can be stocked with a maximum of $15,000 in merchandise at one time. He said on opening day the store held closer to $12,000 because there were some items, such as candy and snacks, Ssldiers eat on missions, that had not yet arrived. He also said that the more the store sells, the more products they will be able to carry.

The first official customer of the PX was 1-133rd Inf. battalion commander U.S. Army Lt. Col. Steven Kremer, from Cherokee, Iowa. He entered the store first to check it out, although an unidentified soldier made the first purchase, rushing to the counter to buy a pack of cigarettes.

Two junior enlisted Ssldiers, U.S. Army Pfc. Gregory Shadlow, a supply specialist from Waterloo, Iowa, and U.S. Army Pfc. Jeremiah Crisel, a chaplain's assistant from Sanborn, Iowa, both soldiers from HHC, 1-133rd Inf., will serve as the official "shopkeepers" of the PX, stocking the store and processing its transactions. At the end of its first day of business, the store had sold more than $750 in merchandise.

Shadlow, a supply specialist, is well-versed in running a store, having previously owned a bar in the civilian sector.

"Running the store is a lot of fun," Shadlow said. "I get to joke around with everybody on base as they make their purchases, which is great."

The PX will be open from 3 to 5 p.m. Monday, Wednesday and Friday, Hunter said, and that when units from the smaller outposts come to the base, they can also schedule it to be open.

LAGHMAN PROVINCE, Afghanistan, Dec. 20, 2010—1st Sgt. Brian Nichols, of Boone, Iowa, the Headquarters and Headquarters Company, 1st Battalion, 133rd Infantry Regiment first sergeant, cuts the ribbon outside the connex trailer which houses the new post exchange at Forward Operating Base Mehtar Lam, Afghanistan. (Photo by U.S. Army Staff Sgt. Ryan C. Matson, Task Force Red Bulls Public Affairs)

ANP stations open, attended by ISAF spokesman

*PANJSHIR PROVINCE, Afghanistan, Dec. 21, 2010—*German army Brig. Gen. Joseph Blotz, International Security Assistance Force spokesperson, and Col. Haji Mohamad Aziz, Shutol Afghan National Police commander, talk before the Afghan National Police station ribbon-cutting ceremony in Shutol District. The ceremony took place at Shutol ANP station to commemorate the construction of four ANP stations in Panjshir: Shutol, Anaba, Rohka and Paryan. Blotz visited Panjshir Valley for the day to attend the monthly Provincial Development Committee meeting, participate in the ANP ceremony, and meet the governor and people in the valley. (Photo by French Army Staff Sgt. Romain Beaulinette, Panjshir Provincial Reconstruction Team)

Preston, USO rocks the house at Bagram Airfield

BAGRAM AIRFIELD, Afghainstan, Dec. 21, 2010–Buddy Jewel and the U.S. Army Band "Downrange" are joined by Nicole Hamilton and Brandy Redman, Dallas Cowboys cheerleaders, during a country performance during the Sgt. Maj. of the Army Hope & Freedom Tour 2010 at Bagram Airfield. (Photo by U.S. Army Spc. James Wilton, Task Force Red Bulls Public Affairs)

By U.S. Army Spc. James Wilton
Task Force Red Bulls Public Affairs

BAGRAM AIRFIELD, Afghanistan, Dec. 21, 2010—U.S. Army Sgt. Maj. Kenneth O. Preston rocked the house at Bagram Airfield with help of the U.S. Army Band "Downrange" and other performers during a USO holiday tour here.

Musical performances, a comedy act and dancing ensued as servicemembers and civilians gathered at the clamshell for the Sergeant Major of the Army Hope & Freedom Tour 2010.

"The office of the Sergeant Major of the Army has had the honor and privilege to sponsor this holiday show for nine years," said Preston. "This is the entertainers' way to say thanks for your service and your sacrifice and for what you're doing for not only our country but what you're doing for the Afghan people."

Musical performances included Kenny Thomas, a former Army Ranger, who was joined by Kevin Lawson, James Jones and Emily West. He, along with Alana Grace, brought the house down with rock performances. Buddy Jewel added a little country flair to the mix.

Leeane Tweeden served as mistress of ceremonies and Chonda Pierce did a comedy act. Two Dallas Cowboy cheerleaders, Nicole Hamilton and Brandy Redman, entertained the servicemembers with a dance routine and joined the musical acts on stage as backup dancers.

This is the second USO-sponsored holiday show to make its way through Afghanistan this month. The performers not only thanked the service members but they shared their own stories of personal experiences or family ties to the military.

"Last year at this time I was standing here on stage and my husband, fiancé at the time, was standing back there in that corner," said Tweeden, who is married to an Air National Guardsman and has been a part of 14 USO shows. "When you go back home tonight and e-mail your families or call them, please thank them for us because, after all, they're what you're fighting for."

The servicemembers in attendance were very thankful for the chance to forget about work for awhile and just enjoy the show.

"On behalf of the 32,850 freedom fighters in RC–East, I would like say thank you," said Command Sgt. Maj. Scott Schroeder, Combined Joint Task Force–101 and Regional Command–East command sergeant major. "I know whether it was 30,000 servicemembers or five that you would still be putting the same amount of energy into the show and we appreciate it and I think that this show was more than adequate."

At the conclusion of the show, servicemembers had a chance to meet the entertainers and receive autographs or personal photos.

Task Force Archer Soldiers carol for Christmas

BAGRAM AIRFIELD, Afghanistan, Dec. 24, 2010–U.S. Army Sgt. Harold Dudley (far left), U.S. Army Chaplain (Capt.) Martha Kester (left) both residents of Des Moines, Iowa; U.S. Army 1st Lt. Cecelia Anderson (center) of Natchitoches, La.; 1st Lt. Sarah Droll (back) of Iowa City, Iowa; all with 334th Brigade Support Battalion, Task Force Archer, sing Christmas carols for the staff and patients Staff Sgt. Heathe N. Craig Joint Theater Hospital. (Photo by U.S. Army Spc. Kristina L. Gupton, Task Force Red Bulls Public Affairs)

BAGRAM AIRFIELD, Afghanistan, Dec. 24, 2010– U.S. Army Chaplain Capt. Martha Kester (far left) of Des Moines, Iowa; U.S. Army 1st Lt. Sarah Droll (left) of Iowa City, Iowa; U.S. Army Staff Sgt. Jackie Malloy (center) of State Center, Iowa; U.S Army Sgt. Jarrod Hogan (center) of Cedar Rapids, Iowa; U.S. Army 1st Lt. Cecelia Anderson (right) of Natchitoches, La.; and U.S. Army Sgt. Harold Dudley (far right) of Des Moines, Iowa; all with 334th Brigade Support Battalion, Task Force Archer, pose in front of the Staff Sgt. Heathe N. Craig Joint Theater Hospital [...] (Photo by U.S. Army Spc. Kristina L. Gupton, Task Force Red Bulls Public Affairs)

Servicemembers celebrate Christmas at COP Najil

LAGHMAN PROVINCE, Afghanistan, Dec. 24, 2010—U.S. Army Spc. Lee Goddard, Company E, 1st Battalion, 133rd Infantry Regiment, left, a truck driver from Dysart, Iowa, serves ham to U.S. Army Sgt. Joshua Anderegg, an infantryman from Garber, Iowa, with Company A, 1-133rd Inf.at Combat Outpost Najil. (Photo by U.S. Army Staff Sgt. Ryan C. Matson, Task Force Red Bulls Public Affairs)

By U.S. Army Staff Sgt. Ryan C. Matson
Task Force Red Bulls Public Affairs

and U.S. Army 1st Lt. Matthew Parrino
Company A, 1st Battalion, 133rd Infantry Regiment

LAGHMAN PROVINCE, Afghanistan, Dec. 24, 2010—The COP is nestled along the base of a mountain, and there is no flat ground; everywhere the servicemembers walk is on a grade. Living conditions are tough, as water for showering and laundry is limited, and the bathrooms are tubes in the ground. There's no Post Exchange to be found here; the Soldiers are just happy to have power.

Despite their tough surroundings, Company A came together to celebrate Christmas and share in some holiday cheer.

"You're out here hanging out with a bunch of people you never thought you would," said U.S. Army Sgt. Kenneth Cain, a squad leader with 2nd Platoon from Dubuque, Iowa. "After a deployment like this, getting shot at together, getting blown up, all that stuff, you dang near consider them family."

Cain, 24, said he does have family here. His younger brother, Kurt, also is an infantryman, is at Forward Operating Base Mehtar Lam, about 25 miles away.

"We've seen each other five or six times now," Cain said. "We make it a point to get a picture every place we're together. Mom likes that."

Cain said on Christmas morning, which is Christmas Eve in the United States due to the 9-and-a-half hour time difference, he got to see his children open some of their Christmas presents.

"They all had their little matching pajamas, on so it was kind of cute," Cain said. "It's a little different, a little difficult with the kids. Santa Claus hasn't come yet, so they opened some presents from their grandparents, aunts, and uncles. I got them a little blow-up deer target with some foam arrows and stuff—it's kind of cool."

This is the second Christmas being deployed for Cain, who also spent a Christmas in Kosovo.

"I'd describe this Christmas as interesting, but definitely worthwhile," Cain said. "We all came here to do a job, all on our own free will, nobody got drafted. I extended for this deployment and we're doing it so people back home can enjoy Christmas and the free life."

The servicemembers took a day off from patrolling the mountainous area around COP Najil to enjoy the holiday. One person who did not have time off, however, was U.S. Army Sgt. Scott Stover, Company E, 1st Battalion, 133rd Infantry Regiment, the lone cook on COP Najil. He was still responsible for feeding several hungry platoons of Soldiers, which was nothing new for him. This time, however, he was cooking two lavish holiday dinners.

"It's tiring," Stover admitted. "You get to the point where you can pretty much do it without any sleep."

Stover, who hails from Strawberry Point, Iowa, and his assistant, U.S. Army Spc. Lee Goddard, Company E, 1-133rd Inf., a truck driver from Dysart, Iowa, prepared two feasts. For lunch, they prepared a dinner of ham and turkey with all the fixings.

Even though Goddard usually works as a truck driver, Stover said, he's learned to cook pretty well.

"I told him when he gets home he'll be able to cook his own meals, no more of that easy mac stuff," Stover joked.

Meanwhile, members of 1st Platoon convoyed to FOB Mehtar Lam, an hour and a half drive south, to pick up mail which was piling up.

When the convoy returned, the rest of the Soldiers from Company A were lining the entrance roadway, waiting for their eight pallets of holiday presents and care packages. They swarmed the trucks like bees on a honeycomb.

That night, Stover had prepared yet another special holiday meal. The

Soldiers were treated to lobster tail, shrimp, crab legs and vegetables for their Christmas Eve dinner.

Yes, they were in a rough and tumble, dangerous place in the mountains of eastern Afghanistan, away from family for the holidays. But the company was doing OK—they had become their own extended family.

LAGHMAN PROVINCE, Afghanistan, Dec. 24, 2010–U.S. Army Pfc. Zach Hanood, a mortarman with Company A, 1st Battalion, 133rd Infantry Regiment, from Reinbeck, Iowa, carries a stack of holiday mail packages down the stairs at Combat Outpost Najil. (Photo by U.S. Army Staff Sgt. Ryan C. Matson, Task Force Red Bulls Public Affairs)

Red Bulls conduct KLE in Ghaziabad

LAGHMAN PROVINCE, Afghanistan, Dec. 26, 2010—U.S. Army 1st Lt. John Dundee (left), 1st platoon leader for Company A, 1st Battalion, 133rd Infantry Regiment, from Waterloo, Iowa, and Afghan National Army Lt. Rastum (right), 1st Company, 1st Kandak, 2nd Brigade, 201st ANA Infantry Corps., talk with a citizen of Ghaziabad. (Photo by U.S. Army Staff Sgt. Ryan C. Matson, Task Force Red Bulls)

By U.S. Army Staff Sgt. Ryan C. Matson
Task Force Red Bulls Public Affairs

LAGHMAN PROVINCE, Afghanistan, Dec. 26, 2010—Whenever someone moves into a neighborhood, it's traditional to go meet one's new neighbors.

In a sense, that's what Company A, 1st Battalion, 133rd Infantry Regiment and 1st Company, 1st Kandak, 2nd Brigade, 201st ANA Infantry Corps soldiers were doing when they conducted a Key Leader Engagement in the town of Ghaziabad.

"This was the first time we had been to this particular village; we really didn't have any information on it," said U.S. Army Staff Sgt. Kevin Ott, an infantryman with Company A, 1-133rd Inf., from Moline, Ill., who is also trained in civil affairs and performs that role on missions. "We went there and introduced ourselves and tried to identify the key leaders of the village. They always try to feel you out on the first visit."

The mission was a joint patrol between ANA and their coalition counterparts, said U.S. Army 1st Lt. John Dundee, 1st platoon leader for Company A, 1-133rd Inf., who led the mission from the coalition side. He said the mission is typical of a daily patrol the units conduct together. Dundee said that while the village of Ghaziabad has not presented any problems for Afghan or coalition forces thus far, Watangatu, a nearby village, has been a haven of enemy activity.

"We also wanted to talk with the people and find out what they know about insurgent activity in the area or the Improvised Explosive Devices that have been detonated a mile or so away from them," said Dundee, a native of Waterloo, Iowa. "We try to gather as much information as we can. They gave us a lot of points on where the enemy goes to or where they come from."

The town is about six miles south of Combat Outpost Najil, where Company A has been deployed since November and is one of several small villages on the way to Mehtar Lam, the next large village. Prior to the coalition's presence in the area, the route to Mehtar Lam had been unpaved.

Khir Mohammed, one of the elders who spoke with Ott, expressed gratitude from the townspeople to the Afghan and coalition forces, saying the paved road cuts the trip time from Ghaziabad to Mehtar Lam from a full day's travel, to an hour trip. "This helps thousands of our people," Mohammed said.

Ott said the road is now theirs, and in order to keep the free flow of travel open and to protect the people of the village, the townspeople need to contact the coalition when they see enemies planting IEDs on it.

Mohammed also expressed concerns of his townspeople. Though Ghaziabad is large and well-developed compared to many other towns, Mohammed said the town would like to eventually put in a school of their own, because many of the children go to school in Watangatu, a dangerous area. Mohammed also expressed concern over the distance between the town and medical facilities. Ott said it was important to go to Ghaziabad to show the people the ANA and coalition forces are there to help secure the area. "We don't know what the villagers have heard about us, and unless we go there, we can't tell them who we are and what we're about," he said.

Dundee also said he was pleased with the mission, as the villagers were very open and receptive to the Soldiers, whereas in the past, getting people from a village to speak openly may take several visits. Though it was only an initial meeting, the Afghan and coalition forces opened a line of communications with another village in the area.

LAGHMAN PROVINCE, Afghanistan, Dec. 26, 2010—U.S. Army Pfc. David Feldman (right), an infantryman from Dubuque, Iowa, with Company A, 1st Battalion, 133rd Infantry Regiment, photographs one of the citizens of Ghaziabad. (Photo by U.S. Army Staff Sgt. Ryan C. Matson, Task Force Red Bulls)

LAGHMAN PROVINCE, Afghanistan, Dec. 26, 2010—U.S. Army Staff Sgt. Robert Ott (left), an infantryman trained in civil affairs with Company A, 1st Battalion, 133rd Infantry Regiment, talks with village elder Khir Mohammed (right) in the village of Ghaziabad. Ott, who hails from Moline, Ill., and the other Soldiers of Company A conducted a Key Leader Engagement with the Afghan National Army to assess the villager's needs and opinion on the coalition. (Photo by U.S. Army Staff Sgt. Ryan C. Matson, Task Force Red Bulls)

Panjshir PRT talks power with Shast villagers

PANJSHIR PROVINCE, Afghanistan, Dec. 27, 2010—Scott Davis (center left), U.S. Army Corps of Engineers construction representative with Panjshir PRT and an Omaha, Neb., native, U.S. Air Force Capt. Brian Jackson (center right), Panjshir Provincial Reconstruction Team engineering lead and a South Haven, Mich., native, Daniel Fredrickson (far right), U.S. Army Corps of Engineers member with Panjshir Provincial Reconstruction Team and a Battleground, Wash., native, and an afghan interpreter walk approximately 1.5 miles to check a canal's general condition and size in Rokha District. The canal will be used to channel water for a micro-hydro dam system. Members from the PRT visited the Shast village to discuss the concerns in the village and the best way to distribute power from the micro-hydro system. (Photo by French Army Staff Sgt. Romain Beaulinette, Panjshir Provincial Reconstruction Team)

PANJSHIR PROVINCE, Afghanistan, Dec. 27, 2010—U.S. Air Force Lt. Col. Joseph Blevins (right), Panjshir Provincial Reconstruction Team commander and an Oregonia, Ohio, native, meets Gul Haidar, the Shast village elder and a former Mujahedeen commander, in Rokha District. Members from the PRT visited the Shast village to discuss the concerns in the village and the best way to distribute power from the micro-hydro system. (Photo by French Army Staff Sgt. Romain Beaulinette, Panjshir Provincial Reconstruction Team)

PANJSHIR PROVINCE, Afghanistan, Dec. 27, 2010—Panjshir Provincial Reconstruction Team members meet with Gul Haidar, the Shast village elder and a former Mujahedeen commander, along with Shast villagers and former Mujahedeen members in Rokha District. The PRT commander, sergeant major, civil affairs and engineering teams visited the Shast village to discuss the concerns in the village. One issue discussed was the best way to distribute power from the micro-hydro dam system. (Photo by French Army Staff Sgt. Romain Beaulinette, Panjshir Provincial Reconstruction Team)

Task Force Ironman fights off attack on COP Najil

*LAGHMAN PROVINCE, Afghanistan, Dec. 29, 2010—*U.S. Army Sgt. Kenneth Cain, a squad leader with Company A, 1st Battalion, 133rd Infantry Regiment, Task Force Ironman, part of the 2nd Brigade Combat Team, 34th Infantry Division, Task Force Red Bulls, from Dubuque, Iowa, looks for enemy activity following an attack on Combat Outpost Najil. The attack, the largest on the COP to that point, was quickly brought to an end without any injuries to U.S. forces with the help of close-air support. (Photo by U.S. Army Staff Sgt. Ryan C. Matson, Task Force Red Bulls Public Affairs)

*LAGHMAN PROVINCE, Afghanistan, Dec. 29, 2010—*Pieces of a 60 mm mortar shell recovered from the mountainside behind Combat Outpost Najil after an attack. The attack was the largest against the COP since the Soldiers from Company A, 1st Battalion, 133rd Infantry Regiment, Task Force Ironman, part of the 2nd Brigade Combat Team, 34th Infantry Division, Task Force Red Bulls took over operations. Five mortar shells were fired on the COP from insurgent forces, as well as small arms fire. The attack was quickly extinguished with the help of close-air support without any injuries to U.S. Soldiers. (Photo by U.S. Army Staff Sgt. Ryan C. Matson, Task Force Red Bulls Public Affairs)

U.S. veterinarians learn Afghan CV-RDL capabilities

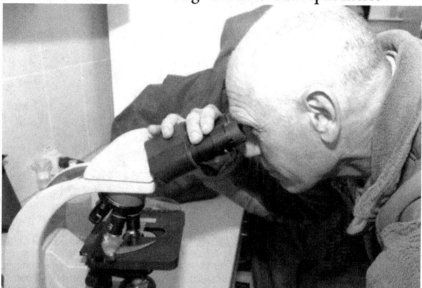

KABUL, Afghanistan, Dec. 28, 2010–U.S. Army Maj. Loren Adams, a New Liberty, Iowa, resident and a veterinarian with the Iowa Agribusiness Development Team examines an anthrax slide through a microscope in the Central Veterinary Research and Diagnostics Lab in Kabul here during a tour. The tour gave a group of U.S. Army vets a better understanding of the lab's capabilities which they will pass on to the Afghan veterinarians they work with, in their respective provinces. (Photo by U.S. Army Spc. James Wilton, Task Force Red Bulls Public Affairs)

By U.S. Army Spc. James Wilton
Task Force Red Bulls Public Affairs

KABUL, Afghanistan, Dec. 28, 2010—A group of U.S. Army veterinarians visited the Afghan Central Veterinary Research and Development Lab here, in order to better understand its capabilities.

The visit included U.S. Army representatives from the Kentucky Agribusiness Development Team II, the Iowa Agribusiness Development Team, the 62nd Cooperative Medical Assistance Brigade and the 411th Civil Affairs Battalion.

The knowledge gained from the visit will help the veterinarians design their workshops, where they train and work with Afghan vets on the provincial and district level. The Kentucky ADT-II works with vets from Panjshir, Parwan, and Kapisa provinces, where the Iowa ADT and 411th work with vets in Kunar and Kandahar.

The tour was guided by Dr. Gulam Mohammad Ziay, the director of Animal Health and Welfare at CV RDL, and Dr. Daad Mohammad Amir, the

Chief Executive Technical Director for the Dutch Committee for Afghanistan, VetServ. Dr. Mohibullah Halimi, the Director General of Animal Health and Production from the Afghan Ministry of Agriculture Irrigations and Livestock, also attended.

"Local vets are key players in responding to animal disease, a constant threat to Afghanistan, which is largely an agricultural country," said U.S. Army Col. James G. Floyd, a Shreveport, La., native and a veterinarian with the Kentucky ADT-II. "Most Afghan families outside of urban areas keep livestock, and in order to prevent disease in these animals, vets in those locations must reliably be able to diagnose their causes."

The CV RDL, which opened in 2009, is the main laboratory controlling 13 provincial labs and six regional labs in Afghanistan. The labs are used to diagnose and document diseases in livestock and report the findings to the MAIL. Fast, proper detection and documentation of these issues helps to ensure the livelihood and health of the Afghan people.

"This is about the future of Afghanistan," said Ziay. "The country of Afghanistan needs to establish a standardized system designed to properly track and take samples from livestock, then test and diagnose diseases, reporting the finding to the government and we have done that; all that is left is implementation."

The CV RDL confirms the diagnosis made in the field by Afghan vets in the smaller provincial and regional labs, as well as conducting training and drafting standardized regulations for those facilities. The facility has departments specializing in histopathology, toxicology, biochemistry, drug analysis, public health and a school to train laboratory technicians. The public health department deals with monitoring and testing products for import and export making sure they're safe for human consumption or use.

Red Bull Soldiers train with ANA, ANP

BAGRAM AIRFIELD, Afghanistan, Dec. 29, 2010—Troop B, 1st Squadron, 113th Cavalry Regiment squad leader, U.S. Army Staff Sgt. Paul Deugan, an Ankeny, Iowa, resident, observes an Afghan National Police officer practice rifle techniques here at Bagram Airfield. Soldiers of Troop B trained with the Afghan National Army and the police to prepare for upcoming joint missions. (Photo by U.S. Army Staff Sgt. Ashlee Lolkus, Task Force Red Bulls Public Affairs)

BAGRAM AIRFIELD, Dec. 29, 2010—U.S. Army Sgt. Jason Stoos, an Ankeny, Iowa, resident, instructs Afghan National Police officers on room clearing techniques here on Bagram Airfield. Soldiers of Troop B, 1st Squadron, 113th Cavalry Regiment trained with the ANA and the Afghan National Police to prepare for upcoming joint missions. Photo by U.S. Army Staff Sgt. Ashlee Lolkus, Task Force Red Bulls Public Affairs)

BAGRAM AIRFIELD, Afghanistan, Dec. 29, 2010—U.S. Army Spc. Thomas Sesker (center, standing), an Ogden, Iowa, resident, shows Afghan National Army soldiers how to conduct a personnel search using U.S. Army Spc. Jason Kincel of Oskaloosa, Iowa, as a demonstrator on Bagram Airfield. Sesker, a vehicle .50-caliber machine gunner, and Kincel, a vehicle driver, are both part of 1st Platoon, Troop B, 1st Squadron of the 113th Cavalry Regiment. [...] (Photo by U.S. Army Staff Sgt. Ashlee Lolkus, Task Force Red Bulls Public Affairs)

Panjshir PRT engineers inspect Paryan road

PANJSHIR PROVINCE, Afghanistan, Dec. 29, 2010—U.S. Air Force 2nd Lt. Phil Compton of Doty, Wash., and U.S. Air Force Tech. Sgt. Eric Garcia of Corpus Christi, Texas, both engineers with Panjshir Provincial Reconstruction Team, check the quality of a bridge under construction on the main road in Paryan District. Panjshir PRT engineers conduct weekly quality control checks on Panjshir road projects to ensure the quality of construction meets work requirements. (Photo by French Army Staff Sgt. Romain Beaulinette, Panjshir Provincial Reconstruction Team)

PANJSHIR PROVINCE, Afghanistan, Dec. 29, 2010—U.S. Air Force 2nd Lt. Phil Compton of Doty, Wash., Panjshir Provincial Reconstruction Team engineer, and Panjshir PRT local Afghan engineer Abid Wardak check the structural integrity of the retaining wall supporting bridge entry way in Paryan District. [...] (Photo by French Army Staff Sgt. Romain Beaulinette, Panjshir Provincial Reconstruction Team)

Red Bulls patrol area around COP Najil

LAGHMAN PROVINCE, Afghanistan, Dec. 30, 2011—The village of Daratah sits in northeastern Afghanistan. Soldiers from Company A, 1st Battalion, 133rd Infantry Regiment, Task Force Ironman, part of the 2nd Brigade Combat Team, 34th Infantry Division, Task Force Red Bulls, conducted a Key Leader Engagement with a village elder, as well as a mounted and dismounted patrol through several other hot spots around Combat Outpost Najil here. The patrol was a joint venture with Afghan National Army Soldiers from 1st Company, 1st Kandak, 2nd Brigade, 201st ANA Infantry Corps. (Photo by U.S. Army Staff Sgt. Ryan C. Matson, Task Force Red Bulls Public Affairs)

LAGHMAN PROVINCE, Afghanistan Dec. 30, 2011—Soldiers from Company A, 1st Battalion, 133rd Infantry Regiment, Task Force Ironman, out of Dubuque, Iowa, cross a creek near the town of Khota here. [...] (Photo by U.S. Army Staff Sgt. Ryan C. Matson, Task Force Red Bulls Public Affairs)

LAGHMAN PROVINCE, Afghanistan, Dec. 30, 2011—U.S. Army Capt. Jason Merchant (right), the company commander of Company A, 1st Battalion, 133rd Infantry Regiment, Task Force Ironman, part of the 2nd Brigade Combat Team, 34th Infantry Division, Task Force Red Bulls, from Dysart, Iowa, hands out cards to Afghan security guards near Combat Outpost Najil. The cards were printed with contact information for people to call in the event they see insurgent activity or are harassed by insurgent forces. [...] (Photo by U.S. Army Staff Sgt. Ryan C. Matson, Task Force Red Bulls Public Affairs)

LAGHMAN PROVINCE, Afghanistan, Dec. 30, 2011—U.S. Army Spc. John Rocha, an infantryman with Company A, 1st Battalion, 133rd Infantry Regiment, from Geneseo, Ill., patrols the highway near the village of Kusuk, as a man and his donkey walk by. [...] (Photo by U.S. Army Staff Sgt. Ryan C. Matson, Task Force Red Bulls Public Affairs)

832nd Engineer Company meets village leaders

PARWAN PROVINCE, Afghanistan, Dec. 30, 2010—U.S. Army Sgt. Adam Dean of Morning Sun, Iowa, 832nd Engineer Company combat engineer, attached to 1st Squadron, 113th Cavalry Regiment, speaks with young Afghan boys from the village of Qalah-ye Boland. The engineers visited the village to meet the village malik and discuss security issues within the village. (Photo by U.S. Army Spc. Kristina L. Gupton, Task Force Red Bulls Public Affairs)

PARWAN PROVINCE, Afghanistan, Dec. 30, 2010—U.S. Army Sgt. 1st Class Todd Sackman of Ottumwa, Iowa, 832nd Engineer Company combat engineer, attached to 1st Squadron, 113th Cavalry Regiment, gives fuel to the village malik of Qalah-ye Boland for the generator that provides electricity throughout the village. [...] (Photo by U.S. Army Spc. Kristina L. Gupton, Task Force Red Bulls Public Affairs)

133

PARWAN PROVINCE, Afghanistan, Dec. 30, 2010—U.S. Army Sgt. 1st Class Todd Sackman of Ottumwa, Iowa (center), and Sgt. Adam Dean of Morning Sun, Iowa (left), both combat engineers with 832nd Engineer Company, attached to 1st Squadron, 113th Cavalry Regiment, speak with the village malik of Torkman. The 832nd Engineer Company visited the Qalah-Ye Boland village to conduct an assessment of the village and to discuss security issues they may have. (Photo by U.S. Army Spc. Kristina L. Gupton, Task Force Red Bulls Public Affairs)

PARWAN PROVINCE, Afghanistan, Dec. 30, 2010—U.S. Army Spc. Tyler Hardy of Keokuk, Iowa (right), and Sgt. Shane Jobe of Burlington, Iowa, both combat engineers with 832nd Engineer Company, attached to 1st Squadron, 113th Cavalry Regiment, provide security for fellow Soldiers while conducting a Key Leader Engagement in the village of Qalander Khel. (Photo by U.S. Army Spc. Kristina L. Gupton, Task Force Red Bulls Public Affairs)

JANUARY
2011

Red Bulls look back on year–
from Iowa to Eastern Afghanistan

By U.S. Army Staff Sgt. Ryan C. Matson
Task Force Red Bulls Public Affairs

and U.S. Army 1st Lt. Matthew Parrino
Company A, 1st Battalion, 133rd Infantry Regiment

LAGHMAN PROVINCE, Afghanistan, Jan. 1, 2011—"It's been very interesting."

That's how U.S. Army 1st Sgt. Chris Harrison, the top enlisted Soldier in Company A (nicknamed "Apocalypse" Company), 1st Battalion, 133rd Infantry Regiment, Task Force Ironman, a part of the 2nd Brigade Combat Team, 34th Infantry Division, Task Force Red Bulls, described the whirlwind journey his company has been on for much of the last 12 months, taking them from Dubuque, Iowa, to tiny Combat Outpost Najil in north-eastern Afghanistan here.

The train-up

Harrison, who hails from Cedar Rapids, Iowa, said that the company conducted a lot of training throughout the year, which helped them prepare for the conditions they face at the remote outpost, Najil, their current location.

Soldiers in the company spent the spring and summer months attending various schools to get specialized training in everything from squad designated marksman training, Combat Lifesaver and combatives classes, to schools teaching them to fly an unmanned aircraft system.

The final bit of training, and the part the Soldiers said was the most beneficial, was at the National Training Center in Fort Irwin, Calif., in mid-September. The company stayed in a place called Combat Outpost Nine, in which they had literally nothing. The COP amounted to an empty gravel parking lot, Harrison said. The Soldiers slept on the ground and a Humvee served as their Tactical Operations Center.

The company would receive a mission and often have less than three hours to plan it and disseminate it to the Soldiers before execution. During the exercise, they were also ambushed by about 200 opposing forces soldiers– Soldiers who are stationed at Fort Irwin and know the area.

"They cheated, of course," Staff Sgt. John Oberfoell, a platoon sergeant for Company A, from Dubuque, Iowa, said. "We had .50-caliber machine guns set up in strategic spots, and they didn't die when we shot them. The gear they wear, which is supposed to go off when one of our weapons shoots a blank at them, didn't have any batteries in them! It was mass chaos."

The scenario was meant to depict the absolute worst type of event: a COP being overrun. Although the training seemed harsh at the time, Harrison said it helped his company more than any other training they received leading up to the deployment.

"Everything was totally extreme," Harrison said. "COP Nine set this company up for success. And at every place we went, they put our company's white [rest] days at the end of the cycle. So it was go, go, go, and then on our white days we'd pack and go to the next place and do the same thing, no time off."

"That kind of motivated everybody for here. Everybody's always go, go, go here, too, and we're all kind of used to it. Everything we've done so far has molded our company for success. This is normal for us ..."

Oberfoell laughed.

"It did suck though," he added.

COP Nine to COP Najil

From NTC, the company deployed right into theater. They found themselves at COP Najil, a tiny outpost in the thick of enemy territory on a mountain with a few plywood buildings, plastic pipes in the grounds as urinals, and scarce provisions. Compared to COP Nine, however, it was a paradise, and as soon as they arrived at the end of October, Company A went right to work with the local nationals to make it better. By their third day in country, the unit had begun conducting patrols in the area of operations.

The company also met their Afghan counterparts, the 1st Company, 1st Kandak, 2nd Brigade, 201st ANA Infantry Corps.

"The first couple weeks we heard all these horror stories about how the Afghan National Army was lazy," Oberfoell said. However, he said these rumors were quickly disproven the first time Company A and 1st Company faced enemy contact Nov. 11.

Hellfire Ridge

It was Nov. 11 when Apocalyspe Company and their Afghan partner, 1st Company, travelled north from COP Najil for a Key Leader Engagement in the village of Domlech. After the KLE concluded, some of the Soldiers started taking contact from the area of another nearby village, Kusuk.

The Soldiers soon found themselves in the midst of an ambush and took heavy contact for about ten minutes, including Rocket-Propelled Grenade rounds from one of the houses in the village. The Quick Reaction Force was called out, and the artillery dropped some rounds in response. The fighting continued for about 15 more minutes, at which time Close Air Support responded, ending the conflict. Apache helicopters responded very quickly and fired Hellfire missiles onto one of the mountains where the insurgents were firing from, which the Soldiers now refer to as "Hellfire Ridge." One of the caves the enemy fired from was also hit by CAS, which earned it the nickname of "Hellfire Cave." The ANA stormed into the village after receiving contact to search for those responsible.

By the end of the battle, Company A and their Afghan counterparts had killed 12 insurgents, including a mid-level Taliban leader. The leader was originally incorrectly reported in the press as being captured by a cavalry unit who was not in the AO, Harrison said. He said the unit found out about his death from reports of his, and several other, Taliban funerals the next day. It was one of the largest engagements by this Red Bulls battalion in recent history.

Sniper kill and cache find

At the end of November, the Kansas Agribusiness Development Team was attacked by RPG and small arms fire in the nearby village of Gumret. Company A, who was providing security with the ANA, responded quickly with several gun-trucks returning fire. One of the company's snipers killed the local Taliban's second-in-charge from 1150 yards during this brief engagement.

Another highlight for the company came Dec. 5. Company A's third platoon had come in contact at Watangatu when convoying up to COP Najil from FOB Mehtar Lam, about 20 miles to the South.

The Soldiers cordoned off the area and began searching where they had received contact. U.S. Army Spc. Curtis Blake Jr., an infantryman with Company A from Clinton, Iowa, explained what happened next.

"We were walking through the village of Sigin when a massive amount of gunfire came out from our trucks," Blake recalled. "They were firing at two guys who were setting up an ambush on us with an RPG and a PKM [automatic machine gun].

"We talked with the villagers and one of the guys was literally shaking, he was scared and we knew he knew something about was going on. He actually gave us permission to search the village and we weren't initially finding anything. We had the ANA knocking on doors and we were looking all over the place. We knew they were setting up an Improvised Explosive Device set and we knew from the muzzle flashes where they had been. We found some holes they had dug as fighting positions and some heavy foot traffic around them. We found some rat trails and were crawling around these big rock structures. It was interesting because you could see from these massive rocks that they had perfect cover to look down at us.

"We started looking around that area and the commander found some Battle Dress Uniform pants, which got everybody excited. We continued further on, following some rat trails and found a rock with some writing on it and asked the terp what it meant. We came to find out it was the trademark signature of one of the Taliban leaders in the area, and it was a pretty hot trail.

"Then the ANA started to hoot and yell—they had found this massive trail of biscuit wrappers. There was brass laying all over the place and we found AK-47s, RPGs, a full BDU uniform, a book bag, you name it. It was awesome. Not only did we take away some of their firepower, but we sent a message to them—we're not scared, and we're gonna find you!"

Longest battle claims a brother

On Dec. 11, the company found themselves in another lengthy ambush. They were near Angar Watu, another nearby village, when they started receiving contact from every direction, including heavy RPG fire. Fighting continued for about 40 minutes until the ambush was silenced. The unit again incorporated CAS in bringing an end to the attack.

Company A had no casualties during the engagement; however, one of the ANA soldiers was killed during the battle.

"It was the same as losing one of our own Soldiers," said Capt. Jason Merchant, Company A commander from Dysart, Iowa. "We do everything with these guys, they're our brothers-in-arms."

Company A Soldiers said they have become close with their Afghan counterparts over the past few months.

"They go out on traffic control points and they search every vehicle, they search every person," Oberfoell said. "We're very lucky to work with this group of soldiers."

"They're go-getters," Harrison said. "No doubt about it."

Other attacks

On Dec. 29, the COP suffered its worst attack of the year as four mortars struck. Company A closely monitored the area and called in another air strike on the enemy position, quickly quelling the attack.

The company has also endured numerous Improvised Explosive Device attacks during their time here. Fortunately, only one Soldier, Pfc. Andrew Zimmerman, an infantryman from Atkins, Iowa, suffered any injuries. Zimmerman, who was a gunner on a convoy, was knocked briefly unconscious and received some stitches to his face as a result of one of the IED attacks at Watangatu, a village to the south of COP Najil which has been a haven of such activity.

The future

Company A has endured a lot of tough training, rough conditions and some fights with the enemy during 2010. It's been a long time and a large distance from COP Nine to COP Najil, but these Red Bulls keep charging hard.

Red Bulls patrol IED hotbed

LAGHMAN PROVINCE, Afghanistan, Jan. 1, 2011—U.S. Army Capt. Jason Merchant, the Company A, 1st Battalion, 133rd Infantry Regiment commander from Dysart, Iowa, scans the area while on patrol on a mountainside near the village of Sigin. The soldiers discovered a command wire in a riverbed while on patrol [...] The area, near the Watangatu boys' school, has been an IED hotbed. (Photo by U.S. Army Staff Sgt. Ryan C. Matson, Task Force Red Bulls Public Affairs)

LAGHMAN PROVINCE, Afghanistan, Jan. 1, 2011—U.S. Army Sgt. Kenneth Cain, a squad leader with Company A, 1st Battalion, 133rd Infantry Regiment from Dubuque, Iowa, pauses after digging loose some broken command wire the unit located in a riverbed while on patrol near the village of Sigin. The company had been hit by Improvised Explosive Devices in the area in the past and called out the 744th Ordnance Company's Explosive Ordnance Disposal team to locate an IED, but it was not found. (Photo by U.S. Army Staff Sgt. Ryan C. Matson, Task Force Red Bulls Public Affairs)

Redhorse Soldiers build up base defense

PARWAN PROVINCE, Afghanistan, Jan. 1, 2011—U.S. soldiers with Troop B, 1st Squadron, 113th Cavalry Regiment, Task Force Redhorse, part of the 2nd Brigade Combat Team, 34th Infantry Division, Task Force Red Bulls, pass sandbags down the work line to fortify their fighting positions where they provide security for fellow soldiers. Troop B occupied vehicle patrol base Dandar to build up the base defense and to conduct dismounted patrols through surrounding villages to ensure security of the area. (Photo by U.S. Army Spc. Kristina L. Gupton, Task Force Red Bulls Public Affairs)

PARWAN PROVINCE, Afghanistan, Jan. 1, 2011— U.S. Army Staff Sgt. Paul Deugan (left) of Ankeny, Iowa, and U.S. Army Sgt. Drew Russell (right) of Dubuque, Iowa, both cavalry scouts with Troop B, 1st Squadron, 113th Cavalry Regiment, part of the 2nd Brigade Combat Team, 34th Infantry Division, Task Force Red Bulls, scan their sector of fire, while Russell utilizes an M-249 Squad Automatic Weapon at Vehicle Patrol Base Dandar. [...] (Photo by U.S. Army Spc. Kristina L. Gupton, Task Force Red Bulls Public Affairs)

Red Bulls patrol through Dandar

PARWAN PROVINCE, Afghanistan, Jan. 2, 2011—U.S. Army Sgt. 1st Class Chris Buchness of Leonardtown, Md., an infantryman and 3rd platoon sergeant with Troop B, 1st Squadron, 113th Cavalry Regiment, Task Force Redhorse, part of the 2nd Brigade Combat Team, 34th Infantry Division, Task Force Red Bulls, and fellow soldiers scan the area while on a dismounted patrol through Dandar village. The Task Force Redhorse soldiers conducted the dismount patrol through surrounding villages to ensure security of the area and to conduct a Key Leader Engagement with village elders. (Photo by U.S. Army Spc. Kristina L. Gupton, Task Force Red Bulls Public Affairs)

PARWAN PROVINCE, Afghanistan, Jan. 2, 2011—U.S. Army Spc. John Marks of Dubuque, Iowa, a cannon crewmember with Troop B, 1st Squadron, 113th Cavalry Regiment, Task Force Redhorse, part of the 2nd Brigade Combat Team, 34th Infantry Division, Task Force Red Bulls, utilizes a M-240B machine gun to provide security overwatch for fellow soldiers conducting a Key Leader Engagement in the village of Dandar. Task Force Redhorse soldiers conducted a Key Leader Engagement with village elder to ensure security within the village and to address concerns they may have. (Photo by U.S. Army Spc. Kristina L. Gupton, Task Force Red Bulls Public Affairs)

Provincial governor holds event to meet people

LAGHMAN PROVINCE, Afghanistan, Jan. 2, 2011—U.S. Air Force Lt. Col. John C. Walker (center), native of Jacksonville, Ill., and the Laghman Provincial Reconstruction Team commander, stands with Laghman Provincial Gov. Mohammad Iqbal Azizi (right) at his compound in downtown Mehtar Lam. The governor invited residents of Laghman Province to his "Meet the People" event where he listened to grievances, resolved land disputes and other arguments between people and discussed the future of Laghman Province. (Photo by U.S. Air Force Senior Airman Ronifel S. Yasay, Laghman Provincial Reconstruction Team)

LAGHMAN PROVINCE, Afghanistan, Jan. 2, 2011—Laghman residents discuss grievances and other difficulties with Provincial Gov. Mohammad Iqbal Azizi (center). The governor invited residents of Laghman Province to his "Meet the People" event where he listened to grievances, resolved land disputes and other arguments between people, and discussed the future of Laghman Province. (Photo by U.S. Air Force Senior Airman Ronifel S. Yasay, Laghman Provincial Reconstruction Team)

Redhorse Troop preps for night patrol

PARWAN PROVINCE, Afghanistan, Jan. 2, 2011—Bravo Troop, 1st Squadron, 113th Cavalry Regiment, Task Force Redhorse soldiers, U.S. Army Spc. Daniel Holz (left corner), a medic from Le Mars, Iowa, U.S. Army Spc. Matthew Johnson (left), of Cedar Rapids, Iowa, and U.S. Army Pfc. Matthew Gibson (left center), of Batavia Ill., both cavalry scouts, U.S. Army Spc. Roman Eastman (center) of Akron, Iowa, a fire support specialist and U.S. Army Sgt. 1st Class Taylor Greene (right) of Des Moines, Iowa, a cavalry scout, listen as U.S. Army Sgt. 1st Class Chris Buchness (right corner), of Leonardtown, Md., an infantryman and 3rd Platoon sergeant, gives the mission brief before conducting a night patrol. (Photo by U.S. Army Spc. Kristina L. Gupton, Task Force Red Bulls Public Affairs)

PARWAN PROVINCE, Afghanistan, Jan. 2, 2011—U.S. Army Spc. Roman Eastman of Akron, Iowa, and a fire support specialist with Bravo Troop, 1st Squadron, 113th Cavalry Regiment, Task Force Redhorse, takes a knee as he listens to a mission brief [...] (Photo by U.S. Army Spc. Kristina L. Gupton, Task Force Red Bulls Public Affairs)

PARWAN PROVINCE, Afghanistan, Jan. 2, 2011—U.S. Army Sgt. 1st Class Chris Buchness (right), of Leonardtown, Md., an infantryman and 3rd Platoon sergeant, and U.S. Army Sgt. 1st Class Taylor Greene (left), of Des Moines, Iowa, and a cavalry scout, both with Bravo Troop, 1st Squadron, 113th Cavalry Regiment, brief their soldiers on reaction to contact before conducting a night patrol, Jan. 2. Bravo Troop soldiers conducted a night patrol to ensure security around the Vehicle Patrol Base Dandar. (Photo by U.S. Army Spc. Kristina L. Gupton, Task Force Red Bulls Public Affairs)

Iowa town showers small Afghan school with supplies

*LAGHMAN PROVINCE, Afghanistan, Jan. 3, 2011—*U.S. Army 2nd Lt. Taylor A. Gingrich, an infantry officer from Cedar Falls, Iowa, with Company A, 1st Battalion, 133rd Infantry Regiment, Task Force Ironman, a part of 2nd Brigade Combat Team, 34th Infantry Division, Task Force Red Bulls, draws a smile from a small Afghan boy as Gingrich lets the boy wear his helmet at Quala e' Najil School in Najil. The Soldiers from Company A., as well as Afghan National Army soldiers from 1st Company, 1st Kandak, 2nd Brigade, 201st ANA Infantry Corps, delivered supplies donated by people from the town of Waverly, Iowa, and its surrounding communities. (Photo by U.S. Army Staff Sgt. Ryan C. Matson, Task Force Red Bulls Public Affairs)

By U.S. Army Staff Sgt. Ryan C. Matson
Task Force Red Bulls Public Affairs

LAGHMAN PROVINCE, Afghanistan, Jan. 3, 2011— "I don't deserve to be on the front page of the paper," said U.S. Army Sgt. Derrick Wygle. "My employer does. I just asked for a couple boxes of school supplies."

Wygle, a mortarman with Company A, 1st Battalion, 133rd Infantry Regiment, 2nd Brigade Combat, 34th Infantry Division, is an Applington, Iowa, native who now lives in Waverly.

What Wygle got was nearly 100 boxes of school supplies from the town of Waverly, Iowa, and its surrounding communities.

And he's still counting.

Toward the end of November, Wygle was talking with his wife Ona, who asked him what he wanted for Christmas. In a way, she was asking on behalf of her husband's stateside employer, the Waverly Health Center, where he works as an emergency room unit coordinator. They were making it a project to send him a good present.

"I'm not much of a Christmas guy; to me it's more about family than gifts and there's not much I could use here," Wygle said. "So I said, 'Well, have them send me a box or two of school supplies.'"

The supplies were for children at the local school, Quala e' Najil. It is one of the closest schools to the tiny Combat Outpost Najil where Wygle and his fellow Soldiers from Company A are serving in eastern Afghanistan. In an area that is one of the more dangerous spots in the Laghman Province, Najil is a town where the Soldiers say they usually feel relatively safe, and children walk up and talk to them from the streets.

From there, Wygle, a seven-year veteran of the Iowa National Guard, said his co-workers at the Waverly Health Center approached the local newspaper and asked for donations., who. Wygle said Ona did not tell him about the article in the Bremer County Independent until after it came out and packages started pouring in. He now has the article on a table inside the wooden b-hut in which he and some of the other mortarmen live. Wygle's story is on the front page, with a photo his wife, a photographer, took of him.

To say the response was overwhelming was almost an understatement, Wygle said.

"It's a really good thing," he said. "They said they sent about 20 boxes, 16 of which I've already received, and they have 70 or more on the way! They still continue, today, to get stuff in for these kids. Basically in one month's time, the town of Waverly and its surrounding areas gathered up enough school supplies for all 3,000 kids at the school."

Wygle, other Soldiers from Company A, and Afghan National Army soldiers from 1st Company, 1st Kandak, 2nd Brigade, 201st ANA Infantry Corps, conducted a dismounted patrol to the village of Najil Jan. 3 and delivered the first batch of supplies to the school. The troops were immediately flooded by children, whose teachers herded them back into their classrooms.

At the school, the soldiers took time to interact with the children and toured the school with the principal. About 2,000 boys attend the school in the morning, with another 950 girls attending in the afternoon. The ANA were noticeably happy to line up the children and hand them the supplies.

Wygle said little things make a huge difference to the children, who are very poor. In fact, a good toy for a child in the village is a wire with two wire wheels on it, which they push through the streets.

"We are trying to make sure the kids who don't have things get them," he said. "They're not asking for big things. You give them a pen and it's like you just gave them their first bicycle."

The Iowa support rendered boxes full of pens, pencils, snacks, pads and book bags.

Quala e' Najil school principal Haminullah said he is thankful for the donations from the United States and that they were a good thing because the children are from a country that is poor and war-torn. He said the supplies will help the students get a better education, which will benefit the larger picture.

"Education is the foundation of a strong country," he said.

U.S. Army Maj. Steven Shannon, the Laghman Provincial Reconstruction Team civil affairs team chief who works at COP Najil with the Company A Soldiers, said he has been to the school and met with Haminullah six or seven times. He said one of his planned projects is to renovate the inside of the school and add classrooms to it as well as provide sidewalks on the streets outside for the safety of the children.

In the meantime, Shannon said these school supplies will make a big difference.

"Sgt. Wygle made an impromptu request to his employer for a couple boxes of school supplies and they promoted it and made it a huge effort from the town of Waverly," he said. "I think it's an awesome thing for the town and businesses of Waverly to do. The people really appreciate it, because the standard of living here is pretty low.

"Plus, the word on the work that we do for these people—that word gets out. People communicate here by word of mouth. We've put in for six projects for (Company A) and the word is already out. Elders are starting to come to the COP and talk about their concerns, and we're not going to get anything done here without the elders."

Shannon said though the majority of the supplies came from Bremer County, there were also some donated from a project known as Operation Care.

Wygle said the response was amazing, but it didn't completely surprise him.

"It's kind of an Iowa thing," he said. "It's not just my community; it's all of our communities. They support every single one of our Soldiers here. My employer has always supported me through drills, flood duty, schools, deployments and now this. They really, really stepped up."

Waverly and its surrounding towns have made it clear—they support their Soldiers.

334th BSB keeps Soldiers' lifeline running strong

PARWAN PROVINCE, Afghanistan, Jan. 4, 2011—U.S. Army Spc. Jill Brogan from Sioux City, Iowa, 1st Squadron, 113th Cavalry Regiment, Task Force Redhorse, sorts through boxes in a supply delivery made by Company A, 334th Brigade Support Battalion, Task Force Archer, to Combat Outpost Pushtaysark Jan 4. Both Task Force Redhorse and Task Force Archer are a part of 2nd Brigade Combat Team, 34th Infantry Division, Task Force Red Bulls. (Photo by U.S. Army Spc. James Wilton, Task Force Red Bulls Public Affairs)

By U.S. Army Spc. James Wilton
Task Force Red Bulls Public Affairs

PARWAN PROVINCE, Afghanistan, Jan. 4, 2011–Soldiers stand amidst the morning haze, their banter highlighted by smoke and fog, flowing from their mouths.

Slowly, the scattered groups converge into one mass. Chaplain (Capt.) Martha Kester, a Des Moines, Iowa, resident and the chaplain for the 334th Brigade Support Battalion, Task Force Archer, part of 2nd Brigade Combat Team, 34th Infantry Division, Task Force Red Bulls, recites a small prayer for protection and safe travel.

Company A, 334th BSB, begins every supply logistical package, known as a LOGPAC, this way. On Jan. 4, they went to Combat Outpost Pushtayshark, nicknamed COP Red Hill by a coalition interpreter when asked to translate Pushtayshark. These LOGPACs are just another day for the Soldiers of Company A, but an important part of a COP's lifeline and a morale booster for the Soldiers stationed there.

"It's their sustainment of life," said U.S. Army Sgt. Mike Helton of Van

Meter, Iowa, Company A. "We bring them their food, fuel and other supplies, like ammo. To me, it's just a job, one with good job security and a way we get to help out, where we can."

Building materials and other items used for work or other daily tasks also come out on the LOGPACs.

"I remember our first couple missions out to Red Hill," said U.S. Army Sgt. Josh Pointsett of Bettendorf, Iowa, Company A. "We brought out their containers to store water and the wood they used to build their chow hall. The thankfulness they had in their faces ... made me realize the importance of our job. Without us doing what we're doing, they have nothing."

"LOGPACs, are our lifeline," said U.S. Army 1st Lt. Gerry Holloway of Des Moines, Iowa, platoon leader for Troop C, 1st Squadron, 113th Cavalry Regiment, Task Force Redhorse, also a part of the Task Force Red Bulls, and the unit in charge of Red Hill. "The LOGPACs supply us with the items, 'beans and bullets,' we need in order to complete our mission. They provide a lifeline between the Soldiers and their families bringing the mail out to us. Without that, morale would be considerably less and make accomplishing our mission, a lot more difficult."

Mail, which keeps Soldiers connected with the outside world and brightens the spirits after a long week of missions, is always a favorite item.

"When they get their mail, it's a real morale booster for them," said Pickett.

"When we bring out mail it is one of the best things for their morale," said U.S. Army Staff Sgt. Andy Johnson, a member of Company A, from Victor, Iowa.

The LOGPACs run every few days and return to Company A's home base, Bagram Airfield. The airfield is also the main hub for transportation, which makes the LOGPACs a perfect conduit for Soldiers trying to get a ride before they catch a plane to go on leave.

Company A goes out into dangerous territory on a daily basis to make sure their fellow Soldiers have the supplies they need to conduct missions. They risk contact with enemy forces all for the good of the team, knowing that the important part is keeping that lifeline flowing strong.

Dara District holds ribbon-cutting for Computer Lab

PANJSHIR PROVINCE, Afghanistan, Jan. 5, 2011—Panjshir Deputy Gov. Abdul Rahman Kabiri, Elizabeth Smithwick, the lead field officer U.S. Agency for International Development with Panjshir Provincial Reconstruction Team and Howe, Texas, native, Panjshir Director of Communication Abdul Muneer and Dara District Gov. Malem Sorab cut a ribbon marking the grand opening of the computer lab in Dara District. [...] (Photo by U.S. Air Force Senior Airman Amber Ashcraft, Panjshir Provincial Reconstruction Team)

PANJSHIR PROVINCE, Afghanistan, Jan. 5, 2011—Provided by quick reaction funds from Interagency Provincial Affairs, 20 computers are unveiled at the grand opening of the Dara District computer lab. Classes on the basics of Microsoft Office are held six days a week with 100 individuals already signed up. Panjshir Deputy Gov. Abdul Rahman Kabiri, Panjshir Director of Communication Abdul Muneer and Dara District Gov. Malem Sorab were in attendance, along with members from Panjshir Provincial Reconstruction Team. (Photo by U.S. Air Force Senior Airman Amber Ashcraft, Panjshir (Photo by U.S. Air Force Senior Airman Amber Ashcraft, Panjshir Provincial Reconstruction Team)

Kentucky ADT attends beekeeping course graduation

*KAPISA PROVINCE, Afghanistan, Jan. 6, 2011—*After completing a two-day course on beehives, graduates receive their beehive and supplies in hopes of making honey and splitting their hives in the spring for extra income. (Photo by U.S. Army Spc. Kristina L. Gupton, Task Force Red Bulls Public Affairs)

*KAPISA PROVINCE, Afghanistan, Jan. 6, 2011—*U.S. Army Maj. Bobbie Jo Mayes of Lawrenceburg, Ky., the women's empowerment coordinator with Kentucky Agribusiness Development Team, hands off beekeeping supplies to one of the graduates at the Director's of Agriculture Irrigation and Livestock Compound. Twenty-five women attended a two-day class on how to raise bees in hopes of making honey and splitting their hives in the spring for extra income. (Photo by U.S. Army Spc. Kristina L. Gupton, Task Force Red Bulls Public Affairs)

Tri-provincial midwife program begins in Charikar

PARWAN PROVINCE, Afghanistan, Jan. 6, 2011—Dr. Abdul Qadir (left center), the assembly coordinator and a member of the Afghan Ministry of Health, cuts a ribbon during the inauguration ceremony for a tri-provincial midwife program in Charikar, Afghanistan, Jan. 6. The ribbon is held up by Dr. Raessa Sabir, a provincial council member (far left); U.S. Army 2nd Lt. David Miller (right center) of Oswego, Ill., a member of the Civil-Military Support Team Parwan, 415th Civil Affairs Battalion; and U.S. Army Capt. Felix Gregorian (far right) of North Clemsford, Mass., and a member of the Civil-Military Support Team (CMST) Parwan. (Photo by U.S. Army Spc. James Wilton, Task Force Red Bulls Public Affairs)

By U.S. Army Spc. James Wilton
Task Force Red Bulls Public Affairs

PARWAN PROVINCE, Afghanistan, Jan. 6, 2011—The Afghan Ministry of Health held an inauguration ceremony to mark the start of a tri-provincial midwife program in Charikar.

Sixty female students from Parwan, Panjshir and Kapisa provinces will attend 26 months of instruction before receiving midwife certificates, allowing them to begin work in their local clinics.

The ceremony was attended by the students and instructors as well as important members of the Afghan Ministry of Health including Dr. Abdunl

Qadir who is in charge of the midwife program; Parwan Provincial Gov. Abdul Basir Salangi; Dr. Mohammad Sabegh Saberi with the Ministry of Higher Education of Parwan Province; and Shah Yazdan Parast with the Parwan Province Department of Women Affairs.

Representatives from coalition forces groups involved in the program also attended including Dr. HyunJoo Song, the Korea International Cooperation Agency gender and education specialist who works with the Parwan Provincial Reconstruction Team; U.S. Army 2nd Lt. David Miller of Oswego, Ill., and U.S. Army Capt. Felix Gregorian of North Chelmsford, Mass., both members of the Civil-Military Support Team, 415th Civil Affairs Battalion.

"I would like to thank the Korean and U.S. PRTs for their assistance with this program," Salangi said. "This is a great program for our nation, our sisters and the future of our babies and their health."

The program will consist of instruction in normal childbirth, neonatal care, pediatric care and recognition of emergency situations during childbirth, along with training and classes on other skills which will enhance the students' resumes, in turn, increasing their job opportunities.

"Mothers, sisters, women and ladies, learn and be proud to serve Afghanistan and work from the bottom of your heart, diligently with love and a deep sense of responsibility as you do this service to your country," said Dr. Raessa Sabir a provincial council member specializing in women's rights.

This is the fourth midwife program in Afghanistan and is part of an attempt by the government and coalition forces to decrease the maternal and infant mortality rates and improve the quality of life for the Afghan people. Afghanistan has the second-highest infant and maternal mortality rate in the world due in a large part to the lack of certified health care specialists and proper neonatal care.

"This is a very big and very proud moment in the life of our women and moms," Qadir said. "Out of 100,000 moms giving birth, 16,000 die because of complications; Afghanistan is second in the world for this problem. The training and knowledge you receive from this program will help women and children to survive birth at a higher rate."

The ceremony concluded with a traditional Afghan tea luncheon where attendees gathered to speak about the program and the future of women's rights and women's education in Afghanistan.

"We are very happy for the chance to be a part of this program and give our thanks to the Afghan government and coalition forces for making it possible," said a nurse and student in the midwife program.

PARWAN PROVINCE, Afghanistan, Jan. 6, 2011—Abdul Basir Salangi, the governor of Parwan, speaks to the attendees of the inauguration ceremony for a tri-provincial midwife program in Charikar, Afghanistan. (Photo by U.S. Army Spc. James Wilton, Task Force Red Bulls Public Affairs)

Son visits mother for promotion

PARWAN PROVINCE, Afghanistan, Jan. 6, 2011—U.S. Army Maj. Martin Roemerman (left), a Platte City, Mo., resident and 1st Squadron, 113th Cavalry Regiment, Task Force Redhorse executive officer, stands with U.S. Army Pfc. Eric Fluharty (center), a Sioux City, Iowa, resident and a crew-served weapons gunner for Company B, 1st Battalion, 168th Infantry Regiment, Task Force Lethal, and shakes the hand of U.S. Army Staff Sgt. Renae Myhre, also a Sioux City, Iowa, native and a member of the Female Engagement Team for Troop A, 1-113th Cav., after her promotion. Fluharty, the son of Myhre, attended his mother's promotion ceremony while he was on his way through Bagram Airfield returning from his two-week, mid-tour leave. (Photo by U.S. Army Capt. Timothy A. Creasman, Task Force Redhorse)

PARWAN PROVINCE, Afghanistan, Jan. 6, 2011—U.S. Army Pfc. Eric Fluharty (left), a Sioux City, Iowa, resident and a crew-served weapons gunner for Company B, 1st Battalion, 168th Infantry Regiment, Task Force Lethal, stands with his mother, U.S. Army Staff Sgt. Renae Myhre, a Sioux City, Iowa, native and a member of the Female Engagement Team for Troop A, 1st Squadron, 113th Cavalry Regiment, Task Force Redhorse, a part of the 2nd Brigade Combat Team, 34th Infantry Division, Task Force Red Bulls, after she was promoted here, Jan. 6. [...] (Photo by U.S. Army Capt. Timothy A. Creasman, Task Force Redhorse)

Redhorse focuses on Bagram Security Zone

PARWAN PROVINCE, Afghanistan, Jan. 7, 2011—U.S. Army Spc. Carlos R. Hansen, of Sioux City, Iowa, and fellow Soldiers of the Personal Security Detail for Headquarters and Headquarters Troop, 1st Squadron, 113th Cavalry Regiment, Task Force Redhorse, patrol the villages in the Bagram Security Zone. Task Force Redhorse, part of the 2nd Brigade Combat Team, 34th Infantry Division, Task Force Red Bulls, is in charge of operations in the BSZ and is increasing combat patrols in order to disrupt insurgent activity in the area. (Photo by U.S. Army Staff Sgt. Ashlee Lolkus, Task Force Red Bulls Public Affairs)

By U.S. Army Staff Sgt. Ashlee Lolkus
Task Force Red Bulls Public Affairs

PARWAN PROVINCE, Afghanistan, Jan. 7, 2011—One element taking part in the patrols is the Personal Security Detail of the Headquarters and Headquarters Troop, 1st Squadron, 113th Cavalry, Task Force Redhorse, part of the 2nd Brigade Combat Team, 34th Infantry Division, Task Force Red Bulls. The cavalry PSD, who also provides Quick Reaction Forces for the Bagram area, took to the streets of the BSZ in the towns of Barfikhel, Saka and Janquadam Jan. 7 and conducted a Key Leader Engagement in Nawdeh.

The mission, similar to their normal day-to-day missions, was the first dismounted patrol conducted by these Task Force Redhorse Soldiers since arriving in country last fall.

"What we did today was a combat patrol in the Bagram Security Zone to disrupt the (indirect fire) attacks we've been having lately," said U.S. Army Sgt. Tom Peck, of Sioux City, Iowa, and the PSD Non-Commissioned Officer-in-Charge. "We are trying to increase our presence in the area to deter insurgents from firing IDF at Bagram."

During the patrol, the Task Force Redhorse Soldiers stopped to talk with locals in the area to gauge how the local Afghan National Security Forces have been operating in their area to ensure security of the area.

"We are increasing our reconnaissance and combat patrols in the Bagram area in order to disrupt the insurgents in the area," said U.S. Army Lt. Col. David A. Updegraff, Task Force Redhorse commander and Wauconda, Ill., resident. "Conducting dismounted patrols enables the task force to directly interact with local villagers who aid coalition forces in the fight against insurgents."

Peck said that when speaking with the locals, they said the Afghan National Police and Afghan National Army would walk through the villages almost daily, but they hadn't seen U.S. forces very often. Task Force Redhorse intends to change that by conducting these dismounted patrols to the villages that cannot be reached by road.

"By conducting these patrols, we can interact with the locals, and they can let us know of insurgent activity in the area," said Peck. "We can use that information to get rid of the insurgents and make the community safer, in turn making BAF safer too."

Eliminator mechanics learn new vehicle systems

LAGHMAN PROVINCE, Afghanistan, Jan. 8, 2011—U.S. Army Spc. Derek Farrington (right), from Ames, Iowa, uses a pry bar to remove a tow bar from the hitch of a Mine-Resistant, Ambush-Protected All-Terrain Vehicle at Forward Operating Base Mehtar Lam, Afghanistan, while U.S. Army Pvt. Torin Xaiden from Independence, Iowa, looks on. The two all-wheeled vehicle mechanics, both with Company E, 1st Battalion, 133rd Infantry Regiment, a part of the 2nd Brigade Combat Team, 34th Infantry Division, hauled another M-ATV which was leaking oil, into the garage and fixed the problem before the operator returned with his paperwork. (Photo by U.S. Army Staff Sgt. Ryan C. Matson, Task Force Red Bulls Public Affairs)

By U.S. Army Staff Sgt. Ryan C. Matson
Task Force Red Bulls Public Affairs

LAGHMAN PROVINCE, Afghanistan, Jan. 8, 2011—U.S. Army Spc. Derek Farrington hopped on a massive tire and vaulted up to the engine block of the truck parked in one of the bays in the garage on Forward Operating Base Mehtar Lam in eastern Afghanistan. With his greasy, nicked-up hands, hands that tell a story of a young man hard at work, he held a bottle of degreaser spray.

"Now where is that leak coming from?" he asked himself and the mechanic looking over his shoulder, U.S. Army Pvt. Torin Xaiden.

The two Iowa National Guard all-wheeled mechanics from Company E [nicknamed "Eliminator" Company], 1st Battalion, 133rd Infantry Regiment, sprayed around hoses and different areas of the engine, searching for the leak. Soon they were joined by Ryan Harris, a civilian who works with the mechanics as a service representative from the OshKosh Corporation, the company that makes the Mine-Resistant Ambush-Protected All-Terrain Vehicles (M-ATV) the mechanics were working on.

Together, the Army mechanics and the civilian lifted a bolt from the top of the engine head and found a small, broken seal.

"Ohh!" Farrington, from Ames, Iowa, said, as he noticed the gap and bend in the ring, which usually forms a perfect circle. They had discovered the problem. Two minutes later, they had replaced the ring and the bolt and fixed the oil leak.

This time the mechanics got lucky. They found a simple problem, a broken ring which costs less than a dollar, but one, which if neglected, could have caused enough oil to leak out of the vehicle to burn up the engine and deadline a vehicle worth hundreds of thousands of dollars. They fixed the problem then tested it by revving the engine and monitoring the area to ensure the leak stopped completely, before the vehicle operator returned from the office with the repair paperwork.

Three months ago, the Army mechanics had never worked or driven the huge hunk of steel in front of them. The M-ATV is an MRAP, the new style of vehicle which has replaced the Humvee due to the rough terrain in Afghanistan and its increased ability to resist damage caused by enemy Improvised Explosive Devices. Now, they work on the vehicles daily, keeping platoons of the 34th Infantry and 101st Airborne Division soldiers on the road to execute missions and cart supplies across eastern Afghanistan.

U.S. Army Spc. Jeremy Hofland, another all-wheeled mechanic from Iowa with Company E, 1-133rd Inf., from Winthrop, Iowa, said the mechanics had to learn to maintain and repair four different kinds of MRAP vehicles while deployed: the M-ATV, the MaxxPro series, the Cougar, and the RG-31 models.

This is the first deployment for all three of the young mechanics, who said when they attended their advanced individual training—the training soldiers receive to learn their specific job in the Army after completing basic training—they learned to work on Humvees. They went from working on Humvees, which weigh 10,000 to 14,000 pounds, to MRAPs weighing as much as 25 tons.

"Humvees are actually kind of simple," Hofland said. "You don't have to drop any belly pans to do any services on the vehicles."

The belly pans Hofland referred to are large steel plates on the bottoms of the MRAP vehicles which form a V-shape and are designed to keep the blasts from roadside explosives away from the vehicles and their crew. Hofland said to service different problems on a MRAP, often these plates must be removed.

Hofland said once the plates are removed, the larger vehicles often offer a mechanic more space between parts to make repairs.

The mechanics said after three months, they haven't yet had to perform any major repairs on the vehicles yet. Some of the common tasks the mechanics said they've performed on the vehicles are tire and fluids changes, and routine maintenance checks, as well as replacing chipped window panes. The windows are several panes thick and weigh several hundred pounds each.

"We actually use a forklift to lift the windows into place," Hofland explained. He said changing a tire is also at least a two-man job, as the tires are about three-feet high and weigh 480 pounds. "It's not like the tires on your car," he said. "You definitely wouldn't want one to fall on you."

The mechanics said they learned maintain and repair the MRAPs after arriving in Afghanistan, largely with the help of service representatives from the vehicle's manufacturers. The engines on the MRAPs are made by heavy equipment companies such as Caterpillar, International and Cummins, the mechanics said.

"Having the service reps here has been a huge plus for us," Farrington, from Ames, Iowa, said.

The mechanics said they still repair Humvees, many of which are being phased out and transferred to the Afghan National Army and Afghan Uniformed Police.

The biggest and heaviest of the four MRAP types the mechanics work on is the MaxxPro, but Hofland said his favorite of the four styles is the M-ATV. "I think it's the best one," he said. "It's the lightest one, it's able to go up and down hills better than the other vehicles, and I like its horsepower-to-weight ratio."

The three mechanics said they've enjoyed the challenge of learning and working on the new vehicle systems on the fly.

Farrington and Hofland are second-generation mechanics who said they grew up fixing things with their fathers and always wanted to be mechanics. Hofland said he started on lawn mowers and just kept going. Xaiden said he wasn't sure what he wanted to do until he took the Armed Services Vocational Aptitude Battery test and scored high in the mechanical section.

"I knew I didn't want to fly, I wanted to be on the ground, so I went with wheeled mechanic," Xaiden, a native of Independence, Iowa, said.

Farrington, in particular, is a ball of energy, always on the go and fixing things, which does not go unnoticed by his fellow mechanics.

"I, and a lot of the other guys out there, think he's the best mechanic we've got," Hofland said.

All the mechanics' quick-learning skills on the new vehicles has kept the fleet operating at a high-level of readiness.

"I've worked with four different units in the two-and-a-half years I've been here in Afghanistan," said Harris, who mentored the young mechanics on maintaining the vehicles. "These guys are great; they've made my job here easy."

Laghman PRT visits shops in Mehtar Lam

LAGHMAN PROVINCE, Afghanistan, Jan. 8, 2011—U.S. Air Force Tech. Sgt. John Kuehlthau of Hurlburt Field, Fla., Laghman Provincial Reconstruction Team civil engineering team, and U.S. Air Force Senior Airman Alexandra Davis of Alpine, Texas, Laghman PRT medical specialist, look around at the marketplace in downtown Mehtar Lam. The PRT gathered information through the Afghan marketplace community to find out how the economy is doing and made purchases for themselves. (Photo by U.S. Air Force Senior Airman Ronifel S. Yasay, Laghman Provincial Reconstruction Team)

LAGHMAN PROVINCE, Afghanistan, Jan. 8, 2011—U.S. Army Spc. Matthew Vandelinde of Rosemount, Minn., Laghman Provincial Reconstruction Team civil affairs, looks around at fabric in the marketplace in downtown Mehtar Lam. The PRT gathered information through the Afghan marketplace community to find out how the economy is doing. (Photo by U.S. Air Force Senior Airman Ronifel S. Yasay, Laghman Provincial Reconstruction Team)

ANA, Task Force Lethal stop suspected IED emplaces in Zormat

PAKTYA PROVINCE, Afghanistan—U.S. Army Spc. Chad Summerfield, 3rd Platoon, Company D, 1st Battalion, 168th Infantry Regiment, Task Force Lethal of Dunlap, Iowa, returns fire on insurgents who initiated an attack on the unit and Afghan National Army soldiers Jan 9. (Photo by U.S. Army Sgt. 1st Class Ryan Johnson, Task Force Lethal)

By U.S. Army 1st Lt. Nicholas Rasmussen
Task Force Lethal

PAKTYA PROVINCE, Afghanistan, Jan. 9, 2011—Afghan National Army soldiers and members of 3rd Platoon, Company D, 1st Battalion, 168th Infantry Regiment, Task Force Lethal, prevented the emplacement of Improvised Explosive Devices in Tatanak village, Zormat District, Paktya Province.

ANA and coalition Soldiers spotted insurgents planting an IED on a road south of the village.

Two platoons from Company D, 1168 Inf. and two ANA platoons from 1st Company, 1st Kandak, 2nd Brigade, 203rd ANA Infantry Corps secured the dig site and searched for the insurgents who fled when they were spotted.

The ANA were beginning to search the suspected qalat when small-arms fire was heard from the north.

"We saw the rounds pepper the dirt a couple hundred meters from us," said U.S. Army 1st Lt. William Schlotzhauer of Las Vegas. "It was clearly just harassment fire. (They) just wanted to show that they weren't afraid."

Once the shots ceased, the combined forces used their Mine-Resistant Ambush-Protected Vehicles as moving cover to clear the site where the shots originated. After arriving at the suspected engagement site, security forces searched the immediate vicinity but found nothing.

Combined forces returned to the suspected qalat to search it and question the residents.

During the search ANA found and confiscated a passport used to travel between Pakistan and Afghanistan, more than 40 D cell batteries, wires and other components that could be used to construct IEDs.

An Explosive Ordnance Disposal team destroyed the IED buried in the road outside of Tatanak.

Panjshir ANP conduct refresher training

PANJSHIR PROVINCE, Afghanistan, Jan. 9, 2011—Paryan Afghan National Police trainer Lt. Col. Mohammad Yaseen shakes hands with U.S. Army Master Sgt. Todd Eipperle, senior Non-Commissioned Officer-in-Charge of Task Force Red Bulls' Embedded Training Team in Panjshir, and Marshalltown, Iowa, native, after the "Police Values and Ethics" training in Paryan District. More than 15 ANP members attended the first of 16 classes, taught by Colonel Yaseen. The class is taught to promote awareness of ethical behavior and how it impacts law enforcement. (Photo by U.S. Air Force Senior Airman Amber Ashcraft, Panjshir Provincial Reconstruction Team Public Affairs)

By U.S. Air Force Senior Airman Amber Ashcraft
Panjshir Provincial Reconstruction Team Public Affairs

PANJSHIR PROVINCE, Afghanistan, Jan. 9, 2011—Paryan Afghan National Police began follow-up basic military training classes in Paryan District here Jan. 9.

Recently, more than 15 local ANP members attended the first class on Police Values and Ethics being taught by a Paryan ANP trainer to promote awareness of ethical behavior and how it impacts law enforcement.

"The ANP moved quickly into the training," said U.S. Army Master Sgt. Todd Eipperle, senior Non-Commissioned Officer-in-Charge of the Task Force Red Bulls' embedded training team in Panjshir, and Marshalltown, Iowa, native. "They were eager for class, taking plenty of notes and asking several questions."

The training is a refresher course reinforcing information local ANP learned at Basic Military Training in Kabul.

"Some ANP never see the initial training from BMT again," Eipperle said. "Being retrained and able to actually openly discuss the scenarios and information will help them apply it easier."

When the ETT members began visiting the districts and asking the local ANP if they were conducting training, the response was a resounding no, Eipperle said.

Knowing the local ANP were not being further trained on the basics, the ETT members began researching ways to help.

ETT members started a "train the trainers" course, which they hold every month, using information from the manuals used to instruct the ANP's BMT course. Several district trainers from Panjshir Province attended the week-long class to learn how to train their local ANP.

ETT members aim for the ANP to continue to hold their own classes.

"The idea is to have the ANP sustain the training once we're gone," Eipperle said. "Just as we do annual training in the (U.S.) military to retain what we've been taught, the ANP will be able to continue their training and apply it to every day circumstances."

Two classes are held every month, each class covering a different subject. During the first class, students discussed scenarios and answered questions identifying the unethical behavior in the scenario, the dilemma and how to resolve the dilemma or behavior.

"When they broke into groups, there were many heated discussions," said U.S. Army Spc. Brian Brown, communication specialist with the Task Force Red Bulls ETT in Panjshir, and a Central City, Iowa, native. "Being able to talk about corruption and taking gifts as police officers is not something they discussed in BMT. Here, they were able to apply the training they just learned to everyday scenarios and come up with an ethical answer."

In July, at the end of the 16-class course, there will be a graduation for the ANP who attended, said Eipperle.

"We're hoping that each district will be able to do the same and the ANP will be able to sustain their annual training and become proficient as teachers and students," he said.

Kotalay: a village caught in the middle

LAGHMAN PROVINCE, Afghanistan, Jan. 10, 2011—U.S. Army 1st Lt. Rob Labios, 3rd Platoon leader for Company A, 1st Battalion, 133rd Infantry Regiment, Task Force Ironman, and a native of Davis, Calif., addresses the people of the town of Kotalay during a Key Leader Engagement. Of the four times the company attempted to visit the village, they have been attacked twice from outside the village. The meeting, however, went on without incident. Task Force Ironman is a part of the 2nd Brigade Combat Team, 34th Infantry Division, Task Force Red Bulls, of the Iowa National Guard. (Photo by U.S. Army Staff Sgt. Ryan C. Matson, Task Force Red Bulls Public Affairs)

By U.S. Army Staff Sgt. Ryan C. Matson
Task Force Red Bulls Public Affairs

Note: This is the first of a series of stories detailing the events that transpire in one small village in Afghanistan—the village of Kotalay. The village, or at least the area immediately surrounding it, has been a hotbed of enemy activity for 3rd Platoon, Company A, 1st Battalion, 133rd Infantry Regiment, Task Force Red Bulls. This series will look at the interaction between the platoon and the village each month, just one village of many in Company A's area of operations.

LAGHMAN PROVINCE, Afghanistan, Jan. 10, 2011—North and to the immediate south of the village there have been Improvised Explosive Device attacks. East of the village, U.S. Army and Afghan National Army troops have reacted to a small-arms gunfire attack. The same is true to the west of the village.

In fact, all around the village of Kotalay, in eastern Afghanistan, the Soldiers have encountered enemy activity.

"It's really a village that's caught in the middle," said U.S. Army 2nd Lt. Rob Labios, the platoon leader for 3rd Platoon, Company A, 1st Battalion,

133rd Infantry Regiment. "It's a village sandwiched by the Taliban. I believe the villagers when they say, 'We don't have insurgents here,' but the insurgents are coming from the east and from the west. To the west of Kotalay is the Sygal Valley, where many of the insurgents are."

Labios and his men from 3rd Platoon made a return trip to Kotalay Jan. 10, a village they visited three times before. They faced contact twice.

Their first trip to the village Dec. 12 went as planned. The unit conducted a Key Leader Engagement. Since it was the first one, U.S. Army Sgt. Toby Hall, a civil affairs team leader with Company A, 413th Civil Affairs Bn., said the unit introduced itself to the people of the village.

"It was a basic relationship-building meeting," said Hall, a native of Amarillo, Texas, who has been to Kotalay on three of the platoon's missions to the town. "We asked them how long it had been since the coalition had been there, and they said no one had been in there in forever; they just saw trucks rolling by."

The next two visits were not so friendly. On Dec. 20, 3rd Platoon was headed toward the village from north. Since their home base, Forward Operating Base Mehtar Lam, is south of Kotalay on a road called Route Nebraska, on the first visit, the unit approached from the south. This time, the platoon was headed to Kotalay from Combat Outpost Najil, to the north. The unit was planning to conduct a KLE in the village when they heard shots from the mountainside around Nurem to the west.

"We were able to chase them down," Labios said. "I remember talking to the police chief about Nurem being a place where high value targets and Taliban were conducting meetings, and we know they were watching us."

The next trip to Kotalay the platoon again faced contact and quickly deterred it, potentially saving the lives of coalition forces or innocent civilians, Labios said.

"The third time to Kotalay, we found an IED, found the wires, and were shot at in so doing," Labios said. "We fired back at the enemy and chased them off of the huge mountain they were hiding on to the east of the village."

In addition to the attacks on 3rd Platoon, a provincial reconstruction team was hit by an IED about 100 meters south of the town Dec. 2.

And on Jan. 10, as they walked down the edges of irrigated fields, Labios returned into historically hostile territory. This time, however, he said some progress was made.

Labios admitted the meeting was at times frustrating, but said progress in the town is a long, step-by-step process, and during this KLE, there were numerous small victories. For example, it was the first time Labios said he had a substantial meeting with the town's malik, Gulam Hazrat.

Hazrat said he was responsible for the actions of the people of Kotalay, and that they were not attacking the coalition, it was the insurgents around the village. He invited the coalition to search the homes in the village, and said he only cared about the people in his village.

After listening to the malik speak, Labios implored the leader for more action.

"You can't have the attitude of just protecting your village," Labios told him. "This is your country. If you look out for the villages around you, they will protect you, too. You need to make every effort to give the Afghan National Army, the Afghan Uniformed Police and us any information you can on IEDs or planned attacks in the area. These are all your people. You need to be proactive and do whatever it takes."

After listening to the young lieutenant, Hazrat agreed he could do more.

Hazrat asked for help for his village with projects such as a retaining wall around the village mosque to keep floodwaters out.

As a possible solution, Labios suggested the village sign up for the "Go Green" program.

In the Go Green program, village elders and residents must sign a contract stating they will report insurgent activity in or around their village immediately to their local police at the district center or to the coalition.

Once this paperwork is submitted, the village is placed on a 90-day probationary period. If no insurgent activity occurs within that time, the village moves into "amber" status and is eligible for assistance on projects, such as the retaining wall Hazrat mentioned. However, once a significant act against the coalition occurs, Hall said the village loses its ability for assistance.

"I'll be watching closely to see if they actually submit that paperwork," Labios said.

At just over 5 feet tall, Labios immediately endeared himself to the youngsters of the village. The 24-year-old, who volunteered for this deployment from his hometown of Davis, Calif., was all business in his talk with the elders, but had a quick smile and jokes for the children. Within minutes, it seemed like every child from the 300 families in the village was surrounding him to share a playful exchange with the platoon's leader.

The kids have proven very useful to the platoon in the past. During their one visit to the Sygal Valley, the enemy's proverbial doorstep, a child helped the coalition win the battle against the enemy, said U.S. Army Sgt. 1st Class Kurt Behrens, 3rd Platoon platoon sergeant from Norwalk, Iowa.

"We were doing stops at buildings near a hill and asking people in the buildings, 'Is the Taliban down there?' and they were saying 'Yes,'" Behrens recalled. "Some kid got released from school in the area we were going to, because they knew we were going to be attacked. So the kid walked up to us and told us they closed school because you're going to get attacked."

Solving the problems in Kotalay will definitely not be an easy task, Labios acknowledged. He said he has information the enemy may be visiting the village at night and harassing the people, checking to see if they have called the coalition and taking their phones and breaking them as well as beating the people up. The cell towers throughout northeastern Afghanistan are shut off at night, and it is widely known this is because the Taliban have threatened the lives of the operators.

Meanwhile, Labios said the coalition faces the challenge of dealing with the village ethically while the enemy continues to employ terroristic tactics.

Whatever happens in Kotalay, one thing is certain, Labios and his Soldiers will not stop trying to make it a better place for visitors and city residents.

"If we don't take action against the Taliban together," Labios told Hazrat, "it's your people and your children who will end up getting hurt by their actions. It comes down to the warrior ethos. We've got to keep working and we'll defeat the enemy."

Panjshir projects completed in Dara, Khenj districts

PANJSHIR PROVINCE, Afghanistan, Jan. 11, 2011—(From left) Dara District Deputy Gov. Abdul Hashim, Panjshir Provincial Reconstruction Team commander U.S. Air Force Lt. Col. Joseph Blevins of Oregonia, Ohio, and engineer Ghulam Mahfooz, program management unit director of Panjshir National Solidarity Program, cut a ribbon in honor of the new micro-hydro system in Dara District. (Photo by U.S. Air Force Senior Airman Amber Ashcraft, Panjshir Provincial Reconstruction Team Public Affairs)

By U.S. Air Force 2nd Lt. Ashleigh Peck
Panjshir Provincial Reconstruction Team Public Affairs

PANJSHIR PROVINCE, Afghanistan, Jan. 11, 2011—Leadership from the Provincial Rural Rehabilitation and Development organization and the National Solidarity Program held a ribbon-cutting ceremony representing the completion of four infrastructure projects in Dara and Khenj districts.

The projects included the construction of two micro-hydro systems in Dara, a bridge with a retaining wall, and an irrigation and micro-hydro canal in Khenj.

Dara District Deputy Gov. Abdul Hashim; Panjshir RRD Director Pair Muhammad Yaftali; Panjshir NSP program management unit director, engineer Ghulam Mahfooz; and Panjshir Provincial Reconstruction Team commander U.S. Air Force Lt. Col. Joseph Blevins of Oregonia, Ohio, spoke during the ceremony.

Speakers expressed appreciation for the efforts of the people, the NSP and the PRT.

"If the people and the Non-Governmental Organizations work together, we will have more stable projects like this for the future," said Yaftali through an interpreter.

Preceding the ribbon-cutting ceremony, power production was initiated for the Gaywaj village micro-hydro system in Dara.

"The system will provide power to 136 families," said Mahfooz.

"The Gaywaj village micro-hydro system canal was supported by the Community Development Council and the NSP and the generator was provided by the PRT," said U.S. Army Spc. Aaron Settlemyre, Panjshir PRT civil affairs specialist and Zeeland, Mich., native. "All labor was done by the villagers."

Many families are seeing positive effects from the other three projects as well.

The Dara micro-hydro system in Qale Now Telkho village provides power to 268 families. The new Dahan Riwat bridge and retaining wall in Khenj District provides 312 families access to the main road. The irrigation and micro-hydro canals in Aziz Big Khil and Chek Cheshma villages provide power to 604 families in Khenj District, said Mahfooz.

"We hope to do more projects just like these," said Blevins. "The PRT is always happy to do projects with the NSP through the CDC process because it means it's a project that is important to the people."

PANJSHIR PROVINCE, Afghanistan, Jan. 11, 2011—Gaywaj villagers observe the water flow from the new micro-hydro powerhouse following its ribbon-cutting ceremony in Dara District, Afghanistan. (Photo by U.S. Air Force Senior Airman Amber Ashcraft, Panjshir Provincial Reconstruction Team Public Affairs)

Iowa father, son serve together in Afghanistan

PAKTYA PROVINCE, Afghanistan, Jan. 11, 2011—U.S. Army Pfc. Andrew Starkey and his dad U.S. Army Spc. Steven Starkey, both of Council Bluffs, Iowa, pose for a photo. Both are attached to Company A, 1st Battalion, 168th Infantry Regiment,which is currently deployed to Afghanistan. (Courtesy photo)

By U.S. Army 1st Lt. Nicholas Rasmussen
Task Force Lethal

PAKTYA PROVINCE, Afghanistan, Jan. 11, 2011–Most Soldiers who are deployed miss their homes. But for U.S. Army Spc. Steven Starkey and U.S. Army Pfc. Andrew Starkey, a large part of what the word "home" represents is just a five-minute walk up the hill.

Steven, a 40-year-old mechanic by trade in Council Bluffs, Iowa, works as a wheeled-vehicle mechanic attached to Company A, 1st Battalion, 168th Infantry Regiment, which currently falls under 3rd Brigade Combat Team, 101st Airborne Division. His son Andrew works in Company A's kitchen preparing breakfast, lunch, and dinner seven days a week. Both Starkeys are assigned to Company F, 334th Brigade Support Battalion out of Red Oak, Iowa.

For both Starkeys, joining the Iowa Army National Guard was a choice they made to serve their country and fulfill some personal goals.

Steven enlisted in the active-duty Army in 1989 as a heavy equipment mobile tactical truck wheel mechanic. He was slated to serve during Operation Desert Storm when personal issues at home prevented his involvement.

He was young and dealing with a troubled marriage when his chain of command made the determination to let him remain in the rear as his unit prepared to support Desert Storm.

"Looking back, I don't feel I was mature enough to handle the task at hand," he said, adding that his brief service helped him mature and gave him cause to consider future opportunities for service.

The events of 9/11 reignited a simmering ambition for Steven.

"I felt like I had left something on the table, an obligation I had left incomplete" he said.

So almost 15 years later, he began the process to rejoin the Army, eventually serving with the Iowa National Guard. The process wasn't easy.

Steven had remarried and had three additional children: daughters Ashley and Rachel and stepson Jon when he decided to reenlist for active duty. Despite trying three times, the active Army would not accept his application since he had more than two dependants.

Steven gave up trying for active duty after the third attempt. Then, in Spring of 2007, he met his daughter's soccer coach, a staff sergeant in the Iowa National Guard. The soccer coach informed Steven that the Iowa National Guard had waivers and programs to allow people in situations such as Steven's to join.

"A month after speaking with [the soccer coach], I was at [the Military Entrance Processing Station] swearing in for service," Steven recalled.

A year later, Andrew raised his right hand and made the oath to serve his country, but he had a different reason: his daughter Kyra.

Being in the Iowa Army National Guard has given Andrew a means to provide healthcare and child support to his only daughter.

"I plan to start a savings account with the money I'm making [on deployment] to help pay for her college," said Andrew

Joining the Guard came with some unanticipated benefits for Andrew.

"I see myself grow every day," said Andrew, "whether or not I enjoy it all the time."

Before making his commitment to serve in the Iowa Guard, Andrew had a loose-cannon mentality, as his father put it. He was an unruly youth who often did not think before he acted. That was nine months ago. Now, six months into deployment, Andrew is a much different person.

"He's level-headed and can take criticism constructively like an adult," said Steven, who went on to say witnessing this change has been one of the most rewarding benefits to come out of being on this deployment together.

Steven said sometimes a father has to be a father, regardless of rank, and stick up for his son.

"It's hard to keep the fatherly instinct at bay when I see my son getting in trouble by his boss," said Steven. "I often have to swallow my pride and know my place."

The Starkeys act more like brothers or best friends when talking with one another, calling each other by their last name and making fun of just about anything the other says. Despite being co-located at the same company, the Starkeys still feel as though they could spend more time together.

As trying as some days may get, the Starkeys usually find some time throughout the week to hang out and unwind together, giving them a chance to solidify, in a unique way, a bond that can only be made between a father and son deployed together.

"The one thing that everyone else wants ... we have," said Andrew "A family member on deployment."

Biden joins servicemembers for breakfast

BAGRAM AIRFIELD, Afghanistan, Jan. 12, 2011—Vice President Joe Biden poses for a photo with U.S. Army Sgt. 1st Class Shane Wrage, a Polk City, Iowa, resident and an Afghan National Police liaison with the 2nd Brigade Combat Team, 34th Infantry Division, Task Force Red Bulls, during a visit he made to the Dragon dining facility on Bagram Airfield. (Photo by U.S. Army Staff Sgt. Michael L. Sparks, 17th Public Affairs Detachment)

By U.S. Army Spc. James Wilton
Task Force Red Bulls Public Affairs

BAGRAM AIRFIELD, Afghanistan, Jan. 12, 2011—Vice President Joe Biden dropped in on servicemembers stationed at Bagram Airfield during breakfast at the Dragon dining facility.

The visit came during an unannounced trip to Afghanistan to meet with top U.S. and Afghan personnel about the status of U.S. forces deployed to Afghanistan, and to assess progress toward the transition to Afghan-led security.

The vice president first worked his way to a table of Soldiers and Airmen from his home state of Delaware, grabbing a piece of bacon from the buffet table en route. He joked with servicemembers commenting, "We're kind of neighbors," telling stories of back home and joining in the disappointment over some recent sports setbacks.

"We talked about our love of the Philadelphia Eagles and how they had a disappointing season," said U.S. Army Chief Warrant Officer Chris Cummings, a Dover, Del., native with Combined Joint Task Force 101. "It was good to see some of our civilian leadership come in and express their gratitude for the sacrifices the Soldiers and their families are making."

Once he finished with his fellow Delawareans, Biden worked his way around the room asking troops where they are from, making small talk and thanking them for serving their country. He kept up the conversational and personal feel, sliding in a joke where he could.

"It was a pleasure to get a chance to see Biden, he's a very nice and personable guy," said U.S. Army Spc. Patrick Valant, a Dyersville, Iowa, native and a member of the Headquarters and Headquarters Company of the 2nd Brigade Combat Team, 34th Infantry Division, Task Force Red Bulls. "He jokingly referenced the fact he had lost the caucus in Iowa during the previous election."

The servicemembers were happy to meet the vice president, many posing for pictures or shaking hands with Biden as he visited their table.

"He is a very warm and wonderful person. Talking to him, it's almost like he has known you before," said U.S. Army Sgt. Mildred Batiste, a Middletown, Del., native with the 131st Transportation Company when asked about meeting the vice president. "He asked me where I was from, and I thanked him for the educational policies he put into place because I am a teacher."

Biden made sure to visit with every one of the approximately 500 servicemembers eating breakfast before leaving. On his way out, Biden grabbed a plate of food for the road.

This is the first visit by Biden to Afghanistan as vice president.

Wearing two hats: Civil affairs soldier is professional rodeo cowboy

LAGHMAN PROVINCE, Afghanistan, Jan. 13, 2011—U.S. Army Sgt. Toby Hall, a team leader with Company A, 413th Civil Affairs Battalion out of Lubbock, Texas, stands in front of the mountains outside Forward Operating Base Mehtar Lam holding a belt buckle from a benefit rodeo for his cousin. It is one of the many rodeos Hall, a professional bronco and bullriding cowboy in civilian life from Amarillo, Texas, won. Now, Hall is conducting missions in villages throughout eastern Afghanistan as an Army Reserve civil affairs soldier. (Photo by U.S. Army Staff Sgt. Ryan C. Matson, Task Force Red Bulls Public Affairs)

By U.S. Army Staff Sgt. Ryan C. Matson
Task Force Red Bulls Public Affairs

LAGHMAN PROVINCE, Afghanistan, Jan. 13, 2011—He said he wanted the national anthem to mean something more to him when he heard it at rodeos.

That's why U.S. Army Sgt. Toby Hall, a team leader with Company A, 413th Civil Affairs Battalion out of Lubbock, Texas, said he joined the Army.

"Before I joined, you'd hear the national anthem and hear the speaker talk about soldiers while I was trying to get all fired up to ride a horse or a bull. I'd think to myself, 'Man I'm nothing but a big sissy—they're over there fighting for my country and all I'm doing is getting on some horse that's going to buck for eight seconds,'" Hall said. "That was kind of a reason I joined; I wanted it to mean something more to me when I heard that song play. If it wasn't for us over here, I wouldn't be able to ride back home."

Presently, Hall is a civil affairs soldier deployed to Forward Operating Base Mehtar Lam as part of Task Force Ironman. Ironically, the task force is under the command of the 1st Battalion, 133rd Infantry Regiment, a part of the 2nd Brigade Combat Team, 34th Infantry Division, nicknamed the "Red Bulls."

Back in his hometown of Amarillo, Texas, however, Hall earns his living as a professional rodeo cowboy, competing in the bull riding and bareback bronco riding events. He competes in rodeo circuits throughout Texas and the Midwest, to include the Texas Cowboys Rodeo Association, the Professional Rodeo Cowboys Association, and the Kansas Pro Rodeo Association, for which he is the bareback riding director.

Possibly the only thing about Hall that doesn't scream cowboy is his height. He's about six feet tall, a good height for a movie cowboy, but not the ideal bull rider or bareback bronco rider's build.

"Most of those guys are between 5-feet-6 and 5-feet-8, and 130, maybe 140 pounds," Hall said.

Everything else about Hall is the genuine article. He has a stockpile of 63 cans of Copenhagen in his room and always a dip in his mouth. He has a deep voice with a bit of a Texan twang and though he's very polite and friendly, always laughing, he walks with a bit of a swagger. His room is lined with cowboy magazines, Louis L'Amour books, John Wayne sayings, pictures of family and friends and their horses and ranches. He can talk for hours about country music.

Hall said he's rode in rodeos all his life and he's got the scars, bumps and bruises to prove it. About two inches above his right eye on his forehead is a slanted scar from where a bronco kicked him in the head. His left pinky is mangled into a u-shape and won't straighten anymore. He's broken his nose three times, his right wrist several times on bareback riggings, his finger, his ankle, had a disk in his back pushing against his sciatic nerve and fractured his right leg when a horse stepped on it on the ground. He said the back injury was the worst, and often he'd wake up at night crying.

"To be a cowboy," Hall said, "you gotta be tough."

A family tradition

Hall was born to be a cowboy, literally.

His father, Eddie, was a professional rodeo bull rider for several years, before turning in his spurs to run a construction business in Amarillo. Hall said he always wanted to be like his father and be a cowboy.

"Before I ever got on an animal, I remember being really little and taping a piece of notebook paper onto my back for a rodeo number," Hall said. "I'd be riding around on a little stick pony, except mine bucked! I always knew I wanted to be a cowboy. In a small town in Texas, it's what you did for fun."

He said he climbed aboard his first live animal, a sheep, when he was five years old and won the first rodeo he entered. From there, he progressed to calves, to steers, junior bulls, and finally to the 2,000-pound bulls he rides now. He said when he was a junior in high school, he found his niche, though, riding bareback broncos.

"The rodeo sponsor told me, 'Hey you can ride bulls, you should try bareback horses,'" Hall recalled. He said he immediately enjoyed it and qualified for the Texas high school finals in bareback riding his junior and senior years. Though he loved riding, he said ,in high school, football was more his focus.

Hall said that changed when he got a rodeo scholarship to Tarleton State, in the "cowboy capital of the world," Stephenville, Texas. He said he got offers from the top five rodeo schools in the country, but chose Tarleton State because of its proud tradition and reputation as a top rodeo school.

"I realized I'd rather just have fun and make something of my life by constantly riding on the rodeo circuits," he said.

From Tarleton State, Hall transferred to West Texas A & M, because the rodeo coach's younger brother was a friend of Hall's whom he had always rode with growing up in Amarillo. While still attending West Texas A & M, Hall said he turned professional, getting his rodeo card at the age of 21.

Hall said he rode thousands of horses in thousands of rodeos but there is one horse that sticks out to him. He said his nemesis is a horse named Outlaw, whom he has drawn many times in competitions.

"I hate that horse with a passion," Hall said. "I draw that same horse every time and me and him don't get along. He kicks me off every time I jump on him, no matter how well I'm riding that sucker. He's just really, really strong."

Hall said when he gets back from this deployment, he knows Outlaw will be back in Texas waiting for him, ready to try and buck him off once again.

You have to win to get paid

Hall said he loves the rodeo, because it is a sport like no other. First of all, he said, unlike football, baseball and other American sports, it is a sport that was based on work.

"Cowboys used to break horses and have contests to see who could stay on the longest," Hall said. "That's really how the whole thing started."

He also said he likes the rodeo, and that it is unique, because money is not guaranteed. "That's the difference between rodeo and other pro sports," Hall said. "You don't get paid to lose. Anybody and their dog can buy a permit to enter rodeos once they turn 18. But you have to make so much money professionally before you can actually get your pro card."

But above the thrill of riding a 2,000-pound animal and the uniqueness of the sport, Hall said it is the fellowship with the other riders he enjoys the most. "The main thing I like about the rodeo, though, are the friendships," Hall said. "The cowboys you ride with are your lifelong friends. The only way to travel is by car or by plane, so we'd pile in as many cowboys as we can into a car to make it cheaper to get to the rodeos. We go rodeo to rodeo to rodeo together."

He said cowboys will also help each other out, paying entry fees to the next rodeo for another cowboy when that cowboy had a rough ride and didn't win any money.

"I've done it for other people, and I've had it done for me," he said. "Not everybody can be first."

Better halves

Hall said he has two partners in life: his riding partner, Mark Owens, with whom he's rode for six years; and his fiancee, another soldier, Staff Sgt. Jeanine Pollard. Pollard, who is also a civil affairs team leader in Company A, 413th Civil Affairs Battalion, is one person Hall did not meet through the rodeo, although she grew up on a ranch in Cloud Croft, New Mexico.

Hall said he met Pollard through the Army.

"We realized we liked each other more than friends," he said. "And we've been best friends ever since"

Even though they are deployed to separate parts of Afghanistan, Hall said he talks to Pollard every night possible and their cross paths every now and again in country. He also said her family sends him a lot of care packages.

Pollard said one thing she likes about Hall being a cowboy is she knows he is following his dream.

"I think it's very cool that he's upholding the tradition of being a cowboy," Pollard said. "I like that he's a cowboy and he does what he loves, and I also like that he takes time out to serve his country as well."

Hall said he watched Owens, who is eight years older, ride as a kid when he was growing up in Amarillo and admired him as a rider. However the two did not meet until 2004 at a church rodeo. Hall said he was 19 then and cocky. He had a 12-point lead in the rodeo and was all but guaranteed a victory check. That's when Mark drew a horse named Happy Appy, which he described as "the rankest horse on the circuit."

"So we're at this rodeo and Mark draws Happy Appy, and I'm thinking 'OK, either Mark's going to come really close to tying me if he rides him, or he's gonna get bucked off,'" Hall recalled. "This horse bucks like no other. I've never seen that horse buck that hard, and he's just one of the best horses there is.

"He started bucking his normal trip and he couldn't get Mark off, so he just started doing this crazy stuff I've never even seen this horse do before. He could not get Mark off; Mark just kept spurring him hard. So, Mark got 89 points and beat me by a point! No one was anywhere close to us."

Ever since that day, Hall said he and Owens have been inseparable, as in every day, all day long. They worked at the same company as welders during the week, and went to the rodeo together on weekends. They worked out for the circuit together, lifting weights and running.

Owens said meeting Hall revitalized his career. "I was ready to retire when I met Toby," Owens said. "But we kind of feed off each other; I've had the best years of my career since we became travelling partners."

Hall said he often spent holidays with Owens' family, which he considers like his own. He said he especially misses riding with his friend this year, since Owens made the Prairie Circuit finals.

"Mark said he still likes to rodeo, but since I'm gone, it's not fun like it was," Hall said. "He said it's more like a job to him now."

Owens said he misses his riding partner, also, but he is proud of the things he's doing as a deployed soldier. "I think the commitment it takes to do what he's doing is awesome," Owens said. "Also, the selflessness is amazing; most rodeo cowboys don't have that level of selflessness."

He said the other riders support him whole-heartedly.

"Everywhere I go, I get stopped by somebody and asked how he's doing," Owens said. "The riders always talk about how great it is what he's doing over there."

Hall said he keeps in touch with Owens, and all his fellow cowboys, and follows them as they compete in rodeos back home. He said he loves his job in the Army, particularly serving his country, but can't wait to get back on the circuit when he gets back home.

"As soon as his boots hit the ground," Owens said. "I've got a bunch of PRCA events for us to go to!"

Two dangerous jobs

In Afghanistan, Hall is not riding bulls. Instead, he is riding along with the Red Bulls' infantry soldiers, going out on missions to villages throughout their area of operations.

Hall, who joined the Army Reserve right after he graduated from college with a degree in agricultural engineering in January 2008, tries to assess the climate of the town by talking directly with its people.

"I try to find the village elder or malik and try to find out what they think of us," he said. "I also try to see what kind of problems the village has and if the enemy is there. I have my own way of doing that, that I've been trained to do, without coming straight out and saying 'Where's the Taliban?' I try to build a relationship with these people."

The relationship is key, Hall said, because the people need to know they can trust him and the coalition's soldiers. He said in the past, civil affairs teams built projects in villages just to say they've contributed to the towns. He said his team tries to find ways to help the villagers improve their town and make it more stable in the long-term.

"I try to ask them about their farms, livestock, wells, hydroelectric power, all sorts of things," he said. "Without us going in and talking to them, they're scared to death of us, and I would be to if somebody was rolling through my town in big old trucks with big old guns on them.

"We let them know we're not here to hurt them, we're here to protect them from the Taliban and give them work so they don't have to join the Taliban. I let them know we're not going to be here forever, and we're not giving out handouts, so we ask them, 'What can I do to help you out, so you can do this on your own?' I like that I actually get to interact with the people here, and see first-hand how they lives in their homes."

Travelling to the town involves stepping into any role needed in the convoy. Hall has served as truck commander or gunner on the missions before. Then he and his team dismount and engage the villagers. When the convoy or the dismounted Soldiers take fire, Hall puts aside his civil affairs role to engage the enemy.

"If somebody's shooting at us, I'm not going to stay back and be scared, we'll be right up with the infantry guys doing our thing," Hall said.

As for the rodeo, Hall doesn't see himself quitting riding anytime soon. "It all depends on how tough you are and how long you wanna keep taking that beating," he said. "I'm going to ride until my body won't let me anymore."

18 Redhorse troops earn award for German weapons qualification

BAGRAM AIRFIELD, Afghanistan, Jan. 14, 2011—U.S. Army Pfc. Scott Greene, a soldier with Troop B, 1st Squadron, 113th Cavalry Regiment, Task Force Redhorse, and a resident of Des Moines, Iowa, fires a G-36 German service rifle during the third portion of the Schutzenschnur or German weapons qualification at Bagram Airfield. Task Force Redhorse is part of 2nd Brigade Combat Team, 34th Infantry Division, Task Force Red Bulls, which is deployed to Afghanistan in support of Operation Enduring Freedom. (Photo by U.S. Army Spc. James Wilton, Task Force Red Bulls Public Affairs)

By U.S. Army Spc. James Wilton
Task Force Red Bulls Public Affairs

PARWAN PROVINCE, Afghanistan, Jan. 14, 2011—Eighteen soldiers Task Force Redhorse soldiers earned the right to wear a silver cord with a bronze, silver, or gold badge after qualifying with German weapons at Bagram Airfield.

Forty-three Task Force Redhorse soldiers from Troop B, 1st Squadron, 113th Cavalry Regiment, part of 2nd Brigade Combat Team, 34th Infantry Division, Task Force Red Bulls, conducted a "Schutzenschnur", or German weapons qualification, under the supervision of German soldiers with the 1st NATO Signal Battalion, German Army.

"Even in the German Army, it may take a soldier several times shooting before he earns the badge," said Stabsunteroffizier Diemo Heyer, a German Army soldier assisting with the certification. "The requirements are very difficult and require a lot of practice to be proficient."

To be awarded the Schutzenschnur, participants are tested on their ability to shoot the G-36 German service rifle, P-8 pistol, and MG-3 machine gun from a series of shooting platforms: from a wall supported position into the 300-meter target, prone into the 250-meter target, standing into the 150-meter target and kneeling into the 100-meter target then standing and kneeling reactive fire into the 50-meter target. To pass the test with they must hit the all targets at least once.

The Schutzenschnur is one of a few foreign military awards authorized for wear on the U.S. Army uniform and is only authorized for enlisted. Officers can receive the award but not wear it. The silver cord is worn on the military dress uniform.

"We are very glad to be here on Bagram and have the opportunity to do cross-training with our [International Security Assistance Force] partners," said Oberfeldwebel Helge Krebs, a German Army soldier assisting with the certification. "Having this opportunity will give us a chance to learn about the American Army and allow us to teach you something about our military."

"It is a great opportunity to work with our [International Security Assistance Force] partners and learn the differences between our weapons systems and theirs," said U.S. Army Spc. Jeffery Graham an intelligence analyst attached to Troop B from Charlottesville, Va. "It is also a great opportunity to learn about future integration of their weapons technology into our own systems."

The rifle has a red-dot scope integrated into the top of the power scope. It also includes and an ambidextrous forward charging handle, which allows shooters to perform immediate action to correct a weapons malfunction more easily and without dropping the barrel.

The opportunity gave soldiers a chance to experience different types of weapons systems and also work with their coalition partners to strengthen ties and build bonds. The Schutzenschnur also included a marksman test for the German soldiers on American weapons including the U.S. Army M4 service rifle and the M9 pistol.

"It was exciting to fire a new kind of weapon," U.S. Army Spc. Cody Bunkers from Remsen, Iowa, and a member of Troop B. "This is a new experience for me and the first weapon I have fired outside of U.S., in terms of military service weapons."

"It's a neat opportunity, one that not many National Guard soldiers get to do, it usually only comes about during a deployment situation," said U.S. Army Sgt. Brad McKinney, a member of Troop B and a Le Mars, Iowa, resident.

Task Force Redhorse plans to attempt another Schutzenschnur later in the year if the schedule permits.

Fun fitness while deployed

PANJSHIR PROVINCE, Afghanistan, Jan. 14, 2011—U.S. Air Force members of Panjshir Provincial Reconstruction Team participate in friendly competition during a volleyball game. The PRT holds weekly competitions to boost morale and encourage various forms of fitness. (Photo by U.S. Air Force Senior Airman Amber Ashcraft, Panshir Provincial Reconstruction Team Public Affairs)

PANJSHIR PROVINCE, Afghanistan, Jan. 14, 2011—U.S. Air Force 2nd Lt. Ashleigh Peck, Panjshir Provincial Reconstruction Team Public Affairs Officer, and Beaver Falls, Pa., native, spikes the ball into her opponent's court during a volleyball game. [...] (Photo by U.S. Air Force Senior Airman Amber Ashcraft Panshir Provincial Reconstruction Team Public Affairs)

A joint venture: 64th MPs, Alingar AUP work, patrol together

LAGHMAN PROVINCE, Afghanistan, Jan. 15, 2011—Soldiers from the 64th Military Police Company, 720th Military Police Battalion, walk out of the village of Kachur, Afghanistan, with Alingar District Afghan Uniformed Police and citizens of the village. (Photo by U.S. Army Staff Sgt. Ryan C. Matson, Task Force Red Bulls Public Affairs)

By U.S. Army Staff Sgt. Ryan C. Matson
Task Force Red Bulls Public Affairs

LAGHMAN PROVINCE, Afghanistan, Jan. 15, 2011–They said it was a typical day in their partnership.

The 64th Military Police Company, 720th Military Police Battalion, visited the Alingar District Center Afghan Uniformed Police. The two police units had a meeting with Alingar AUP Police Chief Adam Khan, ate together, worked on vehicles together and ended the day with a joint patrol.

"This is pretty typical for us, we do everything together," said U.S. Army 1st Lt. Malcolm Adler, a platoon leader with the 64th MP who hails from Bronx, N.Y. "We eat together, we sleep in their center, we work together, we train together."

Adler said the company will typically visit the Alingar District Center, which is the equivalent of a police station in the United States, several times a week, often staying there for three or four nights at a time. The company then conducts patrols in towns throughout the Alingar District, which has been

191

named a key terrain area, a location the coalition wants to concentrate their efforts on due to population and other factors.

Adler said the MPs conduct four to five patrols a week with their Afghan partners. He said they have been partnered together since April 2010 as part of Task Force Ironman, conducting more than 100 joint patrols together during that time.

This time out, the police patrolled through the town of Kachur, a village a little over a mile to the south of the district center. Khan chose the village because the police had not been there together in a while.

AUP 1st Lt. Mohammed Hussain is a graduate of the Mehtar Lam Provincial Police Academy and has been a police officer in Afghanistan for more than 20 years. He said the AUP have not had any problems from this particular village, although it is one the enemy is known to pass through in conducting operations against the coalition.

"We went with the Americans to the village of Kachur to talk to the civilian people about their problems," Hussain said. "We asked them about their security problems and about enemies around the village. They said the people will call us, but they don't really have any security concerns, they are partners with the AUP."

Adler said the patrols are important, even if the people in the villages say they feel safe.

"It's how we gain information on enemy activity in the area," he said. "We have to get out there and be policing with the AUP in the area, and ask them if they see any crime ... The villagers will tell us."

Though they did not find any security concerns in Kachur, the people did tell them about some problems in the village concerning their water and school, which Adler said he will forward on to the provincial reconstruction team to look at.

The day began with a meeting between Kahn and Adler and his platoon sergeant, U.S. Army Staff Sgt. Joe Contreras, a native of San Antonio, Texas. The three men discussed the chief's future plans in the area. The chief said the Alingar AUP have been conducting about 14 patrols weekly through villages in the area.

Adler said the AUP have stepped up their independent patrols in the last few weeks and have also recovered numerous Improvised Explosive Devices in the area.

While the meeting transpired, U.S. Army Spc. Carlos Pulido, 64th MP all-wheeled mechanic from Turlock, Calif., took a look at some of the AUP's Humvees. It is a vehicle with which Pulido is very familiar and he said he was able to help them fix some minor problems with the vehicles, such as changing out some bolts in the half shaft and giving the AUP a jack to use to change tires. Pulido was assisted by Alingar AUP Farid Ahmad Malang, platoon sergeant, who helped him carry his tools and service the vehicle. Pulido explained the problems with the vehicles through an interpreter so Malang will know how to fix similar problems in the future.

"They're all pretty good guys," Pulido said of his AUP counterparts. "They all just want to jump in and help."

Adler said when he started working with the police in Alingar in April, they were initially hesitant to get out and patrol with the Americans. In the 10 months he's been here, however, the AUP have become more and more eager to go out with the Americans after having success on joint missions.

"Those AUP will go anywhere with us," Adler said.

Hussain agreed.

"We want to go on joint patrols all the time with the American military police," he said. "It's all we want. It's impressive when we work together. It lets the people know the AUP are out there and are on patrol in Mehtar Lam and here in Alingar."

ANA enforces weapon registration law

PAKTYA PROVINCE, Afghanistan, Jan. 16, 2011—Afghan National Army 1st Lt. Pallawanna, 3rd Company, 1st Kandak, 2nd Brigade, 203rd ANA Infantry Corps inspects for a serial number on an AK-47 owned by a resident of Sar Mast Kheyl village in Zormat District, Paktya Province. (Photo by U.S. Army 1st Lt. Nicholas Rasmussen, Task Force Lethal)

By U.S. Army 1st Lt. Nicholas Rasmussen
Task Force Lethal

PAKTYA PROVINCE, Afghanistan, Jan. 16, 2011—The 1st Company, 3rd Kandak, 2nd Brigade, 203rd ANA Infantry Corps of the Afghan National Army and U.S. Army soldiers with Company C, 1st Battalion, 168th Infantry Regiment visited Sar Mast Kheyl village, Zormat District, Jan. 16.

During the visit, an impromptu meeting was held in which ANA officials urged villagers to call coalition and Afghan forces for help if there is insurgent activity near the village.

Although Afghans are allowed one weapon and a limited amount of ammunition, according to ANA Lt. 1st Pallawanna of the 3rd Company, 1st Kandak, 2nd Brigade, 203rd ANA Infantry Corps, the Government of the Islamic Republic of Afghanistan requires all citizens of Afghanistan who own firearms to register them.

If a citizen is found in possession of an unregistered firearm or excess ammunition, the munitions can be confiscated by ANA, he said.

To demonstrate the legitimacy of his claims, Pallawanna asked the villagers to present their firearms for registration.

Initially only a few villagers presented their weapons, expecting the ANA to take the guns away. But after inspection of the firearms and recording of the serial numbers, the ANA officer returned the guns to the owners.

Witnessing this, other villagers presented their firearms for registration taking comfort in the knowledge the weapon would be returned.

"This is the kind of activity that creates trust between villagers and the ANA," said U.S. Army 2nd Lt. Joel Sage, 3rd Platoon leader of Ankeny, Iowa. "And trust in the ANA ultimately leads to trust in GIRoA."

Red Bulls join service members, civilians in remembering Dr. King

BAGRAM AIRFIELD, Afghanistan, Jan. 17, 2011—Soldiers stationed at Bagram Airfield, here lead fellow service members and civilians in a march around the airfield to honor Dr. Martin Luther King Jr.. The march was a representation of the 54-mile civil rights march Dr. King made from Selma to Montgomery, Ala. in 1965. (Photo by U.S. Army Spc. James Wilton, Task Force Red Bulls Public Affairs)

BAGRAM AIRFIELD, Afghanistan, Jan. 17, 2011—U.S. Army Sgt. 1st Class Chris White, the equal opportunity advocate for the 2nd Brigade Combat Team, 34th Infantry Division, Task Force Red Bulls from Des Moines, Iowa, sings a solo at the Dr. Martin Luther King Jr. Day observance ceremony on Bagram Airfield. Festivities also included a march and a five-kilometer run around BAF. (Photo by U.S. Army Spc. James Wilton, Task Force Red Bulls Public Affairs)

Nuristan PRT, Task Force Red Bulls host two-day shura

NURISTAN PROVINCE, Afghanistan, Jan. 18, 2011—Citizens from Nuristan Province exchange greetings before a shura at the Nurgaram District Center. The two-day shura featured Afghan speakers from the local government as well as the United Nations, who discussed strategies for bringing peace to Nuristan. (Photo by U.S. Army Staff Sgt. Ryan C. Matson, Task Force Red Bulls Public Affairs)

NURISTAN PROVINCE, Afghanistan, Jan. 18, 2011—Wakil Saki (right), Nurgaram District elder, listens to Dr. Abdul Wakil, Nuristan representative for the United National Development Program, at Forward Operating Base Kalagush. The Nuristan Provincial Reconstruction Team and Task Force Ironman, part of the 2nd Brigade Combat Team, 34th Infantry Division, Task Force Red Bulls, sponsored the meeting with civic and government leaders from the Nuristan province. The PRT works with the government of the Islamic Republic of Afghanistan to help bring peace and stability to the region. (Photo by U.S. Air Force Chief Master Sgt. Richard Simonsen, Nuristan Provincial Reconstruction Team Public Affairs)

NURISTAN PROVINCE, Afghanistan, Jan. 18, 2011—Nurgaram Afghan Uniformed Police Chief Capt. Sham Mamood (left) and U.S. Army Capt. Garrett Gingrich of Waterloo, Iowa, commander of Company C, 1st Battalion, 133rd Infantry Regiment, Task Force Ironman, a part of the 2nd Brigade Combat Team, 34th Infantry Division, talk through an interpreter prior to a shura at the Nurgaram District Center. The two-day shura featured Afghan speakers from the local government as well as the United Nations, who discussed strategies for bringing peace to Nuristan. (Photo by U.S. Army Staff Sgt. Ryan C. Matson, Task Force Red Bulls Public Affairs)

NURISTAN PROVINCE, Afghanistan, Jan. 18, 2011—Afghan National Police Gen. Zahid Shams Nuristani (left), commander of the Nuristan province ANP, talks with Dr. Abdul Wakil (center), from the United Nations Development Program, and U.S. Navy Cmdr. Bill Mallory, commanding officer of the Nuristan Provincial Reconstruction Team from Chesapeake, Va. at the conclusion of a two-day shura at the Nurgaram District Center. [...] (Photo by U.S. Army Staff Sgt. Ryan C. Matson, Task Force Red Bulls Public Affairs)

NURISTAN PROVINCE, Afghanistan, Jan. 18, 2011—U.S. Army Lt. Col. Steven Kremer (left) from Cherokee, Iowa, commander of Task Force Ironman, part of the 2nd Brigade Combat Team, 34th Infantry Division, Task Force Red Bulls, and U.S. Army Lt. Col. Roberto Garcia from Chicago, civil-military affairs operations center director for the Nuristan Provincial Reconstruction Team, prepare to enter a meeting with civic and government leaders on Forward Operating Base Kalagush The Nuristan PRT and Task Force Ironman sponsored a two-day shura, which focused on bringing peace to Nuristan. Soldiers from Task Force Ironman operate in three districts of western Nuristan. (Photo by U.S. Air Force Chief Master Sgt. Richard Simonsen, Nuristan Provincial Reconstruction Team Public Affairs)

ANA, Task Force Redhorse spread message of security

PARWAN PROVINCE, Afghanistan, Jan. 19, 2011—Naweed Achmad, an Afghan National Army platoon sergeant with the 1st Company, 3rd Kandak, 1st Brigade, 201st ANA Infantry Corps, speaks to village elders in Sabikhel about the importance of security. Security is everyone's responsibility, said the ANA platoon sergeant. (Photo by U.S. Army Spc. James Wilton, Task Force Red Bulls Public Affairs)

PARWAN PROVINCE, Afghanistan, Jan. 19, 2011—U.S. Army Spc. Jeffery Hall from Carol, Iowa, medic with Troop A, 1st Squadron, 113th Cavalry Regiment, Task Force Redhorse, uses a Hand-Held Interagency Identity Detection Equipment system on an Afghan local national who works on Bagram Airfield during a visit to Sabikhel Jan. 19. The HIIDE system is a biometrics collection tool that helps Task Force Redhorse, which is a part of the 2nd Brigade Combat Team, 34th Infantry Division, Task Force Red Bulls, and other U.S. military forces quickly identify and track known criminals and ensure they aren't hiding among the general population. (Photo by U.S. Army Spc. James Wilton, Task Force Red Bulls Public Affairs)

FET plays vital role in Mayl Valley operations

LAGHMAN PROVINCE, Afghanistan, Jan. 19, 2011—The Female Engagement Team for 1st Battalion, 133rd Infantry Regiment at Forward Operating Base Mehtar Lam, Afghanistan. The team members are (front row, left to right), U.S. Army Pfc. Shannyanne Adame, a truck driver from Bettendorf, Iowa; U.S. Army Spc. Kimberly Lindsey, an administration specialist from Eldora, Iowa; U.S. Army Pvt. Olivia McBride, a production control specialist from West Union, Iowa; (back row, left to right), U.S. Army Capt. Jodi Marti, a company commander from Knoxville, Iowa; U.S. Army Staff Sgt. Jennifer Voegtlin, a combat medic from Altoona, Iowa; U.S. Army Sgt. Shannon Osterholm, a truck driver from Mason City, Iowa; U.S. Army Sgt. Samantha Kauffman, a signal support systems specialist, from West Union, Iowa. All of the soldiers are from Company E, 1st Battalion, 133rd Infantry Regiment, except for Voegtlin, who is from Headquarters and Headquarters Company, 1st Battalion, 133rd Infantry Regiment. The FET members were a key part of a large, highly successful recent mission dubbed "Operation Rockstar." (Photo by U.S. Army Staff Sgt. Ryan Matson, Task Force Red Bulls Public Affairs)

Red Bull Soldiers own the night:
Former NCO patrols dark streets as cavalry officer

PARWAN PROVINCE, Afghanistan, Jan. 19, 2011—U.S. Army 1st Lt. Gerry Holloway, a Melbourn, Iowa, resident and a platoon leader with Troop C, 1st Squadron, 113th Cavalry Regiment, Task Force Redhorse, part of the 2nd Brigade Combat Team, 34th Infantry Division, Task Force Red Bulls, gives a final briefing to his soldiers before heading out on a night patrol. Holloway, a former combat engineer Non-Commissioned Officer turned infantry lieutenant, leads 2nd Platoon on nightly patrols around the Bagram Security Zone. (Photo by U.S. Army Staff Sgt. Ashlee Lolkus, Task Force Red Bulls Public Affairs)

By U.S. Army Staff Sgt. Ashlee Lolkus
Task Force Red Bulls Public Affairs

PARWAN PROVINCE, Afghanistan, Jan. 19, 2011—The graveyard shift.

The shift despised by most requires waking while others are leaving work, working while others sleep and sleeping while the world moves through its normal hustle and bustle of the day. This is the shift with which U.S. Army 1st Lt. Gerry Holloway and his soldiers of 2nd Platoon, Troop C, 1st Squadron, 113th Cavalry Regiment, Task Force Redhorse, are all too familiar.

The moon filled the sky with a bright, smoky haze dotted by a few stars as Holloway stepped out into the brisk night air at Combat Outpost Red Hill, also known as Pushtaysark. The night skies are normally dotted with stars out here because there are no street or store lights shining. This scene is common for most combat outposts in Afghanistan.

"It's a beautiful sight to wake up, step outside and see the stars every morning," said Holloway, a father of five from Melbourn, Iowa. "Of course, our morning is everyone's night time on our shift."

Holloway and his crew consisting of infantrymen, a medic, and a cook, who is one of the company's two Female Engagement Team members, rove and patrol the streets of the surrounding areas looking for insurgent activities and ensuring that the local people are safe throughout the night.

This mission is similar to those he did as a team leader when he deployed to Iraq in 2005 and 2006. He and his team of three conducted convoy security operations in the areas north of Baghdad when he was assigned as a Non-Commissioned Officer in Task Force Redhorse, which is part of 2nd Brigade Combat Team, 34th Infantry Division, Task Force Red Bulls.

"Sometimes I miss being an NCO," he said. "I miss the responsibilities of taking care of soldiers and making sure missions get accomplished. I still ensure that missions get accomplished as an officer, but it's different."

His deep-rooted ties to the NCO corps is evident while on patrol and throughout operations, as Holloway ensures soldiers have their sensitive items, take proper safety precautions, and conduct other tasks for which NCOs are normally responsible.

"As a lieutenant, now I am responsible for developing the plan, and the NCOs in my platoon are in charge of carrying the plan out. Sometimes it's hard to shut that 'NCO' side of me off," he continued. "I really do try to not micromanage, but it's hard."

Holloway decided to try his luck as an officer in early 2007 and applied for a direct commission, which was accepted in October 2008. He said he loves being an officer and considers it one of the best decisions he's ever made.

"The detailed levels of planning are what I enjoy about being an officer," Holloway admitted. "I like to get into the nuts and bolts on how to accomplish a mission. As an NCO, I would get my orders and execute. I get to help build those orders now, and I make sure that my NCOs are following through with them."

"It's a huge step to transition from an NCO to an officer," said U.S. Army Capt. Richard Rush, Troop C commander and Altoona, Iowa, resident who deployed with Holloway when he was an NCO as now as an officer. "I think he's adapted well to the officer environment, It happens a lot when NCOs [transition] to officer, where they still like to operate as NCOs."

The soldiers enjoy Holloway's leadership style.

"When I'm not out on mission, I'm helping out in the kitchen, or I find something to do to keep me busy," said FET member U.S. Army Sgt. Stephanie Bliss, a Sioux City, Iowa, resident. "But, I like going along on missions. I love 2nd Platoon. They are usually the ones to pull me in for missions. Lt. Holloway is not like a lot of officers who joined then became officers. He knows how to talk to soldiers, and he's very low-key. I like it."

Whether as an NCO or as an officer, Holloway continues to take care of his soldiers.

The night patrol came and went, like most nights he and the soldiers of 2nd Platoon go out. As the sun began to rise, the troops headed to Bagram Airfield to conduct vehicle maintenance and get ready for the next mission. Holloway and his troops will be ready to own the night once again.

*PARWAN PROVINCE, Afghanistan, Jan. 19, 2011—*U.S. Army Spc. Joshua Vondrak, of Sioux City, Iowa, and combat medic for 2nd Platoon, Troop C, 1st Squadron, 113th Cavalry Regiment, Task Force Redhorse, part of 2nd Brigade Combat Team, 34th Infantry Division, Task Force Red Bulls, helps set up the tactical formation as the platoon headed out on dismounted patrol. The platoon is assigned the task of patrolling the Bagram Security Zone during the night hours. (Photo by U.S. Army Staff Sgt. Ashlee Lolkus, Task Force Red Bulls Public Affairs)

Iowa Soldiers discuss 'average' days in Afghanistan

NURISTAN PROVINCE, Afghanistan, Jan. 20, 2011—U.S. Army Pfc. Corey Vanotegham, an infantry radio telephone operator from Victor, Iowa, with Company C, 1st Battalion, 133rd Infantry Regiment, Task Force Ironman, smiles as he stands beside a Holstein cow at the farmer's market in Alingar Jan. 20. Vanotegham, who grew up on a dairy farm in Iowa, talked about the day-to-day life of an infantryman in Afghanistan. Task Force Ironman is a part of the 2nd Brigade Combat Team, 34th Infantry Division, Task Force Red Bulls, and the Iowa National Guard. (Photo by U.S. Army Staff Sgt Ryan C. Matson, Task Force Red Bulls Public Affairs)

By U.S. Staff Sgt. Ryan C. Matson
Task Force Red Bulls Public Affairs

and U.S. Army Sgt. Joseph Sawyer
Company C, 1st Battalion, 133rd Infantry Regiment

NURISTAN PROVINCE, Afghanistan, Jan. 20, 2011—For two U.S. Army Soldiers from Iowa, their mission to Alingar District Center with Task Force Red Bulls Jan. 20 felt like just another day in the books. It was just one of the more than 300 they will spend in this mountainous country far from home. However, it was another key ingredient in helping improve Afghanistan's security and economy.

U.S. Army Spc. Jarod Huser and Pfc. Corey Vanotegham, along with the other Soldiers of 1st Platoon, Company C, 133rd Infantry Regiment, visit the Alingar District Center, two or three times a week. Each trip includes several smaller chores or duties depending on the circumstances.

During this mission, the Iowa National Guard Soldiers assigned to the 2nd Brigade Combat Team, 34th Infantry Division, Task Force Red Bulls, provided both transportation and security for a civil affairs officer who is working feverishly to complete a budget that will affect the thousands of Afghan citizens in the area.

"We go to Alingar quite a bit," said U.S. Army Spc. Jarod Huser, an infantry gunner from Ames, Iowa. "For that mission, we did a mounted patrol down to Alingar, checking for roadside bombs along the way, pulling security at all times, watching out for enemy activity, just getting a feel for what's going on in the villages."

Mounted in Mine-Resistant, Ambush-Protected vehicles, the Soldiers convoyed from Combat Outpost Kalagush south through hills and valleys to Alingar. Once there, they positioned themselves tactically throughout the town watching for anything out of the ordinary while U.S. Army Maj. Andrew Dejesse, a civil affairs officer with Company A, 413th Civil Affairs Battalion, from Amarillo, Texas, went to work.

DeJesse spoke with Fetah Mohammad, the Alingar district manager of village affairs, trying to finalize points in a budget plan for the district for the upcoming year, one that was due in three weeks. He also talked at length with the district education director for his recommendations on the budget. There are 72 schools attended by more than 38,000 students, so finalizing the budget was big business, and was the main reason 1st Platoon conducted the mission to Alingar.

While DeJesse was inside talking to the education director, Huser was inside his MRAP manning the gun constantly monitoring for threats around the perimeter of the village using the truck's Common Remotely Operated Weapon Station ("CROWS"). Operating the CROWS equipment, the gunner is not in an external turret potentially exposed to enemy gunfire and IED blasts, but sits inside the vehicle and maneuvers the gun with a joystick while carefully monitoring his surroundings through a camera.

"I love being a gunner," Huser said. "I do the CROWS, but also do open-turret sometimes. I like being able to be up in the truck looking around. I watch for everything, but ridgelines (are) a big thing. I can look through the CROWS and find people up there moving around I wouldn't be able to see with the naked eye."

After DeJesse conducted his business, the Soldiers walked the streets of Alingar with their ANA counterparts.

"Just about every time we go out, we try to get our faces out on the streets," said U.S. Army Pfc. Corey Vanotegham, an infantry radio telephone operator from Victor, Iowa. "People see we're there, that we have a presence and have good intentions. Going out and seeing the people, trying to speak a little

Pashtu with them and seeing what they have to sell is interesting."

After the patrol through the city, the day was not done for the Soldiers from 1st Platoon The Soldiers received word of a possible IED near the town of Tupac. The Soldiers spent almost an hour scouring a steep ridge outside the village and combing the fields along the valley for signs of the device.

The IED was located the following day by another platoon after a tip from another villager. A Soldier walking on a bank of the valley uncovered the IED's command wire. The wire to detonate the device was a copper wire not much thicker than a fishing line, completely buried in the dirt in a valley.

"It's really hard to find an IED, without hitting it," Vanotegham said.

Vanotegham said he likes that there is no "average" mission.

"I like just running missions in general," he said. "The mission to Alingar is somewhat predictable, but then again, it could be unpredictable. At any moment there or on your way back, you could come into enemy contact."

Vanotegham said missions will often change. On this day's mission, in addition to the IED, the Soldiers heard gunshots in the distance and investigated the shots with the local townspeople as they patrolled through the village. The shots were far enough away not to be of any great concern to the Soldiers, but they are typical during operations in the field.

Soldiers must be prepared for anything while out on a mission, he said. At any moment, the Soldiers may receive a mission to climb a 7,000-foot mountain to try and locate an enemy fighting position or indication of enemy presence in the area. They will walk and search for hours and often uncover very little, if anything at all.

"You might not find a goldmine, but if you find any indicator of someone being present who's not supposed to be there, it's worth it," Vanotegham said. "You can't just skip that step, because the one time you do find something, it might save somebody's life."

Besides being together in Afghanistan, both Huser, 22 and Vanotegham, 21, share another common bond. The two Soldiers are both Iowa State University "Cyclone" students.

Huser is a business management major and Vanotegham is an agricultural education major. In fact, Vanotegham said the highlight of this mission for him was seeing a reminder of home, a Holstein cow at the Alingar farmer's market. It was the first Holstein he had seen since arriving in country four months ago. "I had to snap a picture, which I know everybody back home will be commenting about on Facebook," Vanotegham laughed. "It's just something that's kind of neat."

Though the farms here are much smaller and more primitive than those in Iowa, Vanotegham smiled when he thought about the comparisons.

"You see a lot of kids out doing work in the fields or playing in them, just like back home," he said. "There's a lot of crops here I've never seen before, but a lot of the same principles. It's just amazing how they make do with what little they have compared to back home where everything's just so plentiful."

In another seven months or so, Vanotegham and Huser will return to the cornfields of Iowa, but until then it will be many more days and missions like this one, one after another. But one thing is guaranteed, no two will be the same, and these Soldiers will be ready for whatever comes their way.

ANA, Red Bulls find IED

NURISTAN PROVINCE, Afghansistan, Jan. 21, 2011—U.S. Army Spc. Michael
Scarsbrook, an infantryman with Company C, 1st Battalion, 133rd Infantry Regiment, Task
Force Ironman, from Iowa Falls, Iowa, looks down on a spot in Tupac, where his unit had
been attacked by an Improvised Explosive Device two days earlier. Task Force Ironman is
a part of the 2nd Brigade Combat Team, 34th Infantry Division, Task Force Red Bulls.
(Photo by U.S. Army Staff Sgt. Ryan C. Matson, Task Force Red Bulls Public Affairs)

By U.S. Army Staff Sgt. Ryan C. Matson
Task Force Red Bulls Public Affairs

NURISTAN PROVINCE, Afghanistan, Jan. 21, 2011—U.S. Army 1st Lt.
Lucas Peterson, a platoon leader with 2nd platoon, Company C, 1st Battalion,
133rd Infantry Regiment, 2nd Brigade Combat Team, 34th Infantry Division,
had heard it all before.

"We didn't see anything," a villager in the town of Tupac told him as he
talked with a group of villagers in the streets of the town Jan. 21. "The people
come from outside our village."

Peterson said it is frustrating. Two days before, an Improvised Explosive
Device had detonated in Tupac just a few feet in front of one of his platoon's
vehicles. It was a near miss and luckily, none of his soldiers were injured in the
attack. The blast was in the middle of the village by a house but the people said
they had not seen or heard anything.

So, the platoon kept patrolling. They had already walked miles and miles
up and down mountains to get to Tupac, having conducted a Key Leader
Engagement in the town of Nengaresh earlier. They were just about to start

209

the long march back to Forward Operating Base Kalagush, when it happened: someone came forward.

A person in the area approached one of the Afghan National Army soldiers from Weapons Company, 1st Kandak, 2nd Brigade, 201st ANA Infantry Corps, on patrol with Peterson's men, and told the ANA soldiers they had seen a wire. That was all they needed.

An hour or so later, after the soldiers had been walking for seven hours, Peterson slipped and skidded a few feet down a steep slope, in so doing, uncovering the wire, which Weapons Company soldier Shafi Ulah quickly located.

The Afghan and American troops followed the wire down one mountainside and up another together before they found that it led straight to an old blast site along the side of the road which had since been filled with rocks. The site had been used to attack the unit that Company C had replaced. The Explosive Ordnance Disposal team was called out and located then destroyed the IED.

Because the person came forward with the littlest tip, the person potentially saved American and Afghan lives, Peterson said.

The IED obviously took a considerable amount of time to emplace, as the wire was buried up and down two complete steep valley slopes. Still, Peterson and his men have seen this before, yet gotten little information from the villagers, who are intimidated by the Taliban.

"They always say if they see something, they'll call and never do. The story of my life," Peterson, who hails from Ames, Iowa, said with a laugh.

U.S. Army Pfc. Brian Wisor, a 20-year-old infantryman from Ackley, Iowa, was one of the Company C soldiers on the patrol when the IED was located. He said when he started the patrol he didn't really expect to find an IED. Prior to locating the IED, in fact, the big news of the day was that it was the twenty-seventh birthday of squad leader U.S. Army Staff Sgt. Jeff Behan, from Sabula, Iowa.

Peterson said the IED was a pressure-cooker packed with 25 pounds of explosives and was comparably small to some that have been found in the area. Still, the damage it could have done was not inflicted on his soldiers.

"If it would have hit one of our trucks, it probably wouldn't have been too bad," Wisor said. "If it would have hit a person, though, or one of the ANA trucks it wouldn't have been a good deal. It was nice that the people are starting to trust us enough to give us information and we can take care of it, instead of some little kid or [other] innocent person in general finding it."

During the mission, Company C's soldiers walked at least 10 kilometers, starting at Forward Operating Base Kalagush, over a mountain and a couple ridges to the town of Nengaresh, where they conducted a KLE. Peterson said his soldiers had often driven past the town, but never stopped and talked with the people.

"We wanted to put our face out there and talk with the people," Peterson said. "The people said it had been a long time since Americans had been through the area. We stop at their bazaar along the paved road, but had never gone up to the village itself. Having them see us makes everything a little more personal."

"It's nice to get out and interact with the people, and see a different view of the villages," Wisor said.

From there, the soldiers hiked onward, up and down valleys to the town of Tupac. They swept the bridge with a metal detector, as well as the fields near Route Philadelphia, the road going through the center of the village that the unit had been hit on two days earlier. They explored the valleys around the village but found nothing. Peterson estimated they had walked probably eight miles up and down mountains during the day. But they had nothing to show for it until the tip came in.

The patrol was a longer one for the platoon, but is nothing new. Wisor said it was his first mission back from leave, and was a quick re-acclimatization.

"It was a smoker," he said with a laugh.

"I just want people to know my guys are out here working hard," Peterson said.

They say hard work pays off, and this time it did. As the soldiers from Company C huffed back to FOB Kalagush, they heard the EOD team blow up the IED they had found in the distance. Though tired from the gruelling day, hearing the IED detonate and knowing it wouldn't be able to hurt them or an innocent civilian brought a smile to their faces.

Stingray, Ironman troops visit Mangow village, talk security

LAGHMAN PROVINCE, Afghanistan, Jan. 21, 2011—U.S. Army Spc. Mason Lembke of West Union, Iowa, an infantryman with Headquarters and Headquarters Company, 1st Battalion, 133rd Infantry Regiment, Task Force Ironman, a part of the 2nd Brigade Combat Team, 34th Infantry Division, Task Force Red Bulls, and Afghan National Army soldiers provide security during a dismounted patrol through Mangow village. [...] (Photo by U.S. Army Spc. Kristina L. Gupton, Task Force Red Bulls Public Affairs)

LAGHMAN PROVINCE, Afghanistan, Jan. 21, 2011—U.S. Army Staff Sgt. Nick McLaughin of St. Paul, Minn., psychological operations specialist with 319th Tactical Psychological Operations Company, Task Force Stingray, speaks with Mangow village malik. McLaughin visited Mangow village to conduct a Key Leader Engagement with village malik to discuss security and needs the village may have. (Photo by U.S. Army Spc. Kristina L. Gupton, Task Force Red Bulls Public Affairs)

LAGHMAN PROVINCE, Afghanistan, Jan. 21, 2011—U.S. Army Pvt. Zachary Volz of Clive, Iowa, combat medic with Headquarters and Headquarters Company, 1st Battalion, 133rd Infantry Regiment, Task Force Ironman, a part of the 2nd Brigade Combat Team, 34th Infantry Division, Task Force Red Bulls, provides security for fellow soldiers as they conduct a Key Leader Engagement. [...] (Photo by U.S. Army Spc. Kristina L. Gupton, Task Force Red Bulls Public Affairs)

LAGHMAN PROVINCE, Afghanistan, Jan. 21, 2011—U.S. Army Staff Sgt. Nick McLaughin (center) of St. Paul, Minn., and U.S. Army Sgt. Clayton Herman of Minneapolis, Minn., both psychological operations specialists with 319th Tactical Psychological Operations Company, Task Force Stingray, conduct a Key Leader Engagement with village elders and malik of Mangow. They visited the village to speak with elders and the malik to discuss the security within the village. (Photo by U.S. Army Spc. Kristina L. Gupton, Task Force Red Bulls Public Affairs)

DFAC dedicated to fallen Guard Soldier opens for business

PARWAN PROVINCE, Afghanistan, Jan. 22, 2011—U.S. Army Maj. Gen. Raymond Carpenter, the acting director of the Army National Guard, and U.S. Army Lt. Col. John J. Perkins, a Johnston, Iowa, native and the 334th Brigade Support Battalion, Task Force Archer, commander, part of the 2nd Brigade Combat Team, Task Force Red Bulls, cut the ribbon across the entrance of the Grady Dining Facility during the grand opening ceremony on Bagram Airfield Jan. 22. (Photo by U.S. Army Sgt. 1st Class Matthew Arrington, 176th Engineer Brigade)

By U.S. Army Spc. James Wilton
Task Force Red Bulls Public Affairs

BAGRAM AIRFIELD, Afghanistan, Jan. 22, 2011—The grand opening ceremony for the Grady Dining Facility was held at Bagram Airfield's Camp Warrior Jan. 22.

The facility is named after U.S. Army Spc. Ryan "Big Smooth" Grady of Bristow, Okla., an engineer with Company A, Special Troops Battalion, 1st Squadron, 172nd Cavalry Division, 86th Infantry Brigade Combat Team, who was killed in action in Parwan Province last year.

"Spc. Ryan Grady represents to us what the modern National Guard is," said U.S. Army Maj. Gen. Raymond Carpenter the acting director of the Army National Guard. "He joined the guard because he wanted to serve his country."

Carpenter joined U.S. Army Lt. Col. John J. Perkins, a Johnston, Iowa, native and the 334th Brigade Support Battalion, Task Force Archer, commander and master of ceremonies for the event in cutting the ribbon across the entrance to the facility and spoke at the ceremony.

"I believe that he (would) truly appreciate that a facility like this one is available for his fellow Soldiers in a place where so very few creature comforts are available," Carpenter said. "I can only hope that you and the many servicemembers who cross the threshold into this building for years to come can enjoy a reprieve from the seemingly endless mission that we have here in Afghanistan. Today, remember those who came before you and those like Ryan, who paid the ultimate price for what we all hold dear."

The dining facility was under construction during Grady's tour in Afghanistan and received the official name a few months back. The theme of the dining facility is Americana, and includes signs such as "Warrior Bucks" over the coffee station and "Warrior Way" over the sandwich bar.

The ceremony included a meal of steak and lobster for those in attendance and those having lunch after the ceremony. It closed with a dedication to all those who have paid the ultimate price.

"If everyone would stand, I would like to propose a toast," Perkins said. "This is to not only Grady but all the servicemembers who have made the ultimate sacrifice. To our fallen comrades."

Cub Scouts interview ANP officer

PANJSHIR PROVINCE, Afgahnistan, Jan. 22, 2011—Afghan National Police Capt. Sefat Mire left), a training officer for Rokha District, and U.S. Army Master Sgt. Todd Eipperle, senior Non-Commissioned Officer-in-Charge of Task Force Red Bulls Embedded Training Team in Panjshir from Marshalltown, Iowa, speak with Cub Scouts via video teleconference Jan. 22. Cub Scouts from Pack 182, located in Ankeny, Iowa, asked the ANP officer several questions about his life in Afghanistan. Photo by U.S. Air Force Senior Airman Amber Ashcraft, Pansjhir Provincial Reconstruction Team)

By U.S. Air Force Senior Airman Amber Ashcraft
Panjshir Provincial Reconstruction Team

PANJSHIR PROVINCE, Afghanistan, Jan. 22, 2011—With the help of social media, military members overseas are able to easily keep in touch with family and friends back home.

Although many service members take advantage of the capability, it is a rare occurrence when video teleconferencing is used for American children to interview an Afghan National Police officer.

"When I was deployed in 2003, we didn't even have Internet access," said U.S. Army Master Sgt. Todd Eipperle, senior Non-Commissioned Officer-in-Charge of Task Force Red Bulls' Embedded Training Team in Panjshir. "Being able to have a meeting like this, face-to-face, makes the experience even better."

The meeting took place Jan. 22 with Cub Scout Pack 182 from Ankeny, Iowa. The Scouts took turns asking Capt. Sefat Mire, Rokha District ANP training officer, about his life in Afghanistan. They wanted to know what it is like for Mire to be a police officer, what the best part of his job is and if he is able to go home to his family every night.

"Some days, we are very busy and travel, so I come home very late," answered Mire, through an interpreter. "But I enjoy being a police officer."

Eipperle, a Marshalltown, Iowa, native and part of the Iowa Cub Scouts, helped set up the session by sending an e-mail to some of the packs back home asking if they would like to talk with an ANP member.

"There is a 'Language and Culture' award Scouts can get," Eipperle said. "Pack 182 responded they would like to get that award and participate in the meeting."

After speaking with the pack's leader, U.S. Army Lt. Col. Sean Ogelsby, Eipperle found an ANP member to talk with the Scouts.

"Captain Mire was outspoken in our train-the-trainers course and was easy to talk to," Eipperle said. "Having four boys of his own at home, he was excited to participate."

For more than a half hour, the Scouts, Mire and Eipperle exchanged questions and answers through an interpreter about life as Scouts in the U.S. and as ANP in Afghanistan.

"It was good to be able to speak to the Cub Scouts," said Mire. "When the PRT goes on missions here and talks to our children, our children come home and tell their fathers about the good experience they had with the Americans. Afghan children are like American children, we want them to look up to us and have good experiences."

After teaching the Cub Scouts how to say "thank you" and "goodbye," "tashakor" and "huda hafez" respectively, they ended their teleconference.

"When I thanked Capt. Mire for doing this for our boys, he simply replied, 'It's something I will remember forever,'" Eipperle said.

Task Force Ironman, ANA provide Laghman Governor security during shura

LAGHMAN PROVINCE, Afghanistan, Jan. 23, 2011—U.S. Army Lt. Col. Steven Kremer (center), of Cherokee, Iowa, commander of 1st Battalion, 133rd Infantry Regiment, Task Force Ironman, a part of the 2nd Brigade Combat Team, 34th Infantry Division, Task Force Red Bulls, and U.S. Army Lt. Col. John C. Walker (right), of Manhattan, Kan., and the Laghman Provincial Reconstruction Team commander, Task Force Red Bulls, speak with Gov. Mohammad Iqbal Azizi about security provided during a shura in the Gomrai village. The Governor spoke to the villagers of Gomrai about stopping the violence in the villages. (Photo by U.S. Army Spc. Kristina L. Gupton, Task Force Red Bulls Public Affairs)

Joint meeting aims to increase Paktya security

PAKTYA PROVINCE, Afghanistan, Jan. 23, 2011–Gen. Nazar Shah Safi (center), the National Directorate of Security chief, listens as Col. Mahmoud Zazai (right), commander of the Afghan National Army's 1st Kandak, 2nd Brigade, 203rd ANA Infantry Corps discusses the effectiveness of night raids and security force patrols in Zormat District, Paktya Province during a weekly security meeting on Forward Operating Base Gardez, Jan. 23. The U.S. Army's 1st Battalion, 168th Infantry Regiment and Team Paktya initiated the weekly security meetings last month in an effort to coordinate the efforts of the ANSF and coalition forces. (Photo by U.S. Army 1st Lt. Nicholas Rasmussen, Task Force Lethal)

By U.S. Army 1st Lt. Nicholas Rasmussen
Task Force Lethal

PAKTYA PROVINCE, Afghanistan, Jan. 23, 2011—Paktya security and how to improve it was the main topic at a joint security meeting held at Forward Operating Base Gardez.

The newly established weekly meeting included participants from the Afghan National Security Forces, the U.S. Army's 1st Battalion, 168th Infantry Regiment, Paktya Provincial Reconstruction Team, the U.S. Department of State and the United Nations Assistance Mission in Afghanistan.

U.S. Army Lt. Col. Stephen B. Boesen II, a native of Ankeny, Iowa, and commander of the 1-168th Inf., known as Task Force Lethal, helped put together the joint security meeting designed to coordinate the efforts of ANSF and coalition forces in Paktya.

"It gives us a chance to come together and say, 'Hey, we have a problem

219

here, let's talk about how to solve it,'" said Boesen. "The whole purpose of the meeting is to get everyone together in an effort to solve the problems of Patkya. I've seen this meeting in Khowst and Ghazni, and it has worked real well; doing things piecemeal does not work. I've seen it."

One focus of this week's meeting was the practicality and effectiveness of night raids performed within the province.

Brig. Gen. Abdal Rahma Safi, the Paktya chief of police, believes the increased presence of the security forces during the day and night in the past week contributed to the low level of insurgent activity in the province.

"Night raids have been very effective based on the reports I have received," said Safi.

Col. Mahmoud Zazai, commander of the Afghan National Army's 1st Kandak, 2nd Brigade, 203rd ANA Infantry Corps, said the shoulder-to-shoulder operations conducted at night by ANA and coalition forces in Zormat District have been successful at controlling insurgent activity.

"I think night raids work to get insurgent forces out of the area," said Zazai. "We can go places that we couldn't before."

Gen. Nazar Shah Safi, the National Directorate of Security chief, spoke of the practical reasons for the ANSF and coalition forces to conduct night raids.

"Conducting operations during the day has a high likelihood of civilian casualties. If conducted at night, civilians are safe in their houses, and it is easier to capture the target," he said.

Other topics at the meeting included the activity level of insurgent forces, the effectiveness of the ANSF and coalition presence, and the need to sustain recently improved ANSF and coalition forces communication and cooperation.

"We used to not participate in operations, night raids, or air assaults," said Safi. "But now, we cooperate with coalition forces, and civilian casualties have decreased."

Mike O'Brien, State Department representative for the PRT, said the security meeting established by Boesen and Team Paktya has been a positive step to achieving congruency of effort by the ANSF and coalition forces in Paktya.

"We will always be available to conduct joint operations with ANSF and coalition forces," said Col. Rahimi, the executive officer for the Paktya Afghan National Civil Order Police Brigade.

Donated suits help Iowa soldiers fight fires

NURISTAN PROVINCE, Afghanistan, Dec. 28, 2011—A fire rages on Combat Outpost Kalagush, Nuristan Province. The fire started when fuel was struck during a mortar attack on the base. Company C, 1st Battalion, 133rd Infantry Regiment, Task Force Ironman soldiers fought the fire but lost their maintenance building in the process. The Waterloo Fire Rescue in Waterloo, Iowa, donated two fire fighting suits to the volunteer firefighters from Iowa stationed at FOB Kalagush. The suits will enable them to extinguish a fire more quickly in the future. Task Force Ironman is a part of the 2nd Brigade Combat Team, 34th Infantry Division, Task Force Red Bulls of the Iowa National Guard. (Courtesy photo)

By U.S. Army Staff Sgt. Ryan C. Matson
Task Force Red Bulls Public Affairs

NURISTAN PROVINCE, Afghanistan, Jan. 25, 2011—When a person calls a local fire department for help, the hope is firefighters respond as quickly as possible.

But no one knew the Waterloo, Iowa, fire department would respond to a fire more than 4,000 miles away.

That's essentially what happened when the Waterloo Fire Rescue sent two fire fighting suits to Iowa National Guard soldiers of Company C, 1st Battalion, 133rd Infantry Regiment, at Combat Outpost Kalagush in eastern Afghanistan. The soldiers fought a large fire Dec. 28, one in which no soldiers were injured but the base's maintenance building was destroyed.

"I expressed through my wife that we could really use some of the gear we had back home for the jobs we have to potentially do here," said company commander U.S. Army Capt. Garrett Gingrich H., who has been a Waterloo firefighter for three years. "So my fire department, who has been extremely supportive of everything I've done through the military, and with the

221

department as well, without hesitation sent two full sets of turnout gear over here for us to use."

Within two weeks of mentioning that gear would be helpful, Waterloo Fire Rescue sent two sets of turnout gear, consisting of flame-resistant overcoats and pants, gloves, hoods and a fire helmet complete with face shield.

Gingrich, who grew up in Dysart, Iowa, said the Dec. 28 fire was a major fire, which his soldiers, along with the help of the Nuristan Provincial Reconstruction Team's security forces, extinguished. The fire was caused when fuel was struck during a mortar attack on the base. The soldiers worked with what equipment they had—a small pump truck, water buffalos [water-tank trailers], and shovels—to put out the fire. Gingrich said he can't say for certain whether the gear would have saved the maintenance building, but it definitely would have helped.

"The gear is really important because during that fire, the heat was tremendous from the fuel," Gingrich said. "The guys fighting the fire weren't able to get close enough to the fire to keep it from spreading. This greatly increases our ability to get in there and attack a fire. You can get right on it, or closer to it, because you don't feel the heat as much. There's not as much chance you'll get burned or catch on fire, so this gear helps to keep our soldiers safe and helps our overall readiness."

Larger FOBs have dedicated fire departments on base with full-time professional firefighters. At smaller locations like Kalagush, however, there are no assigned fire-fighting assets, so soldiers have to extinguish fires themselves.

Company C Soldiers put out three fires including the large one Dec. 28.

Two of the fires involved shipping containers set ablaze after enemy fire ignited the materials inside. The infantry soldiers, though not firefighters by trade, responded quickly to douse the flames.

As a firefighter, Gingrich knows the risk of fire is still present on the FOB. Like bases throughout the country, many of the buildings are constructed of wood and could be ignited by lightning or any number of other factors. Thanks to the equipment donated by the Waterloo Fire Rescue, the soldiers said they are more prepared to fight a fire should another occur.

One soldier who will be more prepared is U.S. Army Sgt. Joseph Sawyer, an infantry team leader from Davenport, Iowa. A volunteer firefighter for two years, Sawyer is also undergoing emergency medical technician paramedic training and hopes to become a professional firefighter when he returns from this deployment.

Sawyer seemed to sum up the sentiments of the soldiers on the fire response team.

"The main thing I'd like to say is thank you," Sawyer said. "We get a lot of stuff from people back home, and a lot of it we put to use, but this is one of the more generous gifts we've received that we're going to be able to put to good use. So really, all we can say is, thank you."

*NURISTAN PROVINCE, Afghanistan, Jan. 25, 2011—*U.S. Army Capt. Garrett H. Gingrich (left) the commander of Company C, 1st Battalion, 133rd Infantry Regiment, Task Force Ironman from Dysart, Iowa, helps adjust the chin strap on a fire helmet worn by U.S. Army Sgt. Joseph Sawyer, an infantry team leader from Davenport, Iowa, also with Company C, Jan. 25 at Forward Operating Base Kalagush, Afghanistan. The equipment, which consisted of two complete sets of turnout gear, was donated to Company C by the Waterloo Fire Rescue in Waterloo, Iowa. The soldiers have put out two small fires and a larger one since being in country, and the department donated the equipment for the soldier's increased readiness should another occur. Sawyer has served as a volunteer firefighter in Iowa, and hopes to become a professional firefighter when he returns from this deployment. Gingrich is a firefighter with the Waterloo Fire Rescue. Task Force Ironman is a part of the 2nd Brigade Combat Team, 34th Infantry Division, Task Force Red Bulls, of the Iowa National Guard. (Photo by U.S. Army Staff Sgt. Ryan C. Matson, Task Force Red Bulls Public Affairs)

Mountainside security: ANP open new district headquarters

PARWAN PROVINCE, Afghanistan, Jan. 27, 2011—The new Surkhi Parsa District Afghan National Police Headquarters sits on the side of a mountain overlooking a valley in the Surkhi Parsa District. (Photo by U.S. Army Spc. Adam L. Mathis, Task Force Red Bulls Public Affairs)

By U.S. Army Spc. Adam L. Mathis
Task Force Red Bulls Public Affairs

PARWAN PROVINCE, *Afghanistan, Jan. 27, 2011*—It should never have succeeded, but the combined coalition and Afghan efforts resulted in the opening of the Surkhi Parsa District Afghan National Police Headquarters. So many things factored against the construction and completion of this olive-green building: it needed to be built on the side of a mountain where falling dirt from the mountain could bury the structure, the building's mountainside home is in Surkhi Parsa District, far away from materials and some of the skilled laborers needed, and many similar projects failed because of security issues.

"I love it," U.S. Air Force Maj. Christopher Meeker, resident engineer for the Bagram-area U.S. Army Corps of Engineers, said of the new ANP station. "This is why we're here, right? It's beautiful."

Beautiful though it is to him, getting to this opening ceremony involved a lot of frustration. Meeker, of Manito, Ill., said this building presents a challenge found across Afghanistan: the only available place to build is on the side of a mountain.

"The big problem we have in Afghanistan is a mountain, river, or farm," Meeker said. "We can't build on rivers, they don't want us to build on farms, so we end up building all of our buildings on mountainsides like this, which presents some problems in how to control the slopes..."

But as Meeker pointed out, the bulk of the work—and, thus frustration—was borne by the Afghans.

"This one was successful because of the Afghans governing themselves, securing themselves, and doing the construction themselves."

The brunt of this work fell on UCC Budservice Construction & Engineering Company Limited. Karimullah Samadi, deputy general manager for UCC, said they faced several challenges in constructing this headquarters. The site's remote location created problems with materials and labor. Yet it was a project he could be proud of, done by Afghans with the help of U.S. government funds.

"I am proud that we totally used Afghan labor, skilled and unskilled laborers, to construct this project based on the design and the standards that were given to us by the U.S. Army Corps of Engineers," Samadi said. "And really this is a place to be proud [of]."

One thing they can be proud of is additional security. Sayid Jan Mahmoud works in the new station's detention center as a member of the ANA. Mahmoud also comes from Lolinj village, located near the new station and able to receive some security from it.

"I would like to thank all of these countries, all of these coalition forces that participated in building this new building," Mahmoud said through an interpreter. "I feel much [more] secure right now because I see the ANP is beside me."

*PARWAN PROVINCE, Afghanistan, Jan. 27, 2011—*U.S. Army Lt. Col. David A. Updegraff of Wauconda, Ill., commander of 1st Squadron, 113th Cavalry Regiment, Task Force Redhorse, 2nd Brigade Combat Team, 34th Infantry Division, cuts the ribbon at the Surkhi Parsa District police headquarters opening ceremony. The plans for the building were made in 2007, along with several other police stations. The International Security Assistance Force plans to add to the ANP's number, hoping to reach 134,000 members by October. (Photo by U.S. Army Spc. Adam L. Mathis, Task Force Red Bulls Public Affairs)

Press Release: Weapons cache found, destroyed in Laghman
By Task Force Red Bulls Public Affairs

LAGHMAN PROVINCE, Afghanistan, Jan. 28, 2011—A weapons cache consisting of more than 100 anti-personnel mines was found by coalition forces on patrol near the village of Jugi, Mehtar Lam District, Laghman Province Jan. 27. An Explosive Ordnance Disposal team was deployed to the scene and destroyed the cache in place.

The security and safety of Afghan civilians is an important part of every coalition operation. All weapons caches found during these operations are destroyed to ensure they do not harm civilians or military personnel.

"Mines are indiscriminate killers. They don't distinguish between Soldiers or civilians, between men, women or children. We must all work together to eliminate the threat posed by these deadly weapons," said U.S. Army Col. Benjamin J. Corell, commander of the 2nd Brigade Combat Team, 34th Infantry Division, Task Force Red Bulls.

If you see any suspicious activity or know of a weapons cache in your area, please report it. Call the Operations Coordination Center Provincial Tip Line at 079-662-[XXXX] or at 079-397-[XXXX].

Task Force Lethal medics aid injured Paktya boy

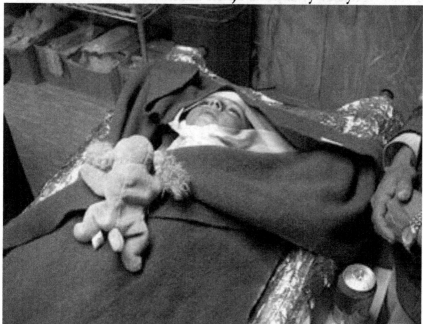

PAKTYA PROVINCE, Afghanistan, Jan. 29, 2011—A boy from Jaji District, Paktya Province, who fell more than 15 feet and struck his head, is stabilized with a cervical collar and kept warm with a wool blanket at the Company A, 1st Battalion, 168th Infantry Regiment, Task Force Lethal aid station at Combat Outpost Herrera, Paktya Province. Medical officials on site monitored the boy's heart rate, blood pressure and other vital signs until transportation to a larger hospital arrived. (Photo by U.S. Army Sgt. John Edwards, Task Force Lethal)

By U.S. Army 1st Lt. Nicholas Rasmussen
Task Force Lethal

PAKTYA PROVINCE, Afghanistan, Jan. 29, 2011—Medics from Company A, 1st Battalion, 168th Infantry Regiment, Task Force Lethal, at Combat Outpost Herrera, Paktya Province, helped care for and evacuate a Jaji village boy, who fell more than 15 feet from a building and landed on his head.

The boy was brought in stable condition to the aid station the day before with swelling in his neck that interfered with his ability to control his arms.

After assessing that the boy's injuries posed a risk to his limbs and possibly life, U.S. Army Sgt. John Edwards of Washington, Iowa, the senior medic at COP Herrera, decided to see the boy after the child had already been seen physicians at the Jaji District Hospital. The doctors there did not have the capability or equipment to properly help the boy.

"If (a patient) has not been seen at the Jaji District Hospital, (normally) we don't allow them onto the COP," said Edwards, explaining the medical rules of engagement for U.S. Army medical personnel. Those rules state coalition forces are not to treat Afghans unless the injury threatens life, limb, or eyesight.

Edwards' actions may have saved the boy from permanent loss of mobility in his arms and even his life.

When word was relayed to Edwards and his team that no air evacuation assets were available due to inclement weather, they realized they were in for a struggle to keep the boy's vital signs stable until advanced care became available.

They tended the boy through the night, regularly checking his pulse, respiratory rate, blood pressure and ability to move his arms.

Medics even played games with the boy, putting on a puppet show and encouraging him to use his hands and arms to grip a ball. After midnight the boy started to show small signs of improvement.

"He started to get some fine motor function of his left arm," said Edwards.

But the boy was still far from recovered.

Edwards noted the boy's arm "pretty much just stayed lying in the same position unless we got him to move it, even then it looked like it took a lot of effort and concentration to do so."

After daybreak, Edwards and Afghan Uniformed Police Col. Shenwary coordinated to have the Jaji Hospital use their ambulance service to transport the child to a hospital in Gardez City.

"When the ambulance arrived, we put him on the spine board and secured him for the trip down to Gardez," said Edwards.

Task Force Red Bulls supply JCOP Pul-e-Sayad

PARWAN PROVINCE, Afghanistan, Jan. 30, 2011—U.S. Army Pfc. Christopher Paine of Hartley, Iowa, a truck driver with 1st Platoon, Company A, 334th Brigade Support Battalion, Task Force Archer, a part of 2nd Brigade Combat Team, 34th Infantry Division, Task Force Red Bulls, puts on his gloves as he gets ready to loosen the straps on supplies brought to Joint Combat Outpost Pul-e-Sayad. Company A visited the JCOP to drop off food, fuel and repair parts. (Photo by U.S. Army Spc. Kristina L. Gupton, Task Force Red Bulls Public Affairs)

PARWAN PROVINCE, Afghanistan, Jan. 30, 2011—U.S. Army Sgt. 1st Class Travis Bougher, of Des Moines, Iowa, the Joint Combat Outpost Pul-e-Sayad mayor and Headquarters Platoon sergeant for Troop A, 1st Squadron, 113th Cavalry Regiment, Task Force Redhorse, a part of 2nd Brigade Combat Team, 34th Infantry Division, Task Force Red Bulls, unloads supplies off of a heavy expanded mobility truck. Soldiers of Company A, 334th Brigade Support Battalion, Task Force Archer, visited the JCOP to deliver food, fuel and repair parts. (Photo by U.S. Army Spc. Kristina L. Gupton, Task Force Red Bulls Public Affairs)

Task Force Rakkasans transfers authority to Task Force Duke

By U.S. Army Staff Sgt. Ben K. Navratil
Task Force Duke Public Affairs

KHOST PROVINCE, Afghanistan, Jan. 30, 2011—The 3rd Brigade Combat Team, 101st Airborne Division, Task Force Rakkasans handed over command of Khowst and Paktya Provinces to 3rd Brigade Combat Team, 1st Infantry Division, Task Force Duke during a Transfer of Authority ceremony at Forward Operating Base Salerno in Khost Province.

The Rakkasans also ceremoniously cased their colors in preparation of their trip back to their home base in Fort Campbell, Ky., while the 3-1st BCT, Task Force Duke from Fort Knox, Ky., uncased their own.

The ceremony was attended by Duke and Rakkasans Soldiers; Brig. Gen. Stephen Townsend, deputy commanding general of Combined Joint Task Force–101; Abdul Jabbar Naeemi, Khowst governor; and several members of the Afghan National Security Forces. It was a great medley of backgrounds, ethnicities and even uniform styles, as the outgoing Rakkasans wore the Army combat uniform, while the Duke Soldiers wore the newer multi-cam uniform.

"The hard work, the sacrifice, the blood of the ANSF and coalition partners have helped meet the conditions for stability in the region," said Naeemi, "and the enemy forces can no longer move freely."

Rakkasans commander U.S. Army Col. Viet X. Luong, of Fort Campbell, Ky., also emphasized the progress made during his unit's rotation here.

"During the early moments of this rotation the Taliban was winning in our provinces," he said. "But this summer, our combined actions started to produce remarkable results. We began to take many enemies out of the fight. The security conditions improved, and we began turning the tide against the Taliban."

Speaking in both English and Pashto, U.S. Army Col. Christopher Toner, commander of Task Force Duke and Topeka, Kan., native, thanked the Rakkasans for their service and sacrifices and pledged his assistance to the ANSF. "Our brothers in the ANSF, we embrace you with a spirit of mutual respect and cooperation," he said. "We are here now to continue the support the Rakkasans have given you over the past 12 months."

As the ceremony drew to a close, Toner promised that he and his Soldiers would help the Afghan people in their fight for their country.

"The Soldiers of the Duke Brigade are committed to using everything in their power to build Afghan capacity for providing security and stability to the region," he said.

ANA tip leads to weapons cache

PAKTYA PROVINCE, Afghanistan, Jan. 31, 2011–U.S. Army Sgt. Michael Jenkins of Ames, Iowa, a team leader for 1st Platoon, Company C, 1st Battalion, 168th Infantry Regiment, poses next to explosive contraband found in Sar Mast Kheyl, Zormat District. Sage and his Afghan National Army partner from the 3rd Company, 1st Kandak, 2nd Brigade, 203rd ANA Infantry Corps found several anti-personnel mines, homemade explosives, Improvised Explosive Device making materials and a significant amount of fertilizer used to create homemade explosives. (Photo by U.S. Army 1st Lt. Joel Sage, Task Force Lethal)

By U.S. Army 1st Lt. Nicholas Rasmussen
Task Force Lethal Public Affairs

PAKTYA PROVINCE, Afghanistan, Jan. 31, 2011—A tip generated by the 3rd Company, 1st Kandak, 2nd Brigade, 203rd ANA Infantry Corps, Afghan National Army pointed ANA and U.S. Army soldiers from Task Force Lethal to a large weapons cache in Sar Mast Kheyl, Zormat District Jan. 31.

The ANA and 1st Platoon of Company C, Task Force Lethal, 1st Battalion, 168th Infantry Regiment, 3rd Brigade, 1st Infantry Division uncovered a significant amount of homemade explosives, Improvised Explosive Device-making materials, several pressure plate IEDs, triggering devices for IEDs and miscellaneous IED parts.

The ANA received the information from a villager during a joint patrol with coalition forces in eastern Zormat a week before the discovery.

While patrolling in a nearby village, the ANA informed coalition forces of the information. As a result, 1st Lt. Khasim, platoon leader for the ANA unit, and U.S. Army 1st Lt. Joel Sage of Ankeny, Iowa, platoon leader of 1st Platoon, Company C, moved their patrols to Sar Mast Kheyl.

While the ANA searched the suspected location for the cache, U.S. Army Sgt. Michael Jenkins of Ames, Iowa, a team leader for 1st Platoon, Company C, was helping provide security. He and his ANA partner saw barbed wire covering a tarp across a field by a nearby structure and decided to investigate.

"He looked around, pulled some brush aside and then I saw the shock on his face," said Jenkins, describing the ANA soldier's inspection.

The soldier looked at Jenkins, saying only, "Boom."

They discovered a vest for carrying equipment and a handful of modified anti-personnel mines reinforced with extra homemade explosives and retrofitted with a pressure plate device.

This find sparked further investigation.

The ANA found switches and wires, IED manufacturing materials, and a significant amount of an illegal fertilizer.

Jenkins was outside the building with a handheld metal detector when the ANA approached Sage and asked for help searching inside.

A small team from 1st Platoon, Company C, including Jenkins, went into the building and began searching.

Inside the building, they found large steel drums and a 55 gallon barrel full of grain. The barrel had a pressure switch hidden inside.

In the end, the ANA, partnered with the U.S. Army, found and removed anti-personnel mines, Improvised Explosive Device manufacturing materials, and ingredients to create homemade explosives.

FEBRUARY
2011

Red Bulls teach ANA vehicle, weapon maintenance

LAGHMAN PROVINCE, Afghanistan, Feb. 1, 2011—U.S. Army Spc. Richard Rawson (left), a field artillery Soldier attached to the scout/sniper platoon of Headquarters and Headquarters Company, 1st Battalion, 133rd Infantry Regiment, Task Force Ironman, from Sioux City, Iowa, shows Afghan National Army soldiers from 2nd Company, 1st Kandak, 2nd Brigade, 201st ANA Infantry Corps how to remove the cover on an air filter during training on the steps of Humvee Preventative Maintenance Checks and Services at Forward Operating Base Mehtar Lam. [...] (Photo by U.S. Army Staff Sgt. Ryan C. Matson, Task Force Red Bulls Public Affairs)

By U.S. Army Staff Sgt. Ryan C. Matson
Task Force Red Bulls Public Affairs

LAGHMAN PROVINCE, Afghanistan, Feb. 1, 2011—The Afghan National Army soldier grabbed the handles on the .50-caliber machine gun, unlocked them and slid them up and off the heavy frame of the weapon at Forward Operating Base Mehtar Lam. His friends from the unit looked over his shoulder, watching him intently from behind.

Removing the handles was the first of many steps in disassembling the weapon. Also watching were U.S. Army Sgt. Leo Pins, a cavalry scout, team leader with the scout/sniper platoon, Headquarters and Headquarters Company, 1st Battalion, 133rd Infantry Regiment, and U.S. Army Spc. Christopher Burke, a field artillery gunner attached to the scout/sniper platoon.

The two U.S. Army Soldiers from the Iowa National Guard's 2nd Brigade Combat Team, 34th Infantry Division, Task Force Red Bulls, taught the ANA soldiers how to disassemble, clean and reassemble the weapon in a two-hour training session the week before.

After training was complete, instructors had the students disassemble and reassemble a weapon. The test was the moment of truth for Afghan soldier Abdul Ahmad, a rifleman with 2nd Company, 1st Kandak, 1st Brigade, 201st ANA Infantry Corps, to see what he had retained from the training.

"The ANA soldiers didn't originally know anything about the .50 cal," Pins said. "So we taught them the basics: how to take the weapon apart and what to look for to make sure it will function correctly. It's been about a week, so all I wanted to see was how much they retained from my first class."

He appreciated the results.

"When I came over here this time, they actually had the bolt completely taken apart, which is something I didn't teach them in the first class. They already figured out how to take it apart and put it back together, so that shows me that in their off time, they've been working with each other to learn more about the weapon, and that they had retained a lot from what we taught them the first week," Pins said.

Piece by piece, for about 10 minutes or so, Ahmad stripped the weapon down, and then carefully put it all back together. Pins and Burke mostly observed the young soldier, but occasionally stepped in to show him a trick for getting a part he was having difficulty with to lock in to place.

"It's pretty impressive, because it takes some of our own Soldiers more than once to even remember half the stuff involved with disassembling and reassembling this weapon," Pins said.

Pins, a native of Dyersville, Iowa, is on his third deployment and has worked with .50-caliber machine guns the last six years.

"I know a lot of the little quirks to make it easier to take this weapon apart," he said. "I've been slowly teaching them what I've learned and a lot of them have picked it up, as well as learned their own ways, which is amazing to see in their second class."

Pins said the ANA soldiers' senior leadership learned the weapon and taught it to their younger soldiers, which Pins said he was happy to see. Ahmad was one of the Soldiers who excelled.

"I watched the Americans take apart the .50 caliber machine gun," Ahmad said. "I watched it very carefully, because I had never touched one before. Now I know how to take it apart and put it back together again, and shoot and clean the weapon. I am happy that I learned that."

After Ahmad had taken the weapon completely apart then reassembled it, he was not done. Burke and Pins watched as the Soldier then checked the headspace and timing to ensure the weapon would fire correctly and was ready for combat.

"They know how to do everything now, and if something happens with that .50-cal., they should know how to fix it," said Burke, of Sioux City, Iowa.

Meanwhile, about 30 yards away, the soldiers from the other half of the ANA platoon were gathered around three of their Humvees. The up-armored vehicles were inherited from the coalition, but now the ANA soldiers are responsible for maintaining and operating the vehicles. That's where U.S. Army Spc. Rene Girasek, a chemical equipment repair specialist with Company E, 1-133rd Inf., and Spc. Richard Rawson, a field artillery gunner attached to the scout/sniper platoon of HHC, came into the picture.

Girasek, who hails from Postville, Iowa, and Rawson, from Sioux City, Iowa, taught the ANA soldiers the step-by-step process of Preventive Maintenance Checks and Services on the Humvees.

"We taught them the three classes of leaks, how to check the fluids, and the steps of (doing preventive maintenance on) the vehicle," Rawson said. "Afterward, we split them into three groups on the vehicles and supervised them while they went over it themselves."

Girasek, who works every day with the mechanics in Company E, has an in-depth knowledge of the vehicles and stressed to the ANA soldiers why proper PMCS are important.

"I tried to explain why it's important to conduct a proper PMCS," Girasek said. "If you go on a mission and your truck dies because it's been leaking and there's no oil in it, it gets overheated or your tires didn't have enough air in them and they go flat, you will not be in a good situation. So we showed them how to conduct PMCS to ensure their truck will work properly."

Rawson said they also showed the soldiers how to switch the vehicle to four-wheel-drive mode in the event they get stuck in the rough Afghan terrain during a mission.

The U.S. Soldiers said they conduct weekly training with their ANA counterparts on everything from vehicle and weapons maintenance to tactical maneuvers. Pins summed up the importance of the training sessions.

"We've been working with these guys for the last two months now, and we go out and do a lot of scout missions," Pins said. "About a month ago we had contact in a village with them and we got to see exactly how they react to that. If we didn't have any type of working relationship with these guys, we probably would have incurred injuries, but by working with these guys and making them our straight-up counterparts, they did an amazing job in the village and we received no casualties."

"It makes us feel more confident to know that, because of our training, they will know what to do to keep this country safe. It's teambuilding. We know if we get into something nasty, the ANA's got our back because they know their job."

How one man makes a difference in Afghanistan

PARWAN PROVINCE, Afghanistan, Feb. 2, 2011—Ghouse Loynab (near left), a human terrain analyst with Human Terrain Team, Task Force Red Bulls, out on patrol with Alpha Troop, 1st Squadron, 113th Infantry Regiment, Task Force Redhorse, a part of 2nd Brigade Combat Team, 34th Infantry Division, Task Force Red Bulls, takes notes as he talks to a villager about governance and development issues. (Photo by U.S. Army Spc. Kristina L. Gupton, Task Force Red Bulls Public Affairs)

By U.S. Army Spc. Adam L. Mathis
Task Force Red Bulls Public Affairs

PARWAN PROVINCE, Afghanistan, Feb. 2, 2011—Rocks were being thrown at U.S. forces. One hit Ghouse Loynab in the head. It was the definition of an unfriendly scenario. One where, in the interests of safety, the American forces with Loynab might have withdrawn from the Afghan village.

However, Loynab, a human terrain analyst with Human Terrain Team, Task Force Red Bulls, had another idea. He recounts his conversation with a village elder that day—a conversation he used to disarm the conflict.

"I said 'So, this is really cool. My dad taught me about Afghanistan, but he never told me that you guys would rock people. Guys, you need to learn, I don't care who you like or who you dislike but when somebody comes into your house, according to the culture, you never ever disrespect your guest,'" said Loynab.

"They were very understanding after that," he finished.

In a war that has come to be less about killing the enemy and more about establishing trust and even friendship with the people, Loynab is a cutting-edge weapon. He is a human terrain analyst, and a man with a foot in both the United States and Afghanistan.

It is how, as a human terrain analyst in Afghanistan, he can shame a village when they abuse Americans.

A job transfer brought his family from Afghanistan to the United States in 1972. After Loynab was born, his father became a successful entrepreneur trying his hand at dry cleaning, cab companies, and the restaurant business. Yet, for all of their success, his father would not let Loynab forget his roots were in Afghanistan.

According to Loynab, his father told him he should respect America all the time, but also respect the culture of Afghanistan from which his grandfather and forefathers came.

He learned English, Spanish, and Dari, and he is learning Pashtu. He also observes the customs of his forefathers' country, kissing his father whenever he greets him. But he is an American. Loynab said he loves his home in Durham, N.C., where he can drive down the street and stop to talk to people, and where his passionately loved Duke Blue Devils basketball team resides.

This mixed background gives him both the credibility and perspective necessary to approach Afghans or confront a rock-throwing village to further the coalition mission.

Loynab explains to Afghans the Americans are there to help them so that one day they can take control of their own country.

Human terrain analysts have been in Afghanistan for years. They work by analyzing statistical data about the population like a social scientist, or by engaging with local leaders.

"I actually have a passion for what I'm doing: One, because I know the job really well now. Two, I know the people, the customs, the culture. And three, you have to be willing to do it," Loynab said.

U.S. Army Maj. Bobbie Jo Mayes, the women's empowerment coordinator with the Kentucky Agribusiness Development Team II from Lawrenceburg, Ky., has worked with Loynab multiple times.

Mayes' job is to provide women with skills in agribusiness that will allow them to make a living wage. Loynab works with Mayes to make that happen, but he has also brought the needy to her attention.

Recently he and his wife, who also works for the coalition in Afghanistan, pointed Mayes to a group of 27 displaced families in desperate need of help.

"These kids look like they have not eaten for months," Mayes said. "Stuff I would never have known about unless they were there."

That is just one way Loynab is able to make a difference. By knowing what his home country can do for the land of his ancestors, he attempts to bridge the cultural and communication gaps, bringing the two sides together and closer to peace.

"(Afghans) need to know this. They need to keep learning this," said Loynab. "We're here to help, to build Afghanistan a better place to live for the Afghan people, and were out."

How to be normal in Afghanistan

By U.S. Army Spc. Adam L. Mathis
Task Force Red Bulls Public Affairs

PARWAN PROVINCE, Afghanistan, Feb. 2, 2011—Is kimchi supposed to be eaten hot or cold?

It is a Saturday morning meeting of friends: a group of people standing around a griddle, waiting as batter turning into pancakes—snow covers the ground and random, oddball statements such as questions are asked about Korean food etiquette when pancakes are being made.

Ignore the uniforms and weapons, and the group could have been standing in a college dorm room or a friend's kitchen. In some ways, they were.

This was the kitchen of U.S. Army Chief Warrant Officer Shawn Kiene of Cedar Rapids, Iowa, the recognized food expert, and the man keeping an eye on the griddle. Kimchi, according to Kiene, can be eaten hot or cold.

"Now those are ready to flip," he said to a Soldier near the griddle. "Joe, you can let Randy do it, he might know something about it."

This is why we need people like Kiene.

It's about more than just a chance for camaraderie or well-made pancakes. By holding a Saturday pancake breakfast, Kiene, a corporate chef in the civilian world, a contracting facilitator and food adviser to the brigade, Headquarters and Headquarters Company, 2nd Brigade Combat Team, 34th Infantry Division, Task Force Red Bulls, in Afghanistan, actually recreates a bit of home. A bit many deployed Soldiers probably don't even realize they miss.

Daily life in Afghanistan is shaped by one constant principle: the mission.

Here, the job must be done or this bit of reconstruction or that mission to stop insurgents won't happen. Some soldiers work at this job for 12 hours a day, some longer. Even during downtime, the mission defines life because it is all that happens during the day.

Back home however, community is rarely about one single thing.

Part of the joy of living with others is in experiencing the talents and knowledge they bring to any situation. The last time you sat in your living room with friends back home, you may have starting talking about sports, but inevitably, someone brought up their pet, their spouse, the car repair they are working on, a book this guy is reading, or a painting that woman is working on.

Talents and hobbies are often thought of as private, almost selfish, things. However, these are the basis of normal life for us. Things that come up in conversation are what drive us. They give us a chance to come together, discuss them and share in them.

A healthy social life is not defined by any one particular interest, but a group of interests people share, or at least are willing to try. Try imagining all of your friends only being interested in watching television and not talking about anything else. Then, try not to jump out a window.

Kiene's pancake breakfast is a challenge. The hobbies we jealously make time for in Afghanistan, the ones we make sure we practice before going to bed, are opportunities to build bridges we had back home.

Your interest in computers, and the latest mod you tried, could be the starting point for a conversation with another guy about his kill record on Halo.

It is about more than just the hobby or the interest itself; it's about being normal in a place that is not normal to us.

Med team leaves Kabul for remote base in southern Nuristan

NURISTAN PROVINCE, Afghanistan, Feb. 2, 2011—U.S. Army Capt. Barbara Krugler (center), a physician assistant from Adel, Iowa, and U.S. Army Sgt. Rachel Hecht (left), a combat medic from Merrill, Iowa, prepare to remove burn dressings from a 3-year-old Afghan girl at Combat Outpost Kalagush. The girl was treated for severe burns before being referred to a children's hospital in Kabul. Krugler and Hecht are part of a medical team from Company C, 334th Brigade Support Battalion, 2nd Brigade Combat Team, 34th Infantry Division, Task Force Red Bulls, and support Company C, 1st Battalion, 133rd Infantry Regiment, also of Task Force Red Bulls. (Photo by U.S. Army Staff Sgt. Jessica Beswick, Task Force Archer)

By U.S. Army Capt. Adrian Sean Taylor
Task Force Archer

NURISTAN PROVINCE, Afghanistan, Feb. 2, 2011—Tucked away in the southern Hindu Kush Mountains sits small Combat Outpost Kalagush. Commanded by U.S. Army Capt. Garrett H. Gingrich, Company C, 1st Battalion, 133rd Infantry Regiment, part of 34th Infantry Division's 2nd

Brigade Combat Team, Task Force Red Bulls, Kalagush is the last U.S.-run forward operating base in Nuristan Province.

"We are a fairly secure base at the moment," said Gingrich of Waterloo, Iowa. "The winter makes it difficult for the insurgents to move around. We expect the insurgency to increase come spring."

In order to help reduce that insurgency, Gingrich said they will continue to work with the locals to build a trusting relationship so they understand that Company C is there to help them.

Along with Company C, there are other components on the base, including the newest addition, a team from Company C, 334th Brigade Support Battalion, known as "Charlie Med," which is also a part of Task Force Red Bulls.

"The base is made up of our infantry company and platoons from active-duty U.S. Army field artillery and military police units," Gingrich said. "The provincial reconstruction team that has been serving here is currently on the way out, and they ran the medical clinic on our base. We are very glad to get an element of Charlie Med. Without them it would severely limit our ability to run missions in this area"

Until last month, the five-person medical team was providing level 2 medical services at Camp Phoenix in the capital city of Kabul. The majority of Charlie Med relocated to Bagram Airfield to establish a level 1-plus medical treatment facility and assist the 334th BSB with convoy support and base operations.

"It is always really sad to leave your best friends behind," said U.S. Army Staff Sgt. Jessica Beswick, senior medic and native of Coralville, Iowa. "There was a little extra anxiety finding out that you are heading to a tiny FOB at the end of the world. We knew little about it except we had heard it had been hit before by insurgents. Our nervousness and anxiety were outweighed by the excitement of taking on a new challenge."

It was a hard transition for the team at first. They joined a treatment facility made up of medical personnel from the Navy and Air Force run by the Nuristan PRT.

"Our systems were very different," explained U.S. Army Sgt. Rachel Hecht, a combat medic from Merrill, Iowa. "We had to learn to mesh with the PRT unit and the infantry company. Infantry units are known to be tight-knit organizations. Their medics train and fight alongside of them. It was hard to come in and say 'here we are, trust us.'"

The main mission of Charlie Med is to run sick-call operations on the base.

"We mainly see U.S. and Afghan Soldiers. We most commonly see young Soldiers with musculoskeletal injuries, due to the heavy equipment they carry while on patrols," explained U.S. Army Capt. Barbara Krugler, the Charlie Med physician assistant and an Adel, Iowa, resident. "We also see contractors and Afghan day workers. The current medical rules of engagement only allow us to see local (Afghans to save) life, limb and eyesight. This is difficult because we do not want to turn anyone away."

"A small girl came in with burns over 50 percent of her body," said Beswick. "She had been treated locally but was in extreme pain. We removed the dry dressings, treated the burns and redressed her wounds. She fell asleep after and her father said it was the first time she slept in over four days."

After U.S. Army medics treat local nationals, they refer them to local hospitals for follow-up treatment.

"We have no idea if they will follow up with the local doctors or not," explained Beswick. "The nearest hospital here is in Kabul. Locals in Nuristan prefer to go to Pakistan and work with Pashtu doctors. We can only hope they continue to get treatment."

The Charlie Med team, serving in Kalagush, finished their transfer with the Nuristan PRT recently and established a level 1 medical treatment facility. They also established good relationships with the contractors, day workers and local shop keepers surrounding the base. Like Gingrich and the infantrymen of Company C, 1-133rd Inf., Charlie Med is preparing for the challenges they will face when spring comes to the Hindu Kush.

Company A goes back into the hornet's nest

LAGHMAN PROVINCE, Afghanistan, Feb. 3, 2011—U.S. Army Sgt. Adam Nielsen, an infantry team leader with Company A, 1st Battalion, 133rd Infantry Regiment, from Cedar Falls, Iowa, points to one of the surrounding mountain ridges his unit took fire from their last time they tried to enter the village of Shebatkyl, Afghanistan. That time, Nielsen's platoon fought through an ambush of enemy forces firing machine guns and rocket-propelled grenades from multiple directions on the surrounding mountains. [...] (Photo by Staff Sgt. Ryan C. Matson, Task Force Red Bulls Public Affairs.)

LAGHMAN PROVINCE, Afghanistan, Feb. 3, 2011—U.S. Army Pfc. Frank Deierling, an infantry soldier from Buffalo, Iowa, with Company A, 1st Battalion, 133rd Infantry Regiment, shows a group of children his 34th Infantry Division "Red Bulls" patch in the village of Shebatkyl, Afghanistan. [...] (Photo by Staff Sgt. Ryan C. Matson, Task Force Red Bulls Public Affairs.)

Company A makes successful return to Shebatkyl

LAGHMAN PROVINCE, Afghanistan, Feb. 3, 2011—U.S. Army Command Sgt. Maj. Marcus Mittvalsky (foreground), Headquarters and Headquarters Company, 1st Battalion, 133rd Infantry Regiment, and the battalion command sergeant major from North Liberty, Iowa, pulls security while U.S. Army 1st Lt. Rob Labios, 3rd Platoon leader from Company A, 1st Bn., 133rd Inf. Regt., from Davis, Calif., talks with a passersby about enemy activity outside the town of Shebatkyl. [...] (Photo by Staff Sgt. Ryan C. Matson, Task Force Red Bulls Public Affairs.)

LAGHMAN PROVINCE, Afghanistan, Feb. 3, 2011—U.S. Army 1st Lt. Rob Labios (center right) 3rd Platoon leader from Company A, 1st Battalion, 133rd Infantry Regiment, from Davis, Calif., conducts a Key Leader Engagement with village elders and townspeople in the town of Shebatkyl. The last time 3rd platoon attempted to go to the village, they were ambushed by enemy forces firing machine guns and Rocket-Propelled Grenades from multiple directions on the surrounding mountains. This time, the Soldiers were able to enter the village and talk with the people there. 1-133rd Inf., Task Force Ironman, is a part of the 2nd Brigade Combat Team, 34th Infantry Division, Task Force Red Bulls, and the Iowa National Guard. (Photo by Staff Sgt. Ryan C. Matson, Task Force Red Bulls Public Affairs.)

LAGHMAN PROVINCE, Afghanistan, Feb. 3, 2011—U.S. Army Sgt. Adam Nielsen (right) an infantry team leader from Cedar Falls, Iowa, and U.S. Army Sgt. Jason Thyne an in fantry team leader from Clinton, Iowa, both of Company A, 1st Battalion, 133rd Infantry Regiment, exchange a high-five after working their way up a steep mountainside outside the village of Shebatkyl. [...] (Photo by Staff Sgt. Ryan C. Matson, Task Force Red Bulls Public Affairs.)

New bunker boosts Afghan guard morale

PAKTYA PROVINCE, Afghanistan, Feb. 3, 2011—Naim, an Afghan Security Guard soldier, monitors people and vehicles entering Forward Operating Base Gardez from a fighting position made by U.S. Army Spc. Nathan Jastorff of Underwood, Iowa, a supply specialist in Headquarters and Headquarters Company, Task Force Lethal, 1st Battalion, 168th Infantry Regiment. The structure was designed and constructed to increase the protection of the ASG while they monitor the front gate of FOB Gardez. (Photo by U.S. Army 1st Lt. Nicholas Rasmussen, Task Force Lethal)

By U.S. Army 1st Lt. Nicholas Rasmussen
Task Force Lethal

PAKTYA PROVINCE, Afghanistan, Feb. 3, 2011—U.S. Army soldiers designed and built a new reinforced tower to protect Afghan security guards as they stand watch at Forward Operating Base Gardez, Paktiya province earlier this month.

The tower plans were created by U.S. Army Spc. Nathan Jastorff, supply specialist, Headquarters Company, Task Force Lethal, 1st Battalion, 168th Infantry Regiment. Guards no longer have to depend on a wooden shack and Plexiglas windows for protection.

A month ago, U.S. Army 1st Sgt. James Cline, the Forward Operating Base mayor, approached Jastorff with an idea.

"Cline wanted a new fighting position with a bunker," Jastorff said. "We knew we wanted steel and we knew we wanted ballistic glass."

Jastorff spent the next few days tossing ideas around in his head.

"I wanted to make something safe," Jastorff said. "Those guards had a wooden shack with half-inch plywood."

After a few days, it came to him. He decided to engineer it to put it on top of the bunker.

Jastorff asked the Oklahoma Agribusiness Development Team for help providing some of the materials, including the steel that would make up a large portion of the tower. He had the headquarter and headquarters company mortar platoon, lead by U.S. Army Sfc. Todd Smiley, take the steel to the firing range and test it against different caliber weapons.

With his hand-drawn schematics and the steel, Jastorff asked the maintenance shop to weld the steel to match his design, which included armored windows scavenged from an old gunner's turret. Jastorff designed it so that a cracked or broken window can easily be removed and replaced with another one.

When the steel was finished, it was mounted on top of a reinforced bunker. With several swings of a sledge hammer, Jastorff and U.S. Army Cpl. Timothy Green got the steel structure to fit.

After two weeks of solid work, the fighting position was complete and put into place, further fortified with sand bags and barriers.

Naim, a security guard said, "This is really safe because it has windows and the metal – it's anti-bullet. The old tower was leaking, and that was not good."

Along with protection from the weather, the reinforced tower will provide the guards security.

"It will give them encouragement to fight, knowing they're safe," Jastorff said.

PAKTYA PROVINCE, Afghanistan, Jan. 31, 2011—U.S. Army Spc. Nathan Jastorff of Underwood, Iowa, with the help of U.S. Army Cpl. Timothy Green of El Paso, Texas, U.S. Army Sgt. Lance Morrow of Council Bluffs, Iowa, and U.S. Army Pvt. Michael Kraught of Des Moines, Iowa, all from Headquarters and Headquarters Company, Task Force Lethal, 1st Battalion, 168th Infantry Regiment, lift the roof for a new, move a roof for a reinforced Afghan Security Guard fighting position near the front gate of Forward Operating Base Gardez. (Photo by U.S. Army 1st Lt. Nicholas Rasmussen, Task Force Lethal)

PAKTYA PROVINCE, Afghanistan, Feb. 2, 2011—U.S. Army Spc. Nathan Jastorff of Underwood, Iowa, and U.S. Army Cpl. Timothy Green of El Paso, Texas, both of Headquarters and Headquarters Company, Task Force Lethal, 1st Battalion, 168th Infantry Regiment, make final measurements before installing a door that will be the final addition to a new fighting position they are building [...] (Photo by U.S. Army 1st Lt. Nicholas Rasmussen, Task Force Lethal)

Kentucky ADT, Afghans conduct sheep study

PARWAN PROVINCE, , Afghanistan, Feb. 3, 2011—Showing how to evaluate a sheep, U.S. Army Col. James G. Floyd of Shreveport, La., the team veterinarian with the Kentucky Agribusiness Development Team II, grips a sheep's head and exposes its teeth to determine its age. The Kentucky ADT II travelled to the Department of Agriculture, Irrigation and Livestock in Parwan Province to prepare for a research project on worms in sheep. (Photo by U.S. Army Spc. Adam L. Mathis, Task Force Red Bulls)

By U.S. Army Spc. Adam L. Mathis
Task Force Red Bulls Public Affairs

PARWAN PROVINCE, Afghanistan, Feb. 3, 2011 –To help move Afghan agriculture forward, U.S. Army Col. James G. Floyd had to become thoroughly familiar with the back end of a sheep during a visit to the Department of Agriculture, Irrigation, and Livestock in Parwan Province.

Floyd, the team veterinarian for the Kentucky Agribusiness Development Team II, demonstrated the proper technique to obtain the necessary fecal matter used to assess the intestinal health of the animal.

Floyd's demonstration was part of a trip by the Kentucky ADT II to the Parwan DAIL to deliver supplies and provide technical advice in preparation for a study of the effects of deworming medicine on Afghan sheep.

Research like this hasn't been done in Afghanistan since the 1970s and is necessary in a country with 20 million sheep and goats.

"If (Afghan farmers) have not dewormed before, they may see a big difference, however we are not sure if deworming makes a big difference in every location," Floyd said.

Floyd's uncertainty is due to the lack of data. He and other U.S. Army military veterinarians found no studies on gastrointestinal worms in Afghan sheep since the mid-1970s. This created a problem: Without data, Floyd and other experts had no way of knowing if deworming treatments should be routinely recommended to improve the health of sheep.

As a result, Floyd and the other veterinarians proposed a deworming study of sheep that could help Afghan farmers and demonstrate to the government the benefit of applied scientific studies in the field.

"We realized we could make this into a project to answer that question ... and get the Afghan government and universities involved," Floyd, of Shreveport, La., said. "We have the goal of demonstrating that this type of research is valid for them to do to generate useful information for the Afghan agriculture."

Generating this information is relatively simple. In three Afghan provinces, three flocks of sheep will be studied. On the first day, the sheep are tagged, weighed, given a physical evaluation and have their feces sampled to determine the amount of worm eggs present. This procedure is repeated ten days later to determine if deworming on the first day effectively reduced the amount of worm eggs. The data and samples will be collected by Afghan collaborators and analyzed at a Bagram Airfield lab.

"It is very helpful," said Sayed Mahmood, animal herd manager for DAIL and in charge of collecting the data in Parwan, through an interpreter. "Afghans keep cattle and sheep for everything."

Floyd hopes that this study has more benefits than just helping sheep. After 30 years of war and devastation in Afghanistan, he hopes this encourages the Afghan people to invest in applied scientific research on farm animals.

"(Afghans) been disrupted for so long that this type of systematic research on animals is pretty well all gone," Floyd said. "So, this is a new thing for Afghan veterinarians and farmers."

Spring plans announced at Panjshir Ag conference

By U.S. Air Force 2nd Lt. Ashleigh Peck
Panjshir Provincial Reconstruction Team

PANJSHIR PROVINCE, Afghanistan, Feb. 3, 2011—More than 150 people gathered at the Astana Guest House here for the 2011 Panjshir Agriculture Conference Feb. 2-3.

Mohammad Asif Rahimi, the Panjshir Minister of Agriculture, Irrigation, and Livestock, was the chief guest and provided the opening remarks to the traders, farmers, producers, government officials and national and provincial media outlets in attendance.

The two-day conference focused on providing Panjshir's farmers an opportunity to articulate their needs in relation to agricultural production, processing and marketing of produce, livestock and product.

"Being the first (conference) for the province, we wanted it to focus on the future," U.S. Army Lt. Col. Jeffrey Casada, Kentucky Agribusiness Development Team II lead from London, Ky. "Ideas were introduced to the farmers on how to increase their income by adding value to their products before leaving the farm."

Also announced, starting in the spring, was the weekly farmers' market in the Bazarak District and Panjshir's first livestock bazaars in Paryan and Shutol districts. "The bazaars should help traders and farmers by bringing animals to a central point and attracting several buyers," Casada said.

The new bazaars will also get a fresh marketing symbol.

"School children from Panjshir will compete to come up with the best logo for Panjshir agricultural products," said Panjshir Director of Agriculture, Irrigation and Livestock Hashmatullah Anyat. "The competition will take place when school begins in March and will be judged by Afghan and local government officials."

Though spring was a large focus, attendees also discussed plans for an Agri-tourism event with a mulberry festival scheduled to be held in the summer.

"With short- and long-term goals voiced and recognized, we feel the agricultural and social lives of Panjshir will increase," said Anyat.

Others in attendance included officials from both the U.S. and Panjshir provincial government; Horticulture Livestock Project members; Roots of Peace members; representatives from the Afghanistan Chamber of Commerce and Industries; and representatives the Accelerating Sustainable Agriculture Program.

"The conference brought national and international attention to Panjshir and we think that will bode well for future projects," said Casada.

Guardians of Peace produces results in Paktya

PAKTYA PROVINCE, Afghanistan, Feb. 5, 2011–U.S. Army Sgt. 1st Class Matthew Smith of Altoona, Iowa, platoon sergeant for 2nd Platoon, Company C, Task Force Lethal, 1st Battalion, 168th Infantry Regiment, helps an Afghan National Army soldier of the 3rd Company, 1st Kandak, 2nd Brigade, 203rd ANA Infantry Corps bag several Improvised Explosive Devices in Zormat District. The items were found after ANA and coalition forces received a tip generated by the Guardians of Peace program. The rest of the munitions in the cache, including a mortar round, a make-shift claymore mine and two anti-tank mines, were destroyed by an Explosive Ordnance Disposal team. (Photo by U.S. Army Sgt. 1st Class Matthew Smith, Company C, Task Force Lethal)

By U.S. Army 1st Lt. Nicholas Rasmussen
Task Force Lethal

PAKTYA PROVINCE, Afghanistan, Feb. 5, 2011—A platoon from the Afghan National Army's 3rd Company, 1st Kandak, 2nd Brigade, 203rd ANA Infantry Corps along with 2nd Platoon of Company C, 1st Battalion, 168th Infantry Regiment, Task Force Lethal of the Iowa Army National Guard, formed a partnership that is already producing meaningful results.

Acting on information gathered from the Guardians of Peace program in Zormat District, the units uncovered two sandbags containing multiple complete Improvised Explosive Devices, one incomplete IED, a large improvised claymore-type mine, a mortar round and two anti-tank mines.

This is one of three caches found in the last week by the 3rd Company and Company C.

"The recent cache finds ... were driven by intelligence gathered by the ANA," said U.S. Army Sgt. 1st Class Matthew Smith of Altoona, Iowa, platoon sergeant for 2nd Platoon, Company C. "The Guardians of Peace tip was a result of the ANA handing out information cards with phone numbers."

Guardians of Peace is a program used by Afghan National Security Forces and coalition forces to receive information about insurgent activity. Local villagers get information from flyers and cards providing instructions on how to contact ANSF and coalition forces if insurgent activity is observed.

When an individual participates, the information is delivered without personally identifying information that may put that person at risk of repercussions by insurgent forces.

A tip was received by the ANA through this program that insurgents were moving explosives and IEDs around an abandoned home close to the Mamuzi health clinic near Bar Janek Kheyl village in eastern Zormat.

The caller kept watch on the activity of the insurgents while the ANA informed 2nd Platoon, Company C, of the situation. The ANA and coalition forces could not act immediately due to weather but spent the day planning what to do as soon as the weather cleared.

The next morning the security forces headed to the Mamuzi clinic.

The ANA searched both the abandoned home as well as some sink holes near it, thinking the pits would be good places to hide things.

First Lt. Pallawanna, a platoon leader for 3rd Company, jumped into one of these sink holes and found fresh footprints. He began digging with his hands then some of his soldiers jumped in to help. After a few minutes, they found something.

"They found two large sandbags," said Smith, commenting on the source of the IED-making materials. "We immediately cleared the area of civilians and sent a small search party to exploit the site."

Once the cache was unearthed the evidence was photographed and the ANA carefully bagged it to avoid contamination.

Before leaving the village, Pallawanna held an impromptu meeting with the primary healthcare provider of the Mamuzi health clinic, the night watchman on duty the night prior, villagers and elders.

Pallawanna showed the elders the contents of the cache, placing emphasis on the land mines.

"This stuff is getting buried in your backyard," explained Pallawanna. His comments focused on the fact that land mines don't discriminate; anyone could be affected by them. He emphasised the need for the villagers to report any insurgent activity they see as any villager could get hurt by the explosives.

The ANA and coalition forces returned to base where an explosive ordinance disposal team destroyed the munitions, and the IEDs were packaged and sent to Bagram Airfield for forensic testing.

Smith and his platoon were happy to do their job working with the ANA.

"Any day that you take eight IEDs out of the fight is a good day for us," said Smith.

Petreaus visits Red Bull Division,
Laghman Province leaders

LAGHMAN PROVINCE, Afghanistan, Feb. 7, 2011—Laghman Province Gov. Mohammad Iqbal Azizi, left, talks with U.S. Army Gen. David H. Petraeus, right, International Security Assistance Force commander, at the governor's compound in Mehtar Lam. The general and the governor agreed that patience is key as the coalition continues to conduct operations in the province. (Photo by U.S. Army Staff Sgt. Ryan C. Matson, Task Force Red Bulls Public Affairs)

By U.S. Army Staff Sgt. Ryan C. Matson
Task Force Red Bulls Public Affairs

LAGHMAN PROVINCE, Afghanistan, Feb. 7, 2011—U.S. Army Gen. David H. Petraeus, International Security Assistance Force commander, met with leaders of the Iowa National Guard's 2nd Brigade Combat Team, 34th Infantry Division, Task Force Red Bulls, in Mehtar Lam, Afghanistan, in a visit that focused on maintaining security in the Laghman Province and increasing economic development in the region.

"I want to assure you that I am not only a 'professor of war' as some journalists in the United States labelled me, I am also a former professor of economics," Petraeus told a group of leaders from the Red Bulls, as well as other military and local government officials, during a lunch hosted by Laghman Province Gov. Mohammad Iqbal Azizi in Mehtar Lam.

"I know that we must not only achieve security—we must then build on that foundation with economic development and improvements in basic services and all the other activities that are necessary for the people to support this government," Patraeus said.

The 1st Battalion, 133rd Infantry Regiment of the Red Bulls is the battlespace owner of Laghman Province and works closely with the Afghan National Army, Afghan National Police, and Afghan Uniformed Police to provide security in the province.

Petreaus began his visit with a meeting between Red Bulls military leaders, as well as leaders of the Laghman Provincial Reconstruction Team, the Kansas Agribusiness Development Team, and other units from nearby Forward Operating Base Mehtar Lam who work with the local population.

Petreaus was briefed on operations the units are conducting with their Afghan counterparts in key terrain areas and throughout the province.

"At the end of the day ... you have to go after the enemy wherever the enemy is—he doesn't care whether it's key terrain or non-key terrain," Petreaus said. "If they can disrupt whatever it is you're doing, that's a problem. We cannot let them have safe-havens anywhere we can prevent it."

After the morning meeting, Petreaus visited with Azizi at his compound. The governor expressed his happiness and gratitude for the coalition's efforts in the province.

"The team working with me is exceeding my expectations," Azizi said. "They are very precise."

Petreaus told the governor the coalition is working to minimize damage to the infrastructure of the province as military operations continue. He said one of the ways he plans to do this is by planting more trees.

"We have destroyed trees as part of military operations, that's something that's inescapable," Petreaus said. "But we will plant many, many more. I am going to have an order that says if you cut one tree, you plant two more somewhere else."

Petreaus said the highlight of his visit to the province was his visit to the Mastoori Girls School in Mehtar Lam, where Azizi took him after their meeting at the governor's compound. There he met some of the more than 2,500 girls who attend the school, as well as one of their teachers.

"The most enjoyable moment of the day for me was seeing the young girls at the school and hearing the excitement in their voices about the education they're now receiving—something that was impossible in the days of the Taliban," Petreaus said.

LAGHMAN PROVINCE, Afghanistan, Feb. 7, 2011—Col. Benjamin J. Corell (left), 2nd Brigade Combat Team, 34th Infantry Division, Task Force Red Bulls commander, U.S. Army Gen. David H. Petraeus (center), International Security Assistance Force commander, and Laghman Province Gov. Mohammad Iqbal Azizi (right), enjoy an Afghan feast together outside the governor's compound in Mehtar Lam. The general met with Red Bulls and local Afghan leaders during his visit to the Laghman Province. (Photo by U.S. Army Staff Sgt. Ryan C. Matson, Task Force Red Bulls Public Affairs)

Iowa National Guard Soldiers cheer Packers to victory from Afghanistan

LAGHMAN PROVINCE, Afghanistan, Feb. 7, 2011—U.S. Army Spc. Chandra Hundley (standing, left), a combat medic from Des Moines, Iowa, and U.S. Army 1st Lt. Billy Habibi (standing, right), a medical operations officer from Des Moines, Iowa, both with Headquarters and Headquarters Company, 1st Battalion, 133rd Infantry Regiment, react after the Green Bay Packers score during the Super Bowl the morning of Feb. 7 at Forward Operating Base Mehtar Lam in northeastern Afghanistan. (Photo by U.S. Army Staff Sgt. Ryan C. Matson, Task Force Red Bulls Public Affairs)

By U.S. Army Staff Sgt. Ryan C. Matson
Task Force Red Bulls Public Affairs

LAGHMAN PROVINCE, Afghanistan, Feb. 7, 2011—It may have been 4 a.m., but the Soldiers gathered at the dining facility on Forward Operating Base Mehtar Lam were far from sleepy.

Instead a crowd of fiery Soldiers were eating chicken wings, jumping up and down, and yelling at the dining facility television screen. It was Super Sunday, Monday morning in northeastern Afghanistan. The Soldiers, primarily from the

1st Battalion, 133rd Infantry Regiment of the Iowa National Guard's 2nd Brigade Combat Team, 34th Infantry Division, Task Force Red Bulls, woke up a little earlier than usual to see a classic confrontation between two of the most storied franchises in the National Football League.

Since Iowa has no NFL team, most of the Soldiers in the dining facility say they root for the closest geographical teams from bordering states—the Chicago Bears, the Minnesota Vikings, the Kansas City Chiefs, and of course, the Green Bay Packers. The Packers fans outnumbered the Steelers fans that morning, although there was still a good representation of fans cheering for the black and gold.

One Packers fan watching the game was U.S. Army 1st Lt. Billy Habibi, who was born in Oshkosh, Wisc. He rocked nervously back and forth in his chair during the commercial break between the third and fourth quarters. The Steelers, down 21-10 at halftime, had closed the gap to 21-17.

"It's a great game," said Habibi, a medical operations officer with Headquarters and Headquarters Company, 1-133rd Inf., who now calls Des Moines, Iowa, home. "The third quarter was terrible for the Packers."

Across from him, wearing a Pittsburgh Steelers cap, U.S. Army Spc. David Brumley, an unmanned aerial vehicle operator from Company B, 2-34th Brigade Special Troops Battalion, from Stuart, Iowa, shook his head.

"I'm gonna say the opposite of that, except for the part about it being a great game," Brumley said. "The first half was terrible."

When asked what they thought would happen, Habibi refused to make a prediction.

"I just know the Packers gotta score," he said. "I don't want to jinx it."

"I'm gonna say 27-21, Steelers," Brumley said.

There were as many as 100 people inside the dining facility to watch the game, but a group of maybe 50 diehards were there from kickoff to the end of regulation. Habibi and Brumley were two of these diehards. Both said they were lifelong fans of their teams. Someone could have almost known exactly what was going on in the game simply by watching their contradictory facial expressions.

But, on this day, it was Habibi who wound up smiling at the end of the game. He and his co-workers and fellow Packers fans from the FOB aid station gathered around the huge Green Bay sign they made for the game to take celebratory pictures after the Packers claimed their fourth NFL title.

Meanwhile, a somber Brumley removed the Pittsburgh flag he had hung on the wall on the opposite side of the television screen.

"That's OK, we already got six (championships.) More than any team," he said as he left the chow hall.

Construction begins on ANA base in Parwan

PARWAN PROVINCE, Afghanistan, Feb. 7, 2011—Afghans haul away the ceremonial golden shovels used to dig the first part of the foundation of an Afghan National Army base at Pushtaysark, also known as Red Hill, in Parwan Province. The facility will be constructed by Afghans with $20 million provided by the United States. (Photo by U.S. Army Spc. Adam L. Mathis, Task Force Red Bulls)

By U.S. Army Spc. Adam L. Mathis
Task Force Red Bulls Public Affairs

PARWAN PROVINCE, Afghanistan, Feb. 7, 2011—A coalition and Afghan vision started becoming reality when golden shovels broke ground on an Afghan National Army base in Parwan Province Feb. 7.

"We're very proud to bring that vision to reality with an Afghan company, Afghan engineers and Afghan laborers," said U.S. Air Force Maj. Christopher Meeker of Manito, Ill., an engineer for the Bagram area U.S. Army Corps of Engineers. "We're going to create 900 jobs in the Parwan economy with this project, and we're very proud of our partnership with the Parwan government and this Afghan contractor."

In a year, the site for the base, located at Pushtaysark, also known as Red Hill, will contain 36 facilities and house 896 ANA troops.

The facility cost approximately $20 million, money provided by the United States. The actual work of constructing the buildings, however, is the responsibility of the Afghans.

"Today I am very glad and happy to lay down the fundamental stone of 6th Kandak of the Afghan National Army in here," said Abdul Basir Salangi, governor of Parwan Province, through a translator. "Of course, if there is no security in a country, there won't be also progress in the fields of education ... and security."

This site was chosen because it occupies a strategic location, allowing troops to defend Parwan Province and Kabul.

Panjshir OCC–P borrows winter plan from Iowa

PANJSHIR PROVINCE, Afghanistan, Feb. 7, 2011—U.S. Army Lt. Col. Tim Glynn, an Ankeny, Iowa, resident and the Panjshir Embedded Training Team commander, instructs members of the Operations Coordination Center–Provincial staff on emergency response planning and operations at the Panjshir OCC–P headquarters. The ETT is part of the 2nd Brigade Combat Team, 34th Infantry Division, Task Force Red Bulls, Glynn, an Iowa Guardsman, used the state of Iowa's Emergency Decision Matrix to help the OCC–P build a written plan for Panjshir Province's winter emergency response. (Photo by U.S. Army Staff Sgt. Ashlee Lolkus, Task Force Red Bulls Public Affairs)

By U.S. Army Staff Sgt. Ashlee Lolkus
Task Force Red Bulls Public Affairs

PANJSHIR PROVINCE, Afghanistan, Feb. 7, 2011—Iowa National Guard Soldiers of the Panjshir Embedded Training Team, 2nd Brigade Combat Team, 34th Infantry Division, Task Force Red Bulls, are currently working with the Operations Coordination Center–Provincial to improve the Panjshir government's emergency winter response planning.

The OCC–P team consists of Afghan National Army, Afghan National Police, and National Directorate of Security officials, who represent their respective agencies for Panjshir Province.

The U.S. Army ETT supports the OCC–P by working with each staff section in plans development and operations.

"We have a plan for emergency situations," ANA Col. Rajab Khan, OCC–P commander, said through an interpreter during a training session. "We have a plan for each agency, and we are working to bring them together."

Under Panjshir's emergency winter response plan structure, the governor has identified who can provide food, shelter and extra clothing. But then, the government waits for external help from agencies in Kabul, said U.S. Army Lt. Col. Tim Glynn, the ETT commander and an Ankeny, Iowa, resident.

The ETT hopes to expand that plan by helping the province take care of itself internally and offered an Emergency Decision Matrix provided by the state of Iowa's emergency response center.

The matrix is a summarized version of the Iowa Emergency Management Response Plan, which is hundreds of pages long. About an eighth of the size of the entire response plan, the matrix offers step-by-step procedures on how Iowa government agencies respond to differing emergencies, including winter weather related issues.

The partnered training has benefited the OCC–P staff and they have enjoyed it, said Khan. "They train us on blizzard response and what we need to do if the snow creates problems," he said. "I want to thank Lt. Col. Glynn and his team for the training, especially the computer training. We have had the computers, but didn't know how to use them until now."

Part of Glynn's plan for emergency response was to help the Afghans build a document with written procedures for differing emergencies, like the Iowa Emergency Decision Matrix.

To help with the process, they also trained their Afghan counterparts how to use the computers, a skill they learned incredibly fast, said Glynn.

"These guys are sharp," said Glynn. "They (were) commanders during the Russian and Taliban wars."

Although building this plan will take time and effort, it will end up being a valuable asset when an emergency happens. "It's painful to go through step-by-step, but once it's complete it will be a great help," Glynn said during the training.

Throughout the afternoon, Glynn discussed the decision making process while using an interpreter to translate the lessons. He asked questions about the importance of saving lives, communication, road clearing and many other aspects of emergency winter response.

The room was full of energy as the staff members responded to each question and participated in the discussion. Glynn jotted down notes on a white board to document the discussion points to add to the written plan.

The training concluded with a rough draft of a plan, with which all participants seemed content. According to the ETT, the Afghan government officials are now a few steps closer in completing their blizzard emergency response plan, in the hope of helping and protecting Afghans.

"They want to help," said Glynn. "They are excited to help."

Panjshir women strengthen communication skills

PANJSHIR PROVINCE, Afghanistan, Feb. 8, 2011–U.S. Army Staff Sgt. Ashlee Lolkus, Task Force Red Bulls Public Affairs Non-Commissioned Officer, and Chandler, Minn., native, shows Rohubza Dousti, a trainer and supervisor at the United Nations Habitat and a Panjshir youth group leader, how to take a proper news photo during a Women's Communication Workshop at the Department of Women's Affairs located in Bazarak District. The two-day training had more than 20 women in attendance and covered writing, photography and public speaking classes. Panjshir Deputy Gov. Abdul Rahman Kabiri presented the women with certificates and congratulations on the second day. (Photo by U.S. Air Force Senior Airman Amber Ashcraft, Panjshir Provincial Reconstruction Team Public Affairs)

By U.S. Army Staff Sgt. Ashlee Lolkus
Task Force Red Bulls Public Affairs

PANJSHIR PROVINCE, Afghanistan. Feb 8, 2011—In a small classroom in the Director of Women's Affairs office, more than 20 women gathered, mostly teachers, for a two-day communications workshop held in Bazarak District here, beginning today.

Shoes were placed outside the door of the classroom, and inside, the room lit up with not only the morning sun pouring through the large-paned windows, but of excited chatter and giggling from the women inside.

Mahtab Farid, a native of Santa Monica, Calif., and public diplomacy officer for the U.S. State Department, was full of energy as she began the

267

training. Farid, who normally works out of Bagram Airfield, came to Panjshir, as she does with many provinces the Regional Command–East supports, to build capacity for Afghan women.

Farid knows the Afghan culture well. She not only has worked in Afghanistan for nearly a year now, but she was also born in nearby Iran.

"Iran and Afghanistan are neighbors, and they share religious and social cultures," she said. "Also, in Iran we speak Farsi, which is very similar to Dari, just a different accent."

Farid began the class with a lesson on introductions. Farid, who is fluent in Farsi, introduced herself, and the Panjshir Provincial Reconstruction Team and Task Force Red Bulls Public Affairs servicemembers, who assisted in the workshop. To learn more about the attendees, Farid had the women pair up and introduce each other to the rest of the group, an exercise requiring them to use their interviewing and public speaking skills.

"The conversation exercise really helped us out," said Naziya Rizai, the principal for Sangona High School in Panjshir, through an interpreter. "The best activities are those that have practical application."

"This session was rough on them. It is hard for them to speak in public," Farid said. "It is important for them to learn good public speaking skills, so that when they need to present themselves in front of important people, they can do well and get the jobs, or grants, or accepted into schools."

Other classes for the workshop included photography and writing skills. By day two of the workshop, the women completed their first assignment: a written proposal on a goal they are working for in their life, whether that was a job request, school attendance, or grant proposals.

"This was a learning opportunity," explained Rizai. "I could use the skills taught to write and speak ... the class resolved some of the written issues the women had."

Farid said she was very proud of the women for working so hard on the assignments.

"Communication in Afghanistan in general is very ineffective due to the wars, the lack of transparency and censorship," said Farid. "When it comes to women affairs, it is much worse because women are not allowed to express themselves freely."

Teaching courses like this two-day seminar is a passion of hers, Farid said. She explained that she loves to visit the communities and help these women in any way she can to give back to Afghanistan and to truly make a difference in their lives.

"My hope is that we can build capacity and provide these women with educational tools," said Farid. "They can use these tools and make something of themselves with what they've learned."

After lunch the second day of the workshop, the women were presented certificates of training. To show community support for the class, Panjshir Deputy Gov. Abdul Rahman Kabiri gave a small speech and thanked Farid and the others for teaching the course. He said he appreciated the respect displayed for their culture by ensuring that the class was for women, by women.

After the men left, the women swirled around the room, sharing laughs and taking pictures before they had to leave.

"If there are classes in the future, on topics like these," said Rizai, "I would most definitely attend again."

Ky. ADT II begins Panjshir sheep parasite project

PANJSHIR PROVINCE, Afghanistan, Feb. 9, 2011–Kentucky Agribusiness Development Team II members, U.S. Army Spc. Justin Allen (left), a London, Ky., native, and U.S. Army Sgt. Nicholas Combs, a Corbin, Ky., native, get to know a lamb at a local farm in Anaba District. The ADT will examine more than 120 pregnant sheep in Panjshir Province, taking fecal samples, age estimates, and FAMACHA-score evel of infection, and body condition scores. The fecal samples will be sent to a partner veterinarian at Bagram Airfield to determine the type and quantity of parasite eggs present in the pregnant sheep. (Photo by U.S. Air Force Senior Airman Amber Ashcraft, Panjshir Provincial Reconstruction Team Public Affairs)

Snow reminds deployed Iowa soldiers of home

BAGRAM AIRFIELD, Afghanistan, Feb. 13, 2011—U.S. Army Sgt. 1st Class Reagan Metcalf, the property book Non-Commissioned Officer for the 2nd Brigade Combat Team, 34th Infantry Division, and Ames, Iowa, resident, shovels snow outside his living quarters. Metcalf spent the afternoon clearing the wet heavy snow from the sidewalks surrounding the brigade headquarters and living areas. More than five inches of snow fell overnight, making some Iowa soldiers miss their snow shoveling duties back home. (Photo by U.S. Capt. Adrian Sean Taylor, Task Force Archer)

Afghan engineers to take more active role in Paktya development projects

By U.S. Air Force Staff Sgt. Barry Loo
Paktya Provincial Reconstruction Team Public Affairs

*PAKTYA PROVINCE, Afghanistan, Feb. 12, 2011—*The Government of the Islamic Republic of Afghanistan will begin taking a more active role in Paktya Provincial Reconstruction Team's development projects.

In the past, GIRoA engineers would help by inspecting projects undergoing construction and would not accept responsibility for maintaining and staffing buildings until the projects were completed.

With every new development project, GIRoA and the PRT will work side by side for the entire development process, including the selection of contractors and identifying project requirements, said U.S. Air Force Capt. Kirk Greene, Paktya PRT and native of Portville, N.Y.

"Now, development will happen in alignment with GIRoA," said Mahfooz Ahmad, Paktya director of economy, "and we like this."

Afghan engineers will be conduct more quality-control visits to construction sites, which Bahai Jan Yar, engineer and Paktya director of sector, hopes will improve the lives of the Afghan people.

"A person can see better with two eyes than one," he said, referring to both Afghan and U.S. engineers conducting inspections. "The quality will get better day by day."

The ultimate goal of the PRT engineers is to pass all development responsibilities over to their Afghan counterparts.

Michael Mihalify of Chassell, Mich., U.S. Army Corps of Engineers, said the Afghan engineers were proactive, concerned, involved, and "trying to make this work."

He said he believes, as do the directors of economy and sector, Afghans should begin fulfilling roles the PRT has been performing since its inception in 2003.

"We're working ourselves out of a job," Greene said.

Engineer soldiers deliver aid to Afghans

PARWAN PROVINCE, Afghanistan, Feb. 14, 2011—An Afghan carrying a child approaches U.S. Army Staff Sgt. Peter Moeller of Atkins, Iowa, a medic with the 832nd Engineer Company, 1st Squadron, 113th Cavalry Regiment, part of the 2nd Brigade Combat Team, 34th Infantry Division, Task Force Red Bulls, for humanitarian aid at Qale-Mussa Pain Middle School in Parwan Province. The humanitarian aid, including clothing, blankets and gloves for children, was donated by the church Moeller's grandmother attends, St. John's Lutheran Church in Newhall, Iowa. (Photo by U.S. Army Spc. Adam L. Mathis, Task Force Red Bulls Public Affairs)

PARWAN PROVINCE, Afghanistan, Feb. 14, 2011—Children crowd around a Mine-Resistant, Ambush-Protected Cougar to receive coats, gloves, blankets and hats from soldiers of the 832nd Engineer Company, 1st Squadron, 113th Cavalry Regiment, Task Force Redhorse, a part of 2nd Brigade Combat Team, 34th Infantry Division, Task Force Red Bulls, at Qale-Mussa Pain Middle School in Parwan Province. [...] (Photo by U.S. Army Spc. Adam L. Mathis, Task Force Red Bulls Public Affairs)

Iowa Soldiers connect with loved ones back home

BAGRAM AIRFIELD, Afghanistan, Feb. 14, 2011—U.S. Army Staff Sgt. David Bloyer of Caroll, Iowa, talks to his wife through a video call program from his living quarters on Bagram Airfield. A little before 7 a.m. in Iowa and 5:30 p.m. in Afghanistan, Bloyer wished his wife, Sasha, and daughter, Skylar, a happy Valentine's Day. Bloyer, an assistant information operations officer and targeting and electronic warfare Non-Commissioned Officer with Headquarters and Headquarters Company, 2nd Brigade Combat Team, 34th Infantry Division, Task Force Red Bulls, has been in Afghanistan since November, but still remains a part of his families lives from afar. (Photo by U.S. Army Staff Sgt. Ashlee Lolkus, Task Force Red Bulls Public Affairs)

By U.S. Army Spc. Adam L. Mathis
Task Force Red Bulls Public Affairs

BAGRAM AIRFIELD, Afghanistan, Feb. 14, 2011—Over a quarter of the earth's surface stands between U.S. Army Staff Sgt. David Bloyer and his wife and daughter. That is more than 7,000 miles and completely different hemispheres. Bagram Airfield is 10-and-a-half hours ahead of his home in Carroll, Iowa.

But Bloyer is there nearly every morning to wake his 1-year-old daughter, Skylar.

Although Afghanistan does not have as many amenities as the United States, Iowa National Guard Soldiers like Bloyer find ways to bridge the distance between Afghanistan and home. Most military installations have come to offer a variety of choices to reach loved ones back home, even for fathers who want to "be there" when their daughter wakes up.

Bloyer uses an Internet-based video calling program to call home a little before 7 a.m. Iowa time. This gives him and his wife, Sasha, time to talk in private. Then, Sasha carries the computer into their daughter's bedroom. "We'll go wake Skylar up together, which is pretty cool because I like being able to see her right when she wakes up," said Bloyer, the assistant information operations officer, and targeting and electronic warfare Non-Commissioned Officer with Headquarters and Headquarters Company, 2nd Brigade Combat Team, 34th Infantry Division, Task Force Red Bulls. "It's one of my favorite things. It's pretty awesome; it's amazing how much she has grown."

To be there every morning for his daughter, Bloyer, who has been in Afghanistan since November, pays for Internet access through an Afghan contractor. Though Morale, Welfare, and Recreation centers offer free Internet, purchasing access offers more privacy.

"It makes it more bearable being able to see your loved ones every day," said Bloyer. "But in another way, it kind of makes you more homesick. (My wife is) like right there, and some days I'm just like, 'Ah, I wish I could just go home.' But, all in all, I would say that it's a blessing, really, to be able to see them every day."

U.S. Army Sgt. Lance Morrow knows that feeling of homesickness. Morrow, a medic with the medical platoon, 1st Battalion, 168th Infantry Regiment, Task Force Lethal, at Forward Operating Base Gardez, has been in Afghanistan since November and keeps in touch with his friends via the Internet, using a social networking site.

"(It's) great for dropping somebody a message or following somebody on their wall. It's easier than sending out constant e-mails to people," said Morrow, of Council Bluffs, Iowa.

While his FOB has a facility for free Internet, Morrow also chooses to purchase it to have personal Internet access in his room.

But, many Soldiers are willing to settle for what the military can provide.

MWR facilities provide free phone calls and Internet. According to Lacey Castleberry, an MWR specialist, on Bagram Airfield in January, 32,550 people used the Internet and 11,993 used the free phone service. These facilities exist at other locations as well.

U.S. Army Spc. Curtis Blake Jr., a radio telephone operator with Company A, 1st Battalion, 133rd Infantry Regiment, Task Force Red Bulls, talks to his girlfriend over a phone provided by the local MWR facility at COP Najil.

"She stays strong, at least when we talk on the phone and stuff," said Blake of Clinton, Iowa. He said talking to her helps reduce the stress.

Like many other Soldiers, staying in touch back home is an emotional release, a chance to communicate with people outside of the Army, and keeps him focused for his work in Afghanistan.

"It's probably one of the few things that keep me sane," Blake joked.

Afghans, Soldiers share poems over radio

PARWAN PROVINCE, Afghanistan, Feb. 16, 2011—U.S. Army Pfc. David Fountain of Ames, Iowa, an intelligence analyst with Headquarters and Headquarters Company, 2nd Brigade Combat Team, 34th Infantry Division, Task Force Red Bulls, reads [an Afghan-language] translation of Robert Frost's "The Road Not Taken." (Photo by U.S. Army Spc. Adam L. Mathis, Task Force Red Bulls Public Affairs)

By U.S. Army Spc. Adam L. Mathis
Task Force Red Bulls Public Affairs

PARWAN PROVINCE, Afghanistan, , Feb. 16, 2011—U.S. Army Pfc. David Fountain sat in a darkened room in Charikar. Candles sat on the table in front of him and a string of colored lights on the wall added to the illumination. A microphone and a group of Afghans waited for him to speak.

"Two roads diverged in a yellow wood," Fountain began.

Beside the intelligence analyst from Ames, Iowa, sat an interpreter, who filled in the pauses with a translation of the poem Fountain was reading, Robert Frost's "The Road Not Taken," for the audience of the Afghan Radio Dunya.

The occasion was a mix of Western and Islamic cultural traditions. Ahmad Anaiesh, who runs Radio Dunya and also read a poem, said the broadcast was part of a two-day celebration to mark Valentine's Day and honor the birth of Muhammad, known as Mawlid al Nabi.

"Today we also share our culture with a society and also with other people in the United States," Anaiesh said through an interpreter.

This mix of cultures was not lost on Fountain. While he often works with data about Afghans, this was his first time to leave Bagram Airfield and experience the culture firsthand.

"I feel, personally, like my eyes were opened to something new, and I think it was a really great overall experience," said Fountain, who is a Soldier with Headquarters and Headquarters Company, 2nd Brigade Combat Team, 34th Infantry Division, Task Force Red Bulls.

The Soldiers who came, however, did not just recite the poetry of others. U.S. Army Spc. Robyn Smalley of Fairfield, Iowa, an intelligence analyst with Company B, 2-34th Brigade Special Troops Battalion, read a poem, titled "Peace" she composed two years ago for International Peace Day.

"Part of the reason I went ahead and decided to choose that poem, even though it was two years old, was because I thought it would be special. I wanted to help bridge that relationship between U.S. citizens and Afghans, and what better subject to speak on than peace?" Smalley said.

*PARWAN PROVINCE, Afghanistan—*U.S. Army Spc. Robyn Smalley of Fairfield, Iowa, an intelligence analyst with Company B, 2-34th Brigade Special Troops Battalion, Task Force Red Bulls, recites her poem, "Peace," which she composed two years ago for International Peace Day. (Photo by U.S. Army Spc. Adam L. Mathis, Task Force Red Bulls Public Affairs)

ANCOP graduate C-IED course prepared to train others

PAKTYA PROVINCE, Afghanistan, Feb. 17, 2011—Col. Muhammed, commander of the Afghan National Civil Order Police in Paktya Province, addresses his soldiers before they graduate from a counter improvised explosive device awareness train-the-trainer course at the Paktya provincial police headquarters in Gardez City. The course trains soldiers to become trainers so they can instruct their units on the precautions needed in responding to IEDs. (Photo by U.S. Army 1st Lt. Nicholas Rasmussen, Task Force Lethal)

By U.S. Army 1st. Lt. Nicholas Rasmussen
Task Force Lethal

PAKTYA PROVINCE, Afghanistan, Feb. 17, 2011—Afghan National Civil Order Policemen proudly displayed their certificates during a graduation ceremony, for the Counter-Improvised Explosive Device awareness train-the-trainer course held at the Paktya provincial police headquarters in Gardez City.

U.S. Army Capt. James Avrams of Logan, Iowa, commander of Headquarters and Headquarters Company, Task Force Lethal, 1st Battalion, 168th Infantry Regiment, helped coordinate training for the Afghan National Security Forces in Paktya Province and arranged for the ANCOP to participate in the C-IED class.

Avrams heard about the class in January and arranged to meet with the organization running the course, a subcontractor called Ronco International.

"(Ronco) primarily put on classes for the Afghan National Army at Forward Operating Base Thunder," said Avrams. "So I said, 'Hey, how about we do an ANCOP only one?' And they were all for it."

The training, conducted at police headquarters for the 4th Brigade, ANCOP, consisted of five days of hands-on classes. Topics included enemy tactics, searching for IEDs, assessing the status of a route, reacting to an IED, reporting an IED and identifying the components of an IED.

The course is designed to accomplish two goals. It provides a basic understanding of IEDs and what to do if one is found and teaches each student the skills to conduct a one-day informational course on IED awareness.

The train-the-trainer feature helps to spread IED awareness significantly throughout the province as graduates of the course share the information with others in their unit.

Col. Muhammed, 4th Brigade, ANCOP commander, has high hopes for the same outcome in Paktya.

"I hope that my soldiers who participated in this class have learned something, and that they will use the information in their operations," said Muhammed.

Sgt. Ja Muhammed, a driver in the ANCOP, is determined to share what he has learned during the C-IED course with more than just members of his unit.

"My target was to come here, learn, and after that, go and teach for my friends and other units and other people who live in the village," said Ja Muhammed.

At the end of the ceremony, graduates packed up the training equipment provided to them as a gift by the instructors and began planning to conduct their first C-IED awareness course.

PAKTYA PROVINCE, Afghanistan, Feb. 17, 2011—A graduate of the first Afghan National Civil Order Police class to finish the Counter-Improvised Explosive Device awareness train-the-trainer class proudly displays his completion certificate to his classmates during a graduation ceremony at the Paktya provincial police headquarters in Gardez City. Each graduate is certified to teach a one-day course on C-IED awareness, a skill they can use to increase the effectiveness of each ANCOP unit. U.S. Army Capt. James Avrams (third from right) from Logan, Iowa, commander of Headquarters and Headquarters platoon, Task Force Lethal, 1st Battalion, 168th Infantry Regiment, initiated the ANCOPs involvement with the C-IED course. (Photo by U.S. Army 1st Lt. Nicholas Rasmussen, Task Force Lethal)

ANA, Red Bulls search Parwai during Operation Brass Monkey

LAGHMAN PROVINCE, Afghanistan, Feb. 19, 2011—U.S. Army Soldiers with Company C, 1st Battalion, 133rd Infantry Regiment, Task Force Ironman, a part of the 2nd Brigade Combat Team, 34th Infantry Division, Task Force Red Bulls, rush to the door of a High-Value Target's residence outside Parwai during Operation Brass Monkey. [...] While they did not nab the High-Value Target they did detain six persons of interest. They also located possible Improvised Explosive Device-making materials and intelligence regarding insurgent operations in the area. (Photo by U.S. Army Staff Sgt. Ryan C. Matson, Task Force Red Bulls Public Affairs)

LAGHMAN PROVINCE, Afghanistan—U.S. Army Maj. Aaron Baugher, from Ankeny, Iowa, the Headquarters and Headquarters Company, 1st Battalion, 133rd Infantry Regiment, Task Force Ironman, battalion operations officer, reads a document he located in a car parked at a High-Value Target's home outside Parwai during Operation Brass Monkey. [...] (Photo by U.S. Army Staff Sgt. Ryan C. Matson, Task Force Red Bulls Public Affairs)

Obrecht brings experience to Cavalry

By Capt. Timothy A. Creasman
Task Force Redhorse

PARWAN PROVINCE, Afghanistan, Feb. 19, 2011—For most captains in the Iowa National Guard, commanding soldiers at the troop or company level is one of the most rewarding jobs of their career. Capt. Kyle Obrecht returns to that rewarding position and brings 12 years of military experience with him.

Obrecht assumed command of Headquarters and Headquarters Troop, 1st Squadron, 113th Cavalry Regiment, Task Force Redhorse, a part of the 2nd Brigade Combat Team, 34th Infantry Division, Task Force Red Bulls, from Capt. Jason Knueven, a Manning, Iowa native, at the Task Force Redhorse headquarters building on Bagram Airfield, here Feb. 19.

"It is an honor to take command for the second time, especially as a Cavalry troop commander because the Cavalry is a tme-honored tradition," said Obrecht, from Council Bluffs, Iowa. "Capt. Knueven did an outstanding job as the HHT commander. I hope to continue serving the soldiers with excellence, as he has done before me."

Knueven held command of HHT for 20 months prior to moving to command Troop A, 1-113 during the cavalry's deployment to Afghanistan. Knueven was responsible for training, equipping and the movement of the headquarters troop and the squadron commander's staff during the pre-mobilization training. He was also responsible for the transition into Afghanistan.

Obrecht works full time as the officer-in-charge for headquarters, 1st Battalion, 168th Infantry Regiment, also a part of the 2-34th BCT. This deployment will be the third in a long line of service, and the second time in command for Obrecht, who served as a platoon leader for 22 months in Iraq when the 1st Battalion, 133rd Infantry Regiment deployed there in 2005. During Obrecht's first command, he spent 18 months as the Company A commander in the 1st Battalion, 168th Infantry Regiment getting that unit prepared for its current deployment to Afghanistan. Before being selected for command of HHT, Obrecht served as a plans officer in the 2-34th BCT plans section.

"We welcome Capt. Obrecht to the squadron and know he will build upon Capt. Knueven's good work," said Lt. Col. David A. Updegraff, the 1-113th Cavalry commander from Cedar Rapids, Iowa. "He will be a strong addition to our team."

ANA, Task Force Lethal conduct joint operation in Zormat

PAKTYA PROVINCE, Afghanistan, Feb. 20, 2011—Members of 1st Company, 1st Kandak, 2nd Brigade, 203rd ANA Infantry Corps Afghan National Army, prepare to dismount and establish blocking positions around an objective to prevent escaping insurgents during an operation to search for Improvised Explosive Device materials in Paktya Province. During the mission, known as Dawn Rider, the ANA partnered with Afghan Uniformed Police, and 3rd Platoon, 615th Military Police Company; and Company D, 1st Battalion, 168th Infantry Regiment, Task Force Lethal. (Photo by U.S. Army 1st Lt. Nicholas Rasmussen, Task Force Lethal)

PAKTYA PROVINCE, Afghanistan—U.S. Army 1st Lt. Justin Schultz (center left) of Council Bluffs, Iowa, and U.S. Army Sgt. Ashley Knopf (center right) of Frankfort, Ind., both members of Company D, 1st Battalion, 168th Infantry Regiment, Task Force Lethal, and soldiers of 1st Company, 1st Kandak of the Afghan National Army ford a river as they move to their blocking position during an operation in Paktya Province. The Afghan and American Soldiers braved winter weather and water obstacles to complete the mission intended to root out a suspected Improvised Explosive Device cell and increase the security of the local populace. (Photo by U.S. Army 1st Lt. Nicholas Rasmussen, Task Force Lethal)

ANSF step it up in Koh-e Sofi with Task Force Redhorse

PARWAN PROVINCE, Afghanistan, Feb. 21, 2011—U.S. soldiers with Troop B, 1st Squadron, 113th Cavalry Regiment, Task Force Redhorse, move into the village of Qual-e Jala here, Feb. 21. Afghan National Army soldiers, Afghan National Police and other assets partnered with Troop B to search the village of Qual-e Jala for targeted individuals in order to 'clear, hold, and build' Koh-e Safi District. While searching the village, the Troop B soldiers and their partners killed one known insurgent, detained four others and also found assorted weapons which they gathered and destroyed. Task Force Redhorse is a part of the 2nd Brigade Combat Team, 34th Infantry Division, also known as Task Force Red Bulls, and maintains security throughout Parwan Province.

By U.S. Army Staff Sgt. Ashlee Lolkus
Task Force Red Bulls Public Affairs

PARWAN PROVINCE, Afghanistan, Feb. 21, 2011—Sounds of CH-47 Chinook helicopter blades chopping the air filled the passengers' ears as they jumped out the back onto a soft dirt field. In the dark, dismounted Soldiers switched-on their night vision devices after the helicopters lifted and flew away, leaving the skies empty except for the bright moon. In the early morning hours, Operation First Snow was finally underway.

As a second round of Chinooks landed, the first group of Soldiers were already moving towards Qual-e Jala to search the compounds for the targeted individual. Soldiers and attachments of Troop B, 1st Squadron, 113th Cavalry Regiment, Task Force Redhorse, a part of the 2nd Brigade Combat Team, 34th Infantry Division, Task Force Red Bulls, took the first steps to clear, hold, and build Koh-e Safi, ridding the area of insurgency one target at a time.

"We went to Qual-e Jala within Koh-e Safi to search for known weapons cache sites, and we wanted to detain a known insurgent we believed was in the area," said U.S. Army Capt. Randall Stanford, a Clive, Iowa, resident and the Troop B commander. "The sources we used didn't work to get our primary objective, so we just continued with our clearing and searching operations."

The company spilt the village and cleared the compounds one by one. Throughout the day, they killed one insurgent, detained four others and found grenades, rockets, landmines and improved explosive device making materials. The Afghan National Army, with minimal guidance, took the lead on the majority of the searches.

U.S. Army 2nd Lt. Andrew Smith, 3rd Platoon leader for Troop B from Iowa City, Iowa, said the ANA soldiers did a great job while they cleared 3rd Platoon's sector of the village.

"We had 10 ANA soldiers with us, and one spoke pretty good English," he said, "which worked out very well because without him we would have had to do a lot of hand signalling. He really helped out."

Stanford said Troop B had trained previously with the Afghan National Army and Afghan National Police that ran the operation with them. He was happy with how much the ANA took the lead in clearing the village.

"They really got in on the questioning of detained individuals," he said. "Without having to go through an interpreter, the ANA had a lot of questions they would fire at them. My interpreter would just have to say 'He's asking this,' and they were asking the right questions. It's good when they can ask the questions and do the searching; we are getting where we need to be which is us backing up and them going forward, and that's happening already."

"We were very satisfied with the cooperation we had with the Bravo Troop," said ANA Lt. Aimal, the executive officer for 3rd Company, 3rd Kandak, 1st Brigade, 201st ANA Infantry Corps. "We did what we came to do and it was very successful. We hope that in the future we have many successful missions like this with other Coalition Forces."

Troop B plans on conducting future operations with the ANA and ANP, Smith said. "I'm looking forward to future partnership with the ANA and ANP because without them our element is so small that it's really difficult to make an impact," he said. "When we have (the Afghan forces) with us, the local Afghans seem to be a little more understanding and accepting of us being there than if it's just us alone."

The mission went off flawlessly, said Stanford. Troop B had planned and briefed the mission for weeks prior to execution, each Soldier knew exactly what his or her task and purpose was. Not only did Troop B have ANA and ANP along on the mission, but they also had a French Operational Mentoring Liaison Team, a Law Enforcement Professional, a Female Engagement Team, Military Working Dogs, and air assets to name a few.

"We had so many assets rolled up into this one mission," Stanford said. "For it to go off as well as it did, and (for us to) find as much stuff as we did, and detain the individuals we did, I couldn't be more proud."

Clearing, holding and improving Koh-e Safi, Qual-e Jala was the first step. Troop B plans to continue throughout the rest of the district to make it a safe place for Afghans to live peacefully.

"We are here to help them," said Smith, "to secure them and to get the guys that are doing harmful things out."

PARWAN PROVINCE, Afghanistan, Feb. 21, 2011—U.S. Army Sgt. Robert Streeter of Newton, Iowa, and soldier with Troop B, 1st Squadron, 113th Cavalry Regiment, Task Force Redhorse, scans a nearby hilltop during a search of the Qual-e Jala village, Afghanistan. (Photo by U.S. Army Staff Sgt. Ashlee Lolkus, Task Force Red Bulls Public Affairs)

Ironman Soldiers share experiences
with Afghan journalists

LAGHMAN PROVINCE, Afghanistan, Feb. 23, 2011—U.S. Army Staff Sgt. Greg Zuercher of Wichita, Kansas, a Kansas Agribusiness Development Team military journalist working with 1st Battalion, 133rd Infantry Regiment, Task Force Ironman, part of 2nd Brigade Combat Team, 34th Infantry Division, Task Force Red Bulls, talks to an Afghan journalist from the Laghman Province during the Afghan Journalism Seminar at the Information, Culture and Youth Center in Mehtar Lam. (Photo by U.S. Army Staff Sgt. Ryan C. Matson, Task Force Red Bulls Public Affairs)

By U.S. Army Staff Sgt. Ryan C. Matson
Task Force Red Bulls Public Affairs

LAGHMAN PROVINCE, Afghanistan, Feb. 23, 2011—If you asked U.S. Army Staff Sgt. Greg Zuercher back in 1984 what he'd be doing today, he probably would have never guessed he'd be in Afghanistan giving tips on news-writing to Afghan journalists.

But that's exactly what the military journalist with the Kansas Agribusiness Development Team was doing at the first Laghman Province Afghan Journalism Seminar in Mehtar Lam. Zuercher, who graduated with a degree in journalism from Kansas State University in 1984, taught a news-writing segment of the two-day professional development seminar. "I tried to show the journalists how they can use a short sentence to draw the reader into the story and then present the facts," said Zuercher of Wichita, Kansas. "I told them that their initial sentence needs to be a grabber; it needs to grab the reader and encourage them to read on."

Zuercher was one of the military journalists who shared their knowledge and tips with their Afghan counterparts during the seminar. About 40 local Afghan journalists, including eight women, attended the seminar. The training was organized by U.S. Air Force 1st Lt. Brittany Martin, a Public Affairs Officer with the Laghman Provincial Reconstruction Team, and a native of Katy, Texas. Both Zuercher and Martin are serving with 1st Battalion, 133rd Infantry Regiment, Task Force Ironman, part of 2nd Brigade Combat Team, 34th Infantry Division, Task Force Red Bulls.

"The Director of Information, Culture and Youth, Fazzinullah Patan, has been proactive in increasing the capability of Laghman's media," Martin said. "We are excited that he allowed us to work with his department to conduct this training, and we look forward to holding follow-on sessions to continue to improve the skills of the local journalists."

On the first day of the seminar, Feb. 22, Mahtab Farid, a native of Santa Monica, Calif., and U.S. State Department public diplomacy officer who has worked as a journalist in the U.S., discussed the elements of writing a solid lead, or introduction, to a news story. She also stressed that the most important factor in any story is to present the truth with confirmed facts from reliable sources.

Zuercher built on this training the second day, and also featured tips on photography from other Ironman journalists. The journalists then separated into working groups in which the Afghan journalists sat down with American military journalists from Task Force Ironman to discuss the leads they had written. During the working group, the Afghans and Americans worked together to formulate questions for the seminar's grand finale, an actual press conference by Laghman Province Director of Forestry, Haji Auhe. When the Task Force Ironman journalists were originally drafting out the seminar, they planned on hosting mock scenarios, but Zuercher thought of a better idea.

"I suggested instead of picking a fictitious story to hold a press conference on, that we chose something that's a real ongoing event," Zuercher said. "I thought of the reforestation program that the Kansas Agribusiness Development Team is hosting, and it turned out to be a good story, and something that we could bring a subject matter expert in to speak on."

That subject matter expert was Auhe, who spoke at length about the reforestation project, which has brought 35,000 new trees to the province already and will bring about 125,000 by its completion. The journalists asked questions on all aspects of the project, from who will care for the new trees, to how long the trees will produce fruit.

Atiquallah Qurashi, a writer for a Laghman Province weekly magazine, was one of the journalists who attended the seminar.

"We learned to report the facts of our story in a concise manner," Qurashi said. "The instructors showed us how to shorten our reports and still get all the facts in. The best part of the seminar for me was that the Americans did not talk to us like students; they talked to us like friends. I will use the things I learned in this seminar every single day on the job."

LAGHMAN PROVINCE, Afghanistan. Feb. 23, 2011—U.S. Air Force 1st Lt. Brittany Martin (right), a Public Affairs Officer from Katy, Texas, with the Laghman Provincial Reconstruction Team working with 1st Battalion, 133rd Infantry Regiment, Task Force Ironman, part of the 2nd Brigade Combat Team, 34th Infantry Division, presents a certificate to an Afghan journalism seminar participant at the Information, Culture and Youth Center in Mehtar Lam. (Photo by U.S. Army Staff Sgt. Ryan C. Matson, Task Force Red Bulls Public Affairs)

Soldiers, AUP remember fallen Afghan brethren

LAGHMAN PROVINCE, Afghanistan, Jan. 15, 2011—Farid Ahmad Malang, left, a squad leader with the Afghan Uniformed Police hands a bolt to U.S. Army Spc. Carlos Pulido, right, an all-wheeled mechanic with the 64th Military Police Company, 720th MP Battalion, from Turlock, Calif. at the Alingar District Center, Alingar, Afghanistan. Ten days later, Malang and three other AUP officers from the Alingar District Center were killed when an Improvised Explosive Device detonated near the village of Tigalam, completely destroying the up-armored Humvee they had been patrolling in. (Photo by U.S. Army Staff Sgt. Ryan C. Matson, Task Force Red Bulls Public Affairs)

By U.S. Army Staff Sgt. Ryan C. Matson
Task Force Red Bulls Public Affairs

LAGHMAN PROVINCE, Afghanistan, Feb. 25, 2011—I am a military journalist, on my second deployment to the Middle East: one to Iraq, this one to Afghanistan.

When I go on missions, I usually try to stay in the background. That is because I'm an extra. I'm the camera guy. Unless I've trained with the unit and have a role in the mission beyond taking pictures and writing their story, I don't want the Soldiers preoccupied with me or doing things differently, it's not safe for them.

But Feb. 25 was one of the rare times I've broken my rule and did something more than just take pictures and ask questions. I went to the Alingar District Center, basically an Afghan police station, and became involved—I gave a grieving father pictures of his son. The father is, and the son was, an Afghan Uniformed Police officer.

On Jan. 25, my friend AUP 1st Lt. Mohammed Hussain, lost his son, Farid Ahmad Malang, and three other AUP officers, Abas Basram, Shafiq, and Kandahar Gul, when a massive 200-pound Improvised Explosive Device detonated completely decimating their up-armored Humvee. The officers were on a proactive patrol through their area of operations near the town of Tigalam.

"The officers who died in the IED bomb were the best officers in the Alingar District Center serving and protecting their people," Hussein told me. He was not crying, but his eyes were full of sorrow, and his voice was different than during previous talks I had with him. It was evident he was still fighting on a daily basis the emotional pain from losing his son.

"My son especially was a brave man. He was like my arm. All the time when we went on patrols, he was trying to protect me. He would never let me take out an IED we'd find, he was the only one who would. He was everything."

This incident hit home to me for a lot of reasons. First of all, in the United States, in Tennessee, I'm a police officer.

Secondly, I saw Hussain and Malang graduate the police academy, the first one held here on a provincial level, Nov. 4, 2010. I saw all four of the officers raise their certificates above their heads and proclaim, "I work for Afghanistan!" in front of the province's government and military officials. It reminded me of why I wanted to join the police force when I left active duty service in 2006. It was the first story I covered when I deployed to Afghanistan, and Hussain was the first person I interviewed. I was lucky to talk to him several times since then.

"The first time I saw you and the other Americans, I was glad," Hussain told me as we sat down to talk about his son and the other officers killed, "because I had found some new friends."

This year, I would be writing about what people are doing, rather than handling the situations myself as an officer. But seeing the Afghan officers graduate still made me feel a sense of camaraderie them, or at least a respect for the profession they had chosen to undertake.

There are a lot of differences between doing the job here in Afghanistan, and rolling around in a squad car back home, but in the end police work comes down to serving and protecting the public.

At home, quite often police work is about talking to people and solving problems. The method of solving a problem may be as simple as listening to a person talk, offering some advice or a number of a service to call, or it may mean carting someone to jail. You still get guns, drugs, chase people, all the stuff you wanted to do when you joined, but an average day for an officer-on-patrol comes down to talking to people and solving their wide array of problems. We usually don't have to worry, thankfully, about bombs blowing up our cruisers, or people shooting at us from mountainsides with automatic weapons or grenade launchers.

The insurgency has always reminded me of a bad street gang. The concepts are the same: they intimidate the people into not talking to authorities and doing what they want done. They terrorize innocent people. The same disdain I feel for people doing those deeds back home is the disdain these officers felt for their enemy here.

The incident also forced me to think of what would have happened had this happened in the United States. Without a doubt, not everybody loves the police back home. However, most people have some level of respect and support for those who try to maintain order and protect the safety of others.

When an officer is killed in the United States, officers come from near and far to their memorials. A convoy of police vehicles with flashing lights may last for miles. The world seems to stop for that moment. The streets are lined with civilians on the route too, and even though it is under tragic circumstances, I think officers can feel the appreciation the public has for what they do.

There will be no parade for the four officers killed here, but their service and dedication is still remembered by the Afghan and American officers who worked with them.

The 64th Military Police Company's 3rd Platoon, out of Fort Hood, Texas, worked and fought side-by-side with the four fallen officers, going on countless missions and patrols with them over the past year. They agreed with Hussain; the four officers killed were the best and brightest of the Alingar DC.

"They really were dedicated to the security of this place," said Sgt. Denver Missel, one of the team leaders in 3rd Platoon from Argyle, Minn. "(They were) hardworking, and they were cheery."

U.S. Army Sgt. Alberto Iglesias, another team leader with 3rd Platoon from South Plainfield, N.J., remembers Malang as being especially cheerful and enthusiastic—always the first one to run and greet his unit's Soldiers each time they visited.

"We called him Walika," Iglesias recalled. "It means 'come here,' but it became his name. As soon as we pulled in the gate he'd start yelling, 'Walika,' so that became his greeting.

"Two days before they died, I gave him one of my knives, because he would find IEDs, and dig them out himself. I told him if you're going to be doing that, at least use this, use something decent. He was always the first one to approach and the first to help, whether it was helping one of the mechanics we brought up to work on a vehicle—he was a squad leader and took care of their vehicles—or whatever we were doing."

"He was a great guy," said U.S. Army Staff Sgt. Joe Contreras, one of the platoon's squad leaders from San Antonio, Texas. "He was involved in everything."

"They were all also always ready to go out and fight, they were all very, very brave," said U.S. Army Sgt. Adam Friday, a team leader from Dover, Del.

Thirty days later, the photographs I gave Hussain of his son with his grandson still visibly shook the 17-year veteran officer. He was pleased to have pictures to remember him by, but he said thinking back on his son's memory will remain happy and still a bit painful all at once. Hussain had nine sons, and three of them followed his chosen profession as an officer. Malang, obviously, was one, and he has another son working at the DC. A third son works as an Afghan National Civil Order Police officer in Kabul, and has expressed interest in coming to Alingar to work with his father as Malang had. Though he can never replace Malang, in the Afghan culture, when one's son or brother dies, it is often a call to service for another family member to continue their legacy.

Meanwhile, Hussain still puts on his uniform and leads the other officers at the Alingar DC on patrols and training, just as he did for 17 years before his son was killed. And though he is grieving, he still presses on with the mission and motivates those around him.

"It's unforgettable for me," Hussain said. "My son was always trying to protect me. He would give some of his salary back to me. He loved working with the coalition forces and had a lot of friends in the MPs. I try to motivate the other AUP to work like my son and the other officers who were killed did in their honor."

Somehow, when I sat down to write this, I couldn't just do the typical news story—who, what, when, where. People read words, they read headlines, they get information or satisfy a curiosity, and then they forget. But these officers should not be forgotten. Both the Afghan Uniformed Police officers and the American military police officers will tell you, they embodied the standard of what an officer here should be.

Two Company E Soldiers re-enlist in Afghanistan

LAGHMAN PROVINCE, AFGHANISTAN, Feb. 26, 2011—U.S. Army Capt. Jodi Marti (left), from Knoxville, Iowa, and the commander of Company E, 1st Battalion, 133rd Infantry Regiment, Task Force Ironman [...] reads the oath of re-enlistment to U.S. Army Spc. Penny Herold (right), an all-wheeled vehicle mechanic from Waukon, Iowa, also with Company E, at Forward Operating Base Mehtar Lam. [...] (Photo By U.S. Army Staff Sgt. Ryan C. Matson, Task Force Red Bulls Public Affairs)

LAGHMAN PROVINCE, AFGHANISTAN—U.S. Army 1st Lt. Clint Holtz (right), from Walnut, Iowa and the executive officer of Company E, 1st Battalion, 133rd Infantry Regiment, Task Force Ironman, [...] reads the oath of re-enlistment to U.S. Army Sgt. Cassidy Howard (left), a truck driver from Milford, Iowa, with the 2168 Transportation Company, assigned to Company E, at Forward Operating Base Mehtar Lam, Feb. 26. [...] (Photo By U.S. Army Staff Sgt. Ryan C. Matson, Task Force Red Bulls Public Affairs)

Tip leads ANA, coalition to weapons cache in Paktya

By U.S. Army 1st Lt. Nicholas Rasmussen
Task Force Lethal

PAKTYA PROVINCE, Afghanistan, Feb. 27, 2011—Acting on a tip, members of the 3rd Company, 1st Kandak, 2nd Brigade, 203rd ANA Infantry Corps, Afghan National Army, alongside 2nd Platoon, Company C, 1st Battalion, 168th Infantry Regiment, Task Force Lethal, uncovered a cache of munitions in a house in Zormat District, Paktya Province.

The tip given to the ANA was generated by the Guardians of Peace program, which allows local villagers to anonymously call Afghan National Security Forces with information about suspicious activity.

Before going to the suspected cache site, 2nd Lt. Malcolm Baraibar, 2nd Platoon leader and native of Fort Dodge, Iowa; and Sgt. 1st Class Matthew Smith from Altoona, Iowa, and the platoon sergeant for 2nd Platoon, conducted joint mission planning with the ANA executive officer, 1st Lt. Hasim.

"We've been working on map reading with the ANA," said Smith. "So a lot of our focus was on planning the route."

When they arrived to the village of Menjawar, the ANA and coalition forces split into two elements.

Baraibar and several ANA soldiers met with the village elders and were very direct with their message.

"We seem to constantly find things that can harm your villagers, ANSF and coalition forces when we come here," Baraibar explained to the elders. He went on to encourage the villagers to use the Guardians of Peace program.

"We can't change what's in the village if we don't know what's happening," he told them.

The second element, lead by 1st Lt. Pallawanna, a platoon leader for the 3rd Company, and Smith, searched the home of the reported weapons cache.

After the ANA performed an initial sweep of the home, coalition forces were allowed in and scanned the interior of the home.

Their search uncovered several boxes of illegal ammunition, anti-personnel mines and other weapons.

The ANA gathered and catalogued all the evidence then questioned and detained two individuals who were brought to the ANA compound.

Acting on tips generated through the Guardians of Peace program during the last few weeks, Company C and the 3rd Company have been methodically and effectively clearing eastern Zormat of enemy weapons, an effort intended to keep violence to a minimum in the coming months.

62nd Medical Brigade visits Panjshir water bottle plant

PANJSHIR PROVINCE, Afghanistan, Feb. 27, 2011—U.S. Army Maj. Robert Paul (center), a Sioux Falls, S.D. native with the Cooperative Medical Assistance team, and his team tour the Panjshir Beverage Industry Ltd. water bottling plant's new equipment in Khenj District. Water the plant bottles is piped in from a natural spring about 4,000 meters from the facility. U.S. Army Master Sgt. Axel Torre, a Carolina, Puerto Rico native, with the 62nd Medical Brigade, U.S. Navy Lt. j.g. Ryan Aylsworth, a Stuart, Fla. Native, with the CMA team, and Paul inspected the re-modeled facility and advised the employees about international sanitation standards, operating procedures, lab schedules and testing. (Photo by U.S. Air Force Senior Airman Amber Ashcraft, Panjshir Provincial Reconstruction Team Public Affairs)

Service members, civilians celebrate Black History Month

BAGRAM AIRFIELD, Afghanistan, Feb. 27, 2011—The Elements of Soul jazz band perform at the Black History Month observance held on Bagram Airfield, while service members and civilians dance and sing to the music. The Enduring Faith Chapel Choir, the Enduring Faith Mime Team and guest speakers also joined the band on stage, to help those in attendance learn about and celebrate African American history. (Photo by U.S. Army Spc. James Wilton, Task Force Red Bulls Public Affairs)

By U.S. Army Spc. James Wilton
Task Force Red Bulls Public Affairs

BAGRAM AIRFIELD, Afghanistan, Feb. 27, 2011—Service members and civilians attended a Black History Month observance held by the 101st Airborne Division, Combined Joint Task Force 101, Equal Opportunity Commission, on Bagram Airfield.

The event was held to teach attendees about the accomplishments and personal courage of African Americans during the Civil War, which was this year's theme, and celebrate how their sacrifices have influenced African Americans in the military today.

"Events like this are so critical because it helps us remember the people that paved the way for folks like me," said U.S. Army Lt. Col. Robert Dummer, 359th Theater Signal Brigade judge advocate and key note speaker for the event. "During the Civil War I couldn't have been a commissioned officer. I am personally thankful for the sacrifices that those people made, so I could have the opportunities that I have today."

Musical acts, including the Elements of Soul jazz band and the Enduring Faith Chapel choir, brought people to their feet dancing and clapping along with the music. The Enduring Faith Chapel Mime Team preformed a piece to cap off the nights entertainment.

Drummer taught those in attendance about figures and battles during the war that may not have received much press but whose impact is still felt today. Soldiers and Airmen also read descriptions of key figures in African American history during the Civil War and asked the crowd, "Who Am I?".

"I was born a slave in 1839, in a slave cabin behind my master's house in Beaufort, South Carolina," said U.S. Army Sgt. Harold Dudley, from Des Moines, Iowa, with the 334th Brigade Support Battalion, Task Force Archer, a part of the 2nd Brigade Combat Team, 34th Infantry Division, Task Force Red Bulls. "As the American Civil War raged, I led a plot that stowed my family and several other slaves aboard the vessel. I and the other slaves were freed. After the war, I was granted a small fortune by Congress for my heroics, and purchased my former owner's home, where I opened a general store."

In that instant, the audience learned about Robert Smalls, who eventually joined the Union Navy and served as a ship pilot.

This event is one of many that the EO commission has planned for the year. The next event, in March, will focus on women's history.

Serving together in the Iowa National Guard: A family affair

By U.S. Army Capt. Adrian Sean Taylor
Task Force Archer

PARWAN PROVINCE, Afghanistan, Feb. 27, 2011—The National Guard has a long history of families serving together to strengthen their community and protect their country. There is no better example of this the family members deployed along with more than 2,800 Iowa Army National Guard Soldiers currently serving in Operation Enduring Freedom, the largest call-up of Iowa forces since World War II.

Among those family members are two brothers serving in two separate task forces in the 34th Infantry Division's 2nd Brigade Combat Team, Task Force Red Bulls, They met recently for a promotion ceremony.

"My brother called me and told me to come and promote him," said U.S. Army Sgt. 1st Class Garry Waldon Jr., of Des Moines, Iowa, and acting first sergeant for the Headquarters and Headquarters Company, 334th Brigade Support Battalion, Task Force Archer, serving at Bagram Airfield. "He's my younger brother. I wouldn't pass that up."

Waldon travelled to Combat Outpost Pul-e-Sayad to promote his brother U.S. Army Sgt. Brandon Corbett, also of Des Moines, Iowa, and a truck commander with Troop A, 1st Squadron, 113th Cavalry Regiment, Task Force Redhorse.

"It helps to have a family member in the Guard," said Waldon. "Although my brother and I have very different jobs, we understand each other. He stops by my office when he is passing through Bagram and uses me to vent."

Family members serving together in the Iowa National Guard seem to be a tradition within the Red Bulls division.

"Sometimes you hear about family members serving together in active duty units, but it is not common," said U.S. Army Col. Benjamin J. Corell, the Task Force Red Bulls commander from Strawberry Point, Iowa. "In the Guard we are responsible for recruiting and we tend to look to family, friends and neighbors."

"Recruiting in the National Guard was not always at 100 percent, like it is today," continued Corell. "I remember when my brigade commander Brig. Gen. Michael Beaman told us to go out and find recruits. He suggested finding people we would feel comfortable going to war with. You are comfortable with your friends and family. In the smaller Iowan communities, service becomes a community tradition."

Even the brigade commander's family follows that tradition. Corell's three sons are all staff sergeants in the Iowa Guard and all served together with their father in 2003 in Sinai.

Corell is currently serving with one of his sons, U.S. Army Staff Sgt. Wade Corell, of Denver, Iowa, and a medical platoon sergeant with a part of the brigade based out of Laghman Province.

Although having multiple family members serving overseas may increase the anxiety of family back home, it gives the deployed Soldiers someone to rely on.

"There are advantages to serving with your sons, although it increases the potential for something bad happening in the family," said Corell. "I have had the opportunity to spend Thanksgiving and Christmas with my sons overseas, and not everyone can do that here."

It's not just fathers, sons, and brothers either. U.S. Army Staff Sgt. Darla Sward of Boone, Iowa, and the maintenance Non-Commissioned Officer-in-Charge of support operations for Task Force Archer, has a very unique situation. She is serving with her son-in-law, U.S. Army Spc. Gabe Lanz, of Des Moines, Iowa, a gunner with Troop B, Task Force Redhorse.

"I like being able to see my son-in-law," said Sward. "We go to lunch together when we can. I even got to go shopping with him once to buy things for my daughter."

For Soldiers who don't have family members serving with them, they still have their squad members there acting as family and bonding just the same. But in almost every unit, one will find brothers and sisters, parents and children, husbands and wives, cousins and friends in the National Guard to serve their communities and serve their nation, together.

MARCH
2011

Task Force Red Bulls donates back packs to Bagram Girls' School

PARWAN PROVINCE, Afghanistan, March 1, 2011—U.S. Army 2nd Lt. Andrew Smith (front) of Iowa City, Iowa, and 3rd Platoon leader, and U.S. Army 1st Sgt. Douglas Wilkens (back) of Hawarden, Iowa, unit first sergeant, both of Troop B, 1st Squadron, 113th Cavalry Regiment, Task Force Redhorse, of the 2nd Brigade Combat Team, 34th Infantry Division, Task Force Red Bulls, give back packs to the young afghan girls of the Bagram Girls' School during a humanitarian assistance delivery, March 1. Soldiers of Troop B donated 500 back packs and 250 radios to the girls school five days before the start of a new school year. (Photo by U.S. Army Spc. Kristina L. Gupton, Task Force Red Bulls Public Affairs)

Dropping In: Company B mortarmen hone skills at Torkham Gate

NANGARHAR PROVINCE, Afghanistan, March 3, 2011—U.S. Army Sgt. Dusty Rhoades (left), a mortarman from Stanley, Iowa, and Spc. Abraham Saleh, a mortarman from Williamsburg, Iowa, both of Company B, 1st Battalion, 133rd Infantry Regiment, relay information from a forward observer on a target to the mortar pit firers at Forward Operating Base Torkham Gate, Afghanistan. The mortars soldiers were practicing registering rounds at Torkham Gate. (Photo by U.S. Army Staff Sgt. Ryan C. Matson, Task Force Red Bulls Public Affairs)

NANGARHAR PROVINCE, Afghanistan, March 3, 2011—U.S. Army Spc. Lance Weiskamp, left, a mortarman from Washburn, Iowa, hangs a mortar round while U.S. Army Staff Sgt. William Mathias, a mortarman from Fairfield, Iowa, both of Company B, 1st Battalion, 133rd Infantry Regiment, looks on at Forward Operating Base Torkham Gate, Afghanistan. The mortars soldiers were practicing registering rounds at Torkham Gate. (Photo by U.S. Army Staff Sgt. Ryan C. Matson, Task Force Red Bulls Public Affairs)

Mail distribution center gets an overhaul

By U.S. Army Spc. Michael Vanpool
101st Sustainment Brigade, 101st Airborne Division Public Affairs

BAGRAM AIRFIELD, Afghanistan, March 3, 2011—Cell phones and the internet offer instant communication across the world, but they cannot replace the simple smile on a soldier's face when a letter or package comes from home.

Recent severe weather created problems for the 90th Human Resources Company, as they moved operations to a new location and battled floodwater from recent rain and snow that threatened to ruin thousands of pounds of mail and packages.

The 90th HR Company recently moved the Bagram Regional Mail Distribution Center to a new location on Bagram Airfield in late January, just a few weeks before. The center processes all mail coming into Afghanistan destined for Regional Commands North, East, Central and West.

It's also located on the one of bases' lower terrain points. Weeks after the move, Afghanistan's infamous winter erupted, hitting BAF with rain and snow. After it subsided, the center was flooded with about six inches of water from the rain and melting snow, which threatened to ruin the mail.

"We had to protect the mail and get the tent fixed," said Maj. Richard Strong, 90th HR Company commander.

The company called in reinforcements to take on the flooding. The 101st Sustainment Brigade, the 90th HR Company's higher headquarters, pulled their resources and gathered additional help.

Task Force Red Bulls, in charge of base operations for Bagram, along with U.S. Air Force civil engineers, extended their assistance to raise the floor of the RDMC to prevent future flooding, said Sgt. 1st Class Phillip Schaffer, brigade plans section Non-Commissioned Officer-in-Charge.

The teams worked together to lay a new floor under the LAMS-A tent of the RMDC. A LAMS-A tent, or large area maintenance shelter-aviation, is a quick-to-erect, deployable maintenance shelter systems for military equipment.

"They're placing big rocks for a solid foundation, with smaller rocks to fill in the holes," Schafer said. "A mat will be placed over the combination of rocks to prevent future flooding of mail operations., Task Force Red Bulls offered their street contractors, consisting of local day workers, to assist with the project "This is something that doesn't happen too often," Schafer said, "The road crew came on the flight line."

The 455th Civil Engineer Squadron built a drainage ditch alongside the RMDC to collect water away from the mail inside, said Air Force Master Sgt. Joe Buck, a heavy equipment journeyman for the 455th CES. The Air Force also helped the local contractors level out the ground with rocks, dirt and sand. We're helping make it better instead of water getting in to the boxes," Buck said.

The stable floor will combat the risk of flooding and provide solid ground for the heavy equipment and massive loads of mail processed daily. "With the ground muddy and wet, we couldn't drive forklifts to move the mail," Strong said.

The 101st Sustainment Brigade oversaw and organized overhauling the flooring, and arranged all the team to work together. "It took quite a bit of coordination between the brigade headquarters, base operations and the Air Force to pull all this together," Shafer said.

Mail operations moved to higher ground during the renovation of the floor. The RMDC continues its mission by sorting and preparing all mail for outward movement if the mail goes to another FOB. "They'll put all Shank mail together or all Jalalabad mail together and palletize it for an aircraft or prepared for a truck," Strong said.

Multinational team trains ANP

BAGRAM AIRFIELD, Afghanistan, March 1, 2011—U.S. Army Spc. Richard Hansen (standing, left), a military police officer with the MP platoon attached to Headquarters and Headquarters Troop, 1st Squadron, 113th Cavalry Regiment, Task Force Redhorse, from Sioux City, Iowa, instructs as the Afghan National Police recruits learn basic marksmanship skills as part of a Joint Police Mentor Training with the Korean Provincial Reconstruction Team, at Bagram Airfield. Task Force Redhorse and the Korean PRT are a part of the 34th Infantry Division's 2nd Brigade Combat Team, Task Force Red Bulls. (Photo by U.S. Army Sgt. Ross Kriegel)

By Second Lt. Brian TeKippe
Task Force Redhorse

BAGRAM AIRFIELD, Afghanistan, March 3, 2011—The automatic rifle fire echoed across the range at Bagram Airfield recently. It was not the familiar pop from an M4 rifle, but a deeper thud of Afghan National Police AK-47 rifles during a culminating event of a two-week training course held by coalition forces. Feb. 19–March 3.

At the end of the course, U.S. Army soldiers from the military police platoon attached to Headquarters and Headquarters Troop, 1st Squadron, 113th Cavalry Regiment, Task Force Redhorse took a group of 18 Afghan National Police to the range for instruction on safety and marksmanship.

"We've seen remarkable improvement from our students in their confidence, understanding of law enforcement duties and tactical proficiency," said U.S. Army Spc. Richard Hansen, an instructor from the MP platoon from South Sioux City, Neb.

During the two-week course, the group of 15 Afghan patrolmen and three officers received instruction on law enforcement duties in a combined effort between the U.S. MP platoon and a Korean Provincial Reconstruction Team

Police Training Team at Bagram Airfield. Task Force Redhorse and the Korean PRT are a part of the 34th Infantry Division's 2nd Brigade Combat Team, Task Force Red Bulls.

The MP platoon gave instruction on weapons training, small-group tactics, and police survival skills to assist the group of ANP to better protect their province from the threats it currently faces. In addition, the Korean team, made up of 10 instructors from the Korean Federal Law Enforcement Academy, provided daily instruction on police ethics, Afghan law and unarmed self-defense among other classes.

Working across cultural barriers and three languages proved to be a daily challenge, according to course instructors, but with the support of many different groups the students were provided with a great training experience.

"So long as everyone wants the same outcome, a stronger Afghan Police force, any obstacle can be overcome,," said U.S. Army Sgt. Ross Kriegel, an MP instructor from Greene, Iowa.

Due to the success of the first class, a second course has been scheduled with an increase in class size and duration. The new, three-week format will allow for an expansion of weapon-handling exercises, incorporation of law enforcement criminal response procedures and exercises in crowd control techniques.

BAGRAM AIRFIELD, Feb. 22, 2011—A Korean Provincial Reconstruction Team instructor teaches Afghan National Police recruits unarmed self-defense during the Joint Police Mentor Training class with the military police platoon attached to Headquarters and Headquarters Troop, 1st Squadron, 113th Cavalry Regiment, Task Force Redhorse, on Bagram Airfield. [...] (Photo by U.S. Army 2nd Lt. Brian TeKippe, Task Force Redhorse)

Panjshir sheep parasite project continues

PANJSHIR PROVINCE, Afghanistan, March 5, 2011—U.S. Army Staff Sgt. Joshua Hancock, assistant Panjshir agricultural lead, Kentucky Agribusiness Development Team II and Monticello, Ky., native, examines a sheep in Khenj District. The Kentucky ADT II examined more than 120 pregnant sheep in three districts and has a seminar planned for April to teach farmers and herders how to use the results to better the health of their flocks. (Photo by U.S. Air Force Senior Airman Amber Ashcraft, Panjshir Provincial Reconstruction Team Public Affairs)

By U.S. Air Force Senior Airman Amber Ashcraft
Panjshir Provincial Reconstruction Team Public Affairs

PANJSHIR PROVINCE, Afghanistan, March 5, 2011—No matter what area of Afghanistan traveled, flocks of sheep and livestock are seen grazing, walking the roads and moving on mountain sides. Agriculture is a key aspect of the country, and with this in mind, U.S. military Agribusiness Development Teams throughout Afghanistan are designated to train and assist the country's veterinarians and farmers.

After months of preparation, the Kentucky Agribusiness Development Team II, a tenant unit with the Panjshir Provincial Reconstruction Team, began a parasite sheep project in Anaba District in early February, continuing on into Rokha and Khenj Districts.

"No matter where the animals are, here, or in the U.S., keeping a good study of flocks of sheep will allow us to determine the correct treatments and keep a better record of the benefits reaped from the treatment," said U.S. Army Staff Sgt. Joshua Hancock, assistant Panjshir agricultural lead for Kentucky ADT II.

The Kentucky ADT tagged, weighed, physically examined and collected feces samples from approximately 120 pregnant sheep throughout the province. Half of the controlled sheep were given fluke and de-wormer to treat and control both gastro-intestinal and pulmonary infections.

"De-worming ewes two to three weeks before lambing is an effective way to reduce transmission of parasites to the lambs," said Hancock, Monticello, Ky., native. "They're in better condition at lambing and produce more milk."

After visiting each district, the team immediately sent the feces samples to the Bagram Airfield lab, where a partner veterinarian examined and determined the type and how many parasite eggs were present in the pregnant sheep. Ten days after the initial visit, ADT members returned to the districts for another examination.

"It's a very productive project for the farmers of Afghanistan," said Afghan Dr. Noor Ali, a Panjshir veterinarian. "The data collected will allow us to show the Panjshir farmers that de-worming their sheep is one of the easiest ways to keep their sheep healthy."

Internal parasites are a threat to sheep health and productivity, added Hancock.

"The parasites cause the loss of large quantities of blood and protein, which results in weakness and anemia," Hancock said. "We use the FAMACHA score card on the eyelids to determine the level of infection. Even if the sheep have a good body score and appear healthy, the build-up of the number of parasites may cause the sheep to lose blood and become very sick."

The Kentucky ADT II began the project showing the veterinarians and farmers how to examine and de-worm their sheep. In the end, the veterinarians and farmers learned to care for the health of the flock on their own.

"Just as every other project we help with in Afghanistan, we want the Afghans to continue to progress on their own," Hancock said.

On April 5 and 6, U.S. Army Col. James G. Floyd, Kentucky ADT II veterinarian, and Shreveport, La., native, is scheduled to hold a discussion on the project's results. Floyd will explain the data generated and the practical payoff from the project to the veterinarians, district extension agents, farmers and herders involved in the project.

Floyd will explain the next steps to using the scientific data collected and also have an open lab about the procedures for finding the results from the fecal samples that were sent to the Bagram Airfield lab.

"Showing the Afghans the results and how we keep records will be a major benefit," Hancock said. "They'll be able to keep track of their flock's health and history much better than before, hopefully taking to heart the benefits of this project."

Soldier improves his home away from home–
Torkham Gate

NANGARHAR PROVINCE, Afghanistan, March 5, 2011—U.S. Army Sgt. Christian Kapler, an infantryman from Oelwein, Iowa, from Company B, 1st Battalion, 133rd Infantry Regiment, talks on a cell phone with his interpreter at Forward Operating Base Torkham Gate. Kapler stays in constant communication with his interpreter for updates on construction projects at the FOB. The Iowa National Guard Soldier and civilian carpenter's work is evident everywhere one sets foot on Torkham Gate. (Photo by U.S. Army Staff Sgt. Ryan C. Matson, Task Force Red Bulls Public Affairs)

By U.S. Army Staff Sgt. Ryan C. Matson
Task Force Red Bulls Public Affairs

NANGARHAR PROVINCE, Afghanistan, March 5, 2011—U.S. Army Sgt. Christian Kapler is a busy man. Anywhere people walk on Forward Operating Base Torkham Gate on the Afghanistan and Pakistan border, they will see something Kapler built, repaired, or improved.

"My dad would say it's genetics," said Kapler, a burly, soft-spoken infantryman from Oelwein, Iowa, with Company B, 1st Battalion, 133rd Infantry Regiment serving as the FOB manager. "My grandfather had a little shop and built everything he had—his house and all. I don't know what he actually did for a job other than build things."

Like his grandfather, Kapler said he enjoys working with his hands.

"I was always tinkering and building things when I was a kid, going to the lumber yard and getting scrap wood and building stuff. I did handyman stuff when I was older, and started going to school at a community college for architecture and contracting, but I kept getting deployed, so I never finished college. I think the unit knows building stuff is the type of thing I excel at."

Torkham Gate has been home to Company B, part of the Iowa National Guard's 2nd Brigade Combat Team, 34th Infantry Division, Task Force Red Bulls, since October, and the base is expanding. Kapler, who supervises 44 Afghan workers of various trades and abilities, is tasked with improving the base.

Kapler said he appreciates the work his crew does, despite what at times is a challenging process of getting supplies and proper tools. He said when his team wants to get something done, they do it quickly.

His company commander, U.S. Army Capt. Kevin Hrodey, from Pleasant Hill, Iowa, said he is impressed with Kapler's accomplishments.

"It is amazing to look at pictures of the FOB from when we first took over operations and then walk around now and see how much it has actually changed," said Hrodey. "It is almost like we are not even in the same place anymore. At the rate Sgt. Kapler is improving this FOB, by the time we go to leave, we'll be leaving a small city instead of a small, remote FOB."

According to Hrodey, people can see the products of Kapler's efforts everywhere they look. His projects have improved all aspects of life on the FOB, from base defense to quality of life to his worker's maintenance facility.

One repair that took some innovation was Kapler's upgrade to the FOB firing range. Before he and his crew got their hands on it, the range was a berm, surrounded by sand-basket barriers, with some old, neglected targets and a few stakes in the ground that marked the distance.

"We use the cardboard from water pallets as target backing," Kapler said.

The older targets were fixed and Kapler's crew installed conduit so targets could be easily replaced once they start deteriorating. He used unserviceable dining facility tables as firing benches, weapons racks, new metal distance markers, a reinforced berm and a camouflage net awning to provide shade.

A 15-year-veteran of the Iowa National Guard, Kapler deployed to Saudi Arabia, Egypt, and Iraq with Company B, and now here to Afghanistan.

He worked construction in Cedar Rapids, Iowa, before becoming a union carpenter. Between deployments, Kapler married an Oelwein, Iowa, woman, and is the proud father of three children. He said he plans to start a tool-rental business when he returns to Iowa, and his wife is taking accounting classes so she can help run the administrative side of the business.

Until he returns, he'll continue his work in Afghanistan.

Top Iowa marksmen train fellow Red Bulls, Afghans at Torkham Gate

NANGARHAR PROVINCE, Afghanistan, March 6, 2011—U.S. Army Pfc. Chris Vega (left), a forward observer from Mason City, Iowa, with the 34th Infantry Division's 2nd Brigade Combat Team in Company B, 1st Battalion, 133rd Infantry Regiment, demonstrates proper shooting stance while U.S. Army Sgt. Martin Ennor (right), an infantry team leader who also serves as his unit's director of marksmanship from Parkersburg, Iowa, also of Company B, instructs a marksmanship class at the range at Forward Operating Base Torkham Gate, Afghanistan. (Photo by U.S. Army Staff Sgt. Ryan C. Matson, Task Force Red Bulls Public Affairs)

By U.S. Army Staff Sgt. Ryan C. Matson
Task Force Red Bulls Public Affairs

NANGARHAR PROVINCE, Afghanistan, March 6, 2011—Two of Iowa's top guns are working with their fellow Soldiers and Afghan counterparts to improve their tactical marksmanship abilities during their yearlong deployment to Afghanistan at Forward Operating Base Torkham Gate.

U.S. Army Sgt. Martin Ennor, an infantry team leader and his unit's director of marksmanship, and U.S. Army Staff Sgt. Jacob Downs, a supply sergeant and weapons instructor, have both won the Governor's 10 Shooting Competition, an annual competition in which military shooters from the Army and Air National Guard, as well as the Army Reserve, compete to determine the 10 best military shooters in the state.

Ennor, from Parkersburg, Iowa, took the top prize in 2008. Downs, from Tipton, Iowa, did the same in last year's competition. Now, the two Soldiers from Company B, 1st Battalion, 133rd Infantry Regiment, 2nd Brigade Combat Team, 34th Infantry Division, Task Force Red Bulls, are working to spread their shooting skills and expertise to other members of the company.

"I like watching the development of each person we train, from where they start out to where they are now," Downs said. "To me it makes me feel they'll be safer when they go outside the wire."

The Soldiers all volunteered for the training, which is usually conducted on their day off, and said the tips Ennor and Downs have shared with them have paid huge dividends in their personal marksmanship abilities.

"It's definitely at least doubled my accuracy and I feel more confident that, if we take contact, I know what to do from running the drills," said U.S. Army Pfc. Richard Reichardt, an infantryman with Company B who has been participating in training sessions led by Ennor and Downs. "I've learned more in two months about shooting from them—the mechanics—than I have in the four years I've been in the military. Plus, you can't beat free training!"

Ennor said he and Downs have both been shooting since childhood, having begun in "the average Iowa family hunter kind of way." They both said shooting calms them down, and helps them to relieve stress.

Neither marksman began shooting with competition in mind. Ennor said his interest peaked in 2007, when he was returning from a 22-month deployment to Iraq.

"What really got me into shooting was being a teacher," he said. "A lot of people say that the best way to learn something is to teach it. You have your shooters, your teachers and your shooters/teachers, the guys who can walk the walk and show people things do work and how they're done."

Ennor, 25, said after returning from Iraq, he was at the demobilization station in Fort McCoy, Wis., when a Small-Arms Readiness Group (SARG) recruiting team was looking for new members. The team trains marksmanship skills to Soldiers about to mobilize. Ennor, who obviously loved shooting and met the recruiter's standard of having consistent high qualification marks at the range, jumped at the chance.

"It was the opportunity to learn something new and get better," Ennor said. "So I signed the paperwork and was off to Fort Bragg two weeks after that. They re-taught me how to shoot, completely revamped everything I had known and made me a better shooter."

With the SARG training, Ennor earned several certifications through the National Rifle Association. He taught students and worked constantly to improve his schools. His SARG team entered the All-Army Shooting Competition in 2008, a month after Ennor had completed SARG school, and won the overall contest in both the pistol and rifle categories. He also completed numerous civilian and military marksmanship training courses.

Ennor said the SARG experience deepened his already intense interest in shooting.

"After (SARG), I knew that working a desk job as a civilian just wasn't going to work for me," Ennor said.

Instead, Ennor decided to completely devote his life to marksmanship training, and started his own business as a personal instructor. In the civilian sector, he now earns his living providing instruction for various military, law enforcement, and civilian clients. It is a passion he shares with his wife, Whitney, who is a female firearms instructor and nursing student in Iowa.

Downs, meanwhile, started as an infantry Soldier and said he just always enjoyed shooting and training. He said his interest in shooting deepened when he decided to try to compete for the Governor's 10, and has grown from there.

"I'm more of a shooter than an instructor," Downs said. "So my training is more 'do as I do.' I can show someone an example of how I shoot, and teach them that way."

This has come in handy when the pair has taught Afghan students here, as well. Ennor said that Downs is the more patient of the two, which is why Downs has had exceptional success teaching the Afghan Security Group members, who also man the gate with Company B. His patience and examples are often able to compensate for a lack of ability to communicate fully.

The instructors said they gear their training here toward combat scenarios. Downs said he and Ennor work on various positions beyond the standard prone, kneeling and standing military firing positions.

"We cover things like the urban prone position, which is basically laying on your side, switching hands and shooting under or over an object, the supine position (shooting from one's back behind cover), as well as various movement and box drills," Downs said. "We also focus a lot on communicating while moving and clearing malfunctions with concise movements."

Ennor said a lot of the drills came from his SARG training as well as from training he and Downs have had throughout their careers.

"A lot of people will get up there and say this is what you have to do because the Army has always trained it this way," Ennor said. "But we not only show Soldiers what to do, we show them why. They start utilizing techniques and get good at it, and see that it works."

"And we're not pressing just one way of doing things, because people have different body types and therefore need to manipulate the weapon the way that works best for them. We're saying, 'you do what works for you 95 percent of the time, in a way that's the most efficient, with the least amount of excessive wasted movement.'"

Downs, 29, said the training they provide is open to any Soldier in any job. In fact, he said some of the Soldiers who shoot the best are those who have not shot very often, because they have less bad habits to break.

"If you come in bull-headed, you're not going to learn anything," Downs said. "You have to come in being open to learning new things."

Ennor said the instructors work with their students on various drills until each one becomes instinctive.

"We don't do this to teach people to qualify on an Army range and to zero," he said. "We do this to teach people lifesaving skills for them to survive in combat. It's almost primal for them now. These things are engrained into their body and their minds. When they are able to perform these skills under stress, under a time-is-life situation, that's when you know that it's been trained to proficiency. It's not something they can learn from a book or a movie or an instructor. They just have to do it until it is completely engrained in their minds."

When Ennor won the Governor's 10 competition in 2008, the competition was set up differently than when Downs won it last year. In 2008, the top five pistol shooters and the top five rifle shooters earned the right to wear the prestigious Governor's 10 tab on their military uniforms. Now, the rifle and pistol scores are combined, so only the best 10 overall shooters earn the tab.

When asked who is the better shot, both Soldiers laughed.

"We don't even know," Ennor said. "We both have our individual strengths and weaknesses."

"And we don't want to find out, either," Downs added, smiling. "We'd be out there shooting for a week!"

Luckily, the two won't have to endure that competition. Instead they said they'll continue to focus on working as a team—a team whose sole goal is to make their fellow Soldiers the best shooters possible.

Red Bulls Soldiers help protect Afghanistan border

NANGARHAR PROVINCE, Afghanistan, March 7, 2011—An Afghan Border Police officer search a bag in a boy's wheelbarrow on the pedestrian walkway at Torkham Gate on the Afghanistan border. (Photo by U.S. Army Staff Sgt. Ryan C. Matson, Task Force Red Bulls Public Affairs)

By U.S. Army Staff Sgt. Ryan C. Matson
Task Force Red Bulls Public Affairs

NANGARHAR PROVINCE, Afghanistan, March 7, 2011—The scene at Torkham Gate in eastern Afghanistan the morning of March 7 was comparable to that of a city at rush hour in the United States.

Dozens of small cars were intermixed in a long line of heavily-decorated, colorful jingle trucks that stretched about a mile from the zero line --the border between Afghanistan and Pakistan.

In the middle of the traffic, a handful of Soldiers from the Iowa National Guard's 2nd Brigade Combat Team, 34th Infantry Division, Task Force Red Bulls. The Soldiers, from Company B, 1st Battalion, 133rd Infantry Regiment, were helping the Afghan Border Police , Afghan Customs Police, and the National Directorate of Security, keep order at the gate.

Though the infantry Soldiers may not be participating in the ground-pounding, door-kicking missions they envisioned for the deployment, they appreciate the mission.

"I enjoy working with the Afghan forces," said U.S. Army Sgt. Casey Ketelson, an infantry team leader from Osage, Iowa, with Company B, 1-133rd Inf.

He said by working closely with NDS, the Afghan intelligence force, the Soldiers can use the information they collect to catch insurgent traffickers and other wanted persons should they try to sneak through. The Afghan agencies help the Soldiers identify certain types of vehicles and people that could be harboring illegal or dangerous items.

About 10,000 people and 1,000 to 2,000 vehicles cross the border between Afghanistan and Pakistan daily at Torkham Gate. Everything from trucks loaded with hundreds of chickens, to people carrying dead relatives who wanted to be buried on the other side of the border, travel through the gate.

Company B's Soldiers help manage the traffic by assisting in various capacities at the gate from security over watch to biometrics collection to vehicle security.

Soldiers help their Afghan counterparts direct vehicles through the checkpoint and randomly select vehicles to be searched to ensure are not carrying contraband or other dangerous materials into the country.

In addition to watching the vehicles, the Soldiers watch the pedestrians and ensure they don't walk into vehicle traffic.

"We try to get pedestrians out of the vehicle routes, or else they plug up traffic and we can't get much accomplished," said U.S. Army Sgt. 1st Class Thomas Boge, an infantry squad leader and the day's sergeant of the guard for Company B, 1-133rd Inf., and an Allison, Iowa, native.

Soldiers working with ABP, also monitor the pedestrian walkway, from both overhead observation posts afoot.

U.S. Army Spc. Chris Linssen, an infantryman from Cedar Rapids, Iowa, said Soldiers provided extra security by having an overhead vantage point.

"We'll watch the (pedestrians) coming in for anything that stands out or doesn't look right," Linssen said.

In addition to physical security, Soldiers collect biometric information on people transiting the border.

U.S. Army Spc. Nathan Valentine is the company's resident expert on collecting biometric information.

"This is the only job I've ever done here," Valentine said. "Other platoons may enter a higher number of people into the system, but we're more selective about the types of people we enter."

He said the Soldiers work closely with their Afghan counterparts when choosing individuals to enter into the system.

To aid in security, the Afghan government is implementing a national identification card and fingerprinting system, which is also being conducted at the gate.

The Soldiers said their biggest obstacle is dealing with the monotony of the job. After a week at the gate they switch to another duty, such as forward operating base defense, for a week. "We try to rotate the Soldiers out between stations to keep them fresh," Ketelson said.

Linssen said people from many countries, not just Afghanistan and

Pakistan, cross the gate with a variety of items. He said the line begins forming before the gate is open.

"At 6 a.m. there will be people crowding on the Pakistan side of the border like they're waiting in line at Walmart on Black Friday," Linssen said.

The Soldiers said they have found items on people entering the gate such as hashish, improperly packaged food goods or items that people haven't paid taxes on. When items like those are found, the ACP seizes them.

The Soldiers said they are not fooling themselves to think they are catching all the contraband coming through the gate. After all, the gate is not the only way to enter the country, simply the most convenient. But they said they do know that every piece of contraband or person they do get could potentially mean a life saved somewhere in the country.

Besides the reward of helping to secure the gate, the Soldiers said there are other perks to working at Torkham Gate. For U.S. Army Spc. Michael Stuart, an infantryman from Anamosa, Iowa, it is getting to sample some of the Afghan food sold by the many vendors in the area.

"This is definitely a perk. The food is great here," Stuart said with a smile as he loaded some lamb, rice and a piece of pan bread onto a plate for lunch.

NANGARHAR PROVINCE, Afghanistan, March 7, 2011—U.S. Army Spc. John Meyer (left), from Iowa City, Iowa, and Spc. Chris Linssen (center), from Cedar Rapids, Iowa, both infantrymen with Company B, 1st Battalion, 133rd Infantry Regiment, 2nd Brigade Combat Team, 34th Infantry Division, Task Force Red Bulls, watch the pedestrian walkway with an Afghan Border Police dog handler (right), at Torkham Gate on the Afghanistan borde. (Photo by U.S. Army Staff Sgt. Ryan C. Matson, Task Force Red Bulls Public Affairs)

80 Afghans begin Korean Vo-tech program

PARWAN PROVINCE, Afghanistan, March 7, 2011—Abdul Basir Salangi, governor of Parwan, speaks to 80 men from Parwan, Kapisa, and Panjshir provinces, Afghanistan, during a ceremony to mark the beginning of their training at the Korean Vocational Training Center on Bagram Airfield. They are the second group to attend the center. The first class had 85 members, 80 of which are currently working on Bagram or in Kabul, Afghanistan. (Photo by U.S. Army Spc. James Wilton, Task Force Red Bulls Public Affairs)

By U.S. Army Spc. James Wilton
Task Force Red Bulls Public Affairs

PARWAN PROVINCE, Afghanistan, March 7, 2011—Eighty Afghan men from Kapisa, Parwan, and Panjshir provinces began the second class at the Korean Vocational Training Center on Bagram Airfield.

The center is funded by the Korean International Cooperation Agency and run in partnership with the Republic of Korea Provincial Reconstruction Team. The center teaches Afghan citizens skills needed for jobs in technical vocational fields. The courses offered at the school include automotive maintenance, construction, electricity, welding and computer. All classes include basic English langue instruction.

"I hope to learn something here, and after that, I will help the people of Afghanistan and my family," said Arab Jan, a student in the computer class at the KVTC. "We passed our exam. Now I want to finish at the school and go get a job."

The KVTC staff also helps graduates find jobs. All 85 students from the first class found employment; 80 are working on Bagram Airfield or in Kabul, Afghanistan, and the other five are instructors with the school.

To study at the center, students must pass an entrance exam to show they have the basic skills and knowledge needed to attend the courses.

"I challenge each of you to stand up and be worthy of the opportunity you have been given," said U.S. Army Col. Benjamin J. Corell, a Strawberry Point, Iowa, native, and commander of 2nd Brigade Combat Team, 34th Infantry Division, Task Force Red Bulls, and a guest speaker at the event. "While many would like to have the opportunity to study and learn a trade here, only a few have been chosen. You...have been given a great opportunity to better yourselves, your families and your country. What you do with this opportunity is up to you."

The KVTC's mission is to provide the training and experience Afghans need to rebuild their infrastructure, support their families and thereby help the people of Afghanistan to improve their future.

"Dear students, you are the future of Afghanistan," said Adbdul Basir Salangi, Parwan Province governor. "Korea and America started out as struggling countries just like Afghanistan, and now they are helping us and our future. These countries are developed now because of their education -- this is the education that you are going to get here. If we try our best then we can develop our country."

Corell said Afghanistan can prosper through programs the KVTC offers.

"What happens here is vitally important to the future of Afghanistan," said Corell. "To truly rebuild this country takes programs and institutions like this, and who better to know and understand this, than the Korean people who themselves had to rebuild their country after a debilitating and destructive conflict. This is how you rebuild a country – one person at a time."

There are many lessons the Koreans can share with the new students including one that Salangi used in his speech.

"To come into this world poor is not our fault, but to go from it poor is our fault," quoted Salangi from a Korean scholar.

Afghan women celebrate a day of their own

PAKTYA PROVINCE, Afghanistan, March 8, 2011—Women and children attend the 2011 Women's Day celebration in Gardez City. Approximately 150 women attended the celebration at the Gardez Municipal Building. (Photo by U.S. Air Force Staff Sgt. Barry Loo, Paktya Provincial Reconstruction Team Public Affairs)

By U.S. Air Force 1st Lt. Sybil Taunton
Paktya Provincial Reconstruction Team Public Affairs

PAKTYA PROVINCE, Afghanistan, March 8, 2011—Officials from the Islamic Republic of Afghanistan highlighted the importance of human rights, education and healthcare during a Women's Day celebration at the municipal building in Gardez.

More than 150 women from the Gardez area, along with delegates from Kabul, including the acting Minister of Public Health, Dr. Suraya Dalil, joined provincial government officials for the ceremony.

Representatives from the Paktya Provincial Reconstruction Team, the 245th Agribusiness Development Team and U.S. Assistance for International Development also attended the ceremony. Halima Kazhan, the Paktya Director of Women's Affairs, started the ceremony by discussing the steady progress that women have been making in the province.

"More women and girls are going to school," said Kazhan. "And more women are getting out of their houses."

A representative from the local Human Rights Commission, Yousaf Malatar, gave a speech about the history of women's rights throughout the world, specifically focusing on Paktya Province.

"In 1975, the United Nations approved women's freedom in Afghanistan," said Malatar. "Then 10 years ago there was nothing for women because of the Taliban."

Dr. Nadir Noori, the Paktya Director of Public Health followed Malatar and discussed the historical significance of women in Islam.

"If we look to the holy Quran, men and women are the same," said Noori.

A group from the Gardez City Girls School performed songs, speakers recited poems delivered several more speeches on the importance of education and better healthcare for the women and girls in the province.

The Religion and Culture Advisor commander for the 203rd ANA Infantry Corps, Col. Waqeb Shah, addressed misconceptions about the treatment of women within the Muslim faith. He then looked into the crowd of women and offered them some words of advice.

"People who think of women as property are not Muslims," said Shah. "Do not look to the men to give you something—take it!"

10th International Women's Day Celebration

BAGRAM AIRFIELD, Afghanistan, March 8, 2011—Service members of Task Force Med-East located on Bagram Airfield at Craig Joint Theater Hospital and Egyptian Col. Tarek Eid, commander of the Egyptian hospital discuss patients in conjunction with a International Women's Day celebrate here. Eid estimated they see 250 to 300 patients each day. The Egyptian hospital has been open for services to surrounding villages since 2003. (Photo by U.S. Army Spc. Kristina L. Gupton, Task Force Red Bulls Public Affairs)

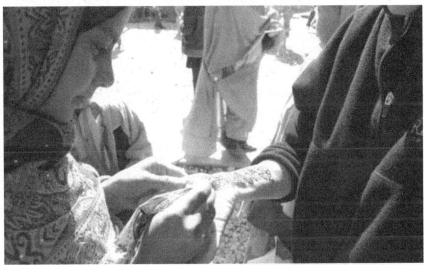

BAGRAM AIRFIELD, Afghanistan, March 8, 2011—A young Afghan girl uses henna to decorate the wrist of one of the many visitors at the Egyptian hospital here on International Women's Day. Afghanistan women have been celebrating womanhood and their rights since the fall of the Taliban in 2001. Women across the world celebrate in honor of mothers, sisters and daughters. (Photo by U.S. Army Spc. Kristina L. Gupton, Task Force Red Bulls Public Affairs)

Panjshir ANP first to receive 30-ton wrecker

PANJSHIR PROVINCE, Afghanistan, March 9, 2011—An Afghan National Police officer directs another ANP officer to move the crane so they can hook it to a Humvee during training on a 30-ton wrecker taught by U.S. Air Force Senior Airman Darin Pugh, Tacoma, Wash., native, and Staff Sgt. Michael Lamonte, Burlington, Conn., native, Panjshir Provincial Reconstruction Team vehicle operators. Panjshir Province was the first to acquire one of ten 30-ton wrecker vehicles that will be issued to Afghan National Security Forces throughout Afghanistan. (Photo by U.S. Air Force Senior Airman Amber Ashcraft, Panjshir Provincial Reconstruction Team Public Affairs)

By U.S. Air Force 2nd Lt. Ashleigh Peck
Panjshir Provincial Reconstruction Team Public Affairs

PANJSHIR PROVINCE, AFGHANISTAN, March 9, 2011—The Afghan National Police in Panjshir Province became the first to acquire one of ten 30-ton wrecker vehicles that will be issued to Afghan National Security Forces throughout Afghanistan.

The ANP worked closely with the Panjshir Embedded Training Team, Forward Operating Base Lion, to address their need for the 30-ton wrecker vehicle.

"Panjshir is full of rough and mountainous terrain where vehicles become disabled and need to be recovered often," said ANP Col. Abdul Qodir, the Panjshir Chief of Traffic. "The truck will be used to get vehicles out of the river and carry destroyed vehicles away from accident scenes."

U.S. Air Force Senior Airman Darin Pugh, a Tacoma, Wash., native, and

U.S. Air Force Staff Sgt. Michael Lamonte, a Burlington, Conn., native, both Panjshir Provincial Reconstruction Team vehicle maintenance members, conducted training on how to operate the 30-ton wrecker for the ANP March 9.

"The training was held on FOB Lion, and it consisted of basic operation in different types of terrain, and introduced basic equipment that came with the vehicle," said Pugh.

Pugh and Lamonte designed a training plan consisting of four training blocks: operation of the vehicle, how to operate the crane, the drag wench and the wheel lift operation.

The training also stressed the importance of safety habits.

"This truck is capable of picking up, towing and fixing other vehicles," said Pugh. "The capabilities of the truck are only limited by the operator's imagination and safe operation."

Although it has many capabilities, without the proper safety procedures, the vehicle would be dangerous to operate, added Qodir.

"Having a vehicle like this is like having a Swiss Army knife in your pocket," said Pugh. "You never know what you're going to use it for. When there's a crisis or accident like a vehicle running off the road into the river, being able to pull that Swiss Army knife out could mean the difference between life and death."

Respected platoon sergeant ends 25-year career with deployment

NANGARHAR PROVINCE, Afghanistan, March 14, 2011—U.S. Army Sgt. 1st Class Patrick Ihns, left, an infantry platoon sergeant, Company B, 1st Battalion, 133rd Infantry Regiment, 2nd Brigade Combat Team, 34th Infantry Division, from Massillon, Iowa, visits with an Afghan boy at the gate at Forward Operating Base Torkham Gate, Afghanistan, in December 2010. Ihns, one of the unit's most respected leaders, will be retiring at the end of the deployment after 25 years of service in the Army. (Photo by U.S. Army Staff Sgt. Ryan C. Matson, Task Force Red Bulls Public Affairs)

By U.S. Army Staff Sgt. Ryan C. Matson
Task Force Red Bulls Public Affairs

NANGARHAR PROVINCE, Afghanistan, March 14, 2011—Some people don't talk much about themselves.

That's the case with Sgt. 1st Class Patrick Ihns, a platoon sergeant with Company B, 1st Battalion, 133rd Infantry Regiment, 2nd Brigade Combat Team, 34th Infantry Division. The 25-year Army veteran may not talk much about himself, but those around him, especially the soldiers he leads, will tell you all you need to know.

"To get a compliment from this guy is just like Christmas," Pfc. Richard Reichardt, an infantryman in Ihns' platoon from Tipton, Iowa, said. "Being in first platoon, you want to strive to do better, because of Sgt. 1st Class Ihns, you don't want to let him down."

Ihns, 44, does not look like someone who has been in the military for a quarter of a century. With six deployments under his belt, he is still leading side-by-side with his soldiers.

"He motivates me—he still kicks, he's still going," U.S. Army Pfc. Scott Suhr, another infantryman from Olin, Iowa, in Ihns' platoon, said "I would have never thought he was in 20-some years."

"If I was in 20 years, I would pray just to be half the soldier he is," Reichardt added.

The soldiers in his platoon said they see Ihns as the type of guy who has been through any situation imaginable and who always remains calm.

"I try to impress on them to always take a second to think before they do something," Ihns said. "A lot of time when something happens, your first reaction is to do whatever you're going to do fast. Sometimes that's not the best idea."

The soldiers in his platoon said they look up to Ihns so much, the worst thing they can imagine is disappointing him.

Ironically, when it came to this deployment, it was Ihns who said he was the one who didn't want to disappoint. Ihns could have retired already. He did not have to go on the deployment, but he didn't want to let his soldiers down.

"There are a lot of good young guys here, who are here for the right reasons," Ihns said. "I talked about whether or not I would retire beforehand ... [but] they were friends with my daughter and graduated with her, and I wouldn't have felt right bailing on them, knowing they're going when I could have went with them."

Ihns, who hails from Massillon, Iowa, and works as an Active Guard Reserve unit readiness Non-Commissioned Officer at the Iowa City, Iowa armory, has 13 years of active-duty service under his belt, but spent the last 12 years with units from the Iowa National Guard's 2nd Brigade Combat Team, 34th Infantry Division. He originally enlisted in 1985 and had a short break in service after his first three years when he said he was a young guy who "thought he knew everything."

He missed the people and camaraderie and came back 14 months later and since deployed to Panama, Saudi Arabia twice, the Sinai Peninsula, and is on his second deployment in Afghanistan. He has been a sniper, and has spent all but a year-and-a-half of those 25 years as an infantryman.

"It's where the rubber meets the road," Ihns said of being an infantryman. "You're it."

The youngest of six children, Ihns said he knew from an early age he wanted to be in the Army. His father also served as a heavy equipment operator.

"It was a way to not to burden my parents, so to speak," he said with a laugh.

He said his favorite time in the military was serving as a squad leader.

"Squad leader's the best job, because you're still more of a doer," Ihns said.

Reichardt said Ihns has taught him the value of loyalty.

"What makes him stick out is he actually cares about his Soldiers," Reichardt said.

"He's very loyal to his platoon. If another sergeant comes up and tries to mess with us for something we're not responsible for, he'll be the first one to come up and be like, 'hey, if you have a problem, come to me.' Most people would be like 'whatever, I don't care.'"

Suhr and Riechardt said Ihns is always there to point out a better way of doing things, without humiliating them.

"If you're willing to learn, he'll teach you everything he knows," Reichardt said.

Ihn's influence on people extends outside the Army.

"He and his wife are always volunteering with things around town, like youth wrestling," said U.S. Army Staff Sgt. Jacob Downs, a supply sergeant with Company B, who lives near Ihns and works with him at the armory. "His kids are older, but he's still there to help the young kids out. And that has extended to his son, too, now he comes down and helps out, also."

At the end of the deployment, the soldiers of first platoon will no longer have their experienced leader with all the answers to look to for guidance, at least not in uniform. He will be retiring when he gets back.

"You're not going to find a better guy than him," said U.S. Army Spc. Lance Weiskamp, a mortarman from Washburn, Iowa, with Company B. "He's the kind of guy you want leading you into combat."

Afghan police, U.S military bond at Panjshir range

PANJSHIR PROVINCE, Afghanistan, March 10, 2011—U.S. Army 1st Lt. Roy Silhanek, Task Force Red Bulls Embedded Training Team operations officer in Panjshir and Tama, Iowa, native, shows Afghan Brig. Gen. Qasim Jangalbagh, Panjshir Provincial Police Chief, how to use the scope on an M4 carbine rifle during weapons qualification in Anaba District. The Panjshir ETT and Law Enforcement Professionals met with several Afghan National Police members at a small arms range to zero their weapons and maintain shooting proficiency. (Photo by U.S. Air Force Senior Airman Amber Ashcraft, Panjshir Provincial Reconstruction Team Public Affairs)

By U.S. Air Force Senior Airman Amber Ashcraft
Panjshir Provincial Reconstruction Team Public Affairs

PANJSHIR PROVINCE, Afghanistan, March 10, 2011—Surrounded by mountains, Anaba District has a large echo effect when a gun blast sounds in the valley. The sound of weapons being discharged over and over also brings many curious onlookers.

More than 30 Afghan National Police watched from a mountainside near a small arms range as several U.S. military and ANP leaders fired M4 carbine rifles at 300 meter targets.

"The ANP joined us for our semi-annual standard weapons qualification," said U.S. Army Sgt. 1st Class Anthony McDavitt, Task Force Red Bulls Embedded Training Team engineer and Police Mentor Team Non-Commissioned Officer-in-Charge. "Someday they'll use the M16, like Afghan National Army has, so familiarization can only help."

He said firing the M4 rifle is similar to the M16.

The ANP, including Afghan Brig. Gen. Qasim Jangalbagh, the Panjshir Provincial Police Chief, observed, the Panjshir ETT and Law Enforcement Professionals performed primary marksmanship instructions before zeroing their weapons.

"Even though I shoot well with the AK-47 rifle, I really enjoyed learning about the M16 rifle and shooting it," said ANP Col. Muhammad Dost, Panjshir's Operations Coordination Center–Provincial deputy commander.

McDavitt, a Davenport, Iowa, native, and marksmanship instructor, ran the range. Along with assisting his team with their semi-annual qualifications, McDavitt will also assist the ANP Basic Academy cadre once a month training cadets at a weapons qualification range.

"The PMT will be joining me in helping implement the Ministry of Interior qualification standards and the Academy cadre's qualification standards for training the cadets," McDavitt said.

The ANP are eager for McDavitt's involvement in the training, said Dost.

"It will be a great benefit to have Sgt. McDavitt help train at the Academy range. He has a lot of knowledge and experience about the range operations. The ANP soldiers are eager to learn," Dost said.

The maintenance standard and weapons system for the AK-47 rifle is very different from that of the M16 series, said McDavitt.

At the end of the day, as the brass from the ammo was picked up, discussions, and jokes commenced about the several hours of training and the results of the bullet-ridden targets.

"Even though the weapons and training are different, at the end of the day, we're able to see the great relationship develop between the Afghan forces and our U.S. military members," said McDavitt. "We get to bond at the range for a few hours, and we all leave with the satisfaction of knowing our counterparts and weapons a little better."

Medic demonstrates bone-injection procedure on roommate

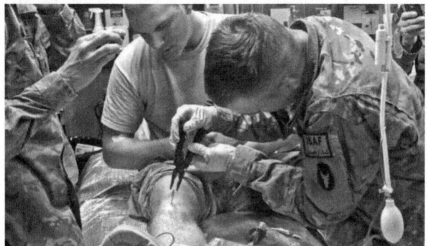

LAGHMAN PROVINCE, Afghanistan, March 10, 2011—U.S. Army Spc. Justin Day, a combat medic from Davenport, Iowa, uses a multi-purpose tool to remove the catheter from a needle injected into the leg of U.S. Army Cpl. Eric Palmer, a combat medic from Fairfeild, Iowa, at the aid station on Forward Operating Base Mehtar Lam. The two medics with Headquarters and Headquarters Company, 1st Battalion, 133rd Infantry Regiment, 2nd Brigade Combat Team, 34th Infantry Division, demonstrated the procedure for fellow medical personnel. (Photo by U.S. Army Capt. Nathan Nicol, Task Force Red Bulls)

By U.S. Army Staff Sgt. Ryan C. Matson
Task Force Red Bulls Public Affairs

NANGARHAR PROVINCE, Afghanistan, March 10, 2011—It's nice to be able to trust your roommate.

U.S. Army Cpl. Eric Palmer trusts 19-year-old U.S. Army Spc. Justin Day, so much he allowed him to drive a needle through his shinbone and pump liquids into it.

"We're roommates; met about a year ago and have been through a lot of medical training together," Palmer said. "I had complete faith in him doing this. We talked to the colonel and he blessed off on it; he thought it would be a good class we could all learn from."

The two combat medics with Headquarters and Headquarters Company, 1st Battalion, 133rd Infantry Regiment, 2nd Brigade Combat Team, 34th Infantry Division, demonstrated an injection of intravenous liquids into the bone of a live patient using a bone injection gun in the aid station at Forward Operating Base Mehtar Lam.

"It was a class on interosseous infusion," explained Palmer, who is an iron worker in his hometown of Fairfield, Iowa. "If we have a patient in a scenario where we're unable to get IV access on them to run fluids into them and they've had a lot of blood loss, we can also run fluids through the bone. The bone marrow will accept the fluid in the same way a vein would."

The medics said the procedure could be used on a Soldier involved in an Improvised Explosive Device explosion who is missing limbs or for heavier people whose veins are not easily accessible. If time was of the essence and the medics could not administer IV fluids, the medics said the interosseous infusion would be the next best option.

"For ... medics, the more tools we have in our toolbox at our disposal to use increases our chances for keeping battlefield casualties alive," Palmer said. "The better trained we are on using these devices on people, the better we can save lives."

Palmer and Day said they have had training on the process, but there was one big difference during this demonstration.

"We had never done training on this on live tissue," said Day, a Davenport, Iowa, native. "It was kind of a big deal ... to inject the fluids into the bone, you have to actually fracture the bone with the (bone injection gun)."

Day explained the process.

"You inject a 15-gauge tropic needle into the bone," he said. "The BIG has a heavy spring which shoots the needle into the bone causing a small fracture. There is a metal catheter around the needle. The needle and the catheter are injected together and then the catheter is pulled out. An extension set for a standard IV is connected, and the fluids are administered inside the bone."

Day injected the needle into a plate of bone known as the tibia plateau by Palmer's shin. The medics said placement of the injection is key because there are arteries inside bones as well as tendons and other things that could be damaged. The Saline fluids are pushed into a cavity inside the bone through a syringe, which is where the pain occurs for the patient, because it breaks apart the marrow.

Palmer, a former wrestler, said he has a pretty high threshold for pain and said when the BIG fractured his bone, it was not painful at all. However, when the liquid was injected into the bone in his leg, he said the level of pain was a 13 on a scale of 1-to-10.

"It did hurt; it's an ungodly pain," Palmer said. "It felt like the bone in my leg expanded to the size of a tanker truck."

The medics administered a small dose of morphine to Palmer, who felt nauseous from the pain. They said in a real-life situation, the patient would be unconscious or medicated prior to the fluid administration or would probably be in so much pain from existing injuries that the bone injection would be an afterthought.

Day, a medic for the scout platoon, said he was not nervous about the procedure because he was confident he could perform the injection correctly. What made him nervous, he said, was the large collaboration of people who watched the process.

"Here I am, a little (specialist), telling our sergeant major and colonel and all these people how this procedure is done," Day said.

Day said he did a lot of research on the device and others like it, such as another emergency bone injector, which is driven into a patient's sternum, prior to using the BIG on his roommate.

"The only reason I didn't let him do the injection into my sternum is because I have a tattoo there I didn't want to get messed up," Palmer said.

One thing was clear from the demonstration: if these medics ever need to apply this emergency procedure in a combat situation, they proved they could do it.

"The only way to find out if something works is to use it," Day said.

Iowa Guardsman keeps professional fighting dream alive while deployed

NANGARHAR PROVINCE, Afghanistan, March 10, 2011—U.S. Army Pfc. Scott Suhr, an infantryman from Olin, Iowa, with Company B, 1st Battalion, 133rd Infantry Regiment, 2nd Brigade Combat Team, 34th Infantry Division works on his punches with help from U.S. Army Pfc. Richard Reichardt, left, infantryman with Company B from Tipton, Iowa, at Forward Operating Base Torkham Gate's gym. Suhr, who fought for the welterweight title in the Mainstream Mixed Martial Arts circuit in Iowa, is not losing sight of his professional fighting aspirations during his year-long deployment to Afghanistan. (Photo by U.S. Army Staff Sgt. Ryan C. Matson, Task Force Red Bulls Public Affairs)

By U.S. Army Staff Sgt. Ryan C. Matson
Task Force Red Bulls Public Affairs

NANGARHAR PROVINCE, Afghanistan, March 10, 2011—On most late nights at Forward Operating Base Torkham Gate, Afghanistan, visitors will find a lone figure in the base gym, kicking a heavy bag over … and over … and over again.

That person is U.S. Army Pfc. Scott Suhr, a 23-year-old infantryman from Olin, Iowa with Company B, 1st Battalion, 133rd Infantry Regiment, 2nd Brigade Combat Team, 1st infantry Division. Suhr, who compiled an 8-4 amateur fight record and fought for a welterweight title, is not giving up on his dream of being a professional mixed martial arts fighter, even if he is several thousand miles and many months away from pursuing that goal again.

"I like fighting more than anything else I've ever done in my life," Suhr said as he reflected on the thrill of cage-fighting for a packed arena. "I've always loved tae kwon do. I love the wrestling. I love the fighting aspect, but as a competition, not a bar brawl. I won't fight someone just to fight them."

Mixed martial arts fighting is the latest in a string of athletic endeavors for Suhr, but he said it is the one sport he is now focused on. To say Suhr was a well-rounded athlete growing up would be an understatement. He played baseball, basketball, football, ran track and wrestled during high school, and, by his own admission, was good at them all.

Suhr said he started wrestling in sixth grade for Aurelia Middle School.

"I liked the individuality aspect of it. It's me and him; I can't make excuses for anything," he said.

"I didn't want to hurt somebody, I just liked the competition. No matter what I participate in, as long as it's competitive, I love it."

By his senior year, he placed third in the state of Iowa in wrestling.

In college, Suhr said he was watching the Ultimate Fighting Championship on TV, when he decided he wanted to give it a try.

"I said to myself, 'These guys have to start off somewhere,'" Suhr recalled. "I noticed a lot of them were wrestlers, and I started looking up online where they were training."

Wrestling was the only aspect of mixed martial arts fighting Suhr had experience with so he hired a muy tai expert as his trainer.

"When I first started training, I could not believe the things he could do," Suhr said. "He was so fast and moved so fluidly. I learned so much from training with him."

After four months, he competed in his first amateur fight.

With several thousand people in the audience, Suhr said he was in awe as he walked to the cage.

"I had butterflies and jitters," he said. "There was a big crowd, loud music, and walking into the cage was almost worse than the state wrestling championships. They shut the cage, and I shook hands with my opponent and the ref was talking to us. The bell rang, and it hit me—this is real!"

Suhr lost that fight in the second round but said he was not discouraged.

"I was motivated, because I knew I could have beaten him," Suhr said. "I knew I could compete at that level."

Suhr said he was immediately in love with mixed martial arts fighting.

"It's so hard, it really does test your body," he said. "In fighting, you've got three 5-minute periods, and you've never been that tired before in your life. The physicality of it is just so much more, the mental game is so much more. You're thinking of what he's going to do, what I'm going to do. You put it all together and it's the ultimate challenge for your body and mind."

He eventually began winning and earned the opportunity to compete for the Burlington Circuit Welterweight Title. Suhr lost the fight but is determined to not only win the next title, but also join the professional circuit when he returns home.

Panjshir residents attend PRT's construction workshop

By U.S. Air Force 2nd Lt. Ashleigh Peck
Panjshir Provincial Reconstruction Team Public Affairs

PANJSHIR PROVINCE, Afghanistan, March 8, 2011—Panjshir Provincial Reconstruction Team engineers conducted its first hands-on construction workshop for 13 locally-owned construction companies.

"After hearing about our construction workshop on the radio station the night before, locals from nine different construction companies showed up an hour early in anticipation that they might be able to join the training and help build a relationship with the Panjshir Provincial Reconstruction Team," said U.S. Air Force 2nd Lt. Phil Compton, PRT Engineer and Doty, Wash., native.

The PRT engineering team began preparing for the construction workshop in January with hopes of mitigating the most common construction errors they have seen in the province.

Compton said workshop was designed with four ideas in mind: to lay out the PRT's expectations for the upcoming construction season; to help contractors close the gap between engineers and project manager and the local unskilled laborers; to create a common reference point for deficiencies discussions; and to allow PRT engineers and contractors to collaborate and network in a consequence-free environment.

The workshop included classroom instruction and hands-on application, including a lesson on working with concrete.

"Everyone here knows these are the basic principles for properly mixing concrete, however we have seen these mistakes on every project that we monitor in the province," Scott Davis, U.S. Army Corps of Engineers construction representative with Panjshir PRT and an Omaha, Neb., native, said to the contractors during the class.

"Having this kind of workshop is very useful for construction engineers," said Haji Ghulam Nabi Yaqoobi, director of Yaqoobi Construction and Road Construction Company, through an interpreter. "It allows us to develop our experience and skills and will help to improve construction in Panjshir Province."

Overall, Compton believes the first two days were a success.

"The contractors were able to perform some hands-on labor, become familiar with the PRT's expectations for rebar and concrete working, and do some collaboration and networking with each other," he said.

Task Force Red Bulls forward repair station keeps Soldiers rolling

By U.S. Army Spc. James Wilton
Task Force Red Bulls Public Affairs

BAGRAM AIRFIELD, Afghanistan, March 11, 2011—The soldiers of Company B, 334th Brigade Support Battalion, Task Force Archer, operate a forward repair station on Bagram Airfield seven days a week to keep all the soldiers of the 2nd Brigade Combat Team, 34th Infantry Division, Task Force Red Bulls, which they are a part of, rolling.

"We provide support to the infantry, cavalry and all soldiers of the brigade making sure their vehicles, their weapons and their radios are running to the best of their ability, all the time," said U.S. Army Staff Sgt. Steven Agnitsch from Wyoming, Iowa, and the maintenance control Non-Commissioned Officer-in-Charge of the Company B forward repair station. "Let's get it in, get it fixed and get it back to the soldiers—that's how I run my shop."

The station has a wheeled vehicle repair area for all vehicles, from Mine-Resistant, Ambushed-Protected vehicles to pick-up trucks used on Bagram. The repair station also has a metal fabrication shop and a communications repair area so maintainers can make repairs on all critical systems on the brigade's vehicles.

"We support the whole brigade with any of its maintenance needs that may come up," said U.S. Army Sgt. Chris Lindahl from Royal, Iowa, a wheeled vehicle mechanic with Company B. "Our job is pretty important [to the soldier in the field] ... we make sure that they have a quality piece of equipment to take outside the wire. Our mission is to make sure that the vehicle they're driving is a reliable one and they have reliable communications so they can get back safe."

"We have had a lot of days where we had 20-plus vehicles in here; it is pretty hectic," said Lindahl. "A couple nights we have had to work pretty late, and the lights were out in the shop, so we had to run some drop cords to generators so we had lights in the shop. We had stuff that had to be done, so we just adjusted fire and did what we had to do to get it finished."

The soldiers who work at the repair station take pride in their job and understand the importance of their mission.

"I have always enjoyed being a mechanic helping the infantry and the Cavalry by keeping their equipment running at top speed, so they can keep on mission," said Agnitsch. "It makes me feel good; I know they can do their job if I do mine."

The other soldiers in the unit share the same sentiment.

"I have been fixing stuff my entire time in the military," said U.S. Army Spc. Kevin Miller from Ankeny, Iowa, a mechanic with Company B. "I am just a simple mechanic, maintaining these trucks is what I do. If these trucks aren't fully mission capable, then the other military personnel here, they can't go out and do their jobs."

The shop handles all types of repairs, from full motor rebuilds to simple jobs called services. Services are fluid- and air-filter changes, coupled with quality assurance and quality control inspections, preformed every 200 to 600 hours and once a year. These services are vital to assure vehicles are in proper working order, according to the maintainers.

"My job is a little monotonous at times but it is fun and important," said Lindahl. "Some days we just do services, but others are challenging like when we get to do the big motor pullouts and assemblies. It has its moments and most of them are good."

The mechanics and metal workers at Company B don't just do this while deployed. Most will do the same job when they return to the United States; the experiences and knowledge they gain will follow them.

"Back home, I work as a mechanic instructor at the National Maintenance Training Center, Camp Dodge, Iowa. Here, I work on MRAPs doing everything I can to make sure that the trucks are fully mission capable and to make sure they are ready to rock and roll at any time," said Miller.

Though it's not glamorous and it's not a typical Army job, Company B's mission is an important one, according to the maintainers.

BAGRAM AIRFIELD, Afghanistan, March 11, 2011—U.S. Army Spc. Mike Lindenburg from Monticello, Iowa, hands a socket wrench to U.S. Army Spc. Kevin Miller from Ankeny, Iowa, both are mechanics with Company B, 334th Brigade Support Battalion, Task Force Archer, a part of the 2nd Brigade Combat Team, 34th Infantry Division, Task Force Red Bulls, while they perform a monthly maintenance check on a mine resistant all terrain vehicle at Company B's forward repair station on Bagram Airfield. (Photo by U.S. Army Sgt. James Wilton, Task Force Red Bulls Public Affairs)

From Day to Night: Alpha Troop's MP Platoon patrols Bagram Security Zone

PARWAN PROVINCE, Afghanistan, March 12, 2011—U.S. Army Sgt. 1st Class Michael Warmenhoven (right) of Marion, Iowa, military police platoon sergeant and U.S. Army Sgt. Adam Berger (left) of Olathe, Kan., an MP attached to Troop A, 1st Squadron, 113th Cavalry Regiment, Task Force Redhorse [...] talk to a villager as they patrol through the villages within the Bagram Security Zone, March 12. (Photo by U.S. Army Spc. Kristina L. Gupton, Task Force Red Bulls Public Affairs)

PARWAN PROVINCE, Afghanistan, March 12, 2011—U.S. Army Sgt. 1st Class. Michael Warmenhoven of Marion, Iowa, Military Police platoon sergeant attached to Troop A, 1st Squadron, 113th Cavalry Regiment, Task Force Redhorse, 2nd Brigade Combat Team, 34th Infantry Division, Task Force Red Bulls, speaks to a young Afghan girl as they patrol through the Bagram Security Zone. (Photo by U.S. Army Spc. Kristina L. Gupton, Task Force Red Bulls Public Affairs)

PARWAN PROVINCE, Afghanistan, March 12, 2011—U.S. Army Spc. Christopher Clark (prone) of Cedar Rapids, Iowa, and U.S. Army Pvt. Jared North (standing) of Ankeny, Iowa, both military policemen attached to Troop A, 1st Squadron, 113th Cavalry Regiment, Task Force Redhorse, 2nd Brigade Combat Team, 34th Infantry Division, Task Force Red Bulls, provide rear security for fellow soldiers while patrolling through the Bagram Security Zone. Members of MP platoon patrol through the villages to ensure security. (Photo by U.S. Army Spc. Kristina L. Gupton, Task Force Red Bulls Public Affairs)

Searching for clues in Wardachi

NANGARHAR PROVINCE, Afghanistan, March 13, 2011—U.S. Army Staff Sgt. Jason Timler (left), an infantry squad leader from Waterloo, Iowa, with Company B, 1st Battalion, 133rd Infantry Regiment, talks with villagers from the town of Wardachi, Afghanistan during a patrol through the area. (Photo by U.S. Army Staff Sgt. Ryan C. Matson, Task Force Red Bulls Public Affairs)

By U.S. Army Staff Sgt. Ryan C. Matson
Task Force Red Bulls Public Affairs

NANGARHAR PROVINCE, Afghanistan, March 13, 2011—On March 4, the Soldiers of Company B, 1st Battalion, 133rd Infantry Regiment, part of the Iowa National Guard's 2nd Brigade Combat Team, 34th Infantry Division, encountered the first instance of indirect fire on Forward Operating Base Torkham Gate in nearly two years.

On March 13, U.S. Army Capt. Kevin Hrodey, Company B's commander from Pleasant Hill, Iowa, decided to look into the attack further on a joint patrol through Wardachi, the point of origin of the attack, with his company's Soldiers and members of the Afghan National Directorate of Security. The patrol was significant, Hrodey said, because it was the first time his unit had been on a patrol exclusively with members of the NDS, the Afghan's intelligence agency. They led the mission from the time the forces arrived in the village, Hrodey said.

"I wanted to go in and conduct an atmospheric with the NDS and find out what was really going on in that village," Hrodey said. "Every time we've dealt with the village in the past, we've come across a very poor bunch of families in there. They say they're not getting supported by their government, that politicians come by and ask them for their money and promise to help them with projects, and then leave and don't come back and they don't know whether the politicians won the election or not."

What Hrodey and his men found was something of a boomtown in Wardachi.

"In the last two months, the town has basically doubled and tripled in size," Staff Sgt. Jason Timler, an infantry squad leader with Company B from Waterloo, Iowa, said. He said that there has been a large influx of refugees from Pakistan who set up camp on the open land surrounding Wardachi. In fact, there is a whole subvillage, Woch Ghrawakay, with 200-300 people who were not there on the company's last patrol through Wardachi a month ago.

The people in Woch Ghrawakay claim they were forced to desert their homes by the military in Pakistan and have crossed the border and set up their village on unoccupied land in Afghanistan.

The company also found a couple large stockades of various supplies— basically outdoor warehouses—in Wardachi. The Soldiers found supplies such as medical and cooking items pushed into caves and checked to ensure there was nothing harmful or illegal in them.

With the amount of smuggling that occurs in the area of Wardachi, there is a high likelihood that many of the goods stored there were illegally smuggled into the village. In fact, the children told of how they are paid a minimal wage to smuggle carts or donkeys of goods back and forth across the passes around Torkham Gate from Afghanistan to Pakistan and vice versa.

Timler said this is basically just a way of life for many villagers along the border.

"A lot of that stuff may not be to harm coalition forces at all, it's just, that's money," Timler, 25, a veteran of two prior deployments, said. "They don't come out and say 'I hate Americans so I'm going to smuggle this through,' it's just, 'I need money to feed a family.'"

While the Soldiers said they are concerned with illegal smuggling, the NDS takes the lead on the investigation and handling of the smuggling, Timler said.

"We're worried about everything illegal, some things more than others," Timler said. "Like a lot of the car parts we found today, we go to NDS on, and they take care of it from there."

There are still many poor villagers throughout Wardachi, but Hrodey and his men also noticed some elaborate construction that cannot be accomplished cheaply in the village. There was even a backhoe in the village.

"We wanted to see who's funding it, because they told us they're not getting any funding from the government, and then all of a sudden there's an economic boom in the village, it's thriving right around the time we get attacked," Hrodey said.

On March 5, some of the company's Soldiers went out to Wardachi and found the area they believe was the point of origin of the three-mortar attack, as well as around the FOB looking for impact sites.

This time around, Timler and his squad talked with some of the locals, who confirmed much of what they had suspected about the attack.

The villagers showed the typical Afghan hospitality to Hrodey and his Soldiers, giving them tea and even cooking them lunch. Hrodey said that just because the attack originated from near the village, the village is known to be involved in smuggling like many border towns and seems to be receiving funding for construction, does not mean the people there are necessarily bad people.

"If the person you're talking to is not a bad guy, but has been coersed or threatened at one point, if you go in and treat them like they're a real person and not a suspect, you're more likely to get some information about what's going on," Hrodey said.

But there is definitely a lot going on in Wardachi, which is why Company B checked it out with the NDS.

"There had been no attacks on the FOB for two years, and then out of the blue two weeks ago we got hit with three mortars," Hrodey said. "The fact that it came and it came from that direction, we had to find out what's going on there. There's a lot going on in that village. They say they need more help, and we don't want them to be influenced by the wrong people."

NANGARHAR PROVINCE, Afghanistan, March 13, 2011—U.S. Army Capt. Kevin Hrodey, center, the commander of Company B, 1st Battalion, 133rd Infantry Regiment, from Pleasant Hill, Iowa, delivers the mission brief before a mission to the town of Wardachi, Afghanistan, near the Afghanistan/Pakistan border as 1st Lt. Torrey Gasch, a fire support officer with Company B from Charlotte, N.C., right, and an officer with the National Directorate of Security looks on. (Photo by U.S. Army Staff Sgt. Ryan C. Matson, Task Force Red Bulls Public Affairs)

NANGARHAR PROVINCE, Afghanistan, March 13, 2011—U.S. Army Pfc. Tyler Sirovy, an infantryman with Company B, 1st Battalion, 133rd Infantry Regiment, from Oskaloosa, Iowa, watches a young boy pass by with a herd of sheep while Sirovy patrols through the town of Wardachi, Afghanistan, near the Afghanistan/Pakistan border. (Photo by U.S. Army Staff Sgt. Ryan C. Matson, Task Force Red Bulls Public Affairs)

347

Displaced Afghan families earn diploma, skills for income

KAPISA PROVINCE, Afghanistan, March 15, 2011—Dr. LisaRe Brooks (left), of Bozeman, Mont., and a social scientist with the Human Terrain Analysis Team, Combined Joint Task Force–101, speaks with displaced women and children of the Tagab District during a visit to the Director of Women's Affairs compound. Brooks and members of the Kentucky Agribusiness Development Team visited the DOWA to present the families with certificates of completion for finishing a two-day honeybee training course. (Photo by U.S. Army Spc. Kristina L. Gupton, Task Force Red Bulls Public Affairs)

Paktya officials address development needs

By U.S. Air Force 1st Lt. Sybil Taunton
Paktya Provincial Reconstruction Team Public Affairs

PAKTYA PROVINCE, Afghanistan, March 15, 2011—Officials from the Government of the Islamic Republic of Afghanistan, including the Paktya provincial governor, district sub-governors and line directors, gathered for a Provincial Development Council meeting at the governor's compound.

Representatives from the Paktya Provincial Reconstruction Team, the 2-45th Agribusiness Development Team and the U.S. Department of State also attended to discuss important development issues with their GIRoA partners.

Juma Khan Hamdard, the provincial governor, opened the meeting by congratulating his fellow Afghans on a new year and shared his wishes for success.

"I want this year to be a safe year and a year of peace," said Hamdard. "I also hope this will be a successful year for the Director of Economy. Line directors have submitted their budgets to their ministries. I hope you all get your money and spend it on good things."

The Director of Economy, Mahfoz Ahmad, explained the process for submitting project proposals and stressed the importance of working through the ministries in Kabul.

"Every line director should be creating proposals and sending them to their line ministers," said Ahmad. "We must increase our opportunities for getting money and projects for all directorates."

One of the major issues addressed during the meeting was the need for higher quality work for development projects.

"Money is being spent on projects, but the quality of work is not good," said Mohammad Ali Sha, the director of the provincial council.

The PRT commander, Air Force Lt. Col. Marchal Magee, of Issaquah, Wash., addressed this issue by explaining the progress being made in the project approval process.

"We have taken a new path on our partnership with our government officials and Afghan security forces to ensure better quality of work on projects throughout the province," said Magee. "We are completely inclusive in making sure we bring them along on all of our missions that fall along their particular lines of effort. We are also working to include the district sub-governors and village elders so they have an opportunity to have their voices heard and to have projects reflect the needs of their communities."

Officials also brought up the need for female dormitories at Paktya University. The deputy chancellor of the university said more women have been interested in attending the school and they are expecting 500 to 600 more female students over the next year, but they do not have the necessary housing.

The director of labor and social affairs, Abdul Samad Muslih, discussed his proposal for expanding vocational training in the province and the positive effect it will have.

"The community will get great benefits from this training," said Muslih.

The director of education presented ideas for new schools, as well as older schools that are in need of repairs, and the director of agriculture, irrigation and livestock, Lelah Zadran, informed the group about all of the new vegetation that will be planted throughout the province in the coming months.

"This year in Paktya Province, we will have more than 4,000 gardens planted," said Zadran.

According to U.S. Army 2nd Lt. Jeff Chavannes, of 1st Battalion, 168th Infantry Regiment, 2nd Brigade, 34th Infantry Division of the Iowa Army National Guard, from Des Moines, Iowa, there will be over 10,000 trees planted throughout the province, as well.

"Our goal is to have the trees planted for Nowruz, the Afghan New Year," said Chavannes.

According to the PRT commander, the event demonstrated the progress being made by Paktya government officials.

"The Provincial Development Council meeting today was a huge step in the right direction to start the New Year off on a good note for our GIRoA partners and to bring much-needed good news to the people of this province," said Magee.

Paktya residents plant trees
to celebrate new year, education

PAKTYA PROVINCE, Afghanistan, March 15, 2011–Zormat residents prepare to plant trees at a school. As part of the Afghan New Year celebration, the Paktya Director of Education, Mihrabudeen Shafaq, organized the tree-planting event for 10 different schools throughout the district. (Photo by U.S. Army Sgt. Ernest Miller, Paktya Provincial Reconstruction Team Civil Affairs)

MP company recalls highs and lows of a long year in Afghanistan

By U.S. Army Staff Sgt. Ryan C. Matson
Task Force Red Bulls Public Affairs

LAGHMAN PROVINCE, Afghanistan, March 16, 2011—Its Soldiers uncovered two huge weapons caches, fought in several firefights, worked hand-in-hand with a unit of Afghan Uniformed Police to help make them a more community-police oriented, proactive force, and lost seven Afghan counterparts along the way.

That, in a nutshell, sums up the last year in Afghanistan for the 3rd Platoon of the 64th Military Police Company, 720th MP Battalion, out of Fort Hood, Texas.

As the platoon's time in country draws to a close, members of the platoon shared their memories—the highs and lows of a long, but eventful year in Afghanistan. "We worked with the AUP to progress them more to a method of community policing," said U.S. Army Staff Sgt. Keith Bachman, 1st Squad leader, 3rd Platoon, 64th MP Company and a Detroit native.

"When we first got here, they were mainly focused on security operations, manning checkpoints and things of that nature," Bachman continued. "Now, we've got them out there interacting with community businesses, village elders, building reports and making apprehensions based on the information they've received from those reports. Community policing has been a successful tool for police in the U.S., and here it helped the AUP go from being a reactionary force to a force that engages the public and is proactive. They're actually preventing crime from happening before it ever occurs by being out there."

The unit arrived at Bagram Airfield, Afghanistan, April 20, and waited five days before discovering their final in-country destination for the next year, Forward Operating Base Mehtar Lam, Afghanistan. The 64th MPs replaced the 984th MP Company from Fort Carson, Col.

"When we got here, the mission for the platoon was to be a Police Training Team for the AUP in the Mehtar Lam, Alishang and Alingar District Centers," said Bachman. "Shortly thereafter, we realized the AUP were capable of conducting missions without additional training. They were already proficient at the tasks we were training them on, so we adopted the role of a Police Mentor Team, which is what we have done since April 27. We pushed them out to do the job they were supposed to be doing."

"It makes sense," said U.S. Army Staff Sgt. Joe Contreras of San Antonio, Texas. "One unit comes in to train; the next comes in to (advise)."

The platoon went right to work with their AUP counterparts. The unit switched their focus on Alingar and Mehtar Lam districts in October, as the two, main key-terrain areas in the area of operations.

Utilizing a proactive, community-policing approach led to several successes for the AUP the platoon they advised, the platoon's Soldiers agreed. This is because the people saw the AUP in the villages doing their jobs, and came forward with information on enemy activity. Whereas when the platoon came here, they said the phone at the district centers seldom rang, the Soldiers said now people regularly call in with information, exhibiting a stronger faith in their police force. This faith from the community has led to several key successes for the AUP and their advisers in 3rd Platoon.

"We had two really big caches that we found," said U.S. Army Sgt. Adam Friday, a team leader from Dover, Del. "One was in Mehtar Lam; the other was in Shamangul village, just south of the city."

The cache the platoon found in the city in September was huge, said Friday. It included several unexploded ordinances, a large amount of mortars, six anti-tank land mines, and shoulder-fired Rocket-Propelled Grenades capable of penetrating coalition armor.

"It was some scary stuff," Friday said. "It was the first real big find for the platoon."

The MPs said they found the cache through working with the AUP, who received a call saying someone may have a bomb in the area. The MP's quick reactionary force escorted the AUP to the area, secured it, and found the cache.

The second big find came in Shamangul Jan. 27 from an undercover source.

"We were on patrol in Mehtar Lam and received a call that there was a cache, but they didn't know exactly where it was," said Troxel. "We had to go and search a big area, pretty much the outer part of the village, and we found 110 toe-poppers (small anti-personnel mines) in a sinkhole."

Along with the caches, the platoon said they also found numerous Improvised Explosive Devices the same way—through information the AUP received from interacting with the local public. The AUP found several more on their own, and even removed many of the IEDs themselves.

"If you look at the statistics, almost 90 percent of the IEDs found in this area were found by the AUP," said U.S. Army 1st Lt. Malcolm Adler, platoon leader from Bronx, N.Y. "They cordon off the site and they'll contact us or EOD, and we'll roll up there and blow it in place, or they'll take it out themselves."

The platoon also endured their share of enemy contact throughout the deployment. Some of these attacks could have been worse had the AUP not alerted the platoon that villagers warned them an attack may be coming.

Contreras said the attacks were a mixed blessing, because although they were attacked, it helped to gain the AUP's confidence in the platoon. The MPs and AUPs fought through about a half dozen enemy attacks, including a three-sided ambush with Rocket-Propelled Grenade fire and numerous incidents of harassment fire, Adler said.

"One of the things we ... learned early on was that we really had to get into something with them before they could trust us," Contreras said. "We got into firefights and that showed them we weren't going to run, we were going to stay there with them and fight, and help them, that we were ready to make an impact."

Besides uncovering caches, IEDs and reacting to contact, the MPs also said they worked with the AUP in handling crime, from heroin trafficking to illegal fishing with explosives. Another highlight the platoon cited was setting up the first police career day with the provisional police headquarters at Mehtar Lam boy's high school in September.

"As a result of that, there were 250 male applicants who expressed an interest in becoming AUP officers," Bachman said. "There was also a follow on career day for females in January, which is a big step in the culture here, with 10 females expressing interest in the AUP."

The platoon also worked with the graduates of the first provincial police academy in the Laghman Province. Unfortunately, some of the graduates also were involved in the low-point of the deployment for the platoon.

That low point came on Jan. 15 when four AUP officers they had worked with were killed in an IED attack near the village of Tigalam. The officers were in an up-armored Humvee on a proactive patrol. The MPs asked if the AUP wanted them to join the patrol, but the AUP said they would be OK on their own. "We were smoking and joking with them the day before, and we asked the chief if they wanted us to go with them, and they told us, 'No, it's our job, our thing,'" said U.S. Army Sgt. Alberto Iglesias, another team leader with 3rd Platoon from South Plainfield, N.J.

"They were really good AUP," he said. "About an hour later we heard one of their trucks had been hit. We geared up and were out there on the scene (fast) and it was ugly, very ugly. They were some of the very best."

The platoon also lost another two of their AUP counterparts earlier in the year in a vehicle borne IED attack in Mehtar Lam, as well as an officer who died in a motorcycle accident during a food run for one of the checkpoints, meaning they lost seven total members of their Afghan team throughout the deployment.

But the year, of course, also had its share of laughs.

"I got sold for two white camels," U.S. Army Spc. Amy Davis, a team leader with 3rd Platoon from Clarksville, Tenn., laughed. "It's funny, because being a female, when I came here, at first the AUP were kind of hesitant to talk to me, but now when I show up, they talk and laugh with me like everybody else."

The platoon said it could not have kept their morale up without the support of people back home. The Adopt-A-Platoon foundation "adopted" 3rd Platoon and sent more than 90 boxes of care items including much-needed personal hygiene items that they said made a huge difference in their year. Besides the support from home, the MPs said volleyball and the gym helped preserve their sanity.

It has been an eventful year-plus for 3rd Platoon, but when asked what the best part of it all was, the response from the Soldiers present was unanimous.

"Going home!" the MPs said, knowing that the end is finally in sight.

832nd Engineers search Sanghar Valley routes for IEDs

LAGHMAN PROVINCE, Afghanistan, March 17, 2011—U.S. Army Spc. Cody Pinkerman, front, a demolition team member of 3rd Platoon, 832nd Engineer Company, 2nd Brigade Combat Team, 34th Infantry Division, Task Force Red Bulls, from Mount Pleasant, Iowa, and U.S. Army Sgt. Mitchell Songer, back, demolition team leader, from Ottumwa, Iowa, trod through some heavy winter wheat searching for Improvised Explosive Device command wires near the town of Sheykhan, Afghanistan. The company had been hit by an Improvised Explosive Device their last two times through the town, which lies in the Sanghar Valley, and the area remains a hotbed of enemy activity. (Photo by U.S. Army Staff Sgt. Ryan C. Matson, Task Force Red Bulls Public Affairs)

By U.S. Army Staff Sgt. Ryan C. Matson
Task Force Red Bulls Public Affairs

NANGARHAR PROVINCE, Afghanistan, March 17, 2011—U.S. Army Soldiers from the 832nd Engineer Company are providing Sanghar Valley, Afghanistan, by clearing routes of Improvised Explosive Devices. While patrolling, the Soldiers pay meticulous attention to their environment to discover any threats that may harm coalition forces or Afghans.

"One of three things is probably going to happen," said U.S. Army Staff Sgt. Donni Rooks, a platoon sergeant from Mount Pleasant, Iowa, with the 832nd Engineer Company, 2nd Brigade Combat Team, 34th Infantry Division, before his company embarked on a route-clearing mission in the Sanghar Valley. "Based on what's been going on in that valley lately, we're either going to come into contact, get blown up, or find something."

Fortunately for the platoon, neither of the first two scenarios occurred. Unfortunately, though, it was not the third either. But this is the painstaking and patience-wearing game that is the life of a combat engineer on a route-clearing mission.

The company was clearing part of the Sanghar Valley, an area where they suffered two Improvised Explosive Device strikes in the past month, the last two times the platoon was in the area. No Americans were injured in the attacks.

Despite being hit their last two times on the route, U.S. Army Spc. Jonathan Meyer, a combat engineer with the 832nd Engineer Company, from Des Moines, Iowa, said he was not nervous during the mission.

"Personally, the first time we got hit, the IED was on my vehicle and after going through that, I wouldn't say I feel safer, but the vehicles that we're in have proven that they can withstand an attack and keep the passengers relatively unscathed," Meyer said. "I'm confident in our equipment."

U.S. Army 1st Lt. Ryan Lett, a platoon leader with the 832nd Engineer Company, from Cedar Rapids, Iowa, was outside the vehicle with three of his Soldiers when the IED detonated. He, also, can have faith in the equipment.

"I think where we happened to be standing at the front of the vehicle, the truck itself deflected most of the blast—I didn't feel a concussion wave or really even feel the ground rumble," he said. "It was one of those weird physics things, I guess."

The route-clearance process is slow and demands the Soldiers maintain strict attention to detail. On this mission, the engineers cleared about a 40-mile stretch of unpaved terrain along Route Philadelphia, which runs parallel in the valley to a paved route. The Soldiers used a variety of Mine-Resistant Ambush-Protected Vehicles to provide security, detect mines and clear them if necessary.

During their time doing route clearance this deployment, the engineers, who are trained in setting explosives, have retrieved and detonated one IED, in January, and been hit by two. One would think that this would frustrate the Soldiers, or sitting in a truck moving so slowly for so long would cause them to lose focus and vigilance. But the importance of what they're doing makes it easy for the 832nd's troops to stay on their toes, Meyer said.

"It's pretty easy to keep your focus when you're trying to avoid getting blown up, or trying to avoid letting your friends get blown up," Meyer said.

Lett agreed.

"I think Staff Sgt. Rooks summed it up when he said, 'Sir, this is a 99 out of 100 business we're in', meaning 99 times when you check something, (there will) be nothing there, but there's always that one time," Lett said. "That's what we're looking for, that one percent."

And that one time, the engineers know, the IED they find could save the lives of the Soldiers and Afghans who travel the routes.

LAGHMAN PROVINCE, Afghanistan, March 17, 2011—U.S. Army 1st Lt. Ryan Lett, right, platoon leader of 3rd Platoon, from Cedar Rapids, Iowa, with the 832nd Engineer Company, 2nd Brigade Combat Team, 34th Infantry Division, Task Force Red Bulls, addresses his troops before a potentially dangerous route-clearing mission of the Sanghar Valley on Route Philadelphia on FOB Mehtar Lam, Afghanistan. (Photo by U.S. Army Staff Sgt. Ryan C. Matson, Task Force Red Bulls Public Affairs)

LAGHMAN PROVINCE, Afghanistan, March 17, 2011—A patrol of Mine-Resistant Ambush-Protected Vehicles as well as Soldiers with the 832nd Engineer Company, 2nd Brigade Combat Team, 34th Infantry Division, Task Force Red Bulls, conduct a route clearance mission through the Sanghar Valley near the village of Sheykan, Afghanistan. (Photo by U.S. Army Staff Sgt. Ryan C. Matson, Task Force Red Bulls Public Affairs)

New ANCOP facility bolsters security in Zormat

PAKTYA PROVINCE, Afghanistan, March 17—Paktya Province Gov. Juma Khan Hamdard cuts the ceremonial ribbon at the newly completed Afghan National Civil Order Police facility in Zormat District. The facility took two years to complete and provided jobs for 200 local Afghans who now have more extensive construction training. (Photo by U.S. Air Force 1st Lt. Sybil Taunton, Paktya Provincial Reconstruction Team Public Affairs)

By U.S. Air Force 1st Lt. Sybil Taunton
Paktya Provincial Reconstruction Team Public Affairs

PAKTYA PROVINCE, Afghanistan, March 17, 2011—Officials from the Government of the Islamic Republic of Afghanistan and the 4th Brigade, Afghan National Civil Order Police, were joined by members of the Paktya Provincial Reconstruction Team; 1st Battalion, 168th Infantry Regiment; and the U.S. Army Corps of Engineers, for a ribbon-cutting ceremony at the newly completed ANCOP facility in Zormat District.

The $13 million project was contracted out by the U.S. Army Corps of Engineers and Combined Security Transition Command–Afghanistan to Proccea Consulting Construction Engineering-Architecture, a Turkish company that provided 200 jobs for local Afghans.

"It has been our honor to assist the ANCOP in expanding their forces, and to assist them in increasing security in Zormat," said U.S. Army Lt. Col. Roger Moore of Atlanta, speaking on behalf of USACE and CSTC-A, during the ribbon-cutting ceremony.

The project took two years to complete and now provides room for the 4th Bde. to house and train 350 ANCOP personnel. The facility also includes a dining facility, latrines, showers, laundry facility, administrative building, well houses and guard towers.

The 4th Brigade ANCOP commander, Col. Muhammed, spoke proudly about the positive effects the facility has made for his unit and Zormat district.

"Our forces are better equipped and better trained. We are prepared to defend our battlespace," said Col. Muhammed.

Paktya Province Gov. Juma Khan Hamdard emphasized the importance of having cooperative village elders to help close the gap between the people and the government. He concluded his speech by focusing on the new ANCOP facility.

"I would like to congratulate the ANCOP commander on the new facility here in Zormat," Hamdard said. "This is now your facility and you must take care of it, because no one will rebuild it for you."

Gulab Shah, Zormat District subgovernor, highlighted the various development projects taking place in the district including a new school, security walls around the clinic and the nearly completed district center, which also contains a new mosque.

"I promise we are doing our best for the people of Zormat," said Shah.

Kapisa forms first Afghan soybean farmers association

KAPISA PROVINCE, Afghanistan, March 17, 2011—Iman Muhammad Arif (far right), Kapisa Director of Agriculture, Irrigation and Livestock, introduces three Afghan soybean farmers who will be on the board of directors for the Kapisa Soybean Farmers Association. Arif famed the announcement during the association's inauguration ceremony at the governor's compound. Gulam Said (center right), is a soybean farmer in Kapisa province who won the Afghan Farmer of the Year award for 2010. (Photo by U.S. Army Spc. James Wilton, Task Force Red Bulls Public Affairs)

By U.S. Army Spc. James Wilton
Task Force Red Bulls Public Affairs

KAPISA PROVINCE, Afghanistan, March 17, 2011—The Afghan Ministry of Agriculture, Irrigation and Livestock, and Nutrition and Education International, held an inauguration ceremony for the Kapisa Soybean Farmers Association at the governor's compound.

"Cooperation among farmers is the key to progress in Kapisa and throughout Afghanistan," said U.S. Army Col. Hunter J. Mathews, from Lexington, Ky., and the Kentucky Agribusiness Development Team commander. "Your formation of a soybean cooperative signals a great day for agriculture in Kapisa. By working together you will share in expertise, funding, and the use of soy processing equipment at a much lower cost than you would as individuals. This cooperation will make a positive difference in your success."

The Kentucky Agribusiness Development Team joined the more than 100 Afghan farmers and representatives from the MAIL and NEI for the ceremony. The Kentucky ADT provided seed and fertilizer to the farmers earlier this year.

"By pulling together and working together, you are helping to turn Kapisa into one of the most progressive and promising agricultural areas in Afghanistan," said Mathews. "When I go home to Kentucky and America, I will speak often of the hard working farmers of Kapisa who have banded together to make this province a more prosperous and productive community."

The MAIL will oversee the association in Kapisa, while the most experienced soybean farmers from the province will serve as directors. Kapisa is the first province to form a soybean farmers association but not the last. Soybeans are currently grown in all Afghan provinces, while northern provinces like Kapisa and Parwan boast the highest production rates.

The MAIL and NEI held a similar ceremony in Parwan Province March 19 for the inauguration of a Parwan Soybean Farmers Association. The Republic of Korea Provincial Reconstruction Team which is funding and building a soy milk factory in the province attended.

NEI, based out of Pasadena, Calif., tested different crops in 2003-2005 for one that would be viable in the Afghan climate and a strong contender in the fight against malnutrition. Soy was selected for its high protein content and ability to flourish here.

This was the first time Afghan farmers had seen or grown soybeans.

"The Kapisa Soybean Farmers Association has joined together in order to educate the people of Afghanistan about the malnutrition and the way to fight it, which is with soy," said Iman Muhammad Arif, Kapisa director of Agriculture, Irrigation and Livestock. "Soybeans can be made into many healthy foods like milk, oil, naan bread and cookies. All of which are healthy and rich in iron and protein."

To help make soy a common food source in homes across the country, NEI provides classes on processing and cooking soybeans to Afghan housewives.

"The fight against malnutrition must be fought in the homes and by each and every person in Afghanistan," said Dr. Steven Kwon, president of NEI. "To rebuild Afghanistan, people have to work hard and study hard. If you make people healthier through better nutrition, then they can work harder and study harder."

He said the high demand and market price of soybeans coupled with the growth potential makes it a viable cash crop; making it a legal alternative to growing opium for Afghan farmers. In 2009, Afghan farmers began producing enough soybeans to compete with other international farmers. These high numbers earned one farmer, Gulam Said, the award of Best Afghan Farmer in 2010.

Kwon said Afghanistan's goal is to produce 300,000 tons of soybeans produced by 2015. He said he believes this is the amount that will end malnutrition in Afghanistan.

"You are making an important step for the future of Afghanistan. Because of you, Kapisa will defeat malnutrition, Afghanistan will defeat malnutrition," said Kwon.

KAPISA PROVINCE, Afghanistan, March 17, 2011—U.S. Army Col. Hunter J. Mathews from Lexington, Ky., and the Kentucky Agribusiness Development Team commander, speaks to Afghan soybean farmers about their farms during the inauguration ceremony for the Afghan Soybean Farmers Association at the Kapisa governor's compound March 17. The Kentucky ADT purchased seed and fertilizer for the farmers earlier this year. (Photo by U.S. Army Spc. James Wilton, Task Force Red Bulls Public Affairs)

ADT shares forestry, animal care techniques in Paktya

By U.S. Army Sgt. John P. Sklaney III
2-45th Agribusiness Development Team

PAKTYA PROVINCE, Afghanistan, March 18, 2011—Afghan officials and Soldiers of the 2-45th Agribusiness Development Team travelled to the Dand Patan district to assess several agricultural products completed over the past year.

U.S. Army Sgt. Maj. Lorn McKinzie, from Depew, Okla., the ADT's senior Non-Commissioned Officer, met with Haji Naiz Mohammed Khalil, the Dand Patan sub-governor, to discuss recently completed projects and future projects in the district.

"The main focus for this part of the year is forestry," said Khalil. "Afghanistan has experienced severe deforestation in the past few decades."

"The ADT plans to assist in planting more than 2,000 trees this year," said McKinzie. "Those trees will provide soil stabilization and ... will result in fruit production."

At the same time, U.S. Army Spc. Jack McComas, from Lawton, Okla., a project manager for the ADT; and U.S. Army Pfc. Cheryl Baldridge, from Prague, Okla., an ADT veterinary specialist, trained nearly 30 local farmers on basic animal husbandry skills.

"The Afghans requested information about local breeds and nutritional values to help their livestock gain and maintain weight," said McComas. "The ADT plans to return and provide the information that the farmers requested."

Mohammad Ali, the Dand Patan agricultural extension agent, requested the training.

"Training is crucial to farmers in the district," said Ali. "With more advanced training, Afghan farmers will be able manage their animals much better and also be able to sustain them, even after the U.S. has left," he said.

Future projects in Dand Patan will include youth livestock training, poultry training, greenhouses, beekeeping and some farmers will also attend Para-Vet training in Gardez. All of the ADT's projects will assist in building sustainable farming methods.

Pelosi, representatives visit Laghman Province

LAGHMAN PROVINCE, Afghanistan, March 20, 2011—U.S. Army Lt. Col. Steven Kremer, left, the commander of 1st Battalion, 133rd Infantry Regiment, from Cherokee, Iowa, greets U.S. Rep. Leonard Boswell, D-Iowa, right, from Iowa's 3rd Congressional District [...] Boswell and several Congressional representatives, including Minority Leader of the House of Representatives Nancy Pelosi, D-Calif., toured the Iowa National Guard's 2nd Brigade Combat Team, 34th Infantry Division, area of operation in Laghman Province, including a visit with Laghman Gov. Mohammad Iqbal Azizi, and to the Mastoori Girl's School in Mehtar Lam. (Photo by U.S. Army Staff Sgt. Ryan C. Matson, Task Force Red Bulls Public Affairs)

LAGHMAN PROVINCE, Afghanistan, March 20, 2011—Congresswoman Nancy Pelosi. D-Calif., minority leader of the U.S. House of Representatives (front); U.S. Army Lt. Col. Steven Kremer (back left), the commander of 1st Battalion, 133rd Infantry Regiment, from Cherokee, Iowa; and U.S. Rep. Leonard Boswell, D-Iowa, (back right), from Iowa's 3rd Congressional District, walk along a line of Mine-Resistant, Ambush-Protected vehicles during a visit to the Laghman Province at Forward Operating Base Mehtar Lam, Afghanistan [...] (Photo by U.S. Army Staff Sgt. Ryan C. Matson)

Guardsmen use civilian skills to build new JDOC

BAGRAM AIRFIELD, Afghanistan, March 20, 2011—U.S. Army Sgt. Kyle Plathe (right), a signal support systems sergeant from Le Mars, Iowa, and Spc. Andrew Johnson, a signal support systems specialist from Bronson, Iowa, both with Headquarters and Headquarters Troop, 1st Squadron, 113th Cavalry Regiment, Task Force Redhorse, a part of the 2nd Brigade Combat Team, 34th Infantry Division, Task Force Red Bulls, install a TV screen at the new joint defense operations center on Bagram Airfield, Afghanistan. (Photo by U.S. Army Spc. James Wilton, Task Force Red Bulls Public Affairs)

By U.S. Army Spc. James Wilton
Task Force Red Bulls Public Affairs

BAGRAM AIRFIELD, Afghanistan, March 20, 2011—Guardsmen often wear two hats when it comes to their civilian and military careers, which gives them a wider range of training and skill sets to draw upon when they tackle a project or problem.

The Iowa National Guard Soldiers with the Information Technology and Communications section, or "S-6," Headquarters and Headquarters Troop, 1st Squadron, 113th Cavalry Regiment, Task Force Redhorse, proved this during the building of a new Joint Defense Operations Center on Bagram Airfield, Afghanistan.

The previous S-6 unit started the plans and construction in July 2010 and finished the foundation before they redeployed.

U.S. Army Capt. Eric Eggers, the 1-113th Cav. S-6 officer from Marshalltown, Iowa, learned about the project when the Cavalry, a part of the 2nd Brigade Combat Team, 34th Infantry Division, Task Force Red Bulls, began their deployment.

Eggers, who works as a project manager in Iowa, said he used his experience to complete the project as quickly and efficiently as possible.

"Having that experience (in project managing) helped me to better run the project here," said Eggers. "The knowledge and experience I gained in Iowa helped me to better assess the project and know what needed to be done, how the project needed to be run for it to work and happen in a timely manner."

The Soldiers completed the project March 15 and transferred operations from the old JDOC the following week.

The younger enlisted Soldiers benefited from the experience of those appointed above them.

U.S. Army Sgt. 1st Class Russell Steffen, the Non-Commissioned Officer-in-Charge of the 1-113th Cav. S-6 section from Sioux City, Iowa, and a member of the Local 231 Electricians Union, took a lead role in completing the project correctly.

"He brought a lot of experience with him, and it is blatantly obvious when he is instructing or teaching that he has done this before and everyone really listens to what he has to say," said U.S. Army Spc. Andrew Johnson, a signal support systems specialist with HHT. "When he was showing us how to lay the terminated ends into the boxes under the workstations, he was showing you have to go [a certain distance] into the terminated end to make a good connection, he was very specific and very detailed about it."

The project itself also lent one Soldier skills toward a future career.

"I did extensive work with physically laying the cable and working with the patch panels, so it is a trade that I now know and can implement, which opens up several job fields when I get back home," said Johnson of Bronson, Iowa, who is studying computer science at Morningside College in Sioux City, Iowa.

Understanding the infrastructure and layout of buildings like the operations center will help Johnson do his job better in the future, said Eggers.

Experience and knowledge go a long way helping Soldiers in their civilian and military careers, but that is not all the JDOC did for those involved in the construction.

"I look at it as an accomplishment. I can take this project and say 'I did something today,'" said Eggers. "Or, when we go home these guys can say 'I built this fantastic JDOC and the guys that came in after us will be able to use it and know that they have it way better than we had it, and that's because of me.'"

Afghan leader discusses future of Afghan security forces

PAKTYA PROVINCE, Afghanistan, March 21, 2011—Afghan Maj. Gen. Gul Nabi Ahmed Zai, 505th Afghan Uniformed Police commander, and U.S. Army Brig. Gen. John Uberti, Combined Joint Task Force–101 and Regional Command–East deputy commanding general for Afghan development, discuss future operations at the AUP zone headquarters to commemorate the Afghan New Year. (Photo by U.S. Army Capt. Kenneth A. Stewart, 17th Public Affairs Detachment)

By U.S. Army Capt. Kenneth A. Stewart
17th Public Affairs Detachment

PAKTYA PROVINCE, Afghanistan, March 21, 2011—Afghan Uniformed Police 505th Zone commander, Maj. Gen. Gul Nabi Ahmed Zai spoke candidly with Deputy Commanding General (Afghan Development), U.S. Army Brig. Gen. John Uberti about the future of Afghan security forces.

The discussion followed tree planting and other Afghan New Year observances at the 505th AUP Zone headquarters.

Ahmed Zai spoke of the transition from purely Afghan Army-led efforts to the need for combined action between the various Afghan National Security Forces and Operations Coordination Centers–Provincial.

"The OCCs were created by presidential decree," said Ahmed Zai. "We need to empower them to conduct missions with unified forces."

Ahmed Zai was referring to a decree from Afghan President Hamid Karzai that created a system of coordination centers tasked with synchronizing the work of the ANSF in response to armed conflict and natural emergencies.

"Operations Coordination Centers should have the authority to respond to emergencies as needed," said Ahmed Zai. "For example, if a region is attacked the OCC should be able to contact units and the send them into the fight."

Uberti recognized the need to train and empower servicemembers serving in the OCC system.

"We need to make sure the ANSF leadership is out their leading," said Uberti. "We have to teach the OCCs how to say yes, when someone asks for help."

Uberti also pointed out the gains made by the ANSF.

"Together the Afghan National Army, the Uniformed Police and the regional commands have made some good decisions throughout the winter," said Uberti.

Ahmed Zai also noted recent ANSF successes throughout the region and discussed the increased cooperation and communication between ANSF forces and the civilian government.

In order to describe the need for good communication and rapid coordination, Ahmed Zai relayed an anecdote from the time of the Afghan monarchy.

"When the king was in power, there was a unit in Kunar Province that witnessed a foreign jet entering Afghan airspace, by the time the chain of command approved the order to shoot down the aircraft, six months had passed," Zai said.

The absurdity of the Ahmed Zai's anecdote was evidence of the enormous progress made by Afghan forces. He said the OCC system broke through layers of bureaucracy and unified diverse service cultures unique to the ANA and the AUP.

Uberti recognized the recent progress and the sacrifices made by Afghan security forces throughout the region.

"In the last week, there has been contact with the enemy .... We have some brave men out there in all our uniforms and we will always remember them," said Uberti.

Ahmed Zai shared Uberti's sentiments and spoke of his great optimism for the future.

"I am very optimistic about our partnership," said Ahmed Zai. "We are working side by side, working for the same goal against our common enemy.

ANA, French, and U.S. conduct joint patrol

PARWAN PROVINCE, Afghanistan, March 21, 2011—Afghan National Army and the French Operational Mentoring Liaison Team join forces with U.S. Army Soldiers with Troop B, 1st Squadron, 113th Cavalry Regiment, 2nd Brigade Combat Team, 34th Infantry Division, Task Force Red Bulls, to conduct a joint dismounted patrol through Qual-e Jala village in the Koh-e Safi District. Troop B partnered with ANA and the French OMLT to check on security within the village and to conduct a Key Leader Engagement with village elders. (Photo by U.S. Army Spc. Kristina L. Gupton, Task Force Red Bulls Public Affairs)

PARWAN PROVINCE, Afghanistan March 21, 2011—Members of the 6th Kandak, 201st ANA Infantry Corps; French Operational Mentoring Liaison Team members; and Troop B, 1st Squadron, 113th Cavalry Regiment, Task Force Redhorse, 2nd Brigade Combat Team, 34th Infantry Division, Task Force Red Bulls, conduct a Key Leader Engagement with village elders Abdul Salam and Faqir in Qual-e Jala village. (U.S. Army Photo by Spc. Kristina L. Gupton, Task Force Red Bulls Public Affairs)

Iowa National Guard's top leadership visit Red Bulls downrange

LAGHMAN PROVINCE, Afghanistan, March 22, 2011—U.S. Army Maj. Gen. Timothy E. Orr (right), the adjutant general of the Iowa National Guard, from Boone, Iowa, talks with U.S. Army Staff Sgt. Jacob Pries (left), an engineer with Headquarters and Headquarters Company, 2nd Brigade Combat Team, 34th Infantry Division, from Davenport, Iowa, and U.S. Army Staff Sgt. Scott Murray Jr. (center), a squad leader from Princeton, Iowa, with Company A, 1st Battalion, 133rd Infantry Regiment, during his visit to Forward Operating Base Mehtar Lam, Afghanistan. (Photo by U.S. Army Staff Sgt. Ryan C. Matson, Task Force Red Bulls Public Affairs)

By U.S. Army Staff Sgt. Ryan C. Matson
Task Force Red Bulls Public Affairs

LAGHMAN PROVINCE, Afghanistan, March 22, 2011—The Iowa National Guard's senior leadership visited their soldiers at Forward Operating Base Mehtar Lam March 22.

U.S. Army Maj. Gen. Timothy E. Orr, the adjutant general of the Iowa National Guard, from Boone, Iowa, and U.S. Army Command Sgt. Maj. John H. Breitsprecker, the senior enlisted leader of the Iowa National Guard, from Altoona, Iowa, arrived at FOB Mehtar Lam to tour the FOB and meet with the Task Force Red Bulls soldiers from the 1st Battalion, 133rd Infantry Regiment, part of the Iowa National Guard's 2nd Brigade Combat Team, 34th Infantry Division.

Orr and Breitsprecker spoke about the soldier's families, the soldiers from the battalion who were injured in the line of duty last month, and things back in Iowa.

"It's great to get a chance to come and see everybody here in Afghanistan, but more importantly to bring a good news report from home. Everyone I run into says tell the troops hello, and thanks for what they're doing everyday," Orr said to soldiers gathered on the FOB. "And I gotta tell you, there isn't anyone who could be more proud of what you're doing than I am."

"You've been working hard, and I know of course the most important thing is your families back at home. The sergeant major and I told you when we sent you off that the number one priority was—you take care of your mission, you take care of each other, and we'll take care of the families. We've worked very hard for those who have come home injured, or in some cases didn't deploy yet because they're still injured, to travel around to ensure they're getting good care and more importantly, that their families are getting taken care of also."

Orr spoke of visiting U.S. Army Spc. Adam Eilers, an infantryman with Company A, 1st Battalion, 133rd Infantry, from Garber, Iowa, one of the three Red Bulls who suffered serious injuries from an Improvised Explosive Device in February. Eilers is currently receiving treatment Walter Reed Medical Center in Washington, D.C.

"He's getting better every day, but he's got a long way to go," Orr said. "We spent Sunday with him and his family and I want to tell you that they're so proud of him and of you. And the support he's getting from his family members and his community, it's a testament of the Ironman team and what you do for each other and how we roll together. I'm proud of what you're doing and I thank you every day for what you and your families do."

Breitsprecker said the communities around Iowa have risen up to support the families of the injured soldiers.

"A lot of times the families want to get out and come to the hospital and don't have the money to go do that, so a lot of communities have banded together to organize some type of activity to raise money to make that possible," Breitsprecker said.

He added representatives of the Iowa National Guard have also met with the employers of injured soldiers to make sure they understand what's going on.

The command sergeant major said family members of deployed soldiers have been following their soldiers through their blogs and media coverage. He said he was impressed with the soldiers attitudes he met during his visit to Mehtar Lam.

"You always see motivation with this Dubuque group—you always see it," Breitsprecker said.

During the visit, Orr and Breitsprecker received a brief from U.S. Army Lt. Col. Steven Kremer, the commander of 1st Battalion, 133rd Infantry, from Cherokee, Iowa. Kremer told them the various ways the battalion has banded together with other members of Task Force Ironman in the Laghman Province to provide security to the province and assist the Afghan government in improving the area in general.

"That's the Iowa way," he said. "Iowans are always making things better."

LAGHMAN PROVINCE, Afghanistan, March 22, 2011—U.S. Army Maj. Gen. Timothy E. Orr (right), the adjutant general of the Iowa National Guard, from Boone, Iowa, talks with U.S. Army Sgt. Robert Wegner (left), a mortarman from Waterloo, Iowa, and U.S. Army 1st Lt. Terry Dunn (center), a platoon leader from Peosta, Iowa, both from 1st Battalion, 133rd Infantry Regiment, during his visit to Forward Operating Base Mehtar Lam, Afghanistan. (Photo by U.S. Army Staff Sgt. Ryan C. Matson, Task Force Red Bulls Public Affairs)

Top IANG leadership visit Soldiers in Afghanistan

BAGRAM AIRFIELD, Afghanistan, March 23, 2011—Maj. Gen. Timothy E. Orr, the Iowa National Guard adjutant general, speaks with Sgt. Benjamin Leuenhagen, a platoon sergeant with Headquarters and Headquarters Troop, 1st Squadron, 113th Cavalry Regiment, and a Sioux City, Iowa, native, during an informal dinner at Bagram Airfield. (Photo by U.S. Army Spc. James Wilton, Task Force Red Bulls Public Affairs)

BAGRAM AIRFIELD, Afghanistan, March 23, 2011—Maj. Gen. Timothy E. Orr, the Iowa National Guard adjutant general, speaks with a group of soldiers from the 2nd Brigade Combat Team, 34th Infantry Division, during an informal dinner at Bagram Airfield. The dinner was held during a visit by top IANG leadership to Afghanistan in order to check on the status of Iowa soldiers deployed in support of Operation Enduring Freedom. (Photo by U.S. Army Spc. James Wilton, Task Force Red Bulls Public Affairs)

BAGRAM AIRFIELD, Afghanistan, March 23, 2011—Command Sgt. Maj. John H. Breitsprecker, the Iowa National Guard senior enlisted adviser, speaks with Spc. Sarah Parsons, a supply specialist with Headquarters and Headquarters Company, 2nd Brigade Combat Team, 34th Infantry Division and an Ames, Iowa, native, during a visit by top IANG leaders to Bagram Airfield. Breitsprecker and Parsons spoke about her transition from the Air to the Army National Guard and the fact that she worked for Breitsprecker's wife while in the Air Guard. (Photo by U.S. Army Spc. James Wilton, Task Force Red Bulls Public Affairs)

Panjshir PRT helps celebrate first day of school in Shutol

By U.S. Air Force Senior Airman Amber Ashcraft
Panjshir Provincial Reconstruction Team Public Affairs

PANJSHIR PROVINCE, Afghanistan, March 23, 2011—In a large hallway on the second floor of a Shutol District boys school, 200 pairs of eyes watched as a small choir of young men sang an old Islamic song about education. Students, teachers and local elders clapped loudly after the young men finished and a praise of "Insha'Allah," or "God willing," was exclaimed.

Panjshir Provincial Reconstruction Team members joined Shutol District natives and Abdul Moqim Halimi, the director of education, for a ceremony commemorating the first day of school today.

"We were excited to attend the ceremony marking the new school year," said U.S. Army Sgt. 1st Class Wayne Wilson, Panjshir PRT civil affairs Non-Commissioned Officer-in-Charge and Homestead, Fla., native. "About nine years ago there were only 34,000 schools in the country but today there are more than 130,000. So helping celebrate a new term in the schools is a great milestone."

Having celebrated Afghanistan's New Year, Nowruz, it was time for more than 50 schools in Panjshir Province to open their doors for the new term. The Shutol school opened its doors to a brand new library with the celebration.

"Though the books were delivered in January, today, being the first day of school, was the perfect opportunity to introduce the new literature to the students; 2,400 reference books were distributed to two boys and two girls schools in Shutol," said Wilson.

The excited children at the ceremony were hushed as their teachers and elders spoke about the importance of knowledge for today's youth.

"The education children have in their developing years is very important for the learning capacity and knowledge they hold as adults," said Halimee. "Everything that they can get a hold of, including these reference books the PRT has given us, will give them knowledge to use in so many ways."

The books given to the schools included new curricula to the Afghan education system. The literature helps prepare children for trade school or college, said 1st Lt. Hakan Togul, the Panjshir PRT civil affairs Officer-in-Charge and Crete, Ill., native.

The civil affairs team is also working on projects to provide basic computer skills to the students and English language skills for more females in the province. "Regardless of the country you are from, helping this generation have a better education helps us all to have a brighter future to look forward to," said Wilson.

Koreans train Afghans in police skills

PARWAN PROVINCE, Afghanistan, March 13, 2011—Afghan National Police officers practice empty hand control skills with Master Cho, a South Korean police instructor, at Bagram Airfield, Afghanistan. (Photo by Won Hyuk Im, Parwan Provincial Reconstruction Team)

By Won Hyuk Im
Parwan Provincial Reconstruction Team

PARWAN PROVINCE, Afghanistan, March 24, 2011—The Parwan Provincial Reconstruction Team and 1st Squadron, 113th Cavalry Regiment, Task Force Redhorse, conducted a three-week training course for 20 Afghan National Police officers and Afghan National Army soldiers from Parwan Province at Bagram Airfield, March 6–March 24.

The course, second one this year, was geared toward preparing trainees for the eventual transition of security responsibility to the Afghan National Security Forces.

The role of the ANP itself is transitional, from mere militia to an effective counter-insurgency force, and in the end professional law enforcement officers who serve and protect the population.

The course curriculum is based upon integrated and diverse requirements taught by 10 Korean police officers with the Parwan PRT; three U.S. Army Military Police officers from Task Force Redhorse, a part of the 2nd Brigade

Combat Team, 34th Infantry Division, Task Force Red Bulls; and one Afghan lawyer. The class has 12 subjects, ranging from marksmanship to police code of ethics, and from empty hand control skills to Afghan police law.

The core lesson for the trainees was straight forward: be the pride of the people you serve. The pride felt by trainers was evident, especially those from the Korean National Police Agency (KNPA).

"Being in Afghanistan is such a prestige," said Mr. Choi, a Korean National police instructor. "Finally, we can give and share."

The South Korean police instructors are proud to contribute to improving law and order in Afghanistan. The KNPA played an important role during the 60-year history of war and reconstruction in South Korea. Because of this, they realize the challenges ahead for the Afghan people.

Discussing the police code of ethics and international human rights with the students shows how challenging this will be. Many ANP officers still accept sharia law and tribal practices rather than the Afghan constitution as their primary source of justice.

Although challenging this belief system raises tough questions from the students, the Parwan PRT believes that it is necessary in order to make progress toward strengthening the rule of law concept in Afghanistan.

A third round of training, with an expanded scope and duration, is currently underway. As a clear sign of progress, in addition to American and Korean trainers, the class includes a number of Afghan instructors from Parwan Province.

Task Force Phoenix supports largest air-assault in RC–East

PARWAN PROVINCE, Afghanistan, March 25, 2011—Afghan National Army (ANA) and U.S. Army Task Force Red Bull Soldiers wait to practice aircraft dismount in blackout conditions March 25. The soldiers used the training during a major joint air-assault mission in Regional Command—East. (Photo by U.S. Army Sgt. Amanda Jo Brown, Task Force Phoenix Public Affairs)

By U.S. Army Sgt. Amanda Jo Brown
Task Force Phoenix Public Affairs

LAGHMAN PROVINCE, Afghanistan, March 25, 2011—Fierce lightning shattered the night sky as a U.S. Army CH-47 Chinook helicopter's 350-pound blades sliced through the air producing a continuous rain of thunder over the otherwise quiet Galuch Valley.

Crews and helicopters from Task Force Phoenix, Task Force Falcon, 10th Combat Aviation Brigade, 10th Mountain Division, provided air transport for a major air-assault mission in Regional Command–East in support of Afghan National Security Forces and Task Force Red Bulls operations.

Task Force Phoenix collaborated with Chinook crews from Task Force Shooter to complete their essential mission: to provide static load training to ANSF and conduct an air assault into the Galuch Valley allowing ANSF and Task Force Red Bull to remove enemy forces and speak with village elders.

"Static load training with (the ANSF) is absolutely critical to the success of our operations," said U.S. Army Lt. Col. Dennis McKernan, Task Force Phoenix, Task Force Falcon commander, and a native of Haddon Township, N.J., "Operating around helicopters is extremely dangerous and any soldier from any country must be trained how to operate on an aircraft to include loading and unloading. The terrain is extremely rugged in Afghanistan. Off-loading soldiers into tight landing zones can be specifically challenging if the soldiers don't know what to do."

To ensure everyone was prepared to off-load an aircraft even in unsatisfactory conditions, Task Force Phoenix and Shooter Chinook crews flew despite lightning. The huge engines quieted their loud roar and the blades slowed to a halt as the crews landed in Combat Outpost Xio Haq and stepped out into the thick darkness.

"Most of the (ANSF) have never been on a CH-47 before. Cold load training allows them to get used to the aircraft and efficient at exiting the ramp when we arrive at the landing zone," said U.S. Army 1st Sgt. Daniel Snyder, Company D, Task Force Phoenix, first sergeant.

The training, conducted in complete darkness, is a simple, but crucial part of a successful air assault. It provides soldiers with familiarity of the aircraft and procedures used during a mission.

Time is of the essence during air assaults with the challenges of rugged terrain, unpredictable weather, and the threat of enemy forces hidden in the shadows, said Snyder.

"You never know what kind of landing zone you will be flying into on a mission," said Snyder, a native of Millington, Mich., "It could have hostiles present, or it could just be a difficult landing where we can only put the back two wheels on the ground. When that happens, there is a lot of stress on the pilots and crew."

"The faster (passengers) exit, the less that can go wrong," added Snyder.

The Chinook crews cycled through the groups just as efficiently as the ANSF absorbed the training.

When the training was complete, the ANSF and Task Force Red Bull Soldiers loaded into the aircraft and prepared to put all of their training into action during the air assault.

The ANSF and Task Force Red Bull Soldiers were all business when it came time to dismount the aircraft into the shadowy mountains surrounding the valley.

"I think it's great that the ANSF are augmented with our forces," said Snyder, "It lets them see what right looks like."

The aviation crews worked diligently to ensure each landing into the mountains was done to standard and done safely regardless of the unique challenges presented by the terrain.

"The greatest hazards were unimproved landing zones that can have large rocks that could damage the aircraft, or steep slopes that are near impossible to land on, unpredictable wind gusts, and enemy personnel (concealed) in the mountain sides and ditches," said Snyder.

With experienced crews manning each helicopter, the Soldiers were confident in the success of the operation.

"Our crews are the best. We purposely stack the crews to best complement each other," said Snyder, "All of us on this mission had done (air assaults) before. It's awesome when you use almost all of your training on one landing and the mission was successful. It's an amazing feeling,"

In a matter of hours, the Chinook crews safely inserted all of the groups into the Galuch Valley with no issues.

As the crews returned to Bagram Airfield, they reflected on a successful joint mission. U.S. Army Sgt. John Colwell, a flight engineer with Headquarters and Headquarters Troop, Task Force Shooter, Task Force Falcon, 10th CAB, 10th Mountain Division, and a native of Phoenix, said he felt the ANSF were very motivated and ready for the mission.

"I feel that (Afghans) will soon be able to obtain their role as defenders in their fight against the forces threatening their country," said Colwell.

PARWAN PROVINCE, Afghanistan, March 25, 2011—U.S. Army 1st Sgt. Daniel Snyder, a CH-47 Chinook flight engineer, briefs Afghan National Army (ANA) soldiers on dismounting aircraft. Snyder, a first sergeant in Company D, Task Force Phoenix, Task Force Falcon, 10th Combat Aviation Brigade, 10th Mountain Division, trained four groups of ANSF soldiers on quick dismounts during air assaults. (Photo by U.S. Army Sgt. Amanda Jo Brown, Task Force Phoenix Public Affairs)

Red Bulls, ANA sweep Galuch Valley, establish joint security center

LAGHMAN PROVINCE, Afghanistan, March 26, 2011—Afghan National Army soldiers from 2nd Kandak, 1st Brigade, 201st ANA Infantry Corps, scour mountain ridges outside the village of Hind Dor, Afghanistan, March 26 during Operation Promethium Puma. (Photo by U.S. Army Staff Sgt. Ryan C. Matson, Task Force Red Bulls Public Affairs)

By U.S. Army Staff Sgt. Ryan C. Matson
Task Force Red Bulls Public Affairs

LAGHMAN PROVINCE, Afghanistan, March 26—An Iowa Army National Guard unit recently wrapped up the largest air-assault operation conducted by the 101st Airborne Division during their year-long deployment to Afghanistan.

Operation Bull Whip began March 25, when the first Soldiers were inserted by air into the southern portion of the Galuch Valley by Task Force Phoenix. The main body of troops entered the northern end of the valley early the next morning. These Soldiers, from 1st Battalion, 133rd Infantry Regiment, Task Force Ironman, a part of the 2nd Brigade Combat Team, 34th Infantry Division, Task Force Red Bulls, and from the French Army, Task Force Lafayette, cleared the valley.

Task Force Lafayette also provided artillery support from Kapisa Province. The 1st Squadron, 113th Cavalry Regiment, Task Force Redhorse, also a part of the 2nd BCT, 34th Inf. Div., provided over watch support from the ridge lines surrounding the valley.

Two platoons from Company A and D of the 1st Battalion, 133rd Infantry Regiment, teamed with an Afghan National Army company from the

2nd Kandak, 1st Brigade, 201st ANA Infantry Corps, cleared the valley on both sides from north to south while the scout platoon and another ANA company provided a blocking position on the southern end.

"The purpose of Bull Whip, was to get a foothold in the Galuch area, to get the government in there, to establish a new district center and really get the government and people connected there," said U.S. Army Lt. Col. Steven Kremer, Puma's ground forces commander, and the 133rd Inf. commander. "Our main mission with Promethium Puma was to get in there and establish the security—defeating the enemy and clearing them from the valley so the government could be established to make that connection with the people."

Laghman Province Gov. Mohammad Iqbal Azizi explained why it was important to bring government to the Galuch Valley.

"The people there had been deprived of the rights of education, health and all services of life by the insurgency," said Azizi. "The people were asking the government of Afghanistan for the physical presence of government there. They were asking for services and the enemy was brutally trying to deprive the people of these kinds of rights, so eventually the president of Afghanistan, President Karzai, approved the district there."

Kremer, a native of Cherokee, Iowa, said the mission was also the first step in providing infrastructure there.

"If you peel the onion back, the underlying issue was also running a set of power lines through the Galuch Valley," said Kremer. "These lines will provide electricity and power to more than 70,000 households throughout the area. The enemy was causing problems and eventually brought this to a halt."

The enemy offered no physical resistance during the operation. Azizi had told the people the government would be coming and leaflets were dropped before the operation began, warning the people troops would be coming.

"They did not come out of the woodwork and fight us, which allowed us to engage the population and conduct shuras to prep them for the government and a big shura at the end of the operation," said Kremer. "We didn't see stiff resistance because we didn't surprise them. They knew the government was coming and the message was sent to the people that we were going to push a security element out there once the district center was approved. They had to make a decision—were they going to stay and fight, or did they believe that we were going to come out there with overwhelming combat power? With the large mass of folks we brought out there and the fact that we air assaulted in, I think the enemy probably made the decision that it was probably best not to fight."

Kremer said the coalition is obviously concerned about enemy supporters still in the valley who may have blended in with the general population. However, he said some of these people who are truly part of the village will see what the future will be like with security and a functioning government. These people will then have a chance to reintegrate as part of the village working with the government rather than trying to disrupt it.

"I don't want to sound like I'm being overly optimistic, but if you can bring enough security and stability for a brief period and the government comes in and starts providing services, the hopes are they will take a leap with the government and see how it works out," said Kremer.

Kremer acknowledged bringing peace and stability to the region will be a long, ongoing process, especially to the northern region of the valley that is more difficult to reach due to the absence of roads and other infrastructure. However, Kremer said now the coalition has the initial foothold in the area it had been seeking.

While the Soldiers were not resisted by the enemy, they did, however, find massive amounts of weapons caches the enemy had been storing in the valley. More than 30 caches were found during the operation, including a slew of weapons, opium stashes, expended munitions for Improvised Explosive Devices, more than a dozen anti-personnel land mines and various pieces of military clothing and communications equipment.

"We told the people to give us the weapons the enemy had been hiding in their villages, because this stuff does not belong to you, it belongs to the army," ANA 1st Lt. Mohammad Sabir-Amiri, an intelligence officer, said. "The people told us where some of the caches were in the villages. We were enthusiastic when we found things because when we found rockets, some of (the U.S.) Soldiers told us the enemy in Iraq had used those same rockets against (coalition) helicopters, and we knew we were finding things that could help prevent that. We were very happy; it was a great achievement."

Sabir-Amiri said the mission was a team effort between Afghan and American Soldiers.

"We worked together—we don't say one group found anything, we say we found it together," Sabir-Amiri said. "One hand alone cannot make a sound, but two hands together can make a great sound. This place is such a dangerous place; we wanted to help one another to make it better. The best thing is that we are all going home safely."

The Soldiers finished clearing objectives in the valley April 2.

Kremer said the ANA and Afghan National Civil Order Police are entering the area to provide long-term security at the joint security center, which will eventually evolve into the government's district center in Galuch Valley.

"The mission has now transitioned into holding the ground that was cleared during the operation in order to allow the government to be established in that area," said U.S. Army Maj. Aaron Baugher, battalion operations officer of the 1-133rd Inf., Task Force Ironman, 2-34th BCT, Task Force Red Bulls, from Ankeny, Iowa.

Kremer said the elders have visited the temporary district center every day since the main shura March 31, and have taken the first steps in working with the government. He said the way the ANA and Red Bulls Soldiers behaved in the villages may have gained the faith of some of the villagers.

"Our Soldiers did a phenomenal job," said Kremer. "They were good to the locals as they went in to their villages. The Afghans, having suffered casualties in the valley in a fight there in the fall, could have gotten emotional as they found caches that included pieces of their equipment from that fight. It could have led to a revengeful situation, but the reality was that the Soldiers did not go that route; they were professional and went into the mind frame that they were there to clear out the bad guys and bring the government to the people."

Azizi agreed. He said he was pleased with the way the Red Bulls and ANA soldiers conducted themselves in clearing the valley.

"I, and the people in general, were highly impressed with the soldiers," said Azizi. "The operation was conducted very professionally. It exceeded my expectations. I am highly impressed with the soldiers in the field in the way that they conducted this operation."

Aziz said the professionalism the soldiers demonstrated helped influence the positive response from the village.

"When I was participating in the shura at the end of the operation with the elders, I did not expect how cordially and very warmly the people would welcome the operation," said Aziz. "Specifically, I was highly impressed with the soldiers in the field. Lt. Col. Kremer and his Soldiers were already having several meetings with the people in the field before the shura. They did so in a friendly manner, and this exceeded the expectations of the people of Afghanistan and the people in that area. It was a very constructive operation."

ANA, coalition forces work side by side during Operation Bull Whip

LAGHMAN PROVINCE, Afghanistan, March 27, 2011—U.S. Army Sgt. Tyler A. Smith of Des Moines, Iowa, a signal support system specialist with the 2nd Brigade Combat Team, 34th Infantry Division, Task Force Red Bulls, monitors radio traffic while at Observation Post Two in Galuch Valley during Operation Bull Whip. Bull Whip is the biggest air-assault mission ever conducted by the 2nd Brigade and the largest conducted by Combined Joint Task Force–101 during its current rotation in Afghanistan. (Photo by U.S. Army Spc. Kristina L. Gupton, Task Force Red Bulls Public Affairs)

LAGHMAN PROVINCE, Afghanistan, March 27, 2011—An Afghan National Army (ANA) soldier scans his sector of fire at Observation Post Two during Operation Bull Whip March 27. ANA soldiers joined Soldiers from the 2nd Brigade Combat Team, 34th Infantry Division, Task Force Red Bulls, in pulling security for the joint Tactical Operations Center at OP Two. Approximately 2,200 troops, including 1,300 Afghan National Security Forces, participated in the operation. (Photo by U.S. Army by Spc. Kristina L. Gupton, Task Force Red Bulls Public Affairs)

Commander witnesses CJTF–101's largest Afghanistan air-assault mission

LAGHMAN PROVINCE, Afghanistan, March 27, 2011—A UH-60 Black Hawk helicopter flies away after dropping off U.S. Army Maj. Gen. John F. Campbell, 101st Airborne Division and Regional Command–East commander, and other members, at Observation Post Two in the Galuch Valley during Operation Bull Whip. Campbell visited the mountain top to check on the status of the largest air-assault mission ever conducted by the 2nd Brigade Combat Team, 34th Infantry Division, Task Force Red Bulls. This air-assault mission also had the distinction of being the largest conducted by the Combined Joint Task Force–101 during its current rotation in Afghanistan. (Photo by U.S. Army Spc. Kristina L. Gupton, Task Force Red Bulls Public Affairs)

LAGHMAN PROVINCE, Afghanistan, March 27, 2011—U.S. Army Capt. Lee Vandewater, of Winterset, Iowa, and an infantry officer with the 2nd Brigade Combat Team, 34th Infantry Division, Task Force Red Bulls, scans his sector of fire at Observation Post Two during Operation Bull Whip [...] (Photo by U.S. Army Spc. Kristina L. Gupton, Task Force Red Bulls Public Affairs)

LAGHMAN PROVINCE, Afghanistan, March 27, 2011—U.S. Army Col. Benjamin J. Corell, of Strawberry Point, Iowa, and the 2nd Brigade Combat Team, 34th Infantry Division, Task Force Red Bulls commander, briefs U.S. Army Maj. Gen. John F. Campbell, 101st Airborne Division and Regional Command–East commander, on operations in the Galuch Valley. Approximately 2,200 Afghan and coalition troops pushed through the Galuch Valley, conducting Key Leader Engagements and searching for weapons caches, to clear the valley of insurgents during Operation Bull Whip. (Photo by U.S. Army Spc. Kristina L. Gupton, Task Force Red Bulls Public Affairs)

Operation Promethium Puma, Day 1: Coalition, ANA soldiers uncover weapons caches in Galuch Valley

LAGHMAN PROVINCE, Afghanistan, March 24, 2011—U.S. Army Capt. Jason Merchant, left, the commander of Company A, 1st Battalion, 133rd Infantry Regiment, Task Force Ironman, 2nd Brigade Combat Team, 34th Infantry Division, Task Force Red Bulls, from Dysart, Iowa, talks over the plan for his unit with Afghan National Army Lt. Col. Shah Alom, 2nd Kandak, 1st Brigade, 201st ANA Infantry Corps, right, at Combat Outpost Xio Haq, during the preparation stages for Operation Promethium Puma. (Photo by U.S. Army Staff Sgt. Ryan C. Matson, Task Force Red Bulls Public Affairs)

By U.S. Army Staff Sgt. Ryan C. Matson
Task Force Red Bulls Public Affairs

and U.S. Army Sgt. Mike Miller
Company A, 1st Battalion, 133rd Infantry Regiment

* Editor's note—This is a three-part series that follows the activities of one platoon. About 30 Soldiers deployed to the remote Combat Outpost Najil, during Operation Promethium Puma, March 26 to April 2. Puma was the ground portion of Operation Bull Whip. This is their story.

NANGARHAR PROVINCE, Afghanistan, March 26, 2011—U.S. Army Capt. Jason Merchant, the Company A, 1st Battalion, 133rd Infantry Regiment, Task Force Ironman, commander, had said it many times before.

"Afghanistan is a hiding place," Merchant, a native of Dysart, Iowa, repeated as he trekked up a steep path in the village of Hind Dor, Afghanistan, March 31. He was referring to the unlimited availability of hiding places for weapons and contraband in the rugged terrain features that make up Afghanistan.

The Soldiers who followed him, members of the company's 2nd Platoon, were on Day Six of Operation Promethium Puma, the ground portion of Operation Bull Whip, the largest air-assault mission conducted by the 101st Airborne Division, Combined Joint Task Force–101, during their year-long deployment to Afghanistan. The mission was conducted with air assets from Task Force Phoenix, a part of the 101st and Soldiers from the Iowa National Guard's 2nd Brigade Combat Team, 34th Infantry Division, Task Force Red Bulls, of which Merchant's Soldiers are a part.

The mission objective was to clear the Galuch Valley from north to south and establish a coalition footprint in the area which is a known insurgent stronghold and training area. Second platoon's mission was to eliminate insurgent forces, weapons and bomb-making materials from the valley. On Day Six, the platoon's Soldiers, weary, dirty, tired and grisly-faced, were still climbing the mountains in search of their targets.

Two other units, one American and one Afghan, attempted to secure the valley in the past year, but, due to heavy enemy resistance, had to withdraw on both occasions.

"The last time the Afghan National Army came in here, they were involved in a big fight and ended up needing to be recovered out of here after taking pretty heavy casualties and losses," said Merchant. "I was anticipating us coming into a pretty heavy fight here in Hind Dor."

But this time, there would be no resistance. Second Platoon, along with several hundred Red Bull and ANA soldiers air-assaulted into the valley in the early morning hours of March 26 without a shot fired. Though they did not face immediate contact, the platoon stayed alert and vigilant, ready for an attack at any time.

Loaded with an average of about 100 pounds of gear, including: food and water, clothing and survival gear in addition to ammunition and weapons systems, the Soldiers climbed dozens of rock walls leading up to the village of Hind Dor.

Once in the village, the platoon split three ways. One squad pulled security while another, teamed with their ANA counterparts, searched the village. The final squad gathered biometrics information on Afghan occupants.

It did not take long for the first discovery to be made. At 8:30 a.m., U.S. Army Pfc. Brett Turner, a Company A, 1-133rd Inf., Task Force Ironman, 2-34th BCT, Task Force Red Bulls forward observer from Johnston, Iowa, was walking along the terraces at the edge of the village when he noticed some overhanging rocks that appeared to have been dug under. He asked another Soldier to check it out.

Turner's suspicions paid off. Under the overhang were two armed rocket-propelled grenades. This was the first cache located in the operation.

"It's been a long time coming, after all the walkabouts with the commander," said Turner. "We've walked some pretty high mountains looking for stuff."

The discovery, the first of his career, was an early birthday present for the young Soldier, who turned 24 the next day. The platoon and the ANA uncovered nearly 20 caches in the valley which was the most out of all the elements involved in the operation.

The platoon provided perimeter security while the ANA searched homes in the village. Second Platoon did not physically enter the villagers' homes, but helped by searching the outside of houses, rock ledges, caves, mountain fighting positions, bushes and exposed structures. The exception to this rule was the Female Engagement Team, military women who search and interview Afghan women in accordance with Islamic culture.

Turner's cache find was relatively small due to the notable absence of men in Hind Dor. Locals said the insurgency had known for a couple weeks of the pending operation and left the valley.

"We pretty much thought they had grabbed everything they were going to use and got the heck out," said U.S. Army Spc. Skyler Moser, a 2nd Platoon Squad Automatic Weapon gunner from Osterdock, Iowa. "We weren't meeting any resistance and we weren't finding anything, so we thought it was all gone."

But it wasn't. A few Soldiers from the platoon, including U.S. Army Staff Sgt. Doug Walwer, a squad leader from Clinton, Iowa, and his weapon's squad, pushed to a small set of buildings outside the main village. One building was on a hilltop and was built up almost like a fort. It was under the building that the alert eyes of the ANA caught the outline of a rocket. After digging under the building, the Soldiers uncovered eight 57 mm Russian rockets.

Five minutes later, the villagers led them into a nearby structure where they found numerous types of explosives, a large chest of foreign army manuals and literature, a spool of copper wire commonly used in the production of Improvised Explosive Devices, artillery shells, magazines, rocket shells, AK-47 and machine gun rounds, RPG heads and other communication and military materials. The Soldiers pulled one item after another from the building. It was "Day One," and the Soldiers netted their first big cache of the operation.

Operation Promethium Puma, Day 2: Battling the elements

NANGARHAR PROVINCE, Afghanistan, March 28, 2011—Afghan National Army Soldiers from 2nd Kandak, 1st Brigade, 201st ANA Infantry Corps, seek cover from a rain and hailstorm in the Galuch Valley, Afghanistan during Operation Promethium Puma. (Photo by U.S. Army Staff Sgt. Ryan C. Matson, Task Force Red Bulls Public Affairs)

By U.S. Army Staff Sgt. Ryan C. Matson
Task Force Red Bulls Public Affairs

and U.S. Army Sgt. Mike Miller
Company A, 1st Battalion, 133rd Infantry Regiment

* Editor's note—This is a three-part series that follows the activities of one platoon. About 30 Soldiers, deployed to the remote Combat Outpost Najil, during Operation Promethium Puma, March 26 to April 2. Puma was the ground portion of Operation Bull Whip. In Part One, they air-assaulted into the Galuch Valley and found their first large cache of the operation.

NANGARHAR PROVINCE, *Afghanistan, March 27, 2011*—The Soldiers of 2nd Platoon, Company A, 1st Battalion, 133rd Infantry Regiment, Task Force Ironman, bedded down for the night on the rocky slope of a mountain. They had climbed through the evening in darkness to get there.

On Day Two, Soldiers endured the most strenuous day of movement during the eight-day operation, according to the Soldiers from 2nd Platoon, Company A., 1-133rd Inf., of the 2nd Brigade Combat Team, 34th Infantry Division, Task Force Red Bulls. It began with a much-needed airdrop of food and supplies. The Soldiers, still carrying heavy packs of gear, scaled a series of steep ridges during a roughly five-mile movement southwest to clear three villages. They found nothing.

The first two days of heavy movement took their toll. Five Soldiers suffered knee or ankle injuries. Many more said they were close to being "broken off." The night would offer no relief.

"We got to our patrol base and got pounded with the winds and rain of 'Hurricane Hind Dor,'" U.S. Army Pfc. Anthony McAndrew, a 2nd Platoon grenadier from Dubuque, Iowa, said. "That was the worst night."

The weather turned out to be the Soldier's most formidable adversary. The second night began with cold, heavy winds before hard rains and hail. The Soldiers struggled to keep warm in their all-weather sleeping bag and covers, ponchos, or in some cases, just sleeping bags. Many displayed signs of hypothermia and two were treated by the platoon medic, U.S. Army Pfc. Zachary Volz, of Des Moines, Iowa.

Soldiers tried to sleep in between guard shifts but many woke up cold and shivering. When day broke for day three of the mission, the Soldiers were not greeted with a sunrise, but rather a final intense two-hour bout of cold rain and hail.

The platoon claimed some of the village's outlying farm shelters, and built fires to raise their core temperatures.

"That's where we shacked up with three cows," said U.S. Army Spc. Skyler Moser, a 2nd Platoon Squad Automatic Weapon gunner, from Osterdock, Iowa.

As the weather improved, so did the Soldier's luck. That morning, as Soldiers took turns drying by the fire, another cache was found. It was discovered because the Soldiers garnered the cooperation of the villagers.

"Right as we got into town, the first house the Afghan National Army hit, there was a cache," said U.S. Army Sgt. Joshua Anderegg, a squad leader from Osterdock, Iowa.

The villagers led the Soldiers and ANA to several other finds, a result of a promise the villagers made during a Key Leader Engagement the day before.

The platoon found a lot of expended rounds, mortars, heroin, TNT and other items.

On Day Four, the mission changed. The original plan called for the platoon to continue pushing south to a medical clinic, which would be the site of a huge peace shura among elders of the Galuch Valley, later that week. It was also the future site of a new district center for the valley.

However, the Soldiers instead found themselves packed, once again, into a CH-47 Chinook helicopter, air-assaulting back to their first objective, the village of Hind Dor. Things would be different in Hind Dor this time around. The first thing they noticed was significantly more males in the village.

An hour after arriving in the town, the voice of U.S. Army 2nd Lt. Taylor A. Gingrich, the platoon's platoon leader from Dysart, Iowa, came across the radio.

"We just found a Degtyaryova-Shpagina Krupnokaliberny, (Soviet heavy machine gun) barrel," he said. "I want to talk to these elders and ask them why they lied to me!"

Gingrich walked into the village courtyard with the massive gun barrel and plopped it down.

Meanwhile, the platoon and ANA continued re-sweeping the village, uncovering three additional RPGs. Second Platoon Soldiers entered the town males, numbering more than 100, into the biometrics system.

The day concluded with a massive meeting in the courtyard.

"I can promise you that my Soldiers are here to help you and not change your way of living," said U.S. Army Capt. Jason Merchant, commander of Company A, 1-133rd Inf., 2-34th BCT, Task Force Red Bulls, from Dysart, Iowa, to the crowd of townspeople. "You have a strong, rich culture. There are elements here in Afghanistan who are enemies of peace and who create instability.

"I need your cooperation to root out these elements of instability and enemies of peace," continued Merchant.

The day concluded with the Soldiers bedding down in the poppy fields surrounding Hind Dor. Many crafted beds from poppy plants to keep them off the cold mud below. It would be another, cold, rainy night for the Soldiers of 2nd Platoon.

Operation Promethium Puma, Day 5: 'The mother lode'

LAGHMAN PROVINCE, Afghanistan, March 30, 2011—U.S. Army Capt. Jason Merchant, the Company A, 1st Battalion, 133rd Infantry Regiment, Task Force Ironman, a part of the 2nd Brigade Combat Team 34th Infantry Division, Task Force Red Bulls, commander of from Dysart, Iowa, looks through pictures of suspected insurgents with assault rifles in a homemade explosives stash found in the village of Hind Dor, Afghanistan, March 30, during Operation Promethium Puma. (Photo by U.S. Army Staff Sgt. Ryan C. Matson, Task Force Red Bulls Public Affairs)

By U.S. Army Staff Sgt. Ryan C. Matson
Task Force Red Bulls Public Affairs

and U.S. Army Sgt. Mike Miller
Company A, 1st Battalion, 133rd Infantry Regiment

* Editor's note—This is a three-part series that follows the activities of one platoon. About 30 Soldiers, deployed to the remote Combat Outpost Najil, during Operation Promethium Puma, March 26 to April 2. Puma was the ground portion of Operation Bull Whip. In Part One, they air-assaulted into the Galuch Valley and found their first large cache of the operation. In Part Two, they continued their mission in the valley, enduring rough conditions.

NANGARHAR PROVINCE, Afghanistan, March 30, 2011—Though the U.S. Army Soldiers would be in the field for three more days, March 30, Day Five, was the last and most substantial day of Operation Promethium Puma for 2nd Platoon, Company A, 1st Battalion, 133rd Infantry Regiment, Task Force Ironman.

With the help from the Afghan National Army soldiers of 2nd Kandak, 1st Brigade, 201st ANA Infantry Corps, March 30 produced what the Soldiers referred to as the "mother lode"—the largest caches found during the entire operation.

The 2nd Platoon, a part of the 2nd Brigade Combat Team 34th Infantry Division, Task Force Red Bulls, separated into two squads, with one searching the eastern side of the Hind Dor Valley, Afghanistan, and the other searching the western side. During the mission, the platoon hiked mountain after mountain in temperatures exceeding 100 degrees. They spent days searching in holes, crevices, caves, rock walls, bushes, ditches, freshly-dug dirt or any number of other hiding places without finding anything, but March 30 would be a different story.

The ANA found the first of eight caches that day in a tree.

"After that, every 10 minutes it seemed like we found something else," said U.S. Army Sgt. Joshua Anderegg, a squad leader from Osterdock, Iowa.

At the end of a very long day, the Explosive Ordnance Disposal team, tasked with destroying the enemy munitions and other material found during the operation, had several duffel bags full of cached items. Even the duffel bags themselves, those of American Soldiers, were found hidden in the houses on the ridge outside Hind Dor. That afternoon, the team laid all the items out on the ground near the platoon's patrol base.

The Soldiers and their ANA counterparts, had found two grenades, hundreds of AK-47 rounds and Pulemyot Kalishnikova machine gun ammunition, gunpowder, 170-milimeter rocket warheads, four 75 mm shells, three Chinese rocket rounds, 12 anti-personnel land mines, six blocks of opium, three U.S. Army combat uniform trousers, five Army duffel bags, three sling-load bags, four British .303 rifles with clips and ammunition, a rocket-launching tube system, as well as various other items.

The platoon found one more cache during the mission, also in a house outside Hind Dor. This cache, though smaller, contained evidence of a homemade explosives lab. There was 150-pounds of illegal fertilizer, military equipment, propellant, gunpowder and other homemade explosives materials, as well as several photos of suspected insurgents holding automatic weapons.

The Soldiers left the Galuch Valley, April 2, after eight days of searching and sweeping. With each day of the mission, the platoon acquired additional pieces of plastic and other material from air drops, and used each piece to improve their sleeping areas. The platoon dug holes, made makeshift tents, and waterproofed their sleeping areas as best they could. They nicknamed the areas "shanty towns."

At night, some Soldiers, with no real access to hot meals other than through the heaters in their meals ready-to-eat, bought food from local farmers. They enjoyed traditional Afghan meals such as goat soup, salted potatoes in sauce, pan bread, and of course Chai tea.

The Soldiers said though they found a large amount of caches in the area, most of the main weapons systems they were looking for remained hidden. A security presence will remain in the area through the implementation of ANA and Afghan Civil Order Police at the new joint security center which had been established after the shura farther south in the Galuch Valley, March 31.

From the standpoint of putting a "footprint" in the valley, the platoon said they accomplished the mission.

"We definitely did that," said Anderegg. "We opened the door for the possibility of security in the area. From that standpoint, the mission was a success."

Provincial governor holds shura in new district

LAGHMAN PROVINCE, Afghanistan, March 31, 2011—Laghman Province Gov. Mohammad Iqbal Azizi greets attendees during a shura held to announce the establishment of the new Bad Pech District government at the district center March 31. The district government will provide a stronger connection between the provincial government and the people in the newly formed district. (Photo by U.S. Air Force Lt. Col. John C. Walker, Laghman Provincial Reconstruction Team)

By U.S. Air Force 2nd Lt. Chase P. McFarland
Laghman Provincial Reconstruction Team

LAGHMAN PROVINCE, Afghanistan, March 31, 2011—On the heels of a successful operation to establish security in the recently approved Bad Pech District, Laghman Province Gov. Mohammad Iqbal Azizi held a peace shura with approximately 300 local village elders and leaders in the newly established district center March 31.

The Afghan-secured shura featured speakers across the spectrum of Laghman's provincial government including the governor, the district's new leadership, security officials, local elders and the director of rural rehabilitation and development.

The shura focused on working to create a promising future for the district and its people. Azizi gave the responsibility for stability and security to the people of the area. He emphasized that security will facilitate the arrival of schools, clinics and other development.

"This is the good way, coming to the peace shura," said Azizi. "Good villages require hard work!"

The successful execution of the shura is another example of the continuously improving capability of Laghman's government officials and security personnel.

"Gov. Azizi's prediction that no shots would be fired during the operation held true, which shows the exceptional job he did shaping the communities in advance of the operation," said U.S. Army Maj. Steven Shannon, Laghman Provincial Reconstruction Team civil affairs officer and Spring Lake, Mich., native.

Laghman Province continues to make strides toward transitioning to complete Afghan leadership. The first step occurs this summer as Mehtar Lam City, the provincial capital, is officially transitioned.

Afghan, coalition forces join in New Year celebration

PAKTYA PROVINCE, Afghanistan, March 26, 2011—Paktya Gov. Alhaj Joma Khan Hamdard meets with U.S. Army Lt. Col. Stephen B. Boesen II of Ankeny, Iowa, commander of the 1st Battalion, 168th Infantry Regiment, Task Force Lethal, at Forward Operating Base Gardez during an Afghan New Year celebration. The gathering was a chance for Afghan and U.S. personnel to celebrate the transition to a new year together. (U.S. Air Force photo by Staff Sgt. Barry Loo, Paktya Provincial Reconstruction Team Public Affairs)

By U.S. Air Force 1st Lt. Sybil Taunton
Paktya Provincial Reconstruction Team Public Affairs

PAKTYA PROVINCE, Afghanistan, March 26, 2011—Government of the Islamic Republic of Afghanistan officials joined members of Paktya Provincial Reconstruction Team; 1st Battalion, 168th Infantry Regiment, Task Force Lethal; and the 2-45th Agribusiness Development Team, for a New Year's celebration at Forward Operating Base Gardez.

The celebration included a chance for coalition forces and GIRoA officials to socialize, eat lunch provided by a local restaurant owner and attend a tree-planting ceremony to symbolize the hope for a new year of success and growth in the province.

"The purpose of the event was to invite our Afghan partners to the FOB to celebrate the New Year," said Michael Obryon, Paktya PRT U.S. Department of State representative from Newburyport, Mass. "It was also an opportunity for us to deepen our relationships and to learn more about the Afghan New Year."

The New Year holiday is a three-day affair in Afghanistan. The first day is the welcoming of the New Year, the second day is for the celebration of education, and the third day is focused on the celebration of agriculture and growth.

The PRT and ADT are partnering with Paktya representatives and Afghan National Security Forces to honor those celebrations by delivering trees, backpacks, school supplies and athletic equipment to various schools throughout the province.

"The good coordination we have with our coalition partners shows great achievement for our province," said Alhaj Joma Khan Hamdard, the provincial governor. "I hope for a peaceful, secure and stable New Year."

PAKTYA PROVINCE, Afghanistan, March 26, 2011—Paktya Gov. Alhaj Joma Khan Hamdard (right) and engineer Lali Zadran (second from left), Paktya director of agriculture and irrigation, plant a tree at Forward Operating Base Gardez during an Afghan New Year celebration. The trees were donated by the 2-45th Agribusiness Development Team as a symbol of growth in the province. (U.S. Air Force photo by Staff Sgt. Barry Loo, Paktya Provincial Reconstruction Team Public Affairs)

Afghan government reaches out to the people

By U.S. Air Force Staff Sgt. Barry Loo
Paktya Provincial Reconstruction Team Public Affairs

PAKTYA PROVINCE, Afghanistan, March 28, 2011—The Government of the Islamic Republic of Afghanistan reached out to residents in Chamkani and surrounding districts within Paktya Province, Afghanistan, March 28.

A delegation of senior provincial government officials, including Paktya Deputy Gov. Abdul Rahman Mangal, met with tribal elders and religious leaders to discuss development, governance, and security in the area.

"In the past, the people knocked on government's doors to ask for help; now, we are coming to your villages and district centers," said Mangal. "We all remember the bad days of the civil war in Afghanistan. Everyone who had authority was killing others and looting other's property. Whatever they could do, they did. Together, we can prevent past experiences of war and conflict."

Villagers commented about the success of the Afghan Local Police, who serve as militiamen for local villages. They also complained about insurgents crossing the border into their territory from Pakistan.

In his speech, Hajji Laiq Mangal, Paktya Provincial Development Council chief, said, "If we have better security, we'll have tourists coming from other countries for site-seeing instead of terrorists."

In response to their security concerns, Afghan Gen. Ghulam Dastagir, Paktya Afghan National Police deputy commander, signed agreements to create new security checkpoints in the region.

Also, the deputy governor addressed the tribal conflicts in the area.

Land disputes and other issues have caused some tribes to violence. GIRoA set up seven shuras throughout the province, partly to help settle such disputes, Mangal said.

If the shuras cannot peacefully resolve the issue, he told them to use the government's judicial process.

"We have judges, we have courts, we have prosecutors, we have a system," he said.

Afghan, U.S. Engineers wrap up construction workshop

By U.S. Air Force Senior Airman Amber Ashcraft
Panjshir Provincial Reconstruction Team Public Affairs

PANJSHIR PROVINCE, Afghanistan, March 28, 2011—The Panjshir Provincial Reconstruction Team engineers concluded a construction workshop for Afghan engineers [...] in the Bazarak Municipality.

Afghans from 13 construction companies received classroom and practical application training during the weeklong workshop. To help prevent common construction errors, they developed knowledge and awareness of useful techniques with the Afghans.

"They've been using such outdated practices that they were actually pretty open to learning proper construction techniques," said Scott Davis, the U.S. Army Corps of Engineers construction representative with the PRT.

The first three classes involved tying and placement of rebar, and proper ways to mix and pour concrete.

"The PRT engineers pointed out deficiencies we knew we had, but didn't know how to fix," said Haji Ghulam Nabi Yaqoobi, director of the Yaqoobi Construction and Road Construction Company, through an interpreter. "So, thanks to the classes they gave, we now have more tools to work with to make our jobs that much better."

The next two days focused on safety and project management.

"One of the things we identified was the lack of safety practices on the job site," said Davis, an Omaha, Neb., native. "Our goal was to educate them in some of the basic safety practices that will decrease the probability of an accident. This goes along the lines of having a clean, organized job site and wearing hard hats, eye protection and proper footwear."

Engineers also stressed the importance of scheduling and project management. "The importance of compiling an accurate schedule and holding to that schedule makes the end-user happy, and makes the contractor more reliable and efficient," said Davis.

On the final day of the workshop, the group gathered around concrete beams to assess their work. A crane lifted the beams and a 15-ton jack applied pressure to assess the breaking point, or faults, in the concrete.

"The testing of the beams showed the Afghan engineers the effects of improper rebar installation, poor concrete mix and cold joints," said U.S. Air Force Capt. Brian Jackson, the Panjshir PRT chief engineer and South Haven, Mich., native. "Showing them the effects of the improper techniques demonstrated the major differences between the application of doing it right and wrong. We're confident that they grasped the training and will have a great take away from the workshop."

Kentucky ADT donates 3,500 evergreens to Panjshir

By U.S. Air Force Senior Airman Amber Ashcraft
Panjshir Provincial Reconstruction Team Public Affairs

PANJSHIR PROVINCE, Afghanistan, March 28, 2011—The Kentucky Agribusiness Development Team II presented Shamir Amiri, director of Panjshir's Directorate of Agriculture, Irrigation and Livestock, with 3,500 evergreen saplings March 28.

"We're very excited to receive these beautiful trees," said Amiri, through an interpreter. "The province is on its way to becoming much greener and more attractive because of the new evergreens."

The six districts and one municipality of Panjshir Province received 500 saplings each, to be planted around schools, district offices and throughout villages.

"We hope the trees will help promote slope stabilization, erosion control and of course aesthetics in the province," said U.S. Army Lt. Col. Jeffrey Casada, the Kentucky ADT lead from London, Ky.

More than 100 villagers and officials attended the Nowruz Tree Planting Ceremony held at the DAIL compound in the Bazarak District.

"Panjshir has a unique opportunity in tourism," said Casada. "The province is already beautiful with the landscape, but the trees flourishing here will make the attraction that much greater."

In addition, reforestation is needed due to the decades of trees being uprooted for firewood and building materials, said Casada.

After the ceremony, district representatives arrived with trucks to take away the trees. The ADT provided the trees, with agreement that communities would provide the tools and labor for planting and upkeep.

"We thank the PRT for helping us celebrate our new year and new spring with these beautiful trees," said Baroukzai. "The people of Panjshir look forward to seeing them grow for many years to come."

Kentucky ADT works to improve Afghan agriculture

By U.S. Army Spc. Adam L. Mathis
Task Force Red Bulls Public Affairs

PARWAN PROVINCE, Afghanistan, March 30, 2011—Approximately 100 Afghans, representing Parwan, Kapisa, and Panjshir Provinces, gathered in the Parwan Directorate of Agriculture, Irrigation, and Livestock building in Charikar.

U.S. Army Lt. Col Aaron Polston had one main message, "We need to get out and teach farmers," he said.

"What we want to do is promote a standard curriculum that we can push out into the high schools so that we can begin to build an educational foundation for agriculture here in Afghanistan," said Polston, the Kentucky Agribusiness Development Team deputy team chief of Greenup, Ky.

The curriculum, purchased by the Kentucky ADT, was developed by Purdue and Kabul Universities and includes lesson plans for an entire school year. It covers agricultural topics from caring for livestock and crops to marketing products.

"It is very enriched with a lot knowledge and a lot of information, and I would like this (to) be included in the programs of our education at the universities and agricultural schools," said Abdul Kabir Farzan, the director of Parwan's DAIL, through an interpreter.

By using a standardized curriculum, the Afghan government will be able to hold teachers accountable if they fail to perform.

"If we want to promote education here in Afghanistan we have to hold teachers to standards, and we have to promote those standards through a basic educational curriculum," said Polston.

The benefit of the new curriculum may reach more than just children. Shahmir Amiri, the director of Panjshir's DAIL, said his province has teams who travel to farms to educate farmers about agriculture. While these teams are very basic, Amiri believes this new curriculum will improve their performance and thereby increase production among the farmers of his province.

The need to increase production is also felt by Muhammad Arifhossini, the director of Kapisa's DAIL. He hopes this program will help educate farmers and expose them to mechanization in agriculture.

"Nowadays, our people want to increase their production in every area, for example, in agriculture and in livestock," said Arifhossini. "(They want) to work better in plant protection and also their cooperative system, which is very important for our farmers to work together with us, and to increase their production, and sell in (the) market."

ROK PRT donates 8 ambulances to Parwan

By U.S. Army Spc. James Wilton
Task Force Red Bulls Public Affairs

PARWAN PROVINCE, Afghanistan, March 30, 2011—The Republic of Korea Provincial Reconstruction Team donated eight new ambulances to the people of Parwan Province in a ceremony at the Green Hotel in Charikar.

Last year, in the Salang District, Parwan Province, 200 people died during an avalanche because they were too far from medical facilities and the district had inadequate emergency transportation, said Soraya Dalil, the acting Minister of Health.

The ROK PRT took on the task of improving the medical care system in the area. The PRT plans to donate a total of 16 ambulances as well as ultrasound equipment and X-ray machines. Four clinics are also planned for the province including one currently under construction in Charikar. In addition, the PRT sent 130 Afghans to Korea in 2010 for medical training and plans on sending another 200 this year. Finally, the PRT is overseeing a midwife training program in Charikar to help alleviate the high number of deaths during childbirth.

"This gift will especially help mothers who are unable to get to the hospital, potentially reducing the number of woman dying from childbirth due to inadequate care," said Dr. Mohammad Qassim Saidi, Parwan Public Health director.

The ambulances will be distributed to six districts which are far from medical facilities or have large populations including Shakyh Ali, Charikar, Salang and Koh-E Safi.

"We have come here with the sincerest intentions for our Afghan friends," said Mr. Kwon, the ROK PRT director. "We will do our best to support Parwan, while working with Gov. Salangi. I will not say reconstruction can be done in a short time. This is a small gift as compared to what we plan to achieve. We can all make a difference day by day. Everyone is a key player in helping Afghanistan."

Parwan Gov. Abdul Salangi thanked the PRT for their overwhelming generosity and their continued support of the Afghan people.

"A strong country requires healthy people," said Salangi. "Do you know anyone who has done this much work?" Salangi said referring to the ROK PRT.

APRIL
2011

Seed company opens soybean processing facility

PARWAN PROVINCE, Afghanistan, April 2, 2011—Haji Abdul Robate Qahir (far left), the Director of the Baston Seed Company, cuts the ribbon across the entrance of his new soybean processing facility in Bagram. Mohammad Sharif Sharif (back left), an engineer with Soy Nutrition Services Afghanistan, Abdul Kabir Farzam (center), the Parwan Director of Agriculture, Irrigation and Livestock, and Shamir Amiri (right), the Panjshir DAIL hold the ribbon for Qahir. (Photo by U.S. Army Spc. James Wilton, Task Force Red Bulls Public Affairs)

By U.S. Army Spc. James Wilton
Task Force Red Bulls Public Affairs

PARWAN PROVINCE, Afghanistan, April 2, 2011—The Baston Seed Company opened the doors of a new soybean processing facility in Bagram.

Local leaders from Panjshir and Parwan provinces, members of Nutrition and Education International and the Kentucky Agribusiness Development Team attended the ceremony.

The building will hold the soy processing equipment donated to the people of Afghanistan by NEI with help from the Kentucky ADT. U.S. and the Baston Seed Company owner, Haji Abdul Robate Qahir, partnered to fund the facility. Baston will buy soybeans from Afghan farmers and clean, dry, and mill them into flour at the new processing facility.

"This soy flour can be added to wheat flour at a 10 percent ratio to create super naan bread," said Col. Hunter J. Mathews the Kentucky ADT commander from Lexington, Ky. "Naan bread that has a great deal of protein content, and that stays fresh for a day longer."

"Soybeans are not the solution to all of Afghanistan's agricultural problems, but they do offer another tool to the local farmer to both feed his family and increase his prosperity," said Mathews. "Your cooperation and support of this new facility is a great sign of progress for the farmers of Afghanistan."

More Afghan farmers started growing soy in place of, or alongside, other more common crops because of its nutritional value and ability to flourish in the local climate. NEI hopes it will be a part of the solution to the nutrition problem in Afghanistan.

"NEI Nutrition was very excited to be a part of the ribbon cutting in Parwan mainly because of the nutritional value that soybeans offer such as milk, flour and food," said Mohammad Sharif Sharif, an engineer with Soy Nutrition Services Afghanistan, a part of NEI.

"Soy is an inexpensive substitute for meat, eggs, and milk, with protein that helps people stay healthy, particularly children and young mothers," said Mathews. "The nutrition from soy beans will help Afghanistan have stronger, healthier people."

NEI will place an expert at the site for the next five years to ensure the equipment works properly and the project stays sustainable.

"Soybean production is important to Afghanistan, as a second crop after wheat and its high protein value," said Abdul Kabir Farzam, the Parwan DAIL. "In addition, the people of Parwan will now have a place to sell their harvest."

He said, Bastan's Soybean Processing building is now open for business and helping to make soybeans a sustainable and profitable crop for Afghan farmers.

PARWAN PROVINCE, Afghanistan, April 2, 2011—Haji Abdul Robate Qahir (far left), the Director of the Baston Seed Company, explains the various types of seeds his company sells to U.S. Army Col. Hunter J. Mathews, the Kentucky Agribusiness Development Team commander and from Lexington, Ky., during a grand opening ceremony for the Baston Soybean processing facility in Bagram. (Photo by U.S. Army Spc. James Wilton, Task Force Red Bulls Public Affairs)

Afghans gather for youth shura

By U.S. Air Force Staff Sgt. Barry Loo
Paktya Provincial Reconstruction Team Public Affairs

PAKTYA PROVINCE, Afghanistan, April 3, 2011—Afghan elders commonly gather to discuss villagers' concerns, but today they gathered with a different type of audience. About 300 residents of Paktya Province, young and old, along with representatives from the Government of the Islamic Republic of Afghanistan and Paktya Provincial Reconstruction Team conducted a youth shura in Gardez City.

"This is the 21st century," said Paktya Deputy Gov. Abdul Rahman Mangal. "The country is looking toward youths to rebuild it."

Shura attendees raised several concerns including unemployment and education.

"Some of our youths smoke hashish because they have no job," a guest speaker said.

In partnership with the Afghan government, U.S. Air Force Lt. Col. Marchal Magee, Paktya PRT commander from Issaquah, Wash., said he will expand vocational training for boys and girls to give them a skill from which they can earn a living wage.

U.S. and Afghan partners are also planning several new projects as part of a new school-year initiative.

"We intend to make four sports grounds in Zormat, Ahmad Abad, Gardez and Chamkani districts for the youths of Paktya," Mangal said.

The PRT will help Afghans distribute backpacks containing school supplies to students throughout the province and provide uniforms and equipment for organized teams, Magee said.

The deputy governor ended the shura with advice for the youth in attendance.

"You must have a goal for success in your life and always try to reach it because life without any goal is nothing," he said.

Task Force Red Bulls search villages for weapons caches

PARWAN PROVINCE, Afghanistan, April 7, 2011—U.S. Army Sgt. Cullen Wurzer, a cavalry scout from Des Moines, Iowa with Troop B, 1st Squadron, 113th Cavalry Regiment, Task Force Redhorse, which is a part 2nd Brigade Combat Team, 34th Infantry Division, Task Force Red Bulls, finds a bag of Rocket-Propelled Grenades and a grenade launcher after searching a compound in Pacha Khak, Afghanistan. Troop B searched the village for weapons caches and conducted a Key Leader Engagement with the village malik. (U.S. Army Photo by Spc. Kristina L. Gupton, Task Force Red Bulls Public Affairs)

Joint effort opens Parwan Operations Coordination Center

PARWAN PROVINCE, Afghanistan—U.S. Army Lt. Col. John Cunningham (left), the 2nd Brigade Combat Team, 34th Infantry Division, Task Force Red Bulls, Parwan Operations Coordination Center–Provincial senior advisor from Fort Dodge, Iowa, speaks to Afghan National Police Brig. Gen. Mir Jaladeen Jamshed, the Regional Command–East Operations Coordination Center–Regional deputy commander, during the dedication ceremony for the new Parwan OCC–P compound in Charikar, April 7. (By U.S. Army Spc. James Wilton, Task Force Red Bulls Public Affairs)

By U.S. Army Spc. James Wilton
Task Force Red Bulls Public Affairs

PARWAN PROVINCE, Afghanistan, April 7, 2011—The Parwan Operations Coordination Center–Provincial compound in Charikar, held a grand opening ceremony April 7 to mark the completion of a remodel and renovation project which started in June 2010.

With Coalition Forces guidance, representatives from the Afghan National Police, Afghan National Army and the Afghan National Directorate of Security work from the OCC–P to coordinate response efforts and disseminate information and intelligence.

The goal is to provide a common operational picture across the Afghan National Security Forces in the province. so agencies can respond to security and emergency situations more effectively. "The new operations center will ultimately serve to increase the capability and capacity of the ANSF and

OCC–P to conduct provincial planning and security response," said U.S. Army Lt. Col. John Cunningham, the 2nd Brigade Combat Team, 34th Infantry Division, Task Force Red Bulls, OCC–P senior advisor from Fort Dodge, Iowa. "It provides a place for successful, combined forces, tactical operations, allowing us to maintain situational awareness of Parwan Province and a common operational picture, security awareness, consequence management and coordinate ANSF response to emergencies."

The renovation included construction of new staff offices, barracks for the Afghan representatives who conduct 24-hour operations, a new operations center, an entry control point for the front gate and four new guard towers for the compound.

"The renovation provided good working and living conditions for the staff officers that work here," said Afghan National Army Maj. Gen. Abdul Jalil Rahimi, the OCC–P commander. "Now all can work together in the same compound and operations center."

The establishment of these Operations Coordination Centers is an important step toward the transition of the security responsibility to the ANSF, he said.

"The equipping of the ANSF is our main goal," said Shahwali, the Parwan Province sub governor. "According to the agreement with the international community, handover of security responsibility from foreign forces is going on in the current year."

Successful integration will increase the capabilities of the ANSF forces and increase the confidence of the local people in their ability to keep them safe, Shahwali said.

"A successful Parwan OCC–P will provide for overall better security for the people of Charikar and Parwan," said Cunningham. "Better security will bring more development and opportunities for jobs, for the local population, ultimately, building the people's trust and confidence in the local security forces and the Government of the Islamic Republic of Afghanistan."

ANSF soldiers graduate covert police training in Gardez

By U.S. Air Force 1st Lt. Sybil Taunton
Paktya Provincial Reconstruction Team Public Affairs

PAKTYA PROVINCE, Afghanistan, April 7, 2011—Eleven Afghan National Security Force soldiers with Task Force Reliance graduated an eight-week covert police training course at Forward Operating Base Gardez, April 7.

Law enforcement professionals, from 1st Battalion, 168th Infantry Regiment, Task Force Lethal, conducted the training, which included covert operations, surveillance, tactical operations, first aid, criminal investigation, interview and interrogation, and Global Positioning Systems.

"They are now a full time operational team that will be based out of FOB Gardez. They are made up of Afghan Uniformed Police, Afghan Border Police (ABP) and Afghan National Civil Order Police," said Barry Ralston, Law Enforcement Professional for Task Force Lethal, from Amarillo, Texas. "We start with partnered, low-level operations to build their confidence until they are ready to operate on their own."

According to Ralston, Task Force Reliance will be incorporated into operations conducted by coalition forces, the Afghan criminal investigation division, the Afghan counter narcotic units and the Afghan National Directorate of Security.

"They are designed to supplement those groups when it comes to surveillance, criminal investigation and taking action on targets," said Ralston. There are not many units like Task Force Reliance operating in Afghanistan, and it is important to have them collecting evidence and building case files as the Afghan Rule of Law system becomes more strict, he said.

"The training you have completed in the last eight weeks is very important to the future of Afghanistan," said Paktya Deputy Gov. Abdul Rahman Mangal, during his speech at the graduation ceremony.

U.S. Army Lt. Col. Stephen B. Boesen II, Task Force Lethal commander, of Ankeny, Iowa, expressed his appreciation for the trainees and his expectations for the graduates. "You are all a shining example of what Afghanistan has to offer," said Boesen. "You have worked hard over the last few weeks and you are ready to take on your special role in protecting the people of Paktya. My request is that you get after the enemy, and stay strong and courageous in your duties."

After receiving their training certificates, the graduates recited an oath and promise to uphold their duties as covert police officials. Each graduate held up their certificate and said they will serve for their country.

"We will try our best to bring peace to our society and to future generations," said one of the graduates.

ADT builds the framework for Panjshir livestock bazaar

By U.S. Air Force 2nd Lt. Ashleigh Peck
Panjshir Provincial Reconstruction Team Public Affairs

PANJSHIR PROVINCE, Afghanistan, April 7, 2011—The Kentucky Agribusiness Development Team II managed the installation of corral panels for a future livestock bazaar in Paryan District.

The first livestock bazaar is planned for June.

"The bazaar should help traders and farmers by bringing animals to a central point and attracting several buyers," said U.S. Army National Guard Lt. Col. Jeffrey Casada, a Kentucky ADT II, Panjshir Provincial Reconstruction Team, lead.

Paryan has the largest amount of livestock in the province and once the bazaar brings those animals to a central location, the corral will bring order to the bazaar.

"The corral, for the livestock, is a way to make the bazaar safer for both humans and animals," said Casada, a London, Ky. native. "It will also make the bazaar look more professional and organized."

The ADT said they were thrilled to work with a local contractor, Mohammad Kabir, to get the corral panels set up for the bazaar.

"I'm very excited about the Paryan livestock bazaar," said Casada. "We've been working on this bazaar for several months and it was an added bonus to the project that we didn't have to go out of the province, or out of the country, to purchase the corral panels."

Kabir welded and set up the metal corral panels at his shop in Anaba District. He then took the panels apart for transportation to the Paryan District Center, forty miles away, where they were assembled for the livestock bazaar.

"Hopefully this project will give Panjshir producers of livestock, fruits, vegetables and nuts a vision for what can be accomplished when they work together," said Casada.

Panjshir PRT attends celebratory Buzkashi game

PANJSHIR PROVINCE, Afghanistan, April 7, 2011—Chapandaz, or Buzkashi players, fight for a calf carcass during a Buzkashi game in Paryan District. More than 1,000 people including local Afghan villagers and Panjshir Provincial Reconstruction Team members attended the event. The chapandaz and their horses go through rigorous training before competing in the game. The goal is to grab the carcass of a goat or calf, clear it of the other players and get it into a target circle to attain points. (Photo by U.S. Air Force Senior Airman Amber Ashcraft, Panjshir Provincial Reconstruction Team Public Affairs)

By U.S. Air Force Senior Airman Amber Ashcraft
Panjshir Provincial Reconstruction Team Public Affairs

PANJSHIR PROVINCE, Afghanistan, April 7, 2011—Panjshir Provincial Reconstruction Team members attended a Buzkashi match in Paryan District, April 7.

Buzkashi, which literally translates to goat dragging, is the national sport of Afghanistan. The crowd consisted of more than a thousand people including local Afghans and several PRT members.

"I've read about the game and seen it portrayed in movies," said U.S. Air Force Lt. Col. Joseph Blevins, the PRT commander and Oregonia, Ohio, native. "You don't truly appreciate the level of intensity involved until you see a match in person."

The game is played on special occasions such as weddings, the Islamic holiday of Eid and Nowruz, or Afghan New Year's.

This particular Buzkashi game was played for the Paryan District Governor Abdul Jalil's son's wedding. Jalil invited members of the PRT to attend the match and help celebrate.

"The PRT is involved in a lot with Panjshir, so I wanted to invite them to something a little more personal to build our friendship," said Jalil through an interpreter.

The chapandaz, or Buzkashi players, and their horses go through rigorous training before competing in the game. The object of the game is to grab the carcass of a goat or calf, clear it of other players and get it into a target circle to attain points. The game can last anywhere from an hour to several days.

This match lasted three hours.

"Being at a Buzkashi game is kind of like being at a NASCAR race, in the middle of a rodeo," said U.S. Air Force Senior Airman Darin Pugh, a PRT vehicle maintenance member, and Tacoma, Wash., native. "It's a truly interactive sport. Not only do the participants need to have their head on a swivel, to find the carcass to score. The onlookers also have to keep theirs rotating as well, to keep from being trampled, as the boundaries and sidelines become intertwined."

The players usually wear heavy clothing and head gear to protect themselves against the other players' whips and boots. The boots usually have high heels that lock into the horse's saddle. This helps the rider lean on the side of the horse while trying to pick up the carcass.

In the end, winners are awarded a chapan (an intricately decorated coat), turbans and cash among other prizes.

"The winner received $4,000," said Jalil, who was also a player in the Buzkashi game. "We're very happy the PRT members were able to attend."

Joint effort builds 2 bridges in 2 days

By U.S. Air Force Staff Sgt. Barry Loo
Paktya Provincial Reconstruction Team Public Affairs

PAKTYA PROVINCE, Afghanistan, April 8, 2011—With guidance from the Paktya Provincial Reconstruction Team, a determined crew of Afghan National Army soldiers and construction workers triumphed over mud, hail and disabled vehicles to complete two bridges in two days to improve the lives of their countrymen in Zormat District, Afghanistan

Altogether, the construction crew experienced four flat tires, one broken axle and a dislodged tractor wheel. But they persevered and continued to build, despite the occasional pummelling from rain and hail.

The bridges will allow villagers to transport produce and other goods in larger trucks and get them to market easier and faster. They also provide quicker access to hospitals and emergency services.

Nick Mohammad, an Afghan laborer, expressed pride in his role in the projects.

"This is serving our country and helping our people," he said, "It's beneficial for the people and effective."

Coalition forces based out of Combat Outpost Zormat funded and provided support for the project.

"We're there simply to make sure all the moving pieces work," said U.S. Army 1st Lt. Tristan Boddicker, a member of the Paktya Provincial Reconstruction Team from Cedar Rapids, Iowa.

Under a cash-for-work program, local workers built the bridges using locally purchased materials. The two bridges cost $2,400 each, he said.

Boddicker said after completing the first bridge, elders and villagers greeted him and expressed their excitement and gratitude for the project.

"They were just totally amazed that in a matter of one day, a full bridge could be built," he said, "they could not stop praising the whole process."

Fill 'er up! Fuelers keep vehicles, aircraft on the go

LAGHMAN PROVINCE, Afghanistan, April 9, 2011—U.S. Army Spc. Brian McCarthy (right), a petroleum supply specialist from West Infield, Maine, with Company E, 310th Task Force Phoenix, in support of 1st Battalion, 133rd Infantry Regiment, 2nd Brigade Combat Team, 34th Infantry Division, fuels a UH-60 Black Hawk helicopter at the Forward Area Refueling Point, Forward Operating Base Mehtar Lam. (Photo by U.S. Army Staff Sgt. Ryan C. Matson, Task Force Red Bulls Public Affairs)

By U.S. Army Staff Sgt. Ryan C. Matson
Task Force Red Bulls Public Affairs

LAGHMAN PROVINCE, Afghanistan, April 9, 2011—Being a U.S. Army petroleum supply specialist, or fueler, is a bit like working at an old-time gas station.

A vehicle pulls up to the pumps, and the crew runs out to fill it up. The only difference for the Army fuelers of Company E, 310th Task Force Phoenix, is that some of the vehicles are helicopters, and they are in Afghanistan.

"Most of what we do is ground fuel for vehicles, but our priority mission is for the birds (Army helicopters)," said U.S. Army Sgt. Matthew Lauilefue, a shift leader of the petroleum supply specialist team from Company E. "We fill up Chinooks, Apaches, Kiowas, and a whole bunch of civilian birds."

Lauilefue, from Honolulu, and his team of fellow fuelers from Fort Drum, N.Y., who run the Forward Area Refueling Point at Forward Operating Base Mehtar Lam, in support of the 1st Battalion, 133rd Infantry Regiment, Task

Force Ironman, 2nd Brigade Combat Team, 34th Infantry Division, Task Force Red Bulls, are coming off a very busy week. They provided the fuel for every bird participating in Operation Bull Whip, which was the largest air-assault mission conducted by the 101st Airborne Division during their year-long deployment to Afghanistan.

During Bull Whip, Company E's fuelers pumped more aircraft fuel than at any other time all year. They refuelled 40 helicopters in a single day.

"We pumped 10,000 gallons of aircraft fuel alone in one day during that mission," said U.S. Army Sgt. Christian Grabowsi, the other shift leader for the petroleum supply specialist team from Company E, and a native of Hinsdale, N.Y.

The fuelers usually pump around 4,000 gallons of fuel in a typical day.

On this day, April 9, the fuelers were having a fairly busy day. A couple Black Hawks came in for fuel, and the fuelers, hearing the helicopters in the distance grabbed their helmets, gloves and eye protection. They were waiting by the fuel points when the helicopters landed. As soon as the Soldiers got back to the shack and removed their gear, they had to put it back on, this time it was a team of Kiowas.

Another responsibility of the fuelers at the Mehtar Lam FARP is re-arming Kiowa helicopters with missiles, rockets and ammunition, but do not handle Apaches.

The fuelers do what is known as a "hot" refuel, meaning they are refuelling the birds with the rotors turning and engines still on. They do this for speed, said Givian.

The fuelers do not know the situation behind the aircraft they are refuelling. While that helicopter may just be delivering some equipment from one base to another, it could also be en route to a medical evacuation or a situation with troops in contact and need to get there.

This means that time is of the essence, so the goal is to get the helicopters refuelled as quickly as possible while still being safe, said U.S. Army Sgt. Rockieve Givian, the fuel team's Non-Commissioned Officer-in-Charge from Atlanta, Ga.

Doing this successfully is how the fuelers are able to make an impact on the battlefield, the fuelers said.

"We know that we're a support element, but at the same time we know when birds are coming in hot that we need to get them loaded, get them moved and get them back in the fight," said Grabowski. "Time on ground is time lost for an infantry unit who may need them."

New sniper rifle fielded at Bagram

BAGRAM AIRFIELD, Afghanistan, April 9, 2011—U.S. Army Staff Sgt. Dennis Long, a mechanic with Headquarters and Headquarters Company, Brigade Special Troops Battalion, 2nd Brigade Combat Team 34th Infantry Division, Task Force Red Bulls, and a native of Williamsburg, Iowa, fires an XM-2010 Sniper Rifle on Bagram Airfield, Afghanistan April 8. The XM-2010 is a new Army-purchased weapon being distributed to sniper teams operating in Afghanistan. (Photo by U.S. Army Sgt. Grant Matthes, Regional Command–East Public Affairs)

By U.S. Army Sgt. Grant Matthes
Regional Command–East Public Affairs

BAGRAM AIRFIELD, Afghanistan, April 9, 2011—Sniper instructors displayed the new XM-2010 Sniper Rifle at Bagram Airfield, Afghanistan to allow service members to look at, shoot and familiarize themselves with the weapon system.

The XM-2010 is a .30-caliber bolt-action rifle with a folding stock, a rail system capable of mounting multiple weapon accessories and uses box magazines that house five rounds.

"They are currently being distributed one per sniper team," said U.S. Army Maj. Tracy Kreuser, Intelligence and Sustainment Company, Headquarters and Headquarters Battalion, 101st Airborne Division force management chief and the division chemical officer. "You don't want the enemy to know you're a sniper, so they added the folding butt stock to make it look more like a regular rifle."

The XM-2010 is a rebuild of the M24 Sniper Rifle and is a good addition to the sniper's arsenal, said Kreuser, a native of Kenosha, Wis.

"They listened to snipers when they built it, so they took everything into account," said U.S. Army Staff Sgt. David Dickson, Company C, 2nd

Battalion, 29th Infantry Regiment sniper instructor, and a native of Southern Pines, N.C. "You can shoot a 10-inch shot group from 1,000 meters."

The XM-2010 will be assigned to sniper teams in Afghanistan before it is distributed to the rest of the Army.

"It is very smooth when shooting the rifle, the scope makes it really easy to accurately hit the target," said U.S. Army Staff Sgt. Dennis Long, Headquarters and Headquarters Company, Brigade Special Troops Battalion, 2nd Brigade Combat Team 34th Infantry Division, Task Force Red Bulls, and a native of Williamsburg, Iowa.

"It's a good system and I am very pleased it was able to be distributed so quickly," said Kreuser. "It's another system that will help us push the enemy back."

Soldier's work integrates Afghan operations

By U.S. Army Spc. Adam L. Mathis
17th Public Affairs Detachment

WARDAK PROVINCE, Afghanistan, April 9, 2011—The screen at the head of the two tables in the Operations Coordination Center–Provincial Wardak displayed statistics about coalition and insurgent activities in the area. Members of various branches of the Afghan National Security Forces listen as one of their countrymen briefed the data. Seated quietly at the table, U.S. Army Lt. Col. Larry Daley listened to his interpreter translate the fruits of his team's labors.

According to Daley, his job as senior U.S. adviser for OCC–P Wardak is the future of the coalition presence in Afghanistan. Since November, Daley of Preston, Minn., attached to the 4th Brigade, 10th Mountain Division, Task Force Patriot, worked to foster better cooperation between the various branches of ANSF and improve their ability to handle security in Wardak Province.

The OCC system

Daley's position in Wardak came about by order of Afghan President Hamid Karzai, who established the OCC system. Originally, the centers coordinated efforts related to elections and natural disasters. The system, however, worked too well to stay within such narrow parameters.

"It has evolved into a way that all of the entities of the Afghan National Security Forces can be integrated for operations and have a unity of effort in securing the population," said U.S. Army Lt. Col. Michael Kelley of Newnan, Ga., Operations Coordination Center–Regional South coalition force commander and senior adviser. OCC–Ps are local agencies that report to the OCC–R in their area.

The coalition presence in the OCCs is that of advisers, Kelley said. Specifically, their job is to aid the various branches of the Afghan security forces as they attempt to work together and share information. As Afghans assume more of what is currently the coalition's job, coalition forces will increasingly assume the role of advisers.

This cooperation is what OCC–R South commander, Afghan National Army Brig. Gen. Muhammad Daood wants to see in the OCC system.

"I hope one day we'll be able to provide security in the whole province," said Daood through an interpreter.

To get there means a lot of drinking for Daley.

"A lot of late night chai sessions is how you get it done," said Daley.

Cooperation

Chai, or tea, is a means to overcoming a problem that sometimes shows up in organizations: lack of communication. The various branches of ANSF have not been sharing the data they collect in Wardak. Daley compared this possessiveness with how the branches of the American military were before the 1980s; each organization had its own set of data and did not necessarily release it to the others.

Drinking tea, an almost ubiquitous custom in Afghanistan, helps Daley develop personal relationships. By establishing friendships and respect between the representatives of various branches of ANSF, Daley is able to improve cooperation.

"Maybe the organizations don't really care for each other a whole lot, but if, as individuals, we can get along, we can make things work, Daley said.

"It's something you've got to work at every day; if you're not working at it every day, you're probably going backwards."

Advising away jobs

Kelley said as the OCCs become more proficient at handling security, there will be less need for coalition troops. Essentially, Daley is advising troops home.

And his work and that of his team is having some success. Recently, Daley began teaching Afghan personnel how to analyze data and ask what is causing those statistics. The result was a desire on the part of some Afghans to learn more.

"We're getting there, it's just taking time to make them sit down and think through very complex problems," said Daley.

Coalition forces donate tents for education

By U.S. Air Force Staff Sgt. Barry Loo
Paktya Provincial Reconstruction Team Public Affairs

PAKTYA PROVINCE, Afghanistan, April 10—Children in Zormat District, Afghanistan, will soon be learning underneath a new roof.

Afghan and coalition forces loaded 25 classroom-size tents onto an Afghan National Army truck, at Combat Outpost Zormat, Afghanistan for distribution to teachers around the district who do not have a building to teach in.

"When the weather is bad, they don't have school," said U.S. Army 1st Lt. Tristan Boddicker, a Soldier of the Paktya Provincial Reconstruction Team from Cedar Rapids, Iowa. "Now they can provide education even during inclement weather."

Coalition forces donated the tents to promote education.

"Education is a right for every human being," said Babrik Haqiar, Zormat director of education.

Haqiar came to COP Zormat to receive the tents and coordinate their transfer to the local education center for further distribution.

Soldiers from the Afghan National Army helped moved the equipment.

"We didn't put on this uniform just to provide security," said ANA Sgt. Rohullah Akhund. "We want to help people and help the children get an education so they can have a better life and have peace."

With the donated tents, the young students in the district will have more protection from the sun and elements.

Haqiar said that beyond being a basic human right, education will also have a rehabilitative effect on Afghanistan.

"It's important for the kids here to go to school so they can rebuild the country," Haqiar said.

Company D fights through ambush in Tengay Mountain Valley

LAGHMAN PROVINCE, Afghanistan, April 11, 2011—U.S. Army Staff Sgt. Chris Brenke (left), the platoon sergeant for 2nd Platoon, 1st Battalion, 133rd Infantry Regiment, Task Force Ironman, a part of the 2nd Brigade Combat Team, 34th Infantry Division, Task Force Red Bulls, laughs after reading an inaccurate report, by the Taliban concerning an ambush on his platoon's convoy the previous day. (Photo by U.S. Army Staff Sgt. Ryan C. Matson, Task Force Red Bulls Public Affairs)

By U.S. Army Staff Sgt. Ryan C. Matson
Task Force Red Bulls Public Affairs

LAGHMAN PROVINCE, Afghanistan, April 11, 2011—The Soldiers from 2nd Platoon, Company D, 1st Battalion, 133rd Infantry Regiment, Task Force Ironman, laughed when they heard the report of the attack.

"The report states: two tanks were hit by artillery shells and a rocket," U.S. Army Staff Sgt. Chris Brenke, 2nd Platoon sergeant from East Dubuque, Ill., read from a printout during the mission briefing April 11. "Both tanks were completely destroyed during the fighting that lasted an hour. The report also said that four American Soldiers were killed and two others wounded. I regret to inform you that four of you guys died yesterday."

The report was from the Taliban Voice of Jihad Online, and was the Taliban's account of what happened the day before in the Tengay Mountain Valley of the Qarghai District. The area is a site of frequent enemy ambushes.

In fact, the majority of the contact Company D has been involved in was

428

in the valley, which 2nd Platoon patrols. Company D is part of the Iowa National Guard's, 2nd Brigade Combat Team, 34th Infantry Division, Task Force Red Bulls, and is stationed at nearby Combat Outpost Xio Haq.

The Soldiers of 2nd Platoon told a very different story.

"Basically, it was a day of a lot of firsts," Brenke said. "It was the first time they hit us in the rain, the first time they hit us with that complex of an attack and the first time from that close."

On a Quick Reaction Force mission, the platoon responded to a call of a burning fuel tanker, said Brenke. A common tactic of the enemy is to shoot at fuel trucks to ignite them, using the burning trucks to draw coalition forces into an ambush. That's exactly what happened April 10.

When the platoon's convoy entered a narrow stretch of highway surrounded by steep cliffs on both sides about 15 miles west of their base, the attack began, said Brenke. Then insurgents launched a barrage of rocket-propelled grenades from the cliff to the south.

"There was about 15 minutes of solid contact, pretty intense fighting," said Brenke. "The RPGs were close. We were firing back with the .50-cal, and they kept fighting. They weren't stopping."

Two of the RPGs struck the middle vehicle, where company commander U.S. Army Capt. Jared Gevock, from Dubuque, Iowa, sat, serving as truck commander. Fortunately, the RPG protective nets on the outside of the vehicles dispersed the grenade blasts, and no Soldiers were injured in the attack.

In fact, the up-armoured Mine-Resistant, Ambush-Protected vehicle suffered battle damage, but was driven back to base. Several other vehicles also suffered bullet holes or chips to their armour, and will need to be repaired, but all were able to return to the base.

When the enemy attacked, first with RPGs, then with machine gun fire, the first four vehicles in the convoy pushed through the ambush. They then returned to assist occupants of the final vehicle, who was under heavy contact. The platoon fought back with .50-caliber machine guns, laying heavy fire and pinning down the enemy in their fighting positions on top of the mountain.

At this time, the enemy started attacking with small arms fire from the cliffs across the road to the north.

"That was pretty smart on their part," Brenke said. "They were pinned down to the south, so the ambushers across the road started attacking us."

U.S. Army Pfc. Joel Mason, a gunner from Cedar Rapids, Iowa, spotted one of the attackers to the north and engaged him, ending the ambush from that side.

"After receiving small arms fire from the south, I saw one of the attackers engage us from the north," Mason said. "We took contact from them, I got positive identification on one of the attackers, confirmed there were no friendly forces in the area, and took him out with the .50-cal."

U.S. Army Spc. Dale Heiser, a CROWS gunner with 2nd Platoon, from Davenport, Iowa, who witnessed Mason's shot through his Crew Remote-Operated Weapon Optics System.

The platoon continued to lay down heavy suppressive fire on the ambushers to the south, keeping constant eyes on six individuals on the mountainside. U.S. Army Staff Sgt. Peter Harder, a forward observer from Huxler, Iowa, called in an air strike on the ambushers.

U.S. forces dropped three bombs, the last one dead on target, according to the platoon, ending the conflict. When all was said and done, three American vehicles suffered repairable battle damage, no American forces were injured and seven insurgent fighters were eliminated, which differed significantly from the Taliban report.

LAGHMAN PROVINCE, Afghanistan, April 11, 2011—U.S. Army Spc. Thomas Egger (left), from Coggin, Iowa, and U.S. Army Pfc. Alex Good, from Fort Dodge, Iowa, both infantry Soldiers with 2nd Platoon, Company D, 1st Battalion, 133rd Infantry Regiment, Task Force Ironman, a part of the 2nd Brigade Combat Team, 34th Infantry Division, Task Force Red Bulls, look at a 7.62 mm round, that was lodged in one of the platoon's vehicles, at Combat Outpost Xio Haq. The platoon fought through an ambush by insurgent forces the day before. (Photo by U.S. Army Staff Sgt. Ryan C. Matson, Task Force Red Bulls Public Affairs)

Company builds relationship with Afghans through supplies

LAGHMAN PROVINCE, Afghanistan, April 13, 2011—U.S. Army Staff Sgt. Peter Harder (left), a forward observer from Huxley, Iowa, and U.S. Army Pfc. Nicolas Howe, an infantry Soldier from Waukon, Iowa, both with 2nd Platoon, Company D, 1st Battalion, 133rd Infantry Regiment, Task Force Ironman, a part of the 2nd Brigade Combat Team, 34th Infantry Division, Task Force Red Bulls, unload lumber from a Mine-Resistant, Ambush-Protected vehicle April 13 in the village of Marshala Kamar. The lumber was used to repair a major bridge in the village. (Photo by U.S. Army Staff Sgt. Ryan C. Matson, Task Force Red Bulls Public Affairs)

By U.S. Army Staff Sgt. Ryan C. Matson
Task Force Red Bulls Public Affairs

LAGHMAN PROVINCE, Afghanistan, April 13, 2011—In what members of 2nd Platoon, Company D, 1st Battalion, 133rd Infantry Regiment, Task Force Ironman, said has been a long, ongoing process, the platoon is one step closer to building a relationship with the nearby village of Marshala Kamar by delivering supplies, April 13.

U.S. Army Staff Sgt. Chris Brenke, from East Dubuque, Ill, visited the village. Brenke is the 2nd Platoon sergeant in 1-133rd Inf., a part of the 2nd Brigade Combat Team, 34th Infantry Division.

"I saw that while the condition of the school was good, they were lacking in school supplies," he said.

The people of the village told him the Afghan government had difficulty providing the school with supplies. So Brenke decided to see what he could do to help. He spoke with his sister-in-law, Nici Hilby, a teacher at the Eleanor Roosevelt School in Dubuque, Iowa, and told her about the school.

Hilby arranged a drive for supplies. People brought extra school supplies during parent-teacher conferences, and in a short period of time, Hilby gathered 20 boxes of supplies. Brenke gave the first two to the Marshala Kamar School principal, Mohammed Umar.

Umar said the supplies will be put to good use.

"These supplies will help our children to become educated," Umar said.

U.S. Army Lt. Garion Ford, 2nd Platoon leader, was impressed with how much the kids have learned at the school with the limited resources they had.

"I was visiting the school, and one of the kids started spouting some English," said Ford, a Knoxville, Tenn., native. "They know English, which means they know it in Pashto as well. They know basic math, because when I first got into the school, I was asking a kid some basic division questions because he knew English really well. He was answering them all in English correctly. It's a testament to Principal Umar."

Ford explained how much the supplies really do help the children.

"Anything helps," said Ford. "I mean, they don't have paper and pens. They have one chalkboard, and they're teaching 300 kids of all grades that way. They all ask for pens, because that is the sign of an educated person here now, so they all want one, it's a thing of pride to have a pen."

"Over here you give a kid a notebook and a pen, and it's Christmas," Brenke added.

The platoon didn't stop with the school supplies. They noticed some of the beams on the village's bridge were becoming worn and needed to be replaced. So 2nd Platoon scoured their supply yard, getting a few pieces of lumber they had on hand that had not been used for any projects, and delivered it to the villagers. "We will use the plywood and lumber to fix our bridge," said Haji Jibar, a village elder. "We want to help these Americans to bring security and peace to our village, because they have come to help rebuild our village and serve our people."

The village, which lies along the banks of the Kabul River, one of the main rivers in Afghanistan, claims about 500 residents. The villagers told 2nd Platoon it had not been visited by coalition forces for more than two years.

Ford said it was initially a challenge to build a rapport with the village.

"The first time we went in there, the females literally ran away scared," said Ford. "Most of the people had never seen an American, besides driving by in up-armoured vehicles."

Ford admitted while the platoon strives to maintain a good relationship with all of the villages in their area of operations, Marshala Kamar was of particular interest to the platoon.

"They were in a gray area, the town could have gone either way," Ford said. "They are a waypoint between the Bad Pech area and the Dergy Valley. The bridge in their town is one of only two in the province you can cross the river on. It's a very important village strategically to have on our side."

The platoon, who arrived in country late October, visited Marshala Kamar seven times now.

Brenke thinks the platoon is slowly and steadily building what they consider to be a good relationship with the town.

ADT sponsors youth poultry training course
By U.S. Army Sgt. John P. Sklaney III
2-45th Agribusiness Development Team

PAKTYA PROVINCE, Afghanistan, April 13, 2011—Afghan government officials from Paktya Province and U.S. Army Soldiers of the 2-45th Agribusiness Development Team attended a graduation ceremony for youth poultry training in Zormat.

Before the ceremony at the Ya Habibullah High School, the 60 students received 20 chickens, a water container, a feeder and 35 kilograms of feed.

Afghan government officials present included Mohammad Zadran, the Director of Agriculture, Irrigation, and Livestock for Paktya Province who spoke of the importance of the training and how to spread the gained knowledge.

"You can help your parents establishing small poultry farms through the training that you received," said Zadran. "Education is the future for sustainable farming methods in Afghanistan."

"Even if the chickens die and the coops burn, the students have the knowledge to start their chicken farming over," said U.S. Army Sgt. Lacy Spanier, from McLoud, Okla., senior female advisor of the ADT. "Knowledge is something that can't be taken away from the students."

Some of the student's parents attended the graduation ceremony and talked of the importance of their child having been selected for the 8-week poultry training. One parent was so excited for the training provided that he brought his tractor, loaded with his son's chicken coop to show off the chickens they plan to raise on their farm.

"I am so proud of my son for completing the training," said the father. "Our chickens have already started to lay eggs and we plan on raising additional chicks."

Mohammad Din, chief of the National Directorate of Security for Zormat, spoke of the need for the Afghans to realize the value of the training they received from their government and also the assistance provided by the United States. "Be thankful for this free training that you have received," said Din. "Many Afghans would be thankful for the training that you have taken part in and of the chickens and other supplies that you were given for completing the training."

"In the future, report bad guys to your local government officials who can take action on your reports," said Din. "Increased security means more and larger projects will be possible in Zormat." The ADT is planning additional youth poultry training programs across the province, along with other agricultural projects.

Medic steps up, saves Afghans' lives

By U.S. Army 1st Lt. Nicholas Rasmussen
Task Force Lethal

PAKTYA PROVINCE, Afghanistan, April 14, 2011—U.S. Army Spc. Matthew Hackett of Omaha, Neb., was treating a Soldier for back pain in the aid station on Combat Outpost Herrera, April 14, when he heard what he said sounded like bubble-wrap being popped followed by a large boom.

"It was like someone punched the wall of the aid station," said Hackett, a medic attached to Company A, 1st Battalion, 168th Infantry Regiment, 2nd Brigade, 34th Infantry Division, Task Force Lethal.

The noises came from an attack at a nearby Afghan Border Police compound, after a suicide bomber and several gunmen left two policemen dead and five wounded.

The injured were brought to COP Herrera for treatment.

"I heard the call on the radio that casualties were coming and moments later the door was getting knocked down," said Hackett.

Hackett and another Company A medic, U.S. Army Spc. Eva Dziengal, of Iowa City, Iowa, had just enough time to prepare their equipment before the incoming casualties began to arrive.

But as the wounded arrived, so did help, in the form of two more medics and three Soldiers certified in combat lifesaving.

Hackett said he is used to taking orders rather than giving them, he said, but as the senior medic on the COP that day, he had to step up and take the lead over the other Soldiers, which was a challenge he faced head on.

"It was a little crazy, my first time being in charge," said Hackett.

Still, Hackett maintained his cool, identifying the needs of each patient on the spot and instructing the medics there to treat them accordingly until a medical evacuation helicopter arrived.

Once stabilized, all five casualties were taken to Forward Operating Base Salerno in Khost Province to be treated at a higher level of hospital care.

Looking back a day after the incident, Hackett said it was helpful that the casualties arrived staggered, instead of all at once.

But it was more than timing that made this medical team successful; it was experience, added Hackett.

"We've dealt with enough trauma in our aid station that everything came natural," he said.

Friends in high places: Company D checks on ANA observation posts

LAGHMAN PROVINCE, Afghanistan, April 15, 2011—U.S. Army Spc. Ahren Blake, a combat medic from Clinton, Iowa, with Company D, 1st Battalion, 133rd Infantry Regiment, Task Force Ironman, a part of the 2nd Brigade Combat Team, 34th Infantry Division, Task Force Red Bulls, holds two puppies he found at an Observation Post in the Aziz Khan Kats mountain valley range near Jalalabad, Afghanistan. The puppies have been living with the Afghan National Army Weapons Company, 2nd Kandak, 1st Brigade, 201st ANA Infantry Corps, which man the OPs that 3rd Platoon visited. (Photo by Ryan C. Matson, Task Force Red Bulls Public Affairs)

By U.S. Army Staff Sgt. Ryan C. Matson
Task Force Red Bulls Public Affairs

LAGHMAN PROVINCE, Afghanistan, April 15, 2011—Soldiers from 3rd Platoon, Company D, 1st Battalion, 133rd Infantry Regiment, Task Force Ironman, climbed up a mountain in the area around the Aziz Khan Kats Mountain Valley near the Duranta Tunnel outside Jalalabad, Afghanistan, to check on their Afghan National Army counterparts who were manning observation posts there.

Three months ago this was a pretty hot area," said U.S. Army 1st Lt. William Hayes, the 3rd platoon, a part of the 2nd Brigade Combat Team, 34th Infantry Division, Task Force Red Bulls, leader. At that time, there were frequent attacks against the ANA, as well as some small-arms fire directed at U.S. forces.

Since the ANA soldiers with Weapons Company, 2nd Kandak, 1st Brigade, 201st ANA Infantry Corps, started manning some observation posts in the area around the clock, attacks have ceased.

There hasn't been an attack in the three months since then,," Hayes said. "There used to be one at least every couple weeks. The OPs have definitely brought stability to the area."

The platoon knows the ANA soldiers well, as they have conducted missions with them for the last three months. The most was an eight-day air assault known as Operation Bull Whip, which took place in the nearby Galuch Valley.

Hayes and his men found the ANA watching the surrounding area, cooking some food and talking. He asked if the soldiers had any security concerns or had seen any enemy activity. The ANA soldiers said, they had not and things had been pretty quiet lately.

When asked if the soldiers had any other concerns, they remarked that they could use some cots, as they had found a lot of snakes in the area lately.

"Does your company commander know about this?" Hayes asked the soldiers. "I'll see if he's tried to do anything. We'll try to work with your leadership to work these supply issues."

The U.S. soldiers then walked to the other checkpoints to check on the ANA soldiers there.

The meeting was briefly interrupted by the sound of machine gunfire over the nearest ridge. The soldiers instantly reacted, taking cover and scanning their sectors. The gunfire sounded as if it had come from one of the CH-47 Chinook helicopters flying through the nearest valley, which was actually part of another unit's area of operations. The soldiers remained vigilant for several minutes while the platoon attempted to contact the other unit. There was no other activity and the soldiers eventually continued on with their mission.

The platoon gave each group of ANA soldiers, at a post, a small transistor radio to listen to, before leaving the OPs.

"Now you can have your dance party," Hayes said as he handed a smiling soldier one of the radios.

The soldiers will stay at the OPs for long periods of time, and the radios will help their morale while they keep the area security, Hayes said.

The platoon's area of operation is unique because it includes Highway 7, the main highway in Afghanistan which runs from Kabul to Jalalabad.

U.S. Army Spc. Matthew Colsch, who patrolled the mountain valley since the unit arrived in late October, said he has seen the infrastructure of the area grow just by watching this highway and the stretches of markets and villages that are cropping up along it.

"We can see a lot more people coming through," Colsch said. "It's a bigger picture of what's going on in the country by just watching the road."

"The main thing we see is the change in technology," continued Colsch.

"Like when we got here, there were not telephone poles, no wires or any of that. They have electricity now. There's been a lot of progress just in the time we've been here."

"I'd say there's a lot [of infrastructure]," U.S. Army Sgt. 1st Class Nicholas Hosch, 3rd platoon's platoon sergeant from Cedar Rapids, Iowa, added. "There's the power lines and there's areas where there was nothing and now there's a lot of families moving back from Pakistan. They're paving the roads off of Highway 7, too, the AO itself has changed a lot just in the time we've been here."

The highlight of the day's patrol, they said, was—by far—a couple of puppies the soldiers found at one of the OPs. Dogs are one of the least-respected animals in Afghanistan, and are often viewed as pests, definitely not pets. These puppies, however, were obviously fed and cared for.

"These guys up here take care of these dogs, because they're really good scout dogs," Hayes said. "They'll bark, at night, if anyone comes around these posts."

For the soldiers of 3rd Platoon, the puppies provided a simple pleasure during a typical mission in Afghanistan.

Sailor brings Boston Marathon to Afghanistan

BAGRAM AIRFIELD, Afghanistan, April 16, 2011—U.S. Navy Lt. Kris Pomplun completes the Boston Marathon shadow race on Bagram Airfield. Pomplun worked closely with the Boston Athletic Association to bring the world-famous race to Afghanistan. (Photo by U.S. Army Sgt. 1st Class J.R. Williams)

By U.S. Army Capt. Jason Beck
210th Mobile Public Affairs Detachment

BAGRAM AIRFIELD, Afghanistan, April 16, 2011—"One percent of the base is awake and ready to go; we're about to wake up the other 99 percent!" said U.S. Army Col. Benjamin J. Corell, commander, 2nd Brigade Combat Team, 34th Infantry Division, Task Force Red Bulls.

Seconds later, a controlled detonation of explosives signaled the beginning of the Boston Marathon on Bagram Airfield for 363 service members and civilians.

For 170 of the participating runners, this was their first marathon. For U.S. Navy Lt. Kris J. Pomplun, aide-de-camp for the senior civilian representative for Regional Command–East, it was more than just a marathon. Pomplun said it was an experience of a lifetime—it was a "bucket list" item.

The "Boston," as it is affectionately referred to by fans, is more than just a 26.2-mile run.

"It's like the Super Bowl, the World Series and the Indy 500 all rolled up into one," said Pomplun.

The run is an annual marathon hosted by the city of Boston, on Patriots'

Day, the third Monday in April. The Boston first began in 1897 and is the world's oldest annual marathon and one of the most popular road races.

Pomplun, who worked closely with the Boston Athletic Association (BAA) to bring the signature marathon to BAF, said he got the idea while doing what he loves.

"I was working out on the treadmill and kind of thinking about how I will miss another Boston," said Pomplun. "Well, maybe I will try and a make a phone call and bring the Boston here to Bagram."

Pomplun said for the past six years the BAA sponsored a shadow race of the Boston Marathon in Iraq. But, since the association had not heard from anyone in Iraq interested in holding it there, they agreed to sponsor a shadow race here in Afghanistan.

"As long as you find yourselves serving abroad to defend our country, it will be our privilege to support your efforts to host the Boston Marathon in Afghanistan," said Thomas S. Grilk, executive director for BAA.

Initially, Pomplun thought this was a great idea, but said he quietly wondered if it would all come together. Once he realized it would happen, Pomplun quickly reached out to another colleague, Chief Warrant Officer Lisa Bryan, who works with Task Force Red Bulls Joint Visitor's Bureau.

Bryan immediately got to work laying out the racecourse and verifying that it was, indeed, 26.2 miles. At first, she and her team used a measuring wheel and walked the nearly eight-mile airfield perimeter. Pomplun had a race map of the base, which was previously used in another marathon several years earlier. But, as is only the case in a combat zone, the map was classified. And, Bagram had grown quite a bit over the several years since the last race. Eventually, Pomplun, Bryan and the others reached out to Army civil engineers who developed detailed computer-aided design drawings.

Once verified, Pomplun sent an e-mail to the BAA and confirmed the course met the race standard.

The association responded by donating everything the 400 racers would receive if they were running the actual Boston Marathon in the States; they sent 400 finisher's medals, T-shirts and race numbers.

To the organizers' surprise, the race filled up in less than three days.

Once word got out the Boston was coming to Bagram, a group of soldiers from Tarin Kowt in Southern Afghanistan reached out and expressed their own desire to run. Pomplun said he wanted to share this amazing experience with as many people as possible and granted them 37 race slots.

While running the racecourse, Pomplun said he would occasionally hear runners talking about how they may not have ever gotten the chance to run the Boston and how much it meant to them.

Pomplun said there were many special moments throughout the race.

However, the one that stands out the most occurred just before the controlled detonation.

Usually, someone is designated to sing the national anthem before a race, but they hadn't planned for it in Bagram.

Pomplun said somewhere amidst the crowd of almost 400 people, one voice, unaccompanied, started singing and was soon joined by all of the others. Each of the 363 participants finished the race.

"While we keep busy each spring with the planning and execution of the annual Boston Marathon, we know that our Armed Services are always busy, always on guard, and always working to keep us safe," said Grilk. "With such devotion to our country and dedication to the defense of the freedoms we enjoy, it has been an honor to support the fine men and women at Bagram Airfield in Afghanistan as they competed in 'The Boston Marathon in Afghanistan.'"

Pomplun said he appreciated all the efforts of the BAA and thanked them for their generosity.

"For that one day [the BAA] gave 400 of us here in Afghanistan an amazing experience —thank you for that gift," said Pomplun.

Grilk agreed, "This year on Patriots' Day at the Boston Marathon we saw many examples of strength and of the determination required to overcome adversity. Adding the efforts of everyone at Bagram to the efforts of those with us here in Boston makes for an even richer story as we look back on the 2011 Boston Marathon."

PRT hosts public affairs training for Paktya officials

By U.S. Air Force Staff Sgt. Barry Loo
Paktya Provincial Reconstruction Team Public Affairs

PAKTYA PROVINCE, Afghanistan, April 16, 2011—A dozen representatives from the Paktya provincial government, including Deputy Governor Abdul Rahman Mangal, attended the workshop on media relations hosted by the Paktya Provincial Reconstruction Team at Forward Operating Base Gardez, Afghanistan.

The workshop provided an opportunity for them to refresh and further develop their skills in conducting interviews and developing public messages for the news media.

U.S. Air Force 1st Lt. Sybil Taunton from West Haven, Utah, used her training and experience as the PRT public affairs officer to lead the workshop.

Taunton emphasized the importance of honesty and the timely release information to the public.

"You all represent the government, and in order to gain the trust of the people the most important thing is to always tell the truth," Taunton said.

Mangal reinforced the importance and Taunton's message to the attendees.

"If any media tries to talk to you, be truthful," Mangal said. "As long as you have good information, you have to deliver it to the people."

Operation Rainbow Valley prevents insurgent movement through Paktya

By U.S. Army 1st Lt. Nicholas Rasmussen
Task Force Lethal

PAKTYA PROVINCE, Afghanistan, April 17, 2011—Rain and mud couldn't stop 1st Battalion, 168th Infantry Regiment, Task Force Lethal, from concluding Operation Rainbow Valley on a high note.

The operation, which occurred in Zormat District, Paktya Province, Afghanistan, resulted in the capture of a known insurgent financier and five additional detainees, the removal of two Improvised Explosive Devices, disruption of supply lines, and denied insurgents freedom of movement throughout Paktya.

Nearly 400 soldiers from the Afghan National Army, Afghan Uniformed Police, and Companies D and C of Task Force Lethal manned six traffic control points day and night. At the same time, route clearance packages 7 and 9 of the 118th Sapper Company cleared the main roads in Zormat searching for insurgent activity and IEDs.

The operation had a good start with one IED found the first day, but activity reached its peak on day two.

Soldiers found a highly-sought insurgent financier on his way home from a market in Gardez City where he worked. Third Platoon, Company D, intercepted the financier as they were moving their Traffic Control Point north along the road. The ANA pulled the truck over and searched the occupants while 3rd Platoon used photographs and other evidence to identify the wanted financier.

Being one of the top men on Task Force Lethal's most wanted list, 3rd Platoon was excited to make the capture.

"It's like a table," said U.S. Army Sgt. 1st Class Ryan Johnson of Griswold, Iowa, platoon sergeant for 3rd Platoon. "If you start taking the legs off the whole thing's going to collapse. This financier was one of those legs, and now the table is wobbling."

The rest of the men in the car were thoroughly searched, and all four were detained and taken to Forward Operating Base Gardez for further questioning.

That evening 1st Platoon, Company D, Task Force Lethal, had a more explosive encounter with the enemy.

Four rounds of indirect fire landed all around 1st Platoon's checkpoint. They also received some small arms fire near the rear truck, which got stuck in the mud while trying to reposition toward the enemy.

"This could not possibly have happened at a worse time," said U.S. Army

Sgt. Daniel Harrison, a squad leader for 1st Platoon from Cedar Rapids, Iowa.

The IDF was seen coming from a house southwest of the TCP. The enemy fire stopped after a few minutes and 1st Platoon recovered the stuck vehicle. Along with their ANA partners and the Task Force Lethal Scout Platoon, 1st Platoon moved to search the home and the area around it.

The coalition forces and ANA detained five individuals inside the home who had explosive residue on their skin. No sign of an indirect fire weapons system was found.

The detainees were taken into custody by the ANA and 1st Platoon returned to their TCP to continue operations.

Aside from the persistent rain, things went smoothly throughout the remainder of the operation. One additional IED was found and removed, and on the last day the sun came out.

Operation Rainbow Valley was successful. The goal to curtail insurgent movement through Paktya Province was accomplished along with the added benefit of capturing a wanted insurgent.

"We've definitely taken the wind out of the sails of the insurgents for a while," said U.S. Army Cpt. Kent Greiner, Company D commander from Nevada, Iowa. "We're striking a nerve with them and we're going to keep striking that nerve to see what happens."

Panjshir PRT engineers assess construction projects

By U.S. Air Force 2nd Lt. Ashleigh Peck
Panjshir Provincial Reconstruction Team Public Affairs

PANJSHIR PROVINCE, Afghanistan, April 17, 2011—Panjshir Provincial Reconstruction Team engineers assessed four active projects in Anaba and Dara districts, April 17.

The projects the PRT engineering team assessed included a district court center, two schools, and a dormitory building.

"With 17 active (construction) projects in the province this was a typical day for us," said U.S. Air Force Tech. Sgt. Eric Garcia, PRT engineering team member and Corpus Christi, Texas, native.

The team inspects each project at least twice a week.

"We try to inspect the projects constantly because each step in a construction project is important," said Daniel Fredrickson, a U.S. Army Corps of Engineers representative with Panjshir PRT and Battleground, Wash., native. "We want to make sure everything is done correctly because once it's done, it's very hard to go back and fix it."

One of the four projects the team evaluated included Molark Morza Shahid Boys School in Abdullah Khil village.

"We wanted to make sure work was started before the river rose so the contractor could have all the materials and supplies here on site to build throughout the entire construction season," said U.S. Air Force Capt. Brian Jackson, the PRT lead engineer and South Haven, Mich., native.

The assessment marked the first time the PRT engineers observed workers on site for the boys school.

"This project looks much better than the last time we were here because there are workers on site and all the necessary equipment and materials have been delivered," said Jackson.

Malem Sorab, the Dara District governor, met the team at the work site.

"We really appreciate the PRT's work with the contractors to get this project started," said Sorab, through an interpreter. "The school we have now only has six classrooms and there are many students."

Molark Morza Shahid will be two stories with 16 classrooms and should be completed by the beginning of the next construction season.

Company B says goodbye to fallen soldier, friend

PAKTYA PROVINCE, Afghanistan, April 18, 2011—The American flag and battalion and company colors wave over the memorial stand for U.S. Army Sgt. Brent M. Maher, on Combat Outpost Dand Patan prior to a memorial service held here today. Maher, an infantryman with 1st Battalion, 168th Infantry Regiment, 2nd Brigade Combat Team, 34th Infantry Division, Task Force Lethal, was killed when an Improvised Explosive Device detonated under his truck in Paktya Province, Afghanistan, April 11. (Photo by U.S. Army Sgt. John P. Sklaney III)

By U.S. Army 1st Lt. Nicholas Rasmussen
2nd Brigade Combat Team, 34th Infantry Division

PAKTYA PROVINCE, Afghanistan, April 18—A memorial service for U.S. Army Sgt. Brent M. Maher was held at Combat Outpost Dand Patan, Afghanistan.

Maher, an infantryman from Honey Creek, Iowa, with Company B, 1st Battalion, 168th Infantry Regiment, 2nd Brigade Combat Team, 34th Infantry Division, Task Force Lethal, was killed April 11 when his vehicle struck an Improvised Explosive Device.

The day began similar to how everyone from Company B was feeling: dreary, cold and wet. Rain fell and the wind blew heavily throughout the morning and most of the afternoon while preparations for the service were completed. However, moments before the service began, the clouds lifted, the wind stopped and the sun began to shine on the small outpost in northern Paktya, in a way reflecting the bright attitude Maher always had.

Most people were a bit frightened when they met Maher initially; he was a tall, burly Iowan who looked as though he could lift a Buick.

447

Talking with him, a person soon found out his good nature was bigger than his stature.

"He was a very intimidating looking man," said U.S. Army Staff Sgt. Zackary Richardson of Orient, Iowa, and Maher's squad leader. "Very quickly I realized that he was just a gentle giant, a big man with a big heart."

"I'm a little guy at 5-foot-7. So, to me, he was 8 feet tall and bulletproof," said U.S. Army Pfc. Bryston Dunkeson of Farragut, Iowa, an intelligence analyst for Company B. "The first time I really interacted with him was on leave."

Dunkeson and Maher spent almost 40 days trying to get home and back to spend their 15-day rest and relaxation leave state-side February of this year. This gave Dunkeson a chance to get to know Maher.

He'd go check on flights at night and early in the morning, hours before the rest of us would wake up, just so we didn't have to.

"He'd do anything for anybody," said Dunkeson.

Likewise, Maher would often give the new guys a hard time. Teasing them about one thing or another was his way of ushering them into the family. "He'd make them earn their stripes," said Richardson.

Members of his company remember Maher as the guy to go to if they had a problem or needed some advice on something.

"I always felt comfortable talking to him," said U.S. Army Spc. Justin Christiansen of Nebraska City, Neb., who was in Maher's truck the day the IED detonated. "He wouldn't say anything to anyone else; it was like a friend talking to a friend with him."

"He truly cared about you," said U.S. Army Spc. Joe Kintsler of Farragut, Iowa, and member of Maher's platoon. "It was natural for him to care about people."

Maher often kept the mood around his platoon and his company as light as possible, either with a joke or with his infectious laughter.

"He was always the first to crack jokes," said Kinstler. "Once he did it, everyone would realize things aren't so bad and joined in."

"He had a dry sense of humor," remembers Christiansen. "He'd try to make jokes with a serious face then you'd see that big smile and you knew he was lying."

"He could draw a crowd," said Kinstler. "You'd hear him laughing and go to find out why and pretty soon the whole platoon would be there having a good time before mission."

Maher loved to hunt, to the point it was the vast majority of conversation for him. The only thing he cherished more was his family. Maher genuinely cared about his fellow man and serving his country.

Service awards Maher received throughout his military career include the

Armed Forces Reserve Medal with "M" device, the Afghanistan Campaign Medal with one Bronze Service Star, two Non-Article five NATO Medals with bronze service star and ISAF clasp, the Navy and Marine Corps Achievement Medal, the Navy Good Conduct Medal, the Sea Service Deployment Ribbon, the Global War on Terrorism Medal, the Korean Service Medal, and the Combat Infantry Badge. Maher was posthumously awarded a Purple Heart, a Bronze Star Medal and promoted from specialist to sergeant.

The evening of his memorial ceremony, Maher's platoon launched a mortar illumination round signed by members of Company B into the night sky over Dand Patan as a final farewell.

PAKTYA PROVINCE, Afghanistan, April 18, 2011—U.S. Army 1st Lt. Michael Anderson of Orlando, Fla., pays his respects to U.S. Army Sgt. Brent M. Maher during a memorial ceremony at combat outpost Dand Patan April 18. Maher, a member of Anderson's platoon in Company B, 1st Battalion, 168th Infantry Regiment, 2nd Brigade, 34th Infantry Division, Task Force Lethal, died April 11 after an Improvised Explosive Device detonated under his vehicle. (Photo by U.S. Army Sgt. John P. Sklaney III)

PARWAN PROVINCE, Afghanistan, April 18, 2011—Company B, 1st Battalion, 168th Infantry Regiment, 2nd Brigade, 34th Infantry Division, Task Force Lethal, holds a moment of silence during a memorial ceremony April 18 for U.S. Army Sgt. Brent M. Maher, who died April 11 after an Improvised Explosive Device detonated under his truck. Three other members of Maher's platoon were injured in the blast. (Photo by U.S. Army Sgt. John P. Sklaney III)

Platoon remembers fallen Iowa Guardsman

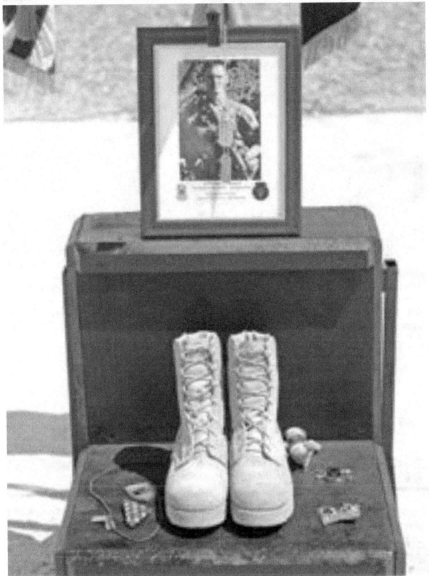

LAGHMAN PROVINCE, Afghanistan, April 18, 2011—Soldiers pay respects through a memorial stand for Spc. Donald Lee Nichols. He was killed in action by an Improvised Explosive Device April 13 in Laghman Province, Afghanistan while serving with Reconnaissance Platoon, Headquarters and Headquarter's Company, 1st Battalion, 133rd Infantry Regiment, 1st Brigade Combat Team, 34th Infantry Division. Nichols' memorial service took place at Forward Operating Base Mehtar Lam April 18. To the right of Nichols' boots is his Donald Duck keychain his platoon mates said he carried with him everywhere. (Photo by U.S. Army Spc. James Wilton, Task Force Red Bulls Public Affairs)

LAGHMAN PROVINCE, Afghanistan, Apr. 18, 2011—U.S. Army Spc. Jacob Ketelaar (left), an infantryman from Waverly, Iowa, and U.S. Army Sgt. Edward Kane (right), a team leader from Portland, Ore., both with the Reconnaissance Platoon, Headquarters and Headquarters Company, 1st Battalion, 133rd Infantry Regiment, 1st Brigade Combat Team, 34th Infantry Division pay their final respects at the memorial stand of Spc. Donald Lee Nichols, who served in their platoon. Nichols' memorial service took place at Forward Operating Base Mehtar Lam, April 18. (Photo by U.S. Army Spc. James Wilton, Task Force Red Bulls Public Affairs)

By U.S. Army Staff Sgt. Ryan C. Matson
Task Force Red Bulls Public Affairs

LAGHMAN PROVINCE, Afghanistan, April 18, 2011—Service members held a memorial ceremony, for U.S. Army Spc. Donald Lee Nichols, who was killed by an Improvised Explosive Device while serving as part of a route clearance security team April 13 in Mehtar Lam District, Afghanistan.

Following the ceremony, members of Nichols' platoon, the Reconnaissance Platoon, part of Headquarters and Headquarters Company, 1st Battalion, 133rd Infantry Regiment, Task Force Ironman, 2nd Brigade Combat Team, 34th Infantry Division, Task Force Red Bulls, gathered to remember not only the Soldier the unit had lost, but the friend and person, as well.

The Soldiers served with their fallen friend on more than 100 combat missions, most of them in the ruggedly mountainous and insurgent-laden area near Combat Outpost Najil.

"When I think about him, I think about how anytime we had really hard missions, and it sucked, he always had something to say that would just make it easier," said U.S. Army Spc. Erik McDonald, a combat medic from Iowa City,

Iowa, with the Reconnaissance Platoon. "You'd be just hating your life, but he'd say something to make it better. I don't think I ever saw him down."

"Sarcasm was his forte," U.S. Army Spc. Kris Henshaw, a sniper with the Reconnaissance Platoon from Sioux City, Iowa, who knew Nichols for two years. "We'd get done climbing a mountain or doing some crazy movement through the night in the freezing cold or whatever, and he'd never complain about it, but he would always have some ridiculous, funny, comment to say at the end of it."

The other Soldiers in the platoon agreed Nichols' sense of humor shined through at all times.

"You could feel completely worthless and tired as hell, and he'd come out with something that would insult you, but still make you laugh," McDonald said.

"He definitely had a way of brightening up the worst situations," said U.S. Army Spc. Nick Williams, a sniper from Muscatine, Iowa.

"He always went above and beyond your expectations of him, and at the worst times and hardest missions, he motivated you," Williams continued. "You just wanted to follow him."

The platoon talked about a time when they were under heavy fire on Hellfire Ridge, a mountain ridge near COP Najil. Bullets were zinging all around Nichols and he tried to make a move to look where they were coming from and three rounds landed inches from him, kicking dirt up in his face. They said he said something likem, "Maybe later," and went back to crouching behind cover.

The platoon remembered when they came under attack in mid-February, after a Mine-Resistant, Ambush-Protected vehicle was flipped by an Improvised Explosive Device, it was Nichols who kept his head and responded first.

"He was rocking the .50-cal, which suppressed the enemy and allowed us to medically evacuate the injured Soldiers," McDonald said.

Another of Nichols' trademarks was a Donald Duck keychain. The Soldiers said he carried it everywhere with him, since they shared the same first name.

U.S. Army Spc. Jacob Ketelaar, an infantryman in the platoon, who knew Nichols since the two attended high school in Ketelaar's hometown, said Nichols had many interests. "He changed them so much," Ketelaar said. "He'd go from wanting to be in the FBI, to being a mechanic, he was ambitious. He had a lot of plans for himself. He was going to move in with his girlfriend and go to school in Iowa City."

More than 100 people attended the ceremony at the small FOB in Laghman Province, Afghanistan. The ceremony began with remarks from the battalion commander, U.S. Army Lt. Col. Steven Kremer, of Cherokee, Iowa. Kremer shared some background on the young Soldier, born in Waterloo, Iowa, was 21 at the time of his death. Nichols graduated in 2009 from Wavery-Shell Rock High School in Iowa, where he was a stellar athlete, especially in wrestling. Shortly after his 18th birthday, Nichols enlisted in the infantry and completed basic training and advanced individual training at Fort Benning, Ga.

"Spc. Nichols has made an impact on everyone here in life and death," Kremer said. "Spc. Nichols is a true testament of being a great American with his decision to support this country, knowing that he would deploy to Afghanistan. Spc. Nichols will be remembered as a hero, a friend and a great Soldier."

Nichols' company commander, U.S. Army Capt. Shane Hunter, from Grundy Center, Iowa, relayed an anecdote of the Soldier's tremendous will and heart.

"Spc. Nichols loved his job as a scout," Hunter said. "It gave him an opportunity to put all of his military skills to the test and be part of a brotherhood that involved operating in the rugged mountains of Laghman Province, Afghanistan. On one mission, Spc. Nichols severely injured his knee but he would not allow anyone to carry his rucksack. He did not want the others to have to carry his weight. He carried the rucksack until finally it had to be taken away from him. That's the kind of Soldier Spc. Nichols was."

"He was the guy who always carried the heaviest load, always," U.S. Army Sgt. James Sherrill, a Reconnaissance Platoon joint fires observer from Johnston, Iowa, who read the scripture during Nichols' ceremony, said. "He carried a M48 and at least 600 rounds and a really heavy bag on top of it all. He would amaze me. He'd be carrying all this stuff, and he might fall and hurt himself, and you would try to take his heavy weapon or his heavy ruck, and he would look you in your face and just say 'No!'"

McDonald said even when he was hurt, Nichols would never quit, and he would carry his fellow Soldiers' gear when they were weighed down, but never allow them to do the same for him.

"Spc. Nichols' love for the United States Army and the members of his platoon was very visible," said U.S. Army 1st Lt. Justin Foote, Nichols platoon leader from New Hartford, Iowa. "It surely will be tough to move on without him. And yet in all of this, we know that our grief is nothing compared to that of his loved ones, his parents, his fiancé and his family."

In accordance with Army tradition, the ceremony concluded with the last roll call, in which U.S. Army 1st Sgt. Brian Nichols, the HHC first sergeant, from Boone, Iowa, called Spc. Nichol's name repeatedly with no answer. After that, volleys were fired by the drill and ceremony team, and Pfc. Jeremiah

Crisel, a chaplain's assistant with HHC from Sanborn, Iowa played Taps on the bugle.

A long line of Soldiers, from all units on the base, passed by to pay their final respects to the fallen Soldier, the first the battalion lost during the deployment to Afghanistan.

His awards and decorations include the Bronze Star Medal, Purple Heart, Army Good Conduct Medal, Afghanistan Campaign Service Medal, Global War on Terrorism Service Medal, North Atlantic Treaty Organization Medal, Armed Forces Reserve Medal with "M" device, National Defense Service Medal, Army Service Ribbon, Overseas Service Ribbon and Combat Infantryman's Badge.

LAGHMAN PROVINCE, Afghanistan, April 18, 2011—U.S. Army Staff Sgt. Nick Rossin (left), a squad leader from Waterloo, Iowa, and Sgt. 1st Class Steven Beireis (right), a platoon sergeant from North Liberty, Iowa, both with the Reconnaissance Platoon, Headquarters and Headquarters Company, 1st Battalion, 133rd Infantry Regiment, Task Force Ironman, 2nd Brigade Combat Team, 34th Infantry Division, Task Force Red Bulls, salute the memorial stand of Spc. Donald Lee Nichols, who served in their platoon Nichols' memorial service took place at Forward Operating Base Mehtar Lam April 18. (Photo by U.S. Army Spc. James Wilton, Task Force Red Bulls Public Affairs)

LAGHMAN PROVINCE, Afghanistan, Apr. 18, 2011—U.S. Army Pfc. Jeremiah Crisel (right), a chaplain's assistant from Sanborn, Iowa, plays Taps on the bugle while U.S. Army Capt. Tony Christoph, a personnel officer from New Hampton, Iowa, both from Headquarters and Headquarters Company, 1st Battalion, 133rd Infantry Regiment, 1st Brigade Combat Team, 34th Infantry Division, Task Force Ironman, salutes at Forward Operating Base Mehtar Lam April 18 during the memorial service for Spc. Donald Lee Nichols, who served with Reconnaissance Platoon, HHC, 1-133rd Inf. (Photo by U.S. Army Spc. James Wilton, Task Force Red Bulls Public Affairs)

Task Force Hurricane takes on ADT mission

BAGRAM AIRFIELD, Afghanistan, April 18, 2011—Col. Neil T. Mullaney, the Kentucky Agribusiness Development Team III commander from Louisville, Ky. speaks during a Transfer of Authority ceremony at Bagram Airfield. The Kentucky ADT III replaced the Kentucky ADT II in the Parwan, Panjshir and Kapisa area of operations. (Photo by U.S. Army Spc. James Wilton, Task Force Red Bulls Public Affairs)

By U.S. Army Spc. James Wilton
Task Force Red Bulls Public Affairs

PARWAN PROVINCE, Afghanistan, April 18, 2011—The Kentucky National Guard's Agribusiness Development Team II, Task Force Ironhorse, welcomed their replacements, the Kentucky ADT III, Task Force Hurricane, during a Transfer of Authority ceremony at Bagram Airfield.

The ADT program began in 2008 and brings 10 to 12 agriculture and agribusiness experts to Afghanistan to teach and mentor local farmers. Supported by a headquarters and security element, the team uses their civilian skills to develop and improve the quality of life for the Afghan people across Regional Command–East, which has eight ADTs, and Regional Command–South, which has one team.

"This has been a long and productive deployment, but ADTs do not work in a vacuum," said U.S. Army Col. Hunter J. Mathews, the Kentucky ADT II commander from Lexington, Ky. "Everything we have been able to accomplish is due to the cooperation and assistance of our partners and friends."

The ADT conducted more than 450 missions on 32 major development projects and 100 quick-impact projects in Parwan, Panjshir, and Kapisa Provinces. These projects restored irrigation canals, improved agricultural education and introduced beekeeping and poultry business skills to women, along with many other projects. The team also worked to strengthen the competency, professionalism and effectiveness of the Afghan government's agriculture officials, which they consider to be there greatest accomplishment.

"The most important thing we did was sitting down with the Director of Irrigation, Agriculture, and Livestock, and working with him to use his staff more effectively, teaching him to get his district-level people out of the office and into the village, helping the local farmers," said Matthews.

It is this focus and expertise, he said, that makes the ADTs so effective-- allowing them to have a large impact on the lives and future of the Afghan people. That level of determination is also evident in the Kentucky ADT III's hope for their rotation through Afghanistan.

"We are going to continue along the same lines of operations that the ADT II has already set in stone, so that we can finish up some of the projects they have already started," said U.S. Air Force Col. Neil T. Mullaney, the Kentucky ADT III commander from Louisville, Ky. "But we want to further develop the youth education. After going to visit the Kapisa Agriculture Institute (KAI) we see a great opportunity there. By focusing more on the younger generations of Afghanistan we think that that will be more fruitful for the long term."

Education is a very important part of ADT III's plan for their deployment, which includes projects in both KAI and the Alberoni University also in Kapisa, said Mullaney.

Continuity is also on the side of the ADT, the fact that the Afghan people see the same patch and hear the same accent when they deal with the Kentucky unit lets them know that they are dealing with the same family. Along with that many of the members from the both units have known each other for many years and have a strong working relationship, which transfers over to a consistent dissemination of information before and after the transfer.

"Additionally two people on his team, left just a year ago with Kentucky ADT I, so he has two guys on his team that know where they're going, know the DAIL and know our provinces," said Mathews, when speaking about the continuity between the groups "I also have one guy from my team, the operations Non-Commissioned Officer that is staying with him. He already knows the procedures and knows who to work with, so that also helps a lot."

This consistency and focus on education means that the new ADT will build on the successes of the pervious unit, break new ground, and create their own milestones as well as pave the way for their brothers in arms, Kentucky ADT IV when they make their way here, in another year.

Bazaar cleanup improves relations, security

PAKTYA PROVINCE, Afghanistan, April 19, 2011—Haji Niaz Mohammed Khallili, sub-governor of Dand Patan and U.S. Army Capt. Brandon Gray, from West Des Moines, Iowa, commander of Company B, 1st Battalion, 168th Infantry Regiment, Task Force Lethal, greet each other during the bazaar clean-up in Dand Patan, Afghanistan. (Photo by U.S. Army Sgt. John P Sklaney III, 2-45th Agribusiness Development Team Public Affairs)

By U.S. Army Sgt. John P Sklaney III
2-45th Agribusiness Development Team Public Affairs

PAKTYA PROVINCE, Afghanistan, April 19, 2011—Task Force Lethal Soldiers and the 2-45th Agribusiness Development Team organized a clean-up day in the Dand Patan village bazaar, employing locals and improving security. The cleanup effort fell under the "Cash-For-Work" program used to infuse cash into an area quickly, with direct results.

Afghan National Security Forces, along with Soldiers from Task Force Lethal, from Company B, 1st Battalion, 168th Infantry Regiment, provided security along the perimeter, while the ADT provided security inside the bazaar. Workers collected more than 500 bags of trash.

"Local children helped improve the appearance of the bazaar and also earned income," said U.S. Army Capt. Brandon Gray, from West Des Moines, Iowa, commander of Company B, 1st Bn., 168th Infantry Regiment, Task Force Lethal. "Another benefit was of the improved sanitation in the bazaar for people of Dand Patan and also visitors."

The C4W programs are limited to less than $5,000 and provide a positive impact to a specific area. C4W focuses on Afghans between 11-18 years of age, because those ages are most susceptible to influence by insurgents or those wishing to destabilize the Afghan government.

"The end result was that for less than $700, the bazaar was cleaned up," said U.S. Army Sgt. Maj. Lorn McKinzie, from Depew, Okla., the senior Non-Commissioned Officer for the ADT. "That money was well spent and directed at those most at risk of being influenced by the insurgents."

"I was pleased with the help in cleaning the bazaar," said Haji Niaz Mohammed Khallili, sub-governor of Dand Patan. "An improved bazaar is important because it brings more money into the community and breaks the cycle of insurgency."

The ADT is planning more projects in Dand Patan, including youth livestock and poultry training, greenhouses, and cool storage facilities.

Task Force Lethal, ANSF distribute 6,000 donated coats to rural Afghans

PAKTYA PROVINCE, Afghanistan—U.S. Army Spc. David Gordy of Ottumwa, Iowa, a member of 1st Battalion, 168th Infantry Regiment, 2nd Brigade, 34th Infantry Division, Task Force Lethal, helps a worker from Gardez City, Paktya Province, unload a truckload of more than 400 boxes full of coats, hats, gloves and scarves on Forward Operating Base Gardez, Afghanistan, March 7. Rapport Afghanistan, a U.S. volunteer group that provides comfort supplies to the rural areas of Afghanistan donated the goods. Task Force Lethal and their Government of Islamic Republic of Afghanistan partners later distributed the winter clothing to local Afghans throughout Paktya Province. (Photo by U.S. Army 1st Lt. Nicholas Rasmussen, Task Force Lethal Public Affairs)

By U.S. Army 1st Lt. Nicholas Rasmussen
Task Force Lethal Public Affairs

PAKTYA PROVINCE, Afghanistan, April 19, 2011—U.S. and Afghan forces handed out hundreds of coats to people living in the rural village of Charwazi, Afghanistan.

All told, Afghan National Army and 1st Platoon, C Company, 1st Battalion, 168th Infantry Regiment, Task Force Lethal, 2nd Brigade Combat Team, 34th Infantry Division, Task Force Red Bulls distributed roughly 6,000 coats to remote Aghan villages since the drive began last year.

"The coats help because many of the homes only have small wood stoves," said an ANA soldier who helped pass out the coats.

A U.S. volunteer group known as Rapport Afghanistan donated the coats, which represented another effort by the group to provide comfort supplies to people in rural areas of Afghanistan.

Months of collecting finally ended March 7, when more than 6,000 coats and 1,500 other clothing items such as gloves and hats were delivered to Forward Operating Base Gardez where Task Force Lethal is based.

Rapport Afghanistan, a Minnesota-based organization, was founded in 2010 by Shawn Mingus, a resident of Chanhassen, Minn., and friend of U.S. Army Lt. Col. Stephen B. Boesen II of Ankeny, Iowa, the Task Force Lethal commander.

Earlier that year, when Mingus heard of Task Force Lethal's upcoming deployment, he contacted Boesen to ask what kind of support he and his task force needed.

"He contemplated for a while and then thought of warm coats, hats and gloves," said Mingus.

Boesen recalled from his previous deployment to Paktya that many people lived and worked around the mountains without warm clothing.

"When I heard him say that I said, 'I'm on it!'" said Mingus.

In March 2010, Rapport Afghanistan began with a board of directors consisting of 10 people, one of whom is originally from nearby Khost Province, Afghanistan.

The group organized volunteers around the United States to collect used coats, hats, gloves, and scarves from their communities.

U.S. Bank pitched in to sponsor coat drives in five major U.S. cities, and organized the shipment of donated items to Minneapolis.

The group continued collections and accepting donations through the spring and summer of 2010.

"I had large, growing piles of coats sitting in my basement from May until November," Mingus said.

It took 50 volunteers two weekends to package, mark, and transfer more than 400 boxes into temporary storage, where they waited for a shipping date.

When Mingus found out where Boesen was going to be stationed, he arranged to have the container delivered directly to his headquarters from Minneapolis, a feat that took more than 15 weeks, and plenty of patience.

The original delivery date in January was delayed significantly due to the weather and other complications that frequently impact a mountainous combat zone. The 400 boxes were divided among each of Task Force Lethal's infantry companies who, with their Afghan national security partners, went to local villages to distribute the coats and warm clothes to Afghans throughout the province.

"We usually hand out 40 to 50 coats at a time," said U.S. Army Pfc. Bryston Dunkeson, an intelligence analyst for Company B, Task Force Lethal and a native of Farragut, Iowa.

"Rapport Afghanistan is a great example of outstanding, grass-root support from volunteers in America who donated time and money for a coat drive to donate warm clothes for the Afghan people who need them," said Boesen.

Panjshir ETT assists investigation

PANJSHIR PROVINCE, Afghanistan, April 20, 2011—U.S. Army Lt. Col. Tim Glynn, Panjshir Embedded Training Team commander and Ankeny, Iowa, resident, talks with Afghan National Police while assisting with an investigation in Khenj District, Afghanistan. The Afghan National Police and National Directorate of Security officials conducted the investigation. (Photo by U.S. Air Force 2nd Lt. Ashleigh Peck, Panjshir Provicial Reconstruction Team)

By U.S. Air Force 2nd Lt. Ashleigh Peck
Panjshir Provicial Reconstruction Team Public Affairs

PANJSHIR PROVINCE, Afghanistan, April 20, 2011—Iowa National Guard soldiers of the Panjshir Embedded Training Team assisted in an investigation in Khenj District, Afghanistan, April 20.

Afghan National Police and the Afghan National Directorate of Security officials conducted the investigation, and the ETT provided additional expertise and equipment. They investigated shots fired at a local ANP officer in Khenj District.

"My team is the first to arrive at the scene of a crime in Panjshir," said anti-terrorism chief with police headquarters, ANP Capt. Ajab Gul, through an interpreter.

Gul worked with NDS for 18 years and has been Panjshir's anti-terrorism chief for the past two years.

"We don't have a lot of basic equipment needed for an investigation," said Gul. "Without ETT, we'd be working with limited supplies and using our bare hands instead of gloves."

Once the initial investigation was complete, the 30-ton recovery vehicle, which the province received from the Ministry of Interior in March, was used to recover the suspect's vehicle which was rolled over in a ditch.

"In the past, the province had to rent a crane and wait for it to come from Parwan, but because Panjshir has the recovery vehicle, the suspect's vehicle was recovered the same day," said U.S. Army Lt. Col. Tim Glynn, the Panjshir ETT commander and Ankeny, Iowa, resident. "This is the first time the recovery vehicle was used in an investigation."

After the suspect's vehicle was secured at the traffic police headquarters, ETT showed the investigations team their technique to take fingerprints.

"The investigation kit we used today for fingerprinting and evidence collection will soon be provided to the ANP with many of the low-cost, high-value materials needed for an investigation," said Glynn. "In May, we will conduct training for the issued equipment so the kits can be used right away."

The kits will include a finger-print case, evidence bags, rubber gloves, law-enforcement labelling material and digital cameras.

"The Afghans do the best with what they have," said Glynn. "We are here to provide them with additional tools and guidance when we can."

Panjshir ETT works with various ANP personnel to continue the working relationship they have developed.

"I am very happy to work with ETT," said Gul. "We meet every week, and whenever we need something, they are there to help."

The Police Mentor Team said they hope their efforts to increase the ANP's basic police skills and procedures will help them better understand their role as a civil security force. But most importantly, they will be able to go home knowing they tried to make Afghanistan a better and safer place for its people.

PANJSHIR PROVINCE, Afghanistan, April 20, 2011—Panjshir's 30-ton recovery vehicle, which the province received from the Ministry of Interior in March, was used to recover a vehicle which rolled over in a ditch in Khenj District, Afghanistan, April 20. (Photo by U.S. Air Force 2nd Lt. Ashleigh Peck, Panjshir Provicial Reconstruction Team Public Affairs)

USAF Prime BEEF engineers build up eastern Afghanistan one COP at a time

LAGHMAN PROVINCE, Afghanistan, April 20, 2011—U.S. Air Force Airman 1st. Class Tyler D. Saulsgiver (front), a structural engineer specialist from Panama, N.Y., and U.S. Air Force Senior Master Sgt. David Sowers, a heavy equipment operator from Staples, Minn., both with the 577th Prime Base Engineer Emergency Force Squadron, sheet the roof of a B-hut building, April 20, at Joint Combat Outpost Xio Haq, Afghanistan. (Photo by U.S. Army Staff Sgt. Ryan C. Matson, Task Force Red Bulls Public Affairs)

By U.S. Army Staff Sgt. Ryan C. Matson
Task Force Red Bulls Public Affairs

LAGHMAN PROVINCE, Afghanistan, April 20, 2011—Two weeks ago, there was nothing there. Today, a crew of eight Airmen from the 577th Prime Base Engineer Emergency Force Squadron swarm all over a row of four 18- by 36-feet plywood buildings—sheeting the roofs, wiring the lights, cutting out the doors.

The plywood buildings are known as B-Huts, and they will serve as living quarters for more soldiers at the tiny, but ever-expanding Joint Combat Outpost Xio Haq, eastern Afghanistan.

"Normally it takes eight or nine days for a B-Hut, but so far we've done all this in a little less than two weeks," said U.S. Air Force Tech. Sgt. Robert Arnold, a structural engineering specialist from Adelanto, Calif., as he pointed to a row of four B-Huts in various states of completion. "We're going pretty fast."

The eight-man team from the Prime BEEF Squadron headed out to JCOP Xio Haq, which is scheduled to go from housing a company-sized element to just less than a battalion-sized element, from their deployment headquarters at Bagram Airfield. Each Airman is trained in a specific trade. Three of the Airmen are structural specialists, trained in carpentry, masonry, roofs, welding and sheet metal fabrication. Two members are heavy equipment operators, one is a heating, ventilation and air conditioning specialist and the team also boasts a plumber and an electrician.

The Airmen can travel anywhere in eastern Afghanistan where work needs to be done, from developed bases to the most remote outposts.

"They send us to the worst-off places to make them better," Arnold said. "We like getting out of BAF as quickly and often as possible, because out here in the field we get to operate as a small team and just focus on the mission, take care of business."

The squadron will hop from base to base or outpost during their six-month deployment, doing any and every type of construction work necessary to improve the area, from grading roads and pouring concrete pads or sidewalks, to building gyms and other buildings.

"You get a sense of pride in the things you've built because you are the mission once you get out here," U.S. Air Force Master Sgt. Kevin Shows, a heating, ventilation and air conditioning specialist from Columbia, Miss., said.

The crew said they build a lot of B-huts, as these buildings are most commonly used for living quarters, but can be adapted to house anything, from latrines to morale, welfare and recreation facilities. The squadron said they don't work off a set of plans on the B-huts. They said the buildings need to fit a set of specifications, but depending on the materials available and the area in which they build the B-huts, the Airmen said they do have a little bit of room to improvise on the buildings.

Arnold said the expeditionary Prime BEEF units are a relatively new organization within the Air Force, with their squadron being the fourth rotation deployed to Afghanistan. He said there are two other Prime BEEF squadrons located in the country.

"Actually the 577th Prime BEEF squadron has only been around a couple years," Arnold said. "Usually they have a REDHORSE [Rapid Engineer Deployable Heavy Operational Repair Squadron Engineers] unit that would come out to do something like this, but this type of work is a bit smaller than what they're used to handling."

Rather than stay at one FOB, these smaller teams travel around to where work needs to be done. So far, Xio Haq is the second stop of the deployment for the team, as they have also built B-huts at FOB Mehtar Lam, also in support of Task Force Ironman, which is comprised of Iowa National Guard soldiers from 1st Battalion, 133rd Infantry Regiment, part of the 2nd Brigade Combat Team, 34th Infantry Division.

The team at Xio Haq includes members from across the United States, including several from the Minneapolis area, one from Mississippi and three from California. They also have a wide array of ages and experiences. For example, while most of the team members work in construction-related fields in the civilian sector, one member, U.S. Air Force Senior Airman Christopher Lange, a structural engineer specialist from Crestline, Calif., is a businessman on the civilian side.

"This lets me learn something new, gives me a change of pace," Lange said. "Usually it would be once a month or a couple weeks a year, but this deployment mission is my big opportunity to go out here and work with these guys, who are the experts. This is my shot to learn my trade in the military, because trying to learn the construction field one weekend a month is really difficult."

The team's lone active-duty member, U.S. Air Force Airman 1st Class Tyler Saulsgiver, a structural engineer specialist from Panama, N.Y., is just 20-years-old.

On April 20, Saulgiver learned to sheet a roof from the team leader, U.S. Air Force Senior Master Sgt. David Sowers. Sowers, from Staples, Minn., has been in the Air Force doing construction work for 31 years, more than a decade longer than the young Airman has been alive.

"I like getting to work with Senior Master Sgt. Sowers," Saulsgiver said. "As you can imagine, I learn a lot from him."

Though the team will travel all over eastern Afghanistan supporting numerous units during their deployment, they said they have particularly enjoyed working with the "Red Bulls" out of Iowa.

"It's a good mix; it's a good fit, said Saulsgiver. "They're just down-home folks just like the rest of us. It's cool to try and make things just a little better here for them."

PRT inspects Laghman agricultural facility

LAGHMAN PROVINCE, Afghanistan, April 20 2011—Laghman Provincial Reconstruction Team engineers inspect a grain milling machine at the Laghman Empowerment Agricultural Facility. The LEAF will provide the people of the Qarghaee District a place to store dry foods and produce. (Photo by U.S. Air Force Senior Airman Ronifel S. Yasay, Laghman Provincial Reconstruction Team)

Speaker attends memorial service for Soldiers killed in Afghanistan

BAGRAM AIRFIELD, Afghanistan, April 21, 2011—Gen. David H. Petraeus (front), International Security Assistance Force commander, House Speaker John Boehner (center) and Command Sgt. Maj. Marvin Hill, ISAF Command Sergeant Major, pay respect to the fallen Soldiers of the 101st Sustainment Brigade. A memorial ceremony for six Soldiers killed in during a suicide bombing at Forward Operating Base Gamberi, Afghanistan, was conducted at Bagram Airfield. (Photo by U.S. Army Spc. Michael Vanpool, 101st Sustainment Brigade Public Affairs)

ROK Chairman visits deployed Korean troops

PARWAN PROVINCE, Afghanistan—Korean Army Gen. Min Koo Han, center, Chairman of Joint Chiefs of Staff of the Republic of Korea, visits a guard post in ROK Provincial Reconstruction Team compound. (Photo by Kim, Byung Ryun, Republic of Korea Ministry of Defense)

By Kim Byung Ryun
Republic of Korea Ministry of Defense

PARWAN PROVINCE, Afghanistan, April 24, 2011—Republic of Korea Army Gen. Min Koo Han, Chairman of ROK Joint Chiefs of Staff, visited deployed troops of the ROK Provincial Reconstruction Team in Parwan Province, Afghanistan. He surveyed the areas of operation and gave soldiers words of encouragement.

"Our deployment to Afghanistan has three meanings," said Han, "contribution to the global world, protection of our citizens, (and) enhancing of our joint operation capabilities.

"It is a must that as one of the major economic powers, we contribute to the global world," Han said.

"Korea ought to contribute to the world as it has become an aid-giving nation from an aid-receiving nation, and that is why we have ROK PRT in Afghanistan"

He said there were 46 nations present in Afghanistan as part of ISAF and the ROK PRT enhances joint operation capabilities. He said the team deserved applause for how well they are accomplishing their mission.

Prior to his visit to ROK PRT, Han met with U.S. Army Gen. David H. Petraeus, International Security Assistance Force commander, in Kabul, Afghanistan, and discussed the current situation in Afghanistan and their mutual interests.

"ROK Army is well-trained, well-prepared, professional and disciplined, and is a great pride to the Koreans," said Petraeus during the meeting. "We are very thankful for what ROK PRT Force and ROK civilians are doing."

Han also visited Bagram Airfield. Upon completion of his visit, Han flew to United Arab Emirates to visit to Korea's Akh Special Force Unit and later to the Gulf of Aden to see the Cheonghae Anti-piracy Unit.

Redhorse Soldiers mourn loss of fallen hero

PARWAN PROVINCE, Afghanistan, April 25, 2011—Commander of Troop A, 1st Squadron, 113th Cavalry Regiment, Task Force Redhorse, 2nd Brigade Combat Team, 34th Infantry Division, Task Force Red Bulls, U.S. Army Capt. Jason Knueven, of Inwood, Iowa, grasps the dog-tags of a fallen hero as U.S. Army Sgt. 1st Class Travis Bentz, A Troop's acting first sergeant of West Des Moines, Iowa, pays his respects during a memorial ceremony at Joint Combat Outpost Pul-e Sayad, Afghanistan, April 25. U.S. Army Staff Sgt. James A. Justice, a squad leader for 1st Platoon, Troop A, of Grimes, Iowa, was killed in action in Kapisa Province during a recovery mission of a downed aircraft April 23. (Photo by U.S. Army Staff Sgt. Ashlee Lolkus, Task Force Red Bulls Public Affairs)

By U.S. Army Staff Sgt. Ashlee Lolkus
Task Force Red Bulls Public Affairs

PARWAN PROVINCE, Afghanistan, April 25, 2011—Soldiers of 1st Squadron, 113th Cavalry Regiment, Task Force Redhorse, 2nd Brigade Combat Team, 34th Infantry Division, Task Force Red Bulls, mourned the loss of a friend and fellow Soldier during a memorial ceremony held at Joint Combat Outpost Pul-e Sayad, Afghanistan.

Soldiers awaiting for the ceremony to begin watched as two OH-58 Kiowa helicopters flew overhead, circling the small JCOP. Pilots of Task Force Phoenix, 10th Combat Aviation Brigade, held out American flags showing their respect to the men and women of Task Force Redhorse as thanks for support received only days prior.

U.S. Army Staff Sgt. James A. Justice, an infantryman from Grimes, Iowa, was killed in action while he and his platoon responded to a downed aircraft April 23 in Alah Say District, Kapisa Province, eastern Afghanistan.

U.S. Army Chief Warrant Officer Terry L. Varnadore II, of Arden, N.C., one of the pilots of the downed aircraft was killed, and the other pilot injured. Two other Task Force Redhorse Soldiers were injured during the recovery mission that day.

With quiet reverence, the Soldiers began the ceremony. The fallen hero's boots, rifle, helmet, and dog-tags, placed atop a small platform, faced an open area on the JCOP. Grieving Soldiers of Troop A, 1-113th Cav., fell into formation and guests lined the area to give a final farewell to a man who will be remembered for being a world-class Non-Commissioned Officer.

Justice, a squad leader of 1st Platoon, Troop A, 1-113th Cav., was originally slated to deploy with the 2-34th BCT in August 2010, but due to medical issues he was held back from deploying. It wasn't until the unit called back to the Iowa National Guard for replacements when Justice went on what would be his fourth deployment. He was in Afghanistan just under a month before his death.

Justice, who enlisted in the Iowa National Guard in 1998, made many friends. Soldiers close to him shared their memories. Many knew him from previous deployments, particularly those from the security force mission in Iraq in 2005.

A long-time friend, U.S. Army Staff Sgt. Doug Stanger of Urbandale, Iowa, and Company Intelligence Support Team NCO for Troop A, 1-113th Cav., served with Justice in Iraq. They were squad leaders together in the same platoon.

"You talk to anybody and they will give you the usual, 'Oh, he was a good guy,' but James really was a good guy," Stanger said. "I was excited ([to hear he was coming as a replacement). I went around and basically told everybody that I could find how lucky we were. I saw him on Bagram Airfield, and I said, 'We would be lucky to have you.' Low and behold he came to Alpha Troop and I just thought how incredibly lucky we were because he is a performer and extremely cool under pressure, especially with all the stuff he went through in Iraq.

"In any situation he was just always calm, never got excited. He didn't sweat the small details," he continued. "And a leader ... Everybody wanted to follow him. In Iraq he could get his guys to do anything he wanted them to do because they just loved him that much and respected him."

"He was probably the best NCO I've ever worked with," said U.S. Army Staff Sgt. Ben Doyle of Menlo, Iowa, and Troop A supply sergeant who deployed with Justice three times. "NCO means a lot of things, but he genuinely, genuinely had care and concern for Soldiers. He cared about Soldiers he was in charge of and their welfare, and that's him in a nutshell. He was a very compassionate guy with a great sense of humor."

"I remember when he first walked into my office, here," Doyle said. "I had heard that he was on Bagram Airfield. He came and found me and walked into my office and I just smiled, and I knew, his smirk, his trademark smirk ... I heard that we were trying to get him at Alpha Troop, and I knew he would have a positive impact on this organization. No question what-so-ever."

Not only did Justice have an impact on the lives of long-time friends, but in the short time he was with Troop A, impacted the lives of the Soldiers with whom he served.

"I learned that he was a determined Soldier the first time we shook hands," said U.S. Army 1st Lt. Peter Choi, Troops A's 1st Platoon leader from Ames, Iowa. "He was determined to make a difference in Afghanistan and to serve his country the best possible way a citizen of the United States can. He made a difference in the platoon in subtle but noticeable ways."

"First Platoon's actions that day changed the dynamics on the battlefield and prevented a situation that could have turned much worse," Choi said during the memorial. "If it wasn't for Staff Sgt. Justice's courage, we would not have been able to make the same impact that we did."

As the ceremony came to a close, every Soldier attending the memorial went up to Justice's display and paid respects, to include members from the French Operational Mentoring Liaison Team and Afghan National Army soldiers based at the JCOP.

Those who knew Justice well held Amanda, his wife, and Caydence, his daughter close in their thoughts.

"I'm thinking about Caydence growing up without the ability to know her father," said Stanger with tears forming in his eyes. "It's going to be tough. My wife and I are definitely thinking about Amanda."

"We are always there for them, no matter what," added Doyle.

Justice's awards include: Bronze Star Medal, Good Conduct Medal, Army Reserve Components Achievement Medal, National Defense Service Medal, Armed Forces Expeditionary Medal, Global War on Terrorism Expeditionary Medal, Global War on Terrorism Service Medal, Iraq Campaign Medal, Non-Commissioned Officer Professional Development Ribbon, Army Service Ribbon, Overseas Service Ribbon (2nd Award), Armed Forces Reserve Medal with M device (3rd Award), Multinational Force and Observers Medal, Combat Action Badge, Air Assault Badge.

PARWAN PROVINCE, Afghanistan, April 25, 2011—Pilots from Task Force Phoenix, 10th Combat Aviation Brigade, 10th Mountain Division, Task Force Falcon, fly their OH-58 Kiowa helicopter over Joint Combat Outpost Pul-e Sayad, Afghanistan, streaming the American flag in respect for the Soldiers of Troop A, 1st Squadron, 113th Cavalry Regiment. The gesture was their final salute to fallen hero U.S. Army Staff Sgt. James A. Justice of Grimes, Iowa, a squad leader for Troop A's 1st Platoon. Justice was killed in action in Kapisa Province during a recovery mission of a downed aircraft April 23. (Photo by U.S. Army Staff Sgt. Ashlee Lolkus, Task Force Red Bulls public affairs)

PARWAN PROVINCE, Afghanistan, April 25, 2011—Soldiers of 1st Squadron, 113th Cavalry Regiment, Task Force Redhorse, 2nd Brigade Combat Team, 34th Infantry Division, Task Force Red Bulls, hold a salute while the national anthem is played during a memorial service for U.S. Army Staff Sgt. James A. Justice of Grimes, Iowa, a squad leader for 1st Platoon, Troop A. [...] (Photo by U.S. Army Staff Sgt. Ashlee Lolkus, Task Force Red Bulls Public Affairs)

Laghman PRT engineers inspect projects, bridges

LAGHMAN PROVINCE, Afghanistan April 25. 2011—U.S. Air Force Capt. Cole Yanish, right, from Nolan, Texas, an engineer assigned to the Laghman Provincial Reconstruction Team, describes project expectations to a local contractor working on the Mia Khan Kats Bridge in Qarghaee District. (Photo by U.S. Air Force Senior Airman Ronifel S. Yasay, Laghman Provincial Reconstruction Team Public Affairs)

Assistant secretaries visit forward troops, talk budget cuts, manpower

BAGRAM AIRFIELD, Afghanistan, April 25, 2011—Assistant Secretary of the Air Force for Manpower and Reserve Affairs Daniel B. Ginsberg speaks to service members attending a dinner at the Dragon Dining Facility on Bagram Airfield, Afghanistan. (Photo by U.S. Army Spc. James Wilton, Task Force Red Bulls)

By U.S. Army Staff Sgt. Ashlee Lolkus
Task Force Red Bulls Public Affairs

BAGRAM AIRFIELD, Afghanistan, April 25, 2011—U.S. Air Force and Army assistant secretaries from the offices of Manpower and Reserve Affairs visited and dined with service members, April 25, at Bagram Air Field, Afghanistan.

Assistant Secretary of the Army for Manpower and Reserve Affairs Thomas R. Lamont, and Assistant Secretary of the Air Force for Manpower and Reserve Affairs Daniel B. Ginsberg visited service members throughout Afghanistan to tour facilities, gauge readiness and talk with service members on ground.

"We want to make sure we are sustaining the force," said Lamont, regarding the purpose of their trip. "We wanted to talk to our commanders and make sure they're getting the type of people (with the critical) skill sets that they need over here ... As manpower folks we have an obligation to see the Army and not sit back in a building and have someone send a report."

Lamont was recently tasked to present a plan to inactivate the Accessions Command, a U.S. Army command established in 2002 that oversees recruiting and initial training of soldiers. The tasking is part of a plan to eventually downsize the military, Lamont said.

While Secretary of Defense Robert Gates has determined the end strength of forces after downsizing, the plan to achieve those results still being worked out, Lamont said. The goal is to make the path gradual so not to put Soldiers at risk of prematurely being moved out of the force.

The Department of Defense is trying to determine how the downsizing would affect the Army Force Generation Model and their boots-on-ground to dwell-time ratio, he said.

"Our intent, and we're really getting there," Lamont explained, "is 1-to-2 (years) on the active side (and) 1-to-4 (years) on the reserve component side. In my recent conversation with the new (Army) chief of staff, Gen. Martin E. Dempsey, he says he still expects us to be able to do it."

Lamont said this will require a balancing act which may require additional drawdown in Iraq and Afghanistan, but the DOD will keep an eye on that balance. Additionally, Lamont hopes to see a 9-month boots-on-ground period for all Army forces in the future and said it is tentatively on the books for fiscal year 2015 pending any changes to their force reduction model.

"It's going to be very complex," he stated.

However, Lamont made it clear they have soldiers' welfare in mind.

"We don't ever want to get to a situation like we had in the 90s, where we told people, 'Thank you for your service but we no longer need you,'" he said.

Ginsberg said if the budgets continue to tighten, they would take care of service members as well as allow combatant commanders the ability to get their job done.

"That's what we do," he said.

"Everybody is an integral part of the fight no matter what (their) job is," Ginsberg explained. "Whether it's installation work, whether it's dropping ordnance on the enemy, everybody is absolutely key to succeeding here in Afghanistan."

Both assistant secretaries said their trip was productive and worth the long hours of travel.

"I'd say they are doing an absolutely phenomenal job meeting all the needs of the nation and just laying it out on the line every day," Ginsberg said about the Airmen he's met while in Afghanistan. "Like their counterparts in the Army, Navy, and the Marine Corps, they're really doing great work."

Kentucky ADT III facilitates Bagram women's shura

PARWAN PROVINCE, Afghanistan, April 27, 2011—Afghan women wash their hands prior to sharing a meal with the Women's Empowerment Team of the Kentucky Agribusiness Development Team III at the Bagram women's shura. (Photo by U.S. Army Pfc. Courtney Ropp, 55th Combat Camera)

Panjshir ANP officers prove their checkpoint operations skills

PANJSHIR PROVINCE, Afghanistan, April 27, 2011—Afghan National Police officers, with the Panjshir Reserve Police Force, practice searching a vehicle with a mirror during a traffic control operations refresher course conducted by the 2nd Brigade Combat Team, 34th Infantry Division, Task Force Red Bulls, Panjshir Embedded Training Team, Police Mentor Team section, at the Provincial Headquarters in Bazarak Municipality, Afghanistan. The PMT conducted the training to prepare the ANP officers for a validation later in the week. (Photo by U.S. Army Spc. James Wilton, Task Force Red Bulls Public Affairs)

By U.S. Army Spc. James Wilton
Task Force Red Bulls Public Affairs

PANJSHIR PROVINCE, Afghanistan, April 30, 2011—The 2nd Brigade Combat Team, 34th Infantry Division, Task Force Red Bulls, Panjshir Embedded Training Team, Police Mentor Team section, started validation exercises for the seven district police agencies in Panjshir Province, Afghanistan.

The exercises will test the Afghan agencies in proper traffic control procedures and checkpoint operations, which the PMT trained the agencies on over the last five weeks.

The first week of training was a "train-the-trainer" week. The team instructed select Afghan police officers on how to teach the classes and practical exercises. Instructors then assisted the newly developed Afghan trainers to teach the techniques and procedures to the rest of the Afghan police officers over a 4-week period.

"I think the style of training that we are doing is working well for them," said U.S. Army Spc. Antonio Rivera, the ETT medic and a PMT member from Des Moines, Iowa. "The combination of the train-the-trainer program, class room and hands-on training, really helps them to catch on to the material."

The validation exercises are the final test to see if the officers have retained the information. During the evaluation, the district police agency receives a call from the Operations Coordination Center–Provincial that smugglers are trying to transport weapons, drugs, or other prohibited items through their district and the police have to set-up a traffic checkpoint and search for the vehicle with only a basic description.

"The training we have done allows us to do the checkpoints better, and we need more of this type of training. It is very important training," said Afghan National Police 1st Lt. Muhammad Naseer, the Paryan Deputy Police commander and the checkpoint supervisor on the first validation exercise, conducted in the Paryan District April 30.

The PMT uses role players, both Afghan and U.S., who go through the checkpoint and evaluate the officers. The role players see if the police are asking the right questions, searching vehicles properly and working in a timely manner. They also look for proper traffic-flow management and use of intelligence sent down from the OCC–P.

"The ANP running the checkpoints asked all the right type of questions and stayed very professional, even adding a few of their own questions," said Naseer. "We learned a lot from the training, and now we are able to do these checkpoints effectively."

The traffic classes are the second installment of the training conducted by the PMT. The first class included Police Values and Ethics plus Use of Force and Human Rights.

"As long as they practice what we teach them, I think they will get proficient at it," said U.S. Army Spc. Brian Brown, ETT signal systems specialist and a PMT member from Central City, Iowa. "The training is helping them, and I really think that they are getting something out of it. But, they have to remember practice is the most important part. It is like us, when we were on our way here we also had to remember to practice, practice, practice, in order to be ready."

The next cycle of training, will focus on First Response, Crime Scene Management, and the importance of Police Presence and Patrolling and is slated to start after all of the district agencies complete their validations.

Program partners PRT, Afghans to complete district water storage tank

By U.S. Army Spc. James Wilton
Task Force Red Bulls Public Affairs

PANJSHIR PROVINCE, Afghanistan, April 30, 2011—The Bazarak Community Development Council with help from the Panjshir Provincial Reconstruction Team's Civil Affairs section finished refurbishing a drinking and irrigation water storage tank for the Bazarak District, Afghanistan.

The project is a part of the "small projects, big impact" program run by the PRT, where up to $5,000 is used to purchase materials for civil reconstruction projects. The Afghan people of the area who will benefit from the project, provide the labor and the remainder of the materials.

"The good thing about this project is with less amounts of money we can help and serve the greater needs of the people," said Abdul Rahman Kabiri, the deputy governor of Panjshir Province, through an interpreter. "The other important part of the project is it gives the people the idea in the future when they have such a project like this that they can do it by themselves and they are aware of the process."

The Afghans point out deficiencies and bring them up to their local CDC who then works with the provincial government to address the problem. The PRT helps this process by donating materials, but the projects are led by the Afghan CDC. Often the people pitch in materials or labor for free to make sure the project is completed.

"These projects show the ingenuity and determination of the Afghan people. When they want something to be done, they get it done," said U.S. Army 1st Lt. Hakan Togul, the PRT Civil Affairs Officer-in-Charge, from Crete, Ill.

The program, designed to build the capacity of the local governments shows the people their government is there to help them and how to use their government channels properly, said Togul.

The tank feeds 45 water faucets from a spring on the top of a nearby mountain supplying 300 families, more than 1,200 people, water for drinking and farming. Plus it will store the water during drier summer months giving them fresh, clean water year-round.

"A lot of the water was wasted before, and they were unable to use it after the spring dried up, but now they can store the water and use it in the future," said Kabiri.

"The water storage tank was completely destroyed, so we brought it back to working condition," said Gulmir, the Bazarak CDC director, through an interpreter. "I am happy to work for my people. Now they have healthy water for drinking. Before, they were using other water sources which were not healthy."

The people of the village often used the river water which can be full of bacteria making it unfit to drink.

The 'small projects, big impact' program is popular among the Afghan people and provides a much needed push in the right direction, according to the PRT.

"I look forward to doing more projects like this with the PRT," said Gulmir. "We need to continue our way and learn to solve the people's problems in the small villages. It is important to do these types of projects which the PRT has been involved in. The small projects help more people than the bigger ones."

The water storage refurbishment is one of eight projects set for the district; many more are planned for the province.

"We are very happy that we can do a little part, and the Afghan people do a big part," said U.S. Air Force Lt. Col. Joseph Blevins, the PRT commander from Oregonia, Ohio. "I hope the people of Panjshir continue to welcome the PRT so we can work together."

MAY
2011

Afghan, Red Bulls medics work together, save Soldier's life

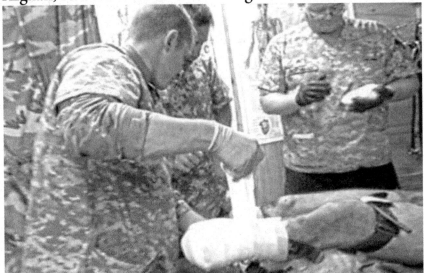

LAGHMAN PROVINCE, Afghanistan, April 18, 2011—U.S. Army Spc. Ahren Blake (left), from Clinton, Iowa; U.S. Army Sgt. Elijah Wright (center), from Janesville, Iowa; and U.S. Army Sgt. Ben Rothman (right), from Independence, Iowa; all combat medics with Headquarters and Headquarters Company, 1st Battalion, 133rd Infantry Regiment, Task Force Ironman, 2nd Brigade Combat Team, 34th Infantry Division, Task Force Red Bulls, treat an Afghan National Army soldier from 1st Kandak, 1st Brigade, 201st ANA Infantry Corps, April 18 at the U.S. aid station on Combat Outpost Xio Haq. The treatment the Afghan and U.S. Army medics gave the soldier saved his life. (Photo by U.S. Army Spc. Bradley Nelson, Task Force Ironman)

By U.S. Army Staff Sgt. Ryan C. Matson
Task Force Red Bulls Public Affairs

LAGHMAN PROVINCE, Afghanistan, May 1, 2011—Afghan National Army medic Sgt. Mohammed Jash summed it up quite simply.

"It's my job," Jash said when asked what he thought, knowing the first aid steps he administered saved the life of a fellow ANA Soldier, both from Weapons Company, 1st Kandak, 1st Brigade, 201st ANA Infantry Corps.

The soldier stepped on an anti-personnel landmine April 18 in the Tengay Mountain Valley, losing his left leg from the shin down. Had it not been for the treatment administered by Jash, the Soldier would have definitely died, said U.S. Army Sgt. Ben Rothman, a medic with Headquarters and Headquarters Company, 1st Battalion, 133rd Inf. Regiment, Task Force Ironman, 2nd Brigade Combat Team, 34th Infantry Division, Task Force Red Bulls, and the Non-Commissioned Officer-in-Charge of the aid station at Combat Outpost Xio Haq.

487

Jash, an ANA medic for two years, said his first action was to stop the bleeding, because medics are trained that stopping the bleeding is the single most urgent part of emergency first-response medical procedures. Jash packed the wound thoroughly with a bandage and applied a tourniquet above the soldier's left knee.

After the Soldier stepped on the land mine, it took his fellow Soldiers more than an hour to evacuate him by carrying him down the mountain. Had Jash's work not been as thorough as it was, the soldier could have bled out during this time.

Jash said he completed three months of medical training from U.S. medics in Kabul. Additionally, Jash said he learns daily from the ANA surgeon and doctor at the ANA aid station on COP Xio Haq, where he works.

After Jash performed the initial lifesaving measures on the casualty, the Soldier was transported to the COP Xio Haq aid station, where Rothman's crew took over treatment. They met the ANA ambulance at the gate and transported the patient to their aid station to await medical evacuation via helicopter.

"Actually he (Jash) did all the work," Rothman, from Independence, Iowa, said. "All we had to do was put an additional tourniquet on the soldier's leg, put a little additional dressing on the wound because there was a little seepage, give him a little medication, and call in the medevac. The work was really already done when he got to us. He was in pretty good shape."

All of the COP Xio Haq medics, all part of HHC, 1-133rd Inf., had a hand in treating the patient, Rothman said. U.S. Army Sgt. Elijah Wright, from Janesville, Iowa, added a second tourniquet on the upper leg and treated the blast damage to the right leg. U.S. Army Spc. Ahren Blake, a combat medic from Clinton, Iowa, added additional packing to the wound and rewrapped it. U.S. Army Spc. Christopher Mollicone, a combat medic from Cedar Falls, Iowa, adjusted the tourniquets on the left leg, assisted Blake with the dressing and took the ANA soldier's vital readings. U.S. Army Pfc. Shane Campfield, a combat medic from Iowa Falls, Iowa, recorded the vital signs, treated the patient's upper left arm and handed the other medics supplies as they needed them, while Rothman administered morphine to the patient and provided the information for the medevac.

The soldier may no longer have his lower left leg. But thanks to the teamwork between Afghan and U.S. medics, he still has his life.

Paktya women gather to voice concerns

PAKTYA PROVINCE, Afghanistan, May 1, 2011–Members of the Paktya Female Engagement Team, including U.S. Air Force Capt. Donna Laulo of the Provincial Reconstruction Team, from Puyallup, Wash. (right), U.S. Army Chief Warrant Officer Jill Graham, from Tahlequah, Okla., and U.S. Army Spc. Crystal Sims, from Duncan, Okla., both of the 2-45th Oklahoma Agribusiness Development Team, and Dunni Goodman of U.S. Assistance for International Development, listen as the Paktya Director of Women's Affairs addresses local women during a shura at the Gardez Women's Development Center, May 1. More than 50 Afghan women attended the shura to address challenges women and children are facing throughout the province. (Photo by U.S. Army Spc. Tobey White, Task Force Duke Public Affairs)

By U.S. Air Force 1st Lt. Sybil Taunton
Paktya Provincial Reconstruction Team Public Affairs

PAKTYA PROVINCE, Afghanistan, May 1, 2011—Women from various districts throughout the conservative Pashtun province of Paktya gathered to voice their concerns at a women's shura hosted by the director of Paktya's Department of Women's Affairs, Halima Khazan, at the Gardez Women's Development Center.

More than 50 women attended the shura and discussed topics including education, healthcare, midwife training and selling products in the local bazaars.

Members of the Paktya Female Engagement Team, which consists of personnel from the Paktya Provincial Reconstruction Team and the 2-45th Oklahoma Agribusiness Development Team from Task Force Duke, officials from U.S. Agency for International Development, as well as representatives from Combined Joint Task Force–101, attended the shura.

"It is the strength of Afghan women that drew me here," said U.S. Army Lt. Col. Kristine Petermann, the Regional Command–East FET program manager, from Harrison Township, Mich. "Someday the rest of the world will know their strength."

According to Khazan, there are local shuras in most districts throughout the province, but representatives rarely come together due to cultural and travel restrictions. In the majority of the Paktya districts, women are required to wear burqas and must have a male family member escort them when leaving their homes.

Paktya Deputy Gov. Abdul Rahman Mangal opened the event.

"The reason we are holding this shura is to discuss all of the issues and problems women in Paktya are facing," said Mangal. "The government is here to help women and their children."

Following his remarks, the deputy governor departed, leaving the women to voice their concerns openly with coalition forces and the director of women's affairs.

A major concern expressed by women from several districts was the need for more schools and teachers so more children can get an education. Khazan said education for women is also very important because a large portion of the female population in Paktya is illiterate.

A woman from the Ahmad Abad District talked about the success of their midwife training program, but also expressed the need for upgrades for the training center. She discussed the lack of understanding between the government- and district-level leadership, and the people in the villages.

"Leaders from the districts need to visit every village and find out what women need," said the woman.

A woman from Gardez area addressed an issue that appeared to hit home with the other women present. Women have gardens, animals, sewing and tailoring skills, and other means of producing items that could help provide a larger income for their families, but they are prohibited from opening shops in local bazaars.

"Women face a lot of challenges, but we are only requesting projects we can actually benefit from," she said.

When all was said and done, the group of women appeared satisfied with the issues addressed. A local Gardez woman who partnered with USAID to initiate projects for women in Paktya Province, said women need to continue taking their concerns to their local women's shura leaders, who will then address those concerns with the director of women's affairs.

"We need to solve each others' issues together as one," she said.

PRT opens all-girl school in Dara District

By U.S. Army Spc. James Wilton
Task Force Red Bulls Public Affairs

PANJSHIR PROVINCE, Afghanistan, May 1, 2011—Members of the Panjshir Provincial Reconstruction Team attended the grand opening ceremony of the Baba Ali Girls School in Dara District, Afghanistan, May 1.

The school can host more than 150 Afghan female students and is a part of a three-school, complex which includes a boy's school.

The Dara Community Development Council, a group of Afghans who address the needs of their community, proposed the school to their local government, but there was no money to fund the project. Hearing this, the PRT decided to take on the endeavour.

"I am very excited and happy that the Panjshir PRT opened the Baba Ali Girls School in this remote district of the Panjshir valley," said Abdul Matin Mubashe, a math and sciences teacher for the Baba Ali School, through an interpreter. "The young girls of the Dara District now have a place to study and learn."

The PRT contracted a local village contractor, Raz Tanha Construction, Road Building and Production Company, to build the 8-classroom school.

"We have an Afghan-first or Panjshir-first policy, if we can find someone capable of doing a project within that community, then we use them to do the work," said U.S. Air Force Lt. Col. Joseph Blevins, the Panjshir PRT commander, and Oregonia, Ohio, native. "The communities really tie in with the PRTs. Our ability to get out and get around and talk to people, and the effectiveness of the government officials really allow us to get a lot more done in Panjshir."

Keeping the money from projects like this in the community helps to rebuild and reinforce the infrastructure. Education is also an important part of that rebuilding and reconstruction effort; it helps increase the knowledge and abilities of the future leaders and builders of Afghanistan, according to the province's education director.

"Education is important to the children of Afghanistan, because they are the future builders of Afghanistan," said Abdul Makim, the Panjshir Province education director, through an interpreter. "That is why I am trying to support the children of Panjshir Province to study and for education. Then they can help to improve the country and our future."

He added, the effort is most needed when it comes to educating the females of Afghanistan, as they are often overlooked.

"Education isn't just important for Afghan society. It is important everywhere around the world, especially here in this very fundamentally religious society," said Makim. "Female education is one thing that was heavily impacted especially during the war years. Therefore, rebuilding female capacity here in Afghanistan is one of our big pushes."

Makim said the PRT's and Afghan government's efforts are making great strides in the fight to rebuild this devastated country, and they go beyond just the construction of schools.

"We are also helping our teachers to learn and grow and become better teachers, through continued education and classes to help them educate our students in modern subjects," said Makim. "These programs and others, both here and outside the country, will make them more knowledgeable and better teachers for the children of Afghanistan."

Improving education of teachers as well as students, both male and female, puts Afghanistan on the right track toward a positive future, said Abdul Rahman Kabiri, the Panjshir deputy governor.

"Schools like this are the first step in the right direction for the people of Afghanistan, and the solution to a problem which is in the education system of Afghanistan," said Kabiri.

"Projects like this school are very important because the children are the foundation of a society, and in America we say the children are our future," said Blevins. "So as long as Americans are welcome in Afghanistan and Panjshir as friends and guests, we will work with you shoulder-by-shoulder, hand-in-hand to do projects like this."

In an uncertain future, hope is what drives a people, and the people of Panjshir have one hope and one request for their children.

"I make this request and hope for the children of Afghanistan, that they will study more and harder so they can improve their country because they are the future builders of Afghanistan and offer a new generation for the community," said Makim.

*PANJSHIR PROVINCE, Afghanistan, May 1, 2011—*Girls from the Baba Ali Girls School sing a song of thanks to the members of the Panjshir provincial government and Panjshir Provincial Reconstruction Team at the school house in Dara District, Afghanistan during a grand opening ceremony. The PRT, a part of the 2nd Brigade Combat Team, 34th Infantry Division, Task Force Red Bulls, contracted the local Raz Tanha Construction Company to build the school in a remote district of Panjshir. (Photo by U.S. Army Spc. James Wilton, Task Force Red Bulls Public Affairs)

Communications Soldiers keep Red Bulls talking

LAGHMAN PROVINCE, Afghanistan, May 1, 2011—U.S. Army Sgt. Samantha Kauffman (right), from West Union, Iowa; and U.S. Army Spc. Josh Klinzman (left), from Iowa City, Iowa, both signal support systems specialists with Headquarters and Headquarters Company, 1st Battalion, 133rd Infantry Regiment, Task Force Ironman, test some vehicle intercom system headsets May 1 in the communications shop at Forward Operating Base Mehtar Lam, Afghanistan. Task Force Ironman is a part of the Iowa National Guard's 2nd Brigade Combat Team, 34th Infantry Division, Task Force Red Bulls. (Photo by U.S. Army Staff Sgt. Ryan C. Matson, Task Force Red Bulls Public Affairs)

By U.S. Army Staff Sgt. Ryan C. Matson
Task Force Red Bulls Public Affairs

and Sgt. Aaron Amos
Headquarters Company, 1st Battalion, 133rd Infantry Regiment

LAGHMAN PROVINCE, Afghanistan, May 1, 2011—Communications Soldiers at Forward Operating Base Mehtar Lam don't have to go looking for work.

"If it has electricity running through it, people will bring it in to commo to fix," said U.S. Army Sgt. Kyle Statema, the Non-Commissioned Officer-in-Charge of the communications section for Headquarters and Headquarters Company, 1st Battalion, 133rd Infantry Regiment, Task Force Ironman, a part of the Iowa National Guard's 2nd Brigade Combat Team, 34th Infantry Division, Task Force Red Bulls, at FOB Mehtar Lam.

Statema, a native of Pella, Iowa, said the communications section or "commo guys," as they are known by their fellow Soldiers, are "jacks of all trades." Though their job is to maintain Army communications equipment, Statema said the commo section often ends up working on anything and everything with a plug and a cord.

"We don't ever tell them no," Statema said. "If we can fix it, we will."

"I like this job because I get to use my brain," said U.S. Army Spc. Josh Klinzman, a signal support systems specialist from Iowa City, Iowa, with HHC.

His boss, Statema, was quick to agree.

"This job will get you thinking," he said.

Statema, a 10-year veteran of the National Guard with three deployments, said the old Army saying is true: You can't shoot or move without communications.

Statema and his Soldiers maintain all Army radio, intercom, navigation and other computer equipment. Statema said there are nine different types of radio systems his Soldiers are responsible for maintaining or repairing.

U.S. Army Sgt. Samantha Kauffman, a signal support systems specialist also with HHC said a large part of the section's day is troubleshooting equipment. "We have vehicles that come in and we'll work on their communications equipment," Kauffman said. "But in between this, we'll have parts in the truck that we'll troubleshoot also. For example, we'll have parts of the blue force tracker that we think may be bad and we'll put them on our test bench and check it out and see for sure whether or not it is that piece of equipment that is bad rather than something else in the system."

"The cool thing with communications is that you're always going to find stuff that you may not know the answer to immediately, but you'll find the answer out. It keeps changing—you're going to keep finding new problems so you have to keep working at it."

The Soldiers said they use tools such as multimeters, radio frequency testing devices and signal testers to troubleshoot equipment. They are trained in the basics of troubleshooting at the United States Army Signal School at Fort Gordon, Ga.

"They taught us how to narrow things down to where a problem exists," Statema said, "but most of our knowledge comes from experience."

The Soldiers said one of the challenges of the job is when they troubleshoot a piece of equipment and still can't find the answer to the problem. "That's the absolute worst," Kauffman said. "It's a terrible feeling to feel defeated by something man-made."

"You feel like you've checked every possible component," Statema said. "And that's when it's nice to have several experienced Soldiers who can take a look at it with a fresh set of eyes, and often figure it out."

Statema said it is rare for a piece of equipment to be broken and no one in the shop can fix it. More often than not, he said, the problems can be fixed easily, such as by just changing a setting on a radio.

Besides troubleshooting and occasionally repairing radio or other equipment, Kauffman said the commo section also makes sure the radios are updated so that Soldiers have secure communications, they ensure radios are always stocked with fresh batteries, and they also train Soldiers on how to do simple troubleshooting themselves, to fix common problems in the field when they occur.

The Soldiers said they also do a little bit of field modification, too. For example, they had a radio antenna which they modified. The inside of the antenna was pulled out of its case, because the cases often snap off and are lost in the field. Instead, the commo section lengthened and modified the antenna so that Soldiers can run it through their body armor or elsewhere.

"It's just stuff we make to help the guys out," Kauffman said. "They said it's more tactical."

Another team maintains and repairs Army computers and the secure Army Internet systems. Problem solving and troubleshooting are a big part of the automation section, as well.

"We'll deal with problems as small as resetting passwords, to somebody bringing in a smoking computer," said U.S. Army Pfc. Michael Shackleton, an information technology specialist from Waterloo, Iowa, also with HHC.

In the section's office, U.S. Army Sgt. Gregg Gott, the automations section Non-Commissioned Officer-in-Charge from Cedar Rapids, Iowa, with HHC, has a stack of different kinds of Rubik's cubes on the edge of his desk. The cubes, which Gott can solve completely in less than three minutes each, are games for someone with the type of problem-solving mindset a person must have to be a good automations Soldier he said.

Shackleton said their job is divided into two main duties.

Shackleton explained. "First there is the automations piece, which deals with computers and software, and then you have network operations which deals more with routers and switches and getting the actual services working."

Above everything else though, just as Soldiers need to be able to talk through radios, the automations section ensures that Soldiers can talk through Army e-mail systems, Shackleton said.

"Our primary focus is making sure that things like the (secure networks) are working because that's how we get the tactical data (from the field)," Shackleton said. "If somebody's in contact we use … secure channels to get the troops support."

Task Force Lethal soldiers earn Purple Heart

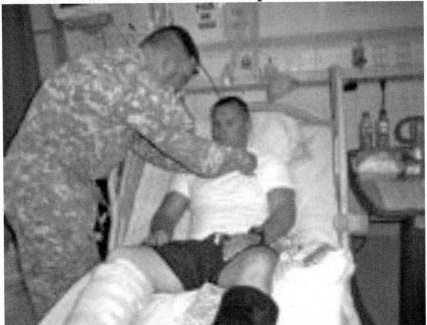

BAGRAM AIRFIELD, Afghanistan, April 30, 2011—U.S. Army Brig. Gen. Warren E Phipps, Regional Command–East and Combined Joint Task Force–101 assistants division commander-support, pins a Purple Heart onto the shirt of U.S. Army Sgt. Matthew Macke, of Cedar Rapids, Iowa, at the Heathe N. Craig Joint Theater Hospital, Bagram Airfield, Afghanistan. Macke, a member of Company C, 1st Battalion, 168th Infantry Regiment, Task Force Lethal was driving the lead vehicle of a mounted combat patrol when an Improvised Explosive Device detonated under his truck April 27. (Photo by U.S. Army Sgt. Brian Maxon, Task Force Lethal)

By U.S. Army 1st Lt. Nicholas Rasmussen
Task Force Lethal

BAGRAM AIRFIELD, Afghanistan, May 2, 2011—U.S. Army Sgt. Matthew Macke of Cedar Rapids, Iowa, a member of Company C, 1st Battalion, 168th Infantry Regiment, 2nd Brigade, 34th Infantry Division, Task Force Lethal, and U.S. Army Spc. Dane Nelsen of Company D, Task Force Lethal, were awarded Purple Hearts April 30 and May 2, respectively, at the Heathe N. Craig Joint Theater Hospital on Bagram Airfield, Afghanistan.

Macke was injured while in the lead vehicle during a mounted combat patrol in Zormat District, Paktya Province, Afghanistan, April 27. An Improvised Explosive Device detonated under his truck, fracturing his right foot and left lower leg. The other U.S. soldiers in the vehicle with Macke were not injured, although the blast severely damaged the vehicle.

"This was the first time in months we haven't found an IED prior to detonation," said U.S. Army Capt. Michael Minard, of Bettendorf, Iowa, Macke's company commander, adding that a locally implemented Guardians of Peace program providing information to coalition and Afghan national security forces has done much to alleviate such explosions.

U.S. Army Brig. Gen. Warren E. Phipps, Regional Command–East and Combined Joint Task Force–101 assistant division commander-support, presented Macke with his Purple Heart award.

Receiving the award was an honor, said Macke. "I look forward to reuniting with my brothers from 2nd Platoon, C Company," he said.

The day after Macke received his award, Nelsen and his platoon were clearing a route near Kowti Kheyl village, Zormat District, when they received small arms and indirect fire. Nelsen was shot in the leg during the fire-fight and was evacuated to Bagram Airfield.

No other coalition forces or ANSF soldiers were injured during the fight.

"We know that there are bad guys in that area," said U.S. Army 1st Sgt. Joedy Dennis, of Alden, Iowa, Company D's first sergeant. "This is the first time we've taken contact up in there."

U.S. Army Maj. Gen. John F. Campbell, Regional Command–East and 101st Airborne Division commander, awarded Nelsen's Purple Heart.

"Now it's just time to recover and get back with my guys who are still risking their lives every day," said Nelsen.

Since Nelsen's injury, Company D completed follow-on operations near Kowti Kheyl, said Dennis.

"It has proved to be beneficial for us, and we took a lot of [insurgent] assets off the battlefield."

Senior NATO Rep visits Panjshir, talks transition

PANJSHIR PROVINCE, Afghanistan, May 3, 2011—Ambassador Simon Gass, the NATO senior civilian representative, walks through the streets of Bazarak District, Afghanistan during a visit to Panjshir Province. The ambassador met with members of the Panjshir Provincial Reconstruction Team and Panjshir's government officials to discuss the pending transition. (Photo by U.S. Army Spc. James Wilton, Task Force Red Bulls Public Affairs)

By U.S. Army Spc. James Wilton
Task Force Red Bulls Public Affairs

PANJSHIR PROVINCE, Afghanistan, May 3, 2011—Ambassador Simon Gass, the NATO senior civilian representative, visited Panjshir Province and met with the Panjshir government, security forces and the Panjshir Provincial Reconstruction Team. Gass discussed the upcoming transition of the province and Panjshir's future.

"I came to Panjshir to see firsthand a province which is going to be one of the very first to transition," said Gass. "I have a very positive impression of the province. When you compare it with Kabul, for example, there is a much greater sense of security here. What you see here is normal life as opposed to the very heavily influenced security atmosphere you see in other places."

"Transition is still going to be a challenge and we need to work on the development and the governance side in order to make sure the Afghan people who live here see a real benefit," Gass continued. "The transition is not going to be easy because it means the PRT will be reducing in size and scope so we are going to have to work in other ways to maintain the peoples' support."

He explained the importance of making sure the people of Panjshir see a benefit from transition and the role the PRT has and will play in that mission.

Members of the Panjshir Provincial Council and representatives from the Afghan Parliament agreed.

"Panjshir will stand as a symbol to all other provinces when it comes to the transition," said Mawlawi Mohamad Faizi, a Panjshir provincial council member. "The international community must understand this and make sure we are helped both economically and politically for this reason. The people of Afghanistan will look to us for guidance on how the transition will go for them."

"No one knows what will happen with the transition, but one thing is for certain, you can't just leave," continued Faizi. "If Afghanistan is left alone as it was in the past, then there will be great disasters and catastrophes. We must continue to work together and build on the progress and successes we have had over the past few years."

Everyone agreed that a continued, joint effort is necessary for the transition to be a success.

"I think Panjshir has great chances. It is a peaceful place, and you see good agricultural production," said Gass. "But like many parts of Afghanistan, there aren't yet jobs for people, so we have to work on the economic and governance side as much as we can to make Panjshir stable as it goes through transition. I think it will be a big challenge, but overall I am optimistic it can be a success. The work the PRT has been doing here over a number of years has certainly contributed to making that possible."

Panjshir PRT engineers survey road to Badakhshan

By U.S. Air Force 2nd Lt. Ashleigh Peck
Panjshir Provincial Reconstruction Team Public Affairs

PANJSHIR PROVINCE, Afghanistan, May 3, 2011—Panjshir Provincial Reconstruction Team engineers surveyed the final portion of the Panjshir Road in Paryan District, Afghanistan.

The PRT engineers conducted the survey to assess the possibility of finishing the Panjshir Road to connect Panjshir and Badakhshan Provinces.

"Completing the road to Badakhshan will contribute to the creation of a corridor of trade in a part of Afghanistan where there is currently no proper access to outside the country," said PRT Director Bill Martin.

Construction of the road began in 2005, when the PRT arrived in Panjshir. The road begins in the southernmost part of the province in Shutol District on the border with Parwan Province and is approximately 130 kilometers (80.6 miles) long. If the final section of road is paved to connect to Badakhshan Province, the road through Panjshir Province will be approximately 145 kilometers (89.9 miles) long.

"If this road is completed, the travel time through all of Panjshir to Badakhshan will be cut down from 24 to four hours," said Abed Wardak, local national engineer with the PRT.

As the PRT engineers traveled to survey the potential road, they assessed the progress and construction of the current road.

"Up to this point, it's been quite a challenge because we're the first to come up here and do any type of paved roadway construction," said U.S. Air Force 2nd Lt. Phil Compton, PRT deputy engineer. "It's great to see this much progress because the previous roadway was so bad that we've had contractors lose equipment during construction just trying to move stuff up here."

When surveying the potential road, the engineers assessed the expected cost of extending the road based on geographical features.

"Our survey included identifying the soil content, slopes and drainage so we can anticipate what the costs are going to be to hire a contractor to construct the roadway," said Compton, from Doty, Wash.

If the road is determined to be necessary and funded, a local contractor will be hired to construct the road. "This project will be good for Panjshir because there are many jobless people here, and this project will create jobs for people," said Wardak.

All Panjshir PRT-funded construction projects require 70 percent of all unskilled labor to be hired within a 20-kilometer (12.4 miles) radius of the project.

"The road gives the unskilled laborers in the local area a chance to work under professionals and build new skills they can apply at home and in their villages," said Compton.

As the road is being constructed, locals will have more job opportunities and once the road is completed, it will enable travel and future trade, he said.

"Some of these people depend on trade for their livelihood," said Compton. "The completion of this road will give locals the opportunity to travel to neighboring provinces to trade in some of the bigger cities and bazaars north of Panjshir."

PANJSHIR PROVINCE, Afghanistan, May 3, 2011—Marty Stanislaus, U.S. Army Corps of Engineers construction representative with Panjshir Provincial Reconstruction team, and Omaha, Neb., native, collects soil from the Panjshir Road in Paryan District, Afghanistan, May 3. The PRT took the samples to Forward Operating Base Lion to be tested. (Photo by U.S. Air Force 2nd Lt. Ashleigh Peck, Panjshir Provincial Reconstruction Team Public Affairs)

U.S. forces train Afghan police in firing fundamentals

PARWAN PROVINCE, Afghanistan, May 4, 2011—U.S. Army Spc. Richard Hansen of South Sioux City, Neb., a military policeman with Headquarters Headquarters Troop, 1st Squadron, 113th Cavalry Regiment, 2nd Brigade Combat Team, 34th Infantry Division, Task Force Red Bulls, shows an Afghan National Policeman a technique to hold the AK-47 in the prone position, during a class at the ANP station in Koh-e Safi, Afghanistan, May 4. (U.S. Army Photo by Spc. Kristina L. Gupton, Task Force Red Bulls Public Affairs)

Task Force Redhorse brings training, confidence to ANP

PARWAN PROVINCE, Afghanistan, May 4, 2011—U.S. Army Spc. Micah Roberts of Washington, Iowa, and cavalry scout with Troop B, 1st Squadron, 113th Cavalry Regiment, Task Force Redhorse, helps an Afghan National Police officer show off his target after rifle range practice outside of Vehicle Patrol Base Dandar in Koh-e Safi District May 4. Soldiers of Task Force Redhorse conducted a five-day accelerated training course to train Koh-e Safi ANP on basic police skills including rifle marksmanship. Task Force Redhorse is a part of the 34th Infantry Division's 2nd Brigade Combat Team and the Iowa National Guard. (Photo by U.S. Army Staff Sgt. Ashlee Lolkus, Task Force Red Bulls Public Affairs)

By U.S. Army Staff Sgt. Ashlee Lolkus
Task Force Red Bulls Public Affairs

PARWAN PROVINCE, Afghanistan, May 5, 2011—Task Force Redhorse military police mentors conducted a 5-day accelerated training course with the Afghan National Police at Vehicle Patrol Base Dandar, located in Koh-e Safi district.

Although it was not the first training session at the ANP station, it was the first conducted since the 86th Infantry Brigade Combat Team, Task Force Wolverine, conducted sessions in 2010, said ANP Lt. Col. Gul Padsha, the ANP station commander.

"We are very thankful for the training," he said through an interpreter. "Every time the Americans come to train, we learn something new."

U.S. Army Sgt. Adam Berger, a Kansas City, Mo., native, who is a Military Policeman attached to Headquarters and Headquarters Troop, 1st Squadron, 113th Cavalry Regiment., and also serves as the Non-

Commissioned Officer-in-Charge of training, said they covered detainee handling, personnel search, handcuffing, control point operations, Improvised Explosive Device awareness, police survival skills, ambush awareness, weapon fundamentals and first aid.

Soldiers from Troop B, 1-113th Cav., a part of the 34th Infantry Division's 2nd Brigade Combat Team, Task Force Red Bulls, assisted the PMT with the training.

"The purpose of the training was to give them the basics," said Berger. "Bravo Troop conducts operations with this group of ANP and plans to work with them more in the future. We are here to familiarize them with the basics, so we can not only advance their skill level and build their confidence, but also make it easier for them to work with the American Soldiers."

One ANP officer, Safi Ulla, who has been an ANP officer for seven years now, said that he especially liked the rifle training.

"We don't normally get target practice," Safi Ulla said through an interpreter. "I really enjoyed being able to fire at targets. The only other time we shoot live ammunition is in combat."

Padsha, said he would like additional training at the ANP station including sessions for the higher ranking ANP officers.

"There are many things that the leadership needs to know, more than regular policemen," he said. "Whatever training the Americans are able to provide will teach us new things."

After the training, Troop B held a graduation ceremony at the ANP station. Task Force Redhorse commander, U.S. Army Lt. Col. David A. Updegraff of Wauconda, Ill., attended the ceremony and praised the ANP's efforts in Koh-e Safi and their partnership with Task Force Redhorse.

The Koh-e Safi District sub-governor, Dr. Abdul Wheed, also attended and said that he appreciated all of their work in Koh-e Safi.

"If the security of Koh-e Safi is strengthened through training events like this," he said through an interpreter, "then the security of Bagram and Kabul will also strengthen."

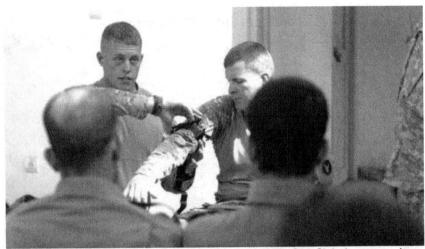

*PARWAN PROVINCE, Afghanistan, May 4, 2011—*U.S. Army Spc. Chris Jesperson of West Des Moines, Iowa, and medic with Troop B, 1st Squadron, 113th Cavalry Regiment, Task Force Redhorse, shows Afghan National Police officers how to apply a tourniquet while using U.S. Army Sgt. Adam Berger's arm as an example at the ANP station outside of Vehicle Patrol Base Dandar in Koh-e Safi District. [...] (Photo by U.S. Army Staff Sgt. Ashlee Lolkus, Task Force Red Bulls Public Affairs)

*PARWAN PROVINCE, Afghanistan, May 4, 2011—*Afghan National Police officer, Safi Ulla, salutes his peers during a graduation ceremony held at the Dandar ANP Station outside of Vehicle Patrol Base Dandar. Also pictured in the background are (from left to right): U.S. Army Lt. Col. David A. Updegraff of Wauconda, Ill., and 1st Squadron, 113th Cavalry Regiment, Task Force Redhorse commander; Parwan sub-governor Dr. Abdul Wheed; ANP station commander Gul Padsha; and U.S. Army 1st Lt. Rodney Brock of Ocean Springs, Miss., and executive officer for Troop B, 1-113th Cav., Task Force Redhorse. [...] (Photo by U.S. Army Staff Sgt. Ashlee Lolkus, Task Force Red Bulls Public Affairs)

Kansas ADT III sponsors agriculture course

LAGHMAN PROVINCE, Afghanistan, May 5, 2011—Dr. Eric Grant Ph.D. (right), U.S. Department of Agriculture senior agricultural expert; U.S. Army 1st Lt. Brian Knipp (center right); agronomist from Hutchinson, Kan.; and U.S. Army Lt. Col. Eric Blankenship (center), the deputy commander of agriculture of Topeka, Kan., all with the Kansas Agribusiness Development Team III, assist in giving certificates of completion to the students of an 11-week course in Applied Agriculture and Animal Science at Mehtar Lam, Afghanistan.. (Photo by U.S. Army Sgt. Kenneth A. Kumle, Kansas Agribusiness Development Team III)

By U.S. Army Sgt. Kenneth A. Kumle
Kansas Agribusiness Development Team III

LAGHMAN PROVINCE, Afghanistan, May 5, 2011—Members of the Kansas Agribusiness Development Team III, participated in the completion ceremony for a course in Applied Agriculture and Animal Science in Mehtar Lam, Afghanistan.

The ceremony was the culminating event for an 11-week course focusing on numerous practical agricultural technologies and techniques that bring the academics from the classroom to the field.

"We have already studied the academic theory of agriculture through Nangarhar University," said Noorzamir, a student. "This course was a good, practical application of those things."

"More than 80 percent of all Afghans base their livelihood on agriculture," said another student, Moneerah Mad. "I'm learning these techniques here so I can go and teach them to other villages."

This course, taught by agricultural professionals sponsored by the Kansas ADT III with the cooperation of the director of the Department of Agriculture, Irrigation and Livestock of Laghman Province and the Nangarhar

University, is vital to the future agricultural growth of the province, according to the ADT.

"I have great hope for the future of Afghanistan because of students like these," said U.S. Army Col. Howard E. Wheeler, commander of the Kansas ADT, from Manhattan, Kan.

Many of these students, scheduled to graduate from Nangarhar University in the next month with a bachelor's degree in agriculture, are looking to the future with plans on pursuing their master's degrees and moving into governance to better serve the people of Afghanistan.

"This course is a gateway for the young agricultural students to get into the agricultural community through the Director of Agriculture, Irrigation, and Livestock," said Dr. Eric Grant, the U.S. Department of Agriculture's senior agricultural expert with the Kansas ADT. "These students are the future agricultural leaders of Afghanistan."

"I want to get a Master of Science degree in agriculture, and through it I can serve my country," said student Mitayyeb. "I'm trying to get even more information, maybe even be a doctor in agriculture so I can better serve my country and my people."

Applied Agriculture and Animal Science courses like this, conducted throughout the country with guidance from organizations like the Kansas ADT will continue to graduate students. With the majority of Afghanistans' livelihood based in agriculture, the graduating students can immediately apply their knowledge once their coursework is complete.

"These students have an enormous amount of opportunity for those that have the knowledge and daring to [seize] it," said Wheeler.

Task Force Red Bulls conduct foot patrol through Bagram

PARWAN PROVINCE, Afghanistan, May 6, 2011—Soldiers with the Personal Security Detail of Headquarters and Headquarters Company, 2nd Brigade Combat Team, 34th Infantry Division, Task Force Red Bulls, head out to conduct a foot patrol around Bagram Airfield. The PSD ensured security within the Bagram Security Zone. (Photo by U.S. Army Spc. Kristina L. Gupton, Task Force Red Bulls Public Affairs)

PARWAN PROVINCE, Afghanistan, May 6, 2011—U.S. Army Spc. Frans Laubscher of Ames, Iowa, a member of the Personal Security Detail of Headquarters and Headquarters Company, 2nd Brigade Combat Team, 34th Infantry Division, Task Force Red Bulls, scans his area during a foot patrol through the Yuzbashi village. (Photo by U.S. Army Spc. Kristina L. Gupton, Task Force Red Bulls Public Affairs)

PARWAN PROVINCE, Afghanistan, May 6, 2011—U.S. Army Spc. Matthew Williams of Eldridge, Iowa, a member of the Personal Security Detail of Headquarters and Headquarters Company, 2nd Brigade Combat Team, 34th Infantry Division, Task Force Red Bulls, writes down the grid of a potential point of origin for indirect fire while out on a foot patrol. (Photo by U.S. Army Spc. Kristina L. Gupton, Task Force Red Bulls Public Affairs)

Nashville lawmen deepen bond through minefield tragedy in Afghanistan

BAGRAM AIRFIELD, Afghanistan, April 14, 2011—U.S. Air Force Staff Sgt. David Terrazas (left), from Lake Orion, Mich.; U.S. Air Force Staff Sgt. Vinny Estes (center), from Pensacola, Fla.; and U.S. Air Force Staff Sgt. Christopher Sargent (right) from Livermore, Calif.; all members of the 455th Expeditionary Security Forces Squadron outside Bagram Airfield, Afghanistan. The three Airmen have been deployed to Afghanistan since April, providing base security to BAF. The three, all of whom serve in the Air National Guard's 118th Security Forces Squadron in Nashville, have experienced the train-up and deployment together, including a patrol through a minefield, in which two fellow Airmen were injured. (Photo by Staff Sgt. Ryan C. Matson, Task Force Red Bulls Public Affairs)

By U.S. Army Staff Sgt. Ryan C. Matson
Task Force Red Bulls Affairs

BAGRAM AIRFIELD, Afghanistan, May 6, 2011—U.S. Air Force Staff Sgt. Christopher Sargent, U.S. Air Force Staff Sgt. David Terrazas, and U.S. Air Force Staff Sgt. Vinny Estes are a pretty tight group.

Back home in the United States, all three are Nashville-area law enforcement officers serving together at Bagram Airfield in Afghanistan as part of the 455th Expeditionary Security Forces Squadron. Here in Afghanistan, however, an early morning tragedy would strengthen their already tight bond.

"It started out like a normal presence/recon patrol," Sargent from Livermore, Calif., recalled. "We had gone and done these patrols numerous times and nothing had happened."

But this day was different.

The team walked through numerous minefields in the past and were comfortable with that; the fields were clearly marked. But on this day, the team responded to a report of an individual digging, a common method for emplacing mines and Improvised Explosive Devices. The field they were in, which bordered the base, was neither marked as a minefield nor indicated as one on a map.

Estes, from Pensacola, Fla., was the point man with a Military Working Dog detachment behind him. Sargent was four men behind the dog handler.

"We were walking through the field," Sargent recalled. "And then two men back from me ... boom!"

A landmine detonated, taking down an Airman.

"I think we were all confused at that moment as to what had happened," Sargent said. He said their instinct was to react to indirect fire, but quickly realized that wasn't what happened.

"There was a big poof of smoke and then an eerie silence," Sargent recalled. "It's just like you hear about: everything slows down drastically. There was the eerie silence and then came the yelling. I looked back and saw [the Airman]. The first thing I noticed was the tattered bone and flesh off his left leg. He was trying to sit up, and his face was ghostly white underneath the black soot."

The squad leader told everyone to get down and a Combat Lifesaver-certified Airman rushed in to provide urgent battlefield care. But the nightmare was not over.

"In a span of what seemed like five minutes, which was actually only a minute and a half, the Military Working Dog handler [stepped on another landmine]," Sargent said. "It's a weird feeling calling for casualty evacuation right outside the wall of the base."

The Airman lost his left foot as a result of the blast. The mine was emplaced 15 feet from the edge of the field and 10 meters from the base in a ditch.

Estes took action to help his injured comrade.

"I heard a boom behind me and all I could see was a black cloud," Estes said. "Then I saw a dog come out, and I saw [the handler]. He was trying to crawl out of the ditch, with black soot all over his face. He couldn't crawl. I reached down and told him to give me his hand and pulled him out. I rolled him over inside the ditch, and started looking for a tourniquet."

Estes put the tourniquet on the Airman's leg, controlled the bleeding and effectively saved him. He performed a two-man carry to evacuate the injured Airmen from the minefield.

Terrazas from Lake Orion, Mich., was inside the base when the incident happened. "I heard an explosion and called the explosive ordnance team to see if they had just done another controlled detonation," he remembered. "That's when I heard [Sargent] come up on the radio and say they had just hit a mine. He was very calm."

"I started responding, and talked to our sniper team to see if they had eyes on the area they were at. Then I heard the second explosion and [Sargent] come back on the radio and said there was a second injury."

"I was thinking about [Estes]," Terrazas said about what went through his head after he got the call. "You start thinking about all the stuff we did, his family, all that. I started getting stretchers together, and at that point didn't know whether they were taking direct fire, being ambushed, or what."

Terrazas and a team of five other Airmen went outside the wire to recover their fellow Airmen, walking through the field with the guidance of the snipers.

"We went out and got the canine handler and the weapons and provided rear security until we got everybody back in," Terrazas said.

"It was a reassuring feeling to see Terrazas ... coming out of the gate to help us," Sargent said.

The team learned later the entire field was heavily mined.

Both Airmen struck by the mines are now recovering at Walter Reed Hospital in Washington, D.C. One Airman, who lost his lower left leg, walked with a walker one week after the incident. In Germany, he got a bedside visit from actress Angelina Jolie, which his fellow Airmen still tease him about.

The three said they believe their ages (Estes is 33; Sargent, 39; and Terrazas, 44), and law enforcement experience, enabled them to remain calm and handle the situation successfully.

"I noticed a big difference in how we responded to the incident," Sargent said. "It was almost to the point where I almost felt a little callous because I wasn't as emotional as the other [Airmen] were. I just think that's just due to our age and experience."

Terrazas agreed.

"Going through the Metro Police academy, as difficult as it was, as much as they beat us down, it actually prepared us for dealing with traumatic experiences like this," he said. Terrazas said their training at the police academy helped them build a wall between emotion and logic, enabling them to take care of the mission at hand and deal with the emotions later.

"Our primary responsibility is the base," Terrazas said, explaining the role of the 455th on Bagram Airfield. "If there is an attack, we lock down the base, secure any holes or breaches, engage and kill the enemy as they attempt to infiltrate the base."

The role of base security means the Airmen must be vigilant, watching where they are walking, knowing where they are, and realizing the people they deal with could be allies or enemies—which, they said, can be a lot like being on patrol back in the United States.

The three, each with about 12 years of military service, have a lot in common besides the minefield tragedy they responded to. All were prior active duty service members, each from different branches. Estes spent nine and a half years on active duty in the Air Force, Terrazas spent eight years in the Marines, including an 18-month deployment. Sargent, meanwhile, spent eight years as an infantry soldier in the Army, including four years in the historic Old Guard drill and ceremony detachment in Arlington.

"You've got three different branches that came together who all work in law enforcement in Davidson County, Tenn., that ended up in the same Guard unit here in Afghanistan," Terrazas said.

About three years ago, each joined the 118th Security Forces Squadron in Nashville. The Metro and Davidson County officers would serve on their respective departments as civilians and come together one weekend a month as members of the same squad at their Air National Guard unit.

What makes the group so tight, Terrazas said, is that each knows he has the other's back, regardless of the situation.

"What we missed most from being prior service is the camaraderie, and we have that amongst the three of us," Terrazas said. "I can't get rid of Estes! We're a band of brothers and we look out for each other."

"There's a common bond there, between military and law enforcement," Sargent added. "Where else do you find a job where people are willing to die for each other?"

Increased cooperation between locals, military leads to several caches

PAKTYA PROVINCE, Afghanistan, May 5, 2011—Afghan National Army soldiers display a cache of six rocket-propelled grenades they found in a home after acting on a tip they received while patrolling through Babeker village, Zormat District, Afghanistan. The ANA and 1st Platoon, Company C, 1st Battalion, 168th Infantry Regiment, Task Force Lethal, 2nd Brigade, 34th Infantry Division, Task Force Red Bulls, also found three Improvised Explosive Devices, and more than 70 rounds of high-caliber ammunition during the patrol. (Photo by U.S. Army 1st Lt. Joel Sage, Task Force Lethal)

By U.S. Army 1st Lt. Nicholas Rasmussen
Task Force Lethal

PAKTYA PROVINCE, Afghanistan, May 9, 2011—With tips from local villagers, U.S. and Afghan forces in Zormat District, Afghanistan, eliminated many weapons caches May 5-9.

Soldiers from the Afghan National Army and Company C, 1st Battalion, 168th Infantry Regiment, Task Force Lethal, 2nd Brigade Combat Team, 34th Infantry Division, Task Force Red Bulls, found 11 rocket-propelled grenades, about 1,000 rounds of varying calibers, two confirmed Improvised Explosive Devices and various other munitions and weapons in the five-day period.

Soldiers found the caches after villagers tipped off the military on the whereabouts of the weapons as part of the Government of the Islamic Republic of Afghanistan's Guardians of Peace program, which rewards Afghans who come forward with information leading to the capture of insurgents or illegal weapons.

The U.S. Soldiers said the work they've been doing to form relationships with the people living in their area of operations led to the increase in amount and quality of the tips received.

"A lot of it has to do with what we did over the winter," said U.S. Army Sgt. Michael Jenkins of Westminster, Md., an intelligence analyst with Company C. "We went out and made friends with the locals."

In one instance, while at a local Madrassa, the Soldiers received a tip that insurgents buried an Improvised Explosive Device near a clinic in Sadar Kheyl village.

"This happens quite a bit," added U.S. Army Spc. Tyler Malom, of Polk City, Iowa, a rifleman in Company C's 1st Platoon. "We'll be out on patrol and somebody will come and tip us off about something in the road."

In another instance, the ANA platoon leader, 1st Lt. Pallawanna, received a phone call about another suspected IED.

Pallawanna and his men investigated the site and found a sack with five mortar rounds, which they brought back to their combat outpost to be destroyed.

"The fact that the ANA were able to gather intelligence and act on it without the support of coalition forces shows their growth as a (company)," remarked U.S. Army Capt. Michael Minard of Bettendorf, Iowa, the commander of Company C.

"The people are really beginning to trust us," said Pallawanna. "You can tell this is true not only because of the number of tips we receive, but also by the way we are received in the villages."

PAKTYA PROVINCE, Afghanistan, May 5, 2011—U.S. Army Sgt. 1st Class Kenneth Cornelius of Bondurant, Iowa, platoon sergeant for 1st Platoon, Company C, 1st Battalion, 168th Infantry Regiment, Task Force Lethal, 2nd Brigade, 34th Infantry Division, Task Force Red Bulls, speaks with villagers through an interpreter, while investigating a report of an Improvised Explosive Device in Zormat District, Afghanistan. The joint patrol found two IEDs, six Rocket-Propelled Grenades, more than 70 rounds of large-caliber ammunition and a hoax IED. (Photo by U.S. Army 1st Lt. Joel Sage, Task Force Lethal)

PAKTYA PROVINCE, Afghanistan, May 5, 2011—U.S. Army Spc. David Nordyke of Ottumwa, Iowa, and an Afghan National Army (ANA) soldier secure the area around an Improvised Explosive Device site in Zormat District, Afghanistan while waiting for an Explosive Ordnance Disposal team to arrive and destroy the IED. [...] (Photo by U.S. Army 1st Lt. Joel Sage, Task Force Lethal)

Task Force Redhorse, ANP conduct joint patrol

PARWAN PROVINCE, Afghanistan, May 9, 2011—U.S. Army Spc. Micah Roberts of Washington, Iowa, a cavalry scout with Troop B, 1st Squadron, 113th Cavalry Regiment, Task Force Redhorse, 2nd Brigade Combat Team, 34th Infantry Division, Task Force Red Bulls, conducts a room search. Troop B conducted the joint foot patrol with ANP to search the village for weapons cache. (Photo by U.S. Army Spc. Kristina L. Gupton, Task Force Red Bulls Public Affairs)

PARWAN PROVINCE, Afghanistan, May 9, 2011—U.S. Army Pfc. Matthew Gibson of Batavia, Ill., a cavalry scout with Troop B, 1st Squadron, 113th Cavalry Regiment, Task Force Redhorse, 2nd Brigade Combat Team, 34th Infantry Division, Task Force Red Bulls, provides security for an Afghan National Policeman while he searches a villager's home. Troop B conducted the joint foot patrol with ANP to search for weapons caches. (Photo by U.S. Army Spc. Kristina L. Gupton, Task Force Red Bulls Public Affairs)

Troop B provides security through the night

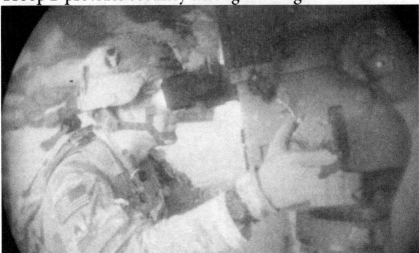

PARWAN PROVINCE, Afghanistan, May 9, 2011—U.S. Army Sgt. Cullen Wurzer of Des Moines, Iowa, and cavalry scout with Troop B, 1st Squadron, 113th Cavalry Regiment, Task Force Redhorse, 2nd Brigade Combat Team, 34th Infantry Division, Task Force Red Bulls, uses a Long Range Advanced Scout System to scan his sector of fire while at Vehicle Patrol Base Dandar, Afghanistan. Troop B maintains security on VPB Dandar while conducting operations in Koh-E Safi District. (Photo by U.S. Army Spc. Kristina L. Gupton, Task Force Red Bulls Public Affairs)

PARWAN PROVINCE, Afghanistan, May 9, 2011—Members of Troop B, 1st Squadron, 113th Cavalry Regiment, Task Force Redhorse, 2nd Brigade Combat Team, 34th Infantry Division, Task Force Red Bulls, prepare to go out on a night patrol in Koh-e Safi District, Afghanistan. Troop B Soldiers conducted a night patrol to ensure security around the vehicle patrol base. Troop B maintains security on VPB Dandar while conducting operations in Koh-E Safi District. (Photo by U.S. Army Spc. Kristina L. Gupton, Task Force Red Bulls Public Affairs)

ADT, non-profit org help orchards take root in Panjshir

By U.S. Army Spc. James Wilton
Task Force Red Bulls Public Affairs

PANJSHIR PROVINCE, Afghanistan, May 9, 2011—The Kentucky Agribusiness Development Team III, attached to the Panjshir Provincial Reconstruction Team and the Roots of Peace, a non-profit organization, donated hundreds of fruit trees to local farmers at the Khenj District Center, Afghanistan, May 9.

The program donated trees to establish six cherry and three apricot orchards that will serve as nurseries. These nurseries, controlled by the Panjshir Directorate of Agriculture, Irrigation, and Livestock, will provide saplings for Afghan farmers and assist in establishing the planned 600 cherry and 100 apricot orchards, over the next two years.

The ROP and Kentucky ADT III, in partnership with the Afghan Ministry of Agriculture, Irrigation and Livestock , also provide workshops at the nurseries that teach Afghan farmers proper growing techniques and the use of pesticides and equipment to improve their growth capacity.

The people gave the program high praise and said they hope efforts will continue.

"The people of Panjshir are eager to work with the ROP and Kentucky ADT program," said Abdul Sabir, the Panjshir DAIL extension agent, through an interpreter. "They love to work on agriculture, and hope that even after this closing ceremony that both organizations will continue to promote agriculture in Panjshir Province."

The Panjshir Valley currently survives on subsistence farming. The program, through the use of high-value crops like cherries and apricots, is designed to turn the valley's basic needs-based fields into sources of income for the farmers.

"Afghanistan does not have a lot of industry or other types of jobs so agriculture is the main source of income for many of its peoples," said Sabir. "If we can increase the development of agriculture in our province and in the country, then we can help the people to make more money and support their families better."

The Kentucky ADT works closely with the MAIL and his provincial and district agents ensuring they will be able to manage the program long after coalition and international aid organizations have left the country.

"The ADT along with the PRT has a unique ability to bring knowledge and experience to the Afghan people through our joint efforts. We hope we can assist Panjshir to be one of the first provinces to transition," said U.S. Army Lt. Col. Blake Settle, the Kentucky ADT commander from Louisville, Ky. "We are bringing everything together and this is the time for the Panjshiries to take the lead in their province."

The Kentucky ADT is also working with Panjshir farmers to create an international market for the fruits and vegetables they produce.

The first step in this process is creating a brand that indentifies the products as being from Panjshir.

"The Panjshir Valley has a very rich agriculture base and produces very high-quality products. People already recognize this quality in many of the Afghan markets, including those in Kabul," said Settle. "We are currently looking at opportunities to brand the name of Panjshir on those products and spread them out into other markets in foreign countries."

PANJSHIR PROVINCE, Afghanistan, May 9. 2011—An Afghan farmer displays a new pair of pruning shears donated by the non-profit organization, Roots of Peace, during a meeting to close a tree donation project at the Khenj District Center, Afghanistan. (Photo by U.S. Army Spc. James Wilton, Task Force Red Bulls Public Affairs)

ROK PRT, Kentucky ADT promote gender equality

By U.S. Army Staff Sgt. Ashlee Lolkus
Task Force Red Bulls Public Affairs

PARWAN PROVINCE, Afghanistan, May 10, 2011—Afghan leaders of the Parwan Province met with the Republic of Korea Provincial Reconstruction Team and members of the Women's Empowerment Team, Kentucky Agribusiness Development Team III, for a gender equality awareness conference at the ROK Charikar Base, Afghanistan.

Attendees learned what the international community considers gender inequality and how important the issue is in other countries, said Dr. Hyunjoo Song, a gender adviser for the ROK PRT.

The segregation of the two sexes, of men and women, is very normal in Afghan society, she continued, but Afghans don't really know that international communities consider the segregation of men and women to be discrimination.

"The training should not take place in one (session), it should take place continuously with the same audience, because it is not easy to change the people's attitudes," said Song.

Education has three components: acquiring skills, transferring knowledge, and changing attitudes. Of these three, changing people's attitudes is the most difficult, according to Song.

"The gender seminar is to change their attitudes," said Song. "That's why we have to have the capacity building seminars with the same audience."

Coalition forces held a similar conference Dec. 14, 2010 in Charikar, where Song spoke to more than 30 participants including attorneys and the mayor about gender awareness.

"The conference was a good experience and I learned a lot," said Mohammad Taher, a deputy director for economics in Parwan Province, through an interpreter. "All of the issues she talked about she is right. Mainly in villages, there is a lot of (discrimination) going on, but big cities are better at respecting women more because they are better educated."

Carmen Tamras, a female linguist with the Parwan PRT from San Jose, Calif., said when they go to the villages to talk to the people, many men will not allow her to talk to the women.

"The men think that since we are westerners that we are going to try to teach their wife inappropriate things, so they don't want them anywhere near us," she explained.

"But when we talk to them and say I am a mother, I am a daughter, or a sister, or a wife, or whatever, show them some pictures of our family, show them that I work really hard and I wouldn't be here if I didn't need to be so they can look at us like a human being just like them ... then they can let us in."

Because talking to the women of the villages can be difficult the Kentucky ADT III takes a different approach.

"We make sure we tie ourselves to the female leadership," said U.S. Army Capt. Carla Getchell of Frankfort, Ky., the Kentucky ADT III women's empowerment coordinator.

At the operational level the Kentucky ADT ties female leadership, such as the director of women's affairs, in with important meetings. They also teach the same kinds of things their male counterparts are teaching to ensure men and women are educated equally on finding resources for their projects.

Like the previous counterparts, Getchell and her team plan to be involved in projects to help Afghan women earn an income through agriculture. Past projects taught widowed and low-income Afghan women how to raise poultry and beekeeping.

"The goal, when setting up the poultry or bee keeping projects, is that coalition forces don't do the training. What we do is assist the local leadership, the female leadership, in resourcing the training," explained Getchell. "They provide the location, and we help them find resources for the training. We are the facilitators in connecting the Afghan (women) with resources available throughout the country."

Song supports the work of the Kentucky ADT III.

"When the women start to make money on their own it empowers them because they will be less dependent on other people," said Song. "It will definitely change their attitudes and change their husbands'. It could change the power structure in the household, it is not common, but it could change."

Combining the work of the PRT and the Kentucky ADT's women's programs, Afghan women may be able to start seeing progress in gender equality, said Getchell.

"I think one of biggest goals of (these gender awareness conferences) is just getting all of the women in the same room so that they are talking," said Getchell. "Networking is huge, and for us, in order to get them to a successful level, they have to know who they can call. Once (they) know the right people to talk to, it's much easier to get (their) job done. We want the line directors to be able to talk to the different leaders they have in their areas so that they can start solving their own problems when they occur."

Song said she intends to keep working on spreading gender awareness.

"I'd wanted to have gender conferences on a regular basis, like every month (after December's conference), but due to the limited mobility and transportation, I couldn't keep the seminars going," said Song. "If the conditions allow it, I will keep the seminars on a regular basis ...."

"In 'sha Alla," she said, meaning, "If God wills it."

ETT improves ANP facilities, abilities

*PANJSHIR PROVINCE, AfghanistanMay 4, 2011—*U.S. Army Maj. Russell Bossard, the Panjshir Embedded Training Team's deputy commander from Pella, Iowa, speaks to Tamim Mohammadi, the owner of Haji Azizullah Mohammad Construction Company, about the electricity refit at the Afghan National Police station in Dara District, Afghanistan. Mohammadi is a Panjshir native, which is an important qualification when the ETT selects contractors for their projects. The ETT is a part of the 2nd Brigade Combat Team, 34th Infantry Division, Task Force Red Bulls. (Photo by U.S. Army Spc. James Wilton, Task Force Red Bulls Public Affairs)

By U.S. Army Spc. James Wilton
Task Force Red Bulls Public Affairs

*PANJSHIR PROVINCE, Afghanistan, May 10, 2011—*The Panjshir Embedded Training Team completed improvements to Afghan National Police facilities in Dara District, May 8 and in Bazarak District, May 10.

The improvements included electrical conduit from generators to the buildings, new fuel tanks, interior lighting and electrical outlets. The Bazarak compound also received new perimeter security lights as a part of the refit.

"The biggest part of our mission is making sure that they're self-sufficient, giving them what they need so they can protect themselves and then expand out to be able to protect the population," said U.S. Army Maj. Russell Bossard from Pella, Iowa, and the Panjshir ETT deputy commander. "If (they) don't have the infrastructure to support the (police) and the mission then (they) can't be successful. So what we are trying to do is improve their facilities so they can be successful."

According to Bossard, the ETT prefers to find local contractors to promote economic growth by keeping money and jobs within the province. The work on the Dara and Bazarak facilities was done by Haji Azizullah Mohammad Construction Company whose owner was from Panjshir.

These improvements, along with other programs, are an important part of the ETT's mission to increase the capacity and effectiveness of the ANSF, Bossard said.

The ETT, which is a part of the 2nd Brigade Combat Team, 34th Infantry Division, Task Force Red Bulls, is also working to improve the security of a few Afghan National Security Forces and Afghan Ministry of Defense storage sites by constructing new fences, barbed wire and guard towers.

"I am very thankful for the work the coalition forces have done for our buildings," said Dara ANP Sgt. Mohammad Aarif, through an interpreter. "Now that we have power and more-secure fences, we can do our job better."

The ETT also plans to start an English language course at the Operations Coordination Center–Provincial.

"The program is designed to help the OCC–P command team in Panjshir communicate and coordinate more effectively with foreign agencies," said Bossard. "The common language within the U.N. is English and most of the OCC–P currently speaks very little, if any."

The team works with the ANSF on a daily basis with training and mentoring programs. Often, they contribute smaller items such as traffic checkpoint operation kits and other supplies Afghan officers need to perform their duty safely.

"Everything the American Soldiers have given us and showed us, allows me to do my job much better," said Aarif. "I joined the ANP in order to help make my province a safer place for the Afghan people."

Future projects the team hopes set in motion are a remodel of the "Lion's Gate," the entrance to Panjshir, which is an important symbol of pride for the people of the valley. They also hope to bring running water to the Dara compound through the installation of a well and storage tank.

Bossard said he thinks these improvements, both present and future, will make the ANSF's facilities more capable of supporting the Afghans security efforts.

Iowans donate to Afghan orphanage

PARWAN PROVINCE, Afghanistan, May 12, 2011—U.S. Army Sgt. Phillip Olson, right, of Estherville, Iowa, and a forward observer in Headquarters and Headquarters Troop, 1st Squadron, 113th Cavalry Regiment, Task Force Redhorse, looks on as a U.S. military interpreter gets boxes ready to distribute donated goods to children at a Charikar orphanage, in eastern Afghanistan. Students of West Middle School in Sioux City, Iowa, collected donations for a class project and sent them to Afghanistan where Iowa National Guard Soldiers distributed them to needy children. Task Force Redhorse is a part of the 34th Infantry Division's 2nd Brigade Combat Team, Task Force Red Bulls. (Photo by U.S. Army Staff Sgt. Ashlee Lolkus, Task Force Red Bulls Public Affairs)

By U.S. Army Staff Sgt. Ashlee Lolkus
Task Force Red Bulls Public Affairs

PARWAN PROVINCE, Afghanistan, May 12, 2011—Off the beaten path, down a few dusty roads in the city of Charikar, Afghanistan, is a small orphanage. The compound is worn with broken windows and bare mattresses. It is filled with young children who have next to nothing. But thanks to an Iowa community, these children will have a few basic necessities that many Americans take for granted.

Soldiers of Headquarters and Headquarters Troop and Troop C, both with 1st Squadron, 113th Cavalry Regiment, Task Force Redhorse, visited the orphanage in Charikar May 12 to hand out a small trailer-ful of goods. The Soldiers deployed with the Iowa National Guard's 2nd Brigade Combat Team, 34th Infantry Division, received boxes upon boxes of necessities from a school in Sioux City, Iowa.

U.S. Army Sgt. Ryan Downs, a cavalry scout from Sioux City, Iowa, with

HHT, said his mother, Christine Poeckes, initiated a shoe drive at West Middle School where she works as an 8th grade English teacher. He said it all started when he was deployed to Iraq and continued five years later here in Afghanistan.

Downs said while deployed to Iraq in 2006, his convoy drove by an orphanage, and he felt he needed to do something for them.

"I e-mailed (my mother) and said, 'Hey, we want to do something.' So, she started collecting clothes and shoes," he said. "And then when we got here, she just said, 'Hey, do you guys want me to collect stuff again?'"

Because Downs works in the squadron's tactical operations center, he didn't have the ability to visit the locals, so he relied on other elements of the squadron for help.

A friend of Downs, who deployed with him to Iraq and helped deliver much need supplies to an orphanage in Iraq, helped get the donations to the kids in Afghanistan as well.

"I have two kids at home and both of them are well off. I kind of wanted to do the same for a bunch of other little kids here, and take care of them. Provide for them, I guess," said U.S. Army Sgt. Tom Peck, a cavalry scout from Sioux City, Iowa, with HHT's Personal Security Detail which goes on regular trips into the Afghan communities. "So, (Downs) and I got together, his mom worked again with the kids at West Middle and got a bunch of shoes sent to us."

The students helped in a big way. Poeckes said her academic mentoring class needed to select a service learning project for the school year to which many students suggested helping needy children. Having donated to the orphanage in Iraq, Poeckes suggested they help raise donations for the kids of Afghanistan.

Poeckes said one of her students came in one day with a clipping from a newspaper that showed two little Afghan girls watching U.S. Soldiers go by ... the little girls had no shoes. "The students came up with different ways to collect donations," she explained. "They completed public service announcements, posters, and public speaking appearances asking for help in collecting. The response was overwhelming."

She said they received more than 300 pairs of shoes in all sizes and varieties along with some socks and various other items. "We had to cut off collecting in order to find ways to ship them. It cost $594 to ship all of those shoes," Poeckes said. "We had some fundraisers and donations from other school activities and sent them off."

Once Downs received all of the packages, they set out to Charikar. Troop C maintained security while Soldiers of HHT's Personal Security Detail distributed the donations.

Downs, Peck and others organized the children in a line to distribute the treats and other goods while the interpreters helped the children fit shoes. After a while, the courtyard was bustling with movement and excitement.

"I think the drop went good," Downs said of the visit to the orphanage. "I mean, kids are kids, right? They looked happy. They looked a little sceptical at first ... I don't know if it's going to change anything, but those kids have shoes now ... and I'm glad we did it."

"I think the kids had a great time with it," said Peck. "I know we had a great time with it as well."

"You can only help so many," he said. But, thanks to the kids of West Middle School's efforts, and Downs' mother, who coordinated the shipping, he continued, the kids of the Charikar orphanage now have shoes that fit and the U.S. Soldiers are able to continue to build trust with the people of Afghanistan.

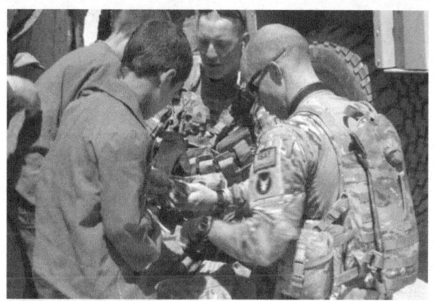

PARWAN PROVINCE, Afghanistan, May 12, 2011—U.S. Army Sgt. Tom Peck and U.S. Army Sgt. Ryan Downs both cavalry scouts from Sioux City, Iowa, in Headquarters and Headquarters Troop, 1st Squadron, 113th Cavalry Regiment, Task Force Redhorse, hand donated goods to young boys at a Charikar orphanage in eastern Afghanistan. Students of West Middle School in Sioux City, Iowa, collected donations for a class project and sent them to Afghanistan where Iowa National Guard Soldiers distributed them to needy children. Task Force Redhorse is a part of the 34th Infantry Division's 2nd Brigade Combat Team, Task Force Red Bulls. (Photo by U.S. Army Staff Sgt. Ashlee Lolkus, Task Force Red Bulls Public Affairs)

Medical training helps ANA treat combat wounded

PAKTYA PROVINCE, Afghanistan, May 10, 2011—Afghan National Army soldiers move a wounded ANA soldier to a medical evacuation helicopter after an Improvised Explosive Device detonated during a patrol in western Zormat District, Paktya Province. The ANA were working with Company D, 1st Battalion, 168th Infantry Regiment, Task Force Lethal, 3rd Brigade, 1st Infantry Division, Task Force Duke, during Operation El Dorado, a continuous, week-long operation to prevent insurgent forces freedom of movement around the province. (Photo by U.S. Army Sgt. John P. Sklaney III, 2-45th Agribusiness Development Team Public Affairs)

PAKTYA PROVINCE, Afghanistan, May 14, 2011—The medical training Afghan National Army soldiers received last winter proved valuable when several were wounded in western Zormat District, Afghanistan, during a week-long operation that ended today.

Wounded during operation El Dorado, their fellow ANA soldiers treated them using the skills they'd practiced during a coalition-led course in January.

Company D, 1st Battalion, 168th Infantry Regiment, Task Force Lethal, 3rd Brigade, 1st Infantry Division, Task Force Duke, developed the Combat Medical Training Course to train the ANA on basic Combat Lifesaver skills.

ANA soldier Abdul Samad used these medical skills May 9 when insurgents attacked an ANA-run traffic control point injuring two ANA soldiers. "I applied a pressure dressing around his shoulder the exact way I trained and practiced in medical classes that I received from the coalition forces," said Samad.

The Afghan soldiers evacuated the two casualties to nearby U.S. Army medics who were with the Personal Security Detail, Headquarters and Headquarters Company, Task Force Lethal, for further treatment.

"When the injured ANA arrived we were happy to see one of them already had a bandage on," said U.S. Army Pfc. William Drayfahl, medic, of Columbus Junction, Iowa.

The PSD medics stabilized both ANA casualties and evacuated them to higher medical care at Forward Operating Base Sharana.

The following day, an improvised explosive device struck an ANA convoy, giving the Afghans another chance to put their skills to work.

This time, they stabilized three injured Afghan soldiers before evacuating them to FOB Salerno for follow-up treatment.

"The ANA stepped up to the challenge and faced their wounded soldiers with confidence and a sense of knowledge," said U.S. Army 1st Sgt. Joedy Dennis of Alden, Iowa, the senior enlisted soldier of Company D.

"There is no doubt in my mind that I would be proud to have one of these ANA trainees take care of me or my soldiers if we were in need of medical assistance due to combat injuries."

PAKTYA PROVINCE, May 10, 2011—Afghan National Army soldier, who suffered a dislocated shoulder after an improvised explosive device detonated, receives treatment from another ANA soldier while being supervised by U.S. Army Pvt. Matthew Wakeen of Davenport, Iowa, a medic for Company D, 1st Battalion, 168th Infantry Regiment, Task Force Lethal, 3rd Brigade, 1st Infantry Division, Task Force Duke, during Operation El Dorado May 10. The ANA soldiers received medical training in an eight-week Combat Medical Training Course led by Company D in January. (Photo by U.S. Army Sgt. 1st Class Ryan Johnson, Task Force Lethal)

Kentucky ADT III dons Red Bull combat patch

By U.S. Army Staff Sgt. Ashlee Lolkus
Task Force Red Bulls Public Affairs

BAGRAM AIRFIELD, Afghanistan, May 14, 2011—Service members with the Kentucky Agribusiness Development Team III conducted their combat patch ceremony, a tradition held by the U.S. Army signifying the recognition of a Soldier's tour-of-duty in a combat zone, on Bagram Airfield, Afghanistan, May 14.

The patch ceremony was unique in that the U.S. Air Force Airmen assigned to the ADT also donned the combat patch, even though it is an Army tradition. To maintain uniformity, Airmen of the of ADT wear the Multicam-patterned Army combat uniform with all the same patches as the Army except on the left-side of their chest they wear "U.S. Air Force" instead.

Because Kentucky ADT III is a part of the 2nd Brigade Combat Team, 34th Infantry Division, Task Force Red Bulls, an Iowa National Guard unit, while in Afghanistan, they are authorized to wear the 34th Infantry Division's "Red Bull" combat patch, which now is fixed to their right shoulder.

"It's interesting to hear the lineage of the patch and the unit that it comes from," said U.S. Air Force Tech. Sgt. Jeffrey Stanley, a Waddy, Ky., native, and Kentucky ADT III security forces Non-Commissioned Officer. He said he was proud to be a part of the unit and its history.

Stanley is on his second deployment. His first was in 2002 to Turkey, with the 20th Fighter Wing out of Shaw Air Force Base, S.C. This was his first combat patch ceremony and the first time he deployed with Army Soldiers.

"It's definitely different learning the Army way," said Stanley. "The way that they do things is a little bit different, but our teams have come together. We've meshed well. We're almost like brothers and sisters now, so it makes things a lot easier as far as learning new things."

"Patching ceremonies are always a great experience," said U.S. Army Sgt. Kathleen Gallagher, a medic from Lexington, Ky., with the ADT. "It's especially wonderful to watch people experience it for the first time."

Gallagher said this is her second deployment; her first was to Iraq in 2008-2009.

"I am very excited to be here in Afghanistan and expect good things from the year ahead," she said.

Much of the unit seems to share the same expectations of the deployment. Gallagher said most of the service members volunteered for the mission so the enthusiasm is usually very high.

"There are 12 Airmen, seven females and the rest are (male) Soldiers from the Kentucky National Guard, from all across the state and from different units, different battalions, commands, brigades," said U.S. Army Command Sgt. Maj. Gordon Blair the Non-Commissioned Officer-in-Charge of the Kentucky ADT III, from Redfox, Ky. "We have probably one of the finest organizations I have ever worked for in my 31 years."

Blair, who joined the active duty Army in 1980, and has since transferred to the Kentucky National Guard works full time for the Guard as a shop supervisor at a field maintenance shop in Jackson, Ky. In Afghanistan he is the Non-Commissioned Officer-in-Charge of the ADT and takes care of the Soldiers and Airmen while they conduct operations throughout Parwan, Panjshir and Kapisa Provinces.

Their mission is to help facilitate the agricultural community in those provinces, Stanley explained. The ADT helps the Afghans by sharing information, providing resources and helping establish connections between the people and their government.

The unit has prepared together as a team since August 2010, and completed their pre-mobilization in both Kentucky and Indiana, which Stanley said helped build the team.

"They've come together over the last 10 months," said Blair. "As a team and a family, they are going to do great things."

"It's an honor just to be on this team and be the NCOIC of this operation," he said. "It is a good moment for me to wear this patch and to do great things for the great people of Afghanistan. I just look forward to the next (few) months here and build on what ADT II did ... and help these people out."

Religious leader sheds positive light on PRT

By U.S. Army Spc. James Wilton
Task Force Red Bulls Public Affairs

PANJSHIR PROVINCE, Afghanistan, May 15—On the eve of the transition, Coalition Forces are shifting their focus to reconstruction and rebuilding of Afghanistan's war-torn infrastructure including the challenging task of gaining the Afghan people's acceptance and trust.

Leading these efforts are the Provincial Reconstruction Teams.

One team, the Panjshir PRT's civil affairs section, is taking an uncommon approach to winning this battle. Through cooperation and continued support of the Panjshir Director of Religious Affairs, Mawlavi Haji Ahmed Halimi, the team said it hopes to shed a positive light on the PRT's mission and inform the Afghan people of their humanitarian efforts.

"We hoped this project would promote the PRT in a different light," said U.S. Army 1st Lt. Hakan Togul, the Panjshir PRT civil affairs Officer-in-Charge from Crete, Ill. "We also thought that through the support of the Panjshir Director of Religious Affairs the people would better understand the role of the PRT."

Halimi said he understands the role the PRT will play and the positive things it can do for his people.

"I think working with the PRT benefits the Afghan people," said Halimi, through an interpreter. "By working with the PRT, I am working for the people because the PRT in Panjshir works for the people."

Halimi worked with the mullahs and religious scholars from the seven Panjshir districts to help the people understand the PRT's intent. He said he hopes the people will realize that the PRT is not there to change their way of life but rather to support it and respect their traditions and culture.

"Right now I am working with the mullahs and religious scholars for peace. We want to remove the bad ideas from the people's thoughts and show them the truth about the PRT," said Halimi. "The PRT and U.S. military came to Afghanistan to help the people. They aren't doing things against their religion, in fact they're helping it, and they just came to Afghanistan to help the people."

A mullah, or religious leader, is a prominent figure in the political and social structure of the fundamental religious society in Afghanistan. Their words and views are highly respected by the people.

"The mullahs go to the mosque five days a week, which means they can pass on the good ideas about the PRT to the people," explained Halimi. "They can help to change the view and ideas of the people about the PRT, letting them know they support their work."

The civil affairs team said they know the importance of working with leaders like Halimi and made a point of doing so when they first got into country. A part of this effort included donating more than 60 loud speakers to the local mosques in every district.

The speakers are used during daily prayer and stand as a physical example of the work the PRT is doing for the people.

"This project helped to show the people that we are not here to intervene with their daily affairs or operations in the province but rather that we are here to help them rebuild and reconstruct their province and way of life," said Togul.

The project received a positive response from the people of the province.

"The reconstruction projects, like the installation of the speaker systems in the mosques, show the people that working with the PRT is a good idea," said Halimi. "The people are happy about the project and the other work the PRT is doing in the province."

"According to the Islamic culture, if groups like the PRT come from other countries to Afghanistan to help the people and do reconstruction or things like that, we welcome them," said Halimi. "But if they come by force and show their power then we don't accept them according to the Islamic rule."

By slowly working with the people through the mullahs, Halimi said he hopes to bring about change to the way they view groups like the PRT.

"We need to work step-by-step, start first in the villages, move to the districts, then the entire province," said Halimi. "Through the support of the mullahs and scholars, we can show the people the benefits of working with the international community."

Halimi's work goes beyond just improving the Afghan's view of groups like the PRT, he said he also wants to help them understand the role that Muslims play in the international community. One way he hopes to do this is through the use of the Internet and other forms of modern technology.

"By working with the new technology that we have available to us, we can connect the Afghan people with the international community, and show them how other Muslims are living, and how they work together for the greater good of the people," said Halimi. "When we show them that, we will not have any problems."

Halimi said he hopes to bring the people of Panjshir and possibly all Afghans into the future. A future which he hopes will be filled with a more informed and accepting population, one that sees the benefits of working with groups like the PRT coming from miles away.

Afghan, U.S. partnership increases security in Paktya

PAKTYA PROVINCE, Afghanistan, May 11, 2011—A CH-47 Chinook carries supplies to a patrol base of Company D, 1st Battalion, 168th Infantry Regiment, Task Force Lethal, 2nd Brigade Combat Team, 34th Infantry Division, Task Force Red Bulls, during operations near the village of Sahak, Afghanistan. The aerial resupply of the patrol base allowed Task Force Lethal to maintain continuous operations during the week-long mission. (Photo by U.S. Army Sgt. John P. Sklaney III, 2-45th Agribusiness Development Team).

By U.S. Army Sgt. John P. Sklaney III
2-45th Agribusiness Development Team

PAKTYA PROVINCE, *Afghanistan, May 16, 2011*—U.S. and Afghan forces completed an operation to increase security and disrupt insurgents' activities in and around Sahak village, Afghanistan.

The operation, called "El Dorado," was a combined mission between 1st Battalion, 168th Infantry Regiment, Task Force Lethal, 2nd Brigade Combat Team, 34th Infantry Division, Task Force Red Bulls, and the 1st Kandak, 2nd Brigade, 203rd ANA Infantry Corps of the Afghan National Army.

ANA Col. Mahmoud Zazai, commander of the 1st Kandak lead Afghan forces during the combined operations.

"U.S. and Afghan forces will work together during all clearing operations," said Zazai. "Combined, the mission will demonstrate the resolve of the Afghan government to provide better and increased security for all Afghans." The operation also tested the ANA's ability to operate for an extended period away from their bases and rely on logistical sustainment and support during the week-long operation.

"Each unit during the mission will be required to keep themselves supplied with not only food and fuel but also any other support such as maintenance or ammunition," said Zazai. "This operation will be a test of our ability to conduct sustained operations with minimal support from the U.S. military."

Task Force Lethal's Company D partnered with the 4th Company, 1st Kandak, 2nd Brigade, 203rd ANA Infantry Corps.

"One of the primary goals of the operation is to place a great deal of pressure upon the enemy," said U.S. Army Lt. Col. Stephen B. Boesen II from Ankeny, Iowa, Task Force Lethal commander. "That pressure will create separation between the insurgents and the local population, and the Afghan and the U.S. military hope to exploit that with future missions and projects that will benefit the locals."

U.S. Army 1st Lt. Chris Burk, a platoon leader in Company D, from Council Bluffs, Iowa, led his platoon during the clearing operations in and around Sahak.

"The mission accomplished many goals by discovering weapon caches, explosives, persons of interest and general security sweeps," said Burk. "In addition, ANA and U.S. forces were able to disrupt the enemy's ability to operate near the village."

Burk's platoon cleared more than four large caches, rounded up more than a dozen insurgents, and confiscated more than 30 unregistered weapons.

Afghan law allows individuals to own weapons as long as they are registered with the Afghan government.

Future combined operations will work to disrupt the insurgents' ability to operate freely, allow for improved security and set the ground conditions for the incoming 279th Infantry Battalion, Task Force Creek, of the Oklahoma Army National Guard, who are scheduled to replace Task Force Lethal this summer.

PAKTYA PROVINCE, Afghanistan, May 11, 2011—U.S. Army Sgt. Seth Hansen of Council Bluffs, Iowa, a squad leader of 2nd Platoon, Company D, 1st Battalion, 168th Infantry Regiment, Task Force Lethal, 2nd Brigade Combat Team, 34th Infantry Division, Task Force Red Bulls, checks for explosive residue left behind on the clothing of a suspect following an Improvised Explosive Device strike on an ANA vehicle. The Afghan National Army detained the suspect after the test came up positive for explosive residue. (Photo by U.S. Army Sgt. John P. Sklaney III, 2-45th Agribusiness Development Team)

Task Force Lethal company fuels the fight

*PAKTYA PROVINCE, Afghanistan, May 12, 2011—*U.S. Army Sgt. Jay Wheeldon, a refuelling specialist, assigned to Company F, 1st Battalion, 168th Infantry Regiment, Task Force Lethal, and native from Missouri Valley, Iowa, refuels a Mine-Resistant, Ambush-Protected vehicle at a checkpoint in Gardez, Afghanistan, May 12. Company F resupplied three checkpoints with rations and fuel daily during an eight-day mission to disrupt Taliban activity. (U.S. Army photo by Staff Sgt. Andrew Guffey, Task Force Duke Public Affairs)

By U.S. Army Staff Sgt. Andrew Guffey
Task Force Duke Public Affairs

*PAKTYA PROVINCE, Afghanistan, May 16, 2011—*U.S. and Afghan National Security Forces completed a week-long operation to expand resupply routes in the Gardez District, Afghanistan.

Company F, 1st Battalion, 168th Infantry Regiment, Task Force Lethal, alongside their partnered ANSF personnel, added three checkpoints to their supply routes, and delivered more than 2,000 gallons of fuel and 4,000 pounds of food and supplies.

Coalition forces set up the checkpoints to keep insurgents from disrupting security force operations and increase security for the local populace who use the roads on a daily basis.

"If we did not get these supplies, we would have to return to base to get refitted which would give the enemy the freedom to move through the area," said U.S. Army Sgt. 1st Class Devin Jepsen, a Schleswig, Iowa, native, and senior Non-Commisioned Officer of 3rd Platoon, Company A, Task Force Lethal.

Company F keeps the rest of the 1-168th Inf. stocked with the supplies they need to operate. This latest operation only represents a fraction of the amount of supplies Company F transported through the area.

Since their arrival in theater in October 2010, they ran more than 80 resupply missions, travelling more than 100,000 miles and delivering 900,000 pounds of supplies throughout Task Force Lethal's area of operations, said U.S. Army Sgt. Eric Wendt, a truck driver from Shelby, Iowa, with Company F.

Spending that much time on the dangerous roads of eastern Afghanistan can't be done alone, so before each supply run, a route clearance patrol checks the road for threats like Improvised Explosive Devices, said Wendt.

"Luckily, we've only been hit by three IEDs since we've been here," he said.

Bridge, retaining wall enhance travel for 6,000

PANJSHIR PROVINCE, Afghanistan, May 16, 2011—Panjshir Provincial Reconstruction Team members, government officials, village elders and Community Development Council members attended a ribbon-cutting ceremony for the Zamankur Footbridge in Anaba District, Afghanistan. The bridge opens a pedestrian pathway to Kapisa Province and provides access for more than 6,000 villagers. (Photo by U.S. Air Force 2nd Lt. Ashleigh Peck, Panjshir Provincial Reconstruction Team Public Affairs)

By U.S. Air Force 2nd Lt. Ashleigh Peck
Panjshir Provincial Reconstruction Team Public Affairs

PANJSHIR PROVINCE, Afghanistan, May 16, 2011—Panjshir Provincial Reconstruction Team members, government officials, village elders and Community Development Council members attended ribbon-cutting ceremonies for a footbridge and a retaining wall in Anaba District, Afghanistan.

"Both projects were joint projects the government, CDC and PRT worked on together," said Anaba District Gov. Gulam Hussein, through an interpreter.

The bridge provides driving and walking access to Kapisa Province through Darband Pass for more than 6,000 villagers.

"Without the footbridge, school children and travelers would have to

543

walk three miles upstream to use the vehicle bridge to get to the other side of the river," said U.S. Army Sgt. Joshua O'Keefe, PRT civil affairs section lead, and Athens, Mich., native.

While the Zamankur Footbridge will open access for pedestrian travel, a retaining wall built for the Froj Bridge will continue to provide a main supply route for vehicles.

"Building a retaining wall for Froj Bridge was a need for the village," said Hussein. "The bridge continues the road for people living on the other side."

The retaining wall began to erode after last year's flooding.

"If erosion of the retaining wall continued, there was a likely chance the road would eventually flood preventing access to the bridge," said O'Keefe.

Once the project was presented to PRT engineers, they conducted a site survey.

"Our government cost-estimate for the project was more than $80,000," said U.S. Air Force Capt. Brian Jackson, PRT engineer lead, and South Haven, Mich., native. "Due to the administration process, it would've taken months to obtain that amount of money."

The PRT gave $5,000 for temporary emergency relief to protect the wall from continued erosion. The villagers used $3,000 to move the debris and used the other $2,000 to start building the retaining wall. Later, the PRT supported the finishing of the project by providing additional funding through permanent relief funds.

"The next time we visited the project site, the villagers explained they only needed $5,000 to finish the project," said U.S. Army 1st Lt. Hakan Togul, PRT civil affairs lead from Crete, Ill. "The emergency relief money was to be a temporary fix, but these villagers used what they had and found a permanent solution," said Togul.

During the ceremony, speakers expressed gratitude for the PRT's assistance and the work of the villagers to complete the project.

"We appreciate all of the hard work done by the people who worked together to complete this project," said Hussein. "We hope this retaining wall will last forever."

While the government gave funds and resources, the villagers provided supplies and labor.

"These projects are textbook examples of the Afghan government, villagers and the PRT working together for the development of Panjshir," said Togul.

Education brings world to hands of Panjshir youth

PANJSHIR PROVINCE, Afghanistan, May 17, 2011—Panjshir Provincial Reconstruction Team members and villagers gather outside the Perengal School preceding the school's ribbon-cutting ceremony in Dara District, Afghanistan. (Photo by U.S. Air Force 2nd Lt. Ashleigh Peck, Panjshir Provincial Reconstruction Team Public Affairs)

By U.S. Air Force 2nd Lt. Ashleigh Peck
Panjshir Provincial Reconstruction Team Public Affairs

PANJSHIR PROVINCE, Afghanistan, May 17, 2011—Panjshir Provincial Reconstruction Team members, government officials, schoolchildren and villagers attended a ribbon-cutting ceremony for the Perengal School in Dara District, Afghanistan.

Children lined the road to the new school to greet visitors as they approached for the ceremony.

Visitors included the provincial deputy governor, a ministry of education representative, the education director, the district governor and the PRT commander.

"Ever since my team and I arrived in Panjshir, we've always felt welcome," said U.S. Air Force Lt. Col. Joseph Blevins, PRT commander. "But I've never felt more welcome than I did today as the school children lined the road to greet us."

The Community Development Council, a group of Afghans who address the needs of their community, brought the need to build the Perengal School to the attention of the PRT who funded the project.

"This valley needed this school and the people here are very thankful for it," said Dara District Gov. Malem Sorab, through an interpreter. "The students used to have to study in rented houses and some were sitting under trees for school lessons."

Construction of the eight-classroom school began in July 2008.

"The school will provide 238 boys a place to continue their lessons," said Perengal School Principal Mahmood Ahmadi, through an interpreter. "We are thankful for this school because it has been built with good quality and high standards."

Ahmadi said he believes there are three fundamentals needed to build capacity for education: a good building, good teachers and good equipment.

"Today this school gives us one of the fundamentals we need for our children to get education," said Panjshir Deputy Gov. Abdul Rahman Kabiri, through an interpreter.

The district governor asked all the people present to help preserve the school and ensure the school achieves its potential.

"We have given you the school. Now, I would like you to help us maintain the school," said Sorab. "I would like the school students to work hard and the director of education to work on building the capacity to bring good quality teachers here."

During the ceremony, boys from the Taza Mahamad Shaheed High School Banner Team sang "Maariff," which means education. The team sang, "We are people of education; education is our job. It doesn't matter if we are male or female but we are responsible for getting knowledge. We are proud of getting an education," relayed through an interpreter.

The PRT commander stressed the importance of working together and working through the government.

"The PRT works with the people through the government to identify projects, and we will continue to do that until we leave," said Blevins from Oregonia, Ohio. "Shana ba shana, dast ba dast," translated to mean shoulder-to-shoulder, hand-in-hand.

The deputy governor reflected on the importance of what has been put in the hands of the youth.

"The holy Quran says that learning is obligatory for every individual, man or woman, because if you are uneducated, you are blind and living in darkness," said Kabiri. "When Allah gives someone education, it means he has all the world in his hand."

Panjshir ANP first to graduate CSI training

PANJSHIR PROVINCE, Afghanistan, May 24, 2011—Afghan National Police members bag evidence and collect fingerprints from a simulated crime scene during a Crime Scene Investigation Class held by Law Enforcement Professionals attached to Panjshir Embedded Training Team in Bazarak Municipality, Panjshir Province, Afghanistan, May 24. The four-day class, funded by the Task Force Red Bulls rule-of-law office, consisted of Afghan rule-of-law criminal procedures, working a crime scene from the beginning through the prosecution in court and collecting and preserving evidence to be presented in court. (Photo by U.S. Air Force Senior Airman Amber Ashcraft, Panjshir Provincial Reconstruction Team Public Affairs)

By U.S. Air Force Senior Airman Amber Ashcraft
Panjshir Provincial Reconstruction Team Public Affairs

PANJSHIR PROVINCE, Afghanistan, May 24, 2011—More than 20 Afghan National Police members from Panjshir Province were the first to graduate from a Crime Scene Investigation class in Bazarak Municipality, Afghanistan.

Task Force Red Bulls rule-of-law office funded the four-day class, held by the Law Enforcement Professionals attached to the Panjshir Embedded Training Team. It consisted of Afghan rule-of-law criminal procedures, crime scene procedures from the initial investigation through the prosecution in court and the physical collection and preservation of evidence to be presented in court.

"Before the graduation, we wanted the class to break into teams and work in simulated crime scenes," said Paul Protzenko, a Law Enforcement

Professional, and Myrtle Beach, S.C., native. "We set up a murder/homicide scene and a breaking/entering situation. The teams used investigation kits and got right to work on collecting evidence and evaluating the crime scenes."

Using the training they learned in the CSI class, the students established specific roles for the investigation, collected biometrics of the witnesses and a victim and obtained evidence from the crime scenes, including weapons and fingerprints.

The students split up their roles in the investigations to include the photographer, evidence collector, witness interviewer and sketch artist. The teams used investigation kits provided by the rule-of-law office to accurately pull up fingerprints and collect all evidence found.

"For the actual time in class being so short, those in attendance were very eager to learn new investigative skills and how to use the kits," Brown said. "This is the first investigative training that went a little more in depth into lifting fingerprints, taking better crime scene photographs and information about ballistics from weapons."

Following the review and evaluation of the investigations, Afghan National Police Brig. Gen. Qasim Jangalbagh, the Panjshir Provincial Police Chief, joined the class to pass out certificates during the graduation.

"I appreciate the instructors for having this crucial training," said Qasim, through an interpreter. "It is very beneficial and I hope for more crimes to be solved with the knowledge of these new skills and resources."

Three more classes will be held to train more than 60 ANP members. Investigation kits will also be signed out to individual units of the members that attended, including the Criminal Investigation Division, Afghan National Directorate of Security, and Counter-Narcotic and Intelligence units.

"When many of us started as investigators, practical training was never given," said ANP Deputy Daber of the CID department at the Provincial Headquarters, through an interpreter. "Now that we all have had more hands-on practice with professionals, we're confident that we'll be able to catch guilty suspects, using the knowledge and kits we attained from the class."

Panjshir school children learn about rule of law

PANJSHIR PROVINCE, Afghanistan, May 24, 2011—U.S. Army Maj. Bill Kelly, Task Force Red Bulls Brigade Judge Advocate, and Norwalk, Iowa, resident, passes out donated school supplies after distributing rule-of-law books to schoolchildren at the Koraba Secondary School in Shutol District, Afghanistan, May 24. (Photo by U.S. Army 1st Lt. James Ostman, Task Force Red Bulls)

By U.S. Air Force 1st Lt. Ashleigh Peck
Panjshir Provincial Reconstruction Team Public Affairs

PANJSHIR PROVINCE, Afghanistan, May 24, 2011—Panjshir Provincial Reconstruction Team members and representatives from the 2nd Brigade Combat Team, 34th Infantry Division, Task Force Red Bulls, distributed 20,000 rule-of-law books and more than 10 boxes of donated school supplies and games to schools in Anaba and Shotol Districts, Afghanistan.

The supplies were incorporated into a Task Force Red Bulls' mission during which the task force and Panjshir Provincial Director of the Department of Education Abdul Muqeem distributed books from a USAID rule of law program that focuses on civics, the Afghan judicial system, constitution and formal law structures.

"The books are to teach the youth about the constitution, government, and importance of following the rule of law," said U.S. Army Capt. Matthew

Kuehl, Task Force Red Bulls' rule-of-law coordinator, and Lake Geneva, Wis., native.

By combining the books with the donated school supplies, the rule of law education program had an even greater impact on students, said Kuehl.

U.S. Army Maj. Bill Kelly, and his civilian employer, the Davis Brown Law firm, one of Iowa's largest law firms supplied the donations.

"Throughout the deployment I had constant offers from members of the firm to help me, our Soldiers or Afghans," said Kelly, Task Force Red Bulls Brigade Judge Advocate, and Norwalk, Iowa, resident.

"We began planning a children's rule of law and constitutional awareness mission, and I thought this would be a great opportunity for the firm to do something that would truly make a difference," he said.

Kelly contacted Courtney Strutt Todd, a Davis Brown associate who specializes in business law, and asked her if she could help collect some basic supplies to hand out with the USAID rule of law books.

Todd and her fellow employees collected more than 10 boxes of supplies and money to cover shipping and the purchase of additional items.

"I was amazed by how much they sent," said Kelly. The shipments included Iowa memorabilia, toys, books, games, treats, movies, DVDs and school supplies. "This definitely made a big difference in the success of our mission and the impact of our rule of law program."

The 20,000 books were part of a total of 50,000 books to be distributed to 30 primary schools in the province within the next month.

"We wanted to bring these books to you to help you learn about law and your government," Kuehl told a classroom of boys in the Anaba Boys High School. "We ask you to study these books because it's important to learn about the law."

The distribution of the law books to the schools was one of many initiatives the Panjshir PRT rule-of-law team initiated to inform villagers of principles of the law.

"We started a rule of law campaign about a year ago to promote public awareness of the formal and informal justice sector by getting information out through the local radio station, newspaper and billboards," said Mahboobullah Nickzad, a local national legal adviser with Panjshir PRT.

While provincial villagers are informed indirectly through local media, the PRT rule-of-law team also holds district leader training classes. In the last two months more than 300 villager elders attended the trainings in five of the province's seven districts.

"We are trying to build the knowledge of the community for a good government with a good understanding of law," said Nickzad.

The PRT rule-of-law team plans to build the knowledge of the community by informing teachers of the province as well. "Sometimes it's hard for kids to understand law so we have come up with a program for teachers which will be held at the Panjshir Teacher Training Institute," said Nickzad. "We plan to train around 800 school teachers to give them a basic understanding of law and the rights of men and women."

The training for the teachers will begin in the next two months and will clarify the relationship between Sharia law and constitutional law.

"Many villagers have the concern that the constitutional law is against Sharia law, and the teacher training course will cover the relationship of the two with a basic introduction of the Afghanistan constitution," said Nackzad. "We want to point out that constitutional law isn't different; it's not anything that goes against Islam."

The Panjshir PRT RoL team said they see the importance of rule of law and strives to inform the public and empower the people.

Panjshir Department of Education Director Abdul Moqim Halimi told Anaba High School students, "You should know the rules, because if you know the rules you can serve your people and be a leader of Afghanistan in the future."

Panjshir PRT helps bring village drinking water

PANJSHIR PROVINCE, Afghanistan, May 24, 2011—U.S. Army 1st Lt. Hakan Togul, Panjshir Provincial Reconstruction Team civil affairs lead and Crete, Ill., native, speaks with a village elder about a project to bring drinking water to Astana village in Bazarak Municipality, Afghanistan. Previously, the village had only irrigation water from the river in the valley at their disposal. The PRT provided materials while the villagers provided the funds for the labor. (Photo by U.S. Air Force Senior Airman Darin Pugh, Panjshir Provincial Reconstruction Team)

By U.S. Air Force Senior Airman Amber Ashcraft
Panjshir Provincial Reconstruction Team Public Affairs

PANJSHIR PROVINCE, Afghanistan, May 24—The Panjshir Provincial Reconstruction Team civil affairs visited a village in Bazarak Municipality, Afghanistan to assess the final stages of a system designed to supply clean drinking water.

According to the PRT, Astana villagers had only irrigation water from the river in the valley at their disposal.

"They previously had no other way to obtain clean water for drinking and cooking," said U.S. Army 1st Lt. Hakan Togul, PRT civil affairs lead and Crete,

Ill., native. "The water from the river is unsanitary and was making some of the villagers sick."

After villagers spoke to the local Community Development Council about the issue, the CDC brought the idea to the PRT civil affairs team.

"We were concerned more villagers would become sick from the conditions of the water," said Idi Mohammad, a CDC member, through an interpreter. "We asked for help from the PRT so this village could have the clean water they needed."

The PRT bought the materials required to build a piping system from a natural mountain spring more than 2,000 meters above the village. The villagers collected funds amongst themselves to help pay for the labor of the workers laying the pipe.

To determine how much water each household is using, engineers will install meters to track water usage.

"The villagers will be charged a small fee for the amount being used and apply the money toward the maintenance of the meters and piping system," said Togul. "They made their own contribution to the upkeep of this project with no prompting from the PRT. This shows great initiative by the village, and it makes me very happy to help."

Laborers from the local area dug and placed the piping.

"The village has gone long enough without proper drinking water, so completing the project as efficiently and as fast as possible is our goal," said Mohammad.

After more than a month of planning and construction, the project is in its final stages of completion. The village expects to have access to clean drinking water within two weeks.

"The Panjshiris are proud people and are concerned about their community," added Togul. "We have a great working relationship, and seeing their dedication to serve themselves to develop their province shows great initiative."

Task Force Red Bulls fight
their largest battle since WWII

NURISTAN PROVINCE, May 25, 2011—U.S. Army Soldiers with the Reconnaissance Platoon, Headquarters and Headquarters Company, 1st Battalion, 133rd Infantry Regiment, Task Force Ironman, 2nd Brigade Combat Team, 34th Infantry Division, Task Force Red Bulls, prepare to board a Ch-47 Chinook helicopter before an air assault into a valley near Do Ab village, Nuristan Province, Afghanistan at Forward Operating Base Mehtar Lam. (Photo by U.S. Army Spc. Kristina L. Gupton, Task Force Red Bulls)

By U.S Army Staff Sgt. Ryan C. Matson
Task Force Red Bulls Public Affairs

NURISTAN PROVINCE, Afghanistan, May 25, 2011—Soldiers of Task Force Red Bulls in Nuristan Province, Afghanistan, fought the largest battle of the 34th Infantry Division since World War II, May 25.

The battle involved only about 40 U.S. service members from the Reconnaissance Platoon from Headquarters and Headquarters Company, and six Soldiers assigned to Company C, both of 1st Battalion, 133rd Infantry Regiment, Task Force Ironman, 2nd Brigade Combat Team, 34th Infantry Division, Task Force Red Bulls, and about 20 of their Afghan counterparts.

Yet this small group of Soldiers thwarted an ambush from an enemy force numbering in the hundreds, killing more than 200 insurgent fighters in an intense battle lasting seven hours. The Soldiers said the most amazing part of the whole conflict, though, there wasn't one coalition forces casualty.

"Everybody there in uniform stepped up and did exactly what they're supposed to do," said U.S. Army Capt. Garrett H. Gingrich, the commander of Company C, 1-133rd Inf., from Dysart, Iowa, and one of six Company C

Soldiers who participated in the battle. "Everybody did their job and it was just an amazing, miraculous thing that nobody (from the coalition) got hurt."

"All I can figure is there was somebody watching over us," U.S. Army Staff Sgt. Luke Chatfield, C Company's joint fires observer from Floyd, Iowa, added.

The battle took place in Do Ab, a village in northern Nuristan Province, about 15 miles north of Combat Outpost Kalagush.

"What some people don't realize is that not every piece of land in our area of operation is reachable by ground or on daily operations," U.S. Army 1st Lt. Justin Foote, platoon leader of the Reconnaissance Platoon, HHC, 1-133rd Inf., said. "This was the premier case of that. None of our guys had ever pushed up to Do Ab, and it had been two to three years since any coalition forces had been up there."

U.S. Army Maj. Aaron Baugher, the battalion operations officer and the battle's senior ground forces commander, explained how Task Force Ironman Soldiers wound up in Do Ab.

"There is a district center in Do AB, which would compare to a county courthouse back in the United States," Baugher explained. "There is also a police headquarters building and a small clinic."

"The reports we received were that the Do Ab Afghan Uniformed Police were attacked by 400 insurgents, and the district center and police observation posts were overrun. There wasn't a lot of information. Initially, our job was to seize back the district center. However, the mission eventually changed to securing the landing zone and some high ground, and getting into a position where we could cover a team of Afghan commandos and U.S. forces, so that they could go ahead and clear Do Ab."

What Baugher did know was that it was 8 a.m., and higher headquarters had given him until 10 a.m. to get some troops to Do Ab to determine what the situation in Do Ab really was.

Baugher summoned the Reconnaissance Platoon, as well as Gingrich and his team from C Company, who immediately flew down to FOB Mehtar Lam from Kalagush to meet with the Recon Platoon.

"They said to be at the flightline in 45 minutes, packed for three days, and that's about all we heard at first," U.S. Army Staff Sgt. Jeremy Buhr, the sniper section leader with Recon Platoon from Waverly, Iowa, recalled. "At the flightline, we found out a little more—that the DC had been taken over by Taliban. Intelligence is sometimes a little skewed and sometimes when they say 400 insurgent fighters they mean more like 50-75, but when we got up there ... I can believe that number. We'd definitely never seen anywhere near the number of enemy fighters that we saw at Do Ab."

Baugher, Foote and his men and Gingrich's team boarded two CH-47 Chinook helicopters to fly to Do Ab. The helicopters landed about 300 meters apart, one to the north one to the south in the only suitable landing zone in the area.

"We saw the terrain we were headed into out the window and it was really, really steep," Buhr recalled. "Physically, the slopes were straight up. It was maybe 150 meters wide east to west in a riverbed; the worst terrain I had ever seen. We could literally only move north toward the district center, or south."

The Recon Platoon Soldiers have climbed hundreds of mountains throughout their year in Afghanistan and said this was "hands down" the worst terrain they had faced. They also said it was the ultimate place for an enemy ambush, which is exactly what happened. Once in the valley, they faced immediate contact.

"As soon as we got off the (helicopter), we took indirect fire from mortars, small-arms fire and Rocket-Propelled Grenades," U.S. Army Spc. Nathan Cunningham, an infantry scout with Recon Platoon recalled.

"The first explosion I heard was an airburst RPG that was aimed at the Chinook, and it was really close," Buhr said. "Every weapons system that the Taliban uses was probably fired at us that day!"

There was nothing to do but seek cover and return fire, the Soldiers said.

"My chalk exited and the first thing we did was immediately run to whatever cover we could find, which ended up being two rocks separated by maybe 30 meters," said U.S. Army Sgt. Edward Kane, an infantry team leader who volunteered for the deployment, and a Portland, Ore., native. "You could run north and south, but the cover was very sparse."

Another problem the Soldiers said they faced was enemy's position. The insurgents held the high ground and were using what is known as plunging fire to shoot over their cover. The coalition forces were in one of the worst positions imaginable.

"So we laid down suppressive fire on all the enemy locations and tried to establish fire superiority, using direct fires, sniper fires, indirect fires with our mortar team," Foote said.

Within 10 minutes, Apache helicopters joined the fight, but the enemy continued to attack.

The Soldiers held off the enemy attack in the landing zone area for the better part of an hour, but knew they needed to move to a better position.

"I made the call that we needed cover and needed to move to a series of khalats, animal pens actually, to the north," Baugher said. "It was the best cover available—other than that we were sitting on the LZ with some boulders just trying to find some cover there with bullets bouncing all around."

The Close Air Support forces gave the Recon Platoon enough of a break in the action via fire superiority to allow the Soldiers to reach the animal pens without much resistance, Foote said.

For six hours the Soldiers, along with their ANA counterparts, fought off the enemy. Meanwhile, the enemy continued to swarm around them in the mountains above, slowly drawing nearer to their positions in the animal pens. The Soldiers did not know it at the time, but the enemy also had heavily fortified fighting positions: chest-high trenches dug into solid rock.

The Soldiers said they continued to fight, but as the enemy drew closer, air assets started to make the difference in the battle. The Joint Terminal Attack Controllers, U.S. Air Force Airmen who communicate with Army and Air Force aircraft from the ground, ran into the open between the khalats to get information from the Soldiers to determine where the rounds were coming from.

"Everybody started helping out the JTACs, calling out distance and direction and stuff," Buhr said. The JTACs used the information to target the enemy positions and called in Close Air Support.

Meanwhile, the Soldiers in the khalats continued to fight and kill the enemy, but the insurgent forces continued to draw nearer. Their shots also became more accurate. A sniper fired within inches of some of the members from Recon Platoon in one of the khlalats.

"There was a little doorway they were zeroed in on, and we continually took sniper fire throughout the whole night," U.S. Army Spc. Aaron McNew, a machine gunner from Cedar Falls, Iowa, said.

"We were surrounded 360-degrees and each squad was fighting their own separate fight at this point," Buhr said.

Foote said the platoon pushed out a squad to an eastern ridgeline which immediately took enemy fire.

"I wasn't up there more than about 10 minutes when I started taking fire from about 25 meters away," Kane said. "I don't think they knew we were there, but they were just trying to shoot in the general direction they thought we were."

"It got to the point where we dropped bombs literally 250 meters from our position because we had the enemy that close," Baugher said.

Dropping massive bombs that close to U.S. forces, just outside the bomb's maximum effective range, left no room for error by the JTAC or the pilots, and was a very difficult decision to make, U.S. Air Force Tech. Sgt. Tavis Delaney, a JTAC with the 116th Air Support Operations Squadron, Washington Air National Guard, said.

Delaney and U.S. Air Force Senior Airman Michael McCaffrey, a JTAC apprentice with the 116th ASOS, based out of Tacoma, Wash., and the U.S. Air Force Tactical Air Control Party with Task Force Ironman, worked with

Chatfield as part of Gingrich's team to hone in on the enemy positions.

"We held them off and the JTACs dropped bombs, and we dropped mortars," Cunningham, who said he shot more than 500 rounds from his machine gun, said. "When it hit, we felt the concussion, and there were rocks raining down on us."

The Soldiers of the Recon Platoon said the bombs were necessary, and made the difference in the battle.

"If they hadn't been there dropping bombs, I don't know that we would have gotten out of that valley," Kane said. "They were getting closer and more accurate."

Baugher said the amount of munitions used demonstrated just how big the engagement was.

"If you looked at just the munitions we dropped, you can see how this was easily the biggest single engagement the division has been in since World War II," Baugher said.

During the operation, close air-support used 500-pound bombs, 105 mm and 40 mm cannon rounds from an AC-130 gunship, hellfire missiles and rockets from the rocket pods. The group troops also expended thousands of rounds. "That's pretty huge."

Chatfield said the efforts of the pilots were crucial in helping save the lives of the infantry fighters on the ground.

"I give a lot of credit to the pilots, both rotary and fixed wing," Chatfield said. "They came in under fire each time we needed them to. They were getting shot at and still were able to get on target time and time again and didn't hesitate. We had (aircraft) come down the valley lower than any fixed wing I've ever seen before, and they were getting shot at there, too, and they didn't care."

After Recon Platoon and Gingrich's small group of Soldiers had fended off the enemy through six hours of fighting, the Afghan commandos and additional American forces arrived in two Chinooks around 7 p.m. There were originally supposed to be two separate drops of reinforcing Soldiers. However, due to the intensity of the gunfire, as well as deteriorating weather conditions, the team of Chinooks only made one run.

"There was a burst from an RPG about 10 meters from where the Chinook was going to land, so it was close," Baugher said.

The Recon Platoon provided cover for the commandos and American forces while they cleared the Do Ab District Center. After a final burst of enemy resistance, the battle ended.

"They got fire for about another hour and a half, maybe two hours after that, and then there was total silence," Baugher said. "We found out later ... the remaining insurgents had broken contact and fled. The Apaches, and AC-130 gunship had dropped a final heavy series of bombs, causing them to finally flee, and preventing additional attacks."

"We spent the next two days securing the district center and doing some patrols through the villages. Not a single shot was fired during that time."

It has been a long year of fighting the enemy for the Soldiers of Recon Platoon. But there is one thing they could all say definitively about the battle at Do Ab.

"Nothing was comparable to this," Foote said. "Nothing."

NURISTAN PROVINCE, May 25, 2011—U.S. Army Soldiers with the Reconnaissance Platoon, Headquarters and Headquarters Company, 1st Battalion, 133rd Infantry Regiment, Task Force Ironman, 2nd Infantry Brigade Combat Team, 34th Mountain Division, Task Force Red Bulls, seek cover and return fire near Do Ab village, Nuristan Province, Afghanistan, after air-assaulting into the valley May 25. (Photo by U.S. Army Spc. Nathan Cunningham, Task Force Ironman)

Ironman truck drivers perform wartime delivery on Black Hawk

LAGHMAN PROVINCE, Afghanistan, May 25, 2011—Soldiers from the 1st Battalion, 133rd Infantry Regiment, Task Force Ironman, a part of the Iowa National Guard's 2nd Brigade Combat Team, 34th Infantry Division, Task Force Red Bulls, load "speedballs"—black bags filled for re-supply missions—at Forward Operating Base Mehtar Lam, Afghanistan. (Photo by U.S. Army Spc. Kristina L. Gupton, Task Force Red Bulls Public Affairs)

By U.S. Army Staff Sgt. Ryan C. Matson
Task Force Red Bulls Public Affairs

LAGHMAN PROVINCE, Afghanistan, May 25, 2011—There is an old Soldier's expression: Don't volunteer for anything.

The theory behind the expression is that a Soldier may not like the duty or detail for which they volunteered.

But even after delivering bags of supplies under heavy enemy-fire to infantry troops engaged in a fierce battle in the mountains of Nuristan Province, U.S. Army Spc. Tyler Parker-Bellinger, a truck driver from Cedar Rapids, Iowa, with Company E, 1st Battalion, 133rd Infantry Regiment, Task Force Ironman, a part of the Iowa National Guard's 2nd Brigade Combat Team, 34th Infantry Division, Task Force Red Bulls, said he would volunteer to do it all again.

"We were up at the flightline helping load the bags," said Parker-Bellinger, who is deployed to Forward Operating Base Mehtar Lam, Afghanistan. "A bird landed and said they needed a couple guys to help unload it. I figured, being a truck driver, I don't get to ride on a helicopter too much, so I said, 'All right.'"

The bags, known as speedballs, are black bags filled with water, food and ammunition sent to troops in heavy contact as part of a quick re-supply mission.

On the afternoon of May 25, Soldiers from the Reconnaissance Platoon, Headquarters and Headquarters Company, 1-133rd Inf., were experiencing heavy contact near Do Ab village, Nuristan Province.

Knowing troops were in contact and pinned down, the entire distribution platoon, along with every available officer and enlisted Soldier, worked on the flightline putting the bags together, Parker-Bellinger said. The hastily-assembled team packaged about 25 bags before helicopters from Company A, 1st Battalion, 169th Combat Aviation Brigade, arrived to deliver the supplies to the troops in contact.

U.S. Army Sgt. Jared Henkle, a truck driver from Cincinnati, Iowa, was one of the Soldiers from Company E's distribution platoon loading bags when the helicopters arrived.

"Spc. Parker-Bellinger and another Soldier were going to go first, but the commander pulled the other Soldier off and put me on it, because she needed a Non-Commissioned Officer ... big enough to throw the bags off the bird," Henkle said. Both he and Parker-Bellinger stand over 6 feet tall and weigh more than 200 pounds.

The pair said the bags weighed several hundred pounds. The bags of water contained 14 cases each and ammunition speedballs contained in excess of 1,000 rounds of 5.65, .320 and 7.62 mm rounds.

Henkle said the crew chief kept the experience calm with humor.

"They were real laid back about it when we took off," Henkle said. "The gunner on my side asked what we did in the Army and we told them we were truck drivers."

"He said, 'Oh this will kind of be the same thing. You deliver supplies, we deliver supplies, kind of the same deal.'"

Henkle said he and Parker-Bellinger started hearing gunfire as the helicopter was about 20 yards from landing. "Just hearing that much fire and knowing you're about to be landing in the middle of it ... that's when it all kind of hit me," Henkle said. "We knew it was hot up there, but we didn't know it would be right by the landing zone like that.

"Once we got to the designated landing zone, immediately there was small arms fire, medium arms fire, and Rocket-Propelled Grenade fire," Parker-Bellinger said.

At that point, the two said, only one thing was on their minds—get the supplies out as quickly as possible. "Once the doors opened, I couldn't even tell you that I heard much of anything, we were just throwing bags as fast as we could," said Henkle.

"We got out nine of the 10 bags before our bird took off," Parker-Bellinger. "The other bird didn't even unload anything because they were taking so much fire."

Both helicopters returned safely to FOB Mehtar Lam, but the second helicopter sustained small-arms damage to the engine and rear fuselage.

Henkle said the gunners could not return fire due to the steep elevation of the valley around them, which prevented them from getting positive identification the insurgent's location. Instead, several of the crew chiefs left their guns and helped unload the supplies. Parker-Bellinger and Henkle threw the bags from inside the aircraft, while the crew chiefs exited the aircraft to assist them.

The crew reported seeing numerous RPGs fired at the aircraft, and rounds landing within feet of the aircraft and personnel. Henkle said the gunner heard rounds hitting the ground right behind him, and when he returned to the base he was visibly shaking. During the unloading of the aircraft, an RPG also landed within 50 yards of the aircraft.

"We heard sort of a muffled explosion, and saw the black smoke," Henkle said.

Henkle and Parker-Bellinger said they were not on the ground more than a minute, yet it was one of the most intense moments of their lives. The two, who have completed about 120 convoy missions through northeastern Afghanistan, had been in convoys which took fire, but both said they had never experienced an attack of that magnitude.

"We were talking about it later," Henkle said. "And with all the adrenaline, those bags were a lot lighter when we were throwing them off the birds than when we were loading them up!"

Due to the damage to the aircraft, as well as an imminent storm, the crews did not return for a second resupply.

U.S. Army Capt. Jodi Marti of Knoxville, Iowa, Henkle and Parker-Bellinger's company commander, said she was proud of her Soldiers' performance. "When they got back and landed, the air mission commander raved about how well they did and said he'd love to take them back if they could come back for a return trip, which didn't end up happening," she said.

"I'm very proud of them. They jumped right up and even though they might not have known exactly what they were getting into, they went anyway, and when they got to the task at hand, they never hesitated, and did what they went up there to do. Not too bad for a couple of truck drivers from Iowa!"

Kansas ADT-III conducts spur ride

LAGHMAN PROVINCE, Afghanistan, May 25, 2011—Spur-holders U.S. Army Staff Sgt. Ryan L. Pierce of Newton, Kan. (left front), a squad leader for the 3/6 Kansas Cavalry Agribusiness Development Team-III; and Sgt. 1st Class Eric Kaltenborn from Manhattan, Kan. (left rear), the Security Platoon sergeant also with the ADT, watch as spur ride candidate U.S. Air Force Senior Airman Melissa Hidalgo Mendez demonstrates her weapon skills with the M16 rifle during her trek through the spur-ride conducted on Forward Operating Base Mehtar Lam, Afghanistan. Hidalgo, an Air Force medic from Topeka, Kan. became the first female Air Force National Guardsman out of Kansas to earn her spurs with the cavalry by completing the spur ride. (Photo by U.S. Air Force Senior Airman Ronifel S. Yasay, Laghman Provincial Reconstruction Team)

LAGHMAN PROVINCE, Afghanistan, May 25, 2011—A soldier wearing the Cavalry Stetson is silhouetted by the morning sun at Forward Operating Base Mehtar Lam, Afghanistan, while candidates compete in a spur ride to earn the right to wear their Stetson. Following successful completion of the competition, participants earned the honor of wearing the traditional Cavalry Stetson and spurs at official Armor and Cavalry functions. (Photo by U.S. Air Force Senior Airman Ronifel S. Yasay, Laghman Provincial Reconstruction Team)

LAGHMAN PROVINCE, Afghanistan, May 25, 2011—Spur ride candidate, U.S. Army Sgt. Paul Olson of Manhattan, Kan. (center), a truck gunner, raises his arm in celebration as he and teammates 1st Lt. Benjamin Pimpl from Olpe, Kan. (left rear), the Security Platoon leader; and Sgt. 1st Class James M. Swafford of Emporia, Kan. (right), the senior maintenance officer; all with the 3/6 Kansas Cavalry Agribusiness Development Team-III, finish the last of their ruck-march iterations on Forward Operating Base Mehtar Lam, Afghanistan, May 25. Because of Olson's enthusiasm, the other spur ride candidates voted Olson as the most-motivated candidate. (Photo by U.S. Army Staff Sgt. Brandon Schultz, 3/6 Kansas Cavalry Agribusiness Development Team-III)

Guard CSM visits troops in Afghanistan

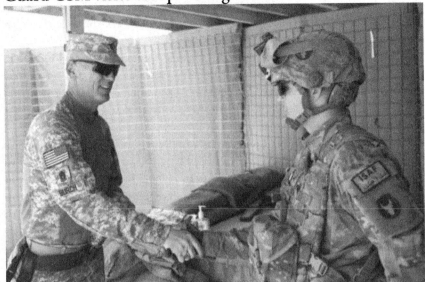

PARWAN PROVINCE, Afghanistan, May 27, 2011—Command Sgt. Maj. Richard J. Burch, the command sergeant major of the Army National Guard and Lincoln, Neb. native, shakes the hand of Spc. Vernon Moore, a military policeman and gunner from Washington, Iowa, with Headquarters and Headquarters Troop, 1st Squadron, 113th Cavalry Regiment, Task Force Redhorse, a part of the 2nd Brigade Combat Team, 34th Infantry Division, at the entry control point on Joint Combat Outpost Pul-e-Sayad, Afghanistan. Burch visited the JCOP during a battlefield rotation he conducted with Command Sgt. Maj. of the Army Raymond F. Chandler, the senior enlisted Soldier for the Army. (Photo by U.S. Army Spc. James Wilton, Task Force Red Bulls Public Affairs)

By U.S. Army Spc. James Wilton
Task Force Red Bulls Public Affairs

PARWAN PROVINCE, Afghanistan May 27, 2011 —U.S. Army Command Sgt. Maj. Richard J. Burch, the command sergeant major of the Army National Guard and Lincoln, Neb. native, visited Soldiers from Troop A, 1st Squadron, 113th Cavalry Regiment at Joint Combat Outpost Pul-e-Sayad, Afghanistan May 27.

The visit was a part of a battlefield circulation Burch and Command Sgt. Maj. of the Army Raymond F. Chandler, the senior enlisted Soldier of the Army, conducted in Afghanistan over the past week.

"The main reason the Sergeant Major of the Army and I came out was to talk with the leadership and the Soldiers to make sure we are working on the right things back in D.C. to help them in their missions here in Afghanistan and making sure that they're prepared, equipped, trained and ready to conduct the missions that are expected of them here in theater."

Burch spoke with the Task Force Redhorse Soldiers, a part of the 2nd Brigade Combat Team, 34th Infantry Division, Task Force Red Bulls, about life on the JCOP, their plans for the future, and whether they keep up with family back home.

The Soldiers had a range of questions for Burch, including those regarding changes in uniform standards, the effect of the active force draw down on National Guard troops, and the upcoming change to the Army Physical Fitness Test. Burch addressed these concerns during an informal sit down at the JCOP's dining facility.

"The biggest thing that anyone in a leadership position needs to make sure and relay to the Soldiers is that we want to hear what is important to them, and we are working on those issues to try and help make the quality of life for the Soldiers better," said Burch. "We must ensure that our focus is on the Soldiers, the units and the missions that they are going to be expected to participate in. These things must receive our attention so we can make sure that we are doing the right things to best prepare them for the future."

The Soldiers said they appreciated his insights.

"I think his comments and answers had a positive impact on the Soldiers," said U.S. Army 1st Sgt. Chad Schweitzberger, the Troop A first sergeant from Moville, Iowa. "It seems we are serving in the Iowa National Guard and the U.S. Army in a time where there are a lot of questions about the present and future. These questions seem to be on everyone's minds, so it was great he was here to provide us with some of his insight on the topics."

Answering Soldiers' questions is only part of visits like these. They also help to connect Soldiers with the Army's higher-level leadership.

"Solders see their leadership in pictures on walls, read articles about their leadership in magazines and on the Internet, when they get an opportunity to meet them in person it adds something more to it," said Schweitzberger. "I think the Soldiers have a better appreciation for leadership after the visit is over. It shows the Soldiers, he cares enough to come and see how they are living and conducting day-to-day operations."

Burch said, like many leaders in the armed forces, does care about his troops and their families and he wanted to make sure they were aware of that.

"We obviously recognize the scarifies that the families and employers are making and we want to make it perfectly clear that we know that we can't do what we are doing these days in Afghanistan and Iraq without their continued support and continued understanding," said Burch. "The big picture can't happen without that support of those families and employers out there."

On a final note, Burch touched on a subject that is troubling him and many leaders through out the U.S. military.

"The National Guard and the Army as a whole has experienced a very troubling spike in suicides in 2010," said Burch. "There are so many stressors that impact our soldiers and our families out there and the military is part of those stressors that hit them. We don't want to continue to be part of the problem we want to be part of the solution."

Emphasis on communication and seeking out assistance is needed in order to not let things like financial or relationship trouble get to a point where Soldiers think they have no other way out, Burch explained.

"It is not all about always being ready for the missions, it is about being there and being ready to assist the Soldiers and the families in there times of need," said Burch. "Whatever it might be... we are here and always ready to be there for them, to help them out."

Dand Patan cooks keep it hot

By U.S. Army Staff Sgt. Ashlee Lolkus
Task Force Red Bulls Public Affairs

PAKTYA PROVINCE, Afghanistan, May 28, 2011—In the '80s, a U.S. Army recruiting commercial said, "In the Army, we do more before 9 a.m. than most people do all day."

That is the reality for the food service Non-Commissioned Officers of Company B, 1st Battalion, 168th Infantry Regiment, Task Force Lethal, charged with feeding Soldiers at Combat Outpost Dand Patan.

U.S. Army Sgt. Antonio Santiago IV of Boone, Iowa, and U.S. Army Sgt. Jeremy Ewoldt of Persia, Iowa, are responsible for feeding the Soldiers of Company B, a part of the Iowa National Guard's 2nd Brigade Combat Team, 34th Infantry Division, Task Force Red Bulls.

"We cook 336 meals a day, seven days a week," said Ewoldt. "We do three hots a day."

"Never done an MRE lunch!" Santiago said matter-of-factly.

"The whole time we've been here. We've never done MREs," Ewoldt repeated.

The three "hots" Ewoldt mentioned are the three hot meals they serve the Soldiers each day. This saves the Soldiers the trouble of having to eat an MRE. A "Meal, Ready-to-Eat" is a type of prepackaged tactical ration that serves one Soldier.

MREs have never been very popular with service members, a fact not lost on Santiago and Ewoldt. They said they believe most Soldiers appreciate having hot meals for every meal, although it's not something their fellow Soldiers are vocal about.

Ewoldt, having served 19-and-a-half years as both an infantryman and a cook understands that you don't always get recognition being a cook in the military.

"Being able to see this situation from both sides, I can recognize that they are just focused on their mission," said Ewoldt. "It's not a glamorous job, so many (infantrymen) don't really notice it," he said of the meals they prepare. "We've been fortunate to have some kitchen patrol help who take notice to the amount of work we put in, and that's come as the deployment has gone along...

"They bust our chops, but it's guaranteed: if you're with the infantry, they're going to bust your chops," Ewoldt said with a smile.

U.S. Army 1st Sgt. Christopher Casey of Neola, Iowa, and the senior enlisted Soldier of Company B. said the infantry soldiers may grumble from time to time about the menu, the available snacks or having to perform KP duty, but they appreciate the hot meals. "It doesn't matter what happened on a mission or whatever they did that day ... they know they have a good, hot meal waiting for them at the end of the day," Casey said.

Ewoldt said he plans the meals out a couple weeks in advance and orders the food re-supply based on that plan.

"It helps to have people give suggestions as well," he said. "Someone suggested grilled sandwiches the other day and they were a hit. Everyone loved them because they were hot off the grill."

Santiago has worked in the food service industry since he was 16, and served as cook for all of his five years with the National Guard. He said getting used to being with the infantry has been a challenge. He was previously assigned to the 3655th Maintenance Company out of Camp Dodge, Iowa, before he volunteered to deploy to Afghanistan.

"I've been trying to volunteer for a deployment for the past two to three years and I finally got lucky to get on this one," Santiago said. He said there were differences between serving with the maintenance unit and serving with the infantry.

"It's different," Santiago said about being a cook in Afghanistan. "We don't have as much equipment here as we do stateside, so it makes things a lot more challenging. That, plus with the work space we have, it's not really big. But, overall, it's not too bad."

Casey said the cooks bring variety to the table.

"Sgt. Ewoldt is a more seasoned veteran with lots of experience and Sgt. Santiago is the young, energetic NCO who keeps Soldiers entertained," said Casey.

Despite the differences in age and experience, the team of two said they work well together. They rotate the breakfast shifts to allow the other a few extra hours of rest. Even so, the two Soldiers don't get much down-time. A 15-or-more hour day is pretty common for them, and they do it day after day, but still manage to help the infantry company manage base operations if needed.

"If they need us for something else, they know that they can come and get us; even if it's for something like Entry Control Point duty or whatever," said Ewoldt.

Not only do they help with the base operations, Santiago has even helped the infantrymen on their daily missions.

"I've actually been on three missions. I'm stoked!" Santiago said. "I've been wanting to go on more, because I don't want to be (stuck on the base)."

Helping out around the COP and with missions allows the two to break up the monotony of the life of a cook in the Army, but they said they know their main mission is what is most important.

"I have told the cooks that the meals they prepare are the highest contributing factor to Soldier morale," said Casey.

PAKTYA PROVINCE, Afghanistan, May 28, 2011 —U.S. Army Sgt. Jeremy Ewoldt, native of Persia, Iowa, and one of two American food service Non-Commissioned Officers for Combat Outpost Dand Patan, Afghanistan, shows a contracted Afghan worker around the kitchen trailer unit May 28. Although Ewoldt is a part of Company F, 334th Brigade Support Battalion, he mainly supports Company B, 1st Battalion, 168th Infantry Regiment, both a part of 2nd Brigade Combat Team, 34th Infantry Division, Task Force Red Bulls. (Photo by U.S. Army Staff Sgt. Ashlee Lolkus, Task Force Red Bulls Public Affairs)

Operation Care donates goods to Afghans, Soldiers

BAGRAM AIRFIELD, Afghanistan, May 29, 2011—U.S. Army Sgt. 1st Class Heidi Lansing, a land management Non-Commissioned Officer from Ely, Iowa, with Company B, 334th Brigade Support Battalion, Task Force Archer, a part of the 2nd Brigade Combat Team, 34th Infantry Division, Task Force Red Bulls, distributes Operation Care humanitarian aid packages to an Afghan woman at Bagram Airfield, Afghanistan May 29. (U.S. Army photo by Spc. James Wilton, Task Force Red Bulls Public Affairs)

By U.S. Army Spc. James Wilton
Task Force Red Bulls Public Affairs

BAGRAM AIRFIELD, Afghanistan, May 29, 2011—Service members volunteering with Operation Care distributed more than 150 care packages filled with basic necessity items to Afghans exiting the entry control point near the Egyptian Hospital on Bagram Airfield, Afghanistan.

U.S. humanitarian organizations and personnel stationed on Bagram donated the items in the packages.

"We know that we aren't going to win the war by kicking down doors," said U.S. Army Staff Sgt. Derek Melendez a 1st Cavalry Division, Combined Joint Task Force–1 intelligence sergeant and the assistant director of Operation Care, from Philadelphia. "The way we are going to win is through the support of the people, so we provide what little amenities that we can and try to build a stronger relationship with the locals here in Bagram."

Operation Care is dedicated to the welfare of both the people of Afghanistan and International Security Assistance Forces, according to their mission statement. [The effort is] deployed by ISAF to fight the insurgency.

Clothing, food, pens, pencils, schoolbooks and other school supplies are a big part of what the program distributes to the Afghan people. Amidst the poverty-stricken families, items like this are often considered frivolous but according to Melendez, the children would disagree.

"The kids are more vocal and they will tell you that they don't have things like books," said Melendez. "For them, it means being able to go to school and have the basic supplies and things that they need to just be a student."

The volunteers don't let this request go unheard, and the Afghan children make sure they know how grateful they are, he said.

"They're always happy and excited when we come," said Melendez. "They're always very grateful, saying thanks for the help that we provide to them."

This gratitude, while more than enough payment, is not the only reason the service members said they take the time out of their day to help the program.

"It is a way to give back and help out. I feel that there is a part of Afghanistan that I didn't get to see," said U.S. Army Sgt. 1st Class Heidi Lansing, a land management Non-Commissioned Officer from Ely, Iowa, part of Company B, 334th Brigade Support Battalion, Task Force Archer, a part of the 2nd Brigade Combat Team, 34th Infantry Division, Task Force Red Bulls. "I volunteer in order to do something and help out where I can, it is an aspect of our military jobs that I enjoy."

Selfless service and doing what is right are common themes among the volunteers but some said they have more personal reasons.

"I grew up without a lot of things, so for me (it's about being able) to give back and not have a kid go to school without a book or spend a winter without a warm coat and the basic necessities that we take for granted," said Melendez. "I think it is a good thing to do, giving back to the people. No matter what country you are in."

The program distributes packages to more than just locals. They also send basic supplies out to service members stationed at remote outposts.

"I think that the packages let the Soldiers know that somebody cares for them," said Lansing. "We put the basics into the packages what many of the Soldiers without Post Exchanges can't get. So I am pretty sure that they are grateful for what we send them."

The volunteers work with Operation Care in their off-time three days a week, to sort and assemble the packages for distribution. They said they do it because they know how important the items are to both the Afghans and service members. "What I have learned since I have been working with Operation Care is the overwhelming generosity of the American people," said

Lansing. "We get so many packages from individuals to large organizations or groups."

Lansing makes sure all the contributors know their donations are appreciated.

"I write thank you letters to all the people and organizations telling them how much everything they are sending means to the Soldiers and Afghan people," she said.

The distributions occur once every 30 days, but the program needs volunteers through the week to prep the items.

For more information or to volunteer, visit www.operation careafghanistan.net.

Panjshir promotes tourism development

PANJSHIR PROVINCE, Afghanistan, May 28, 2011—Katherine Haddon, Agence France Presse Kabul Bureau Chief, takes a picture at Bambarda Pass in Paryan District, Afghanistan. Haddon, along with more than 20 other international media and tourism experts attended the two-day Panjshir Tourism Development Conference to become familiar with tourism opportunities in the province and network with potential partners. (Photo by U.S. Air Force Senior Airman Amber Ashcraft, Panjshir Provincial Reconstruction Team Public Affairs)

By U.S. Air Force Senior Airman Amber Ashcraft
Panjshir Provincial Reconstruction Team Public Affairs

PANJSHIR PROVINCE, Afghanistan, May 29, 2011—International media representatives, tourism experts, and Afghan officials made up the more than 50 attendees to the two-day Panjshir Tourism Development Conference May 28- 29.

Officials held the conference to attract investors and tour operators to Panjshir as a tourism destination, taking advantage of its natural beauty, the proximity to the country's capital and the overall security, said Bill Martin, Panjshir Provincial Reconstruction Team director and Arlington, Va., native.

"The main idea of the conference was to stimulate the interest in tourism development and social opportunities for the province," said Martin. "With a goal of increased local jobs and income, we wanted to look at tourism in a way that minimizes cultural and environmental impacts."

The first day, visitors flew in to Shahr Bland village in Paryan District,

574

the northern most district in Panjshir and began their tour of the province with a breakfast with District Gov. Abdul Jalil and local elders.

Spending their day in Panjshir as tourists themselves, the group traveled south to see the many views of the mountain-filled province centered around the Panjshir River. The group also stopped at a local bazaar and Ahmad Shah Massoud's Tomb.

"This place has great natural beauty with amazing mountains, a beautiful river and fresh air," said Marshall Ferrin, Afghan Investment Support Agency senior investment advisor. "There is a great potential for outdoor activities in Panjshir, and I'm sure our adventurer friends here will see that opportunity."

Throughout the day, the Panjshir PRT escorted the group and spoke with them about their experiences in the province.

"Though we're here on a deployment, we've still been able to be out in the valley among the people and learn about their culture," said U.S. Air Force Senior Airman Darin Pugh, Panjshir PRT vehicle operator and Tacoma, Wash., native. "Thinking about the prospect of being able to come back to Afghanistan in the future and vacation to Panjshir is pretty cool."

Deputy Gov. Abdul Rahman Kabiri hosted the group for a traditional Afghan dinner at the governor's compound.

"I believe the most appealing areas for tourism here are the outdoor activities," said Peter Jouvenal, co-owner of Gandamack Lodge in Kabul, Afghanistan and London native. "Fishing, kayaking, mountain biking, hiking-it's all here!"

The second day of the conference took place in the great hall of the newly dedicated Massoud Technical and Vocational School. The Panjshir Provincial Government supported by AISA and Panjshir PRT hosted the event.

Since Afghanistan has not had an active tourism industry for more than thirty years, Afghan government officials raised the need to create public awareness about tourism's benefits.

"We truly believe we have the capacity of attracting tourists to Panjshir," said Afghanistan Deputy Minister for Tourism Nabi Farahi, through an interpreter. "With support from our international colleagues and the Panjshiris utilizing their resources from the valley, the campaign for developing tourism here will hopefully be a success."

Participants brought up Panjshir's historic and natural attraction opportunities repeatedly.

"Think about why people travel; not only for sightseeing, but also for their health, for sports and cultural events," said John Heather, U.S. Agency for International Development officer and tourism development expert, to the conference attendees. "Bazarak Municipality may play a very important role in this. It has a government seat, a guesthouse, and easy access to restaurants, the river, and Massoud's Tomb. The soccer stadium that has the capacity for 18,000 spectators is literally right across the street."

"Imagine using the stadium's large potential to attract national teams for their summer practices; athletes like to train in high altitudes. Imagine what the fans can do in the valley, while they're not watching their favorite teams. With Panjshir having such a famous history of fighting the Soviets, and the Taliban under the leadership of Ahmad Shah Massoud, Massoud's Tomb will be an incredible attraction as well," he added.

Panjshir needs investments in hotel and restaurant infrastructure, designation of park and picnic areas, signage for historic and natural points of interest and linkages between outside investors and local residents, said Martin.

"As a PRT, we have spent most of our time and effort building up the basic infrastructure for the province. Now we believe it's time, and it's possible, for the private sector to work with the provincial authorities to develop tourism here. The United States will have a long-term development relationship with Panjshir and Afghanistan; we believe that tourism is a realistic approach to developing the economy of the province further," he said.

One of the issues addressed by numerous speakers during the conference was the support needed by the local community.

"One of the main things we need to work on is a public awareness campaign," said Kabiri. "Tourists are not coming here to take things from us or make fun of our culture."

The deputy minister stressed tourism is a way to preserve one's culture; not take away from it and it's vital that locals understand that.

"Our duty is to secure and save our culture; tourism plays an important role in the economic development of a country," said Farahi. "Introduction of this to our culture is very important."

He said the conference provided a first step in making tourism in Panjshir a reality.

"We're very excited about the prospects for tourism in Panjshir," said Kabiri. "We're looking forward to our colleagues from far places seeing how beautiful Panjshir is and showing them the many opportunities we have for them to invest."

Sweat earns pride, money for wounded warriors

BAGRAM AIRFIELD, Afghhanistan, May 29, 2011—U.S. Army Spc. Ashley O'Hearn (left), a brigade aviation operations specialist from Pipestone, Minn., shouts words of encouragement to U.S. Army Staff Sgt. Brenda Caldwell a supply sergeant from Omaha, Neb., Both are with the Iowa National Guard, 2nd Brigade Combat Team, 34th Infantry Division, Task Force Red Bulls. Caldwell is completing a round of push-ups during a Memorial Day "Murph" CrossFit workout at the clamshell gym on Bagram Airfield [...] (Photo by U.S. Army Spc. James Wilton, Task Force Red Bulls Public Affairs)

BAGRAM AIRFIELD, Afghhanistan, May 29, 2011—U.S. Army Sgt. Michael Sullivan, an Iowa National Guard, 2nd Brigade Combat Team, 34th Infantry Division, Task Force Red Bulls operations sergeant from Des Moines, Iowa, conducts a round of squats during a Memorial Day "Murph" CrossFit workout at the clamshell gym on Bagram Airfield [...] (Photo by U.S. Army Spc. James Wilton, Task Force Red Bulls Public Affairs)

BAGRAM AIRFIELD, Afghhanistan, May 29, 2011—U.S. Army Spc. Andrew Miller (left), a fire support specialist from Humboldt, Iowa; U.S. Army Spc. Torey Lasater (center), a brigade aviation operations specialist from Conrad, Iowa; and U.S. Army Maj. Eric Wieland (right), a fires support officer from West Des Moines, Iowa; all with the 2nd Brigade Combat Team, 34th Infantry Division, Task Force Red Bulls, finish their first one-mile run in front of the clamshell gym Bagram Airfield, Afghanistan during the Memorial Day "Murph" fundraiser. (Photo by U.S. Army Spc. James Wilton, Task Force Red Bulls Public Affairs)

PRT, GIRoA, ANSF build trust, distribute supplies in Paktya

PAKTYA PROVINCE, Afghanistan, May 29, 2011 —Afghan National Army soldiers distribute backpacks to young Afghans at the Gardez Orphanage in Gardez City, Afghanistan. The backpacks contained school supplies and humanitarian aid and were used to build trust between the ANA and the local population. (Photo by U.S. Air Force Staff Sgt. Barry Loo, Paktya Provincial Reconstruction Team Public Affairs)

By U.S. Air Force 1st Lt. Sybil Taunton
Paktya Provincial Reconstruction Team Public Affairs

PAKTYA PROVINCE, Afghanistan, May 29, 2011—Officials from the Government of the Islamic Republic of Afghanistan and Afghan National Security Forces handed out school supplies to children at a newly built school in Paktya Province, Afghanistan.

The visit was part of an education initiative between the GIRoA, ANSF, and the Paktya Provincial Reconstruction Team intended to increase trust and support between the local population and their government and military leaders.

The initiative, which kicked off in March, consists of opening ceremonies for new schools and the distribution of school supplies, and will continue through June.

Approximately 4,000 backpacks, cases of pens and pencils and small Afghan Flags, all made in Afghanistan and purchased as a way to infuse the local economy, have been distributed.

Additional school supplies and other items such as toys, clothes and athletic equipment, were donated by people and organizations from the United States.

"The level of support we received from families and organizations in the U.S. was phenomenal," said U.S. Air Force Capt. Donna Laulo, of the PRT from Payulap, Wash. "They sent us enough supplies to fill thousands of backpacks, which shows that our level of commitment to this country goes beyond just our service men and women."

The PRT collected the supplies and put together more than 12,000 backpacks containing basic school supplies, educational coloring books, flags, hand-crank radios and toys.

Mehrabbudin Shfaq, Paktya director of the Department of Education, and his staff coordinated the outreach missions that included visits with the principal of each school, as well as district sub-governors and village elders.

"It is very important for us to improve education in the province, and the children need those supplies," said Shfaq.

Haji Rasool Mohammad, vice president of the Mami Khail Construction Company, also participated in the project.

Mohammad had recently completed renovations to a school in the Jani Khel District, and volunteered to deliver backpacks to the students to celebrate the school's completion.

"People are very poor, and they cannot afford to buy notebooks and supplies," said Mohammad, "I'm very proud to deliver this, and I'm very happy to help the kids."

Religious and cultural advisors from the 203rd ANA Infantry Corps played a major role in the transportation and distribution of the supplies in the Gardez area.

Local ANA and Afghan Uniformed Police units took the lead in distributing the supplies to schools in districts throughout the remainder of the province.

"We didn't put on this uniform just to provide security," said ANA Sgt. Rohullah Akhund of Zormat District. "We want to help people and help the children get an education so they can have a better life and have peace."

JUNE
2011

Coalition forces foster relations between Afghan, U.S. students

PARWAN PROVINCE, Afghanistan, June 6, 2011—Gregory P. Macris, a U.S. State Department foreign service officer currently working with the Parwan Provincial Reconstruction Team, through the use of an interpreter, shows drawings to Afghan students at Number Two City Secondary School, in Charikar District, Afghanistan. U.S. students at Thomas Jefferson Elementary School in Macris' hometown of Falls Church, Va., made the drawings as a part of an art exchange program. (Photo by U.S. Army Spc. James Wilton, Task Force Red Bulls Public Affairs)

By U.S. Army Spc. James Wilton
Task Force Red Bulls Public Affairs

PARWAN PROVINCE, Afghanistan, June 6, 2011—Gregory P. Macris, a U.S. State Department foreign service officer currently working with the Parwan Provincial Reconstruction Team, visited the Number Two City Secondary School, in Charikar District, Afghanistan, June 6 to deliver drawings made for the Afghan students by U.S. second graders from Thomas Jefferson Elementary School in his hometown of Falls Church, Va.

"Today International Security Assistance Forces paid a visit to our school to share the knowledge and talents of students in Charikar and students in U.S.," said Fawzia Hakimi, the Afghan school's principal. "The U.S. students' paintings will encourage our students to work hard."

"I am very thankful for the visiting of ISAF to our school, their assistance is also very useful to us, it will encourage us to study hard and serve for the society," said Sona Sadat, a student at the Afghan school.

The program started with a visit Macris made to Thomas Jefferson Elementary School.

"I visited the class in the states and handed out some supplies," said Macris. "They drew their dogs, their houses and their football teams. The reaction to the art exchange was fantastic."

While visiting with the U.S. students, Macris did more than just ask for drawings, he also talked to them about Afghanistan and taught them a few words in Dari. Macris then brought those pictures with him and shared the pictures and attempts at writing Dari words with the Afghan students.

The Afghan students drew their own images for the U.S. students, which Macris will deliver when he returns to the states. Macris also taught the Afghan children the English words for the pictures they had drawn.

"This visit not only exchanges talent of both students, Afghan and U.S., it also encourages both students to know each other's culture and share their culture and information," said Adellah, a teacher at the Afghan school.

The art exchange is a part of a much larger idea. Macris hopes to one day build a sister city program.

"In the longer term, what I would like to do here is build what we call a sister city relationship between my hometown of Falls Church and Charikar, the capitol of Parwan," said Macris. "Long-term relationships, where the mayors and city council members visit their counterpart's respective cities and talk about things that city fathers have to face every day, things like fostering schools in times of declining budgets, property taxes or trash collection."

Starting a sister city project proved difficult. After running into officials with over-crowded schedules and lack of interest in the idea, Macris' had to rethink his strategy.

"I talked with other people in the sister city program and they said to try and start a smaller relationship," said Macris.

Macris' daughter, a student at Jefferson, suggested starting a smaller relationship with an art exchange program.

"What I am trying to do is start at the school level or even the classroom level," said Macris. "I am trying to create a link between that school and the girl's school here in Charikar."

Macris hopes this relationship will build and spread interest in the program and branch out into other parts of the community, making the idea of the sister city program more appealing to city officials. Macris' hopes the demographic of Falls Church will fuel support for the program.

"The area of Falls Church ... is married with a lot of military families and foreign service families," said Macris. "It is a very worldly city. The students already knew a little bit about Afghanistan, they could even point it out on a map."

They probably had a family member or two that served over here, continued Macris.

"I tell a funny story when I come over here to Afghanistan. In my area of Falls Church, a mile down one road and I can go to the Bamayan restaurant, and a mile up the other road I can go to the Panjshir restaurant," said Macris. "I literally have two Afghan restaurants on either side of me. It's like Parwan being sandwiched by Panjshir and Bamayan."

These two places on opposite sides of the world seem to be made for each other, continued Macris. He said he hopes his efforts will help build a stronger relationship and understanding between the Afghan and American people.

For now, though, the Afghan people are in the midst of trying to rebuild a shattered infrastructure, and in need of more than just a cultural exchange.

"Some of our students are not in a good economic situation, and are not able to buy stationery and other supplies to continue their studies," said Sadat. "We want the Afghan government and ISAF to pay more attention to our problems and supporting us to continue our studies."

Macris knows their plight so he invited along members of the 2nd Brigade Combat Team, 34th Infantry Division, Task Force Red Bulls, to distribute school supplies they collected.

"This humanitarian aid drop is what is going to leave much more of a lasting impression here because they've got a willing spirit but the flesh is weak, so to speak," said Macris. "The resources aren't there, so to be honest this is the thing that will really help."

Another young girl and her brother, with the help of their classmates from St. Francis of Assisi Catholic School in West Des

Moines, Iowa, collected a large amount of the school supplies. Elisabeth Wunn, 10, fourth grade, and Michael Wunn, 8, 2nd grade are the children of U.S. Army Maj. Michael Wunn from Clive, Iowa. Wunn is the Public Affairs Officer for 2nd Brigade Combat Team, 34th Infantry Division, Task Force Red Bulls.

Wunn's deployment has been difficult on his two oldest children. To help them understand, he visited their classrooms, and taught the students about Afghanistan and what the children were like. He explained that they were just like U.S. children, and enjoyed the same things, like coloring and soccer, but that they lived different, impoverished lives.

"We also talked about how soldiers have to make sacrifices as a part of their duties and how they make a difference in the world through their work," said Wunn. "The kids thought this was neat and they wanted to know how they could help out. So I suggested that they could collect school supplies and soccer balls to send to the kids in Afghanistan."

"I am happy, ISAF give me color pencils and a pen," said Ferdaws, 6, a student at the Afghan school. "I hope I will get toys in future." He later found out about the soccer balls and was ecstatic.

"Now through this exchange we've connected kids from Afghanistan, Falls Church, and West Des Moines," said Wunn. "That's pretty amazing if you think about it. What a great way to expand their horizons and learn a little about kids from other parts of the world."

The future of the program is uncertain, but through the minds and hearts of young children the program has a chance, said Macris. He said he will do all he can to make sure it comes to fruition.

"I am not sure what the next step will be, but when I go back to the states, my goal is to start working from that end to build this relationship," said Macris. "I know my successor quite well and he is coming here to continue to the work from this end, so I am thinking if we can do a little push/pull we can move this thing along."

PARWAN PROVINCE, Afghanistan, June 6, 2011—U.S. Army Maj. Michael Wunn from Clive, Iowa, a Public Affairs Officer with 2nd Brigade Combat Team, 34th Infantry Division, Task Force Red Bulls Public, passes out markers his children and other students of St. Francis of Assisi Catholic School in West Des Moines, Iowa, collected. (Photo by U.S. Army Spc. James Wilton, Task Force Red Bulls Public Affairs)

PARWAN PROVINCE, Afghanistan, June 6, 2011—An Afghan student at Number Two City Secondary School, Parwan Province, Afghanistan, shows off the drawing she made for students of Thomas Jefferson Elementary School, Falls Church, Va., during a visit from International Security Assistance Forces. (Photo by U.S. Army Spc. James Wilton, Task Force Red Bulls Public Affairs)

Panjshir PRT restores canal, drinking water

PANJSHIR PROVINCE, Afghanistan, June 1, 2011—U.S. Air Force Lt. Col. Joseph Blevins, Panjshir Provincial Reconstruction Team commander and Oregonia, Ohio, native, speaks with Community Development Council member Zianlar Bostan about projects in the Shutol District, Afghanistan June 1. A cement canal in Dehe Kalan village running from the river in to four villages downstream is being rebuilt after the previous year's spring floods damaged it. The canal allows the villages to have a consistent flow of irrigation and drinking water. (Photo by U.S. Air Force Senior Airman Amber Ashcraft, Panjshir Provincial Reconstruction Team Public Affairs)

By U.S. Air Force Senior Airman Amber Ashcraft
Panjshir Provincial Reconstruction Team Public Affairs

PANJSHIR PROVINCE, Afghanistan, June 6, 2011—High spring flooding damaged the canal last year.

"The canal helped provide more than 200 families in four villages with irrigation and drinking water," said U.S. Army Sgt. Joshua O'Keefe, Panjshir Provincial Reconstruction Team civil affairs team sergeant and Athens, Mich. native. "Many of the families were going to relocate due to the fact they would have no water for their spring crops."

The PRT civil affairs team learned of the damaged canal when they were checking the quality of other projects in Shutol District in December.

"The district governor ended up asking if we could help fund fixing the canal, since so many families were without water," said O'Keefe. "After identifying the problem areas, we were able to support it with bulk funds."

The PRT delivered cement and supplies in January, but the cement could not be poured due to the weather conditions and temperatures.

"This section of the district became a priority," said Shutol District Sector Director Gulabuddin, through an interpreter. "These villages are so far from the main road and river, they were out of water for quite some time. We needed to get the canal fixed as soon as possible."

When the weather started to warm in early March, the villagers teamed together and used gabion baskets left over from previous district-led projects to build a foundation that would reach above where the spring water would rise.

"Before the foundation was built, the villagers used a wooden frame and sheet metal troughs that ran all the way to the villages," said O'Keefe. "Though it leaked a lot, it was a temporary fix until the cement could properly be poured."

When the Panjshir PRT civil affairs team visited Dehe Kalan village again mid-spring, the project started taking shape.

"Many villagers would help out as often as they could," said Gulabuddin. "They would gather the large rocks blocking the way of the canal and take them out. They, too, wanted the canal to be finished as quickly as possible."

Though Shutol is the first district in the province, it sits far back from the main road that travels through Panjshir.

"This river affects so many families that are in this part of the district," said Community Development Council member Zianlar Bostan, through an interpreter. "We are very happy that this canal is being built better than before. We hope it lasts a long time."

Kapisa women's leaders propose a new plan

KAPISA PROVINCE, Afghanistan, June 7, 2011—U.S. Army Capt. Carla Getchell, a women's empowerment coordinator from Frankfort, Ky. with the Kentucky Agribusiness Development Team III, and the Department of Women's Affairs Director Saifora Kohistani listen June 7 at the Department of Women's Affairs compound in Kapisa province, Afghanistan, as Kapisa Family Economics Director Sulhaila Kohistani explains her plans for getting food-drying boxes to use as training aides for Kapisa women. (Photo by U.S. Army Staff Sgt. Ashlee Lolkus, Task Force Red Bulls Public Affairs)

KAPISA PROVINCE, Afghanistan, June 7, 2011—U.S. Army Capt. Carla Getchell, Kentucky Agribusiness Development Team III women's empowerment coordinator from Frankfort, Ky., and the Kapisa Family Economics Director Sulhaila Kohistani calculate the cost of food-drying boxes June 7 at the Department of Women's Affairs compound, Kapisa Province, Afghanistan. (Photo by U.S. Army Staff Sgt. Ashlee Lolkus, Task Force Red Bulls Public Affairs)

U.S. Army Military Police remember
Sgt. Joshua D. Powell

By U.S. Army Staff Sgt. Ryan C. Matson
Task Force Red Bulls public affairs

LAGHMAN PROVINCE, Afghanistan, June 10, 2011—The music from the sound system, Pearl Jam's "Just Breathe," served as a somber reminder of the day's occasion.

"Yes I understand that every life must end; As we sit alone, I know someday we must go..."

The 164th Military Police Company selected the music for the memorial ceremony of Sgt. Joshua D. Powell, a team leader from Tyler, Texas. Powell was one of four military police officers from the 164th Military Police Company, 793rd Military Police Battalion, 3rd Maneuver Enhancement Brigade killed when an Improvised Explosive Device detonated June 4 outside the village of Khanda in Laghman Province, Afghanistan. Also killed were: Sgt. Devin A. Snyder of Cohockton, N.Y.; Sgt. Christopher R. Bell, of Saint Joseph, Mich.; and Spc. Robert L. Voakes, Jr. of Hancock, Mich.

Powell's experience included three years of military service and two deployments, one of which was to Afghanistan where he was wounded and decorated for valor.

"With only one year of dwell time from his last deployment, Sgt. Powell selflessly volunteered at the first opportunity to redeploy and serve alongside his brothers and sisters in arms yet again. Sgt. Powell seamlessly transitioned from the 164th MP Company rear detachment, to our forward-deployed 3rd Platoon in Mehtar Lam. Upon arrival Sgt. Powell immediately took charge as a team leader and quickly established his roots within the platoon—demonstrating his uncanny ability to become an invaluable part of the team in a very short amount of time," Powell's company commander, U.S. Army Capt. Christopher Gehri, from Anchorage, Alaska, recalled.

The other members of Powell's platoon described him as a person who lived for the excitement of deploying and who always wanted to be outside the wire. His experience and knowledge also made him extremely respected amongst his peers.

"Like most of us here, I only had the honor to know Sgt. Powell for a short amount of time," U.S. Army Spc. Jacob Blackburn, from Fairbanks, Alaska, a military police officer and one of Powell's soldiers in the 164th, said during the remarks he offered during the ceremony.

"However, in the time I had the opportunity to work for him, I learned more from him than any of my previous leaders. He was a very humble, yet professional NCO. He was extremely knowledgeable of the way things work while we are serving downrange. I would like it to be known that Sgt. Powell's knowledge, advice and stories of his past deployments not only prepared us as soldiers, but enlightened us and gave us insight as to what to expect."

Other soldiers remembered a lighter side of Powell.

"Let me tell you about Sgt. Powell," Sgt. Jonathan Enlow, a team leader with the 164th from Tahlequah, Okla., said. "He was probably the most country bumpkin/closet genius I ever met. He had a very distinctive drawl, and always walked around with an incessant grin. He had a crazy laugh that always made everyone else laugh."

"He was goofy, but intelligent. And when it came to a mission, there was nothing he couldn't be entrusted with, he was the consummate professional, and I don't know anybody that was more disciplined. Here was this guy who was extremely goofy and liked to have a good time, but everything he did demanded discipline."

"He loved his job," Staff Sgt. Vincent Vetterkind, a squad leader with the 164th from Wausau, Wis., added. "He ate, slept, and dreamed the Army."

Powell was born Sept. 8, 1982 in Tyler, Texas, and joined the Army in 2004. He had served with the 984th MP Company, Fort Carson, Colo., and served as a squad leader, team leader, and Military Police patrolman.

His military awards include the Purple Heart, Bronze Star, Army Commendation with "V" device, Army Commendation Medal, Army Achievement Medal, Valorous Unit Award, Army Good Conduct Medal, National Defense Service Medal, Afghanistan Campaign Medal, Global War on Terrorism Medal, Global War on Terrorism Expeditionary Medal, Army Service Ribbon, Overseas Ribbon, North Atlantic Treaty Organization Medal and the Combat Action Badge.

He is survived by his wife.

U.S. Army Sgt. Christopher Bell remembered by fellow MPs

By U.S. Army Staff Sgt. Ryan C. Matson
Task Force Red Bulls public affairs

LAGHMAN PROVINCE, Afghanistan, June 10, 2011– "By the book."
That's the way his friends in the 164th Military Police Company, 793rd Military Police Battalion, 3rd Maneuver Enhancement Brigade. described U.S. Army Sgt. Christopher R. Bell of Saint Joseph, Mich., when they described the fallen MP June 10 on Forward Operating Base Mehtar Lam, Afghanistan.

Bell was one of four Military Police officers from the 164th MP Company killed when an Improvised Explosive Device detonated June 4 outside Khanda village, Laghman Province, Afghanistan. Also killed were: Sgt. Devin A. Snyder of Cohockton, N.Y.; Sgt. Joshua D. Powell of Tyler, Texas; and Spc. Robert L. Voakes, Jr. of Hancock, Mich.

"He was a walking Army regulation," said Spc. Victor Franco, from Tampa, Fla.

"His thing was that as long as something was done by the book, it was done right," said Staff Sgt. Vincent Vetterkind, a squad leader with the 164th MP Company from Wausau, Wis. "He looked at it as, if the Army actually worked the way the regulations state, it can be the greatest organization in history, and if people don't do that, they're screwing it up. Do it the way it says, do it the way it says."

Bell's commander, Capt. Christopher Gehri, of Anchorage, Alaska, said Bell was extremely tactically and technically proficient, and could recite information from field manuals as well as Army regulations.

"From the very beginning, Sgt. Bell demonstrated a maturity well beyond his years," Gehri said. "He demanded hard work, opportunities to grow and professionally develop, and held his peers accountable 100 percent of the time. Sgt. Bell thrived on all things Army. Disciplined, determined problem-solver and critical thinker—these are the words and traits that will always resound in my mind when I think of Sgt. Bell. He never deviated from a standard."

The soldiers in his platoon all said his dedication was unparalleled.

"He was one of the most passionate people I ever met in my life," Vetterkind said. "His short-term goal was to be promoted to sergeant, which happened posthumously, and his long-term goal was to be sergeant major of the Army, and I have no doubt he would have done it, absolutely none. He was a natural leader."

He competed in 22 boards, and won them all.

Still, with all his professionalism and his disciplined nature, Bell did have a softer side.

"He liked 'chick flicks,'" Pfc. Stacey Jordan, from Belmont, N.Y., remembered with a smile. "He used to watch them with me and Sgt. Snyder. He loved the movie *The Notebook*. He wouldn't care if someone would tease him about them either. He would say, 'I don't care, they're fun, they're good movies!'"

The soldiers also said he was always there to listen to them and assist with their problems. Still, they said, if they were wrong, he would hear them out and tell them why they were wrong, often reciting a regulation.

Bell was born Jan. 5, 1990, in Saint Joseph, Mich., and joined the Army in 2008. He served as a team leader, gunner, driver, and Military Police patrolman with the 164th. His military awards include the Purple Heart, Bronze Star Medal, National Defense Service Medal, Afghanistan Campaign Medal, Global War on Terrorism Medal, Army Service Ribbon, Overseas Service Ribbon, North Atlantic Treaty Organization Medal, and the Combat Action Badge.

He is survived by his wife, and daughter Lana Bell.

"Sgt. Bell spoke often of his wife and their 1-year-old daughter, " Gehri said. "If you asked him about his family, he would tell you that there could be no more perfect of a family than that he and his wife had created."

One thing that showed through was the respect Bell's soldiers had for him.

"Sgt. Bell was the best leader I had in my military career," an emotional Spc. Justin Tobener from Tracy, Calif., said in his remarks recalling his fallen sergeant.

"I remember talking to Sgt. Bell for three or four hours just a couple days before this happened," Vetterkind recalled. "And I remember him saying all that he wanted to do was just make a difference. That's what he wanted to do, in ever way and every day. This was the only thing that could stop him."

Fallen U.S. Army Sgt. Devin A. Snyder remembered

By U.S. Army Staff Sgt. Ryan C. Matson
Task Force Red Bulls Public Affairs

LAGHMAN PROVINCE, Afghanistan, June 10, 2011—Friends gathered June 10, to remember U.S. Army Sgt. Devin A. Snyder, a military police officer from Cohockton, N.Y. who was one of four Military Police officers from the 164th Military Police Company, 793rd Military Police Battalion, 3rd Maneuver Enhancement Brigade killed when an Improvised Explosive Device detonated June 4 outside the village of Khanda in Laghman Province, Afghanistan.

Also killed were: U.S. Army Sgt. Joshua D. Powell of Tyler, Texas; U.S. Army Sgt. Christopher R. Bell of Saint Joseph, Mich.; and U.S. Army Spc. Robert L. Voakes, Jr. of Hancock, Mich, and civilian Brett Benton of Dry Ridge, Ky.

Her friends laughed when they thought of her clumsiness. "She was extremely clumsy," Sgt. Jonathan Enlow, a team leader from Tahlequah, Okla., remembered with a soft chuckle.

"Every time she turned around it seemed she had a new bruise. I used to joke that she could trip over a single sheet of paper!"

"You heard something fall and you knew she was near," U.S. Army Staff Sgt. Vincent Vetterkind, a squad leader from Wausau, Wis., said with a smile. "You'd laugh at her, and she'd start laughing too."

The MPs said she was as good-natured about her clumsiness as everything else in her life.

"She would walk into barriers, or trip over little rocks or just her own feet and then kind of smile and look behind her and act like there was something there she tripped over," Enlow said. "She was always the first to smile."

"She was someone who was always able to bring a smile out from everybody else, too," Vetterkind added. "She had the ability to make people laugh or make them feel better if they were having a bad day."

In reality, the 5-foot-10-tall, thin Snyder, who some in her platoon nicknamed "Olive Oyl," was an excellent athlete. She was a star soccer player and a high-school track champion.

Her friends also described her as superstitious (she would never use a white lighter because she thought it was bad luck) and a bit paranoid, especially after she once found a bug in some Afghan food she was eating.

The other MPs recalled how Snyder fought to go on the deployment with them. She had a physical profile dealing with a circulation condition, but was able to convince the doctors that the condition would be no more of a problem overseas than it was in Alaska and eventually got it lifted.

"She would not give up on coming on this deployment," Vetterkind said. "She would fight tooth and nail."

"She always cared more about what was right rather than what was more convenient," Enlow added. "She wanted to be a good Soldier, and she was."

The Soldiers remembered how she had a tough time adjusting to the weather in Alaska, where the 164th is headquartered.

"She wasn't an Alaska person," Enlow said. "She hated the cold and the snow and said she wanted to move to Georgia."

Still, Enlow and the other Soldiers said she always found a way to have fun and do things with her fellow Soldiers, such as buying a pink four-wheeler to ride with them.

"She loved tattoos," U.S. Army Spc. Jeremy Johnson, a military policeman from Chickasha, Okla., recalled. "She had a half-sleeve of tattoos on one arm and talked about making it a full-sleeve on one arm and then getting one on the other arm, too. I kept giving her a hard time, telling her that someplace in all those tattoos, she should hide 'Waldo.'"

She was born in Virginia Beach, Va., Aug. 7, 1990, and joined the Army as an MP in 2008 immediately after finishing high school. She served as a team leader, driver, gunner, and patrolman with the 164th, which deployed to Afghanistan in March.

Her awards include the Purple Heart, Bronze Star Medal, National Defense Service Medal, Afghanistan Campaign Medal, Global War on Terrorism Medal, Army Service Ribbon, Overseas Ribbon, North Atlantic Treaty Organization Medal, and the Combat Action Badge.

She is survived by her mother and father.

It was clear that Snyder was loved by her fellow Soldiers.

Thinking of her friend, U.S. Army Pfc. Stacey Jordan, a military police officer from Belmont, N.Y., stared down at the table before her with eyes filled with sadness.

"She was my best friend," Jordan said. "We were always together; she was like my sister. She will be missed."

Fallen U.S. Army Spc. Robert L. Voakes remembered

By U.S. Army Staff Sgt. Ryan C. Matson
Task Force Red Bulls Public Affairs

LAGHMAN PROVINCE, Afghanistan, June 10, 2011—Soldiers from the 164th Military Police Company, 793rd Military Police Battalion, 3rd Maneuver Enhancement Brigade, remembered their fallen comrade, U.S. Army Spc. Robert L. Voakes, Jr., from Hancock, Mich, June 10 on Forward Operating Base Mehtar Lam, Afghanistan.

Voakes was one of four Military Police officers from the 164th killed when an Improvised Explosive Device detonated June 4 outside the village of Khanda in Laghman Province, Afghanistan. Also killed were: U.S. Army Sgt. Christopher R. Bell of Saint Joseph, Mich.; U.S. Army Sgt. Devin A. Snyder of Cohockton, N.Y.; and U.S. Army Sgt. Joshua D. Powell of Tyler, Texas.

"He always made you laugh," his friend and fellow Military Police officer in the platoon, U.S. Army Spc. Victor Franco, from Tampa, Fla., recalled with a smile.

U.S. Army Capt. Christopher Gehri, from Anchorage, Alaska, Voakes' company commander with the 164th, also spoke of the young Soldier's sense of humor.

"Spc. Voakes chose his words carefully, more often than not, at the exact right time to let his fellow Soldiers have a laugh," Gehri said during the ceremony. "His word was always good enough. His actions were above reproach."

U.S. Army Sgt. Jonathan Enlow, a team leader with the 164th from Tahlequah, Okla., agreed.

"He was quiet, but not because he didn't know what to say or didn't want to say it, but he just was reserved," Enlow said. "But he was always on the periphery watching. And he always had a comeback, he was very witty. He was waiting to say something and when he let it loose, you had nothing you could say."

U.S. Army Spc. Colton Oslund, from Stillman Valley, Ill., another military police officer with the 164th who spoke about Voakes at the memorial ceremony, remembered something different about Voakes.

"I remember Spc. Voakes always talking about his Cadillac," Oslund recalled.

He loved that car, and I'd like to think that somewhere Voakes is driving around in a 24-karat-gold Cadillac with 24s, the truck bumpin' and watching over us."

Voakes was born in Hancock, Mich., Feb. 26, 1990, and joined the U.S. Army in 2009. He served as military policeman, driver, and gunner.

"He had been my gunner, and he was an excellent gunner, he was just flat out on it," U.S. Army Staff Sgt. Vincent Vetterkind, a squad leader with the 164th from Wausau, Wis., said.

But what all Soldiers seemed to remember most about Voakes was his tremendous pride for his Native American heritage. In fact they say he was planning to take his mid-tour leave to attend a Native American function back at his tribe, and aspired to being a reservation police officer.

"He was Native American and very proud of that heritage," Oslund said. "He told his squad leader that he and one of his brothers were the only two from his tribe that had been to Afghanistan and in combat. His family was very proud of him for his service."

"He had a huge flag of his tribe in his room," Franco added. "He would get very upset if you told him you thought he was anything else than Native American."

Perhaps Gehri summed it up when he said, "Spc. Voakes was proud of his Native American heritage, and the Keweenaw—his tribe. They were an important part of his life. He was a warrior."

His military awards include the Purple Heart, Bronze Star Medal, National Defense Service Medal, Afghanistan Campaign Medal, Global War on Terrorism Medal, Army Service Ribbon, Overseas Ribbon, North Atlantic Treaty Organization Medal and the Combat Action Badge.

Voakes is survived by his father.

Company completes final patrols of deployment

LAGHMAN PROVINCE, Afghanistan, June 14, 2011—U.S. Army Spc. John Rocha, an infantry team leader, wrapping up his second deployment to Afghanistan, from Geneseo, Ill., Company A, 1st Battalion, 133rd Infantry Regiment, Task Force Ironman, 2nd Brigade Combat Team, 34th Infantry Division, Task Force Red Bulls, watches as a curious villager observes a combined forces convoy near the town of Watangatu in Laghman Province, Afghanistan. It was one of the final patrols for Rocha and the soldiers of Company A, who spent the year deployed to Combat Outpost Najil, one of the smallest and most remote locations where soldiers from Task Force Ironman served during their deployment. (Photo by U.S. Army Capt. Jason Beck, 210th Mobile Public Affairs Detachment)

LAGHMAN PROVINCE, Afghanistan, June 15, 2011—U.S. Army Sgt. Anthony Meyers, middle, a team leader from Clinton, Iowa, shows U.S. Army Spc. Aaron Williams, right, a machine gunner from Council Bluffs, Iowa, and U.S. Army Spc. Jesse Sprank, left, a squad designated marksman from Bellevue, Iowa, all with Company A, 1st Battalion, 133rd Infantry Regiment, Task Force Ironman, 2nd Brigade Combat Team, 34th Infantry Division, Task Force Red Bulls, a landmark in the distance outside the town of Dumlum, Laghman Province, Afghanistan, outside Combat Outpost Najil. (Photo by U.S. Army Staff Sgt. Ryan C. Matson, Task Force Red Bulls Public Affairs)

Red Bulls complete successful tour at COP Najil

LAGHMAN PROVINCE, Afghanistan, June 15, 2011—U.S. Army Pfc. Elisha Bottleman (right), a machine gunner from Edgewood, Iowa, with Company A, 1st Battalion, 133rd Infantry Regiment, Task Force Ironman, 2nd Brigade Combat Team, 34th Infantry Division, Task Force Red Bulls, leads a group of Company A soldiers down a hill in northeastern Afghanistan, outside Combat Outpost Najil, Afghanistan. (Photo by U.S. Army Capt. Jason Beck, 210th Mobile Public Affairs Detachment)

By U.S. Army Staff Sgt. Ryan C. Matson
Task Force Red Bulls Public Affairs

LAGHMAN PROVINCE, Afghanistan, June 15, 2011—U.S. Army Spc. John Rocha wiped the sweat from his sun-beaten face and then took another step through the river valley. It was another 100-plus degree day in northeastern Afghanistan.

Rocha and his fellow soldiers combed the rugged terrain along the narrow highway, looking for enemy threats for what they hoped was the last of hundreds of combat patrols through the area.

When Rocha, an infantry team leader from Geneseo, Ill., and the other soldiers from Company A, 1st Battalion, 133rd Infantry Regiment, Task Force Ironman, 2nd Brigade Combat Team, 34th Infantry Division, Task Force Red Bulls, arrived in Laghman Province, Afghanistan, Oct. 31, 2010. Eight months ago, traveling the length of this road was a dangerous undertaking, and rarely attempted.

The soldiers deployed to Combat Outpost Najil, a small, remote base in the mountains of the Alishang Valley. The road follows the valley south to the province's capital city, Mehtar Lam, about 20 miles away. The sphere of influence around COP Najil was only about five square kilometers. Traveling beyond that meant almost certain enemy contact.

"I wanted to expand the security bubble around the COP and ensure freedom of movement on the main supply route," U.S. Army Capt. Jason Merchant, the commander of Company A, from Dysart, Iowa, said.

Merchant said his philosophy when engaging the enemy was simple.

"Relentless pursuit was my intention," Merchant said.

However, Merchant said aggressive combat action and patrolling were only half the equation for bringing security to the Alishang Valley.

"I have to have a unit that can deliver overwhelming force, but one that is also compassionate," Merchant said. "Connecting with the civilian population supports our security bubble."

To connect with the people, Iowa troops used techniques ranging from simple handshakes and gestures while on patrol, to coordinating meetings among local leaders.

Merchant said gaining the trust of the local people was a challenge, but among the most important accomplishments of his company during the deployment. To do this, Merchant said he focused on a mindset of not simply giving the locals projects or making empty promises, but focusing on self reliance.

This sentiment was echoed by Merchant's Afghan counterpart at COP Najil, Afghan National Army Capt. Abdul Quader, 1st Company, 2nd Kandak, 1st Brigade, 201st ANA Infantry Corps. "The groups that were here before us promised the locals a lot of things, so when we came here they didn't know us," Quader said. "When we said something, we'd do it; we wouldn't promise anything unless we were going to do it."

"The people saw that Capt. Merchant and his soldiers respected Afghan culture and traditions. For example, they didn't enter homes without permission, or stop people on the street without a reason. If you respect the people, they will respect you."

Gaining the trust of the people enabled Merchant to gather information about enemy activity from them and respond to it. Whereas Merchant said at the beginning of the deployment, no one would share this information with his men, now it has become the difference in maintaining security in his area.

Merchant paraphrased a Mao Tse Tung quote, "Insurgents are like fish in the ocean and the ocean is the people. They hide amongst the population."

Company A even used what Merchant referred to as a "dark period" to strengthen ties between the coalition and the local populace. After some civilians were accidentally killed in a military operation, Merchant said his soldiers spent a lot of time and effort to rebuild rapport and trust with the citizens, eventually turning the town into an ally against terrorism.

Merchant said he did this by treating the incident with the same consideration as if had happened in his hometown.

Merchant attributed much of the success in the area to having a strong partnership with the ANA.

"It takes an aggressive leader to succeed in this area; Capt. Quader is that guy," Merchant said.

The feeling was mutual for Quader.

"We have a common enemy in worldwide terrorism," Quader said. "When Capt. Merchant and I started working together in Najil, there were a lot of insurgents in the area. Now, there are a lot less insurgents."

Over the last year, the ANA have stood shoulder-to-shoulder with Company A to accomplish the mission. Almost all patrols have featured an even number of Afghan and American soldiers.

Though his company inherited a COP that lacked a lot of basic amenities such as showers and latrines, Merchant said he couldn't have asked for a better group of soldiers to go through the deployment with.

The soldiers, mostly from northeastern Iowa and surrounding areas, said they are proud of their accomplishments at Najil.

"I like to think that we helped the people here," said U.S. Army Pvt. Carl Roth, a grenadier from East Dubuque, Ill. "I think we gave them some peace of mind and made them feel safe to live their lives."

Rocha, on his second deployment to Afghanistan, said he feels reducing the enemy's freedom of maneuver was Company A's biggest achievement.

"Our unit did a good job of finding the middle-ground between aggressiveness and working with the civilian population," he said.

By the time Company A leaves Najil, Merchant said the company's area of operation and influence will have expanded from 5 square kilometers to more than 170.

Although the highway to Mehtar Lam is still potentially dangerous, it is now regularly traveled by both civilians and military convoys without incident.

"The security and training we provided have set the conditions for the ANA to be able to take over so we don't wind up here again," Merchant said.

Soldier takes bullet to helmet, walks away unscathed

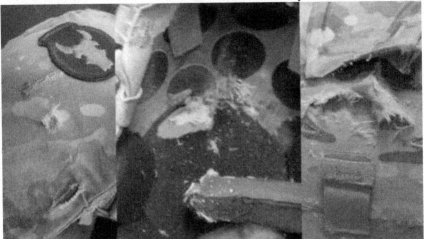

BAGRAM AIRFIELD, Afghanistan, June 13, 2011—U.S. Army Spc. Tom Albers' helmet after taking a round of enemy fire. The entrance point of the round in the front of the helmet (left), the damage caused on the interior of the helmet, its path was under the pad and the rear (center), the exit point and damage to the cover and back of the helmet (right). (Photo by U.S. Army Spc. James Wilton, Task Force Red Bulls Public Affairs)

By U.S. Army Spc. James Wilton
Task Force Red Bulls Public Affairs

BAGRAM AIRFIELD, Afghanistan, June 13, 2011—"There is something I need to tell you" are not the words any mother wants to hear from her son who is deployed to Afghanistan.

This time U.S. Army Spc. Tom Albers, a Troop C, 1st Squadron, 113th Cavalry Regiment, Task Force Redhorse, driver and infantryman from Alton, Iowa, had good news, considering the alternative.

"I am fine and healthy and not hurt, everything is OK but," said Albers to his mother over the phone, "I have been shot in the helmet."

"You were wearing the helmet right," his mother responded, said Albers.

The phone call was made from Craig Joint Theater Hospital on Bagram Airfield, Afghanistan, May 28.

Albers and his team were conducting a dismounted joint presence patrol earlier that day in Parwan Province when the Afghan National Police officers they were teamed with spotted an individual they knew to be associated with insurgent forces. While searching a hillside for the individual, the team came under fire.

"My head cleared the hill ... I saw a house on my right and as I was in the middle of saying 'Hey I got a house over here,' when I heard the first shot," said

603

Albers "It felt something hit me in the side of the helmet and was knocked to the ground. It felt like someone had hit me in the head with a wooden baseball bat."

The team quickly took cover and responded with fire on the building. Albers was momentarily stunned, but after checking himself and realizing he was still alive, he regained his bearings and took up a position to return fire.

"I laid there for what seemed like five minutes but realized later that it was just a couple of seconds, I thought to myself, "Am I dying? No I don't really think so," Albers said. "Felt my head, no blood or anything, so I thought 'okay what just happened to me?' I was confused but I turned around and started laying down fire from the direction it had come from."

Albers and the Joint Terminal Attack Controller were on one side of the building while the rest of the team was 50 to 100 meters away on the other side. They were taking heavy fire so they decided to pull back and join the rest of the team.

"I was just getting plinked at, rounds were hitting in a consistent, natural firing rhythm, but I look up at Albers and his position is just getting obliterated, he was covered in dust," said U.S. Air Force Staff Sgt. Jason Roland, the 116th Air Support Operations Squadron (ASOS) JTAC from Tacoma, Wash., who was attached to Albers' team that day. "Someone was going full-auto on his position, so I yelled up at him and told him to move."

The group provided suppressive fire so Albers and Roland could pull back and regroup with the rest of team who were taking cover behind a building and wall.

"It really surprised me, from the moment I thought, 'OK, I am fine, and there is no blood running down my face,' until after we met up with the lieutenant, I don't really remember anything," said Albers. "I think that is because I wasn't thinking, I was reacting, doing what needed to be done; covering fire, moving back, whatever it was. I think that was all because of our training, muscle memory kicked in. It made me think, all that time we spent training wasn't stupid, it wasn't pointless, it is needed and it works."

Albers reacted like he was trained to, and he seemed responsive and aware said Roland. The only part that seemed strange to his fellow team member was a question he kept asking.

"Albers did fine, the only thing that was funny is as we fell back, I realized something is little weird with Albers. He keeps asking about his helmet," said Roland. "It feels like something hit his helmet, he wants me to look at his helmet, I say 'I don't care about your helmet, I want you to (watch) to the north because if we get attacked they're going to come from the North.'"

The team called in air support and enemy fire subsided enough to assess the situation. One ANP suffered a wound to his backside, so medics were called to attend to him. Albers even assisted the medic with the other injured teammate.

"At that time, the medic had time to check on Albers and he realizes that he got shot in the helmet," said Roland. "He passes this on to the lieutenant who decides it is time to pull back."

As they began pulling out, Albers said he finally realized the seriousness of what just happened. "I was pulling security and just keep thinking to myself, 'I just got shot in the head,' I would hear something and move and again think, 'I just got shot in the head, what just happened?'" said Albers.

The events that day stuck in his mind for days to come said Albers. They serve as a reminder to stay vigilant. The smile on his face at the hospital, would also serve as a reminder to enjoy every day, no matter how tough.

Medics evacuated Albers, and after hospital staff gave him a battery of tests, they found him to be perfectly healthy, minus a small burn mark across the top of his head.

The patrol that day was a normal day for any infantryman with risks every soldier has a chance of facing. Albers knew this, but he wanted to be in the military ever since he could remember.

"According to my parents I have wanted to join the military since I could talk, it was either Marines, Air Force, this, that," said Albers.

When he was 17, Albers spoke with a recruiter, who is now a first sergeant in the same squadron, and decided the time was right. Now 20, he said he feels the deployment is going well and has enjoyed every part of his three-year military career. Albers is the only member of his large family currently in the military, but his father and grandfather are both veterans.

"My favorite part is the camaraderie, especially after this incident. Everyone has been very supportive," said Albers. "They are all like my brothers now."

The team takes their roles as brothers very seriously. They watched over him at first, making sure he was doing all right.

"Everyone was cool about it. Everyone was here for me, making sure I was OK and if I had to talk to anybody they were here for me," said Albers "We joke around about it, now that I they know I am fine, and now that I got the Purple Heart, 'Oh the one-upper, had to get the Purple Heart.'"

Albers' 15 minutes of fame is a big part of the jokes shared about the team. These simple actions prove to Albers that they care and also help him to not take the incident too seriously. His family has also helped to keep him smiling about the incident.

"My nephew, Talon, got on his mom's (social media page) and sent me a message, 'I am glad you're OK, but no more messing around, that was scary, don't be messing around anymore,'" said Albers.

The 1st Squadron, 113th Cavalry, will be in Afghanistan for another month or two, and after, Albers said he is looking forward to spending time with family and friends and going back to school when he returns.

The shot has not deterred his desire to be in the military, and he plans to reenlist when his current contract ends. Albers plans to stay in the infantry and has hopes to move up in the ranks becoming a squad or platoon sergeant.

The helmet, which will be sent to his house after military officials examine it, will serve as a good training tool to teach his Soldiers the importance of proper wear of their protective equipment or at the very least, keep their heads down.

BAGRAM AIRFIELD, Afghanistan, June 13, 2011—U.S. Army Spc. Tom Albers, 20, of Troop C, 1st Squadron, 113th Cavalry Regiment, Task Force Redhorse, a part of the 2nd Brigade Combat Team, 34th Infantry Division, Task Force Red Bulls, and infantryman from Alton, Iowa, stands outside the Troop C command office, healthy, happy, and ready for battle even after taking a round of enemy fire to the helmet two weeks prior. (Photo by U.S. Army Spc. James Wilton, Task Force Red Bulls Public Affairs)

ANSF, Ironman stand fast:
A glimpse of Bad Pech after Operation Bull Whip

LAGHMAN PROVINCE, Afghanistan, June 17, 2011—An Afghan National Civil Order Policeman stands outside his shared living quarters near the Bad Pech District, Afghanistan. After the valley was swept by Afghan National Security Forces and coalition forces back in Operation Bull Whip last March, a joint combat outpost and district center was established to create a government presence in the newly established Bad Pech District. As the facilities are not plentiful for the ANSF, they make do with the tents created from American re-supply parachutes collected during the sweep of the valley. (Photo By U.S. Army Staff Sgt. Ashlee Lolkus, Task Force Red Bulls Public Affairs)

By U.S. Army Staff Sgt. Ashlee Lolkus
Task Force Red Bulls Public Affairs

LAGHMAN PROVINCE, Afghanistan, June 17, 2011—In a dusty, hot valley in the center of eastern Afghanistan, Afghan National Security Forces and U.S. soldiers worked to bring security to the province's newest district.

To bring the Government of the Islamic Republic of Afghanistan into Pech Valley, a partnered operation began last March to sweep the valley of insurgents, establish a district center and bring development to the people.

Former Alingar District sub-governor, Haji Alif Shah, now sub-governor of the new Bad Pech District, said he feels for the people and will do his job properly and shared his thoughts on that process.

"Even though it's now summer time, the winter is coming," Shah said. "We need offices for the personnel of the district, the Afghan National Police, the municipality."

He said security is good since the forces have been in the area, but they need to get resources in place.

"We need the same things that other districts have," he said. One of the beginning stages is establishing security. "We need to take care of our military set-up before they can help the people."

U.S. Army Capt. Kevin Hrodey, commander of Company B, 1st Battalion, 133rd Infantry Regiment, Task Force Ironman, 2nd Brigade Combat Team, 34th Infantry Division, Task Force Red Bulls, from Pleasant Hill, Iowa, agreed with Shah and met with the ANSF leaders on nearly a daily basis to discuss the security situation and other needs.

"I think generally everybody has the same goal," he said. "Everyone wants to see the district succeed. I think they've got the right people in place. A lot of times it takes a little help and nudging them in the right direction in order to make something work, but everybody has the same goal in mind."

"I am very happy to be working with Capt. Hrodey and the Americans," said Afghan National Army Capt. Walli, with 1st Kandak, 2nd Brigade, 201st Corps. "We work together for everything. He and his men help to bring a good situation here. We have been out in the villages and they are also happy we are here to bring security to the area."

"Everybody I talk to; locals in the villages, they are happy we are here," confirmed Hrodey. "Happy that they can finally see some faces of the government, and government just needs a kick start. It can't be expected to work over night; it's going to be a process."

"I heard from the people around here," Walli said, "that they think the district center is temporary because we don't even have a water pump for ourselves and living in tents."

Shah said he heard the same sentiments from the people.

"I think a big thing is that no one is used to these types of conditions," Hrodey said. "They are used to having buildings, but here they are, thrown in the middle of nowhere, living in houses dug out of the ground built with parachutes and post pickets .... It's a whole new world out here. It's taken them time to adapt and adjust to their new mission, same as us."

Hrodey said, "These guys are making do with what they have. They are making do because they believe in it."

"For whatever we are responsible for in the area and what we are able to do, we will take care of," said Shah. "We don't want the people to question and blame us for not doing something for them.

"The last 10 years, there was no security in this area; this district was away from the provincial center," said Shah. "There has been no construction development, no agricultural development, and no schools. When there is no school or education that is where the security problems come up."

"[The district center is] supposed to have a director of education, director of agriculture, all these different people to build the staff for the sub-governor, and they don't have that yet. That is a key part that is still missing," Hrodey said.

Shah said they are working with coalition forces regarding these issues. The largest issues are the basics: roads, electricity and structures for the district center.

All of these things take time, but the sub-governor, ANSF and coalition forces continue to work together to make sure eastern Afghanistan's newest district is taken care of.

"This district will succeed," Hrodey said, "if they get the people out here and the programs in place."

Two Brothers, Two Valleys
Gingrich brothers answer call to serve

NURISTAN PROVINCE, Afghanistan, June 19, 2011—U.S. Army Capt. Garrett H. Gingrich, commander of Company C, 1st Battalion, 133rd Infantry Regiment, Task Force Ironman, 2nd Brigade Combat Team, 34th Infantry Division, Task Force Red Bulls, from Waterloo, Iowa, shows a bracelet, which memorializes two of his Soldiers killed in action in a previous deployment—U.S. Army Staff Sgt. Scott E. Nisely and Spc. Kampha B. Sourivong. Separated by roughly 15 miles, he and his brother serve in two of the most demanding provinces in northeastern Afghanistan. (Photo by U.S. Army Capt. Jason Beck, 210th Mobile Public Affairs Detachment)

By U.S. Army Capt. Jason Beck
210th Mobile Public Affairs Detachment

BAGRAM, *Afghanistan, June 19, 2011*—Once again, the Gingrich boys answered the call to serve their country in combat.

The pair, Capt. Garrett H. Gingrich, commander of Company C, 1st Battalion, 133rd Infantry Regiment, from Waterloo, Iowa, and 2nd Lt. Taylor A. Gingrich, a platoon leader with Company A, 1st Battalion, 133rd Infantry Regiment from Cedar Falls, Iowa, both part of Task Force Ironman, 2nd Brigade Combat Team, 34th Infantry Division, Task Force Red Bulls, previously served alongside one another in Iraq for 22 months—the longest U.S. Army deployment during Operation Iraqi Freedom.

At the time, Garrett was a second lieutenant with the same company he now commands; Taylor, served as a combat medic for Company B, 1-133rd Infantry Regiment

Separated by roughly fifteen miles, the brothers now serve in two of the most demanding provinces in northeastern Afghanistan. Garrett is based out of Combat Outpost Kalagush in Nuristan Province, which borders Pakistan and operates near the Alingar Valley. Taylor is based out of Combat Outpost Najil in Laghman Province, which borders Nuristan to the southwest. Taylor mainly operates in the Alishang Valley.

It's a long way from the small town of Dysart, Iowa, where the brothers were raised.

"My family and I grew up in Dysart, Iowa. Where we are from, it's all small-town farming communities," said Taylor.

"If anyone needed any help with manual labor, they would always come and ask for the Gingrich boys."

Both brothers credit their parents for setting the standard and passing along a strong work ethic. Deb, their mother, is the director for an Emergency Room back in Iowa and their father, Craig, serves as a paramedic serves in the same hospital.

"Mom is the epitome of a leader," said Taylor. "It takes a strong-willed woman to run an ER"

As for his father, Taylor said, "Dad is now 60, and works harder than both me and Garrett."

Garrett added, "Among the values our parents passed along were do the right thing and get to know people."

For Taylor, doing the right thing means not cutting corners. "You can never cut corners; as leaders we must do the right thing every time to ensure the safety of our Soldiers and the citizens here in our area of operations," said Taylor.

On a recent mounted convoy to Mehtar Lam, Taylor dismounted elements of his platoon to clear several danger zones of Improvised Explosive Devices. Though no IEDs were found, he admitted it must be done every time. "You cannot let the enemy dictate your next move. I will dismount every time, because the one time you don't is the one time you may end up losing a Soldier due to complacency."

Those same values are what Garrett said served him well in a recent conflict in the village of Do Ab, which is located approximately 15 miles north of FOB Kalagush. Over the course of about seven hours, Garrett and approximately 40 U.S. servicemembers, and 20 of their Afghan counterparts, thwarted an ambush and killed more than 200 insurgent fighters. It was the largest battle for the Iowa National Guard's "Red Bull" since World War II.

Garrett said his unit could not have done what they did that day in Do Ab, if they had not gotten to know their Afghan counterparts and trusted one another to do the right thing.

"It is part of our mission to develop strong relationships with the Afghan National Army, the Afghan National Police, and others here in order to support them establish security," said Garrett.

"As for my own leaders," Garrett continued, "I trust them to make the right decision, because I know them, understand how they think and see them do it every day."

Both brothers call and keep up with one another as much as possible - sometimes seeking advice, others times just to make sure the other is all right.

"When Garrett was up in Do Ab, I monitored the situation here at COP Najil; needless to say, I was worried," said Taylor.

"I'm always concerned. Both valleys are not completely safe. My concern is for my Soldiers and my brother," said Garrett. "Both companies have been through a lot. I will be relieved when my Soldiers are able to return home and Taylor leaves here as well."

Garrett knows the dangers of combat all too well. During his previous deployment to Iraq, one of his Soldiers was killed.

"When we were in Iraq, Garrett lost one of his squad leaders to small-arms fire. Garrett still wears a bracelet with the Soldier's name on it. We still pray for that Soldier and his family every Thanksgiving and Christmas," said Taylor. "I saw how it changed Garrett, and I hope I don't have to go through the same thing."

Garrett has passed a lot of what he has learned on to his younger brother, Taylor.

"Garrett has been a mentor for me. If I have questions, I call him," said Taylor. "He is why I became an infantry officer; I'm his biggest fan."

But, just as much as Garrett has been a mentor for Taylor, so too has Taylor been one for Garrett.

"I am proud of Taylor. He has truly established himself as an outstanding leader in his platoon," said Garrett. "As we've grown older, we've gotten a lot closer. He is as much of a role model for me."

Both Garrett and Taylor say serving together in combat has made things easier.

"It's easier doing a lot of the things I do here, because I know my brother is here with me sucking it up too," said Taylor.

"Being deployed together has changed us; we've gone through the same things and have grown a lot closer," said Garrett.

LAGHMAN PROVINCE, Afghanistan—U.S. Army 2nd Lt. Taylor A. Gingrich, a platoon leader with Company A, 1st Battalion, 133rd Infantry Regiment, Task Force Ironman, 2nd Brigade Combat Team, 34th Infantry Division, Task Force Red Bulls, from Cedar Falls, Iowa, returns to his Mine-Resistant, Ambush-Protected vehicle after he and his Soldiers cleared the site of a previously detonated Improvised Explosive Device while on a mounted convoy to Mehtar Lam. Separated by roughly 15 miles, he and his brother serve in two of the most demanding provinces in northeastern Afghanistan. (Photo by U.S. Army Capt. Jason Beck, 210th Mobile Public Affairs Detachment)

NURISTAN PROVINCE, Afghanistan—U.S. Army Capt. Garrett H. Gingrich, commander of Company C, 1st Battalion, 133rd Infantry Regiment, Task Force Ironman, 2nd Brigade Combat Team, 34th Infantry Division, Task Force Red Bulls, from Waterloo, Iowa, discusses the plans for an upcoming mission with a couple of his Afghan National Army counterparts on Combat Outpost Kalagush. Separated by roughly 15 miles, he and his brother serve in two of the most demanding provinces in northeastern Afghanistan. (Photo by U.S. Army Capt. Jason Beck, 210th Mobile Public Affairs Detachment)

Chaplain gives final sermon from Afghanistan

LAGHMAN PROVINCE, Afghanistan, June 26, 2011—U.S. Army Chaplain (Capt.) Michael Willer, from Webster City, Iowa, the battalion chaplain for 1st Battalion, 133rd Infantry Regiment, Task Force Ironman, part of the Iowa National Guard's 2nd Brigade Combat Team, 34th Infantry Division, Task Force Red Bulls, talks to soldiers during his final sermon of his deployment at the chapel on Forward Operating Base Mehtar Lam in Laghman Province, Afghanistan. (Photo by U.S. Army Staff Sgt. Ryan C. Matson, Task Force Red Bulls Public Affairs)

By U.S. Army Staff Sgt. Ryan C. Matson
Task Force Red Bulls Public Affairs

LAGHMAN PROVINCE, Afghanistan, June 26, 2011—With 16 people in attendance, the chapel at Forward Operating Base Mehtar Lam, Afghanistan, was nearly at capacity June 26.

Fifteen soldiers and one civilian seated folding chairs listened as U.S. Army Chaplain (Capt.) Michael Willer, the battalion chaplain for 1st Battalion, 133rd Infantry Regiment, Task Force Ironman, part of the Iowa National Guard's 2nd Brigade Combat Team, 34th Infantry Division, Task Force Red Bulls, gave his final sermon of the unit's deployment.

"The record here is 23, and that was on Easter," Willer said with a warm smile. "So attendance has been between two and 23 on Sundays."

For the past eight months, Willer has been preaching from the connex chapel. Actually, it is two connexes joined together, or a "doublewide," but the chapel doesn't occupy all the space.

"There's also a closet in here and a barbershop," Willer explained. "I get my haircut there all the time. You can get your haircut and worship in the same spot all before lunch. Occasionally, the Afghan barber will leave his music on Saturday night before he leaves, so we'll enjoy Middle Eastern music through the wall while we worship."

Though it may not be a fancy church, Willer said he is fond of the chapel.

"Even though it is two connexes put together—even though there's a birds nest in the wall and they get loud at times," Willer said with a laugh, "it's still a chapel; it's still holy ground."

Willer's final sermon in Afghanistan focused on Psalm 150, his favorite, he said. Willer said it is his favorite because it breaks down the why and the how of worshiping. During the sermon, he discussed how people often worship or have other routines in their lives which they forget how and why they do them.

To illustrate this point, Willer spoke about a woman who cooked a delicious ham every Sunday after church, each time she cut the ends off the ham. When a friend asked the woman why she cut the ends off the ham, and if doing that gave the ham its delicious flavor. The woman admitted she did not know and that her mother had always done it that way. When the woman asked her mother why she cut the ends off her hams, her mother told her "it didn't fit in the pan I had to cook it in."

In the front row of the chapel was one of Willer's regular attendees, U.S. Army Sgt. Toby Hall, a civil affairs team leader with Company A, 413th Civil Affairs Battalion, assigned to the 2nd Brigade Combat Team, 34th Infantry Division, Task Force Red Bulls, from Amarillo, Texas. Hall said he has attended all but three or four of Willer's services this year, either because he was on leave or on a mission.

He said he likes Willer's "laid-back style," and how he relates to the soldiers in the battalion, despite not having been a career soldier.

"He's a down-to-earth guy," Hall said. "When you talk to him, you don't have to feel like you're walking on eggshells because you're talking to a messenger of God. He's a normal human being, and he doesn't ever try to act like anything else. He's funny, and he doesn't just sit in his office and use the cross against everybody that walks in because they cuss or something like that. He knows he's in a war zone and he knows that he's with soldiers and everybody's not perfect."

Willer does far more than hold a Saturday night and Sunday morning service. He handles Red Cross messages for soldiers, and has the difficult task of holding memorial services as well. He also travels between the other forward operating bases and combat outposts were the Red Bulls have soldiers, tending to their religious needs. He said numerous soldiers at the smaller and more remote FOBs and COPs in Laghman Province have brought their bibles and read them regularly, as well as host prayer groups and bible studies on their own to keep the faith.

Just traveling around has been a "big deal" to Willer, he said.

"Just seeing the changes in the countryside from one place to another— from here to say Torkham Gate or Najil has been a huge highlight for me," Willer said. "It really does change over a short distance."

Willer, a lifelong Iowan, serves as a preacher outside of the military, also. He went to college at the University of Iowa before attending seminary and went straight from college into the ministry.

He has only been a chaplain for four years. Willer said his calling into the Iowa National Guard came not from above, but from an article in the Des Moines Register.

"About a year before I got in, the Des Moines Register ran a full page article on the fact that the Iowa National Guard had a shortage of chaplains— they had 16 slots and only seven were taken," Willer, now 41, recalled. "When I read that, it really just bothered me that I was still young enough that I could be doing something and that I wasn't. My wife and I went through like a week or two process of praying about it and asking ourselves what that meant, and we came to the conclusion that if they needed chaplains there was not a reason I shouldn't do it."

Willer will return home to Webster City, Iowa, where he preaches at a church, as well as in a neighboring town. While he was gone, a retired pastor from the church filled in for him.

This is Willer's first deployment, and he said it has been a different experience preaching for soldiers instead of civilians. "It's been different in that the life challenges that people here face," he said. "People are away from their families and separation is difficult. People's prayer concerns tend not to be so much for the soldiers here, but for their loved ones back home. Church here is really lifting up our prayers for our loved ones back home in that they're able to carry on and be alright without us there."

His churchgoers are overall much younger, too, Willer said.

"A lot of them are 18, 19, and some of them have never been away from home," he said. "So the soldiers here have experienced things for the very first time. Back home, when you go through ups and downs, you have friends and family that are close; here, your family are your friends that you deployed with."

Willer said helping soldiers deal with the emotional separation of being away from family, as well as dealing with it himself, is one of the challenges he faced during his deployment as a chaplain. The other, he said, has been dealing with the role of performing memorial services for fallen soldiers.

"I've done funerals back home, but many of them were for older people who had lived out life," he said. "Here, the memorial services I've done have been for young people that had a full life ahead of them and felt called to serve their country and gave their life serving it. That's a very emotional, and humbling thing to be part of for someone like that."

He said his year in Afghanistan has given him a new perspective to return to the U.S. with.

"I think that being in a country like this and seeing what we have in the States and how blessed we are compared to what the people here have, and yet they're still happy here. It's given me a new perspective to take back," Willer said. "In the nine months that I've been here, that's kind of a struggle that I've had."

Still, through the good times and the bad times, Willer said he doesn't regret his year here.

"Each person that came through this church has given me memories that I'll keep for a long time," Willer said. "It truly is a blessing and a calling from God to be here and help others keep the faith while they are separated from their families during the deployment. I would do it all again in a heartbeat, because it really has been a life-changing experience."

JULY 2011
& AFTER

Washington ANG guide air strikes, turns tide during major battle

LAGHMAN PROVINCE, Afghanistan, June 18, 2011—U.S. Air Force Senior Airman Michael McAffrey from Tacoma, Wash., a Joint Terminal Attack Controller with the 116th Air Support Operations Squadron (ASOS), Washington Air National Guard, patrols alongside a field near Khanda village, Laghman Province, Afghanistan. The efforts of McAffrey and the other JTACs from the 116th ASOS were credited by members of the Reconnaissance Platoon, 1st Battalion, 133rd Infantry Regiment, Task Force Ironman, 2nd Brigade Combat Team, 34th Mountain Division, Task Force Red Bulls, as being the difference in the battle of Do Ab May 25 and with saving many of the soldier's lives that day. (Photo by U.S. Army Staff Sgt. Ryan C. Matson, Task Force Red Bulls Public Affairs)

By U.S. Army Staff Sgt. Ryan C. Matson
Task Force Red Bulls Public Affairs

NURISTAN PROVINCE, Afghanistan, July 2, 2011—U.S. Air Force Airmen from the Washington Air National Guard directed multiple airstrikes May 25 helping a significantly outnumbered U.S. Army and Afghan National Security Forces unit fight through an ambush and free a district center from insurgents.

Joint Terminal Attack Controllers (JTAC) from the 116th Air Support Operations Squadron (ASOS), in communication with coalition fighter and bomber aircraft, directed aerial attack on enemy positions while U.S. and Afghan soldiers fought to drive insurgents from Do Ab, a tiny village in Nuristan Province, Afghanistan.

It was the largest battle ever fought by members of the Washington Air National Guard, and one of the most significant battles in the last 10 years of the war in Afghanistan, according to soldiers who fought in the battle.

Approximately 40 U.S. service members, including two JTAC Airmen, and about 20 of their Afghan counterparts went to Do Ab after intelligence reports indicated insurgents overran the district center.

The Airmen and Soldiers from the 1st Battalion, 133rd Infantry Regiment, Task Force Ironman, 2nd Brigade Combat Team, 34th Infantry Division, Task Force Red Bulls, fought through a massive ambush from an enemy force numbering in the hundreds, killing more than 100 insurgent fighters in an intense 7-hour battle.

The service members involved said the most amazing part of the whole conflict, though, was there was not one Coalition casualty. The Airmen from the Washington ANG were the key to the battle, they added.

"If they hadn't been there dropping bombs, I don't know that we would have gotten out of that valley," U.S. Army Sgt. Edward Kane, an infantry team leader from Portland, Ore., with the Reconnaissance Platoon, Headquarters and Headquarters Company, 1st Battalion, 133rd Infantry Regiment, Task Force Ironman, said. "The enemy was getting closer, and their shots were getting more accurate."

The Airmen spoke modestly of their involvement in the mission.

"We were very lucky," U.S. Air Force Tech. Sgt. Tavis Delaney, a JTAC with the 116th ASOS, from Tacoma, Wash., said.

Delaney and U.S. Air Force Senior Airman Michael McCaffrey, a JTAC apprentice with the 116th ASOS, were the two specially trained members of the U.S. Air Force Tactical Air Control Party inserted with the U.S. Army soldiers from the Recon Platoon that day.

The Army leadership and rank-and-file members the JTAC Airmen support said there was much more than luck at work during the fight.

JTACs are trained to work alongside U.S. Army soldiers to control precision air strikes on the enemy. In Afghanistan, their work is critical to saving U.S. and Afghan military lives, said Delaney and McCaffrey's team leader, U.S. Air Force Maj. Raed Gyekis, the 116th's Air Liaison Officer from Tacoma, Wash.

He said the training and preparation a JTAC undergoes is strenuous, combining many of the top specialized schools from both the Army and Air Force.

The geography of the valley made it extremely challenging for coalition forces.

"This is a fairly remote valley, surrounded by high canyon walls. It had been a while, nearly two years, since any American forces had been there," said U.S. Air Force Lt. Col. Chris Adamson, 116th ASOS squadron commander from Tacoma, Wash. "Do Ab is a remote area with a small district center, comparable to a small town courthouse in America. Not much else is there."

Adamson said his Airmen and the 1-133rd's soldiers faced a lot of uncertainty pertaining to the mission.

"We received several reports indicating that the local Afghan police had been overrun by 400 to 500 Taliban fighters, but the information was of questionable value. Delaney and McCaffrey were embedded with the Army platoon sent to secure the district center."

"The mission came down quickly," recalled Gyekis. "Headquarters wanted to know what the situation in Do Ab really was. Our Army unit had very little time between notification and mission execution."

"Maj. Gyekis told me to grab Mac and be ready to go for a three-day mission, at the helicopter, in 52 minutes," recalled Delaney, the lead JTAC from the 116th ASOS.

Delaney and McCaffrey boarded the two CH-47 Chinook helicopters with the platoon. When the helicopters touched down in the narrow canyon floor next to a rushing river, the Airmen said knew they were tactically in one of the worst possible spots to be ambushed from. The Soldiers and Airmen were in a valley surrounded by steep canyon walls. It was, however, the only suitable landing zone in the narrow canyon.

"There was no good cover or concealment on the landing zone," said U.S. Army 1st Lt. Justin Foote, of New Hartford, Iowa, the platoon leader for Recon Platoon. "We had enemy mortar rounds exploding all around us and tracer rounds splitting our formation."

The 116th ASOS JTACs have navigated some of the most difficult terrain in eastern Afghanistan, in the shadow of the Hindu Kush mountain range.

"This was some of the worst," recalls Delaney, "and exactly where I would choose to place an ambush if I was the enemy."

Which is exactly what happened.

"As soon as we got off the helicopters, we started taking fire from every direction ... Rocket-Propelled Grenades, AK-47, machine guns and mortars," McCaffrey said. "They held all the high ground surrounding the landing zone."

For the Army, there was nothing to do but seek cover and return fire. Nonetheless, cover was sparse, and the enemy was so high above the coalition forces, they could use plunging fire to shoot over what little cover the Soldiers had. The JTACs, knew these first minutes were critical for their unit's survival.

"The Army laid down suppressive fire on all the enemy locations, while Delaney and McCaffrey hastily requested more firepower," recalled U.S. Air Force Master Sgt. Rob Lee from Tacoma, Wash., another 116th ASOS JTAC, who was working the headquarters' radios. Lee relayed their urgent requests and quickly got Navy and Air Force strike aircraft overhead to support his pinned-down teammates.

Within a short time, while under fire, Delaney began to guide jets to drop the first bombs onto the heavily-armed enemy surrounding his embattled unit. The bombs continued to fall for the next seven hours.

Meanwhile, Apache and Kiowa attack helicopters also joined the fight, but the enemy continued to attack. The soldiers fended off the enemy attack in the landing zone area for the better part of an hour before moving to a better position.

With Delaney and McCaffrey guiding bombs onto the enemy positions, the small infantry force escaped the open landing zone. They took cover in a nearby series of abandoned Afghan khalats (mud huts) and rock-walled animal pens.

For six hours, they, along with their Afghan National Army counterparts, fought off the enemy. Meanwhile, the enemy continued to swarm around them in the mountains above, slowly drawing nearer to their positions in the animal pens. The soldiers did not know it at the time, but the enemy had heavily fortified fighting positions: trenches dug into solid rocks that were chest-high.

The soldiers said they continued to fight, but as the enemy drew closer, the air strikes began to take their toll on the overwhelming enemy force that had them surrounded and pinned down.

Despite a deadly hail of bullets kicking up dust at their feet and RPGs exploding nearby, Delaney and McCaffrey continuously ran between the khalats to figure out where the greatest threats were coming from and then control airstrikes on top of the advancing enemy fighters' intent on killing them.

The Taliban targeted the JTACs each time they sprinted across open ground.

"Every time Sgt. Delaney lifted his foot, a bullet kicked up dust in the footprint he had just left," McCaffrey said.

Meanwhile, Airmen at FOB Mehtar Lam did their best to support their fellow Airmen in the fight in the valley at Do Ab.

"We loaded a bunch of emergency helicopter resupply 'speedballs' full of more ammo, water and food for the guys," said U.S. Air Force Master Sgt. Dave Glisson from Tacoma, Wash., a 116th ASOS member helping push assistance forward to Delaney and McCaffrey. "But only a few were successful getting dropped off due to the heavy amount of gunfire in the battle. Several aircraft were shot up in the effort."

"It got to the point where the enemy had maneuvered within 200 meters of the team," recalled U.S. Air Force Tech. Sgt. Jaime Medina, another 116th

ASOS JTAC from Tacoma, Wash. "Tavis made the gutsy call to recommend a danger-close mission to the ground commander."

Dropping massive bombs that close to U.S. forces, just outside the bomb's maximum effective range, left no room for error by the pilots, and was a very difficult decision to make. "It had to be done, however," said Delaney. "We were in direct danger of being overrun."

The bombs shook the entire team.

"We felt it hit, rocks flew by our heads, dust erupted everywhere and all sound seemed to stop for several seconds," remembers McCaffrey.

The Soldiers and Airmen said the bombs made the difference in the battle.

The efforts of the pilots were also crucial to helping save the lives of the platoon, added U.S. Army Staff Sgt. Luke Chatfield, a joint fires observer from Floyd, Iowa, with Company C, 1st Battalion, 133rd Infantry Regiment, Task Force Ironman, who worked hand in hand with the JTACs during the battle.

"I give a lot of credit to the pilots, both helicopter and jet," Chatfield said. "They came in under fire each time we needed them to, and they were getting shot at and still were able to get on target time and time again and didn't hesitate. We had fixed-wing come down the valley lower than any fixed wing I've ever seen before, and they were getting shot at there, too, and they didn't care."

Air Force and Army aircraft dropped a large number of munitions including 18 bombs, more than 20 large-caliber cannon rounds from an AC-130 gunship, Hellfire missiles, and rockets. The ground troops also expended thousands of rounds.

"The 116th ASOS and Washington ANG have had members deployed nearly continuously since Sept. 11, 2001," Gyekis said, "We have members who humbly wear the Silver Star, Bronze Star, Purple Heart, and other awards for valour for their service to the nation. What these two did that day is right up there with the very best of those."

After a final burst of enemy resistance, the battle ended, almost as suddenly as it began. "For the next several days, we secured the district center and conducted patrols through the villages," recalled Delaney. "We didn't receive any more gun shots."

Adamson said the two Airmen had not only survived a well-laid ambush, but they had turned the tables on the enemy. They used their wits and skills to bring air power to bear on an overwhelming enemy force, and in the end, their actions were pivotal to bringing every single one of their brothers-in-arms home. All of the men of the platoon were pulled out three days afterward, exhausted and humbled by their good fortune.

"I couldn't be prouder of what our Washington Guardsmen did to bring those soldiers home safely to their families," Adamson said.

"What Delaney and McCaffrey did that day was both extraordinary, as well as expected from each of our JTACs," said Gyekis. "We spend years preparing for days like this. They were the right men, in the right spot, at the right time. We train so that each of our team could be thrown into a meat grinder like Do Ab and do what those two did. We are fortunate to have a lot of men of their caliber in our unit ... and they were all jumping at the chance to hop on a helicopter and get up there and help Tavis and Mike out during this battle."

The day after the platoon returned to their forward operating base, several of the Army soldiers and leadership individually approached Delaney and McCaffrey's team leader, Gyekis.

"Your two JTACs saved our lives," they told him. Gyekis recalled how one of them had tears in his eyes when he recounted the story, and how his wife and children had Delaney and McCaffrey to thank for his safe return.

"Those soldiers' words," Delaney said, "are the highest compliment you could ever pay one of our JTACs."

Iowa National Guard Soldier killed in Afghanistan: Another Iowa Soldier wounded in the attack

For Immediate Release
Iowa National Guard Public Affairs

CAMP DODGE, JOHNSTON, IOWA, July 9, 2011—The Iowa National Guard regrets to announce the death of Sgt. 1st Class Terryl L. Pasker, 39, of Cedar Rapids, Iowa. Pasker was killed by an Afghan National Directorate of Security officer during a mounted patrol, Saturday, July 9, in Panjshir (pan jeer) Province, Afghanistan at approximately 9:30 a.m., local Afghanistan time. As Pasker conducted the mounted patrol, the security officer stopped Pasker's vehicle, then shot and killed both Pasker and a civilian in the vehicle. Master Sgt. Todd Eipperle (EPP er lee) of Marshalltown, Iowa, driving an armored vehicle in front of Pasker, stopped as soon as the shots were fired, and exchanged gunfire with the Afghan security officer, killing the security officer. Eipperle was wounded in the attack.

Pasker was assigned to Company B, 334th Brigade Support Battalion, 2nd Brigade Combat Team, 34th Infantry Division, Iowa Army National Guard, Cedar Rapids, Iowa. Eipperle is assigned to the Headquarters and Headquarters Company, 2nd Brigade Combat Team, 34th Infantry Division, Iowa Army National Guard, Boone, Iowa, and is currently receiving medical treatment at a U.S. Army facility in Afghanistan. The attack is under investigation.

Pasker was born Feb. 26, 1972 in Anamosa, Iowa and graduated from Lisbon (Iowa) High School in 1990. He enlisted in the U.S. Army in July 1990 and joined the Iowa Army National Guard in April 1995. Pasker was serving as an Electronic Maintenance Supervisor during his current deployment. He previously deployed to Afghanistan for Operation Enduring Freedom in 2004.

Pasker was part of the approximately 2,800 members of the 2nd Brigade Combat Team, 34th Infantry Division deployed to Afghanistan. These Iowa Soldiers reported to their mobilization station at Camp Shelby, Miss. in Aug. 2010 for additional training and preparation before departing for the Afghanistan theater of operations. The unit arrived in Afghanistan in November 2010, where the Soldiers provide full-spectrum operations in a combat theater, including lethal and non-lethal capabilities, support to Afghan National Army and Police units, and assistance to humanitarian relief initiatives.

Pasker is survived by his wife, Erica of Cedar Rapids; his mother and father, Mary and David Pasker, of Blairstown; brother Andrew Pasker of Lisbon; and sisters Christine Ross of Oakland, Tenn. and Rebecca Southard of Salem, Ore. [...]

First Team remembers the fallen

FORT HOOD, Texas, May 30, 2012—Mary Pasker, a Gold Star family member, traces the name of her son, Sgt. 1st Class Terryl L. Pasker, who was killed in action July 9, 2011 in eastern Afghanistan, after the 1st Cavalry Division's Memorial Re-dedication Ceremony on Cooper Field. (Photo by U.S. Army Sgt. Kimberly Browne, 1st Cavalry Division Public Affairs)

By Sgt. Kimberly Browne
Headquarters, 1st Cavalry Division Public Affairs

FORT HOOD, Texas, May 30, 2011—As the face of war continues to change, the promise of remembering our fallen is something the 1st Cavalry Division has held on to and continues to show with each passing deployment.

America's First Team honored their fallen from Iraq and Afghanistan during a Memorial Rededication Ceremony, May 30 on Cooper Field.

The ink-black granite memorial bears witness to all that lost their lives while deployed with the division in support of Operation Iraqi Freedom and Operation New Dawn in Iraq, and Operation Enduring Freedom in Afghanistan.

"It's a beautiful monument and it's nice to see that you're honoring the soldiers," said Mary Pasker, Gold Star mother of Sgt. 1st Class Terryl Pasker.

Terryl, who served with the 2nd Brigade Combat Team, 34th Infantry Division, Iowa National Guard, was killed-in-action July 9, 2011 in eastern Afghanistan.

"By commissioning this monument, we have charged these stones to keep vigil over the memory of our fallen," said Maj. Gen. Dan Allyn, commanding general of the 1st Cavalry Division. "And in turn they charge us never to waiver in our commitment to honoring the legacy of their precious charges."

Names of the 17 U.S. soldiers from Operation New Dawn were engraved into the original, horseshoe-shaped monument, along with an additional campaign stone that details the mission that closed the war in Iraq.

OND began, Sept. 1, 2010, and marked the end of military action in Iraq. A little over two years later on Dec. 15, 2011, OND concluded more than eight years of combat. On Dec. 18, 2011, soldiers of the First Team's own 3rd Brigade Combat Team were the last to leave Iraqi territory and cross into Kuwait.

Just to the east, three new memorial walls now stand to remember those lost during the division's latest deployment to eastern Afghanistan for Operation Enduring Freedom.

OEF and the Global War on Terror were sights unseen and a historical first for the Cav. The division headquarters took over authority May 19, 2011 from the 101st Airborne Division (Air Assault) of Combined Joint Task Force–1, Regional Command–East, headquartered in Bagram, Afghanistan.

"Captured on these stones are the names of soldiers from ten brigades and eight divisions within our Army," Allyn said. "The sacrifice of sailors and Airmen from the U.S. Navy and Air Force is also recorded, as well as the names of Service Members from three allied countries who served with the First Team and CJTF–1 in Afghanistan."

The new OEF walls contain the names of 104 U.S. Service Members and civilians; 39 coalition partners, to include Poland, France and Jordan; and two Military Working Dogs.

These additions carry on a legacy to remember the fallen. This legacy now physically connects the heroes of today's wars with their brethren from nearly half a century ago.

"The granite is from the same quarry in India that was used for the Vietnam Memorial," said retired Command Sgt. Maj. Dennis Webster, president of the 1st Cavalry Division Association. "This is the best division memorial that I have yet to see."

The division's memorial was first dedicated April 4, 2006 and is rededicated following every deployment of the division's, to honor those who have served and given the ultimate sacrifice.

"The nation that forgets its defenders will itself be forgotten."—Calvin Collidge

GLOSSARY

Acronyms are words constructed with the first letters of words and are pronounced as a word themselves. For example: "Light Amplification by Stimulated Emission of Radiation," becomes "LASER." Initialisms are constructed similarly to acronyms, but each letter is pronounced individually. Initialisms below are presented as punctuated in the following examples: "F.B.I." and "C.I.A."

AAFES ("AY-fees"): Army and Air Force Exchange Service
A.D.T.: Agribusiness Development Team
A.K.: *Avtomat Kalashnikova*, Soviet-era designation indicating the weapon manufacturer Kalashnikov, from which the family of assault rifles commonly known as the "A.K.-47" gets its name.
ALO ("AY-low") Air Liaison Officer
A.N.A.: Afghan National Army
ANCOP ("AN-kahp"): Afghan National Civil Order Police
A.N.P.: Afghan National Police
A.N.S.F.: Afghan National Security Forces
A.O.: Area of Operations
A.P.F.T.: Army Physical Fitness Test
ASOS ("AY-sahws"): Air Support Operations Squadron
A.U.P.: Afghan Uniformed Police
BAF ("Baff"): Bagram Airfield
BAT-HIIDE ("BAT-HYE-d"): Biometric Automated Toolset (BAT) and Handheld Interagency Identity Detection Equipment (HIIDE).
B.C.T.: Brigade Combat Team
Bde.: Brigade
BEEF: Base Engineer Emergency Force
B.I.G.: Bone Injection Gun
B.M.T.: Basic Military Training
B.S.B.: Brigade Support Battalion
B.S.O.: Base Support Operations
B.S.T.B.: Brigade Special Troops Battalion
B.S.Z.: Bagram Security Zone
C4W: "Cash for Work"
CAS ("Kaz"): Close Air Support
CERP ("Surp"): Commander's Emergency Response Program
C.I.E.D.: Counter-Improvised Explosive Device
C.I.D.: Criminal Investigation Division
CIST ("Sist"): Company Intelligence Support Team
C.J.T.F.: Combined Joint Task Force
C.L.P: Combat Logistics Patrols
C.L.S.: Combat Lifesaver
C.M.S.T.: Civil-Military Support Team
Coalition: Involves group of U.S., NATO, and other nations' military forces.
COIN ("KOY-en"): COunterINsurgency
Combined: Involves more than one nation's military.
COP ("Kahp"): Combat Outpost

C.P.: Command Post
C-RAM ("SEE-ram"): Counter Rocket, Artillery, and Mortar
CROWS ("Krohz") Common Remotely Operated Weapon Station
C.S.I.: Crime Scene Investigation
C.S.S.B.: Combat Sustainment Support Battalion
CSTC–A ("See-STICK-ah"): Combined Security Transition Assistance–Afghanistan
C.V.-R.D.L: Central Veterinary Research and Diagnostics Lab
DAIL ("Dayl"): Directorate of Agriculture, Irrigation and Livestock
DFAC ("DEE-fack"): Dining Facility
DShK ("DOOSH-kah"): *Degtyaryova-Shpagina Krupnokaliberny*; Soviet-era heavy machine gun.
D.O.D.: Department of Defense
DOWA ("DOW-ah"): Department of Women's Affairs
DVIDS ("DIH-vids"): Defense Video & Imagery Distribution System
E.C.P.: Entry Control Point
E.O.D.: Explosive Ordnance Disposal
E.T.T.: Embedded Training Team
FAMACHA ("Fah-mah-chah"): FAffa MAlan CHArt; graduated method of selecting sheep for deworming treatment.
FARP ("Farp"): Foward Arming and Refueling Point
FET: Female Engagement Team
FOB: Forward Operating Base
GIRoA ("jye-ROH-ah"): Government of the Islamic Republic of Afghanistan
GWOT ("JEE-waht"): Global War on Terror
H.H.C.: Headquarters and Headquarters Company
I.B.C.T.: Infantry Brigade Combat Team
I.E.D.: Improvised Explosive Device
I.A.N.G.: Iowa National Guard
I.D.F.: Indirect Fire
ISAF ("EYE-saf"): International Security Assistance Force
Joint: Involves more than one branch of U.S. military service.
JTAC ("JAY-tack"): Joint Terminal Attack Controller
JDOC ("JAY-dock"): Joint Defense Operations Center
K.L.E.: Key Leader Engagement
K.N.P.A.: Korean National Police Agency
K.V.T.C.: Korean Vocational Training Center
LEP ("Lehp"): Law Enforcement Professional
LRAS ("ELL-raz"): Long Range Advanced Scout System
LOGPAC: Logistics Package
JCOP ("JAY-kop"): Joint Combat Outpost
LOGPAC: LOGistics PACkage
L.Z.: Landing Zone
MAIL ("Mayl"): Ministry of Agriculture, Irrigation and Livestock
M-A.T.V. ("EM-A.T.V."): Mine-Resistant, Ambush-Protected All-Terrain Vehicle
MEPS ("Mehps"): Military Entrance Processing Station
M-RAP ("EM-rap") Mine-Resistant, Ambush-Protected
M.R.E.: Meal, Ready-to-Eat. A packaged, single-serving military ration.
M.P.: Military Police

MPAD ("EM-pad") Mobile Public Affairs Detachment
M.W.D.: Military Working Dog
NATO ("NAY-toh"): North Atlantic Treaty Organization
N.C.O.: Non-Commissioned Officer
N.C.O.I.C.: Non-Commissioned Officer-in-Charge
N.G.O.: Non-Governmental Organization
N.D.S.: National Directorate of Security
N.T.C.: National Training Center, Fort Irwin, Calif.
O.C.C.–P.: Operations Coordination Center–Provincial
O.C.C.–R.: Operations Coordination Center–Regional
O.E.F.: Operation Enduring Freedom
O.I.C.: Officer-in-Charge
O.I.F.: Operation Iraqi Freedom
OMLT ("AHM-let"): Operational Mentoring Liaison Team
O.N.D.: Operation New Dawn
O.P.: Observation Post
P.A.N.C.O.: Public Affairs Non-Commissioned Officer
P.A.O.: Public Affairs Officer
P.K. or P.K.M.: *Pulemyot Kalashnikova*; a Soviet-era machine gun.
P.M.C.S.: Preventive Maintenance Checks and Services
P.M.T: Police Mentor Team
Prime BEEF: Prime Base Engineer Emergency Force
P.R.T.: Provincial Reconstruction Team
P.S.D.: Personal Security Detail
P.X.: Post Exchange, a military store
Q.R.F.: Quick Reaction Force
REDHORSE: Rapid Engineer Deployable Heavy Operational Repair Squadron Engineers
R.C.–Capital: Regional Command–Capital
R.C.–E: Regional Command–East
RIP ("Rihp"): Relief in Place
R.M.D.C.: Regional Mail Distribution Center
R.O.K.: Republic of Korea
R.O.P.: Roots of Peace
R.P.G.: Rocket-Propelled Grenade
SAW ("Saw"): Squad Automatic Weapon
SARG ("SAR-guh"): Small-Arms Readiness Group
SNAFU ("SNAH-foo"): Situation Normal, All F---ed Up
T.C.P.: Traffic Control Point
T.F.: Task Force, a temporary, ad hoc organization
TIC ("Tick"): Troops-in-Contact
TOA ("TOH-ah"): Transfer of Authority
TOC ("Tahk"): Tactical Operations Center
U.N.: United Nations
UPAR ("YOU-par"): Unit Public Affairs Representative
U.S.A.C.E.: United States Army Corps of Engineers
U.S.A.I.D.: United States Agency for International Development
U.S.O.: United Service Organizations
V.P.B. Vehicle Patrol Base

INDEX

ABOUT THE EDITOR

In 2010, Randy Brown was preparing for deployment to Eastern Afghanistan as a member of the Iowa Army National Guard's 2nd Brigade Combat Team (BCT), 34th Infantry "Red Bull" Division. Since its organization in 1917, the division has historically comprised citizen-soldiers from Minnesota, Iowa, North and South Dakota, and other Midwestern states. In news reports, the 2010 deployment of more than 3,000 was billed as the largest activation of Iowa troops since World War II.

After a paperwork SNAFU dropped Brown from the deployment list only days before federal mobilization, he continued to serve until December 2010, when he retired with 20 years of military service. His military career included an overseas peacekeeping mission in 2003 with the Iowa National Guard's 1st Battalion, 133rd Infantry Regiment (1-133rd Inf.).

He then went to Afghanistan anyway, embedding with Iowa's Red Bull units as a civilian journalist in May-June 2011. A former editor of Iowa community and metro newspapers, as well as national trade and consumer magazines, he is now a freelancer based in Central Iowa.

He writes about military topics at: www.redbullrising.com.

Brown is author of the poetry collection "Welcome to FOB Haiku: War Poems from Inside the Wire" (Middle West Press, 2015). For more information, visit: www.fobhaiku.com.

Brown was the 2015 winner of the inaugural Madigan Award for humorous military-themed writing, presented by Negative Capability Press, Mobile, Ala. He was the 2012 winner of the Military Reporters and Editors' (M.R.E.) independent-blogging category, and was a finalist in the Milblogging.com awards' veteran (2011) and reporter (2012) categories.

He is the current poetry editor at the literary journal *As You Were*, published twice a year by the non-profit Military Experience & the Arts. He is also a member of Military Reporters & Editors, the Military Writers Guild, and the Military Writers Society of America.

NOTES ON EDITING

This collection assembles and collates U.S. government-generated content as it first appeared on Defense Video & Imagery Distribution System (DVIDS), the now-defunct Combined Joint Task Force–101 (CJTF–101) and "Iowa Red Bulls" websites, and other online venues. Generally, producers of this content were the public affairs teams of:

- The Iowa National Guard's 2nd Brigade Combat Team (B.C.T.), 34th Infantry "Red Bull" Division, deployed to Eastern Afghanistan from November 2010 to July 2011. During this deployment, the 2-34th BCT was known as "Task Force Red Bulls."
- Those Agribusiness Development Teams (ADT) and Provincial Reconstruction Teams (PRT) operating within Area of Operations (AO) Red Bulls.
- Unit Public Affairs Representatives (UPAR) of the Iowa National Guard's 1st Battalion, 168th Infantry Regiment (1-168th Inf.), "Task Force Lethal," operating separately from Task Force Red Bulls in Paktya Province.

When first published, these articles and photographs were cleared for public release by their respective release authorities, and free of copyright. As such, civilian news providers were free to feature the content in newspapers, newscasts, and websites.

Photographs originally appeared in color. They were converted to black and white for this book. Photographs were selected based upon a number of factors, including story-telling content, depiction of named individuals, and successful conversion to low-resolution, black-and-white printing. Many, but not all, photographs released by Task Force Red Bulls are included here.

The editor sought to optimize future historians' potential use of this content as a primary source material by presenting articles mostly as they were published, with the following notes and exceptions:

- The U.S. Army's idiosyncratic insistence of capitalizing "Soldier" in public affairs content was left intact. To match this practice, the editor also capitalized the term "Airman" on all references.
- Headlines, including sometimes obscure military jargon, also remain mostly unchanged. Where possible, acronyms in headlines were "unpacked" to improve readability and ease-of-understanding.
- Datelines were changed to more accurately reflect chronology of the deployment. In DVIDS parlance, datelines are now "dates taken," rather than "dates posted." In civilian terms, datelines are the dates the articles were written or photographed, rather the dates they were filed, posted, and/or published.

- For consistency, "Parwan Province" datelines that took place on Bagram Airfield were standardized to read "Bagram Airfield." Datelines that took place outside Bagram Airfield, including the village of Bagram and/or the "Bagram Security Zone," were standardized to "Parwan Province."
- Military ranks were changed to conform to Associated Press style.
- In order to better more effectively index named individuals, full-names were standardized across all references. For example, an individual originally appearing in separate articles as both "Sgt. Jim Doe" and "Sgt. James Doe II" is now presented solely as the latter. Afghan names were also standardized.
- In many instances, references to named members of Afghan National Security Forces include only rank and last name. This reflects the original reporting.
- Unit names were standardized, in the index, to a format such as "Company A, 1st Battalion, 133rd Infantry Regiment." It was the practice, however, for some companies to locally take on non-standard designations. Examples include "Eliminator" (in place of the standard NATO phonetic alphabet "Echo") and "Apocalypse" (rather than "Alpha").
- Use of the word "Kandak" to refer to battalion-sized Afghan military formations was made uniform across all content. However, use of the related abbreviation "Coy" was replaced with the term "Company."
- U.S. units were indexed down to battalion/squadron level. Company-/troop-sized units are listed with their higher headquarters. Afghan units are indexed down to the company level.
- Certain fluidly constructed terms and acronyms, such as "Operations Coordination Center–Provincial" (OCC–P) and "Mine-Resistant, Ambush-Protected" (M-RAP), were standardized.
- Terms and acronyms such as "Improvised Explosive Device (IED)" "Rocket-Propelled Grenade (RPG)" were also more consistently capitalized.
- Some proper names were also standardized. Examples include "Bull Whip" (vs. "Bullwhip") and "Task Force Redhorse" (vs. "Task Force Red Horse.').
- Place names were standardized. Example: "Pad Pakh" and "Bad Pech" now appear as the latter in all references. Other standardized names include: "Gulach," "Panjshir," "Pul-e-Sayad," and "Koh-e Safi."
- Information added or deleted by the book's editor are indicated in brackets. Information added by the original writer are indicated in parentheses. Task Force Red Bulls "editors' notes" are unchanged.

DID YOU ENJOY THIS BOOK?

Tell your friends and family about it, or post your thoughts via social media sites, like Facebook and Twitter! On-line communites that serve military families, veterans, and service members are also ideal places to help spread the word. about this book, and others like it!

Share a quick review on websites for other readers, such as Goodreads.com. Or offer a few of your impressions on national bookseller websites, such as Amazon.com, or Barnesandnoble.com.

Better yet, recommend the title to your favorite local librarian, military historian, museum gift store manager, or independent bookseller!

We appreciate your support! In future projects, we'll continue to look for new Middle Western stories and voices to share with our readers. Like the motto of the 34th Infantry "Red Bull" Division says: "Attack! Attack! Attack!"

You can write us at:

Middle West Press LLC
P.O. Box 31099
Johnston, Iowa 50131-9428

Or visit:
www.middlewestpress.com

CPSIA information can be obtained
at www.ICGtesting.com
Printed in the USA
FSOW04n0847261216
28845FS